THE MAKING OF KINGDOMS

Anglo-Saxon Studies in Archaeology and History 10

Papers from the 47th Sachsensymposium
York, September 1996

Edited by

Tania Dickinson and David Griffiths

Oxford University Committee for Archaeology
1999

Published by the Oxford University Committee for Archaeology
Institute of Archaeology
Beaumont Street
Oxford

Distributed by Oxbow Books
Park End Place, Oxford, OX1 1HN

Distributed in North America by
The David Brown Book Compnay
PO Box 511, Oakville, CT 06779

ISBN 0 947816 93 3
ISSN 0264 5254

The cover illustration is of three gold figures from Sorte Muld, Bornholm, Denmark (see p. 178)

Typeset by Oxbow Books
Printed in Great Britain
at the Short Run Press
Exeter

Foreword

Anglo-Saxon Studies in Archaeology and History is an annual series concerned with the archaeology and history of England and its neighbours during the Anglo-Saxon period.

ASSAH offers researchers an opportunity to publish new work in a flexible format which allows diversity in length, style or geographical spread of contributions. Papers placing Anglo-Saxon England in its international context, including contemporary themes in neighbouring countries, will receive as warm a welcome as papers on England itself.

ASSAH 10 is wholly devoted to the publication of papers from the 47th International Sachsensymposium, 'The Making of Kingdoms', held at the University of York in September 1996 (see Introduction).

ASSAH's internet home-page, with information on the availability and content of volumes, can be found at: http://users.ox.ac.uk/~assah/

Papers submitted to ASSAH must be internally consistent, accurate and readable without detailed specialist knowledge. All papers are commented upon by academic referees. Volume 11 has already received a number of submissions, and Volume 12 is at its early planning stage.

The Editor of ASSAH, The Organiser of the 47th Sachsensymposium, and the Oxford University Committee for Archaeology would like to record their gratitude to the Aurelius Charitable Trust, the Council for British Archaeology and the University of York for the financial support which this volume has received from these sources.

David Griffiths
Institute of Archaeology
36 Beaumont Street
Oxford OX1 2PG

Email: david.griffiths@archaeology.oxford.ac.uk

Contributors

Morten Axboe
Bredevej 87, DK-2830, Virum, Denmark

Charlotte Fabech
Department of Prehistoric Archaeology, University of Aarhus, Moesgård, DK-8270 Højbjerg, Denmark

Helen Geake
Norfolk Museums Service, Castle Museum, Norwich, N21 3JU, UK

Danny Gerrets
Department of Archaeology, State University of Groningen, Poststraat 6, 9712 ER Groningen, The Netherlands

Anders Götherström
The Archaeological Research Laboratory, Greens villa, Stockholm University, S-106 91, Stockholm, Sweden

Lotte Hedeager
Department of Nordic Archaeology, Institute of Archaeology, Art History and Numismatics, University of Oslo, Frederiks gate 3, N-0164 Oslo, Norway

Anthonie Heidinga
Department of European Archaeology, University of Amsterdam, Nieuwe Prinsengracht, 1018 VZ Amsterdam, The Netherlands

Nicholas Higham
Department of History, University of Manchester, Oxford Road, Manchester, M13 9PL, UK

John Hines
School of History and Archaeology, University of Wales, Cardiff, PO Box 909, Cardiff CF1 3XU, UK

Karen Høilund Nielsen
Byagervej 160, 1mf, DK-8330 Beder, Denmark

Jan-Peder Lamm
Statens Historiska Muséer, Box 5428, S-114 84 Stockholm, Sweden

Kevin Leahy
Scunthorpe Museum and Art Gallery, Oswald Road, Scunthorpe DN15 7BD, UK

Kerstin Lidén
The Archaeological Research Laboratory, Greens villa, Stockholm University, S-106 91, Stockholm, Sweden

Bente Magnus
Lainus Cultural Heritage Consultants, Saltmätargt. 6, S-111 60 Stockholm, Sweden

Ulf Näsman
Department of Prehistoric Archaeology, University of Aarhus, Moesgård, DK-8270 Højbjerg, Denmark

Lucas Quensel-von Kalben
Kummerfelder Str. 1, D-25494 Borstel-Hohenraden, Germany

Julian Richards
Department of Archaeology, University of York, King's Manor, York YO1 7EP, UK

Jytte Ringtved
Department of Prehistoric Archaeology, University of Aarhus, Moesgård, DK-8270 Højbjerg, Denmark

Marianne Schauman-Lönnqvist
National Board of Antiquities, PO Box 913, Helsinki, Finland

Christopher Scull
English Heritage, 23, Savile Row, London, W1X 1AB, UK

Nick Stoodley
207 Farley Lane, Upper Slackstead, Braishfield, Hampshire, SO51 0QL, UK

Margrethe Watt
Bornholms Museum, Box 126, DK-3700 Rönne, Denmark

Barbara Yorke
King Alfred's College of Higher Education, Winchester, SO22 4NR, UK

Contents

Part III. Identifying kingdoms in the mind

Introduction

ASSAH 10 is dedicated to publication of papers delivered to the 47th Sachsensymposium, held in York in September 1996, on the theme of 'The Making of Kingdoms'. The conference focused on the formative period for north-west European kingdoms, that is the Late Roman and Early Medieval periods (*c*. AD 300–900) and brought together scholars working both as individuals and as part of current national projects, such as the Danish 'From tribe to state', the Swedish 'Svealand in the Vendel and Viking Periods' and the Dutch 'From Scheldt to Weser. Frisia in north-western European perspective'. While the papers draw on data from distinct, albeit geographically and culturally linked, regions around the North Sea and Baltic, few concentrate directly on the identity or history of specific kingdoms (though cf. Heidinga and Gerrets on Frisia, Axboe on Denmark, Leahy on Lindsey and Hines on Middle Anglia). Rather debate has turned less on 'whether this is' or 'where is' a kingdom and more on how the structures of early kingdoms can be accessed archaeologically and historically. For these reasons the papers are presented thematically not regionally, so that interconnections and resonances, which rebound between them, are maximised, and readers are invited to draw comparisons and contrasts between research from different areas or different substantive starting points. Readers with particular regional interests should still be able to pick out papers of relevance to them.

Part I presents five papers concerned with general models and research agenda derived from archaeology and history. The first three offer frameworks for the archaeological study of Denmark, Frisia and Anglo-Saxon England (Näsman, Heidinga and Scull respectively) and provide context for the papers which follow in Parts II and III, including more particular studies of settlements, burials, art styles and jewellery as well as surveys of individual kingdoms. They are supported by two papers by historians of Anglo-Saxon England: Yorke summarises the now salutary perspective taken towards the earliest records for Anglo-Saxon kingship, and Higham synthesises his readings of the evidence for overkingship – *imperium* – in fifth- to seventh-century England. From Part I two leading agendas emerge which are then explored through the papers in Parts II and III.

Part II is concerned with the search for kingdoms on the ground. Key issues are the control and mobilisation of resources through economic, social and territorial organisation, and they are explored in a number of ways. The first four papers are all concerned with problems of characterising political units in terms of their centres and territories. Fabech and Ringtved tackle these in two explicitly complementary studies of Denmark. Their papers are further complemented by Schauman-Lönnqvist's analysis of putative polities in south-west Finland on the basis of rich burials and by Richards' critique of the archaeological evidence for Middle Saxon centres of production and consumption in Northumbria. The potential of burial studies to yield social information is developed further in the next three papers. Lidén and Götherström explore how the molecular biology of skeletal remains can provide a novel route to such information for the Vendel Period in Sweden. Quensel-von Kalben and Stoodley use more familiar methods of burial analysis to investigate the social structuring of elite groups in southern England: the former examines the role of Christianity in defining Late Romano-British opposition to the establishment of Saxon polities and the latter examines how changing household structure correlates with increased social stratification in seventh-century Wessex. Themes raised in all these papers are variously illustrated in four surveys of particular areas or kingdoms which conclude Part II – Axboe on Denmark, Gerrets on Westergo, Leahy on Lindsey and Hines on the Cambridgeshire Region.

Part III is directed towards identifying kingdoms in the mind. The special repertoire of Scandinavian and Anglo-Saxon art styles and jewellery is viewed in the context of post-processualist themes about the role of material culture in negotiating and legitimising social relationships. Political programmes – kings and kingship – are seen as constructed and supported through symbolic appeal to sources of authority. Hedeager, Lamm and Magnus all invoke a shamanistic Odin cult and cosmology, expressed on bracteates and Salin's Style I and, by inference, in ritual enactment, as the key means by which Scandinavian kingships were ideologically underpinned in the late fifth and early sixth centuries. The iconography of gold foil figures (*guldgubber*) suggests that this tradition lived on through the sixth and seventh centuries, but Watt's careful study also points to a Late Roman or Merovingian contribution to northern conceptions of kingship. And Høilund Nielsen argues that from the later sixth century wider dynastic authority was promoted through the development of Salin's Style II, with differences in its uptake, in this case in England, reflecting its capacity to serve the differing affiliations and political agenda of regional elite. But, as Geake finally reminds us, the dominant style-statement of seventh-century grave-goods in England was not to northern gods or descent, but to Rome and Byzantium – the ultimately 'tried and tested' authority for those who aspired to *imperium*.

***

The 47th Sachsensymposium could not have taken place without the generous support of a number of institutions. As organiser of the symposium, I should like to thank the British Academy, the British Archaeological Association, the Centre for Medieval Studies (University of York) and the Goethe Institut (York) for financial assistance, and the Department of Archaeology (University of York), the York Archaeological Trust, the Yorkshire Museum and the York Visitor and Conference Bureau for additional help. I should also like to thank Oxford University Committee for Archaeology, and the Editor of ASSAH, for making Volume 10 available so that what was a stimulating and pleasurable event for participants can, in part, be shared with a wider audience.

Tania Dickinson
Symposium Organiser
Department of Archaeology
University of York
King's Manor
York YO1 7EP

Anglo-Saxon Studies in Archaeology and History 10, 1999

The Ethnogenesis of the Danes and the Making of a Danish kingdom

Ulf Näsman

Since the 1970s Danish archaeologists and historians have shown a growing interest in the question of whether it is possible to understand the background of the Danish kingdom as it appears for the first time in the written sources from the Viking Age; that is whether it is possible to give a coherent picture of the development of South Scandinavian societies from the Birth of Christ to the conversion to Christianity in the tenth century, the traditional end of the Viking Age and beginning of the Scandinavian Middle Ages.

The Danish Research Council launched a research programme called 'From Tribe to State in Denmark', which aimed to understand the formation of the Danish kingdom by studying the interaction between economic, social and political circumstances from the Roman period to the Viking Age (Mortensen and Rasmussen (eds) 1988; 1991; Näsman 1997). The basis of the programme consisted of many new and important finds made by Danish archaeologists during the last decades. The large sacrifices of war booty at Ejsbøl and Illerup as well as the many dated underwater barriers in Danish fjords and bays were important evidence of conflict and war. Excavations and analyses of cemeteries and settlements had revealed that major changes took place in economy and social structure. Studies of hoards and sacrifices as well as analyses of pictorial art revealed changes in cult, religion and ideology.

But the many investigations of social, economic and military conditions had to be put into a general framework, which of course encompasses the political organisation of society. To achieve such a goal, the bases of method and theory had to be clarified, which led naturally to the main problem: whether it is possible for archaeology to investigate political organisations, the development of which of course ran parallel to and interacted with the economic and social changes. Danish archaeologists have often studied economic and social conditions of past societies, but only a few (e.g. Hedeager 1980; 1992; Randsborg 1980; 1991; J. Jensen 1982) have dared to address the complicated question of the development of polities from tribes to kingdoms, which was the theme of the 47th Sachsensymposium, 'The Making of Kingdoms'. The research programme 'From Tribe to State in Denmark' had this intention.

To run such a programme, one must be convinced that archaeologists can write history and one must have a firm idea how to do it. There must be a belief that archaeology has methods to develop the interpretation of material culture into more or less well-founded pictures of social structures and political conditions. Archaeological sources do not tell the story by themselves – a fact that historians never stop telling us. The information concealed in material culture has to be transmitted through a theoretical lens and manipulated by various methods, historical analogy being the most important (Wylie 1985; Näsman 1988a).

Two themes have been brought into focus:

1) the ethnogenesis of the Nordic peoples: the formation of the tribes that appear in the few and difficult written sources of the first millennium AD;
2) the making of the three Nordic kingdoms: Denmark, Norway and Sweden.

In Denmark, research into these questions intensified through the 1980s and 1990s. This seems – after New Archaeology and all that – to be a quite natural new turn in the spiral of research, and similar tendencies are observable also in Norway, where one thinks of Bjørn Myhre's project on the Borre region in south Norway (Myhre 1992), and in Sweden where Frands Herschend and Birgit Arrhenius have launched the Svealand project, focusing on the famous boat-grave cemeteries at Valsgärde and Vendel.

A problem with this kind of long-term research is its inherent teleological perspective: the natural goal of research is of course the states of Denmark, Norway and Sweden, or to be more precise and less anachronistic, the kingdoms of the Danes, the Norwegians and the Swedes, respectively. One has to beware the dangers of the evolutionary trap and unilinear thinking (Claessen 1983). The project 'From Tribe to State' reveals its teleological vision in the title, so it is essential for me to emphasise that a Danish kingdom is not a self-evident formation but the result of a series of concrete historical circumstances.

One has to remember that there have been alternative possibilities at several occasions. If one believes in the broad processes of history, one can say that there have been forks in the development where society could have taken a new direction and, if you believe in the role of the individual, you can talk about cross-roads where rulers had to make a choice.

When archaeologists today ask these questions, they are in fact investigating the possibilities of carrying out analyses of political and social circumstances by archaeological means. By studying changes over time, hypotheses about the cause of change have to be made, and thus basic archaeological ideas about social development are investigated. The limits of archaeology as an historical discipline are thus tested.

In almost all of Scandinavia the periods from the Roman Iron Age to the Viking Age are prehistoric; in fact prehistory lingered on till the thirteenth century in several regions. But some parts of late prehistoric Scandinavia, and certainly South Scandinavia, deserve to be labelled protohistoric. Nevertheless, Scandinavian archaeologists often forget or ignore the fact that the first millennium AD is an historical period in large parts of Europe, and, unfortunately, the Scandinavian development is too often evaluated in isolation from the rest of Europe. This is despite the fact that material culture studied by archaeology clearly demonstrates that interaction with continental as well as insular powers continuously influenced the social development of Scandinavia. Thus it is necessary that the approach to Scandinavian late prehistory includes an historical dimension and a European perspective.

Outside the Roman Empire the first to fifth centuries AD were a period of reaction against and adaptation to Mediterranean civilisation. Historically, this implies that the development in Denmark during the 'Roman Iron Age' has also to be viewed from the perspective of the Germanic-Roman interaction. The Migration period of Scandinavia cannot be understood without paying regard to the strong impact of Byzantium and the Germanic-Roman successor kingdoms that can be traced in almost every part of Europe. Social transformations of continental and insular Germanic societies which were influenced by the successor kingdoms are described in written sources, and many of these changes were certainly paralleled in Scandinavia. The Germanic language affiliation, great similarities in material culture, the obvious connections to other European peoples that archaeology can demonstrate, all these certainly indicate that the questions about Danish ethnogenesis and the Danish kingdom will find their answer in a European context. The headline 'The Germanic attempts at organisation' used by Le Goff (1988) to characterise the Frankish realm can without difficulty be applied to a description of Scandinavia in the Merovingian period and the Viking Age. South Scandinavia was linked to France and Germany, as well as to England. The Danish development was certainly part of a common west European trajectory.

In the protohistorical first millennium AD in South Scandinavia it is necessary to employ cross-disciplinary co-operation between archaeologists, historians, historians of religion, historical geographers and scholars of place-names and also of sciences like botany, geology, etc. Without the written sources and without the co-operation of historians and linguists, Danish archaeologists would not be able to talk about 'Danes' and could not have any idea that they belonged to peoples talking 'Germanic' languages. In fact the social and political system of the Scandinavian Iron Age societies could be understood only in very general terms. The best possibility of interpreting the archaeological record of South Scandinavia is by analogy with historians' interpretations of other more or less contemporary Germanic peoples, based on descriptions in the written sources. Fundamental in this respect is Reinhard Wenskus' monumental book *Stammesbildung und Verfassung* (1961). And the application and development of his ideas by Herwig Wolfram and others are also very useful (e.g. Pohl 1980; Wolfram 1988; Heather 1991). In brief, Wenskus' thesis is that the many small Germanic tribes of the Early Roman Iron Age were pressurised by Nomadic peoples, by the Roman expansion and not least by internal competition, and were thus forced into larger units – tribal confederations. Loosely united to begin with, many confederations soon became dominated by one tribe. This hegemony was won by military and political means. Within the framework of such confederations, the first continental kingdoms developed, for instance the Frankish Merovingian realm (e.g. Zöllner 1970; James 1988; Wood 1994). The process of amalgamation described by Wenskus is in fact very similar to the process of 'peer polity interaction' as described in a book by Colin Renfrew and John Cherry (1986).

The English word 'kingdom' corresponds in Scandinavian languages to *kongedømme*, but we have also another useful concept *kungarike*. *Rike* is related to the Germanic word *reiks*, a high-ranking leader, and it means 'dominion', 'rule' over people, and in a transferred sense only the concept is applied to the territory settled by the people, that is the 'country' or 'state'. Dominions could be of different kind, however: kingdom, chiefdom, duchy, county, etc. A super-regional dominion is a kingdom, a regional dominion is a chiefdom, a duchy, a county, etc. Many regional rulers are in fact former kings or so-called petty kings of small realms. In a kingdom, chieftains and petty kings can survive as regional and local leaders, but eventually they are often replaced by royal agents (on kingdoms, see in this context Wolfram 1971; Schlesinger 1973; Sawyer and Wood 1977; Sawyer 1978; Bassett 1989; Yorke 1990.

Today, archaeological long-term study of Scandinavian societies in the first millennium AD has laid new ground on which scholars have to build their image of the making of the Danish kingdom. So I will now briefly describe some of the results and focus on changes in the material that I find significant for the study of

Danish ethnogenesis and the making of the kingdom.

One of the most important results is that is has been possible to bridge the gap of the 'Dark Ages' during the fifth to eighth centuries and connect the relatively full archaeological and historical record of the Viking Age to the very rich archaeology of the Roman Iron Age (Näsman 1991a–b). Until recently the Migration and Merovingian periods appeared as a hiatus because of their poor and one-sided archaeological material. Consequently, Danish scholars had great problems in describing the development in the centuries preceding the appearance of the kingdom in the written sources at the end of the eighth century. The lack of sources was interpreted as the result of a social crisis of considerable importance followed by population decrease and settlement abandonment (discussion summarised in Näsman 1988b). But recent pollen-analytical studies of the cultural landscape, for instance, do not support this view (Berglund (ed.) 1991; Aaby 1993) and also archaeological research during the last twenty years has improved the source situation (Näsman 1991b). It is especially the progress of settlement archaeology that has enabled Danish, German and Swedish archaeologists to paint a new picture of the formation of the pre-Viking and Viking Danish kingdom. Today one can say that the changes in the record of the fourth to eighth centuries probably reflect a period of rapid social transformation, but not necessarily one of crisis.

The rural settlement

From a base already established in the Late Bronze Age, agriculture in South Scandinavia developed through small steps to form the present cultural landscape. Based on changes in the well studied settlement pattern of Jutland, archaeologists can point to two periods of settlement change in the first millennium AD, one around 200 and the other around 700 (Hvass 1988; 1993). Both seem to represent a rural expansion, while the Migration period is considered to be a period of stabilisation (looked at positively) or stagnation (looked at negatively). The development of farmsteads in Jutland from the pre-Roman Iron Age to the turn of the first millennium is summarised in Figure 1. The changes around 200 led to larger farms, each with a large fenced-off yard with more buildings, including a long dwelling-cum-byre house. The changes around 700 entailed much larger farmyards, more buildings and a new house construction, all set in the well-planned setting of seemingly regulated hamlets. In general, settlements developed:

- from a subsistence economy to a more centralised system aiming at the production of a large surplus,
- from farms within a common fence to individual farmsteads in hamlets and villages, each with their own fence,

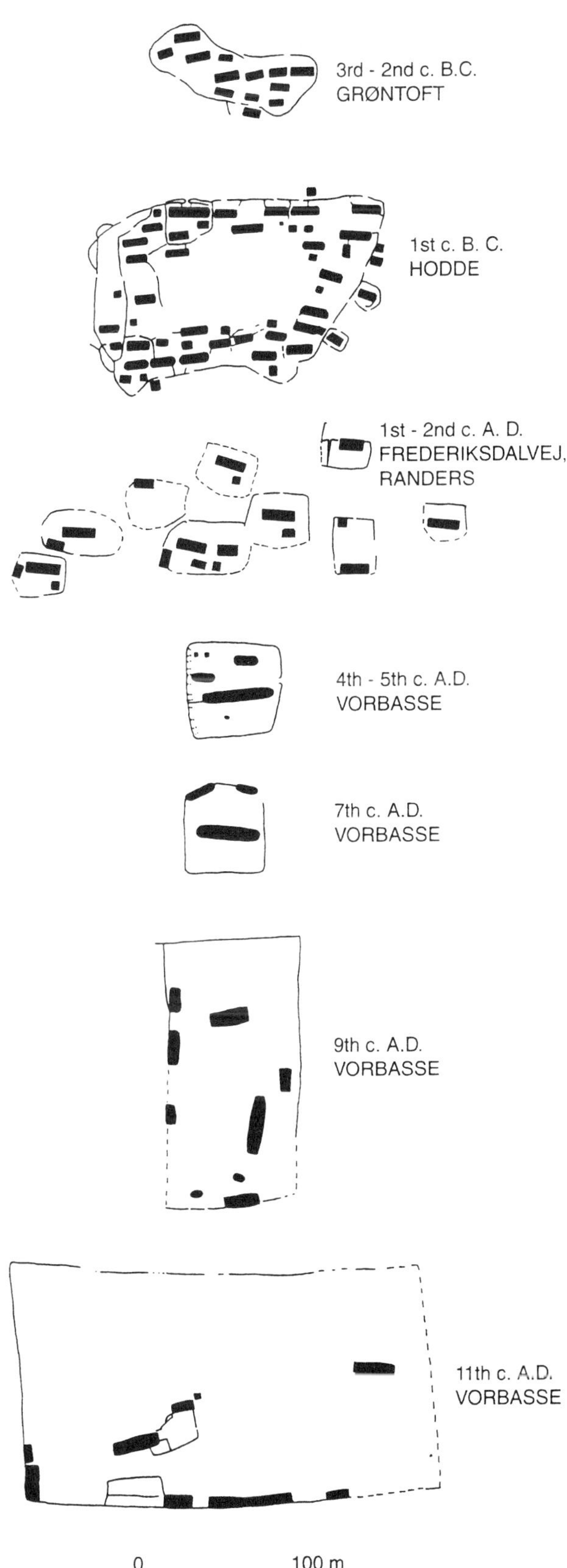

Fig. 1 The general development of settlement in Jutland. For the third century BC to the second century AD the whole hamlet is shown; for hamlets dating from the fourth to eleventh centuries AD only the plan of a single farmstead is shown. After Hvass 1993.

- from small family farms to large farmsteads and manors,
- from chieftain's farms standing alone or within a hamlet fence to manors at hamlets that were run by the magnate himself or a farm-manager (*bryde*).

The study of building tradition and inter-site organisation demonstrates a long continuity and conservative tradition reaching back into the Bronze Age. It has to be emphasised that the development by and large follows that of the north-western continental plain area down to the Rhine (Waterbolk 1991; Zimmermann 1991; 1992). For instance, the lay-out of a hamlet of seven farms at Vorbasse in the eighth to ninth centuries shows a regulated, well planned settlement that is fairly similar to hamlets in the northern parts of the Carolingian empire, for instance at Kootwijk just north of the Rhine (Heidinga 1987). The evidence of farm buildings does not support any idea that ordinary Danes were more barbaric than Franks, Frisians or Anglo-Saxons or that their agriculture was less productive. Today we are able to follow long continuities in the cultural landscape, and many settlement archaeologists presume that the historical pattern of church villages, hamlets and single farms has its roots as far back as the Migration period or the Late Roman period (Callmer 1992; Fabech and Ringtved 1995; L. Jørgensen 1995a–b).

The development of chiefdoms and kingdoms means the mobilisation of resources into a centralised political system. Power is accumulation and use of resources. It now seems certain that the elite of Denmark could base their social and military position on a surplus, and that this surplus was growing. Technology was improved and rural produce increased, especially from the eighth century onwards, and this expansion continued through the Viking Age and did not end until the end of the High Middle Ages (Myrdal 1985; 1988; Berglund 1991). It is the surplus created by this expansion that could carry the late Viking and high medieval Danish kingdom with its administration, military power, church, towns, etc.

Trade and exchange

In this context, the theme of trade and exchange is primarily interesting because it reveals the origin and intensity of foreign influences on internal developments, and thus it shows in which direction to look for analogies in support of attempts to understand the social structure of the period in question. Secondarily, it is relevant because knowledge about how the surplus available was used in trade contributes to our understanding of both the economic system and the social structure as well as the interaction between them.

In the Late Roman Iron Age and the Migration period there was, in Scandinavia, a prestige-goods exchange that reached, through various middlemen, regions all over Europe from the Black Sea to the North Sea (Hansen 1987; Hedeager 1988; Näsman 1991c). The connections to Central Europe and to the east were broken in the sixth century, not to be reopened till the Viking Age. This change gave the Danish region a key position between the North Sea and the Baltic, between the Continent and Scandinavia proper (Näsman 1986). The end of the eastern connections is a main cause of the dominating position that was held by the Merovingian culture in the development of Scandinavian material culture, supplemented later in the Viking Age by influences from the insular area as well as from the Carolingians and Ottonian Saxony. The effect of strong Frankish impact on Scandinavian culture can hardly be overestimated (Ørsnes 1970; Vierck 1981; Steuer 1987a) and, indeed, its effect must also be considered on phenomena outside the reach of normal archaeological methods, as for instance on political organisation (cf. L. Jørgensen 1995b).

In this way South Scandinavia gradually became part of a commercial zone in west Europe, as revealed in the eighth century by the distribution of sceattas (Fig. 2): the so-called Wodan-monster type has a significant concentration in Ribe, the earliest proto-urban site in South Scandinavia (S. Jensen 1992). This distribution pattern can be supplemented by the distribution of lava quernstones from the Rhine (L.C. Nielsen 1987, fig. 23; Steuer 1987b, fig. 10) and other imports to enhance the impression of Denmark's inclusion in the Frankish-Frisian North Sea market (Wood 1983). The growing trade with the west is certainly an important element in the making of the Danish kingdom, and in the Viking Age the rapid urbanisation in the late tenth and eleventh century demonstrates that Denmark gained great profit from its dominating position in the North Sea – Baltic trade network (Andrén 1989).

Central places, proto-towns, and early towns

The first Scandinavian, complex central settlement appeared already in the third century, in the Late Roman Iron Age, at Gudme, Funen, and it included a beach market at Lundeborg (Nielsen *et al.* 1994). Further central sites appeared in the course of the following centuries, and thus the number of contemporary central-places grew rapidly. By the year 700 they are found in virtually every settlement area of South Scandinavia (Callmer 1994; Ulriksen 1994). These sites were not only trading stations, as most were labelled a few years ago, but many of them were also certainly centres that fulfilled important political, social and religious functions (Näsman 1991d). Many of them seem to have served as manorial residences.

Thus an increasing complexity in the settlement pattern accompanies the changing structure of the rural settlement and the increasing agrarian production. In fact, the elite of the centres based their power on the mobilisation of the rural surplus; at the same time, one

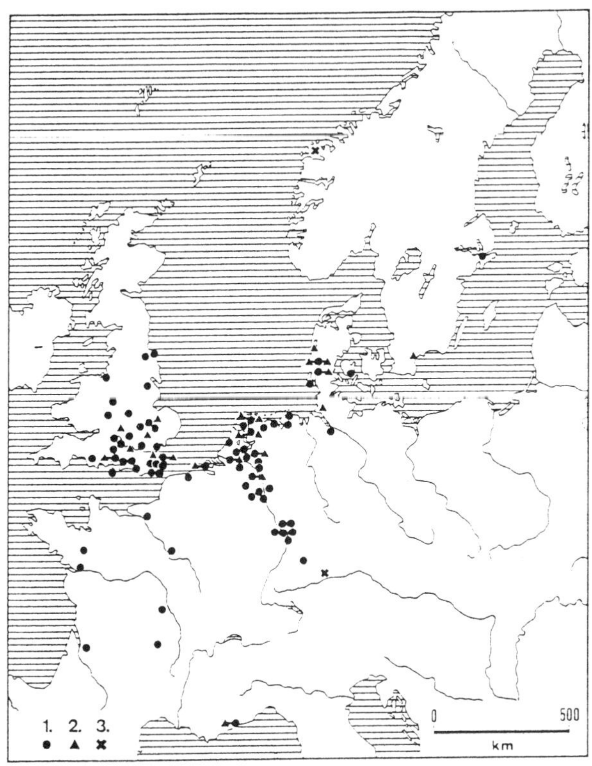

Fig. 2 A distribution map of sceattas demonstrates the growth of a North Sea market, including South Scandinavia. 1: Porcupine type; 2: Wodan-Monster type; 3: other types. After Steuer 1987b with a porcupine sceatta found at Gudme added.

can say that the stimulus to produce a rural surplus probably came from an increasing demand of the elite at the centres.

The number of new central-places did not grew so fast in the Viking Age. What happened in this period is rather that some are replaced by other sites, and that urbanisation began which meant that the old central-places lost their position and were replaced by towns like Hedeby, Ribe, Århus, and so on (Jensen and Watt 1993; Jensen 1993). Hedeby and Ribe are the first urbanised settlements in Denmark, and excavations show that they started in the eighth century, a little later than the famous emporia Quentovic, Dorestad, Hamwic and Ipswic of the Franks, Frisians and Anglo-Saxons; their lay-out, buildings, etc. are, however, quite similar (cf. Hodges 1982).

So today it must be concluded that at the threshold to the Viking Age Scandinavian societies had a much more advanced economic system and a much more complex social organisation than was believed only fifteen years ago. This growth of central places started in the Late Roman period, the speed of development increased in the Migration period and culminated around 700. After this a qualitative change started and urbanisation began slowly to replace the central settlements with the proto-towns and early towns of the Viking Age.

Warfare

Forty-seven sacrifices of spoils-of-war at twenty-eight sites demonstrate frequent warfare in South Scandinavia from *c.* 200 to *c.* 500 A.D. (Fig. 3). These finds are evidence of conflicts over resources and peoples as well as the territories settled by them. Perhaps control of the communication channels through South Scandinavia was a main goal. But raids by King Hugleik and other Danes against the Merovingian realm in the sixth century reveal that the military expeditions were not restricted to Nordic waters (Wood 1983). Recent analyses of the military equipment of the sacrificed spoils-of-war demonstrate that the warriors of the period were not an unorganised 'wild bunch', but properly trained soldiers with a command structure and considerable knowledge of the tactics of contemporary warfare (Ilkjær 1993).

The defence of threatened peoples is archaeologically demonstrated by fortifications, dykes and underwater barriers as well as ring-forts (M.S. Jørgensen 1988; Rieck *et al.* 1993). The datings cluster in two periods, the Late Roman-Early Migration period (third to fifth centuries) and the Viking Age (tenth to eleventh centuries). The first is contemporary with the many sacrifices of spoils-of war, the second with a period when written sources are available (Fig. 4). The first period could be characterised as one of tribal warfare, in which the many polities were forced to join larger confederations through the pressure of endemic warfare and conquests (for the concepts, see Halsall 1989). In this period, the inhabitants of South Scandinavia too were 'peoples in arms', as Herwig Wolfram has expressed it (Wolfram 1988, 7). In the archaeological record, the indicators of war seem to disappear after AD 500, not to reappear in large numbers till the Viking Age. Was this period a *Pax Danorum*, as suggested by Ian Wood (1983)? I think that the silent archaeological record indeed could indicate that the Danes had won almost total hegemony in the eastern North Sea basin and the south-western Baltic. So endemic warfare ceased and wars of conquest became less frequent. Thus this phase can be understood as a period of consolidation between an early phase of tribal warfare and a later phase in which the territorial defence of the Danish kingdom becomes visible in the record.

The wars between Denmark and the Carolingian empire in the ninth century are the first wars in Denmark to be mentioned in the written record. But archaeology demonstrates the presence of serious military threats to Denmark in the centuries before: the throwing up of the first dyke at Danevirke in the late seventh century as well as reinforcements of the dyke and the building of a barrier in the Schlei Fjord in AD 737 and the building in AD 726 of a canal across the island of Samsø at the approach to the Danish Belts (H.H. Andersen 1993; A.N. Jørgensen 1995). The strategic localisation of these defence works reveals that the threats were met with a military organisation including both navy and army. This is perhaps the first appearance of a national defence organisation similar to

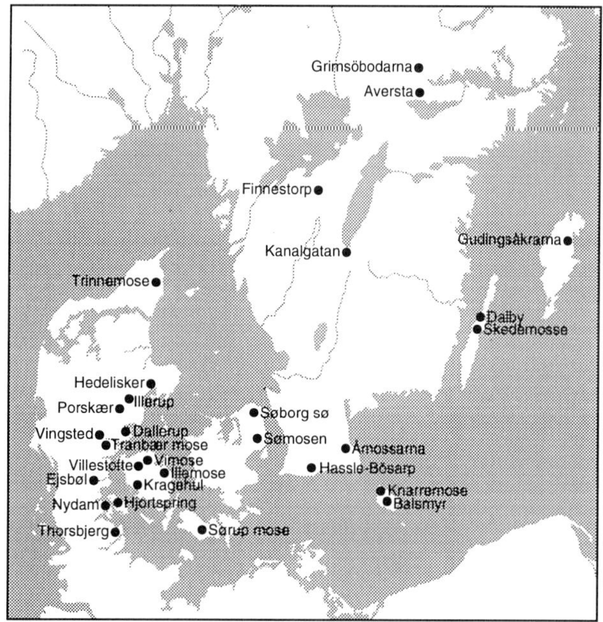

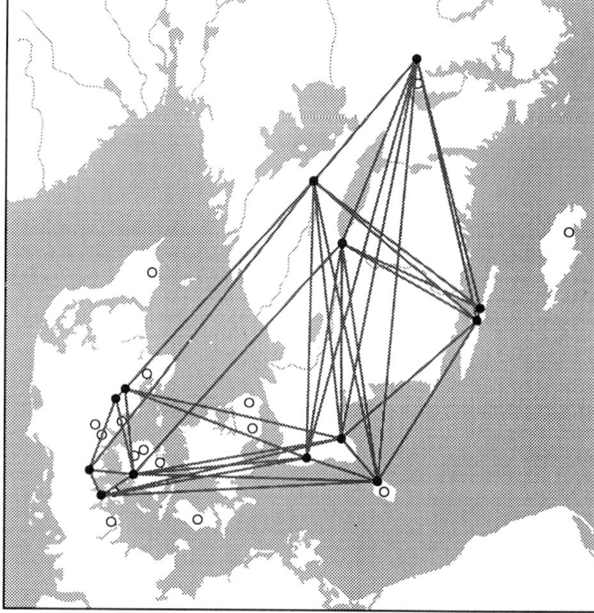

Fig. 3a–b Distribution maps of all sites with booty sacrifices in Scandinavia. To the left (a) place names of all sites. To the right (b) the sacrifices representing battles of the fifth century (filled circles) are connected with lines to give an image of the war zone of the century. After Fabech 1996.

the so-called *leding* (levy) of the Viking Age (Lund 1996). So the first mention of Danish fleets and armies in the Frankish annals after AD 800 must not be taken as the first Danish activity in the military theatre of the South Baltic and the North Sea. According to explicit texts the ninth-century wars are clearly national wars, either wars of conquest on a large scale between kingdoms, primarily with the Franks, or civil wars which for a large part seem to be triggered off by the same aggressive Frankish diplomacy. The archaeological record indicates that warfare now was quite different from war in the Roman and Migration periods.

Thus the two phases of fortifications mirror two different military political situations: in the Late Roman and Migration periods they are tribal wars and conflicts over resource control; in the Late Merovingian period and the Viking Age they concern a Danish kingdom's territorial defence against external attempts at conquest.

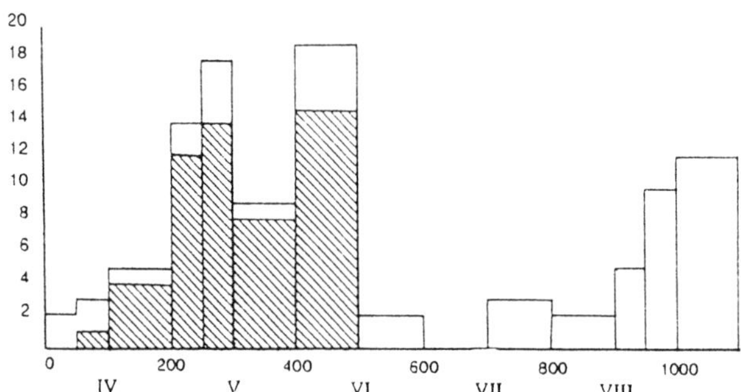

Fig. 4 A sketch of the frequency of 'war indicators' in the record. Booty sacrifices are represented by the hatched area. Other war indicators are dated fortifications, ship blockages and battles mentioned in written sources. Weapon graves are excluded, since they seem rather to reflect internal conflicts of a social rather than a martial character. IV: Early Roman Iron Age; V: Late Roman Iron Age; VI: Migration period; VII: Merovingian period; VIII: Viking Age. After Näsman 1994.

Religious changes

The conversion to Christianity is often considered a major turning point in Scandinavian history. And in a way it was, of course. But the importance of Christianisation is heavily overestimated in Scandinavian history. Almost everything observable in the High Middle Ages has been explained by it. But modern archaeology has been able to demonstrate that most of these phenomena started to develop before the official conversion. The conversion was simply a step, and not even the last one, in a process that had started long before. A result of this is that the paganism of Scandinavia must not mislead us into believing that the Scandinavians were barbarians (in the modern sense; in contemporary sources pagan is identical with barbarian).

Charlotte Fabech has published a diagram (Fig. 5) which shows how a great change in cult practice took place around AD 500 when the use of bogs and lakes for offerings stopped. Instead religious objects are found

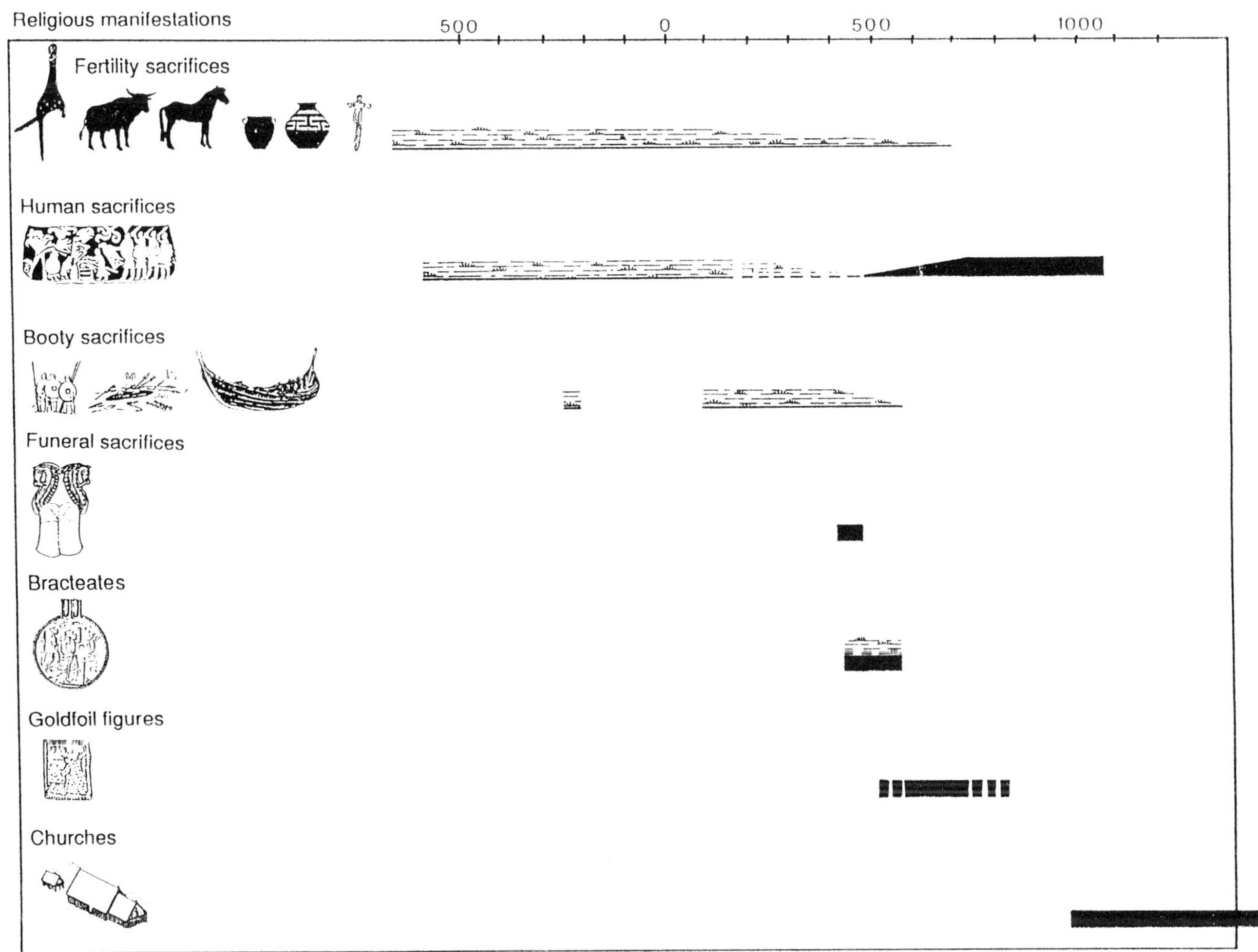

Fig. 5 Sketch demonstrating the distribution over time of religious manifestations in the archaeological record of South Scandinavia. Sacrifices in wet land are marked with bog hatching, finds from dry land are marked in black. A cult site discontinuity is seen in the Migration period, a religious discontinuity at the conversion. After Fabech 1991.

hoarded in settlement contexts, sometimes – and this is a new phenomenon that appears at this time – in the postholes of the great halls of the magnates (Herschend 1993). This indicates a change whereby the elite has taken over the control of religion in a new way: they have made a personal institution of religious practice. Plausibly the elite had won this new position on the basis of their achievements during the period of warfare during the third to fifth centuries. The close link between cult and elite continued unbroken after Christianisation, that is the church was built by the magnate and on his ground (Nyborg 1993). So indeed we have a kind of cult-site continuity from the pagan period into the Christian era (cf. O. Olsen 1986). A great break took place in the Migration period, however, and it is associated with other social and political changes that in an archaeological perspective seem more radical than those at the conversion in the tenth century. It is after the fifth century that the archaeological material demonstrates a close link between cult and magnates, chieftains and kings. This is certainly one important element in the formation of a Danish kingdom.

Political development

Analyses of material culture reveal that South Scandinavia in the Early Roman Iron Age consisted of many small regions (Ringtved 1988), perhaps as many as fifteen, and on the basis of written sources like Tacitus and Ptolemy one can guess that they correspond to tribal areas. In the Late Roman Iron Age and the Migration period the formation of a South Scandinavian super-region can be discerned, but it still seems subdivided into a small number of distinguishable culture zones, perhaps not more than seven, and, again, on the basis of written sources like Jordanes and Procopius, one can guess that the small tribes had joined into larger confederations precisely as on the Continent.

In my opinion and in the opinion of other Danish archaeologists (cf. Hedeager 1992), a Danish kingdom had appeared not later than the end of the Migration period, in the sixth century. On the basis of the well-studied material culture of the early Merovingian period (Ørsnes 1970; K.H. Nielsen 1991), one can assume that it had its core area in central Denmark – South Jutland, Funen, and Sjælland – with a close periphery of North Jutland, south Halland, Scania, Blekinge and Bornholm. Probably more loosely attached to the Danish hegemony was a more distant periphery in South Sweden.

So the Danish kingdom already had a history of at least a couple of centuries when it first appeared in the Frankish chronicles at the end of the eighth century. On an archaeological basis, there is no reason at all to believe that the Danish elite and their kings were ignorant about what was happening in Europe before the first written evidence proves that they were in fact very well-informed (cf. Wamers 1994). Certainly they could cope with the problems that appeared. And the earliest written evidence supports such a view.

Danish involvement in European politics is first clearly observable in 777 when the rebellious Saxon leader Widukind instead of appearing at a meeting called at Paderborn by Charlemagne took refuge in the land of King Sigfred, king of the Danes. In 782 Sigfred sent representatives to a meeting with Charlemagne at Lippe. Space does not allow more examples to be given, so this must suffice to support the archaeologically reasonable assumption that the Danish kingdom was a political and military actor on the North European scene long before the Viking Age. In the light of the new archaeological picture of the Danes and their kingdom there is no reason to uphold the historians' traditional picture of the Danes as a barbaric horde of looters.

In the light of all these arguments, three phases can be described (Fig. 6):

Roman Iron Age: Tribal societies with chieftains or small kings.

Late Roman Iron Age, Migration period, and early Merovingian period: A process of amalgamation started and warfare characterises the period. The result is the formation of tribal confederations with an overlord and subordinate regional kings. Written sources speak in favour of the Danes as the people who eventually won hegemony over South Scandinavia in the sixth to seventh centuries.

Late Merovingian period and Viking Age: A process began in which local chieftains were replaced by royal agents. The last area to be integrated under direct Danish royal rule, in the reign of Svend Forkbeard, was probably Scania.

Thus the making of Medieval Denmark was finished.

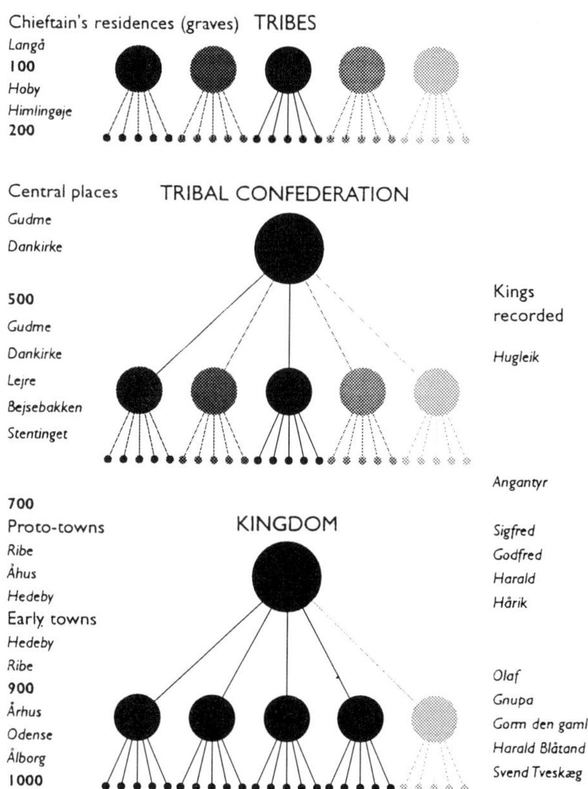

Fig. 6 Sketch covering three hypothetical phases in the development of South Scandinavian polities into a Danish kingdom. To the left important sites with finds indicating a central position in contemporary social and political development, and to the right some of the rulers mentioned in the written sources. After Näsman 1997.

Final remarks

As a result of archaeological achievements in the last decades, a number of traditional views about Scandinavian late prehistory appear less likely, or rather erroneous. It is not true that Scandinavia stepped out of the *coulisse* of obscurity to enter the west European socio-political scene only at the very beginning of the Viking Age. It is an exaggeration that Christianisation was a decisive historical turning-point. It is an underestimation that the pagans were incapable of organisation and that a formation of a Danish kingdom therefore is unthinkable before the late Viking Age.

The Christianisation was only one step in a long, unstable winding staircase leading to the Scandinavian Middle Ages. A Danish kingdom probably already existed in the late Migration period. Archaeological studies of settlement hierarchies and military history demonstrate that the barbarians certainly could organise themselves long before the conversion. In my opinion, the main contribution which the Scandinavians made to 'the formation of Europe' was not their conversion but their commercial and political activities during the preceding centuries, when the Scandinavians became integrated as a periphery of the Merovingian west (Näsman 1998).

Unfortunately, the ethnogenesis of the Danes is beyond the reach of study, but a rough hypothesis may be formulated. The Danes were one of several tribes in the

Roman Iron Age, somewhere in South Scandinavia. Events outside the Scandinavian scene were of fundamental importance for the possibility of the Danish *gens* to grow in power in the Late Roman and Migration periods. The Danes could already during the early Merovingian period usurp power over all important channels of communication between the Baltic and the North Sea, between Scandinavia proper and the Continent. On the basis of this key position, a kingdom was created. Its survival was by no means a matter of course. In their continued efforts to secure the Danish position against the attacks of neighbours, capable kings established the borders of high medieval Denmark in the course of the Viking Age.

References

Aaby, Bent 1993: 'Man and the environment', in Hvass, S. and Storgaard, B. (eds.) *Digging into the Past. 25 Years of Archaeology in Denmark* (Copenhagen/Højbjerg), 16–19.

Andersen, H. Hellmuth 1993: 'Nye Danevirke-undersøgelser', *Sønderjysk Månedsskrift* 1993/11, 307–312.

Andrén, Anders 1989: 'The early town in Scandinavia', in Randsborg, K. (ed.) *The Birth of Europe: Archaeology and Social Development in the First Millennium A.D.*, Analecta Romana Instituti Danici. Suppl. 16 (Rome), 173–177.

Bassett, S. (ed.) 1989: *The Origins of Anglo-Saxon Kingdoms* (London).

Berglund, Björn E. (ed.) 1991: *The Cultural Landscape during 6000 years in Southern Sweden – the Ystad Project*, Ecological Bulletins 41 (Lund).

Callmer, Johan 1992: 'From Bronze Age dispersed settlements to medieval village in the Krageholm area', in Larsson, L. *et al.* (eds.) *The Archaeology of the Cultural Landscape. Fieldwork and Research in a South Swedish Rural Region*, Acta Archaeologica Lundensia Ser. in 4° 19 (Stockholm/Lund), 395–410.

Callmer, Johan 1994: 'Urbanization in Scandinavia and the Baltic region *c.* AD 700–1100', in Ambrosiani, B. and Clarke, H. (eds.) *Developments around the Baltic and the North Sea in the Viking Age*, The Twelfth Viking Congress/Birka Studies 3 (Stockholm), 50–90.

Claessen, Henri 1983: 'Kinship, chiefdom, and reciprocity – on the use of anthropological concepts in archaeology', in Brandt, R. and Slofstra, J. (eds.) *Roman and Native in the Low Countries – Spheres of Interaction*, Brit. Arch. Rep. Internat. Ser. 184 (Oxford), 211–222.

Fabech, Charlotte 1991: 'Booty sacrifices in Southern Scandinavia: a reassessment', in Garwood, P. *et al.* (eds.) *Sacred and Profane*, Oxford University Committee for Archaeology Monograph 32 (Oxford), 88–94.

Fabech, Charlotte 1996: 'Booty sacrifices in Southern Scandinavia – a history of warfare and ideology', in *Roman Reflections* (Rome), 135–138.

Fabech, Charlotte and Ringtved, Jytte 1995: 'Magtens geografi i Sydskandinavien', in Resi, H.G (ed.) *Produksjon og Samfunn. Om Erverv, Spesialisering og Bosetning i Norden i 1. årtusind e.Kr.*, Universitets Oldsaksamling. Varia 30 (Oslo), 11–37 and Summary.

Halsall, Guy 1989: 'Anthropology and the study of pre-conquest warfare and society: the ritual war in Anglo-Saxon England', in Hawkes, S.C. (ed.) *Weapons and Warfare in Anglo-Saxon England* (Oxford), 155–177.

Hansen, Ulla Lund 1987: *Römischer Import im Norden*, Nordiske Fortidsminder B 10 (Copenhagen).

Heather, Peter 1991: *Goths and Romans 332–489* (Oxford).

Hedeager, Lotte 1980: 'Besiedlung, soziale Struktur und politische Struktur in der älteren und jüngren Kaiserzeit Ostdänemarks', *Praehistorische Zeitschrift* 55/1, 38–109.

Hedeager, Lotte 1988: 'Money economy and prestige economy in the Roman Iron Age', in Hårdh, B. *et al.* (eds.) *Trade and Exchange in Prehistory. Studies in Honour of Berta Stjernquist*, Acta Archaeologica Lundensia, Ser. in 8° 16 (Lund), 148–153.

Hedeager, Lotte 1992: *Iron-Age Societies. From Tribe to State in Northern Europe, 500 BC to AD 700* (Oxford).

Heidinga, Anthonie 1987: *Medieval Settlement and Economy North of the Lower Rhine. Archaeology and History of Kootwijk and the Veluwe*, Cingula 9 (Assens).

Herschend, Frands 1993: 'The origin of the hall in southern Scandinavia', *Tor* 25, 175–199.

Hodges, Richard 1982: *Dark Age Economics* (London).

Hvass, Steen 1988: 'The status of the Iron Age settlement in Denmark', in Bierma, M. *et al.* (eds.) *Arheologie en Landschap*, [Festschrift to H.T. Waterbolk] (Groningen), 97–132.

Hvass, Steen 1993: 'The Iron Age and the Viking Period: Settlement', in Hvass, S. and Storgaard, B. (eds.) *Digging into the Past. 25 Years of Archaeology in Denmark* (Copenhagen/ Højbjerg), 187–194.

Ilkjær, Jørgen 1993: *Illerup Ådal 3–4. Die Gürtel*, Jysk Arkæologisk Selskabs Skrifter 25/3–4 (Højbjerg/Århus).

James, Edward 1988: *The Franks* (Oxford).

Jensen, Jørgen 1982: *The Prehistory of Denmark* (London/New York).

Jensen, Stig 1992: *The Vikings of Ribe* (Ribe).

Jensen, Stig 1993: 'Early towns', in Hvass, S. and Storgaard, B. (eds.) *Digging into the Past. 25 Years of Archaeology in Denmark* (Copenhagen/ Højbjerg), 202–205.

Jensen, Stig and Watt, Margrethe 1993: 'Trading sites and central places', in Hvass, S. and Storgaard, B. (eds.) *Digging into the Past. 25 Years of Archaeology in Denmark* (Copenhagen/ Højbjerg), 195–201.

Jørgensen, Anne Nørgård 1995: 'New investigations of the Kanhave Canal', *Maritime Archaeology Newsletter* 5, 9–15.

Jørgensen, Lars 1995a: 'The warrior aristocracy of Gudme? The emergence of landed aristocracy in Late Iron Age Denmark', in Resi, H.G. (ed.) *Produksjon og Samfunn. Om Erverv, Spesialisering og Bosetning i Norden i 1. årtusind e.Kr.*, Universitets Oldsaksamling. Varia 30 (Oslo), 205–220 and Summary.

Jørgensen, Lars 1995b: 'Stormandssæder og skattefund i 3. – 12. århundrede', *Fortid og Nutid* 1995/2, 83–110.

Jørgensen, Mogens Schou 1988: 'Vej, vejstrøg og vejspærring. Jernalderens landfærdsel', in Mortensen, P. and Rasmussen, B. (eds.) *Fra Stamme til Stat i Danmark. 1 Jernalderens Samfund*, Jysk Arkæologisk Selskabs Skrifter 22/1 (Højbjerg/Århus), 101–116 and Summary.

Le Goff, Jacques 1988: *Medieval Civilization 400–1500* (Oxford) [1st ed. 1964 *La Civilisation de l'Occident Médiéval*. Paris].

Lund, Niels 1996: *Lið, Leding and Landeværn* (Roskilde, Vikingeskibshallen).

Mortensen, Peder and Rasmussen, Birgit M. (eds.) 1988: *Fra Stamme til Stat i Danmark. 1 Jernalderens Samfund*, Jysk Arkæologisk Selskabs Skrifter 22/1 (Højbjerg/Århus). Summaries.

Mortensen, Peder and Rasmussen, Birgit M. (eds.) 1991: *Fra Stamme til Stat i Danmark. 2 Høvdingesamfund og kongemagt*, Jysk Arkæologisk Selskabs Skrifter 22/2 (Højbjerg/Århus). Summaries.

Myhre, Bjørn 1992: 'The royal cemetery at Borre. Vestfold', in M.O.H. Carver (ed.) *The Age of Sutton Hoo* (Woodbridge), 301–313 and pls. 19–22.

Myrdal, Janken 1985: *Medeltidens Åkerbruk*, Nordiske museets Handlingar 105 (Stockholm). Summary.

Myrdal, Janken 1988: 'Agrarteknik och samhälle under två tusen år', in Näsman, U. and Lund, J. (eds.) *Folkevandringstiden i Norden. En Krisetid mellem ældre og yngre Jernalder?* (Århus), 187–220.

Näsman, Ulf 1986: 'Vendel period glass from Eketorp-II, Öland, Sweden', *Acta Archaeologica* 55 (for 1984), 55–116.

Näsman, Ulf 1988a: 'Analogislutning i nordisk jernalderarkæologi', in Mortensen, P. and Rasmussen, B. (eds.) *Fra Stamme til Stat i Danmark. 1 Jernalderens Stammesamfund,* Jysk Arkæologisk Selskabs Skrifter 22/1 (Højbjerg/Århus), 123–140 and Summary.

Näsman, Ulf 1988b: 'Den folkvandringstida krisen i Sydskandinavien?', in Näsman, U. and Lund, J. (eds.) *Folkevandringstiden i Norden. En krisetid mellem ældre og yngre jernalder?* (Århus), 227–255.

Näsman, Ulf 1991a: 'Det syvende århundrede', in Mortensen, P. and Rasmussen, B. (eds.) *Fra Stamme til Stat i Danmark. 2 Høvdingesamfund og Kongemagt*, Jysk Arkæologisk Selskabs Skrifter 22/2 (Højbjerg/Århus), 165–177. Summary.

Näsman, Ulf 1991b: 'The Germanic Iron Age and Viking Age in Danish archaeology since 1976', *Journal of Danish Archaeology* 8 (for 1989), 159–187.

Näsman, Ulf 1991c: 'Sea trade during the Scandinavian Iron Age', in Crumlin-Pedersen, O. and Hansen, K. (eds.) *Aspects of Maritime Scandinavia AD 200–1200* (Roskilde, Vikingeskibshallen), 23–40.

Näsman, Ulf 1991d: 'Some comments on the symposium A Social organization and regional variation, Sandbjerg Manor, April 1989', in Fabech, C. and Ringtved, J. (eds.) *Samfundsfunds Organisation og Regional Variation*, Jysk Arkælogisk Selskabs Skrifter 27 (Højbjerg/Århus), 328–333.

Näsman, Ulf 1994: 'The Iron Age graves of Öland – representative of what?', in Stjernquist, B. (ed.) *Prehistoric Graves as a Source of Information*, Kungl. Vitterhets Historie och Antikvitets Akdemiens Konferenser 29 (Stockholm), 15–30.

Näsman, Ulf 1997: 'Från region till rike – från stam till stat', in Krøger, F. (ed.) *Riksamling: Kongemakt og Høvdingemakt*, Karmøyseminaret 1996 (Karmøy), 46–65, refs. 110–114.

Näsman, Ulf 1998: 'The Scandinavians' view on Europe in the Migration Period', in Larsson, L. and Stjernquist, B. (eds.) *World-View of Prehistoric Man* [Festschrift to Gad Rausing] (Lund), KUHAA Konferenser 40 (Stockholm), 103–121.

Nielsen, Karen Høilund 1991: 'Centrum og periferi i 6.–8. årh.', in Mortensen, P. and Rasmussen, B. (eds.) *Fra Stamme til Stat i Danmark. 2 Høvdingesamfund og Kungemagt*, Jysk Arkæologisk Selskabs Skrifter 22/2 (Højbjerg/Århus), 127–154 and Summary.

Nielsen, Leif Chr. 1987: 'Omgård. The Viking Age water-mill complex', *Acta Archaeologica* 57 (for 1986), 177–204.

Nielsen, Poul Otto, Randsborg, Klavs and Thrane, Henrik (eds.) 1994: *The Archaeology of Gudme and Lundeborg*, Arkæologiske Studier 10 (Copenhagen).

Nyborg, Ebbe 1993: 'Church and cloister', in Hvass, S. and Storgaard, B. (eds.) *Digging into the Past. 25 Years of Archaeology in Denmark* (Copenhagen/Højbjerg), 242–247.

Olsen, Olaf 1986: 'Is there a relationship between pagan and Christian places of worship in Scandinavia', in Butler, L.A.S and Morris, R.K. (eds.) *The Anglo-Saxon Church*, Council of British Archaeology. Research Reports 60 (London), 126–130.

Ørsnes, Mogens 1970: 'Südskandinavische Ornamentik in der jüngeren germanischen Eisenzeit', *Acta Archaeologica* 40 (for1969), 1–121.

Pohl, Walter 1980: 'Die Gepiden und die Gentes an der mittleren Donau nach dem Zerfall des Attilareiches', in Wolfram, H. and Daim, F. (eds.) *Die Völker an der mittleren und unteren Donau im fünften und sechsten Jahrhundert*, Österreichischen Akademie der Wissenschaften. Veröffentlichungen der Kommission für Frühmittelalterforschung 4 (Wien), 239–305.

Randsborg, Klavs 1980: *The Viking Age in Denmark. The Formation of a State* (London).

Randsborg, Klavs 1991: *The First Millennium A.D. in Europe and the Mediterranean* (Cambridge).

Renfrew, Colin and Cherry, John F. (eds.) 1986: *Peer Polity Interaction and Socio-political Change* (Cambridge).

Rieck, Flemming, Andersen, Steen W. and Roesdahl, Else 1993: 'Territorial defence', in Hvass, S. and Storgaard, B. (eds.) *Digging into the Past. 25 Years of Archaeology in Denmark* (Copenhagen/Højbjerg), 210–214.

Ringtved, Jytte 1988: 'Regionalitet. Et jysk eskempel fra yngre romertid og ældre germanertid', in Mortensen, P. and Rasmussen, B. (eds.) *Fra Stamme til Stat i Danmark. 1 Jernalderens Stammesamfund*, Jysk Arkæologisk Selskabs Skrifter 22/1 (Højbjerg/Århus), 37–52 and Summary.

Sawyer, Peter H. 1978: *From Roman Britain to Norman England* (London).

Sawyer, Peter H. and Wood, Ian N. (eds.) 1977: *Early Medieval Kingship* (Leeds).

Schlesinger, Walter 1973: 'Über germanisches Heerkönigtum', in Schlesinger, W. *Das Königtum* (Lindau/Konstanz), 05–141 [first publ. in *Beiträge zur deutschen Verfassungsgeschichte des Mittelalters* 1, Göttingen, 1963, 53ff].

Steuer, Heiko 1987a: 'Helm und Ringschwert', *Studien zur Sachsenforschung* 6, 189–236.

Steuer, Heiko 1987b: 'Der Handel der Wikingerzeit zwischen Nord- und Westeuropa aufgrund archäologischer Zeugnisse', in Düwel, K. *et al.* (eds.) *Untersuchungen zu Handel und Verkehr der vor- und frühgeschichtlichen Zeit in Mittel- und Nordeuropa. IV Der Handel der Karolinger- und Wikingerzeit*, Abhandlungen d .Akad. d. Wissenschaften, Phil.-Hist. Kl. III, 156 (Göttingen), 113–197.

Ulriksen, Jens 1994: 'Danish sites and settlements with a maritime context AD 200–1200',. *Antiquity* 68, 797–811.

Vierck, Hayo 1981: 'Imitatio imperii und interpretatio germanica vor der Wikingerzeit', in Zeitler, R. (ed.) *Les Pays du Nord et Byzance*, Figura N.S. 19 (Uppsala), 64–113.

Wamers, Egon 1994: 'König im Grenzland. Neue Analyse des Bootkammergrabes von Haiðaby', *Acta Archaeologica* 65, 1–56.

Waterbolk, H. T. 1991: 'Das mittelalterliche Siedlungswesen in Drenthe', in Böhme, H.W. (ed.) *Siedlungen und Landesausbau zur Salierzeit. 1. In den nördlichen Landschaften des Reiches* (Sigmaringen), 47–108.

Wenskus, Reinhard 1961: *Stammesbildung und Verfassung* (Cologne) [2nd ed. 1977].

Wolfram, Herwig 1971: 'The shaping of the early medieval kingdom', *Viator* 1 (for 1970), 1–20.

Wolfram, Herwig 1988: *History of the Goths* (Los Angeles).

Wood, Ian 1983: *The Merovingian North Sea* (Alingsås).

Wood, Ian 1994: *The Merovingian Kingdoms 450–571* (London/New York).

Wylie, Alison 1985: 'The reaction against analogy', in Schiffer, M.B. (ed.) *Advances in Archaeological Method and Theory* 8 (London/New York), 63–111.

Yorke, Barbara 1990: *Kings and Kingdoms of Early Anglo-Saxon England* (London) [2nd ed. 1992].

Zimmermann, W. Haio 1991: 'Die früh- bis hochmittelalterliche Wüstung Dalem', in Böhme, H.W. (ed.) *Siedlungen und Landesausbau zur Salierzeit. 1. In den nördlichen Landschaften des Reiches* (Sigmaringen), 37–46.

Zimmermann, W. Haio 1992: *Die Siedlungen des 1. bis 6. Jahrhunderts nach Christus von Flögeln-Eekhöltjen, Niedersachsen. Die Bauformen und ihre Funktionen*, Probleme der Küstenforschung im südlichen Nordseegebiet 19 (Hildesheim).

Zöllner, Erich 1970: *Geschichte der Franken bis zur Mitte des 6. Jahrhundert* (München).

Anglo-Saxon Studies in Archaeology and History 10, 1999

The Frisian Achievement in the First Millennium AD

Anthonie Heidinga

Introduction[1]

The title of this paper may sound rather pompous, as if the Frisians are to be sold on the archaeological market. In a way they are, for my intention is indeed to draw international attention to the somewhat neglected part of the southern North Sea coast which was called Frisia in the early Middle Ages. I have to admit that I am trying to sell an unfinished product – the project which I am introducing here was only recently started – but the data now available justify the label 'achievement'. During the early Middle Ages Frisia appeared on the European stage, being the intermediary between the Continent, England and Scandinavia. Thus a full understanding of what happened here provides a major contribution to North-western European history.

Although there is ample literature about Frisians, the Frisian region, Frisian trade, Frisian language, etc., and the shelves of the museums sag under the weight of the archaeological finds collected in the area, the picture of protohistoric Frisia has remained vague. As far as the Dutch part of it is concerned, most archaeological research in the coastal wetlands has focused on specific regions or sites, been merely descriptive or has dealt with man-environment relations from a processual viewpoint. A coherent and holistic picture of the whole region, which also paid attention to socio-political and cultural processes seen from a historical-anthropological point of view, is still missing.

Another obstacle in the way of a coherent view of the Frisian past is the fact that the data from the Dutch part, on the one hand, and those from the German coastal area, on the other (in particular the remarkable results in the field of settlement archaeology), have never been really interconnected, in spite of the good relationship between archaeologists from both sides of the border.

In the few general studies on the Frisians (Halbertsma 1965–1966; 1982; 1989; Russchen 1967; Blok 1979; Lebecq 1983) archaeology in fact plays a minor role, which is partly excusable for there is a severe lack of published and recently evaluated data. One aspect of Frisian history, however, has always drawn national and international attention: the early-medieval long-distance trade and its impressive manifestation at the famous *emporium* of Dorestad, which has been excavated during the last decades (Van Es 1990; Van Es and Hessing 1994, 82–119, 184–94). Research in this field, however, almost bypasses Frisia itself. So the role of Dorestad is mainly seen in its Frankish and international context, and we meet the historically known Frisian tradesmen in all parts of Europe but hardly ever in their homeland. The socio-political and economic background and the context 'at home' of this economic upheaval has remained under-exposed, as has the interaction of Frisia with the outside world in general,and not exclusively in commercial terms. So Frisia, which even before the rise of Dorestad must have had an important intermediary position between the Frankish realm and the emerging polities in England and Scandinavia, wrongly remained in the periphery of attention in the international discourse on the transformation of the Western and Northern European world in the first millennium AD.

This is one of the reasons why a multidisciplinary project called *From Scheldt to Weser. Frisia in Northwest-European perspective (3rd–10th century)* was initiated in 1995 by the three archaeological institutes active in the field of the protohistory of the Dutch coastal region: the **Groningen Institute of Archaeology** (GIA) of the State University of Groningen, the **Institute for Pre- and Protohistoric Archaeology** (IPP) of the University of Amsterdam and the **State Service for Archaeological Investigations** (ROB). The aim of this joint enterprise is to arrive at a coherent picture of the developments in the region from the late Roman period to the beginning of the later Middle Ages, by asking relevant questions, integrating available data, stimulating new research and by creating an international forum of discussion for archaeologists and representatives of related disciplines. The keywords of the project are *communication*, in the sense of every form of interaction between people and their social, natural and supernatural environment, and *identity*, that is the 'membership' of any social, ethnic or other group. A central issue of the project is the understanding of the growth of political and economic power in the area which culminated in the seventh century, according to Martin Carver 'probably the most intriguing period in European history' (Carver 1993, 39).

In my paper and in the contribution in this volume by my fellow-researcher in the project, Danny Gerrets, only some aspects of the project can be dealt with. Inevitably there is some overlap, but I shall try to elucidate the more general aspects, whilst he looks at Frisia from a northern viewpoint, that is the *terp* region, where a key site for Frisian archaeology has recently been excavated.

The transformation of the Frisian world: a short outline

During the first millennium AD a remarkable transformation took place in the coastal area of the present Netherlands and adjacent Northern Germany, a realm which I shall provisionally call *Frisia* (the justification for which will follow). It is even questionable whether one can speak of a transformation, for while the contrast between before and after is distinct, in the presumed transitional phase darkness if not emptiness prevails: if anywhere, here in the Low Countries the Migration Period marks a real break in history. During the Iron Age and Roman period this soggy edge of the European continent was fairly densely populated, but there is little evidence that the important political and cultural developments taking place beyond the Frisian horizon had any lasting effect on the introvert, seemingly egalitarian and isolated societies beyond the river Rhine – the people whom the Romans called *Frisii*. Even the impact of *romanitas* was superficial, as far as the *translimes* part of the region is concerned (Van Es 1965–1966; 1972). In the late Roman period the 'Frisians' were also strikingly absent from the arena of political growth amongst the Germanic tribes beyond the *limes*. Although some human activities in the fourth or even fifth century are attested in some parts of Frisia, the overall picture is one of depopulation on a large scale from the third century onwards. Anyway, the demographic basis for any form of political organization other than on a very local scale was lacking. In this sense the Frisians no longer existed. End of story – but remarkably not of the Frisians.

After the 'pause' of the Migration period we see quite a different picture. Step by step the region again filled up with people, partly due to the natural growth of surviving groups, but mainly to immigration, as seems to have been the case in the fifth century in the northern salt-marshes (Gerrets, this volume). In contrast to the old Frisians, the new ones, in particular those from the northern salt-marshes, soon participated actively in international networks, which in the seventh to ninth centuries culminated in the pivotal position of the Frisians in the traffic and exchange between the Frankish realm, England and Scandinavia. The present state of archaeological information suggests that this development was hatched in the *terp* region of the province of Friesland in the fifth century. From the later sixth century onwards and especially in the first half of the seventh century, gold and other luxury goods flowed in, probably mainly from the Frankish area (Knol 1993), a particular Frisian style of jewellery was developed which combined Scandinavian taste with Anglo-Saxon (Kentish) technology (Mazo Karras 1985; Gerrets, this volume), and from the late sixth century coins were probably already being minted somewhere in the region (Arent Pol, pers. comm.). This may have been the start of the flourishing but anonymous Frisian coinage of the following centuries in the coastal area outside Dorestad.

Less clear is the situation in the western part of Frisia in the early Merovingian period. Perhaps as early as the late sixth century, settlements involved in interregional exchange were established near the mouth of the rivers Rhine and Scheldt (Bult and Hallewas 1990; Besteman 1990; Van Heeringen, Henderikx and Mars 1995, 42–9). And in the central river area, at the fork of river Rhine and river Lek, Dorestad came into being, developing from some landing facilities and a mint at a former Roman castellum in the first half of the seventh century to the largest trading centre of Northwest Europe in the eighth century (Van Es 1990; Van Es and Hessing 1994, 82–119). From then on the Frisians appear in the spotlight of history as a dominant group of middlemen in the long-distance trade on the Rhine and the North Sea, attested in trading centres as far as Birka in the south, York in the west and Strasbourg in the south, if not as far as Rome, where a Frisian pilgrim colony was founded in 779 (a survey in: Lebecq 1983). The disintegration of the Carolingian empire and the repeated Viking raids, which resulted in the downfall of Dorestad, put an end to the heyday of Frisian trade, but the inhabitants of the North Sea shores remained active in commerce and shipping, though under other conditions and partly under other names. There is, in a manner of speaking, a line running from this *unique group of middlemen* from the early Middle Ages, as Richards Hodges called them (Hodges 1977, 209) to the Dutch entrepreneurs in the seventeenth century, who also knew how to translate their maritime skill and the geographically key position of the Dutch delta into money and power. The Frisian achievement in the early Middle Ages can be seen as a sign that economic power in Europe was to shift from the Continent to the maritime nations of the northwest.

I have introduced the Frisians here deliberately from a one-sided demographic and economic viewpoint and in a descriptive way. Now we have to answer the 'how' and 'why' of Frisian achievement, which leads us inevitably to other spheres of life, the socio-political conditions in particular, to the European context and to the unique environment in which the Frisians operated. I shall give here a provisional comment on the landscape as a

Fig. 1 The world as known by the Frisians in the eighth to ninth centuries. Indicated are the Frisian homeland and trading centres in Europe which were visited by Frisian merchants (drawing IPP, Amsterdam).

conditional factor and on the nature and socio-political background of Frisian trade. But before doing so, I have to explain who the 'Frisians' were.

Frisia and the Frisians: territoriality and ethnicity

The geographical scope of the project, from Scheldt to Weser, is not merely an arbitrary demarcation of the proposed research area, for it refers implicitly to the territory between Sincfal (a former stream south of the Scheldt) and the Weser in which Frisian law was applicable according to the *Lex Frisionum* which Charlemagne had recorded in about 804. The suggestion is that we are dealing with people who not only shared the same name and law, but were indeed an ethnic unity, or *gens*. The problem is that 'emic' information is missing, so we do not know if the Frisians themselves were aware of an ethnic communality. This jurisdictive territory could have been the product of ethnic classification by the Franks[2], possibly an occasional construction to create unity within the recently conquered coastal districts, which now formed one *ducatus*. The tripartite division of this territory, in which the central area – the present province of Friesland – had a special position, suggests, however, that it originated from pre-Frankish conditions (Halbertsma 1965–1966, 74). It probably reflects an historical extension of the Frisian sphere of influence to the west and to the east. Other explanations are possible, however.

It is significant that all necessary conditions for *gens*-formation are apparent in Frisia before the Frankish annexation in the eighth century. Scholars like Reinhard Wenskus and Patrick Geary (Wenskus 1961; Geary 1983) have demonstrated that in the Migration period and early Middle Ages political power and warfare were indispensable conditions for tribal formation and also that ethnic affinity was confined to the upper strata of society, that is the free warriors who 'acquired their identity through their adherence to particular royal or ducal families alongside whom they fought and whose traditions they adopted' (Geary 1983, 22). Thus a relativily small group, the king and his *Gefolgschaft*, which could be ethnically mixed, generated and reproduced the *gens* by a set of traditions (the myth of a common origin in the first place), symbols and rituals. This model is very well applicable to the Frisian situation. Here indeed a strong military leadership existed in the seventh century. The Frisian kings (the Franks called them *duces*, which however does not exclude kingship: the Latin terminology only suggests a relationship to an overlord, whether a Frank or a Frisian – see for instance Bassett 1989) were able to conquer the former Frankish territories of the central river area (including the Roman fortresses of Utrecht and Dorestad) and the coastal districts south of the river Rhine (so-called *Frisia citerior*). Their last king, Radbod, succeeded in resisting Frankish expansion to the north till his death in 719. The power of these seventh-century leaders probably stretched far beyond the central river area in which they are historically mentioned, may be even beyond the Weser border, which was in fact a Frankish frontline. As Danny Gerrets demonstrates in his paper, political power, thus the *gens* of Frisians, was born in the *terp* region, in Westergo, but it came to maturity by the expansion to the south and by the confrontation with 'others', in this case the Franks. Success in warfare and the immediate contact with the Frankish rulers, whom they met on equal terms, probably resulted in the consolidation of the power of these Frisian kings who now had their residence in former Roman state property, the *castellum* of Utrecht. But the last step to fashionable European kingship, that of conversion to Christianity, was never taken.

Frisian ethnicity has mainly been regarded as a given, objective phenomenon, a complex of properties (like language) and attitudes by which the people of coastal areas felt themselves to be Frisians. Frisians of this kind would have existed from the Iron Age till the present day. Indeed, Frisian tribes, the *Frisii majores* and *Frisii minores*, situated in the Frisian *terp* area and in North Holland, were already mentioned by Tacitus, there are references of Frisians as invaders of England by Procopius (Lebecq 1983, 108) and the inhabitants of *Frisia* (or *Fresia*), that is the coastal wetlands from Flanders to the Danish border, were called Frisians since the eighth century. But, as was said before, we do not know how these 'Frisians' defined themselves. Apart from phases of *gens* formation on a higher level, as described above, the 'we-perception' of most of the people did not exceed the boundaries of their immediate environment. Of course, a certain persistence of traditions and language in a wider area may have existed (and it did), but these correspondences were not necessarily expressions of ethnicity. Ethnicity was a dynamic and situational construct, as Patrick Geary put it (Geary 1983), and so were the means of communicating ethnic identity.

The remarkable persistence of the name 'Frisians' has always been regarded as a proof of ethnic continuity (see Gerrets, this volume). Now that we must conclude that the Frisians of the Roman period are virtually separated from their early medieval namesakes by a severe demographic dip, there is a problem. The name, which might have been prestigious, was apparently appropriated by new *gens* builders who were seeking legitimation.[3] For some reason the name remained useful for a long time, but it should be realised that it covered different categories of people (members of a tribe, inhabitants of a region called Friesland, traders, stubborn peasants opposing central authority, etc.) and was used in different contexts during history. And it should be repeated, as far as the first millennium is concerned, that only the perception of outsiders is known. Therefore, research on identity and communication in a broader sense is likely to be more fruitful for archaeology than searching after ethnic Frisians.

A maritime society in a maritime landscape

Of particular interest is the understanding of how Frisian society functioned as a maritime nation living in a maritime landscape which consisted mainly of wetlands. How, for instance, was this society affected by the fact that a segment (particularly the young mature males) was periodically away from home, lived temporarily in a very special *Gefolgschaft*-like band, travelled not only between trade-centres but also between different cultural systems and probably acted in different social roles? Frisian culture must have been influenced by the dichotomy of isolation as far as life on the remote salt-marshes is concerned, on the one hand, and of a high degree of cosmopolitanism, on the other. This is just one aspect of a society which stood with one foot on land and with the other in the water. The essence is that we are dealing with a *maritime* cultural landscape, which requires a conceptual framework that differs greatly from the models with which archaeologists are used to working.[4] Generally speaking, water (the sea, rivers and lakes) puts its stamp not only on settlement patterns and subsistence economy but must also have a great effect on communication with the outside world, social structures, mentality and the perception of time and space. Living near the water does not always lead to maritime behaviour, but the fact that most settlements in the area were accessible by water shows the strong relationship of the Frisians with the maritime landscape. Early medieval Frisia, thus defined by waterways, must be described as a maritime network. The ship played a major role as the medium of all kinds of communication and must also have had an important symbolic meaning as is shown by the fact that it is regularly depicted on the coins minted at Dorestad. It is conceivable that the ship also figured as a prestige item in gift exchange and other ritual contexts like burial practices. A most interesting aspect is the fact that political structure must also have been determined by the ship as the main medium of communication. The *circuit* of kings who visited their residences or directly consumed hospitality from their people, thus the geographically limited basis of early medieval kingship (see for instance Charles-Edwards 1989), had completely different dimensions in a maritime realm, as Viking Age Norse kingship illustrates. In this field a lot of work has to be done, however, for hardly anything is archaeologically known yet about Frisian shipping, ships or their symbolic meanings.

A few words about the 'land side' of the cultural landscape of the Frisians. Although there was a certain diversity of environmental conditions and agrarian practices, it is justified to say that economy was dominated here by cattle-breeding. This fact too is meaningful in the light of Frisian activities, for in such stock-breeding societies a high degree of mobility of people and ample conditions for raiding and commercial activities were generally provided for (Slicher van Bath 1965).

Environmental conditions and the favourable geographic position of Frisia – it was the natural gateway of the Continent to the North Sea countries – can only partly explain the remarkable role of the Frisians in long-distance exchange. It is obvious that Frisian 'trade' owed its success to the macro- economic and political developments in Northwestern Europe from the seventh century onwards, in the Frankish realm in particular. On the other hand, internal socio-political processes in Frisia itself must also have been at stake.

Wealth, power and exchange

Within the scope of this paper I can only hint at some of the problems concerning the nature of exchange or trade and its relation to political power. Historically and archaeologically, Frisian trade emanated from darkness in the eighth century, when it took place under the protection and control of the Frankish king and the church of Utrecht in 'visible' special-purpose settlements like Dorestad (Lebecq 1992). No doubt an important change took place in Northern European economic strategies in this period, resulting in large scale commodity exchange (not only of valuables but also of bulk goods from the royal and monastic demesnes) and the emergence of *emporia* and tolls. The question is, however, whether long-distance trade as such was born or reborn then as an important new step on the evolutionary ladder, a point of view taken by Richard Hodges and others but rejected by Martin Carver on convincing grounds (Hodges 1977; 1982; Carver 1993, 41–62). The Gudme-Lundeborg complex on Fünen in Denmark (third to sixth century), for instance, suggests that the Germanic elites from the North fed their *thesaurus* not only by means of occasional plunder, gifts and tributes, but disposed as well of a regular supply of goods as early as the Migration period (Thrane 1987; Thomsen 1991). Whether we are dealing with trade or with a well-organized tribute system, all the elements of the port-of-trade system were already there, though placed in a specific ritual setting. This example suggests that gift-exchange and commodity exchange, which are often seen as mutually exclusive phases in evolution, were in fact interconnected. Trade was the hidden counterpart of gift-exchange. In the historical and literary sources (like *Beowulf*) it is non-existent or strongly under-exposed, because it did not fit into the *Weltanschauung* of contemporaries, especially not that of the church (Gurevich 1990).

It is hardly conceivable that the Frisian trade of the eighth century emerged from nothing: there must already have been networks and forms of exchange, which is actually proven by the imported gold and huge quantities of Frankish pottery in the *terp* region from the sixth century onwards. It is questionable, however, whether real trade, thus commodity exchange, was at stake already and whether the Frisians actually went to the European 'market' with their own salt, cloth, combs, etc. or with foreign products as early as the sixth century. It is more likely that most of the gold (especially coins) arrived here in this period in the context of gift-exchange and treaties. Dark Age Frisian elites probably owed a great deal of their wealth to their position as allies of their mighty neighbours, the Merovingians (the Frisian-Merovingian coalition against the Swedish ruler Hygelac, who raided the north of Austrasia in about 523 (Halbertsma 1989, 8–9), proves that this sort of relationship really existed). It is quite possible that by this sort of investment the Franks created Frisian power and, in a wider sense, tribal formation, as the Roman empire did before with regard to their barbarian neighbours beyond the *limes*. The 'income' from their position as federates would have enabled the Frisian leaders to participate in the elite-networks around the North Sea, which in some way also led to commercial activities. It goes too far, however, to speak of 'the Merovingian North Sea', as Wood does (Wood 1983).

A final question: the relation between trade and kingship. There is a tendency among Dutch and German scholars to depict early medieval Frisia as a sort of *Bauern-Republik*. Thus local big farmers would have organized trade as independent entrepreneurs (Ellmers 1977, 16–29, 266–270; Schmid 1991, 15). This view may be applicable to the situation in the later Middle Ages, but conflicts strongly with the ideas we have of the Germanic societies of the early Middle Ages, in which the lord/king is supposed to have played a central redistributive role. And it is in conflict with historical reality: we have not only the Frankish king protecting and controlling Frisian trade in the eighth to ninth century, but also Frisian kings in the previous century, who were to be found then in the very region of Dorestad. These facts at least suggest that trade and political power were interconnected, even in Frisia.

Abbreviation

BROB = Berichten van de Rijksdienst voor het Oudheidkundig Bodemonderzoek.

Notes

1. This paper goes into some aspects of the archaeology and history of the Frisian region which are dealt with in general in: Heidinga, H.A. 1997, *Frisia in the First Millennium. An Outline*, Utrecht. I refer the reader to this book for additional information and ample literature on the subject.
2. Jos Bazelmans (post-graduate member of the research group of the Frisia project) is preparing a paper on the subject of ascribed ethnicity in the case of the Frisians.
3. The transmission of ancient, prestigious tribal names without the existance of ethnic continuity in the proper sense is proven in other cases. Walther Pohl pointed, for instance, to the Avars, whose name dates back to the times of Herodotus (Pohl 1991, 79).
4. In Danish archaeology, however, the importance of the maritime cultural landscape has been recognized for years. In 1993, the *Research Centre for Maritime Archaeology* of the National Museum started an ambitious project on this subject (see Crumlin-Pedersen 1991; 1996).

References

Bassett, S. (ed.) 1989a: *The Origins of Anglo-Saxon Kingdoms*, (London).

Bassett, S. 1989b: 'In search of the origins of Anglo-Saxon kingdoms', in Bassett 1989a, 3–27.

Besteman, J.C. 1990: 'North-Holland AD 400–1200: turning tide or tide turned?', in Besteman, J.C., Bos, J.M. and Heidinga, H.A. (eds), *Medieval Archaeology in the Netherlands. Studies presented to H.H. van Regteren Altena*, (Assen/Maastricht), 91–120.

Blok, D.P. 1979: *De Franken in Nederland*, 3rd ed. (Haarlem).

Bult, E.J. and Hallewas, D.P. 1990: 'Archaeological evidence for the early-medieval settlement around the Meuse and Rhine deltas up to ca AD 1000', in Besteman, J.C., Bos, J.M. and Heidinga, H.A. (eds), *Medieval Archaeology in the Netherlands. Studies presented to H.H. van Regteren Altena* (Assen/Maastricht), 1–90.

Carver, M.O.H. 1993: *Arguments in Stone. Archaeological Research and the European Town in the First Millennium*, Oxbow Monograph 29 (Oxford).

Charles-Edwards, Th. 1989: 'Early medieval kingships in the British isles', in Bassett 1989a, 28–39.

Crumlin-Pedersen, O. (ed.) 1991: *Aspects of Maritime Scandinavia, AD 200–1200*, Proceedings of the Nordic Seminar on Maritime Aspects of Archaeology, Roskilde, 13th–15th March, 1989 (Roskilde).

Crumlin-Pedersen, O. 1996: *Archaeology and the Sea*, 18e Kroonvoordracht, (Amsterdam).

Ellmers, D. 1972: *Frühmittelalterliche Handelsschiffahrt im Mittel- und Nordeuropa*, (Neumünster).

Ellmers, D. 1985: 'Die Bedeutung der Friesen für die Handelsverbindungen des Ostseeraumes bis zur Wikingerzeit', in Lindquist, S.- O. (ed.), *Society and Trade in the Baltic during the Viking Age*, Acta Visbyensia 7 (Visby), 7–54.

Es, W.A. van 1965–1966: 'Friesland in Roman times', *BROB* 15–16, 37–68.

Es, W.A. van 1972: *De Romeinen in Nederland* (Bussum).

Es, W.A. van 1990: 'Dorestad centred', in Besteman, J.C., Bos, J.M. and Heidinga, H.A. (eds), *Medieval Archaeology in the Netherlands. Studies presented to H.H. van Regteren Altena* (Assen/Maastricht), 151–182.

Es, W.A. van and Hessing, W.A.M. (eds) 1994: *Romeinen, Friezen en Franken in het hart van Nederland, van Trajectum tot Dorestad 50 v.C.–900 n.C.* (Utrecht/Amersfoort).

Geary, P.J. 1983: 'Ethnic identity as a situational construct in the early middle ages', *Mitteilungen der Anthropologischen Gesellschaft in Wien* 113, 15–26.

Gurevich, A.J. 1990: 'The Merchant', in Le Goff, J. (ed.), *The Medieval World* (London), 243–284.

Halbertsma, H. 1965–1966: 'The Frisian Kingdom', *BROB* 15–16, 69–108.

Halbertsma, H. 1982: *Frieslands Oudheid*, diss. Groningen.

Halbertsma, H. 1989: 'Herinneringen aan St. Willibrord in Friesland', in Kiesel, G. and Schroeder, J. (eds), *Willibrord, Apostel der Niederlande, Gründer der Abtei Echternach* (Luxembourg), 42–68.

Heeringen, R.M. van, Henderikx, P.A. and Mars, A. (eds) 1995: *Vroeg-Middeleeuwse ringwalburgen in Zeeland* (Goes).

Heidinga, H.A. 1997: *Frisia in the First Millennium. An Outline* (Utrecht).

Hodges, R. 1977: 'Trade and urban origins in Dark Age England: an archaeological critique of the evidence', *BROB* 27, 191–215.

Hodges, R. 1982: *Dark Age Economics: the Origins of Towns and Trade, 600–1000 AD* (London).

Knol, E. 1993: *De Noordnederlandse Kustlanden in de Vroege Middeleeuwen*, diss. VU Amsterdam.

Lebecq, S. 1983: *Marchands et Navigateurs Frisons du Haut Moyen Age*, 2 vols. (Lille).

Lebecq, S. 1992: 'The Frisian trade in the Dark Ages. A Frisian or a Frankish/Frisian trade?', *Rotterdam Papers* 7, 7–16.

Mazo Karras, M. 1985: 'Seventh-century jewellery from Frisia: a re-examination', *Anglo-Saxon Studies in Archaeology and History* 4, 159–177.

Pohl, W. 1991: 'Conceptions of ethnicity in Early Medieval studies', *Archaeologia Polona* 29, 39–49.

Russchen, A. 1967: *New light on Dark Age Frisia* (Drachten).

Schmid, P. 1991: 'Mittelalterliche Besiedlung, Deich- und Landesausbau im niedersächsischen Marschgebiet', in Böhme, H.W. (ed.), *Siedlungen und Landesausbau zur Salierzeit, Teil 1: in den nördlichen Landschaften des Reiches* (Sigmaringen), 9–36.

Slicher van Bath, B.H. 1965: 'The economic and social conditions in the Frisian districts from 900 to 1500', *A.A.G. Bijdragen* 13, 97–133.

Thomsen, P.O. 1991: 'Lundeborg: a trading centre from the 3rd–7th century AD', in Crumlin-Pedersen 1991, 133–144.

Thrane, H. 1987: 'Das Gudme-Problem und die Gudme-Untersuchung', *Frühmittelalterliche Studien* 21, 1–48.

Wenskus, R. 1961: *Stammesbildung und Verfassung. Das Werden der frühmittelalterlichen Gentes* (Köln-Graz).

Wood, I. 1983: *The Merovingian North Sea* (Alingsas).

Anglo-Saxon Studies in Archaeology and History 10, 1999

Social Archaeology and Anglo-Saxon Kingdom Origins

Christopher Scull

Introduction

The written sources for Anglo-Saxon England attest the existence of kingdoms by the seventh century, ruled by kings who claimed continental Germanic ancestry (Kirby 1991; Yorke 1990). Evidence that this threshold of historical visibility genuinely coincides with a watershed of social and political development may be found in aspects of the archaeological record from the late sixth century which appear to be consistent with a new degree of social differentiation and political centralisation: in particular princely burial; the development of a settlement hierarchy, indicative of territorial authority and formalised surplus extraction; and the existence from the early seventh century of special commercial or trading settlements – *wics* or *emporia* – which may be linked to the centralisation of economic and political power (Arnold 1988; Carver 1989; Scull 1992; 1993).

There is, however, little written evidence for Anglo-Saxon society or polity before the seventh century (Dumville 1989; Yorke 1993). The question of kingdom origins therefore has to be studied across the interface of history, dependent on written sources, and pre- or proto-history, for which archaeology is the main source. The issue can be approached from two directions: the fifth and sixth centuries may be viewed retrospectively from the apparent security of later written sources, or they may be tackled directly through the archaeological record using generalising models of social and political development (Bassett 1989b; Carver 1989; Scull 1992).

Both approaches have their limitations, especially if applied insensitively. Simple historical retrospection risks serious anachronism, while uncritical application of general models may mask complexity and diversity (Scull 1992, 66–67). It is also pointless to pretend that generalising approaches stand outside historical research and retrospective argument: it is difficult to see otherwise how the specifics of time and place might be addressed, and in any case much general theory was itself developed within a framework of historical enquiry. Without the historical record it is unlikely that we would be talking about kingdoms, nor would we be confident about locating the territorial interests of regional elites, much less linking these with named dynasties and individuals.

The complexities of interpretation are therefore compounded by the relationship between historical and archaeological data. Detailed integration of both data sets is desirable, but this is far off – if indeed it can ever be achieved. The archaeology of the fifth and sixth centuries stands for the most part outside the limited framework of historical narrative and must therefore be addressed on its own terms. This position has been challenged (Richards 1987, 201–202; Alcock 1988), but this does not alter the limitations of the written sources. There is agreement that a reliable historical context for archaeological material cannot be ignored: in question is the level at which this might exist, and how it might be related to the archaeological record.

Another effect of this inter-disciplinary divide is that scholars might be tempted to huddle safely on one side or the other. For example, the great majority of contributions to *The Origins of Anglo-Saxon Kingdoms* (Bassett 1989a), a benchmark publication, concentrate on the seventh century and later, and upon written sources, at the expense of the archaeological evidence for the fifth and sixth centuries and the extensive theoretical literature generated by processual or social archaeology. This reflects an earlier intellectual attitude widespread in Anglo-Saxon studies: processual archaeology was initially resisted or ignored, and – in marked contrast to approaches to the Iron Age and Migration Period in Denmark and Scandinavia – there has been little explicit use and development of processual models or perspectives in Anglo-Saxon archaeology.

The reasons for this are worth considering. There has been a genuine feeling that such approaches were inappropriate and unnecessary: kingdoms were taken as a given, and the historical framework gave plausible explanations – conquest and consolidation – for their origins and development. It was also relevant that much influential literature on state formation dealt with the origins of early states in – for example – Meso-America, Mesopotamia, and the Bronze-Age Aegean, societies where the physical expressions of social and political stratification conformed to modern perceptions of what a state should look like, but where this was sufficiently far removed from the evidence for Anglo-Saxon England to make the application of general models of social and political evolution appear unattractive. A further complicating factor has been the continuing debate in literature on state formation over matters of definition and taxonomy. Tenth- and eleventh-century England has been considered a state society (Campbell 1975; Hodges 1982, 189–93), but it may also be argued that after Rome the state in northern Europe has been exclusively a phenomenon of the sixteenth century and later (Fenger 1991, 294). Claessen and Skalník (1979) confronted such problems by refining the developmental taxonomy (the early state, of which three types may distinguished: the inchoate early state, the typical early state, and the transitional early state) but even so it is not clear that English society of the seventh and eighth centuries would fit satisfactorily into any single category despite clear evidence for social and political complexity and for regional and wider hegemony.

The Early State Module

That there was a genuine basis for some of the reservations about the applicability of processual models to early England can be illustrated by the example of the Early State Module (ESM) (Renfrew 1974; 1975; Renfrew and Level 1979; Fig. 1). This influential evolutionary and spatial model has been widely used for other places and periods but there has only been one major attempt to apply it to the origins of Anglo-Saxon kingdoms (Arnold 1988, 175–88, fig. 5.5) and this is not wholly successful.

The model predicts the emergence of territorial statelets (ESMs) each with a settlement hierarchy focused on a central place, whose integration generates higher-order political units; the area of such statelets is most often around 1500 sq km, and the mean distance between the central places of neighbouring entities is approximately 40 km. However, the fifth to ninth centuries in England were a time when the functions which would have been integrated in an urban central place system in Roman Britain or Late Medieval England were in fact devolved among a range of rural settlements, with political centralisation focused on central persons rather than central places. This may be seen in the periodic centres of peripatetic kingship (Austin 1986); the possibility that political authority was invested primarily in people rather than territory (Davies and Vierck 1974, 228–29); the articulation of lordship and jurisdiction; and the social organisation of production and exchange through a rural structure of multiple or complex estates (Hooke 1986; Blair 1989; Hines 1994; Scull 1997).

The ESMs defined by Arnold for southern England in the sixth and seventh centuries are centred not on settlements but on rich burials (Arnold 1988, fig. 5.5; Fig. 2). Translating Last Resting Place into Central Place

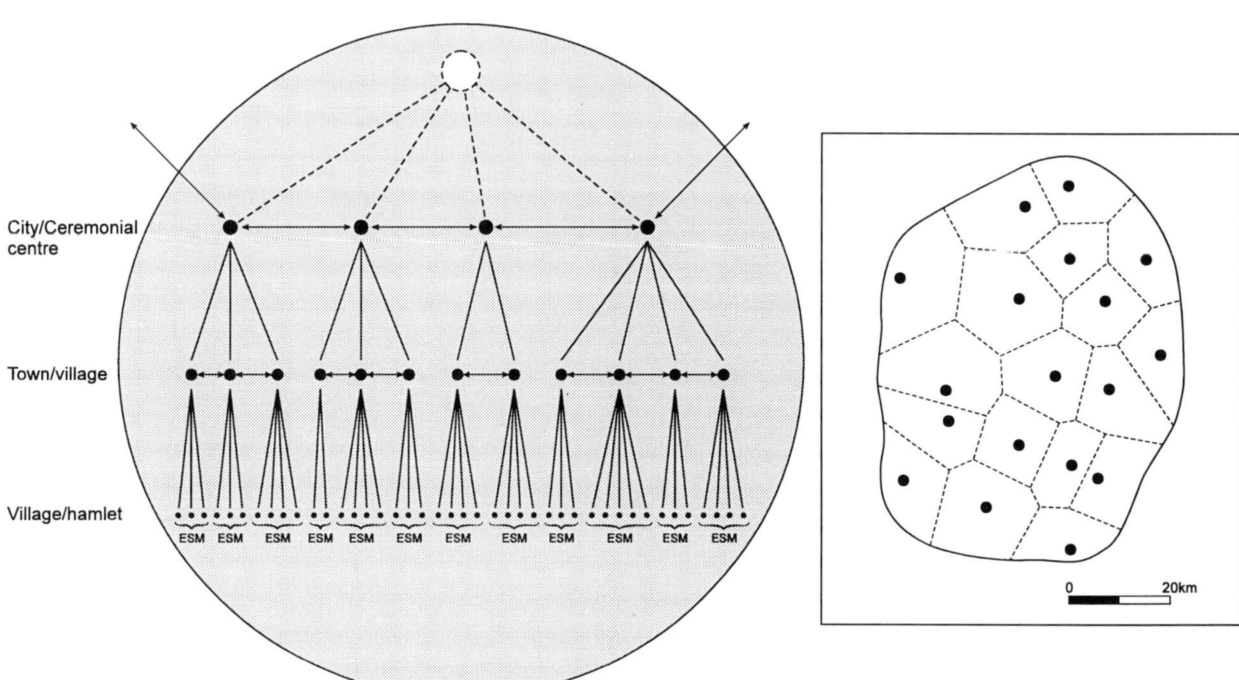

Fig. 1 The Early State Module, showing the place of ESMs within an early civilisation (left) and the idealised territorial structure of an early civilisation with the territories and centres of ESMs indicated (right). After Renfrew 1975, figs. 2 and 6.

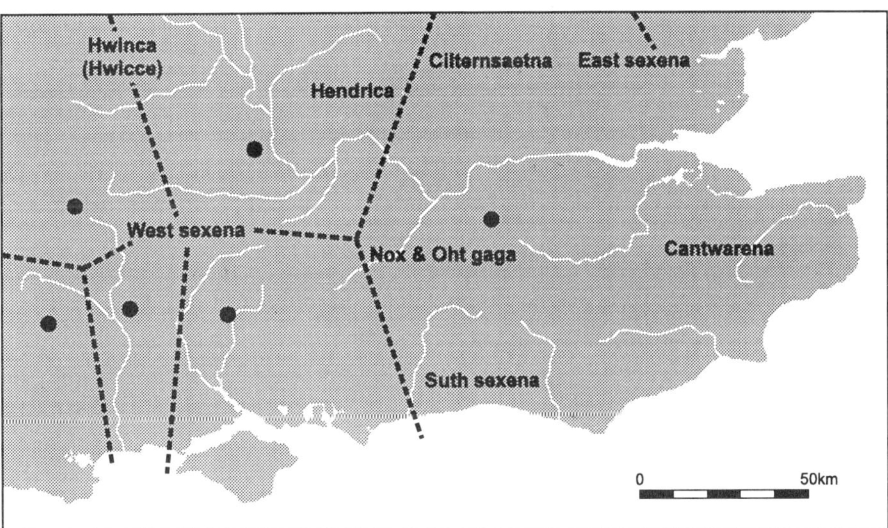

Fig. 2 South-east England in the later seventh century showing territories defined by constructing Theissen Polygons around rich graves against groups assessed at 2000 hides or more in Tribal Hidage. After Arnold 1988, fig. 5.5 and Davies and Vierck 1974.

in this way negates the basis of the spatial model unless it can be demonstrated that all these graves are the burials of regional elites (which appears unlikely on other archaeological grounds) and that there is so exclusive, close and consistent a link between the graves of regional elites and a single regional central place that the former can be assumed to represent the latter. As yet no such link can be demonstrated and, as noted above, it may be erroneous to think of early kingdoms having a single permanent central place. The territories defined for the later seventh century fit poorly with the approximate location of political groupings recorded in Tribal Hidage (Fig. 2). This may be exacerbated by the incomplete archaeological sample and the possibility that elite burial practice was not uniform, church burial having replaced richly-furnished princely burial as the preferred option for kings by this time (Deliyannis 1995).

Thus, while it is easy to accept that many of the principles which lie behind the ESM might apply to England in the fifth to seventh centuries, it is more difficult to accept the applicability of this specific spatial expression of social and political organisation and its connection to some stage in a simple hierarchy of socio-political sophistication. Power and authority are cultural constructs and neither their expression nor their articulation is uniform in human societies. A site such as Gudme in Denmark, interpreted as a multi-functional central place with a supra-regional importance (Nielsen *et al.* 1994), might be presented quite convincingly as the focus of an ESM but nothing comparable is known from England. A good case can be made that the royal vill at Yeavering was both a pagan, then a Christian, cult centre and periodically an elite residence and meeting place, but as a royal vill or estate *caput* it may be presented as only one of many in the Northumbrian kingdom. The supposed heart of the East Anglian kingdom in south-east Suffolk provides a good example of the problems encountered when seeking integrated central places. There is archaeological, historical and toponymic evidence for a royal vill, elite burial ground and cult centre within 6 km of each other on the River Deben, but the main port-of-trade at Ipswich is 19 km as the crow flies from the royal vill at Rendlesham, on another navigable estuary (H.E. iii, 22; Warner 1985; Fig. 3).

Constructing Thiessen Polygons around the known major trading places of the eighth century defines territories from the archaeological evidence alone which broadly correspond to known political geography (Fig. 4). However, Renfrew's model is explicit in predicting that ports-of-trade will be established only after the ESM has emerged (Renfrew 1975), and the territories are rather larger than those predicted by the ESM model and cut across known political groupings of the seventh century. The territories defined by this exercise would thus appear to represent a level of political and territorial integration beyond that of the ESM, but for which it is difficult to define constituent or antecedent ESMs. These examples illustrate the difficulties encountered in attempting to apply the model to the available data for fifth- to eighth-century England: specifically, that a simple spatial approach which defines polities from centres is compromised if single centres cannot be identified.

Social dynamics and Anglo-Saxon kingdom origins

It would be unwise to reject the principles behind the ESM out of hand, but it is clear that it cannot be applied usefully to the explanation of Anglo-Saxon kingdom

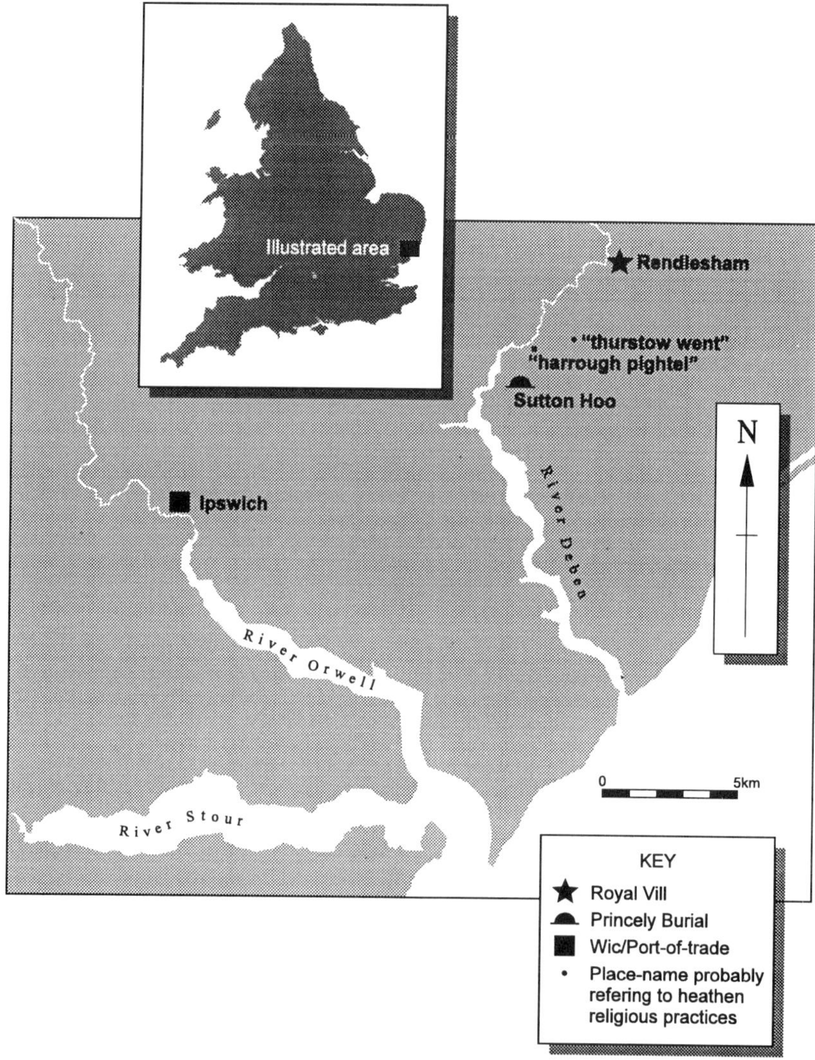

Fig. 3 South-east Suffolk in the seventh century: evidence for sites with some central-place functions.

origins without modification, and that other approaches are required. Two main questions may be identified: how did elite individuals or elite lineages establish and perpetuate lordship and hegemony? and how did elites emerge in the first place, and what social transformations were associated with these processes? What follows by way of an answer to these questions in the next two sections is based upon more detailed discussions which have been published elsewhere (Scull 1993; 1995).

Peer competition and competitive exclusion

At present the most influential model of Anglo-Saxon kingdom origins is that put forward by Bassett (1989b). This proposes competition between local political groupings with the winners becoming progressively more powerful, the process culminating in the establishment of regional chiefdoms and eventually in the establishment of the authority of a single dynasty over a wide area. This is a back-projection of early history, notably the dynastic conflicts chronicled by Bede in the *Historia Ecclesiastica*, but it also tallies well with some theoretical positions on state formation, in particular in its adoption of the Darwinian doctrine of competitive exclusion (Carneiro 1978). If this model is accepted, and if Tribal Hidage is to be considered a seventh-century document, then the picture represented by Tribal Hidage may be interpreted as a palimpsest of the levels of regional hegemony and overlordship established through such a process, which may in turn be linked to the hierarchy of *reges*, *subreguli* and *principes* recorded by Bede (Campbell 1979). The smallest units recorded in Tribal Hidage may give some indication of the sort of local polity with which the process of competition began, but caution is necessary here: some local political entities of the seventh century may have been new creations (Yorke, this volume).

Models of peer-competition and competitive exclusion have been applied more widely to Migration-period Europe and to other periods. They provide a plausible trajectory of development and a mechanism – conflict –

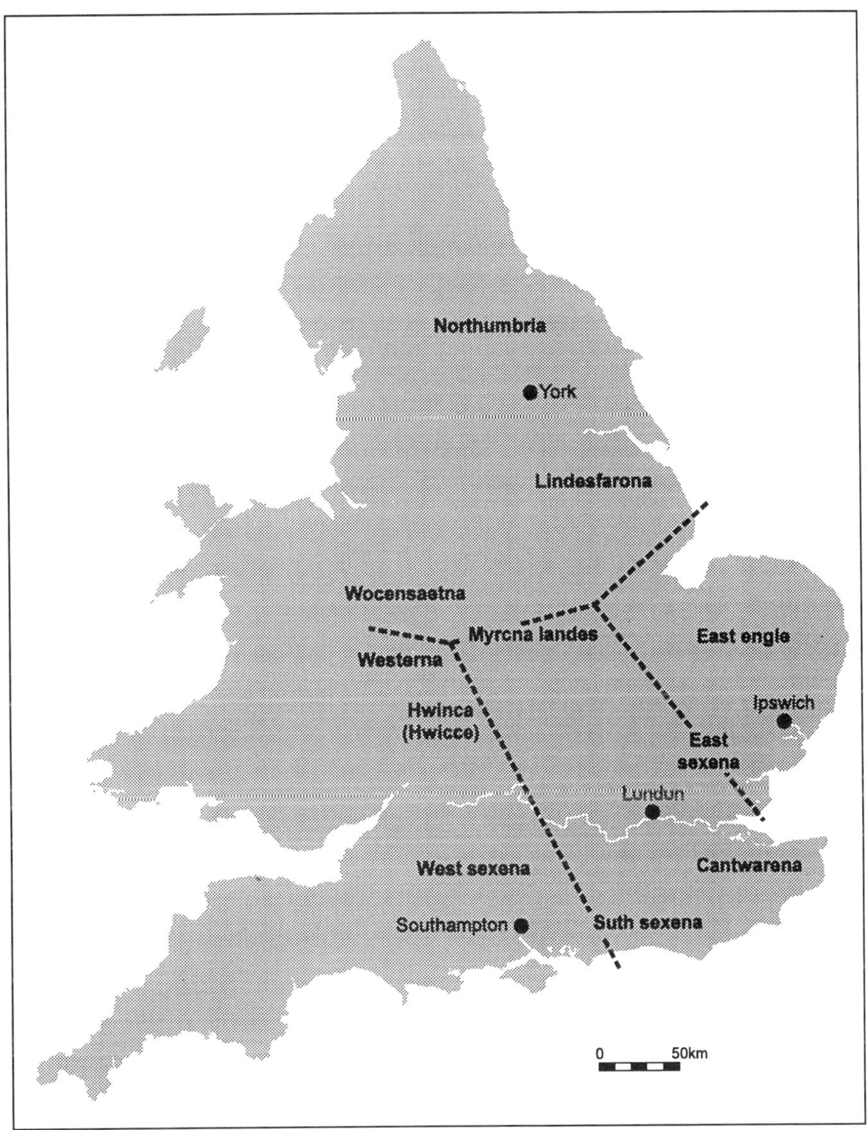

*Fig. 4 England in the seventh and eighth centuries showing territories defined by constructing Thiessen Polygons around major trading settlements (*wics *or* emporia*) known from archaeological evidence alone against major political entities (Northumbria and groups assessed at 7000 hides or more in Tribal Hidage).*

through which dynastic power was established. However, such a process must have been fuelled by, and precipitated, other changes, and such competition presupposes an existing degree of social and political complexity. Social and political transformations are themselves the aggregates of individual actions and relationships, and if long-term developments are to be understood we must consider the social and economic dynamics which may have operated at the level of the individual, lineage and kin group but which when aggregated generated larger-scale change.

The evidence for community and social structure over much of southern and eastern England in the fifth and sixth centuries is consistent with a model of broadly-equal, internally-ranked patrilineal and patrilocal descent groups farming or exploiting ancestral territories. The cemetery evidence suggests unequal social relations, but this appears to be more marked within communities than between them. A number of axes of inequality may be identified: ranking by lineage or position within a lineage, and differentiation by age, gender or cultural identity (Scull 1993).

These societies appear to have been structured in ways which would allow development along the lines predicted by models of peer competition. There is, however, little clear evidence for regional or paramount elites before the later sixth century. This may be explained by the suggestion that local chieftaincies established through such competition were likely to have been personal and impermanent. Thus we might expect some accentuation of social ranking but no marked social stratification until one such group was able to establish a more stable paramount status. This is the most plausible context for princely burials, whose appearance in the archaeological record is broadly contemporary with other phenomena consistent with emergent social stratification and more stable political centralisation. These can be attributed to attempts by new paramount elites to consolidate and perpetuate new configurations of power and authority, and to legitimise a new status. Such transitions might be effected in a number of ways, all of which may have constituted axes of competition, and all of which can be addressed to a greater or lesser extent through the archaeological record (indeed, many are examined in detail in other contributions to this volume): manipulation of external political and exchange contacts; manipulation of symbolism and ideology, of which princely burial is itself an aspect; manipulation of the past, descent, and ethnic or cultural identity; and manipulation of the means of production through changes in landholding and territorial organisation (Scull 1993, 76–77; 1995, 77–79). The close relationship between kings and the church in the seventh century may also have been a relevant factor (Mayr-Harting 1972). Conversion was targeted at elites, and so it may have been very much in the Church's interest to maintain the status quo as found even if this kingdom structure was a new phenomenon. Conversely, the introduction of Christianity from Rome offered the new paramount elites a powerful package of ideology and symbolism which might be used in strategies of legitimation.

Status, landholding, and socio-political change

Some models of social and political development in the fifth and sixth centuries have privileged the competitive acquisition and redistribution of exotica through inter-regional exchange as a causal mechanism (Arnold 1980, 81–82, 138–39; 1982, 128). However, the importance of land as a social resource fundamental to status and power must be emphasized. Charles-Edwards (1972) has discussed the links between the territorialization of authority and changes in relationship between status and landholding in pre-Viking England. Put simply, he argued that in early Anglo-Saxon society status as a free man (which may be taken to include at least a nuclear family and dependants, which might include slaves and clients) depended upon a minimum landholding, and that if this was not available status by birth could not be perpetuated. This hypothesis generates some interesting predictions if applied to the post-migration circumstances of the fifth and sixth centuries.

Assuming any population increase, there would be a social imperative towards territorial expansion as individuals in each new generation required sufficient land to maintain their status by birth. Such expansion would be more rapid if we assume primogeniture, but even with partible inheritance the bottom threshold would be reached sooner or later and more land would be required. Any limit on territorial expansion – physical or political – would lead to pressure on land as a social resource. One result of this might be external conflict between local groups or chiefdoms. Another, internal result might be to increase the number of higher-status individuals dependent upon a local chieftain or clan head in a client:lord relationship, a process which would concentrate political power and, indirectly, control of land in fewer and fewer hands. Either would enhance or accelerate the social and political dynamics whereby a group or individual might eventually establish a wider regional hegemony (Scull 1993, 77–79). Such pressure on land as a social resource might be triggered by a relatively small increase in a particular social segment of the population: it would not require gross population increase on a scale which would precipitate pressure on land as a subsistence resource, for which there is in any case no evidence.

This model works best if it is accepted that there was some movement of population from the continent to Britain in the fifth century: the starting point for the process would therefore be a populated landscape, but one in which the opportunity existed to take land or to establish lordship over its existing inhabitants. This raises the question of how social evolutionary perspectives and migration theory might be integrated to provide a more sophisticated understanding of the social and political developments behind the emergence of the Anglo-Saxon kingdoms. It must be emphasized that neither post-Roman British society, nor the continental parent societies of the Germanic incomers, can be regarded as pristine societies, and it should be recognised that migration might have established inequalities not only between incomers and the indigenous population but also within the immigrant populations. One example of this is the way in which power or privilege might accrue from a claim to first-comer status. In politically fissile societies this might be viewed as a powerful motive to migration, and if subsequent contact with the homeland was structured by kinship and co-residence ties these could be manipulated to reinforce a special status. Later Anglo-Saxon royal genealogies suggest that continental ancestry was an important legitimizing claim, and the self-perception of a small number of key individuals – apex families – might therefore form the 'kernel of tradition' around which a wider political identity might be constructed (Scull 1995, 77–79). There is little or no direct evidence for the territorial extent of local chiefdoms in the fifth and sixth centuries, but there is evidence from eastern England to suggest that some expressions of cultural identity became increasingly uniform from the later fifth century (Høilund Nielsen 1997, 86–87). If, as seems likely, political competition was linked to the construction of identities, this phenomenon would be consistent with the establishment of larger polities as predicted by models of peer-competition.

Conclusions

The ranked societies of the fifth and sixth centuries were capable of political integration to the extent that would support local chieftains and an impermanent or cyclical regional hegemony, but the establishment and maintenance of any permanent regional overlordship required, and precipitated or accelerated, permanent social and political change. Thus the origins of the Anglo-Saxon kingdoms are to be sought not so much in the factors governing the long-term evolution of complex societies, as some conventional processual analyses have suggested, but in the relatively short-term transformations within such societies (Scull 1992; 1993). It is important to understand processes of state formation, but we should not make the mistake of automatically defining kingdoms as states, or treating kingship as unchanging. Some local chieftains of the fifth or sixth centuries may have considered themselves kings, but we may doubt whether they would have been recognised as such by the major rulers of the seventh century, or by contemporary Frankish monarchs.

The two models outlined above are complementary, emphasizing respectively external competition and internal social dynamics. Both are explicitly processual, but both are driven by social considerations – the need to maintain and reproduce rank and status – and so attempt at a simple level to integrate general processes, human actions and the archaeological record. Their social basis is the local descent group and the conical clan, whose place in the model of peer-competition and competitive exclusion is analogous to that of the ESM in Renfrew's model for the evolution of civilisations, but whose spatial expression is different and less amenable to simple definition. A number of the most useful generalising models available to archaeology in recent years were originally formulated for times and conditions other than those for which they have been adapted: Smith's dendritic central place model and core-periphery models are two examples (Smith 1976; Wallerstein 1974). The attitude of processual theory to traditional early medieval archaeology has been characterised as throwing the baby out with the bathwater, but in its response to general theory traditional Anglo-Saxon archaeology has been guilty of the same. While the ESM may not be useful in the context of fifth- to eighth-century England the two alternative models outlined above suggest that the critical application of processual approaches is still likely to prove rewarding in seeking the origins of Anglo-Saxon kingdoms, and that there need be no contradiction between processual and post-processual archaeologies.

Acknowledgements
I should like to thank colleagues who attended the York *Sachsenymposium* for comment on the original draft of this contribution, Tania Dickinson and David Griffiths for the invitation to include it in the published proceedings of the conference, and Vince Griffin of the Central Archaeology Service, English Heritage, who prepared the illustrations.

Abbreviation

H.E. = Colgrave and Mynors 1969

References

Alcock, L. 1988: 'The activities of potentates in Celtic Britain, AD 500–800', in Driscoll, S.T. and Nieke M.R. (eds.) *Power and Politics in Early Medieval Britain and Ireland*, Edinburgh University Press (Edinburgh), 22–46.

Arnold, C.J. 1980: 'Wealth and social structure: a matter of life and death', in Rahtz, P., Dickinson, T. and Watts, L. (eds.) *Anglo-Saxon Cemeteries 1979*, Brit. Arch. Ser. Brit. Ser. 82 (Oxford), 81–142.

Arnold, C.J. 1982: 'Stress as a stimulus for socio-economic change: England in the seventh century', in Renfrew, C. and Shennan, S. (eds.), *Ranking, Resource and Exchange: Aspects of the Archaeology of Early European Society*, Cambridge University Press (Cambridge), 124–31.

Arnold, C.J. 1988: *An Archaeology of the Early Anglo-Saxon Kingdoms*, Croom Helm (London).

Austin, D. 1986: 'Central Place Theory and the Middle Ages', in Grant, E. (ed.) *Central Places, Archaeology and History*, Sheffield University Department of Archaeology and Prehistory (Sheffield,), 95–103.

Bassett, S. 1989a: *The Origins of Anglo-Saxon Kingdoms*, Leicester University Press (London).

Bassett, S. 1989b: 'In search of the origins of Anglo-Saxon kingdoms', in Bassett, S. (ed.) *The Origins of Anglo-Saxon Kingdoms*, Leicester University Press (London), 1–27.

Blair, J. 1989: 'Frithuwold's kingdom and the origins of Surrey', in Bassett, S. (ed.) *The Origins of Anglo-Saxon Kingdoms*, Leicester University Press (London), 141–58.

Campbell, J. 1975: 'Observations on English government from the tenth to the twelfth century', *Trans. Royal Hist. Soc.* 5th series 25, 39–54.

Campbell, J. 1979: *Bede's Reges and Principes*, Jarrow Lecture.

Carneiro, R.L. 1978: 'Political expansion as an expression of the principle of competitive exclusion', in Cohen, R. and Service, E.R. (eds.) *Origins of the State: the Anthropology of Political Evolution*, Institute for the Study of Human Issues (Philadelphia).

Carver, M.O.H. 1989: 'Kingship and material culture in early Anglo-Saxon East Anglia', in Bassett, S. (ed.) *The Origins of Anglo-Saxon Kingdoms*, Leicester University Press (London), 141–58.

Charles-Edwards, T. 1972: 'Kinship, status and the origins of the hide', *Past and Present* 56, 3–33.

Claessen, H.J.M. and Skalník, P. 1979: 'The early state: theories and hypotheses', in Claessen, H.J.M. and Skalník, P. (eds.) *The Early State*, Mouton Publishers (The Hague).

Colgrave, B. and Mynors, R.A.B. 1969: *Bede's Ecclesiastical History of the English People*, Oxford University Press (Oxford).

Davies, W. and Vierck, H. 1974: 'The contexts of Tribal Hidage: social aggregates and settlement patterns', *Frühmittelalterliche Studien* 8, 223–93.

Deliyannis, D. 1995: 'Church burial in Anglo-Saxon England: the prerogative of kings', *Frühmittelalterliche Studien* 29, 96–119.

Dumville, D.N. 1989: 'Essex, Middle Anglia and the expansion of Mercia in the south Midlands', in Bassett, S. (ed.) *The Origins of Anglo-Saxon Kingdoms*, Leicester University Press (London), 123–40

Fenger, A.O. 1991: 'Fra stammeret til statsbegreb', in Mortensen, P. and Rasmussen, B.M. (eds.), *Fra stamme til stat i Danmark 2: høvdingesamfund og kongemagt*, Århus University Press (Århus), 289–96.

Hines, J, 1994: 'North-Sea trade and the proto-urban sequence', *Archaeologia Polona* 32, 7–26.

Hodges, R. 1982: *Dark Age Economics: the Origins of Towns and Trade AD 600–1000*, Duckworth (London) .

Høilund Nielsen, K. 1997: 'The schism of Anglo-Saxon chronology', in Jensen, C.K. and Høilund Nielsen, K. (eds.), *Burial and Society: the Chronological and Social Analysis of Archaeological Burial Data*, Århus University Press (Århus), 71–99.

Hooke, D. 1986: 'Territorial organisation in the Anglo-Saxon West Midlands: Central Places, Central Areas', in Grant, E. (ed.) *Central Places, Archaeology and History*, Sheffield University Department of Archaeology and Prehistory (Sheffield), 79–93.

Kirby, D.P. 1991: *The Earliest English Kings*, Routledge (London).

Mayr-Harting, H. 1972: *The Coming of Christianity to Anglo-Saxon England*, Batsford (London).

Nielsen, P.O., Randsborg, K. and Thrane, H. (eds.) 1994: *The Archaeology of Gudme and Lundeborg*, Akademisk Forlag, Universitetsforlaget i København (Copenhagen).

Richards, J.D. 1987: *The Significance of Form and Function of Anglo-Saxon Cremation Urns*, Brit. Arch. Rep. Brit. Ser. 166 (Oxford).

Renfrew, C. 1974: 'Space, time and polity', in Rowlands, M. and Friedman, J. (eds.) *The Evolution of Social Systems*, Duckworth (London), 89–114.

Renfrew, C. 1975: 'Trade as action at a distance', in Sabloff, J.A. and Lamberg-Karlovsky, C.C. (eds.) *Ancient Civilisation and Trade*, University of New Mexico Press (Albuquerque), 3–59.

Renfrew, C. and Level, E.V. 1979: 'Exploring dominance: predicting polities from centres', in Renfrew, C. and Cooke, K.L. (eds.) *Transformations, Mathematical Approaches to Culture Change*, Academic Press (New York), 145–68.

Scull, C.J. 1992: 'Before Sutton Hoo: structures of power and society in early East Anglia', in Carver, M.O.H. (ed.) *The Age of Sutton Hoo: the Seventh Century in North-western Europe*, Boydell Press (Woodbridge), 3–23.

Scull, C.J. 1993: 'Archaeology, early Anglo-Saxon society and the origins of Anglo-Saxon kingdoms', *Anglo-Saxon Stud. Archaeol. Hist.* 6, 65–82.

Scull, C.J. 1995: 'Approaches to material culture and social dynamics of the lMigration Period in eastern England', in Bintliffe, J. and Hamerow, H. (eds.), *Europe between Late Antiquity and the Middle Ages: Recent Archaelogical and Historical Research in Western and Southern Europe*, Brit. Arch. Rep. Int. Ser. 617 (Oxford), 71–83.

Scull, C.J. 1997: 'Urban centres in pre-Viking England?', in Hines, J. (ed.), *The Anglo-Saxons from the Migration Period to the Eighth Century: an Ethnographical Perspective*, Boydell and Brewer (Woodbridge), in press.

Smith, C.A. 1976: 'Exchange systems and the spatial distribution of elites: the organisation of stratification in agrarian societies', in Smith, C.A. (ed.), *Regional Analysis*, Vol. 2, Academic Press (New York), 309–74.

Warner, P. 1985: 'Documentary survey', *Bull. Sutton Hoo Res. Comm.* 3, 17–21.

Wallerstein, I. 1974: *The Modern World System*, Academic Press (London).

Yorke, B. 1990: *Kings and Kingdoms of Early Anglo-Saxon England*, Seaby (London).

Yorke, B. 1993: 'Fact or fiction? The written evidence for the fifth and sixth centuries AD', *Anglo-Saxon Stud. Archaeol. Hist.* 6, 45–50.

The Origins of Anglo-Saxon Kingdoms: The Contribution of Written Sources

Barbara Yorke

Kings and kingdoms are one of the more accessible topics for historians of Middle Saxon England, but unfortunately for us the first Anglo-Saxon kings and the formation of the earliest kingdoms occurred before the keeping of records became commonplace in Anglo-Saxon England. Earlier attempts to fit archaeological evidence into a framework of documents purporting to depict what occurred in the fifth and sixth centuries have been discredited (e.g. Myres 1969). This has led many archaeologists to question the value and reliability of all written texts for the early Anglo-Saxon period, but in fact they still have a considerable potential if properly understood and used judiciously.

The Anglo-Saxon Origin Myths

The traditional accounts of the arrival of Hengist and Horsa, Cerdic and Cynric, Ælle and his three sons, and Stuf and Wihtgar have rightly been rejected as simple accounts of events in the fifth and sixth centuries (Sims-Williams 1983a; Yorke 1993). Thanks partly to the use of the type of anthropological parallels which have had such an important part to play in developing archaeological approaches to the Early Middle Ages, we can now recognise these not so much as early attempts at narrative history, but as examples of Germanic oral tradition whereby the creation of new kingdoms and dynasties was validated and explained (Goody 1968). Although myths of this type are part of the Anglo-Saxons' common Germanic inheritance (Wenskus 1961), they were not static entities, but could be refined to suit changing political circumstances. The inclusion of foundation myths for Kent, the South Saxons and the Jutes of Wight and Hampshire in the ninth-century *Anglo-Saxon Chronicle* underscores the fact that the descendants of Cerdic and Cynric had become the masters of all these former kingdoms (Scharer 1996, 178–85). One might cite as a parallel how King Alfred's declaration that he was drawing upon the lawcodes of Æthelbert of Kent and Offa of Mercia, as well as that of his ancestor King Ine, for the production of his own lawcode could be seen as buttressing his claim to be ruler of all the Anglo-Saxons (Keynes and Lapidge 1983, 164, 305–6). The foundation accounts are of considerable interest for the study of early medieval propaganda and political thought, but they are not realistic depictions of either the *adventus* or the creation of kingdoms. But even these sources may throw us the occasional nugget; for instance, the tradition of Port and his two sons may represent the foundation myth of a dynasty in southern Hampshire (identified by Bede as a Jutish province) that otherwise has gone unrecorded (Yorke 1989).

Needless to say, the dates attached to these foundation accounts cannot be accepted either as reliable survivals from a pre-Christian era. They would have been added when the oral accounts were adapted to an annal format and that may have occurred, for the *Chronicle* entries, as late as the end of the ninth century (Bately 1978). With annals all events that one wants to record have to be assigned to a particular year, but everything we know about Germanic oral sources makes it very unlikely that any versions which emerged from the pre-literate past had dates attached, and, of course, before conversion to Christianity the Anglo-Saxons would not have known of the *anno domini* system of dating (use of which in England may have been pioneered by Bede) (Harrison 1976). A detailed study by David Dumville has shown not only that the pre-Christian dates allotted to the West Saxon kings in the *Anglo-Saxon Chronicle* cannot be correct, but that they have been manipulated to achieve specific ends (Dumville 1985). It is in fact unlikely that any specific dates have survived from the pre-Christian era in later Anglo-Saxon sources. Recent studies have shown that information Bede received from Canterbury about the dates of King Æthelbert seem to have been incorrect, caused perhaps by confusion of his age at death with the number of years he had ruled (Wood 1983; Brooks 1989). If there was confusion at the oldest centre of Anglo-Saxon Christianity about the chronology of the first Anglo-Saxon king to be converted, it does not inspire much confidence in any other supposedly early Kentish dates, let alone those for other Anglo-Saxon kingdoms.

Sources written in the fifth and sixth centuries

Although there are no contemporary Anglo-Saxon sources for the fifth and sixth centuries, there are contemporary writings from other societies in northern Europe. The *De Excidio Britanniae* of Gildas has continued to be the subject of much attention, and its account of a revolt by Saxon federates provides a potential model for how the transition from Roman Britain to Anglo-Saxon England occurred (Winterbottom 1978). There is still a lack of consensus though about when and where Gildas wrote, how his relative dating is to be realised in absolute terms or, indeed, whether his account does provide a reliable guide to events of the subRoman period (Sims-Williams 1983b; Lapidge and Dumville 1984; Higham 1994). These matters will not be pursued further here as there is ample literature available, but it should be noted that Gildas's account is important not only for the Anglo-Saxon *adventus* and the existence of British kingdoms, but also for what he implies about Anglo-Saxon communities at the time he wrote, as Nicholas Higham has discussed recently (Higham 1994; this volume).

Also relevant for Britain in the fifth and sixth centuries are writings from Gaul. The *Gallic Chronicle* and the *Vita* of St Germanus of Auxerre have attracted particular attention, though not complete agreement on how they should be interpreted (Thompson 1984; Wood 1984; Jones and Casey 1988; Burgess 1990). Other writers like Gregory of Tours and Sidonius Apollinaris have not received so much attention in this context. It is true that they do not give us much detail about Britain as such; observations by Gregory of Tours on events in Anglo-Saxon England are restricted to the marriage of 'the son of a certain king in Kent' to a Frankish princess (Krusch and Levison (ed.) 1951, IV, 26 and IX, 26) – though these have been of great importance in amending Bede's dates for Æthelbert of Kent, as discussed above. What Gregory and Sidonius do provide is information about the 'Saxons' (a term which embraces all non-Frankish Germans from the North Sea zones) operating in Francia and in the Channel (Wood 1983; Yorke forthcoming). They depict 'Saxons' behaving like the Vikings of later centuries, raiding the Channel throughout the fifth and sixth centuries, establishing colonies and bases within Francia, including on the Channel coast, and on occasion 'lending' their armies to assist Frankish leaders and factions. There are potentially important implications here for how the 'Saxons' may have behaved on the English side of the Channel as well, with raiding, and perhaps the establishment of bases by the raiders, continuing through much of the sixth century. The identification in Frankish sources of 'Saxon' bases in Normandy, opposite the two Jutish provinces of Kent and the Solent region of southern Hampshire and the Isle of Wight, must be significant for understanding contacts between England and Francia in the sixth century (Lorren 1980; Welch 1991), and may provide part of the background to Frankish claims to hegemony in southern England which Ian Wood has explored (Wood 1983).

Written sources of the seventh and eighth centuries

With the advent of Christianity which was accepted by all the Anglo-Saxon kingdoms in the course of the seventh century, the historian is at least given more to do as the number of written records increases, though whether interpretation is easier because of that is a moot point. The surviving sources contain relatively few references to the sixth century as such, not so much because of distaste for a period of paganism, but because, as was discussed above, information coming from that period belonged to a different thought-world with different ways of configuring the past from the Christian-classical tradition. What we might hope to be able to do from the Anglo-Saxon sources for the seventh and eighth centuries is to reconstruct the political situation at the beginning of the seventh century which could be presumed to have been the result of events in the sixth century. But how far can historians be sure that they know what the political map of the early seventh century was? We have very few sources that were composed in the early seventh century. Pride of place must go to the lawcode of King Æthelbert of Kent (d. 616) which Patrick Wormald has recently affirmed as 'a presentation in a new cultural medium of basically traditional law' (Wormald 1995, 974). Here we may have the best opportunity provided by a seventh-century source of a window back into the sixth century. Later seventh-century lawcodes survive from the reigns of Hlothere and Eadric of Kent (673–85), Wihtred of Kent (issued in 695) and Ine of Wessex (issued between 688 and 694) (Attenborough 1922). Comparison of these lawcodes with those of Æthelbert allows us to see how rapidly kings were developing their powers in the course of the seventh century, for instance, by increasing their responsibilities for law and order and profiting from fines and other judicial payments as a result (Wormald 1995). We must be aware that by the end of the seventh century there had been substantial developments in the office of king and perhaps in the form of kingdoms as well.

In the last quarter of the seventh century the range of documentation increases with the first surviving charters and the earliest narrative sources in the form of saints' Lives. But our dominant source for events in the seventh century is, of course, the *Historia Ecclesiastica* of Bede which was completed in 731 or 2. The point need not be laboured here that Bede was an extremely erudite scholar who had particular aims in writing which are likely to have affected his presentation of material. But although the *Historia Ecclesiastica* is not a straightforward work to use, we should not ignore the fact that Bede used language with great precision (e.g. Fanning 1991), and that his belief that in his own day, as in Old Testament times, God spoke to men through the pattern of events (Ray 1976; McClure 1983) meant that these events must be reported as accurately as possible so that they could be properly interpreted.

If in some respects Bede's work can be seen as the Bible of the seventh and eighth centuries, we must be aware of the danger, that like the Bible, it may be cited selectively to support specific hypotheses. One of the myths about seventh- and eighth-century written records is that they support the idea of large numbers of small kingdoms in Anglo-Saxon England in the early seventh century which by 700 had lost their independence and been incorporated into larger kingdoms as *regiones*. The sources do not rule out the possibility that smaller kingdoms may once have existed, but nor do they provide positive support for the contention that they were once widespread. It is certainly not proven that every *regio* (subdivision of a larger kingdom) had a king; no *-ingas* unit, however large, is represented as having its own ruler in a seventh- or eighth-century source. Bede believed that kings controlled areas equivalent in size to later counties and shires (or one could say Roman *civitates*) and which consisted of several *regiones*. The larger *-ingas* groups and other *regiones* when we get to see them in documented contexts appear primarily as administrative units on which tribute and other payments might be levied, which might pass between royal houses in the negotiations that ended wars, and which might become the *parochiae* of early minsters (Yorke 1999). In 779, for instance, when King Offa of Mercia defeated King Cynewulf of Wessex in a battle, Cynewulf was obliged to cede to him *Bensingtun* (Benson, Oxon) and various other *tunas* with their dependent districts in the upper Thames valley. Benson and Cookham (the only other *tun* involved in this transaction that can be identified by name) were administrative centres for the surrounding areas and possessed minster churches (Blair 1994). One cannot categorically say that these had never been independent, self-governing units with their own leaders, but nor is there any evidence which compels us to interpret them in this way. Even although Benson is a 'people' name, incorporating the element *-ingas*, that need not mean, in the wise words of James Campbell, that there was 'anything primitive or "tribal" about such names. There may be; but the Anglo-Saxons gave "people" names to areas and governmental divisions to which later centuries would have given "area" names. What sounds like a tribe may have been only an administrative district' (Campbell 1979, 48).

In 1989 Steven Bassett provided an entertaining, and often cited, knock-out football league analogy for the competition between kingdoms in the early Anglo-Saxon period which has become in danger of being accepted rather too literally (Bassett 1989, 26–7). Although there is a certain truth in big kingdoms growing by 'knocking out' the smaller, the history of Anglo-Saxon kingdoms in the seventh and eighth centuries was not one of simple linear growth. Many 'lesser league' kingdoms like Kent or that of the South Saxons can be shown to have had considerable stability for at least 150 years under their own native rulers. The predatory actions of Mercian kings in the eighth century which ended their independence are not necessarily a continuation of forms of overlordship in the seventh century, but rather seem to represent a new departure in royal aggrandisement. While warfare in the seventh and eighth centuries might certainly be the result of aggression *between* kingdoms, the written sources also reveal considerable armed conflict *within* kingdoms between rival claimants for the throne who might be either closely related to one another or from different branches of a royal house.

The apparently plentiful subkingdoms of the seventh century need not indicate a plethora of formerly self-governing units which had been incorporated by more successful neighbours. Subkingdoms could be the result of one kingdom taking over another as in the well-documented case of Deira becoming a subkingdom of Bernicia, ruled by princes of the Bernician royal house, prior to the full incorporation of Deira into Bernicia and the formation of the kingdom of Northumbria (Blair 1947; Yorke 1990, 74–81). But other subkingdoms seem to have been the creation of regnal practices or dynastic politics and might be both short-lived and individualistic. One might cite here Wulfhere's creation of a subkingdom in Surrey and adjoining areas for his kinsman Frithuwold in the 670s from various *regiones* which seem to have been only temporarily brought together for this purpose and which split-up to follow different histories again when his rule ceased (Blair 1989).

Looking at regnal practices in seventh- and eighth-century Anglo-Saxon England one is struck by the variety of forms one finds. Some kingdoms like Mercia or Northumbria seem to have had only one king at a time, but in others various patterns of joint kingship were followed (Dumville 1989; Yorke 1990, 167–71). In Kent there seems to have been regularly a senior king based in east Kent and a junior partner in the west of the province who were generally closely related (Yorke 1983; Brooks 1989, 67–74). Among the East and West Saxons it is harder to identify consistent territorialisation; the number of kings ruling together seems to have fluctuated and rulers might be only distantly related to one another (Yorke 1990, 52–4, 142–6). The Hwicce, on the other hand, seem to have had a number of instances of brothers ruling jointly, but with no sign a division of power between them (Finberg 1972, 167–80; Sims-Williams 1990). The adoption of Christianity, and thus of common forms of documentation in all the Anglo-Saxon kingdoms, may conceal other variations in the way kingdoms were organised, and differences may have been even more marked in 600 than they were in 700 (Keynes 1995).

One concomitant of these variations in regnal practice could be that they stem at least in part from variations in the way kingdoms originated. It is unlikely that there is a common format which can account for the origins of all the Anglo-Saxon kingdoms (Bassett 1989). There may be a place for both the hypothesis derived from Gildas, of the leaders of federate forces rebelling against their former masters and taking over their provinces, and the type of model based on settlement dynamics leading to ranked societies which Chris Scull has developed in detail for East Anglia (Scull 1992; 1993). Other possibilities should be considered as well including the intervention, perhaps after the main period of *adventus*, of 'pirate' warbands or exiled princes from other parts of *Germania*. Sam Newton would prefer to interpret the origin of the royal house of East Anglia in this way, based on his reading of *Beowulf* (Newton 1993). A model on these lines could also be developed through analogy with later Viking activity (Coupland 1995).

Perhaps one should also consider whether Bede's famous tripartite division of the settlers into Angles, Saxons and Jutes might be relevant to the question of kingdom origins (Colgrave and Mynors 1969, I, 15, 50–1). In the seventh century regnal practice of the two Saxon kingdoms of the East and West Saxons can be distinguished from that of their Anglian and Jutish neighbours by a pronounced tendency for the names of kings to alliterate with those of their founder king (Sledd/Cerdic) and by a form of multiple kingship which might result in very distant cousins ruling at the same time (Yorke 1990, 52–4, 142–6). Archaeological and dialect evidence also supports the significance of the threefold division (Hines 1990). It can be seen as well in the names of *regiones*: those in Jutish areas have the suffix *-ware*; Saxon areas favour the use of *-ingas*; Anglian areas include some *-ingas*, but also *-saetan* compounds and simple nouns derived from names of rivers or other topographical features (e.g. Gyrwe) (Cox 1975–6). How far the Anglian, Saxon and Jutish divide also had a political dimension is an issue which has yet to be explored fully. It is tempting to argue that this was the case for the Jutes whose provinces in Kent and the Isle of Wight shared Frankish connections and commanded the two areas of southern England with the shortest channel crossings to Francia and lay opposite 'Saxon' colonies on the facing Frankish shores (Yorke forthcoming). Was there some essentially different 'political' experience between Anglian and Saxon areas in the sixth century which had been obscured by the time written records began? Alan Vince's demonstration of a close correlation between the boundary between Saxon and Anglian areas and the borders of two late Roman provinces of Flavia and Maxima Caesariensis suggests some profitable lines for future investigation (Alan Vince at the 47th Sachsensymposium).

We are not at the stage where definite conclusions can be presented about the origins of kingdoms in Anglo-Saxon England, not least because there is so much about the subRoman period which is still the subject of controversy and often of radically different interpretations. When the balance of power shifted from British to Germanic control in eastern and southern England would seem to be a crucial matter, together with the issue of how much of the administrative infrastructure that can be discerned in the seventh-century Anglo-Saxon kingdoms was based on subRoman arrangements, as some scholars have argued (Gelling 1967; Foard 1985; Balkwill 1993; Dark 1994, 137–71). We also need to decide whether the question of the origins of kingdoms needs to be separated from the history of Germanic settlement in Britain and the identification of the earliest units of resource management ('estates'). There may be a danger of confusing separate issues here, and the question remains worth asking of whether one would be able to deduce from archaeological evidence the existence of kingdoms if their presence was not known from written sources. Unlike the Anglo-Saxons we do not have to see the history of the royal houses as the embodiment of the history of their provinces. But we still remain uncertain whether kingdoms grew naturally out of the earliest colonies or were the unnatural creations of roving warleaders who imposed themselves upon settled communities. There is not necessarily going to be one model to serve all, and the origins of Anglo-Saxon kingdoms may have been more diverse than we often care to think. However, if a consensus is ever reached it will need to draw upon both archaeological evidence and written sources; the contribution of the latter is not exhausted yet.

References

Attenborough, F.L. (ed.) 1922: *The Laws of the Earliest English Kings*, Cambridge University Press (Cambridge).

Balkwill, C.J. 1993: 'Old English wic and the origin of the hundred', *Landscape History* 15, 5–11.

Bassett, S. 1989: 'In search of the origins of Anglo-Saxon kingdoms', in Bassett (ed.)1989, 3–27.

Bassett, S. (ed.) 1989: *The Origins of Anglo-Saxon Kingdoms*, Leicester University Press (London)

Bately, J. 1978: 'The compilation of the Anglo-Saxon Chronicle, 60BC to AD890: vocabulary as evidence', *Proc. Brit. Acad.* 64, 93–129.

Blair, J. 1989: 'Frithuwold's kingdom and the origins of Surrey', in Bassett (ed.)1989, 97–107.

Blair, J. 1994: *Anglo-Saxon Oxfordshire*, Alan Sutton (Stroud), 26–7, 49–52.

Blair, P. Hunter 1947: 'The origins of Northumbria', *Archaeologia Aeliana* 4th series, 25, 1–51.

Brooks, N. 1989: 'The creation and early structure of the kingdom of Kent', in Bassett (ed.) 1989, 55–74.

Burgess, R.W. 1990: 'The Dark Ages return to fifth-century Britain: the "restored" Gallic Chronicle exploded', *Britannia* 21, 185–96.

Campbell, J. 1979: 'Bede's words for places', in Sawyer, P. (ed.) *Names, Words, and Graves: Early Medieval Settlement*, University of Leeds (Leeds), 34–54.

Colgrave, B. and Mynors, R.A.B. 1969: *Bede's Ecclesiastical History of the English People*, Oxford University Press (Oxford).

Coupland, S. 1995: 'The Vikings in Francia and Anglo-Saxon England to 911', in McKitterick, R. (ed.) *The New Cambridge Medieval History II, c.700–c.900*, Cambridge University Press (Cambridge), 190–201.

Cox, B. 1995–6: 'Place-names of the earliest English records', *English Place-Name Society Journal* 8, 12–66.

Dark, K. 1994: *Civitas to Kingdom. British Political Continuity 300–800*, Leicester University Press (London).

Dumville, D.N. 1985: 'The West Saxon Genealogical Regnal List and the chronology of early Wessex', *Peritia* 4, 21–66.

Dumville, D.N. 1989: 'Essex, Middle Anglia and the expansion of Mercia in the south-east Midlands', in Bassett (ed.) 1989, 123–40.

Fanning, S. 1991: 'Bede, Imperium and the Bretwaldas', *Speculum* 66, 1–26.

Finberg, H.P.R. 1972: *The Early Charters of the West Midlands* (2nd ed.), Leicester University Press (Leicester).

Foard, G. 1985: 'The administrative organization of Northamptonshire in the Saxon period', *ASSAH* 4, 185–222.

Gelling, M. 1967: 'English place-names derived from the compound *wicham*', *Medieval Archaeol.* 11, 87–104.

Goody, J. (ed.) 1968: *Literacy in Traditional Societies*, Cambridge University Press (Cambridge).

Harrison, K. 1976: *The Framework of Anglo-Saxon History to A.D. 900*, Cambridge University Press (Cambridge).

Higham, N. 1994: *The English Conquest. Gildas and Britain in the Fifth Century*, Manchester University Press (Manchester).

Hines, J. 1990: 'Archaeology, philology and the *adventus Saxonum vel Anglorum*', in Bammesberger, A. and Wollmann, A. (eds.) *Britain 400–600: Language and History*, Carl Winter Verlag (Heidelberg), 17–36.

Jones, M. and Casey, J. 1988: 'The Gallic Chronicle restored: a chronology for the Anglo-Saxon invasions and the end of Roman Britain', *Britannia* 19, 367–98.

Keynes, S. 1995: 'England, 700–900', in McKitterick, R. (ed.) *The New Cambridge Medieval History II, c.700–c.900*, Cambridge University Press (Cambridge), 18–42.

Keynes, S. and Lapidge, M. (eds.) 1983: *Alfred the Great. Asser's Life of King Alfred and Other Contemporary Sources*, Penguin Books (Harmondsworth).

Krusch, B. and Levison, W. (eds.) 1951: Gregory of Tours, *Decem Libri Historiarum, Monumenta Germaniae Historica, Scriptores Rerum Merovingicarum* 1.1. (Hannover).

Lapidge, M. and Dumville, D.N. (eds.) 1984: *Gildas: New Approaches*, Boydell and Brewer (Woodbridge).

Lorren, C. 1980: 'Des Saxons en Basse-Normandie au VI siècle?', *Studien zur Sachsenforschung* 2, 231–59.

McClure, J. 1983: 'Bede's Old Testament Kings', in Wormald, P. (ed.) *Ideal and Reality in Frankish and Anglo-Saxon Society*, Basil Blackwell (Oxford), 76–98.

Myres, J.N.L. 1969: *Anglo-Saxon Pottery and the Settlement of England*, Clarendon Press (Oxford).

Newton, S. 1993: *The Origins of Beowulf*, Boydell Press (Woodbridge).

Ray, R.D. 1976: 'Bede the exegete as historian', in Bonner, G. (ed.) *Famulus Christi*, SPCK (London), 125–40.

Scharer, A. 1996: 'The writing of history at King Alfred's court', *Early Medieval Europe* 5, 177–206.

Scull, C. 1992: 'Before Sutton Hoo: structures of power and society in early East Anglia', in Carver, M. (ed.) *The Age of Sutton Hoo*, Boydell Press (Woodbridge), 3–24.

Scull, C. 1993: 'Archaeology, early Anglo-Saxon society and the origins of Anglo-Saxon kingdoms', *ASSAH* 6, 65–82.

Sims-Williams, P. 1983a: 'The settlement of England in Bede and the *Chronicle*', *Anglo-Saxon England* 12, 1–41.

Sims-Williams, P. 1983b: 'Gildas and the Anglo-Saxons', *Cambridge Medieval Celtic Studies* 6,1–30.

Sims-Williams, P. 1990: *Religion and Literature in Western England, 600–800*, Cambridge University Press (Cambridge).

Thompson, E.A. 1984: *St Germanus of Auxerre and the End of Roman Britain*, Boydell and Brewer (Woodbridge).

Welch, M. 1991: 'Contacts across the Channel between the fifth and seventh centuries: a review of the archaeological evidence', *Studien zur Sachsenforschung* 7, 261–9.

Wenskus, R. 1961: *Stammesbildung und Verfassung: das Werden der frühmittelalterlichen Gentes*, Bohlau Verlag (Köln).

Winterbottom, M. (ed. and trans.) 1978: *Gildas; The Ruin of Britain and Other Documents*, Phillimore (Chichester), ch. 23–6.

Wood, I.N. 1983: *The Merovingian North Sea*, Viktoria Bokförlag (Alingsås).

Wood, I.N. 1984: 'The end of Roman Britain: continental evidence and parallels', in Lapidge and Dumville (eds.) 1984, 1–26.

Wormald, P. 1995: '*Inter cetera bona...genti suae*: law-making and peace-keeping in the earliest English kingdoms', *Setttimane di Studio del Centro Italiano di Studi Sill Alto Medioevo* 42, 963–93.

Yorke, B.A.E. 1983: 'Joint kingship in Kent c.560–785', *Archaeologia Cantiana* 99, 1–19.

Yorke, B.A.E. 1989: 'The Jutes of Hampshire and Wight and the origins of Wessex', in Bassett (ed.) 1989, 84–96.

Yorke, B.A.E. 1990: *Kings and Kingdoms of Early Anglo-Saxon England*, Seaby Books (London).

Yorke, B.A.E. 1993: 'Fact or Fiction? The written evidence for the fifth and sixth centuries AD', *ASSAH* 6, 1–6.

Yorke, B.A.E. 1999: 'Political and ethnic identity: a case study of Anglo-Saxon practice', in Frazer, B. and Tyrell, A. (eds.) *Social Identity in Early Medieval Britain and Ireland*, Leicester University Press (London), in press.

Yorke, B.A.E. forthcoming: 'Gregory of Tours and sixth-century Anglo-Saxon England', in Mitchell, K. and Wood, I.N. (eds.) *The World of Gregory of Tours*, E.J. Brill (Leiden).

Anglo-Saxon Studies in Archaeology and History 10, 1999

Imperium in Early Britain: Rhetoric and Reality in the writings of Gildas and Bede

Nick Higham

Neither Gildas nor Bede set out to describe the political structures of their own communities, but each wrote from a contemporary perspective and something of the current political context naturally became embedded in the work each produced. That of Bede is the later and by far the more transparent: it is in various ways possible to establish the relationship between his vision of recent insular society and the reality upon which it was based with some confidence. Gildas, in contrast, wrote a far more opaque and polemical work, devoid of dates and spatial indicators, albeit one which specifically addressed contemporary objectives (as *DEB*, I). The task of disentangling and interpreting his purposes from his flights of rhetoric poses much greater problems today for those wishing to reconstruct the political systems of his generation or those of his parents and grandparents.[1]

To Gildas, first, therefore: following traditions already firmly entrenched in the *Seven Histories* of Orosius (Wright 1985; Kerlouégan 1987, 81–5; Arnaud-Lindet 1991), he used the terms *rex* and *imperator* for Roman emperors and both *regnum* and *imperium* for 'imperial rule' or 'empire'. Only *imperator* and *imperium*, however, occur exclusively in the *De Excidio Britanniae* in this context. Both words are used in such a way as to imply a degree of legitimacy and moral rectitude. The nearest thing to an exception is Gildas's use of *imperium* with reference to the evil Magnus Maximus (*DEB*, XIII), but he was careful to qualify it with *iniquissimus* ('most iniquitous'), so differentiating it from more legitimate examples, and remarked his unfitness to even show the insignia of an *imperator*. Magnus Maximus's career was, therefore, treated by Gildas as the moral interface between legitimate Roman *imperatores* and illegitimate British rulers, and the point at which language appropriate to Roman imperial authority gave way to less deferential terms for those exercising rule over Britain. Gildas was not alone in adopting this position: although he included detail which had come from some other source, he followed Orosius's characterization of Maximus and others closely. In the *Seven Histories* (VII, xxxiv, 9, 10; xxxv, 2, 3, 10), Orosius viewed Maximus as a virtuous man who would have been worthy of imperial status had he not seized it contrary to his own oath, and treated him variously as a *tyrannus* and as *imperator*. Similarly, a string of *tyranni* – including the British Gratian and Constantine, contested unsuccessfully with Honorius *imperator* for control of the western empire (VII, xl, 4, 5; xlii, 3, 4, 6, 7, 9, xv).

The authority of later figures in the *DEB* was restricted to Britain and Gildas generally termed them *tyranni*. Kings active in the present and addressed in *DEB* XXVII to LXXV provide the least problematic examples of these. Gildas took upon himself the role of a biblical prophet, duty bound by God to test contemporaries and condemn unjust kingship and a compromised priesthood. His strictures offer a mirror image of the just king and legitimate clergy whose virtues might encourage God to protect His people (see also Brooks 1983/4; Bachrach 1988). Even so, in between the two extremes of legitimate Roman *imperatores* and British *tyranni* were various unnamed *rectores* ('governors' or 'rulers') and *duces* ('military leaders'), both past and present, whom Gildas treated with considerably more respect (Higham 1994, 151–9, 189).

When attempting to reconstruct the fall of Britain, therefore, Gildas envisaged legitimate Roman imperial rule giving way to the wicked empire of Magnus Maximus. When that fell, he envisaged a Britain bereft of soldiers and without Roman governors (*DEB*, XIV) but still operative as a single political unit: it was, for example, 'Britain' which then sent legates with letters to Rome to appeal for military protection (*DEB*, XV, 1). Gildas's conceptualisation of this period of self-government leans heavily on existing literature – not least Revelations and the Aeneid – and seriously misrepresents the resumption of imperial control post-Maximus, yet there is an historical reality behind the political vision. Britain had a long history of sporadic self-rule prior to AD400 which invariably featured unified control under a quasi-imperial figure (such as Clodius Albinus, Carausius, Allectus). Successive British imperial candidates put up by the insular army early in the fifth century culminated in the meteoric career of Constantine III, who attempted to wrest the Gallic Prefecture (including Britain) from Honorius's supine grip in the years 407–10 (Thompson 1977), much as Magnus Maximus had done a generation earlier from Gratian. In 410–11 Honorius regained Gaul but had not the resources to restore active control of the British diocese. An imperial reconquest must often have seemed imminent on occasion right up to Aetius's death in 454.

Given the precedents and what we know of Constantine III, Gildas was probably correct in representing a pan-diocesan authority descending intact. His brief flirtation with this process featured unnamed tyrants who ruled and were killed successively, in a context which encompassed 'Britain' and 'everyone'. These may well represent Gildas's treatment of Constantine's family and their opponents, of whom he had arguably read in Orosius's *Seven Histories* (VII, xl, 4–7; xlii, 1–6). This brought Gildas down the years to the anonymous figure of a *superbus tyrannus* whom we, following Bede (*HE*, I, 14), know as Vortigern (for the pun, see Jackson 1982, 35–6). The *superbus tyrannus* is portrayed as a pan-British ruler at the point when he met with his councillors and devised a plan to protect the 'fatherland' (*patria*: a term used by Gildas as synonymous with erstwhile Roman Britain), which involved employing Saxon mercenaries. His advisors were 'the silly princes of Zoan' who gave 'foolish advice to Pharaoh'. Related references suggest that Gildas thought of these 'silly princes' as if the forerunners of the kings of his own day, so his image of 'Vortigern' is suggestive of a diocesan ruler presiding over a council of tribal or regional aristocrats (Higham,1994, 38–9).[2] Vortigern was, however, the last British figure whom Gildas treated as if ruler of all of what had been Roman Britain. By contrast, the idealised hero-figure of Ambrosius Aurelianus (*DEB*, XXV, 3), who resisted the Saxon rebels, was represented as a leader of only a fragment of the Britons and accorded no official title, despite his fundamental position within Gildas's providential vision of the history of his own people.

Gildas's text does, therefore, suggest a cut-off for the political unity of sub-Roman Britain which coincides with what Professor Edward Thompson long-since dubbed 'the war of the Saxon federates' (Thompson 1979) and even implies that it was that war that brought it to an end. In his own times, Gildas portrayed parts of western Britain as ruled by five kings whose moral shortcomings were such that he termed them tyrants and railed against them (*DEB*, XXVII–XXXVI). They were not, however, entirely equal, although Gildas highlighted their individual responsibilities for their own moral shortcomings and the consequent displeasure of God. Rather, Maglocunus, the 'dragon of the isle' – so Satan in Revelations – was given very different treatment to that of the other four which implied his greater power and regality (Higham 1992). This suggests that he was their senior in status, although how this difference manifested itself in practice is unclear. Either a sort of 'overkingship' or, minimally, a degree of differential status, apparently existed in Wales and the South West when Gildas was writing but it was not obviously formalised.

There are hints of an unequal political relationship between Maglocunus and some still greater military leader: Maglocunus was, for example, only 'greater than many in power' and 'almost the most powerful general in Britain' (*DEB*, XXXIII, 1, 2). The identity of the more powerful figure who is implicit in the text is not established, but association of the British tyrants with a 'devil-father' figure (*DEB*, LXVII,2; CVII, 4; the phrase recurs in CIX, 3 but there unambiguously refers to Satan) may imply that Gildas had a Saxon leader in mind. The terminology would certainly be apt since he characterised Vortigern's Saxon mercenaries as barbarians, animals, convicts, heathen and devils during his description of their rebellion and the ravaging of Britain (*DEB*, XXIII–XXVI). Even so, Gildas depicted Satan as welcomed by the Britons even before the arrival of the Saxons (XXI, 3), so his meaning is likely to have been both literal and metaphorical.

The church was clearly integral to social organisation and control in Gildas's Britain, as one might expect on the basis of parallels from elsewhere in western Europe (e.g. Wood, 1994, 71–87). Gildas's condemnation of churchmen uses a whole suite of Old Testament texts. Some criticise clerical willingness to associate themselves with God's enemies. To an extent these are the British kings but they arguably also include devil-like barbarian unbelievers, whom he had already characterised via the oppressors of the Israelites in the Old Testament. Take for example *DEB*, LXX, 2 (paraphrasing parts of Judges, XI, 30–40): 'Which, in order to lay low the innumerable thousands of the Gentiles, enemies to the people of God [the Britons in this context], sacrificed his own daughter (by which is understood his own pleasure) because she came to meet the victorious army with drum and dancing (that is, carnal pleasures), in payment of a vow?' Although Gildas envisaged that Maglocunus had been reclaimed by the devil when he reneged on his monastic vows (*DEB*, XXXIV, 3), the Saxons were the abomination who were 'hated by God and men' (*DEB*, XXIII, 1), and the likelier to be referred to herein.

Even at the time of writing, Gildas retained a strong image of 'the fatherland' – *patria* – which he used only in the singular but on twenty-one separate occasions in this text for a territory which was inhabited by the *cives* – 'citizens' – who were apparently the Christian Britons of intramural Britain (Higham 1994, 10, 38; Dumville 1995, 183) It was that same *patria* which Vortigern had sought to protect by employing Saxon mercenaries (*DEB*, XXIII, 1), so it had a political reality at least to that date. He likewise used such terms as *Britannia*, 'provinces' and *rectores* – which seems at least on occasion to translate as 'provincial governors' – all in a contemporary context. One or more treaties governed relations between Britons and Saxons, again apparently in a universal context (*DEB*, XCII, 3). Such treatment implies the survival of a diocesan-centric vision of British society even up to the date of authorship, yet it was a society which had long been detached from Rome and which had had some sort of history as a British successor state. Furthermore, it could even evince loyalty and a degree of nationalist fervour in a quintessentially British Latin author such as Gildas, which suggests that the idea of a British nation retained a significant degree of social and cultural identity at the time of writing.

However hesitant our understanding of Gildas's *De Excidio*, therefore, there is evidence scattered through it which implies that the society with which he was familiar retained some sort of image of, and pride in, its own ethnicity and cultural identity. This sense of identity found expression in Latin as a language of elite intercourse, such political concepts as 'citizens' and 'fatherland' and a shared vision of a just and God-fearing society. The island home of the Britons was eulogised in terms reminiscent of the Garden of Eden or the Land of Canaan (*DEB*, III) and Gildas's vision was certainly universal rather than parochial. British identity acquired added definition from the exclusion of other insular peoples such as Saxons, Picts and Scots, who were accorded less than human status and were not perceived as Christians. From Gildas's perspective, the Britons were a people chosen by God, who were presently suffering divine punishment via the scourge of the Saxons on account of their sins. Yet his work reveals that the idea of a British people and even a single civil community survived, ready to rise once more just as soon as it had returned to obedience to the Lord and earnt redemption thereby.

***

Bede's treatment of *imperium* is far easier to grasp. Looking back to a distant Roman rule of Britain (*HE*, I, 2–11), he envisaged a situation in which the Britons were ruled by their own sub-kings under the broad umbrella of the *regnum* of the Roman emperors and the Roman people (e.g. *HE*, I, 4). Provincial governors do not feature in his text. In this respect, his treatment of the imperial past depended heavily on his perception of the present and the ladder of unequal royal authority with which he was himself familiar.[3] In consequence, it offers valuable insights into those same perceptions. Bede's treatment of various later English 'overkings' was sufficiently detailed to allow us at least to sketch out the extent of their influence and identify the main factors which underpinned their power. Their *imperium* was like that of the Romans in the sense that they had some sort of power over other kings and other peoples – and this last is an important aspect of Bede's use of the term which is sometimes neglected (Fanning 1991). Some English 'overkings' had power over Britons as well as various English peoples and kingdoms (*provinciae*), and some also over Picts and Scots (as *HE*, II, 5).

Although he forebore to describe Hengist and Horsa as kings (*HE*, I, 15), Bede seems to have had no real vision of English political practice prior to kingship. His famous listing of *imperium*-wielding kings (II, 5) necessarily pushes back his assumption that 'overkingship' existed into the 570s, if not earlier: indeed, a literal acceptance of the *ASC* would push Ælle's *imperium* back to 477–91 (against which view, see Sims-Williams 1983). An early emergence of English kingship would seem to find some support in Procopius's story of an insular Anglian army campaigning in the Rhineland around 550, under the leadership of a king's son and intent on avenging a slight to an English king's daughter (*History of the Wars*, VIII, 20). Given the military character of early English kingship, it presumably evolved quickly out of the leadership of warbands in the settlement era of the fifth century. 'Overkingship' perhaps originated in the greater authority of whichever military leaders were accorded precedence and acknowledged as leaders of more than a single *comitas*, or succeded in extracting tribute from the largest number of rivals – both British and English. Since 'overkingship' was not systematically institutionalised in the early seventh century, it seems likely that it was even more ephemeral and *ad hoc* at an earlier date and based on personal reputation above all else. Even so, Bede did have some vision of dynastic origins, noting Ida, for example, as the first Bernician king of his line and attempting to date his activities to the mid-sixth century. For what it is worth, therefore, Bede apparently favoured the view that particular lineages established exclusive rights to royal status during the course of the sixth century, but that does not require that other dynasties had not already held similar positions of power: Bede's various horizons do not, therefore, provide terminal dates for the inception of English kingship *per se*, but of specific royal dynasties beyond whom he was decreasingly capable of recovering the remote past.

By the seventh century, the most important single factor underpinning 'overkingship' in most documented instances was a significant military victory. Many great 'overkings', such as Raedwald or Oswald, seem to have become hegemons immediately after achieving a spectacular success in battle over a powerful and feared opponent (*HE* II, 12; III, 1). Such presumably led contemporaries to view them as particularly god-favoured. The less likely the win, perhaps the greater the impact. In consequence, other kings sought their protection and recognised their superiority. When every king did this – as occurred for example according to Bede following Edwin's victory over the West Saxons in 626 – then the resulting 'overkingship' was universal – with or without the Picts and Scots. It was certainly not only the people who had been defeated who recognised the superiority of an 'overking' – and Edwin's influence over the see of Canterbury in the period 627–33 provides a good example in support of this point (*HE*, II, 17). So too does Bede's notice in passing of Oswald's hegemony over Sussex and

Wessex (*HE*, III, 7; IV, 14), when he is only known to have defeated and killed a Welsh king near the Roman wall.

Several kings clearly established substantial military reputations by repeated victories: the obvious examples are Æthelfrith of the Bernicians and Penda of the Mercians, although Bede forebore to use the term *imperium* of either for transparently rhetorical reasons.

War was not, however, the only method used by even non-Christian kings to attain or sustain superiority. Æthelfrith's presumed responsibility for the development of a spectacular royal centre at Yeavering looks very much like an initiative designed to enhance his own imperial pretensions – and the timber theatre is very suggestive of royal ceremonial (Hope-Taylor 1977, 158–61). Æthelberht perhaps used the Roman architecture of Canterbury for similar purposes and the settings occupied by these two contemporary 'overkings' have some similarities. Additionally, Æthelfrith was one of many kings who used marriage as a strategy to reinforce the expansion of his power. His usurpation of the Deiran kingship *c.* 604 was legitimised by marriage to a princess of the local royal house, who then passed on her own dynastic interest to their sons, Oswald and Oswiu, both of whom eventually became kings of the *Deiri* and could claim to be descendants of a Deiran king (*HE*, III, 6). For the future, power in the north would be contested by two interrelated dynasties with whom different regional communities continued to identify their own interests (Yorke 1990, 78), but the marriage was a first step in the creation of Northumbria.

Some kings delegated regional authority to their close kin. Penda used his son Peada as a means to consolidate control of Middle Anglia (*HE*, III, 21), Saeberht ruled the East Saxons under the *potestas* of his uncle Æthelberht of Kent (II, 3) and two related sub-kings successively ruled Deira under Oswiu, who also established *principes* in Mercia, against whom local *duces* revolted in favour of their own dynasty in 658 (III, 24). The *Life of Wilfrid* reveals the presence of sub-kings and ealdormen in various parts of Northumbria and Bede refers to similar figures in Wessex. The creation of sub-kingships for members of the royal kin was a potent means of imposing the authority of a powerful dynast on communities which had alternative traditions of royal authority, and so of binding them into a growing kingship.

Not all early 'overkings' are known to have had a military reputation based on victory. The principal exception is Æthelberht of Kent, whom Bede failed to credit with any sort of warlike activity. Unless this is a matter of poor data, his 'overkingship' seems to have depended on amities forged by marriage during his father's reign with the Franks and East Saxons. It seems pertinent to contrast the aggressive characteristics of Æthelfrith's more warlike regime in the north with the more diplomatic approach to political issues of his southern contemporary, Æthelberht of Kent. It is also worth noting that, of these two, it was the regime which was short on military kudos but strong on diplomatic links which first sought to reinforce its status via Christian ideas about authority and organisation. Æthelberht's entire reign seems to have involved a partnership with successive bishops based at or very near his court – first the Frankish Liudhard and then the Italians Augustine and Laurence, with Mellitus and Iustus deployed as dependent agents in outlying provinces.[4] Æthelberht's new willingness to accept baptism in the mid-590s was arguably calculated to respond to a shift in the balance of power in Francia in favour of the militant and ostentatiously Catholic King Childibert and his sons (Wood 1994). However, his new Christian identity and the influx of an entire cohort of foreign clergy gave him access to the hierarchical organisation of the Christian clerisy, its monotheistic ideology, its regularisation of ritual and its top-down vision of authority, all of which offered opportunities to enhance his own power and perhaps even expand his hegemony still further. The baptism of Raedwald of the East Angles at Canterbury looks very much like an exercise in the reinforcement of 'overkingship' *vis-à-vis* a powerful, mature and peripheral, subordinate king. Sæberht's baptism was probably a similar event (Angenendt 1986). Æthelberht clearly learnt very early that rituals such as adult baptism or the consecration of a church offered new and potent means to both reinforce and advertise his own position, within his own core people and outside. Augustine's putative dealings with the British clergy in the west are likely to have been promoted by the king as a vehicle for the expansion of his own superiority over British kings. Æthelberht's written law-code arguably reflected his desire to project himself as a 'real' king who was visibly doing kingly things: publication of new tranches of Salic law had been among the last political acts of King Childibert during the years 594–6 (*MGH, Leges*, IV, i, 269–73; Wood 1994, 107) and Æthelberht may well have taken the idea from one of the several Frankish clergy who arrived at his court from what had been Childibert's territories (dispatched by the Merovingians at Gregory's request: Gregory *Epist.* VI, 49, trans. *EHD*, I, 790–1), who would have been better placed than Italians to prepare a document in Old English. Experimentation with coinage was another feature of Æthelberht's reign which offered some potential to reinforce and advertise his kingship and his new cult (Werner 1991). Æthelberht was a king who understood the value of showmanship to a regime and one also who was prepared to experiment with new methods of enhancing his own power.

In the north, a generation later, each of Edwin, Oswald and then Oswiu all used Christian cult within a wider package of strategies designed to embed and extend their own hegemonies. The baptismal sites associated with Edwin and his development of York as a new ritual centre for his regime reveal much about the organisational geography of his power. Oswald placed Bamburgh and

Lindisfarne at the centre of his alternative polity, which replaced Edwin's Roman bishop with a rival, Irish sacerdotal authority in alliance with his own dynasty. The establishment under royal patronage and protection of a uniform ritual with a single calendar of festivals and ceremonial sites which could be endlessly replicated offered kings the capacity to refocus society on their own palace complexes and marginalise alternative but less manageable sources of authority – such as non-Christian shrines. Subordinate priests offered great kings agents through whom they could seek to supervise their neighbours and provide themselves with information. The journeying of Bishop Cedd of the East Saxons backwards and forwards to the north and the courts of its kings, his patrons, is an apt example (*HE*, III, 22). Edwin's forcible export of Christianity to the East Angles in the late 620s provides a clear indication of his concern to use cult as a vehicle to control that recently dominant dynasty and reduce it to client status (*HE*, II, 15). His correspondence with the papacy as the king responsible for both Canterbury and York reflects his determination to impose himself on the Christian clergy of both English synods, and Pope Honorius was prepared to legitimise his pretensions in order to further conversion (*HE*, II, 17). Oswiu received similarly valuable diplomatic support and a great cache of relics from the papacy when he united English Christendom under the authority of Rome in 664 (*HE*, III, 29).

Bede, of course, viewed royal support of missionary activity as spiritually motivated, but that is most unlikely to have been the whole of the story. This is not to suggest that kings were cynical manipulators of Christian priests. Rather, both they and the missionaries recognised the potential for mutual benefit which co-operation afforded. During the conversion period kings divide between those who attempted to inflict their religious affiliation on other kings and those who did not. Those doing the inflicting were always *imperium*-wielding kings, although such was not a requirement of that status.

One of the central issues behind the mid-seventh-century contest for overall hegemony was its extent, and this has all sorts of knock-on implications as regards ethnicity and state formation in Britain. The geographical centre of Britain lies in the north Pennines – Haltwhistle is often quoted. If the Bernician dynasty was to emerge as dominant, that would affect Strathclyde, Dalriada and Pictland as much as southern England, and kings such as Oswiu and his sons were certainly active in advancing Englishness northwards across much of what is now Scotland. It was in part Pictish success in repulsing the hegemonal pretensions of the Bernician dynasty that enabled the Mercians to detach the south from Northumbrian influence.

The end result was Christian kingship among the English, with the greater 'overkingships' of the north and Midlands developing into Northumbrian and Southumbrian realms which mirrored, if rather inaccurately, the two synods which Gregory had envisaged in 601, but which only became permanently established immediately following Bede's death. The ideas about government with which Christianity was associated enhanced the non-military aspects of English kingship and helped consolidate ever greater power in the hands of *imperium*-wielding kings. In the regions over which they had more certain power, many erstwhile client-kingships were demoted to the status of provinces under the rule of ealdormen and aristocracies. The see-saw battle for universal hegemony of the mid-seventh century died away after 685 and the death of Ecgfrith, leaving Mercian power virtually unchallenged in central and southern England.

Bede noted that, in the present, Kent, the East Saxons, East Angles, West Saxons, the Hwicce, Lindsey and other southern *provinciae* unnamed were subject to Æthelbald of the Mercians (*HE*, V, 23), but the Hwicce and Lindsey were by then little more than dioceses within an expanding Mercia and others were likewise to succumb during the eighth century. The last surviving charter of an autonomous Hwiccan king is dated 693, and the first of a Hwiccan *sub-regulus* 706 (Sawyer 1968, nos. 53, 54). Earlier 'overkingship' was often personal and impermanent – at least outside the confines of the better established regional agglomerations of kingships. The new, bloated kingdoms of Mercia, Northumbria and to a lesser extent Wessex were comparatively permanent and individually more powerful than had been the more localised kingships of a century earlier, and politics were far less fluid in consequence. Temporary *imperium* was, therefore, giving way to a handful of larger, consolidated English states, the largest two of which had been the most successful hegemonal powers of the previous century. Although imperial claims were to remain part of the rhetoric of English kings up to the Norman Conquest and beyond, the type of hegemony which Bede began to contextualise *c*. 600 changed during the period he was discussing and was coming to a close by the time he wrote. It evolved during the conversion period, transforming into something rather different as kings seized on Christian ideas about organisation, authority and government and applied those to their own needs. An Æthelfrith warrior-king of *c*. 600 was far removed from the coin-minting, tax-collecting, church-founding, law-issuing, synod-presiding kings of late seventh- and eighth-century England. English kingship had developed a long way during the saga of Bede's conversion story and the process of state formation was well advanced by the point at which he finished.

Notes

1. All references to Gildas's work are to Winterbottom (ed.) 1978. Comments herein on Gildas's *De Excidio Britanniae* précis discussion at far greater length in Higham 1994. There is a useful discussion of some aspects of Gildas's political vision in Dumville 1995, but this contribution is seriously compromised by the author's commitment to a northern context for Gildas and his work. That view was offered in its most developed form by Thompson (1979, 216–18). Its inadequacies were explored in detail in Higham 1994, 90–6 and I would suggest that it is now untenable. See also now Snyder 1998, published since this paper was written.
2. For the rhetorical constructs linking Vortigern's councillors with the British kings who were Gildas's contemporaries, see *DEB*, XXIII, 2; XXXVII, 2. For discussion, see Higham 1994, 38, 156, 205–6. Several earlier writers have also argued for a pan-British context for Vortigern's authority: e.g. Frere 1974, 411–12. There is a current tendency to assume that tribal territories (*civitates*) are the largest social and political units descending from Roman Britain appropriate to discussion of political continuity in the fifth century: see most obviously Dark 1994 and also Dumville 1995, 180–1. While it seems reasonably certain that some tribal regions did survive into early medieval England, the assumption that larger units had no role after *c*.410–20 is at odds with the literary evidence, which in contrast offers no support for this use of the term *civitas*. To Gildas, *civitates* were towns (*DEB*, III, 2; XIX, 3) and approximately synonymous with *urbes* (XVIII, 2) and *coloniae* (XXIV, 3). There is no hint of any use of *civitas* for autonomous tribal territory in his text, while he does refer to a variety of other units, including provinces.
3. Discussion is based on the text edited in Colgrave and Mynors 1969. My comments on Bede's vision of 'overkingship' are more fully expressed in Higham 1995.
4. These comments précis discussion in Higham 1997.

Bibliography

Angenendt, A. 1986: 'The conversion of the Anglo-Saxons considered against the background of the early medieval mission', *Settimane di Studi Sull'Alto Medioevo* 32 (2), 755–66.

Arnaud-Lindet, Marie-Pierre. (ed.) 1991: *Orose Histoires (Contre les Paiens)*, 3 (Paris).

Bachrach, B.S. 1988: 'Gildas, Vortigern and constitutionality in sub-Roman Britain', *Nottingham Medieval Studies* 32, 126–40.

Bede: see Colgrave and Mynors.

Brooks, D.A. 1983/4: 'Gildas' *De excidio Britanniae*: its revolutionary meaning and purpose', *Studia Celtica* 18/19, 1–10.

Colgrave, B. 1927: *The Life of Bishop Wilfrid by Eddius Stephanus*, Cambridge University Press (Cambridge).

Colgrave, B. and Mynors, R.A.B. (eds.) 1969: *Bede: Ecclesiastical History of the English People*, Oxford University Press (Oxford).

Dark, K. R. 1994: *Civitas to Kingdom: British Political Continuity 300–800*, Leicester University Press (London).

Dewing, H.B. (ed. and transl.) 1928: *Procopius: History of the Wars*. Loeb (London/New York).

Dumville, D.N. 1995: 'The idea of government in sub-Roman Britain', in Ausenda, G. (ed.), *After Empire: Towards an Ethnology of Europe's Barbarians*, Boydell Press (Woodbridge), 177–204.

Eckhardt, K.A. (ed.) 1962: *Pactus Legis Salicae, Monumenta Germaniae Historica, Leges Nationum Germanicarum* 4 (1) (Hannover), 1–236.

EHD: see Whitelock.

Ewald, P. and Hartmann, L.M. 1887–90: *Gregory I: Register*, in *Monumenta Germaniae Historica, Epistolae* i, 2 (Berlin).

Fanning, S. 1991: 'Bede, *Imperium* and the Bretwaldas', *Speculum*, 66, 1–26.

Frere, S.S. 1974: *Britannia*, Oxford University Press (Oxford).

Gildas: see Winterbottom.

Gregory *Epist.*: see Ewald and Hartmann.

Higham, N.J. 1992: 'Medieval "overkingship" in Wales: the earliest evidence', *Welsh History Review* 16,145–59.

Higham, N.J. 1994: *The English Conquest: Gildas and Britain in the Fifth Century*, Manchester University Press (Manchester/New York).

Higham, N.J. 1995: *An English Empire: Bede and the Early Anglo-Saxon Kings*, Manchester University Press (Manchester/New York).

Higham, N.J. 1997: *The Convert Kings: Power and Religious Affiliation in Early Anglo-Saxon England*, Manchester University Press (Manchester/New York).

Hope-Taylor, B. 1977: *Yeavering: An Anglo-British Centre of Early Northumbria*, HMSO (London).

Jackson, K. 1982: '*Varia*: II. Gildas and the names of the British princes', *Cambridge Medieval Celtic Studies* 3, 30–40.

Kerlouégan, F. 1987: *Le De Excidio Britanniae de Gildas: Les Destinées de la Culture Latine dans l'Ile de Bretagne au VI siecle*, Sorbonne (Paris).

Life of Wilfrid: see Colgrave.

MGH: Leges: see Eckhardt.

Orosius: see Arnaud-Lindet.

Procopius: *History of the Wars*: see Dewing.

Sawyer, P.H. 1968: *Anglo-Saxon Charter: An Annotated List and Bibliography*, Royal Historical Society (London).

Sims-Williams, P. 1983: 'Gildas and the Anglo-Saxons', *Cambridge Medieval Celtic Studies* 6, 9–25.

Snyder, C.A. 1998: *An Age of Tyrants: Britain and the Britons A.D. 400 600*, Pennsylvania State University Press (Pennsylvania).

Thompson, E.A. 1977: 'Britain, A.D. 406–10', *Britannia* 8, 303–318.

Thompson, E.A. 1979: 'Gildas and the history of Britain', *Britannia* 10: 203–26.

Werner, M. 1991: 'The Liudhard Medalet', *Anglo-Saxon England* 20, 7–41.

Whitelock, D. (ed.) 1979: *English Historical Documents* I, 2nd ed., Routledge (London/New York).

Winterbottom, M. (ed.), 1978: *Gildas, The Ruin of Britain and other Documents*, Phillimore (Chichester).

Wood, I. 1994: *The Merovingian Kingdoms 450–751*, Longman (Harlow).

Wright, N. 1985: 'Did Gildas read Orosius?', *Cambridge Medieval Celtic Studies* 9, 31–42.

Yorke, B. 1990: *Kings and Kingdoms of Early Anglo-Saxon England*,

Organising the Landscape. A matter of production, power, and religion

Charlotte Fabech

In Denmark, detector surveying has brought to light many new settlements from the late Scandinavian Iron Age (third–eleventh century), characterised by a wealth of metal finds. This has changed our impression of this period radically, and has led to a resurgence of interest in the question of the social and political role played by central Nordic localities during the Late Iron Age. Places like Helgö in Lake Mälaren, Dankirke in Jutland, Gudme/ Lundeborg on Funen and Sorte Muld on Bornholm occupy the forefront of attention (Lundström 1988; Ramqvist 1990; Fabech and Ringtved 1995; Hansen 1990;1991; Thrane 1992; 1993; Thomsen *et al.* 1993; Nielsen *et al.* 1994; Jørgensen 1995b; Watt 1991). Gold, silver, craft products and imported objects occur in outstandingly large quantities in these few places. The result is that they have been given paramount positions in Scandinavian polities, positions dominating all surrounding regions. But is this impression misleading? The widespread distribution of die-linked Nordic gold bracteates as well as goldsmith's work from the continent demonstrates that fifth and sixth century Scandinavia had plenty of small political constellations, each with its own paramount centre (Fig. 1).

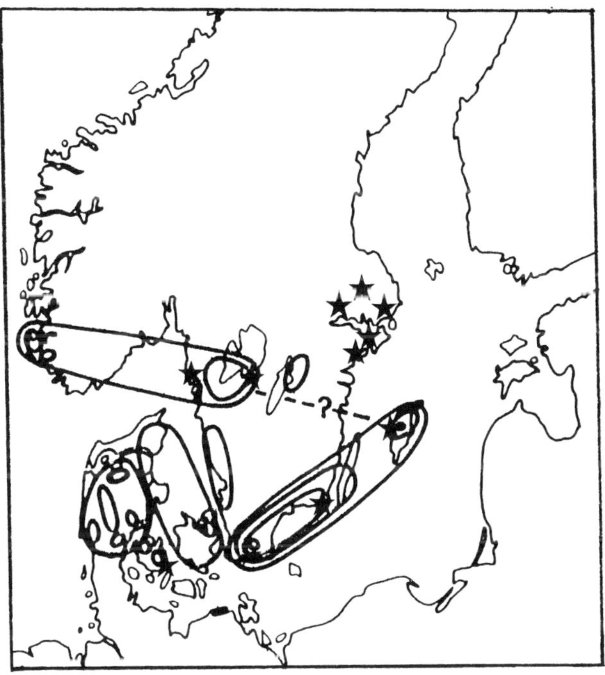

Fig. 1 Distribution of die-linked gold bracteates as well as goldsmith's work from the continent (after Andrén 1991 and Fabech 1994).

The number of sites characterised by material rich in small finds is rapidly increasing. In the years to come, we have to expect that many new sites comparable to Dankirke and Gudme will appear. Therefore the time seems ripe to rewrite the settlement history of the first millennium radically, supplying it with a more differentiated version both with regard to the economy and the social and political conditions. In a new history we have to be careful not to overestimate the significance of sites already well known and published, nor to give them hegemonic positions over more or less large parts of Scandinavia (Ringtved 1991; see also Ringtved, this volume). Instead, we have to increase our knowledge about newly found sites and their landscape setting, as well as continue to localise new central settlements. It is necessary to get a more representative sample in order to estimate how large an area a centre controlled and how far it was to the next centre. What kind of organisation of the landscape formed the backdrop to these centres? Does it reflect a structure consisting of several normal rural settlements and a few larger and richer centres, or is it an expression of a system in which power was widely distributed in the landscape, so that we have to expect many normal rural sites as well as a considerable number of more or less rich centres? Should we expect the centres to be distributed as densely as High and Late Medieval manors and church villages, or were they fewer? Not until we have got an understanding of these topographic circumstances will it be possible for us to grasp the organisation of the polities of South Scandinavia.

Concepts like central-place, aristocratic residence, elite settlement, centre of wealth, magnate manor, magnate farm, trading site, centre of power, cult site, sanctuary, etc. are all used as self-evident in papers on new finds from the Migration and Merovingian periods. But does the varied terminology really reflect as many different types of settlement? Or do we have to see them as a demonstration of the fact that the investigation of these sites is in its initial phase, and that our concepts are thus not yet well-defined? It is obvious that we, the archaeologists, desperately need a clarifying debate in order to find concepts that are both understandable and appreciable for non-archaeologists.

Continuity or discontinuity?

The centres of power have been characterised by Ulf Näsman as settlements that housed several functions: we can expect that they functioned as cult site, aristocratic or royal residence, craft working area, trading site and military base, and that they fulfilled super-regional functions within cult and justice (Näsman 1991a and b). Such characteristics correspond in reality quite well to the basic functions of the central-places of the thirteenth century: administrative, legal, military, ideological and economic (Harrison 1997). Thus we could ask ourselves whether the centres of the High Middle Ages (twelfth to thirteenth centuries) have their origin in Viking and pre-Viking periods.

Investigations of aristocratic sites during the first millennium indicate that there is a connection between the centre complexes of the Late Iron Age and the High Medieval manorial estates. This connection has to be considered as a continuity between the power centres of the two periods (Fabech 1994; Fabech and Ringtved 1995; Jørgensen 1995a; Brink 1996; Riddersporre 1996). The medieval noblemen with manor and church thus cannot be seen as a result of a plundering economy of the Viking Age or the formation of a Christian kingdom in the tenth to eleventh centuries, as is often believed (Lindqvist 1988). We can only understand them if we trace their origin back to the disintegration of the Early Iron Age tribal society, with its collective ideology, after which the appearance of a new society allowed the individual to step forward.

Our impression of considerable continuity in function and significance between centres of the Late Iron Age and those of the High Middle Ages finds support in the development of the Iron Age sacrificial customs as reflected in finds from lakes and bogs. This development goes from individual sacrifices of pottery, food or ornaments, which have traditions going back to the Stone Age, to large communal manifestations, such as human and war booty sacrifices, and ultimately to the cessation of the wet land offerings at the end of the sixth century (Fabech 1994). The conclusions of my study of Iron Age sacrificial customs thus indicate that the sacral role, which was played by wetland sites through thousands of years, came to an end in the sixth century. This would suggest that important ideological changes took place in the Migration period. It is interesting to note that from about the year 400 and before the cessation of the long-lasting sacrificial custom, we see new religious manifestations appearing. For example, gold bracteates are found in wetlands as well as on dry land, and in both cases seem connected to settlements of some importance. From the sixth century a new find category of supposed sacral significance appears: the gold foil figures. With one exception they are found on dry land. The find spots of gold bracteates and gold foil figures show some congruence, and can furthermore be associated with some of the most important settlements of the period. That many of these early centres did not lose their importance is evinced by the fact that medieval manors and churches often are found at them (Fig. 2). The change in sacrificial customs is also reflected in the few written sources and in the place-name material (Fabech 1994,170).

The changes in offering practice in the fifth to sixth centuries coincide with the introduction of a hall building at the magnate residences (Herschend 1993). These exceptional buildings lack the usual household waste, traces of stock raising and simple crafts. They correspond to the hall Heorot as described in Beowulf, an account that gives an idea of the significance of the hall for the reputation of the rulers: here feasts, banquets, and gift-giving took place (Herschend 1992; 1993).

After the cessation of the use of wet lands for offerings, cult rituals moved not only to the magnate halls. Two recent excavations in Sweden, at Borg in Östergötland (Lindeblad 1997; Nielsen 1997) and Sanda in Uppland (Åqvist 1996), have revealed cult houses near the hall building. The words *hørg*, *harg* and *hov*, found in written sources, have at last got an archaeological counterpart. In years to come we have to expect that a number of new sites will produce evidence of halls as well as of cult houses or cult sites connected with the manorial residence.

The evidence taken together gives indeed a strong impression of an ideological change during the Migration period, the making of a new society. A society in which power has been separated from the old tribal community and now become personified in a ruler, in much the same way as the hall was separated from the daily life of its rural setting, as Frands Herschend has demonstrated.

This change can be illustrated tentatively by an example from Denmark, recently investigated by Torben Egeberg Hansen (1996). In a small area around Dejbjerg in Western Jutland we can follow the settlement development from several small rural settlements with a local offering bog in the Early Iron Age to a hamlet with a magnate farm-cum-hall in the Late Iron Age and Viking Age, and in the High Middle Ages we find a village with a nobleman's manor and church. The sacrifices in the bog, the two famous prestigious wagons as well as pottery and some wooden objects, seem to come to an end about 400 A.D., contemporary with the building of the magnate hall (Fig. 3). The magnate residence is situated at toft no. 1 on the old cadastral map. It is thought-provoking that the 500-years younger church and manor are situated on

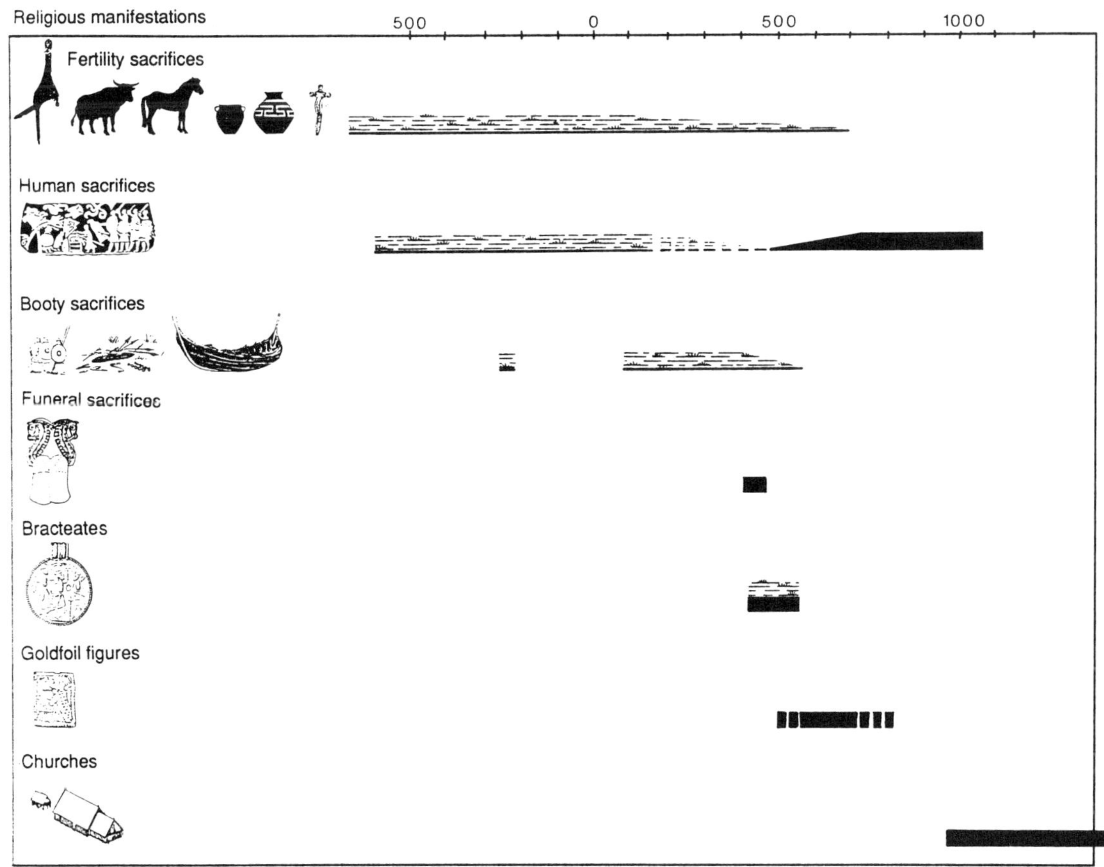

Fig. 2 Tentative chronology of the various types of religious manifestations in southern Scandinavia. Sacrifices in wetland are marked with bog-signature. Manifestations on dry land are marked with black.

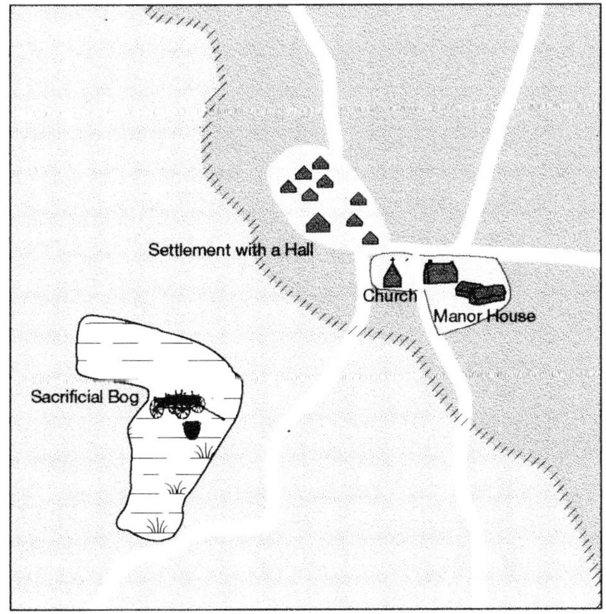

Fig. 3 Dejbjerg in Jutland with sacred bog used in the Early Iron Age till the Migration period, a magnate residence at a hamlet dating to the Migration period, and hamlet with a manor and a church in the High Middle Ages (after T. E. Hansen 1996).

the same toft as the Migration period hall (Torben Egeberg Hansen, pers. comm.). Investigations have not been made to study what the settlement looked like in-between the Migration period and the High Middle Ages, but a number of stray finds and a hoard of a blacksmith's equipment found in the area between the Migration period hall and the medieval church and dating to the Viking Age (T. E. Hansen 1990) indicate that the development in Dejbjerg might have resembled that of Bjäresjö in Scania. At Bjäresjö multidisciplinary research has demonstrated how a magnate farm with a hall from the Viking Age through a number of phases became a manor with a church in the Middle Ages (Skansjö, Riddersporre and Reisnert 1989; Callmer 1992).

Thus, we can today sketch a development from hamlet with magnate farm-cum-hall to hamlet with manor-cum-church, and the inevitable consequence is that in order to understand the structure and origin of medieval estates we have to find the starting-point of investigation as early as the transition from the Early to the Late Iron Age in the fourth–sixth centuries. The sketched development is now found at a number of sites, but this does not mean that this trajectory is the only one possible. On the basis of investigations at Bjäresjö, Lisbjerg, and Uppåkra, we know already today that a Viking Age manor did not necessarily develop continuously to form the centre of a medieval estate. The large farm at Bjäresjö became a medieval manor, and later it moved out of the hamlet to a defensible position where the manor Bjersjöholm is still to be found, but the large farm at Lisbjerg came into the possession of the Aarhus bishop, and the large farm at Uppåkra was paid as compensation by its owner to the king, who in 1085 A.D. bestowed it on the cathedral of Lund, so they never developed into medieval manors (Skansjö, Riddersporre and Reisnert 1989; Jeppesen and Madsen 1997; Riddersporre 1996).

Different landscapes

If we look at geographical central-place models like Christaller's central-place theory, we get a logical model based mainly on distances (Christaller 1966). It shows a regular but complicated system with settlements at several levels. It helps us to realise that settlement systems can be very complex, but it cannot explain why the sites are placed exactly where they are. It shows us that we have to expect many different sites interconnected, but it does not help us to find them.

South Scandinavia has multifarious landscape types and thus the natural resources furnished the basis for various life forms with consequent differentiation of settlement and production. In this way the natural landscape gave different conditions for man's exploitation. From this background we can expect central places and magnate farms to differ in situation, form, and expression depending on type of landscape and resources. The question is, however, whether the rich sites – the central places – have had the same function and significance in spite of different geographical settings and different economy, or whether we will find similar material representation regardless of physical setting. In other words, is it reasonable to expect that all central places have a similar background, function, and significance in all areas of South Scandinavia? In order to address this problem, we have to describe, classify, and compare the different settlements.

An important first step is to work out a social and political hierarchy of the archaeological localities on the basis of their contents and function (Fabech and Ringtved 1995). To look for the position of a site in the hierarchy it is necessary to work on at least three levels: local, regional, and super-regional. A place that holds a central position on a local level could be insignificant in a super-regional perspective.

Figure 4 shows an attempt to structure the small finds in this way. Yet one may more appropriately speak of a hierarchy of settlements, for instance with a division into three levels. The pyramid illustrates the simple observation that there are very few of the supposed localities which have more than a regional significance, a larger number

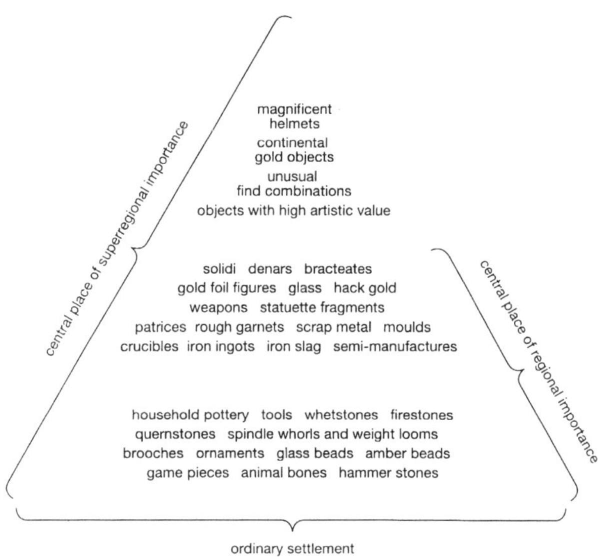

Fig. 4 Attempt to assign levels for settlement materials from the Later Iron Age. (Fabech and Ringtved 1995).

of sites have a more normal wealth, and a broad basis of settlements where only the production of everyday goods can be traced. How can we discover the few forgotten paramount centres? One strategy might be to take a closer look at places which have yielded gold finds.

An unusual gold find can indicate where to find important settlements (Fabech 1991) – we can say that the distribution of gold finds outlines the power of the Migration period landscape in the same way as manorial and royal estates outline the political geography of the Middle Ages. Rich graves, runic stones, and silver hoards show the same in the Viking Age (Fig. 5). The figure tries to list features which are characteristic of central places in the Migration and early Merovingian periods, and corresponding places in the Viking Age/High Middle Ages. If more indicators occur at the same locality and in at least two periods, it suggests the existence of a place with structural continuity.

Interdisciplinarity

Cultural landscapes are very complex, and our only possibility for revealing their past reality is to adduce more or less fragmentary sources from several different disciplines. Thus an interdisciplinary approach is required, in which several incomplete sources are related to one another. Only by means of a collation and interpretation of overlapping sources will it be possible to obtain a picture which can mirror the prehistoric whole.

Certain place-names indicate where to look for the forgotten and hidden but not completely vanished central places of the past (Brink 1996). Place-names belong to a type of source of immense importance in settlement study,

INDICATORS OF CENTRAL PLACES
IN THE MIGRATION PERIOD

ARCHAEOLOGICAL FINDS
continental gold objects
gold bracteates
gold foil figures
golden sword mountings
finds from workshops (precious metal)
scrap silver hoard
weapons

ARCHAEOLOGICAL STRUCTURES
hall building
larger contemporary settlement
larger cemetery
landing site

POSITION IN CULTURAL LANDSCAPE
position in relation to communication
favourable position in relation to resources
the settlement and its different functions dispersed over a larger area

PLACE NAMES
sacral
organizational

STRUCTURAL CONTINUITY (Viking Age/Middle Ages)
runic stones
silver treasures
early romanic churches (magnate church)
chapels
manor houses
royal estates
manorial estates

Fig. 5 Indicators of a central place. The figure tries to list features which are characteristic of central places in the Germanic Period and for corresponding places in the Viking Age/Early Middle Age. If several indicators occur in the same locality and in both periods, it suggests the existence there of a place with structural continuity.

Fig. 6 An example of a so-called name setting, Falbygden in Västergötland, Sweden (after Brink 1997). Settlements are marked with ■. Gold finds from the Roman Iron Age and Migration period are marked with a ★.

but without the support of the geographical, archaeological, and historical setting, the results will remain hypothetical.

Particular place-names appear often in so-called place-name settings. The Swedish onomatologist and settlement historian Stefan Brink considers these name settings as indicators of power centres or administrative centres (Brink 1997). Similar place-name settings are found all over Scandinavia, but they are not to be expected everywhere or anywhere. So it is interesting to note certain coincidence with the find-spots of Migration period gold finds. It is characteristic that the centre in such a setting often has a name like *-tuna*, *-husby*, or *-sala*. Surrounding the centre we find hamlets or farmsteads, some of them with names indicating specific functions: in cult and law, in military organisation and defence, etc. The example shows a name setting in the central settlement area Falbygden in the province of Västergötland in west Sweden (Fig. 6). In this area many magnificent Migration period gold finds have been made: for instance the three-ringed collar from Ålleberg (Holmqvist 1980) and heavy currency rings from Gudhem. There are central sites with names like Saleby – the hamlet with a hall, the *-tuna*-names Tunhem and Sätuna, sacral names indicating sites with sanctuaries like Göteve, Kinneve, Gudhem and Friggeråker, names indicating the social role of the inhabitants like Smedby and Karleby, and names like Vårskal, Vårtofta, etc. which indicate watch-out points in a defence system in the south. How can we understand the background of these names that certainly are of different age? Do the names show that Late Iron Age power was represented in the area by an unbroken chain of centres, each and everyone of them revealing itself with a place-name and archaeological small-finds, or have we to consider the possibility that they cluster in few short periods in which power was manifested in the landscape, separated by periods without a power present that could leave such traces? Only new multi-disciplinary investigations can solve the problem.

It is important to emphasise that the space of South

Scandinavian society was not only determined by nature, but was a social setting too. Personal relations and initiatives, and the power and charisma of some few individuals determined when sites that appear to be equal competed for status as central place, and when the access to traded goods, craft products, as well as sacral and communicative functions were fought for. Consequently, we cannot look upon the landscape simply as a topographic and economic frame around the settlements; it is essential to grasp the mental landscape if we are searching for the landscape of power.

From an example found in the Icelandic sagas (Egil's Saga, Sturlubok and Landnamabok) Frands Herschend has demonstrated that social relations were of decisive importance for the organisation of settlements in a landscape (Herschend 1994). I will give a short summary of his paper. After a feud with King Harald Fine-hair, Skalagrim and his father Kveldulf are forced to settle in Iceland. They sail with two ships. Kveldulf dies on his ship during the voyage but it is arranged for his coffin to be put into the sea, so that, if the coffin land in Iceland, his son could chose to settle where it came ashore. Skalagrim built a farm close to the spot where his father's body had put in (Fig. 7). He calls his farm Borg which means hill or height but at that time was connected with socially dominating farms. Grim is the foremost of the shipmates and he is given a farm opposite to Borg on the southern side of the fjord. Six other shipmates or men are each granted a farm, and these farms form a crescent around Borg. Skalagrim makes two more farmsteads for himself and puts an anonymous, but not autonomous, household in each. In addition to the secondary farms he creates five production units, where stock breeding, salmon fishing, hunting and iron production is important. Skalagrim invites an honourable and rich man Olaf to settle in his district, and Skalagrim's father-in-law, Yngvar, who has been driven out of Norway, is also settled in a very good site.

Skalagrim's achievement is depicted as an ideal *landnam* – we see the chieftain as the powerful leader, who arranges both his own farmstead and his dominion in the region. This way of arranging a settlement in virgin land might indeed reflect a Scandinavian way of thinking about settlement organisation. The problem is, however, how to identify such a pattern in South Scandinavia where the land was more or less fully occupied long before the birth of Christ. Nevertheless, we must consider the possibility that similar ideas are a backdrop of the settlement pattern of the Late Iron Age-Viking Age Scandinavia. Herschend´s study emphasises my point that in order to understand the function and significance of any settlement we have to investigate its surrounding context.

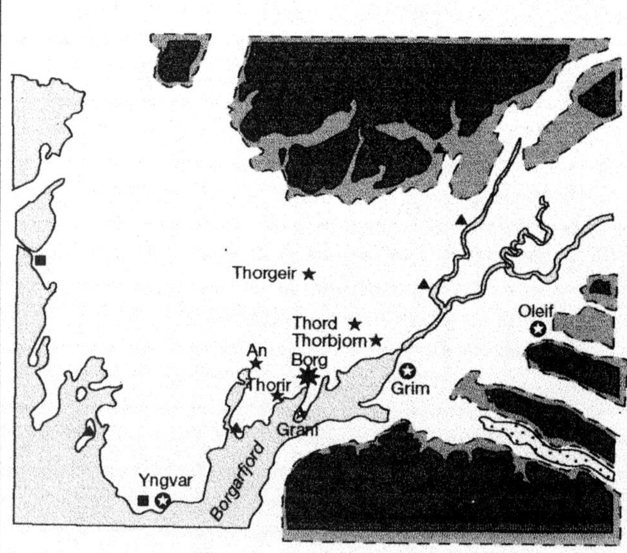

Fig. 7 A map of Skalagrim's settlement at Borgarfjord, Iceland. ✱ Skallagrim's farm. ✪ Farms of Yngvar, Grim and Oleif. ■ Farms belonging to Borg. ★ Farms belonging to freemen and freed men. ▲ Sites for pursuing animal husbandry, fishing, hunting and iron production (Frands Herschend 1994).

Central places – a model

The concept central place stands here for settlements with a rich and varied find material. It represents sites that in the Iron Age fulfilled different functions. At present it is difficult to differentiate between various functions on the basis of the available archaeological material. But we can surmise that they served as residence of the paramount leader and his/her attached specialists with a variety of functions that included monopoly of force, economic management, craft production, and ceremonial legitimisation of power. The manufacture of special wealth in such places served strategically to link together and control the society economically as well as symbolically.

The locality in Denmark which ranks highest for its wealth and exceptional finds is Gudme (Thrane 1992; 1993; Nielsen *et al.* 1994; Fabech and Ringtved 1995; Jørgensen 1995b). The site has also been the most intensively investigated and is therefore the natural starting-point for discussing the structure and the function of wealthy settings. Recently new investigations have brought forward many new sites, which supplement and emphasise our ideas about the appearance and function of such places. In sum we have now a generalised picture of the general traits of a central place. Our knowledge about Gudme and other central places or magnate farms, e.g. Helgö, Slöinge, Borg and Uppåkra in Sweden, and Sorte Muld, Dankirke, Dejbjerg, Strøby and Kalmargården in Denmark, makes it possible to attempt a general model (Fig. 8) for a central place in South Scandinavia (Lundström 1988; Ramqvist 1990; Fabech & Ringtved 1995; Lundqvist 1997; Lindeblad 1997; Stjernquist 1994; 1995; Riddersporre 1996; Watt 1991; Hansen 1990; 1991; T. E. Hansen 1990; 1996; Tornbjerg 1994; Jørgensen 1995a; Jørgensen and Pedersen 1996).

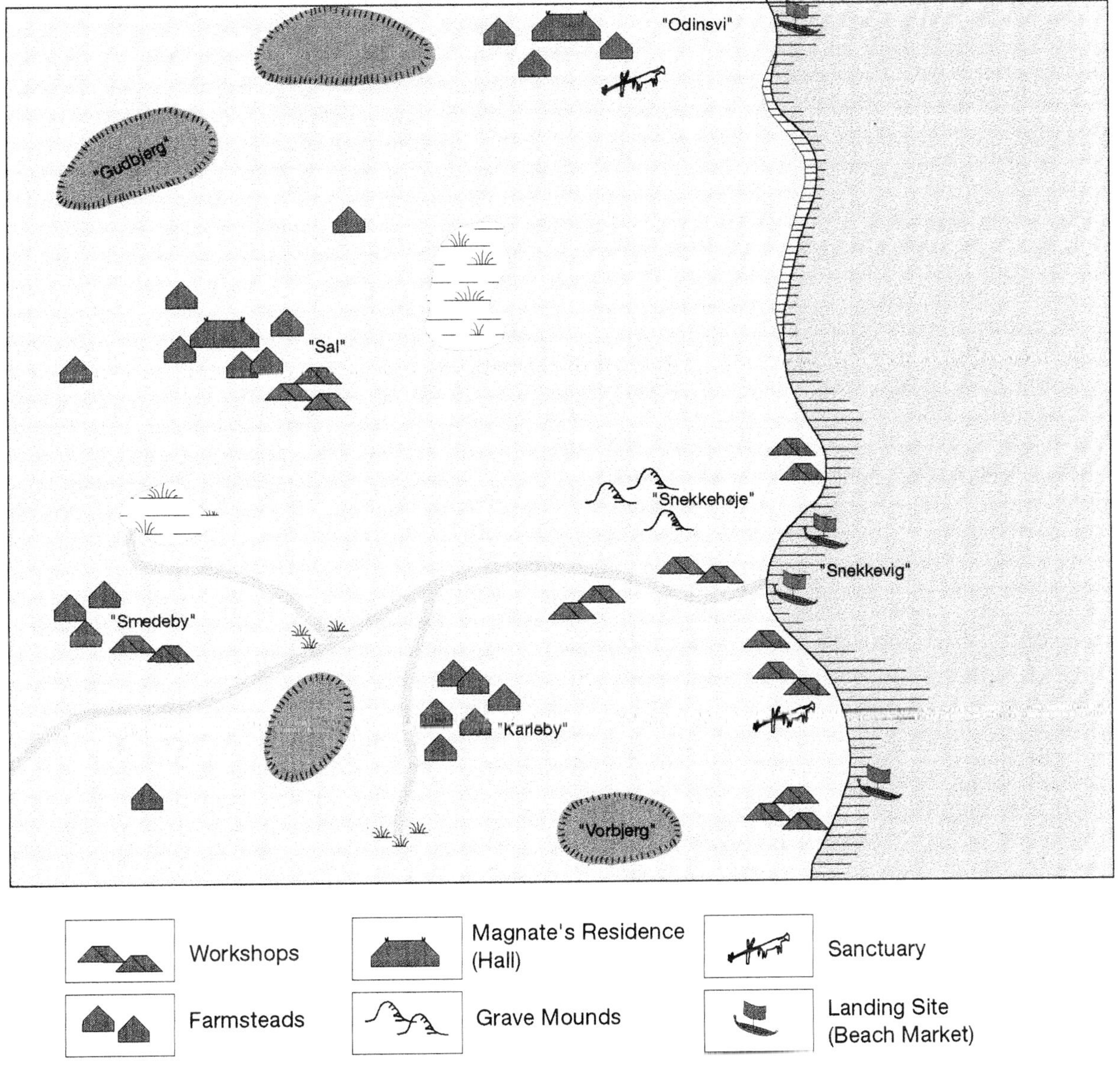

Fig. 8 Attempt to provide a general model of a central place in South Scandinavia.

A central place seems to include both a proper centre and several satellite settlements. Besides hamlets with ordinary houses we find magnate residences with hall and production areas, cult building/site/shrine and trading-places. It is characteristic that the settlements are found scattered in a landscape which can be naturally divided up by wet areas, hills and ridges. The central place does form a cluster and it is consequently not represented by a single spot.

The status and function of a central place is indicated by a combination of several phenomena. Finds of symbols of power and religion, for example gold mounting for swords, gold bracteates, gold foil figures, bronze statuettes, animal figures, coins, etc. Very often the name of the place itself has a sacral place-name such as Gudhem, Odinsvi, Torslund, Lund, or Vi – indicating that the site was the home of a god/the gods or a sacred place – or such a name is found at other sites or natural formations in the vicinity. In the surroundings of sacral names, we often find names indicating a special building or the role of the inhabitants, like Sal, Tuna, Karleby, Rinkeby, and Smedby (Sørensen 1992, Brink 1996; 1997).

It is characteristic that many sites are localised a few kilometres from the coast, at which one or more ports and landing places are to be found. The only one that has been archaeologically investigated in South Scandinavia is found at Lundeborg a few kilometres from Gudme, and here a large and rich material of small finds tells us that exchange and manufacture were important activities. The site seems to have been a periodical beach market. In combination with the other sites in the Gudme region, a settled space appears, a "settlement area" attached to a "centre".

Only a few of the known central places can be dated

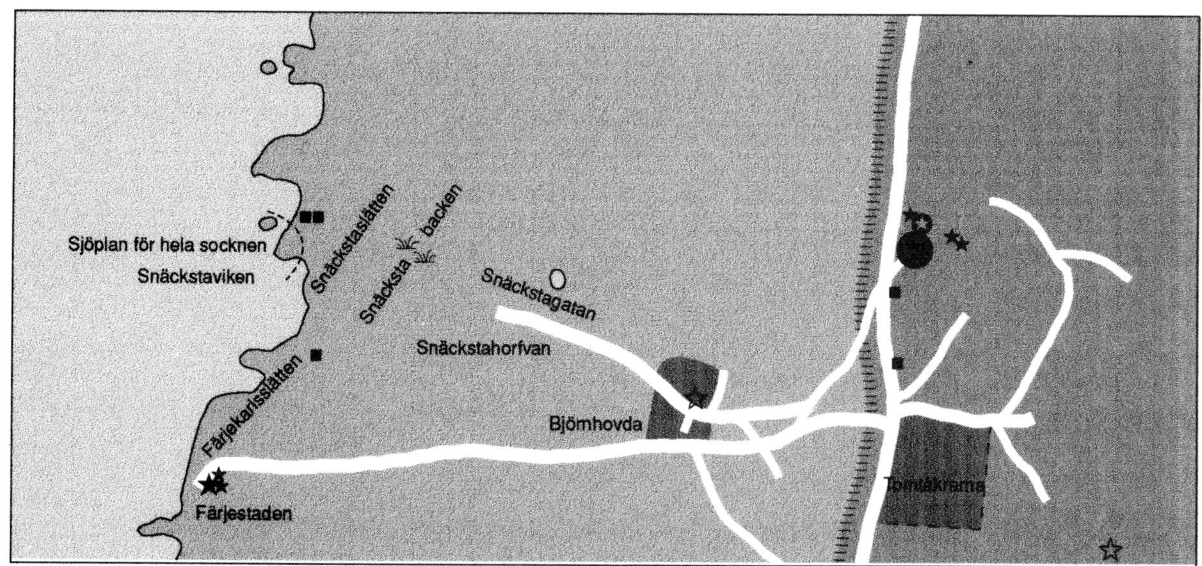

Fig. 9 Map of the Björnhovda area on west Öland, Sweden. The find spot of the famous Björnhovda patrices is marked with ✪, gold finds with ★, the Färjestaden gold collar with ★, Late Iron Age settlements with ●, Viking Age silver hoards with ☆, Iron Age graves with ■.

to the Late Roman Iron Age (third–fourth century) while a large number does not appear till the seventh century. Many of them continue through the Viking Age to appear as medieval manors, church villages or towns. Only new archaeological excavations and geographical investigations of cadastral maps can settle the question whether in general there is a functional continuity between the central settlements and harbours of the Migration period and the High Medieval manors and churches.

Splendid finds and their interpretation

Investigations of the rich sites are necessary and of great importance, if we shall comprehend the aristocratic sites of the Migration and Merovingian periods. But we are only at a beginning – we know too little about them, their function, significance and internal relations, and we have just begun to study the many new settlements and the interpretation of them. We have to be careful not to use our present knowledge as a stereotype, we must not go too far in our interpretations too early, and we must not use these sites and their splendid finds to illustrate the history of the past without sufficient knowledge about them and their context.

The famous patrices found at Björnhovda in Torslunda parish on the Baltic island Öland is a good example. They are used, as pointed out by Ulf Erik Hagberg, over and over again to illustrate papers on the power symbols of the Migration and Merovingian periods: the helmet and the sword (Hagberg 1976). But few have considered where they were found and in which context. This is surprising, considering that Björnhovda until now is the only site in Scandinavia where we have evidence of the making of helmets like those in Valsgärde, Vendel and Sutton Hoo. A short introduction to the site raises questions that in my opinion we have to answer.

Björnhovda is placed on the west plain of Öland, just above the main crossing to the medieval town Kalmar on mainland Sweden (Fig. 9). The present village is situated in the middle of a broad plain below a marked escarpment, on top of which the main road runs and along which most of the ancient cemeteries are placed. But, as Sölve Göransson, the historical geographer, has demonstrated, this was not its original position (Göransson 1968). The ancient tofts of the village are still to be seen in the fields east of the escarpment at the road crossing. Just north of the old tofts the patrices were found. An excavation at the site revealed occupation layers, remains of large buildings, and traces of bronze casting. In the same field a hoard of solidi coins and gold rods has been found.

At the Sound of Kalmar we find the Ferry Stead, Färjestaden, but a place-name, Snäckstaviken – the bay at the site of ships – is reflected also in field names and the name of a road from Björnhovda to the sea, indicating that a landing place once was here. A stone circle and standing stones at the bay support such a view (Carlsson 1987). One of Sweden's three famous gold collars, a golden breloque, and a solidus have been found just south of the bay.

Björnhovda-Snäcksta is located between the church villages Algutsrum and Torslunda in the richest and most important settled area on Öland (Fig. 10). In the Björnhovda area we may expect the main centre of the whole island in the Migration and Merovingian periods (Herschend 1980; Näsman 1997). The place name Torslunda

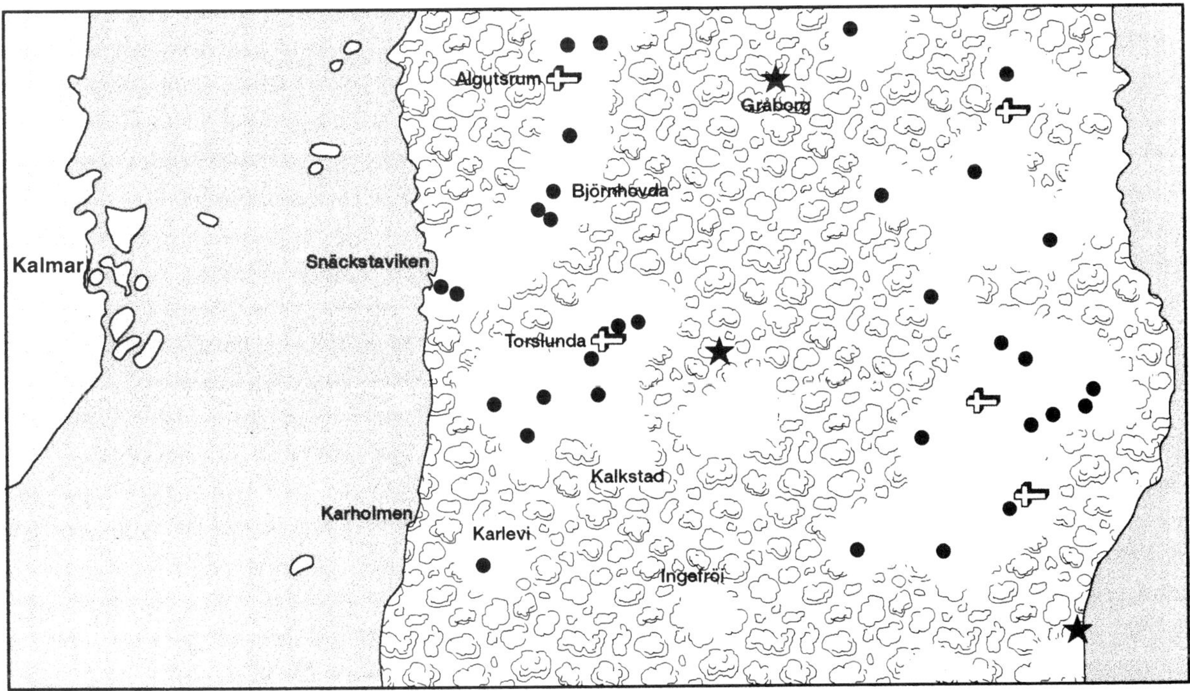

Fig. 10 Björnhovda and surroundings. Gold finds are marked with ●, ring-forts with ★. The white areas show the extent of the open settled regions of the Migration period, as suggested by Edgren and Herschend 1982.

and the field name Ingefrøi indicate a central position in cult and ritual (Hallberg 1985; Hellberg 1986). Björnhovda probably did not loose its importance in the Viking Age entirely, as indicated by two Viking Age silver hoards, arm- and neck-rings as well as Cufic coins. A continued organisational importance of the area may be seen in the place-name complex Karlestad (Kalkstad), Karlevi and Karholmen, indicating the settlement, cult site and landing site of Viking Age warriors.

We get the impression that Björnhovda through the whole of the later half of the first millennium housed a magnate's residence, including specialised crafts and a landing place at Snäcksta. But a church was never built here as far as we know; the Romanesque stone churches were built in the neighbouring villages Algutsrum and Torslunda. Whether this reflects a decline or not is an unsettled question that needs further investigations of the cadastral sources.

The super-regional relations between Öland and the mainland must have been of great importance. Bulk goods to be exchanged might have been wood, iron and agricultural produce. The regions must have had a mutual interest in controlling the traffic through the Sound of Kalmar. The shortest crossing to Öland is between Kalmar and Snäcksta/Färjestaden. The Björnhovda site certainly fit in here: on both sides of the crossing, we can expect to find a central place. In the historical period the main centre of the Möre region was the Kalmar area (Blomkvist 1979,168 ff.), but some functions of this centre have roots in the Roman Iron Age and the Migration period as revealed by denars and solidi found here (Herschend 1980).

The Bay of Snäcksta must be regarded not only as an important crossing between Öland and the mainland. Its location at the sailing route between the continent and the central Swedish Mälaren area, as well as Finland, must also be considered. In a period when raids and war were not isolated events but rather the state of things, and before real state power was able to protect and secure marketplaces, roads and sea routes, it was important that the maritime and commercial centres of the time were sacrosanct sites too. The site Björnhovda-Snäcksta can be seen as such a sacred refuge and maritime junction.

The example demonstrates that an investigation of the landscape context of fine finds, *in casu* the patrices and the gold collar, gives us information that tells us much more than the finds themselves can tell and that it enables us to relate the finds to other sources in the area, archaeological as well as historical.

I hope that my examples have demonstrated that we are at the beginning of new insights into the settlement pattern of the first millennium A.D., that we still have a long distance to cover, and that we have to be careful not to cling to old views and opinions that can influence our models and hypotheses, nor to draw too rapid conclusions on too weak evidence. We have to work together, across the gaps between institutions and disciplines. This way of working raises often more questions than it answers, but new knowledge is created, and unanswered questions are the fuel of future research.

References

Andrén, A. 1991: 'Guld och makt – en tolkning av de skandinaviska guldbrakteaternas funktion', in Fabech, C. and Ringtved, J. (eds), *Samfundsorganisation og regional variation. Norden i romersk jernalder og folkevandringstid*, Jysk arkæologisk selskabs skrifter 27 (Højbjerg/Århus), 245–256. Summary.

Blomkvist, N. 1979: 'Kalmars uppkomst och äldsta tid', in Hammerström, I. (ed.), *Kalmar stads historia I* (Kalmar), 167–310.

Brink, S. 1996: 'Political and social structures in early Scandinavia', *Tor* 28, 235–281.

Brink, S. 1997: 'Västsvenska namnmiljöanalyser', in Strandberg, S. (ed.), *Ortnamn i språk och samhälle. Hyllningsskrift till Lars Hellberg*, Acta Universitatis Upsaliensis, Nomina Germanica, Arkiv för germansk namnforskning 22 (Uppsala), 61–84.

Carlsson, D. 1987: 'Äldre hamnar – ett hotat kulturarv', *Fornvännen* 82, 6–18. Summary.

Callmer, J. 1992: 'A contribution to the prehistory and early history of the south Scandinavian manor. The Bjäresjö investigations', in Larsson, L, Callmer, J. and Stjernquist, B. (eds), *The Archaeology of the Cultural Landscape. Field Work and Research in a South Swedish Rural Region*, Acta Archaeologica Lundensia Ser. in 4° No 19 (Stockholm), 411–457.

Christaller, W. 1966: *Central Places in Southern Germany*, trans. by C.W. Baskin, Prentice-Hall (Englewood Cliffs, NJ).

Edgren, B. and Herschend, F. 1982: 'Arkeologisk ekonomi och ekonomisk arkeologi', *Fornvännen* 77/1: 7–21. Summary.

Fabech, C. 1991: 'Samfundsorganisation, religiøse ceremonier og regional variation', in Fabech, C. and Ringtved, J. (eds), *Samfundsorganisation og regional variation. Norden i romersk jernalder og folkevandringstid*, Jysk arkæologisk selskabs skrifter 27 (Højbjerg/Århus), 283–303.

Fabech, C. 1994: 'Reading society from the cultural landscape: South Scandinavia between sacral and political pwer', in Nielsen, P.O., Randsborg, K. and Thrane, H. (eds),*The Archaeology of Gudme and Lundeborg*, Arkæologiske Studier 10 (Copenhagen).

Fabech, C. and Ringtved, J. 1995: 'Magtens geografi i Sydskandinavien', in Resi, H.G. (ed.), *Produksjon og samfunn. Om erverv, spesialisering og bosetning i Norden i 1. årtusind e.Kr.*, Universitets Oldsaksamling. Varia 30 (Oslo), 11–37. Summary.

Göransson, S. 1968: 'Björnhovda och Håkantorp. Fallet med de "försvunna" Ölandsbyarna', *Särtryck ur forskningsrapporter från Kulturgeografiska institutionen, Nr. 10*, Uppsala universitet, 48–77.

Hagberg, U.E. 1976: 'Fundort und Fundgebiet der Modeln von Torslunda', *Frühmittelalterliche Studien* 10, 323–349.

Hallberg, G. 1985: *Ortnamn på Öland* (Stockholm).

Hansen, H.J. 1990: 'Dankirke', *Kuml* (for 1988–89), 201–247. Zusammenfassung.

Hansen, H.J. 1991: 'Dankirke. En myte i dansk arkæologi', in Fabech, C. and Ringtved, J. (eds), *Samfundsorganisation og regional variation. Norden i romersk jernalder og folkevandringstid*, Jysk arkæologisk selskabs skrifter 27 (Højbjerg/Århus), 15–23.

Hansen, T.E. 1990: 'En vikingetids værktøjskasse', *Kuml* (for 1988–89), 311–24 and Summary.

Hansen, T.E. 1996: 'Et jernalderhus med drikkeglas i Dejbjerg, Vestjylland' *Kuml* (for 1993–1994), 211–237. Summary.

Harrison, D. 1997: 'Centralorter i historisk forskning om tidig medeltid', in Callmer, J. and Rosengren, E. (eds) "*...gick Grendel att söka det höga huset...*" *Arkeologiska källor till aristokratiska miljöer i Skandinavien under yngra järnålder*, Hallands länsmuseums skrifter 9 (Halmstad).

Hellberg, L. 1986: '"Ingefreds sten' och häradsindelningen på Öland"', Festschrift für Oskar Bandle, *Beiträge zur Nordischen Philologie* 15, 19–29.

Herschend, F. 1980: 'Två studier i öländska guldfynd', *Tor* 18 (for 1978–1979), 33–294. Summary.

Herschend, F. 1992: 'Beowulf and St. Sabas: the tension between the individual and the collective in the Germanic Society around 500 A.D.',*Tor* 24,145–164.

Herschend, F. 1993: 'The origin of the hall in Southern Scandinavia', *Tor* 25,175–199.

Herschend, F. 1994: 'Models of petty rulership: two early settlements in Iceland', *Tor* 26, 163–191.

Holmqvist, Wilhelm 1980: *Guldhalskragarna* (Stockholm).

Jeppesen, J. and Madsen, Hans J. 1997: 'Trækirke og stormandshal i Lisbjerg', *Kuml* (for 1995–96), 149–171. Summary.

Jørgensen, L. 1995a: 'Stormandssæder og skattefund i 3. – 12. århundrede', *Fortid og nutid* 1995/2, 83–110.

Jørgensen, L. 1995b: 'The warrior aristocracy of Gudme? The emergence of landed aristocracy in Late Iron Age Denmark', in Resi, H.G. (ed.), *Produksjon og samfunn. Om erverv, spesialisering og bosetning i Norden i 1. årtusind e.Kr.*, Universitets Oldsaksamling. Varia 30 (Oslo), 205–220. Summary.

Jørgensen, L. and Pedersen, L. 1996: 'Vikinger ved Tissø', *Nationalmuseets arbejdsmark* 1996: 22–36. Summary.

Lindeblad, K. 1997: 'The town and the three farms', in Anderssson, H., Carelli, P. and Ersgaard, L. (eds), *Visions of the Past*, Lund Studies in Medieval Archaeology 19, 491–512.

Lindkvist, T. 1988: *Plundring, skatter och den feodala statens framväxt*, Opuscula historica Upsaliensia 1 (Uppsala).

Lundqvist, L. 1997: 'Central places and central areas in the Late Iron Age. Some examples from south-western Sweden', in Anderssson, H., Carelli, P. and Ersgaard, L. (eds), *Visions of the Past*, Lund Studies in Medieval Archaeology 19, 179–98.

Lundström, A. (ed.) 1988: *Thirteen Studies on Helgö*, The Museum of National Antiquities Studies 7 (Stockholm).

Nielsen, A-L. 1997: 'Pagan cultic and votive acts at Borg', in Anderssson, H., Carelli, P. and Ersgaard, L. (eds), *Visions of the Past*, Lund Studies in Medieval Archaeology 19, 373–92

Nielsen, P.O., Randsborg, K. and Thrane, H. (eds) 1994: *The Archaeology of Gudme and Lundeborg*, Arkæologiske Studier 10 (Copenhagen).

Näsman, U. 1991a: 'Nogle bemærkninger om det nordiske symposium "Samfundsorganisation og Regional Variation" på Sandbjerg Slot den 11. – 15. april 1989', in Fabech, C. and Ringtved, J. (eds), *Samfundsorganisation og regional variation. Norden i romersk jernalder og folkevandringstid*, Jysk arkæologisk selskabs skrifter 27 (Højbjerg/Århus), 321–333.

Näsman, U. 1991b: 'Det syvende århundrede – et mørkt tidsrum i ny belysning', in Mortensen, P. and Rasmussen, B.M. (eds), *Høvdingesamfund og Kongemagt. Fra Stamme til Stat i Danmark, 2*, Jysk Arkæologisk Selskabs Skrifter 22,2, 165–178.

Näsman, U. 1997 Strategies and tactics in Migration period defence. I: A. Nørgård Jørgensen (red.) *Military Aspects of Scandinavian Society in a European Perspective AD 1–1300.* København: 1997 146–155.

Ramqvist, P.H. 1990: 'Helgö. Unikt handelscentrum eller vanlig bondgård?', *Fornvännen* 85, 57–67.

Riddersporre, M. 1996: 'Uppåkra – en diskussion med utgångspunkt i de äldsta lantmäterikartorna', *Meta* 1996/3, 13–32.

Ringtved, J. 1991: 'Fremmede genstande på Sejlflodgravpladsen, Nordjylland. Importens lokale kontekst', in Fabech, C. and Ringtved, J. (eds), *Samfundsorganisation og regional variation. Norden i romersk jernalder og folkevandringstid*, Jysk arkæologisk selskabs skrifter 27 (Højbjerg/Århus), 47–73.

Skansjö, S., Riddersporre, M. and Reisnert, A. 1989: 'Huvudgårdar i källmaterialet', in Andersson, H. and Anglert, M. (eds), *By, huvudgård och kyrka. Studier i Ystadområdets medeltid*, Lund Studies in Medieval Archaeology 5 (Lund), 71–133.

Stjernquist, B. 1994: 'Uppåkra, ett bebyggelsescentrum i Skåne under järnålderen', *Fra Luristan til Lusehøj. Festskrift til Henrik Thrane i anledning af 60-års dagen* Fynske Minder. Særtryk 1994, Odense Bys Museer, 99–116.

Stjernquist, B. 1995. 'Uppåkra, a central place in Skåne during the Iron Age', *Lund Archaeological Reports* 1, 89–120.

Sørensen, J. Kousgård 1992: 'Haupttypen sakraler Ortsnamen Südskandinaviens', in Hauck, K. (ed.), *Der historische Horizont der Götterbild-Amulette aus der Übergangsepoche von der Spätantike zum Frühmittelalter. Bericht über das Colloquium vom 28. 11.–1. 12. 1988 in der Werner-Reimers-Stiftung, Bad Homburg*, Abhandlungen der Akademie der Wissenschaften in Göttingen, Philologisch-Historische Klasse, Dritte Folge, Nr. 200 (Göttingen), 228–240 and fold-out map.

Thomsen, P.O., Blæsild, B., Hardt, N. and Michaelsen, K. Kjer 1993: *Lundeborg – en handelsplads fra jernalderen*, Skrifter fra Svendborg and Omegns Museum, Bd. 2.

Thrane, H. 1992: 'Das Reichtumszentrum Gudme in der Völkerwanderungszeit Fünens', in Hauck, K. (ed.): *Der historische Horizont der Götterbild-Amulette aus der Übergangsepoche von der Spätantike zum Frühmittelalter. Bericht über das Colloquium vom 28. 11.–1. 12. 1988 in der Werner-Reimers-Stiftung, Bad Homburg*, Abhandlungen der Akademie der Wissenschaften in Göttingen, Philologisch-Historische Klasse, Dritte Folge, Nr. 200 (Göttingen), 299–380.

Thrane, H. 1993: *Guld, guder og godtfolk – et magtcentrum fra jernalderen ved Gudme og Lundeborg*, Nationalmuseet (Copenhagen).

Tornbjerg, S.Å. 1994: 'Danefæ', *Årbog for Køge museum* (for 1993), 95–96.

Watt, M. 1991: 'Sorte Muld', in Mortensen, P. and Rasmussen, B.M. (eds), *Høvdingesamfund og Kongemagt. Fra Stamme til Stat i Danmark, 2*, Jysk Arkæologisk Selskabs Skrifter 22,2, 89–107. Summary.

Åqvist, C. 1996: 'Hall och harg – det rituella rummet', in Engdal, K. and Kaliff, A. (eds), *Religion från stenålder till medeltid*, Riksantikvarieämbetet, Arkeologiska undersökningar Skrifter 19 (Linköping), 105–120.

Anglo-Saxon Studies in Archaeology and History 10, 1999

The geography of power: South Scandinavia before the Danish kingdom

Jytte Ringtved

For many years studies of Germanic societies focused on delimiting culture areas, political or claimed ethnic groups. Observed similarities and differences between these were seen as the results of diffusion or migration. Later a general shift towards the economic and functional aspects of these societies developed, which favoured explanations in terms of continuity and peaceful development. In the north European plain this was promoted by large-scale settlement excavations which revealed everyday rural life. For more than a decade now, many efforts have been made to engage with issues concerning the elite members of society and with political development. Hereby focus has shifted towards the initiative of the individual person, towards competition and war, dominion and conquest. In Denmark this has been encouraged by two important factors: one is the renewed excavations in and results from the impressive booty sacrifices, the other is the enormous growth in the finds of metalwork from around AD 200 and onwards. This is due in turn to the extensive use of metal detectors by amateurs and the ability of Danish archaeologists to integrate these into the antiquarian system.

In the Nordic Countries the elite and their concomitant milieu in the landscape have recently become extremely topical. A number of contributions are now available coinciding with the appearance of methodological advances in the subject (Näsman 1991a; Herchend 1993; Fabech and Ringtved 1995; L. Jørgensen 1995; Brink 1996; Lundqvist *et al.* 1996). But what is perhaps slightly overlooked is the fact that elite milieus are one dimension of society – geographically as well as socially – and groups identified by their culture another. If we are to address the geography of power we must study both dimensions in relation to each other. This is not to advocate a revival of the tribal studies of former times. But if we study elites in a presumed cultural vacuum we will surely miss important tools of interpretation.

It is not easy to give an overview of the process leading to the formation of the Danish kingdom in the later part of the first millennium AD (see Näsman 1997 and this volume). Some problems stem from periods of few and uneven sources; others are methodological in nature, caused by the difficulty of making history with almost no help from written sources. No doubt a Danish kingdom had been formed by the eighth and ninth centuries AD, as revealed by archaeological as well as written sources, but its origin still lies in a rather dim light. Archaeologically a new homogeneity in the south Scandinavian material came into being in the late sixth and seventh century, most likely reflecting the establishment of an overall political structure or political dominance by the Danes. The formative period in advance of this seems to be the preceding centuries – the third to fifth/sixth centuries, which in archaeological terms equals the Late Roman period and the Migration period.

One of the few contemporary authors to mention Scandinavia is the Byzantine diplomat, Procopius, writing in the 550s. Unfortunately he was more interested in describing Scandinavia (his Thule) beyond those areas occupied by the Danes. To this end he enumerates thirteen different tribes, each with a king. The tribal names found in Jordanes' *Getica* have striking similarities to present-day landscapes in Norway and Sweden north of Scania and are here tentatively mapped by Per Ramqvist (1991) (Fig. 1). Transferring the picture of segregated tribal areas from north to south Scandinavia cannot be done directly. The morphology and vegetational history of the south does not allow for such obvious barriers in the landscape as in the hilly and forested north. Also, as is argued below, it seems that the south had gone through a development similar to that on the continent, where Germanic tribes aggregated into larger confederations. Tacitus and Ptolemy provide information on a number of comparable tribes which in the Early Roman period could have been situated within present-day Denmark, whereas subsequently only Jutes, Angles and Danes played a role. During the fifth and sixth centuries the Danes must have already bordered on to the North Sea as they had direct contact with the Franks and are mentioned several times in the Frankish sources. At this stage their central kingship or overlordship in the region was established.

Suggestions about the political structure of the third to fifth/sixth centuries

A number of suggestions about the political structure of this period have been made in recent years. They range from strong tendencies to unification and centralisation of power to a dispersed structure involving many small units, autonomous or paying tribute to the more influential ones. The latter has been advocated for the later part of the period by Johan Callmer on the basis of the map in Figure 2, which shows the presumed settled areas (in black) divided by non-occupied territory (Callmer 1991, 268 fig. 5). In the Danish area the distribution is based on the place-name evidence (cf. Clausen 1916). Callmer argues that this settlement pattern represents a political system similar to the one that can be inferred from the context of Tribal Hidage, as this is presented to us by W. Davies and H. Vierck (1974). A similar suggestion has been made for the political development of the central Netherlands in the fifth to seventh centuries AD (Heidinga 1990, 36). It is founded in a settlement pattern consisting of isolated nuclear districts divided by no man's land (Heidinga 1990, 13). Strong contributory causes for this can be found in the physical and geographical conditions, just as the accessibility of the nuclear districts play a role in the development of larger ethnic and political units. In this respect the Netherlands seem to compare better with the northern rather than southern part of Scandinavia.

The other interpretational trend, which stresses tendencies towards unification and centralisation at an supra-regional level, may here be represented by the map of Eliza Fonnesbech-Sandberg (Fig. 3). On the basis of the gold items of the period she argues that the Gudme site on Funen is the only centre of power in the Migration period and that the rest of present-day Denmark is to be seen as a periphery to Gudme (Fonnesbech-Sandberg 1991, 243). The characteristics of the so-called centre at Gudme can be recapitulated as: a small region with great richness, with one or more beach markets, with several sacral place-names and, at the focal point, the large cemetery of Møllegårdsmarken and the Gudme settlement itself (J. K. Sørensen 1985; Hauck 1987; 1992; Thrane 1992; 1993; Thomsen *et al.* 1993; P. O. Nielsen *et al.* 1994; P. Ø. Sørensen 1994). In turn this last element is a very large agrarian settlement where various crafts have been performed. It is rich in metal finds including items of precious metal, high quality jewellery, imports and symbols of power such as the ring-studs of solid gold for sword hilts. Recently a hall-building has been discovered and this, together with the rich finds and the symbols of power, signals the presence of a king or a regional leader. The combined political and religious function of the leader stands out through the sacred character of the site, as indicated by the place-names.

Another example of the same approach – the centre and periphery – could be Ulla Lund Hansen's presentation of the Stevns-area on Zealand. Because of its rich gravefinds, including its large number of Roman imports, it is thought to have ruled minor centres on Zealand and to have influenced the rest of Scandinavia through its monopoly of imports (Fig. 4) (U. L. Hansen 1988; 1995; Randsborg 1987; cf. an earlier presentation in Hedeager 1980). The bulk of the rich finds from Stevns date from an early part of the Late Roman period (Eggers period C1b). It should be mentioned that the suggested political centre at Stevns has been doubted, as rich gravefinds within an area do not automatically constitute an absolute standard for political leadership. Besides burial customs and religious beliefs, the presence or absence of such finds depends on the need to manifest the leading positions. Therefore rich gravefinds may often indicate conflict and rivalry and hence political instability (Steuer 1978, 472 ,481; Hedeager 1993, 127ff.)

Fig. 1 Possible settlement areas of the thirteen Scandinavian tribes north of Scania, mentioned by Procopius. After Ramqvist 1991, fig. 1.

Questions need to be asked about these centre-periphery interpretations: are the centres mentioned of supra-regional importance with – as has been suggested (U. L. Hansen 1994, 57f.) – one coming into power after the other, Stevns very early in the Late Roman period and Gudme taking over from there? Or are they ex-

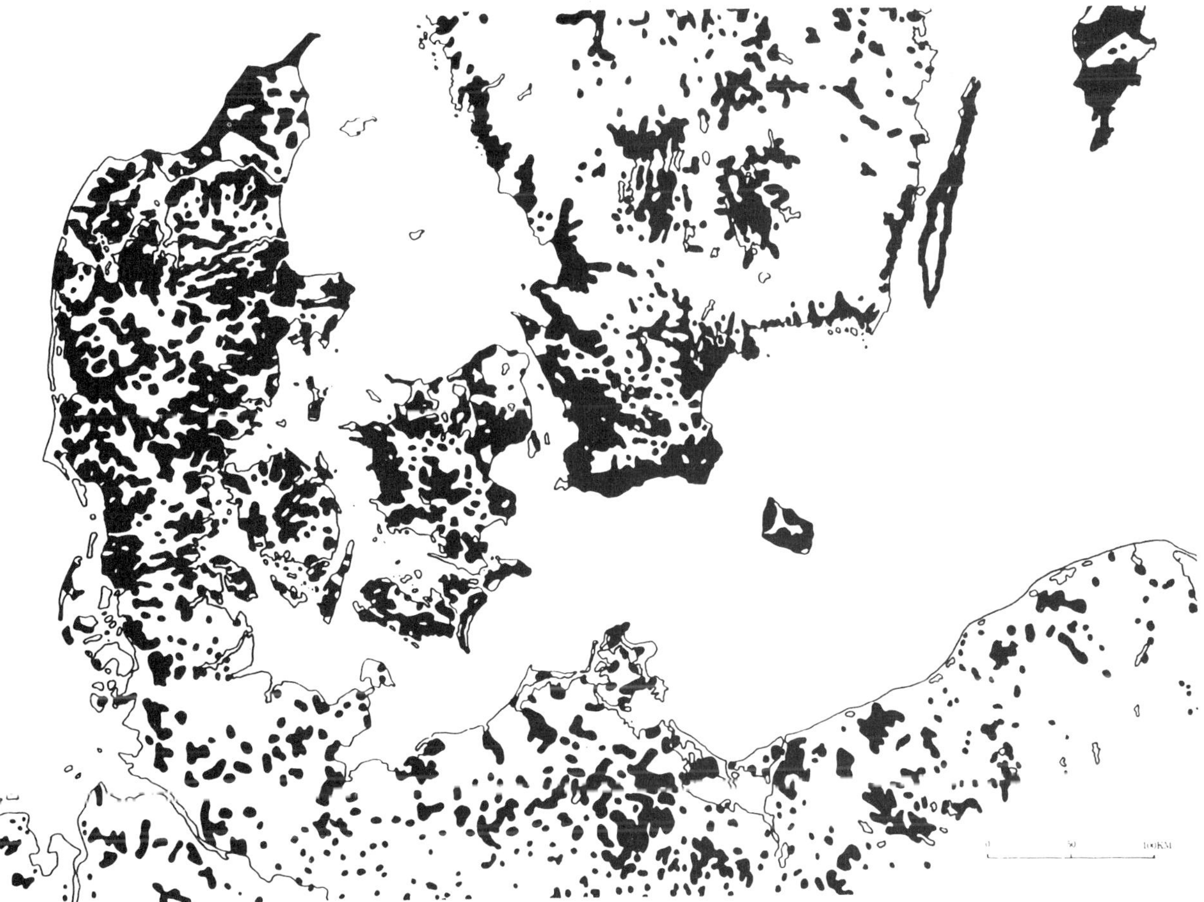

Fig. 2 Possible settlement areas in southern Scandinavia c. *AD 500–1000 (in black). After Callmer 1991, fig. 5.*

pressions only of rich families or regional leadership? In short, what kind of power and influence might have been exerted by the Germanic societies in these periods and what may the archaeological correlates be?

General political geography. An attempt

In my opinion south Scandinavia went through a political development parallel to those of West-Germanic societies on the continent. As with the examples of the Franks, the Alamanni and perhaps the Saxons, larger confederations seem to have grown from segmented, tribal societies leading to Early Medieval kingdoms. As it is important to understand the nature of the power exerted, the arguments in favour of this will be presented in short in the following discussion.

The assignation of the south Scandinavian development to this west European trend of course needs a coherent view and the support of all available sources. Still we will not get far without leaning on two basic assumptions: first, that the identities of tribes and peoples were founded in and upheld by their leaders, which explains why group identity might change very suddenly when leaders are replaced or adopt a new cultural orientation (Wenskus 1977, 54ff.); and second that such identities might be expressed in material culture (though neither always nor necessarily).

On the basis of the situation in Jutland, the tribal societies of the last centuries BC and the first centuries AD seem to be small units marked by distinct cultural traits which make them stand out from neighbouring societies (cf. Heidinga 1987). To be ascribed social relevance a multitude of characteristics from more spheres of society should be testified. In a comparative analysis of a couple of these units, variations in political structure and wider geographical orientation have likewise been suggested (Hedeager and Kristiansen 1982, 120ff.). In the peninsula at least four, and perhaps as many as nine, different regional groups appear. We need more comparative studies to decide the strength and congruence of regional variations in this period, but the results of the afore-mentioned analysis seem to imply the existence of a relatively high number of polities.

Moving into the Late Roman and the Migration periods (from middle second to middle sixth century), a tendency towards larger and relatively less distinct regional groups can be seen. Using a similar premise to those applied to the preceding centuries, only two regional groups show up. They divide Jutland into a northern part and a mid-southern part (Fig. 5) (Ringtved 1988a; 1988b). On closer examination general similarities within and differences between the social structure of these groups can be deduced.

In practice, the change in regional patterns seems to reflect the amalgamation of the smaller tribes into confederations, followed by adoption of a common group identity at a geographically wider level. It cannot here be argued at length, but a few points should be emphasised. The continuity of some of the outstandingly rich milieux, for example, speaks against completely new societal constellations, but in support of amalgamations. From northern Jutland could be mentioned the Års-area, encompassing in the early period the fortified settlement in the bog of Borremose and the Gundestrup silver cauldron, and mixed gold deposits including bracteates in the later (Hines 1989, 199). Another example can be found in the landscape of Vendsyssel in the area of Kraghede and Stentinget (Ringtved 1991), testifying to continuity within more than one of the old tribal contributors to the presumed confederation. As to the southern regional group more studies need to be undertaken, but one example from Dejbjerg has been produced (T. E. Hansen 1996; cf. also Fabech, this volume). The elite milieu at Dejbjerg is, however, perhaps not quite so high-ranking or influential as the other examples mentioned. Continuity of inhabitants can furthermore be seen by the preservation of the old tribal names in the designations

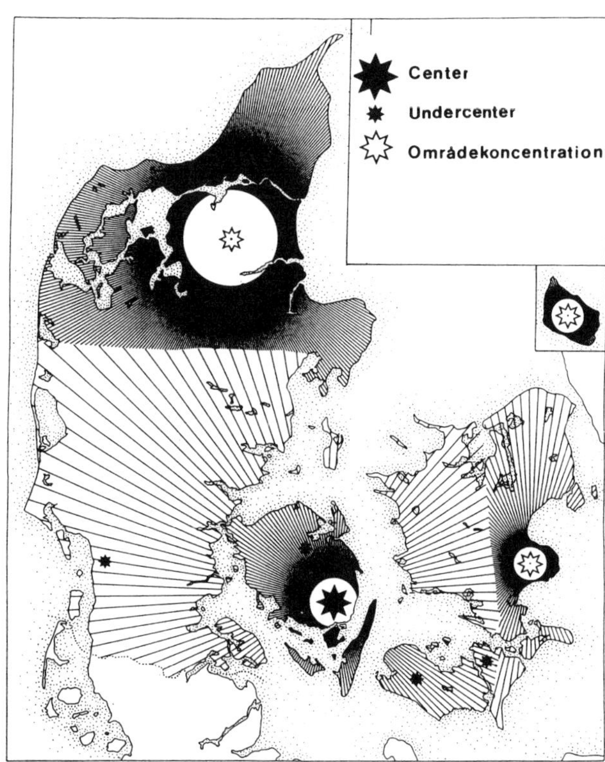

Fig. 3 Suggested political geography of Denmark in the Migration period. Large black star: centre. Small black star: secondary centre. Open star: area-concentration. After Fonnesbech-Sandberg 1991, fig. 8.

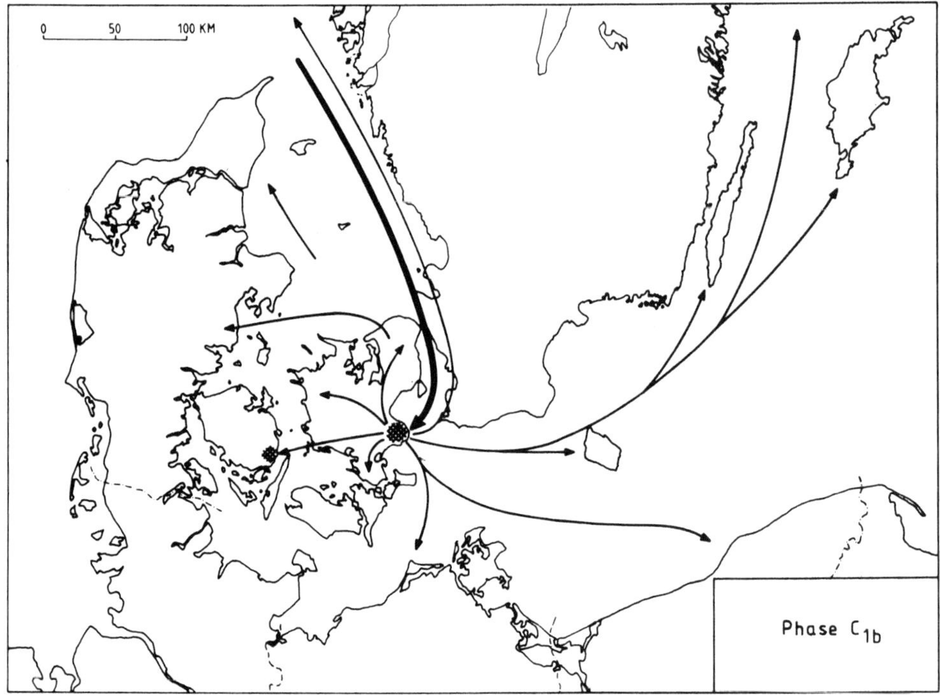

Fig. 4 The suggested centre of Stevns on Zealand (a trade centre) based on the supply of Roman imports. These are distributed to secondary centres on Zealand and to other areas. After U. L. Hansen 1988, fig. 1.

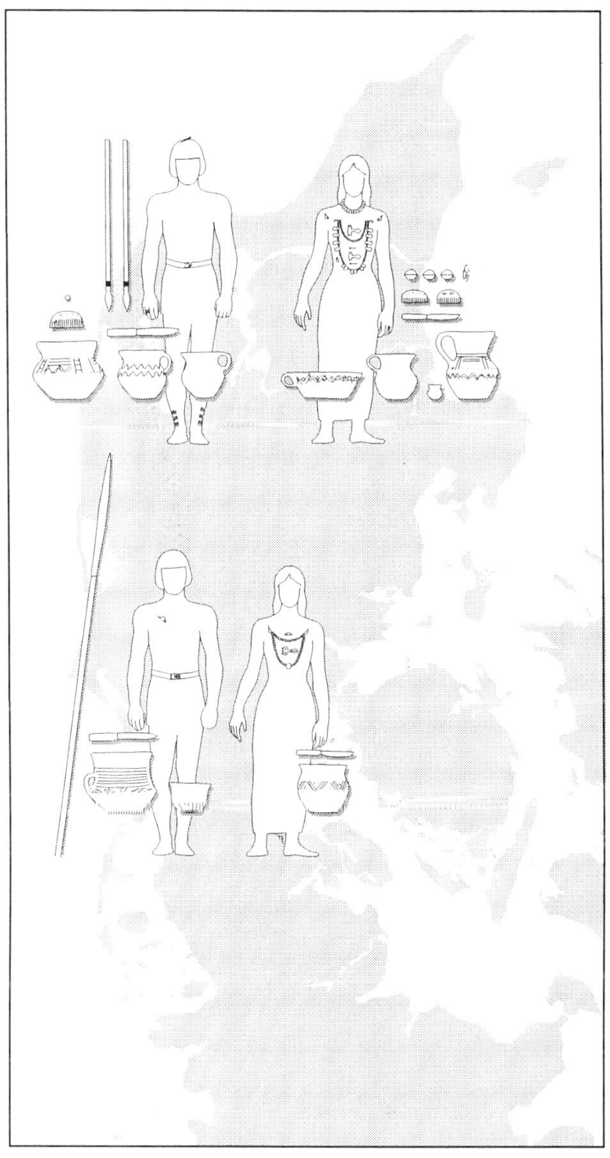

Fig. 5 Regional differences in gravefinds exemplified by male and female equipment from the fourth century AD. After Ringtved 1993.

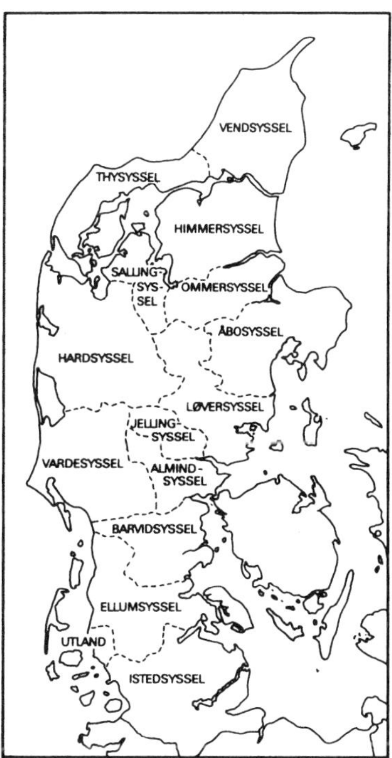

Fig. 6 In Jutland the earliest known administrative division consists of districts called 'sysler'. It presumably antedates Christianity. Drawing J. Kraglund, Skalk *after Fenger 1989, 41.*

for the various landscapes and later administrative units, such as the Cimbri, the Teutoni, the Vandalii and the Harudi in the districts of Himmersyssel, Thysyssel, Vendsyssel and Hardsyssel respectively (Fig. 6) (Wenskus 1977, 73, cf. 522). Not surprisingly, vague echoes of the material culture of the old tribal regions can be found in the larger groupings. Continuity of rich milieus and of tribal names seems to be more pronounced in the north Jutlandic regional group.

What has yet to be argued for is the rise of the Danish kingdom at the end of, or subsequent to, the Migration period. As this question seems to involve further trajectories in the areas which contributed to the kingdom, I will leave it until after an examination of north Jutland as an example of the regional approach.

In search of the actual political geography

Returning to the two scenarios stated at the beginning – in short, the centralised versus the dispersed societal model – the general impression speaks for the former. But only a corner of the veil which covers the actual political geography has yet been lifted. An obvious obstacle is the inability of the archaeological sources to reveal political hierarchy in its many forms. If we look to contemporary Germanic societies for inspiration, we see a network of interrelated societies, some of which are subject to direct, others to indirect, political dominance. Direct dominance, in the form of conquest or subjugation by replacing parts of the local elite, is of course most likely to show up archaeologically. Hegemony, or submission to clientship, may not bring about any internal changes at all (Wenskus 1977, 445ff.). The recent debate between Heiko Steuer and Ross Samson about the effect of Frankish hegemony over Alamannia around AD 500 emphasises the fact that the extent of material correlations can always be questioned (Samson 1994; Steuer 1994). And clientship and the paying of tribute may also take many forms, covering a whole range of obligations, just as it may take place on more than one front at any one time (Wenskus 1977, 446f.; Wood 1983, 11).

A weak point in the empirical quest for dominance seems to be that interpretations are based on premises of a standardised culture, or put in other words: in the search for centres and peripheries, the cultural code of the centre is assumed to be valid for the whole area under study. This means that peripheries are judged by the presence or, as it is, the absence of the same item or find category that is defining the centre. This does not take into consideration that local or regional traditions exist which influence the cultural codes and the depositional manners (Näsman 1984, 28ff.). And even though the material culture as such may be very alike over large distances, societies may be structured differently and, for one thing, their need to display affluence may vary considerably. It is therefore necessary as a basis for further conclusions to consider a region by its own standards and to evaluate how impact from outside is transformed within the local milieu. So a thorough source criticism and a regional approach must be prerequisites of such studies.

The regional approach: North Jutland

As an example of the regional approach I choose to sketch here the characteristics of the northern part of Jutland in the Migration period. As already stated, differences exist between it and the middle and southern parts of Jutland. It is a profound difference, which manifests itself in pottery styles, burials, sacrifices, housebuilding, the organisation of settlements, etc. (cf. Fig. 5). Within north Jutland variations are less pronounced and the region is here looked upon as having a common cultural code.

The setting

The natural geography of north Jutland immediately reveals the special topography of this region. It is characterised by many small enclaves of habitable land divided by the strait of the Liim Fjord, by deep cut valleys and by large tracts of wetlands. Having been heavily suppressed by the massif of the last glacier, the land is still uplifting. As a consequence large stretches consist of low-lying raised sea bed where meadows and peatbogs have developed. In the first millennium AD the contours of the land had approached what we see today, but, without the effect of drainage and reclamation, the low-lying areas would have only been passable with great difficulty and the landscape would have been highly split up. Even in historic times the inhabitants of the various morainic hill-formations were designated *holmboere* (= inhabitants of islets).

The strait of the Liim Fjord itself likewise deserves attention. It is an extraordinarily large, protected stretch of water and, with its many branches, reaches deep into the interior of Jutland. Its configuration has changed many times which has made the Liim Fjord in turn a fjord and a strait. In the first millennium, it can be argued, three ways into this system existed: in the east, at Hals (as today), to the west, south of the present entrance canal, and from a northerly direction into the central part of the waterway (Fig. 7) (Fabech and Ringtved 1993; Møller 1986).

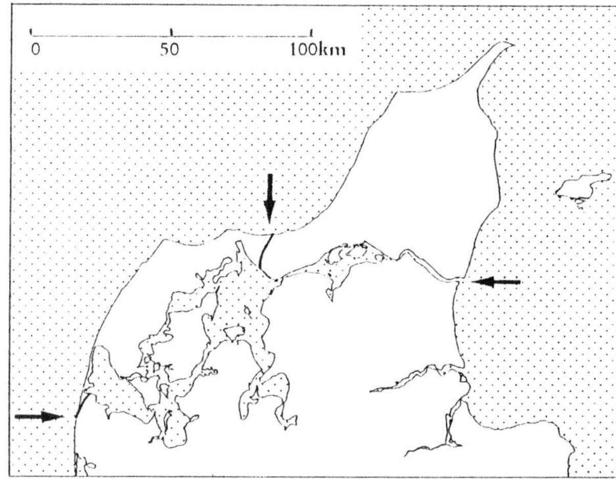

Fig. 7 The Liim Fjord with the three likely passages into the water-system in the first millennium AD. They give access to and from the North Sea to the west, Skagerrak to the north and Kattegat to the east.

The archaeology

Being excellent as a means of communication, and the land just the opposite, no wonder the Liim Fjord became an important waterway. Going by the fjord was also a means to avoid navigation along parts of the dangerous North Sea coast and around the Skaw Reef. Archaeologically the coast of the fjord attracts attention. Along the narrow channel of the eastern part intensive metal detector surveys and archaeological investigations have produced interesting new insights (Christensen and Johansen 1993, 200f.). Many large settlements, rich in metal objects, have been found, not exactly at the waterline, but on the height of the hills bordering on the fjord (Fig. 8). One of these settlements certainly begins in the Late Roman period, more supervene in the Migration period, and the bulk of the material stems from the Merovingian and Viking periods. This type of settlement contrasts with what is known from other parts of south Scandinavia in that it forms an extremely dense pattern, while the sites are strikingly poor in precious metal and thereby items of the highest quality and prestige.

In general, however, North Jutland has a fair share of the Migration period gold (see e.g. Fonnesbech-Sandberg 1988, 140; Hedeager 1992, 65 and 186), of which a large part was made into symbols of high prestige and value. Conspicuous are the golden neckrings of the region, one of which is the heaviest and proclaimed perhaps the most noble ornament from the Danish Iron Age (Brøndsted 1960, 292). In contrast to other parts of south Scandinavia almost all the golden rings are deposited away from the settlement areas in the wetlands, which are so charac-

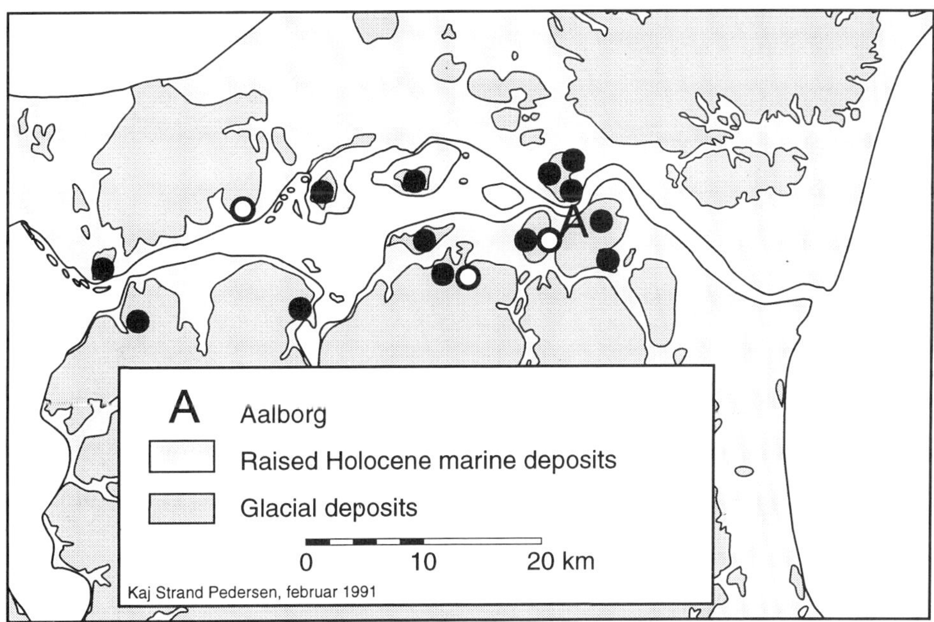

Fig. 8 Settlements rich in metal objects from the eastern part of the Liim Fjord from the Late Roman to the Medieval period. ●: known from excavations or more finds by metal detector surveys. ❍: possible settlement indicated by one or a few finds. The city of Aalborg was founded in the Viking period on sand bars in the low-lying area directly on the coast. Based on Christensen and Johansen 1993, supplemented by E. Johansen (pers. comm.).

teristic of the region. As such they are part of a prominent depositional category in north Jutland encompassing also brooches and other items (Geisslinger 1967, Abb. 1,3 at p. 24). The use of wetlands for depositing had taken place continuously from the Bronze Age onwards but by this time it had mainly ceased in the rest of south Scandinavia and been replaced by depositions on dry land.

Cemeteries and gravefinds furnished with personal equipment and ornaments are also known from north Jutland during the Migration period. The general south Scandinavian tendency was, however, for gravegoods to diminish progressively through the Late Roman and Migration periods, making presumed Migration period graves almost undetectable and certainly inadequate for detailed social analysis. In the whole of this period north Jutish combinations of gravegoods form categories which are distinct for this region (Ringtved 1988a, 146ff.). Compared to south Jutland less emphasis is put on weapons and the status of weapon-bearing men in the better equipped male graves. More weight, on the other hand, is put on basic kinship-relations in terms of the dichotomies of child – adult, male – female. This pattern decreases, however, in the Migration period in favour of mere status and richness, but at the same time in the south funerals are not even used to signal, for or against, such structures of society – they are now empty or almost empty of gravegoods.

In the context of the north Jutlandic development, what may the implications of these special traits be? As a starting point we see the co-occurrence of sacral place-names and gold deposits or other specially valuable objects, indicating that power and cult goes together here as it does in Gudme. These focal points in the landscape are also near traffic-corridors or junctions for water-and sea routes, revealing the central functions performed here (Fig. 9) (Ringtved 1991, 65ff.). But in comparison to Gudme another political attitude is exerted, exemplified by the wetland deposits. These are relicts of a sacrificial practice which had mostly been given up by this time in the southern parts of Denmark. This reorientation goes together with a change from individual and collective offerings in communal wetlands to religious manifestations solely on dry land related to the dwellings of noblemen (Fabech 1991, 288 fig. 3; see also Fabech this volume, fig. 2; individual vs. collective offerings see Herschend 1991, 36). The change of practice may be seen as a consequence of the shift from an older legitimisation of a mythical tribal ancestry to the legitimisation of leading families by divine ancestry – as it is suggested to us from the iconography of the bracteates and the later gold foil figures. On the former, we see the pantheon of the old Norse mythology and the mighty Odin depicted with symbols of worldly leadership. On the latter, the representation has quite convincingly been linked to the Norse hierogamy myth of the divine marriage: the hierogamy between a god and a woman of the giants has provided the basis for the royal houses (Steinsland 1990). This elevated status of the new leaders seems not to have been consolidated in north Jutland and in this respect the region exhibits a unique political development. Put in social terms, the new Migration period society embodies a transformation from a leadership embedded

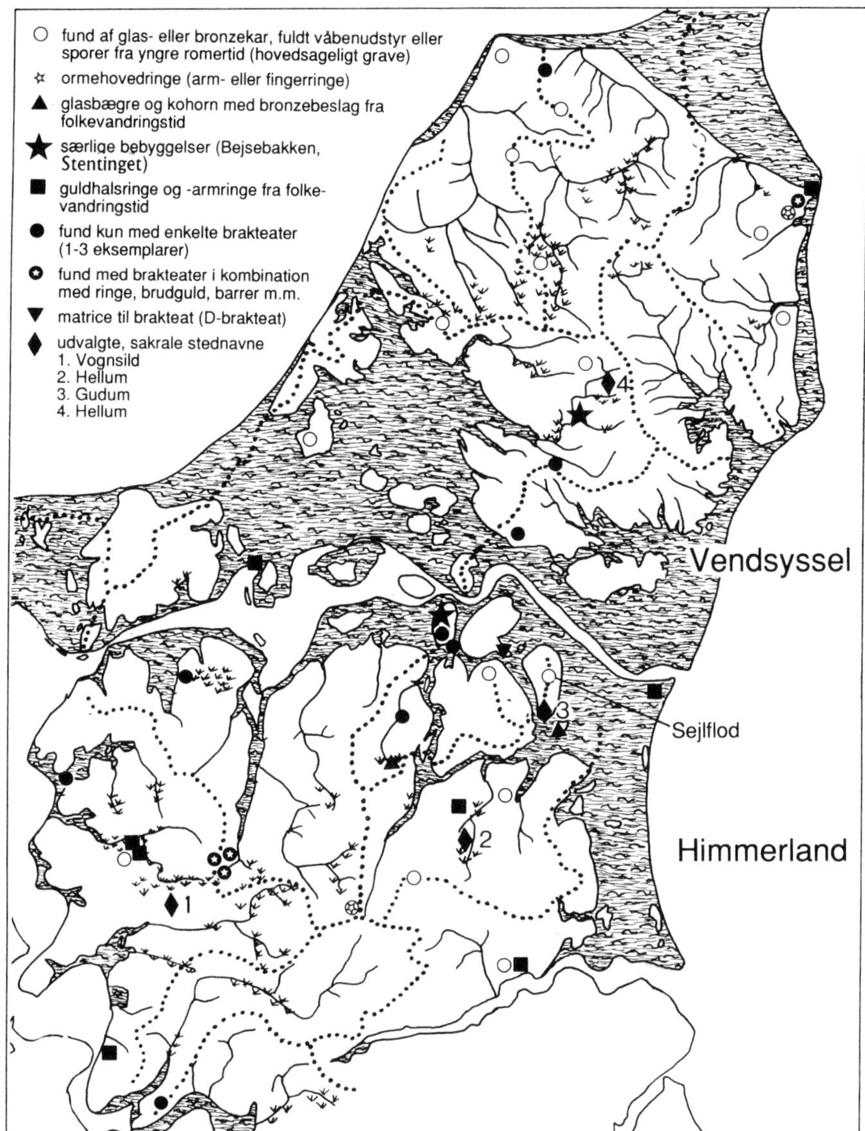

Fig. 9 Map of Vendsyssel and Himmersyssel (Himmerland) with important assemblages from the elite social environments of the Late Roman and Migration periods. ○: glass or bronze vessels, weapons or spurs from the Late Roman period. ☆: snake-headed rings. ▲: glass-beakers and oxhorns with bronze mountings. ★: settlements of the most exceptional character (status 1991). ■: gold neck- and armrings from the Migration period. ●: 1–3 bracteates. ✪: bracteates in combination with rings, cut gochld, ingots, etc. ▼: die for D-bracteate. ♦: selected sacral toponyms. Dot-and-dash line: watersheds. After Ringtved 1991, fig. 35.

in the local community and related to status within and between lineages to a system with more emphasis on status and power-structure beyond the local context. The elite is no longer bearer of the tribal traditions, but bearer of the elite traditions in a wider society. It forms the basis of a more definite centralisation of power. The hypothesis of a divergent development within the north Jutlandic area was based on the prolonged tradition of collective offerings. Another side of the same matter is the lack of gold and high-status items at elite settlements, put into the ground as private depositions in and around the houses. This is a major constituent part of the rich milieu at Gudme. The hypothesis of a weakly-developed north Jutlandic leadership may also be supported by the dense network of the afore-mentioned settlements, mirroring perhaps a less developed pyramidal structure within the elite, and by the continued political need to manifest positions by display in funeral customs.

If this rough sketch is accepted, it can be argued that it reflects a diverging social and political development within the north Jutlandic region compared to south Jutland and most likely also to other parts of south

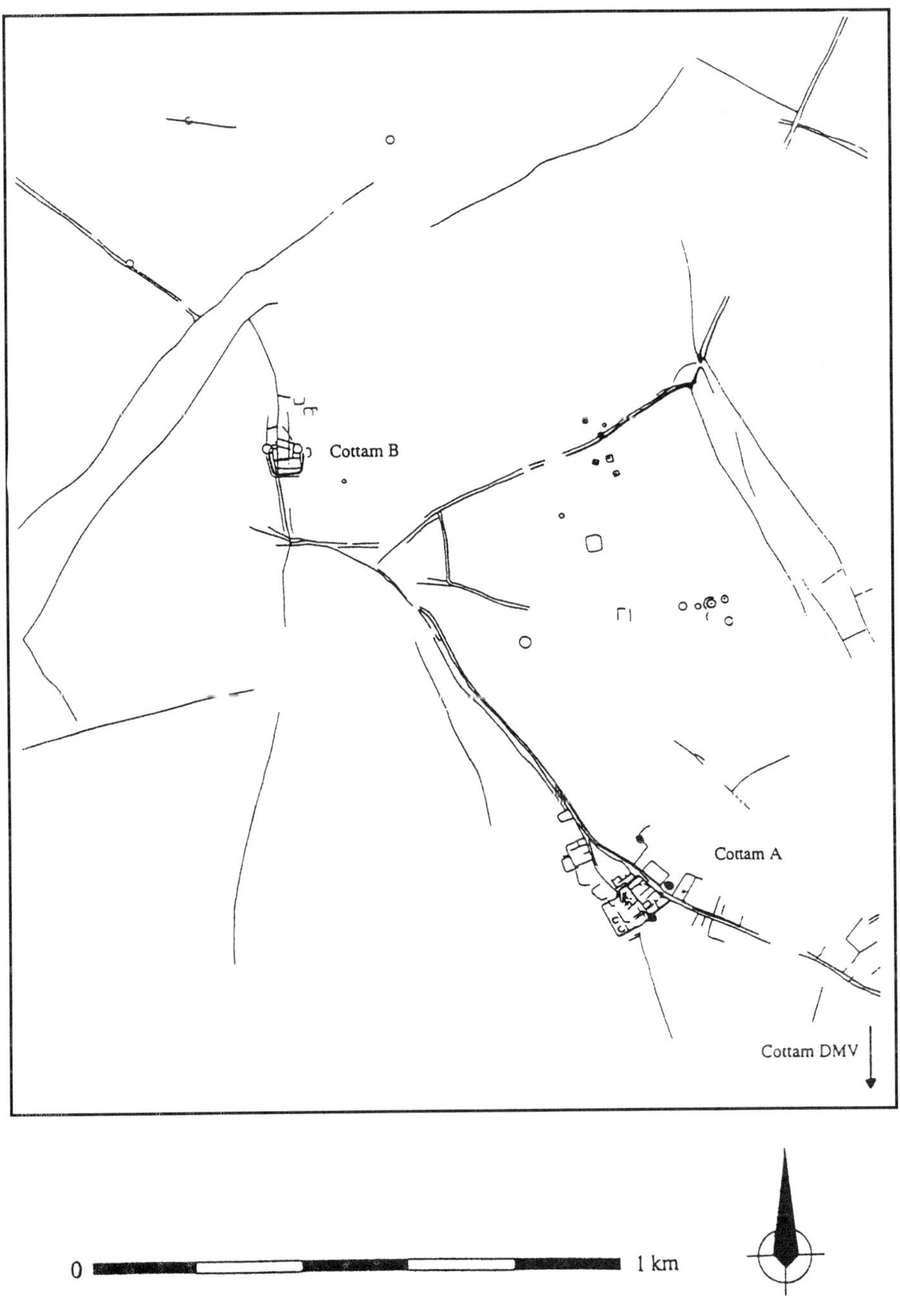

Fig. 2 Cottam crop mark sites A and B and DMV

mark enclosures and a re-examination of the large number of undated enclosures known from the Yorkshire Wolds and beyond (Figs. 3–4). It is anticipated that far more may turn out to be of early medieval rather than of Iron Age or Romano-British date.

Second, the productive site at Cottam B was revealed, on excavation, to have the structural features, including pits and posthole buildings, and material debris that one would expect of a normal settlement site. There was little to suggest that this was a periodic market or trading community. The site had been created as a result of deep ploughing which had disturbed the Anglo-Saxon cultural layers. This ploughing was removing the upper levels of the crop mark features and distributing the debris into the plough zone. Nevertheless, the question remains as to whether this debris is richer and more plentiful than one would expect of a 'typical' Middle Saxon settlement.

In order to resolve this it is necessary to compare the density of metal detector finds from Cottam and other so-called 'productive sites' with the finds densities of nearby excavated sites. If the productive sites are somehow special or of particularly high status then they should yield more metalwork than other settlements.

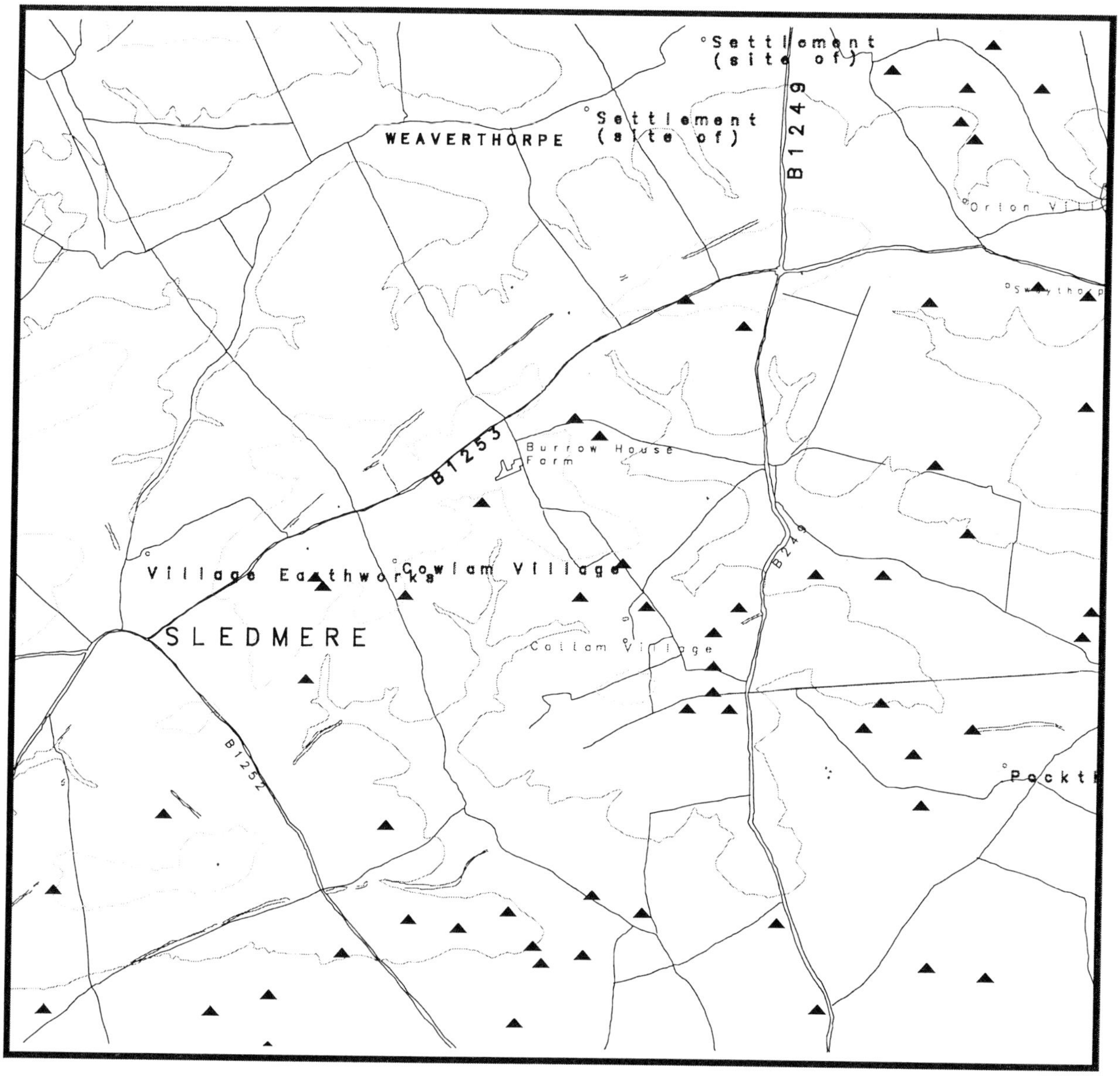

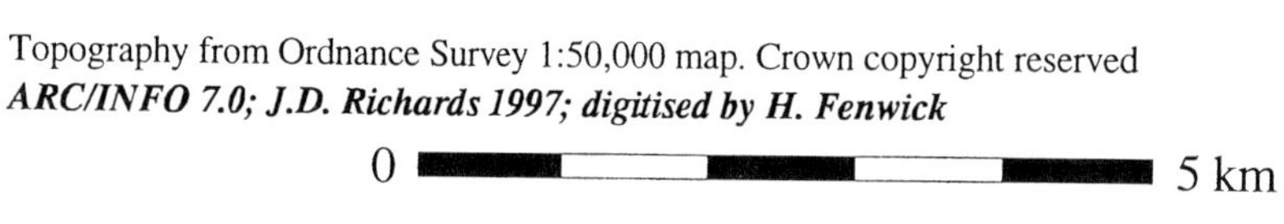

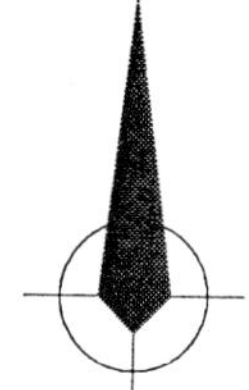

Fig. 3 Cottam environs: undated crop mark sites

Wharram Percy

A second Middle Saxon settlement has been excavated at Wharram Percy, some 8 miles due west of Cottam. Wharram Percy is better known for Beresford and Hurst's examination of the Deserted Medieval Village, but its early settlement history may turn out to be as significant. Middle Saxon activity is spread over much of the area of the medieval village, but is concentrated on the plateau (Fig. 5). In 1975, a two-post sunken-featured building was excavated by Gustav Milne on the northern fringes of the medieval village. The finds from its fill included a Northumbrian sceat of *c*.750 and a sherd of Tating-type ware, of the late eighth or early ninth centuries (Milne and Richards 1992, 5–12). During 1980–84 Philip Rahtz identified two sunken-featured buildings cut into a Roman hollow-way, immediately south of the North Manor (Milne and Richards 1992, 86–8). These were originally described as sixth century (Hurst 1984, 82), largely on

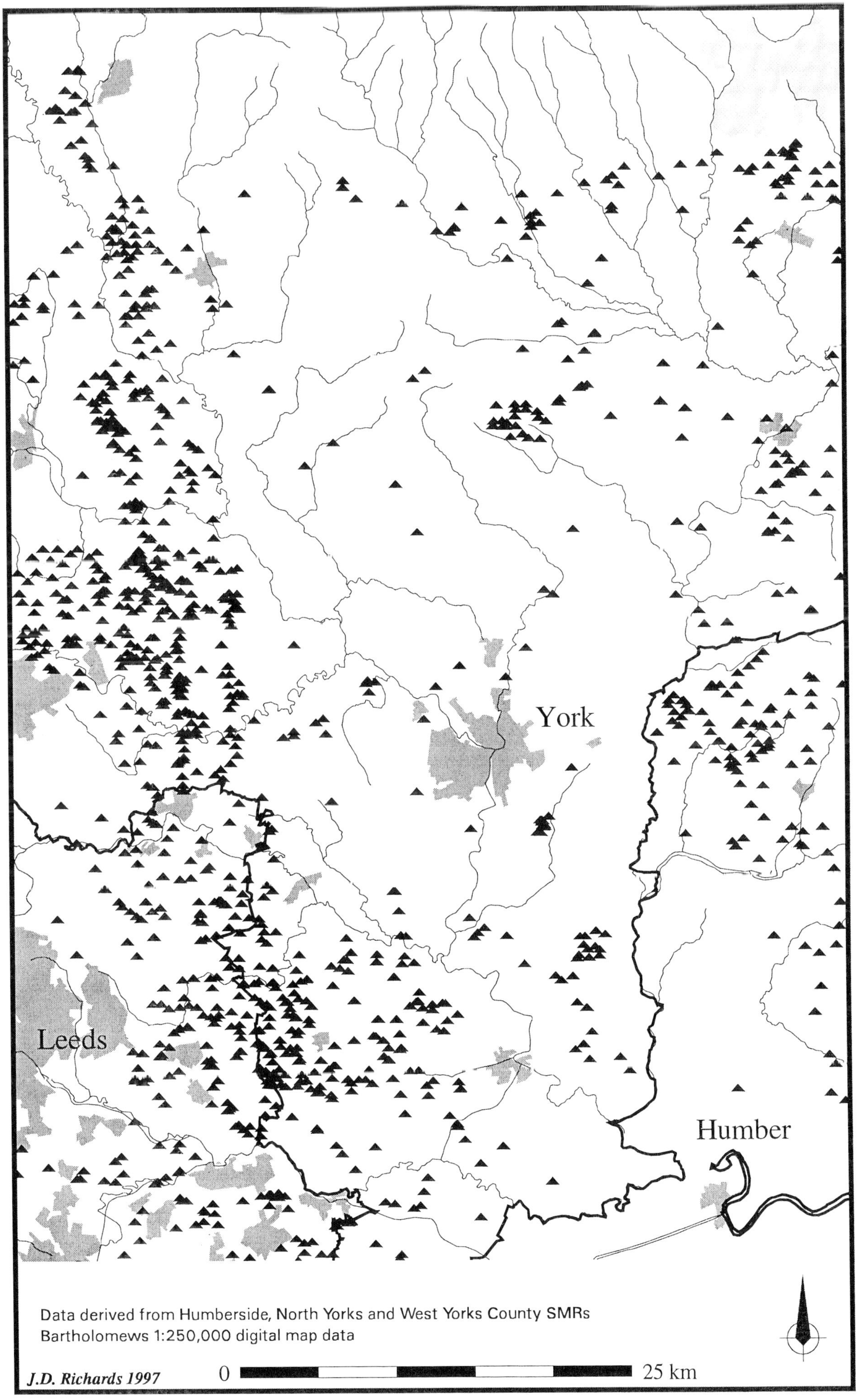

Fig. 4 York environs: undated crop mark sites

the basis of a strike-a-light for which sixth-century parallels were quoted, but it has been suggested that they could also be later (Milne and Richards 1992, 93). In 1989–90 a fourth sunken structure was identified cut into a Romano-British field boundary ditch. The associated midden deposit provided evidence for non-ferrous metal-working, with both crucibles and clay moulds, including a mould fragment with interlace ornament dated on stylistic grounds to the late eighth or early ninth centuries (Milne and Richards 1992, 59–66) and a fragment of a stone cross-head dated to the eighth century (Milne and Richards 1992, 43)

Further Middle Saxon finds have been made in other parts of the Guardianship area, including a second eighth-century cross fragment, a styca and a ninth-century strap-end from the plateau immediately above the church, and a number of stycas and sceattas from the church excavation itself. The spread of these finds led me to conclude, in 1992, that 'Middle Saxon Wharram may have been as extensive as the post-Conquest village'. I also noted that the nature of the finds assemblage, 'including stone sculpture, imported Tating-type ware, and copper-alloy metalworking, confirms the high status nature of Middle Saxon occupation at Wharram', speculating that the village might have had a possible ecclesiastical foundation (Milne and Richards 1992, 94).

The most intensive Middle Saxon occupation, however, was on the site of the later medieval South Manor house, where a Middle Saxon timber hall and smithy have been excavated (Stamper and Croft forthcoming). The South Manor site plays a critical role in any discussion of the nature of Middle Saxon occupation at Wharram Percy, and of its development into the post-Conquest village. Of all the Middle Saxon sites it is the only one which was still occupied in the post-Conquest period, and furthermore, as the site of one of the two manor houses, it clearly had a special status in the later eleventh and twelfth centuries.

There is no firm evidence for major early Anglo-Saxon activity in the South Manor area; most of the Anglo-Saxon pottery recovered from the South Manor site is probably seventh- or eighth-century. This is confirmed by the radiocarbon dating where the four samples from features associated with the smithy all fall within the calibrated date range of AD 600–1010 at the 68 per cent confidence limits. A silver sceat of *c.* AD 700–710 is probably the earliest datable contemporary object, but two sword pommels and a seventh- or eighth-century hilt guard are also probably contemporary with the Middle Saxon settlement, and are particularly diagnostic of its high status. The ceramic assemblage also suggests high status. One or two wares may have come from well outside the local region. These include five sherds of Ipswich ware, the most northerly location for this type, although not much further north of the assemblage at Flixborough which contains some 300 sherds. The pottery also includes ten black-burnished vessels imported from northern France, dated to the seventh to ninth centuries, as well as the Tating-type ware sherd mentioned above. Hitherto, these continental imports have mainly been found at *wic* trading sites such as Hamwic, Ispwich, London and York. Where they occur on rural sites, such as at Brandon and Barking, this tends to be attributed to the high status of the settlements, even to a monastic function, although continental imports have not been recognised at Flixborough. Many of the stone artefacts were also imported from overseas, including a large number of the hone stones, and some Mayen lava quern stones.

Overall, therefore, the finds assemblage from the South Manor supports the picture of high status Middle Saxon occupation. How does it compare with a 'productive site'? At first sight, the absolute numbers of a few diagnostic categories of finds appear to be rather low when compared with Cottam (Table 1). Thus, from the South Manor there is only one eighth-century coin, one strap end, and 11 copper alloy pins, whereas metal-detector finds from Cottam B include 4 eighth-century coins, 34 strap ends, and 63 copper alloy pins. Only the number of iron knives is equivalent and, given the presence of an iron smithy at the South Manor, the relatively high numbers of knives at Wharram is not unexpected. Similarly, from another metal-detector site now known as South Newbald (Leahy forthcoming) there are some 72 eighth-century coins, about 20 strap ends, and 60 pins. However, such figures have to be understood in the context that in each case the metal-detector users have intensively worked an area of

Table 1 Total numbers of selected categories of finds from Middle Saxon sites in Northumbria

	Eighth-century coins	Ninth-century coins	Copper-alloy strap ends	Copper-alloy dress pins	Iron knives
Cottam B	4	29+	34	63	40
South Newbald	72	101	20+	60	0
Wharram Percy: South Manor	1	0	1	11	*c* 45
Flixborough	29	39	22	445	313
Hartlepool	2	0	1	4	0
Whitby	17	100+	14	114	?
Fishergate, York	18	15	5	74	57

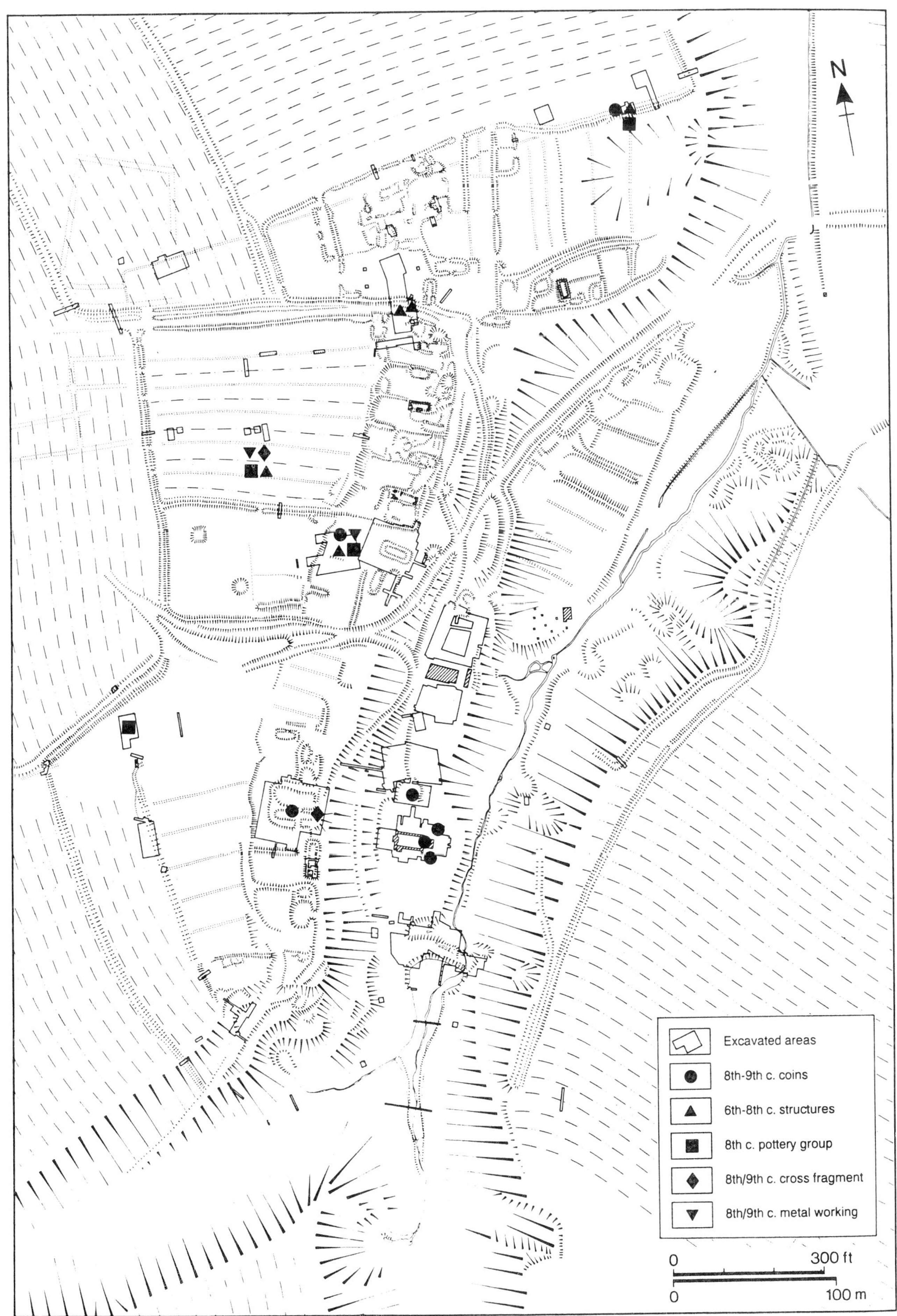

Fig. 5 Wharram Percy: Middle Saxon finds (from Milne and Richards, fig. 44)

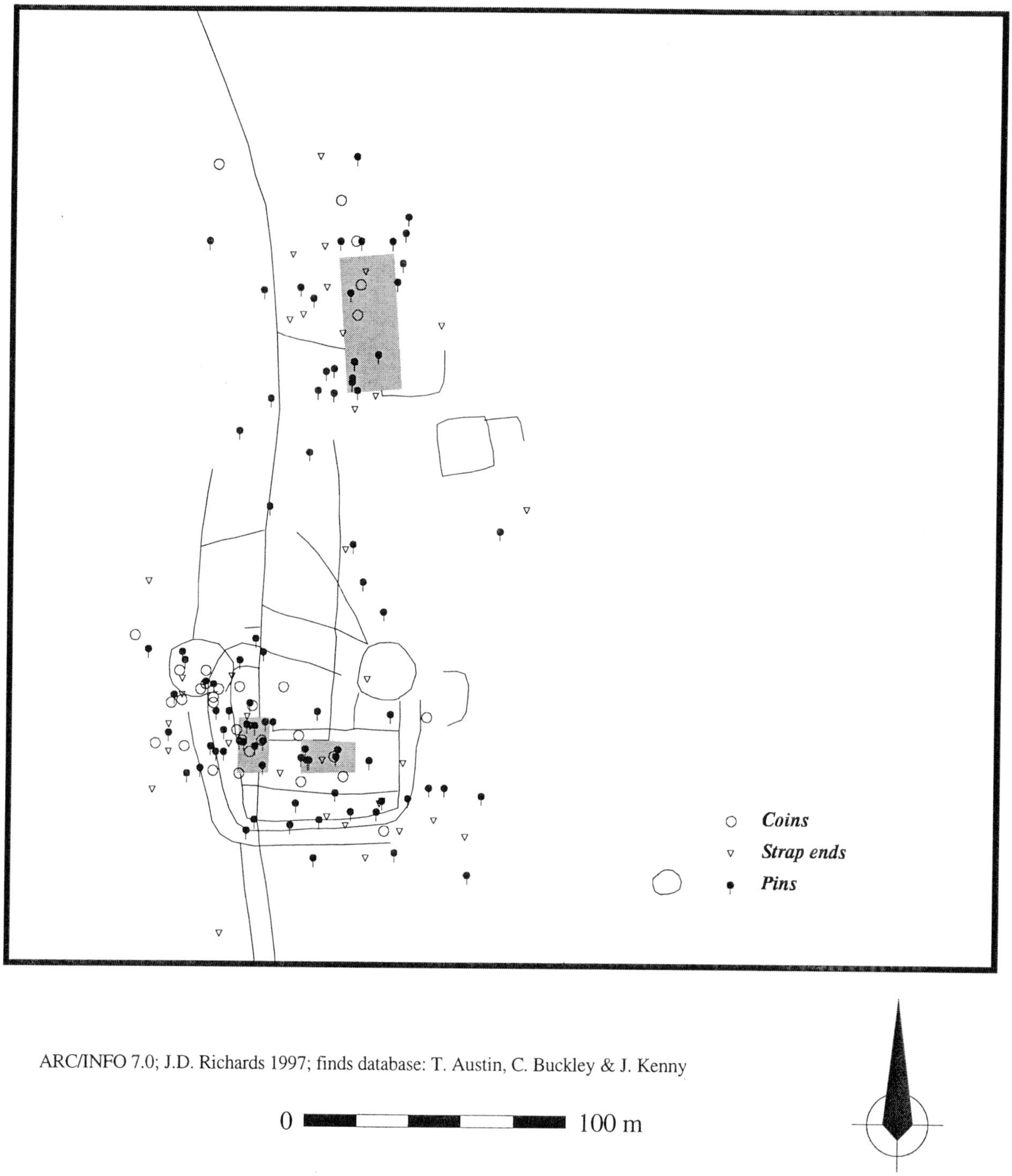

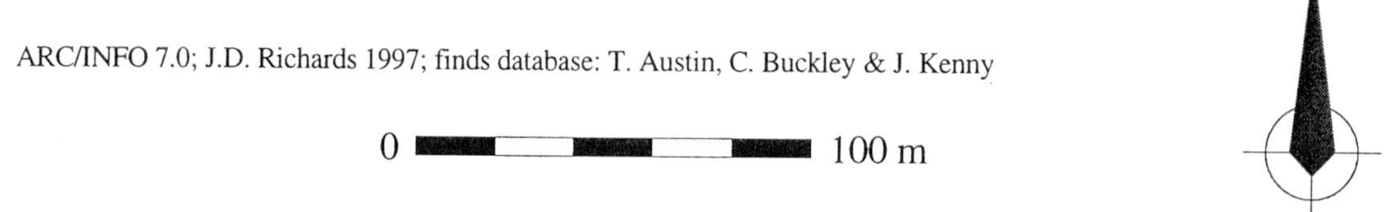

Fig.6 Cottam B: selected metal detector and excavation finds. Shaded areas represent excavated areas.

c.30,000m^2, and that in the case of South Newbald, at least, the site is now considered to be 'worked-out', with modern agricultural practices having brought most of the metalwork into the plough soil. At Cottam, excavation has led to the recovery of some further finds, but not in high numbers (Fig. 6). At Wharram, by contrast, only a fraction of the settlement area, estimated at *c*.6 per cent (Beresford and Hurst 1991, 131), has been dug and the rest is undisturbed by modern ploughing or metal detecting.

The South Manor sites comprise an excavated area of *c*.900m^2 but it has been suggested that Middle Saxon finds are widely distributed within the Guardianship area, having been recovered from a number of interventions. If, rather than take the absolute number of finds, we base comparison on the relative density of these indicators we find that Wharram Percy is also a 'productive site' with the figures for the average density of finds per 100m^2 within the range of those for South Newbald and Cottam

Table 2 Average density of finds per 100m²

	Approximate area invest-igated (m²)	Eighth-century coins	Ninth-century coins	Copper-alloy strap ends	Copper-alloy dress pins	Iron knives
Cottam B	30,000	0.01	0.1	0.11	0.21	0.13
South Newbald	30,000	0.24	0.37	*c* 0.07	0.2	0.0
Wharram Percy: South Manor	900	0.11	0.0	0.11	1.22	*c* 5.0
Flixborough	4,000	0.73	0.98	0.55	11.13	7.83
Hartlepool	1,500	0.13	0.0	0.07	0.27	0.0
Whitby	5,000	0.34	*c* 2.0	0.28	2.28	?
Fishergate, York	2,500	0.72	0.6	0.2	2.96	2.28

(Table 2). Thus the density of strap ends at Wharram is identical to that at Cottam B, and higher than that at South Newbald. If the density for the South Manor is reasonably assumed to continue throughout the area of Middle Saxon settlement at Wharram, and if one ploughed and then metal detected the scheduled area then one might expect to find some thirty strap ends! With eleven copper-alloy dress pins from the South Manor excavations Wharram also has a considerably higher density of these artefacts than both Cottam B and South Newbald.

In comparison with the possible monastic site at Flixborough and the known Middle Saxon monastery at Whitby, however, both Wharram and the 'productive sites' fare rather poorly, having significantly lower densities of most of the chosen artefact types. Flixborough is clearly unusual, with high proportions of eighth- and ninth-century coins, five times the density of strap ends and at least ten times the number of dress pins. Whitby also has much greater densities of metalwork than Cottam or Wharram but, with the exception of ninth-century coins which simply reflect Whitby's survival beyond Flixborough, it has lower densities than the Humber site (Peers and Radford 1943). Hartlepool, on the other hand, has densities which are comparable with both Cottam and South Newbald, apart from the lack of ninth-century coins which is explained by its abandonment in the later eighth century (Daniels 1988, 175). Had it been ploughed and metal-detected over a number of years then, like Wharram, it could have been seen as a 'productive site'.

The artefact densities for the 'productive sites' are lower than for the excavation of the urban *wic* site at Fishergate in York (Rogers 1993). The density of coins at Fishergate is comparable to that of Flixborough, although the proportions of strap ends and dress pins are lower, being comparable with the figures from Whitby, although still ten times higher than either Cottam or South Newbald.

There are also differences between the 'productive sites'. Indeed, for some categories of artefact there are greater divergences within the 'productive site' category than between it and other types of site. For example, the complete absence of iron knives at South Newbald clearly separates it from Cottam. Given the same group of detectorists were involved on both sites this is not simply a product of different collection policies. Rather, the 'productive site' category is masking several types of site.

Conclusion

So, in conclusion, there is nothing special about 'productive sites', other than the way in which they have been discovered. The term is meaningless and should be abandoned. Indeed, from the figures presented above it is clear that the densities of metalwork recovered from the 'productive sites' are in fact lower than those known from both monastic sites such as Whitby and Flixborough, and *wic* sites such as Fishergate. On the other hand, they are little different from what has been seen as a high status Middle Saxon settlement at Wharram Percy.

The 'productive sites' do not have the densities of finds and especially coins associated with the trading site at Fishergate. There is no special reason to view them as periodic market sites. Indeed, there is nothing about the location of Cottam which would lead one to view it as a central place. Rather this level of concentration of coinage and metalwork has to be seen as a feature of all Middle Saxon sites so far examined. It should perhaps be seen in the context of the evolution of the Anglo-Saxon kingdoms, the development of lordship and a tributary economy.

References

Beresford, M. and Hurst, J.G. 1990: *Wharram Percy: Deserted Medieval Village* (London).

Daniels, R. 1988: 'The Anglo-Saxon monastery at Church Close, Hartlepool, Cleveland', *Archaeological Journal* 145, 158–210.

Haldenby, D. 1990: 'An Anglian site on the Yorkshire Wolds', *Yorkshire Archaeological Journal* 62, 51–63.

Haldenby, D. 1992: 'An Anglian site on the Yorkshire Wolds', *Yorkshire Archaeological Journal* 64, 25–39.

Haldenby, D. 1994: 'An Anglian site on the Yorkshire Wolds – Part III', *Yorkshire Archaeological Journal* 66.

Hodges, R. 1982: *Dark Age Economics* (London).

Hurst, J.G. 1984: 'The Wharram Research Project: results to 1983', *Medieval Archaeology*, 28, 77–111.

Leahy, K. forthcoming: 'Middle Anglo-Saxon metalwork from South Newbald and the "Productive Site" phenomenon in Yorkshire'.

Milne, G. and Richards, J.D. 1992: *Wharram: A Study of Settlement on the Yorkshire Wolds, VII. Two Anglo-Saxon Buildings and Associated Finds*, York University Archaeological Publications 9 (York).

Newman, J. 1995: 'Metal Detector Finds and Fieldwork on Anglo-Saxon Sites in Suffolk', *Anglo-Saxon Studies in Archaeology and History* 8, Oxford University Committee for Archaeology, 87–93.

Newman, J. forthcoming: 'Barham, Suffolk – Middle Saxon market or meeting place?', in Metcalf, D.M. and Blackburn, M. (eds), *Productive Sites of the Middle Saxon Period, Proceedings of the 12th Oxford Coin Symposium.*

Peers, C.R. and Radford, C.A.R. 1943: 'The Saxon monastery of Whitby', *Archaeologia* 89, 27–88.

Richards, J.D. forthcoming: 'Cottam: Anglian and Anglo-Scandinavian Settlement on the Yorkshire Wolds', *Archaeological Journal.*

Rogers, N.S.H. 1993: *Anglian and Other Finds from Fishergate. The Archaeology of York* 17/9, Council for British Archaeology (York).

Stamper, P.A. and Croft, R.A. forthcoming: *Wharram: A Study of Settlement on the Yorkshire Wolds, VIII. The South Manor Area Excavations*, York University Archaeological Publications 10 (York).

Wade, K. 1984: 'Barham' (excavation summary), in Martin, E, Plouviez, J. and Ross, H. (eds), 'Archaeology in Suffolk', *Proceedings of the Suffolk Institite of Archaeology* 35, 326.

Anglo-Saxon Studies in Archaeology and History 10, 1999

The Archaeology of Rank, by means of Diet, Gender and Kinship

Kerstin Lidén and Anders Götherström

This paper discusses and exemplifies the possibilities of studying the archaeology of rank by means of diet, gender and kinship using scientific methods. The methods employed are stable isotope, trace element, and DNA analyses on bone. The study is part of a larger project concerning the power structures within the central parts of Svealand during the Vendel and Viking period. Initial preliminary results are very positive concerning the identification of rank as well as kinship analysis.

Introduction

This study is part of a larger project called Svealand in the Vendel and Viking periods (SIV) which is a collaboration between the two universities in Uppsala and Stockholm. The project's aim is to analyse and understand power structures within the central parts of Svealand during the Vendel and Viking periods (Arrhenius and Herschend 1995).

Old research within this area, derived from literary sources, was based on the conception that Svealand was a single centrally governed kingdom ruled by a king seated in old Uppsala. These literary sources have been re-evaluated and criticised, however, to the point that they no longer are seen as contemporary or reliable for use as sources for the understanding of the events in early Svealand (e.g. Lönnroth 1977, Moberg 1941, Sawyer 1991). That the large mounds in old Uppsala were erected for kings or members belonging to a dynasty have now been confirmed, however, by the recent analyses of the material found in the east and west mounds analysed by Birgit Arrhenius and Torstein Sjøvold where remains of a 12 year-old infant prince had been buried with items that can be judged as true regalia (Arrhenius and Sjøvold 1995). This indicates that the kingship in old Uppsala at this time, the first half of the sixth century, had some kind of hereditary status, since the age of the prince indicates that he must have been too young to achieve that status by himself. However, it is still not known how these kings were related to the rest of the Svealand.

Earlier and present archaeological work in and around Svealand has tended to focus on mercantile centres, such as Birka (Ambrosiani 1996; Holmquist-Olausson 1993), whereas less is known of smaller settlements depending on agricultural subsistence.

Key sites in this project are the big farms, Vendel situated some 30 km north of old Uppsala and Valsgärde situated just north of old Uppsala (Fig. 1). These are sites famous for their boat cemeteries which were excavated in the early 1900s and where settlements have now also been found (Isaksson 1997, Norr & Sundkvist 1997). The excavations at these two sites, taking place annually during spring and fall, will hopefully clarify the relation between centre and periphery, enable us to tie together our understanding of the political nature of early Svealand, its chronology and its pattern of settlement and social stratification, and thus provide information on whether the development within these areas was synchronous or if there were two independent power centres (Arrhenius and Herschend 1995).

Our part in this project is called 'the kinship project' and deals with nutrition and DNA analysis, where the main focus is on studying the archaeology of rank by means of diet, gender and kinship.

Material and methods

It has often been observed that mortuary data and treatment in death are closely related to social position in life, but treatment is also influenced by ideology, particularly the meaning and significance of death both for the one who died and for those who are left. However, as biological features are not part of the mortuary ritual

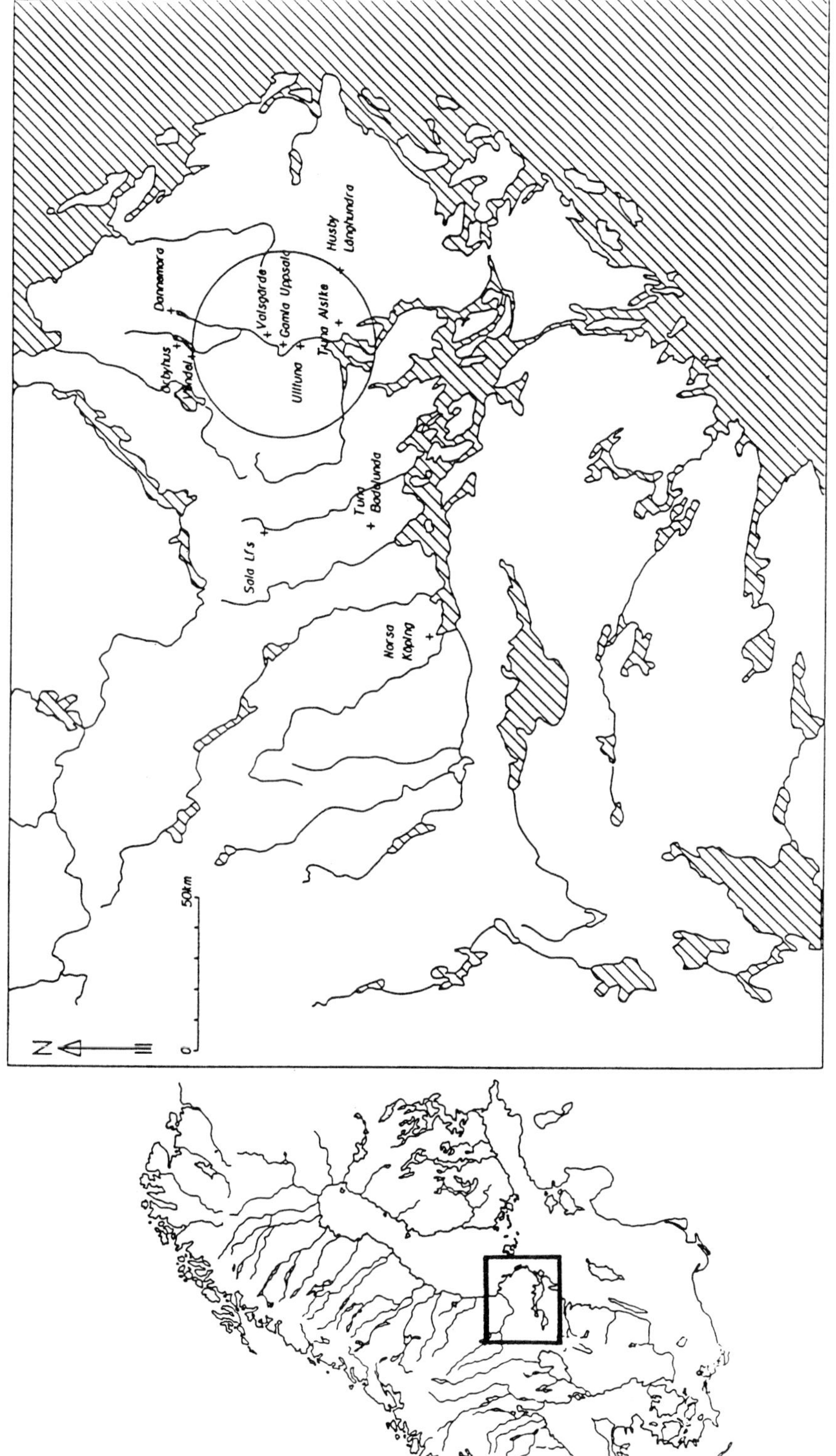

Fig. 1 Map of Sweden with the key sites in the project 'Svealand in the Vendel and Viking Periods' marked.

but may affect the choice of burial treatment, they can provide a starting point to distinguish variations in burial treatment (Wason 1994).

We work with mortuary data, primarily with human skeletal remains. Identifying the sex of individuals from prehistoric cemeteries is crucial for a subsequent analysis of the social and biological structure, for example ranking, of ancient societies (Wason 1994). Once sex is determined, males and females can be compared with regard to nutritional status, diet, physical stress, life expectancy, and material status.

The most common way by far of performing sex determinations is morphological analysis of the skeleton, the second way is the identification of gender indicating artefacts. This is not always completely satisfactory, however. But the problem of sex identification of non-complete skeletons, very young individuals and cremated bones can now be overcome by the use of molecular sex identification (Hummel and Hermann 1991, Götherström *et al.* 1997b). Here X and Y chromosome specific sequences, based on the amelogenin sequence, are used for molecular sex identification. We extract DNA for sex identification according to Lidén *et al.* (1997) where collagen and other proteins are broken down with a guanidium treatment, DNA is extracted with a phosphate buffer and finally purified by silica. We have noticed that this kind of phosphate extraction is a good method when dealing with a hydroxyapatite rich material (Götherström and Lidén 1996). The molecular sex identification is then performed by PCR, the amelogenin sequence (Götherström *et al.* 1999), as well as a Y-specific repeat (Witt and Erickson 1989), are amplified and the pattern on the gel is then used for the identification.

In order to establish archaeological rank we use dietary analysis, material status and kinship. Diet is a well known indicator of rank and has, as such, been used in archaeological studies (Schoeninger 1979; Schutowski 1994; Schutowski and Herrmann 1996). Differential access to different food sources such as protein or specific crops is traced in the skeletal remains of humans. Here we use stable isotope and trace element analyses on bone which provide information on the major food sources in the diet (Schoeninger and DeNiro 1984; Tuross *et al.* 1994; Lidén 1996).

We use stable carbon and nitrogen isotopes from bone collagen to differentiate from where the protein digested originates. That is carbon isotopes indicate whether the protein originates from marine resources and nitrogen isotopes from which trophic level in the food chain the protein comes. Collagen was extracted according to Brown *et al.* (1988) where high molecular remnants are selected for. The isotopes were measured using an Optima Fison mass spectrometer with a precision of <0.1%, and are given as $\delta^{13}C=(Ru/Rs-1)x1000\%$, where Ru and Rs are the respective $^{13}C/^{12}C$ ratios for the unknown and the standard (PDB limestone for carbon and AIR for nitrogen). The values expected for each isotope should therefore be similar to those seen in an analysis of two Neolithic populations originating from megalith burials (Fig. 2; Lidén 1995), where there is a difference between the populations in both carbon and nitrogen isotopes indicating a different origin for their main food sources. It is also clear that there was a difference in diet within a population: food resources were not distributed equally within the populations, and particularly not within the coastal population.

Kinship is also of utmost interest when discussing problems concerning the making of kingdoms in order to discriminate between inherited and acquired rank. 'It is rather common that where high status is achieved, this avenue to prestige and power is open only to males, while when ranking is strongly hereditary, women are often included in a more comprehensive rank system, and are more likely to hold the higher status' (Wason 1994:98). This would thus be reflected in the proportion of high status female to male burials. In the case of multiple burials it is of interest to know whether those persons buried together were related in some way. Since a child is given half of its genome from its mother and half of its genome from the father it is possible to identify a mother–father–child relation in a burial.

We have based our kinship analysis on a micro satellite (actin) identified at the *cardiac muscle actin gene* locus positioned on the 15th chromosome and published by Litt and Luty (1989). The result of a molecular sex determination in grave 23a, from the Middle Neolithic cemetery Ajvide, Gotland, provided not only new information on the sex of the individual but also demonstrated its relationship to individual 23b,

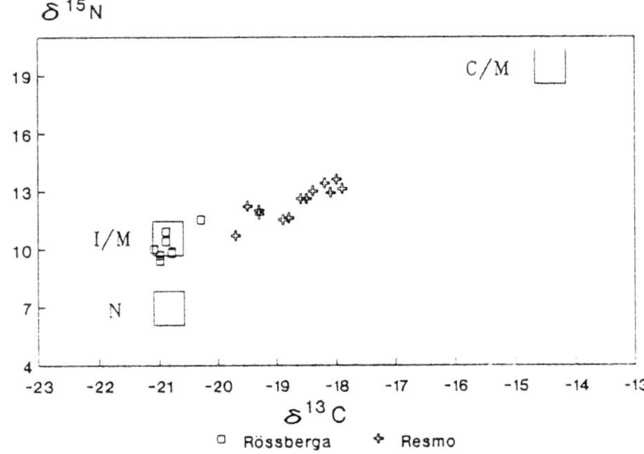

Fig. 2 Expected isotope values for populations feeding on different resources, i.e. marine versus terrestrial protein and low versus high trophic protein. The sites represent two Swedish megalith populations, one coastal (Resmo) and one inland (Rössberga). The boxes denote the expected end values respectively for a population living entirely on terrestrial or marine protein; C/M = coastal mesolithic; I/M = inland mesolithic; N = neolithic (from Lidén 1995).

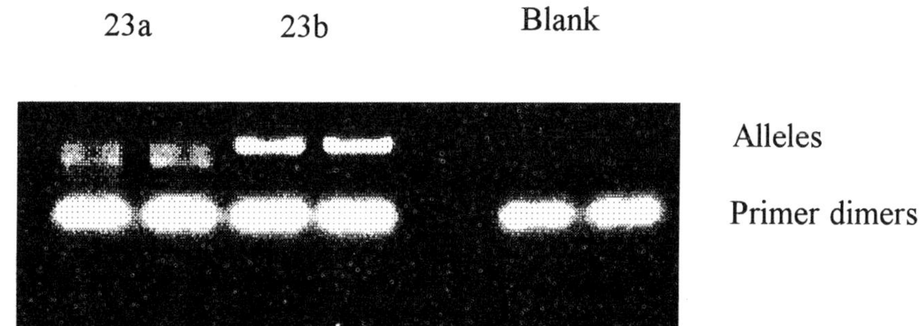

Fig. 3 Kinship analysis of the two individuals, 23 a and 23 b, from the Neolithic cemetery at Ajvide, Gotland, Sweden. The analysis is based on a micro satellite the cardiac muscle actin gene, *positioned on the 15th chromosome.*

Table 1 Osteological (Arrhenius 1990) and molecular sex identifications (#from Malmström 1995), stable isotope values in ‰ and trace element values in ppm (Arrhenius 1990), on the individuals buried at the boat grave cemetery in Tuna, Alsike parish, Uppland, Sweden.

Sample	**Age**	**Ost. sex**	**Mol. sex**	**δ^{13}C**	**δ^{15}N**	**Cu**	**Zn**	**Se**
Tuna III, **34**	Ad	M	?	–20.1	14.0	16.1	184	2.7
Tuna XI, **35**	Ad	M	?	–20.8	14.7	15.9	118	2.7
Tuna VIb, **36**	Ad	F	F?#	–20.6	13.4	–	99	3.7
Tuna IV, **37**	Ad	F?	M?	–20.5	13.7	0.8	119	7.2
Tuna I, **38**	Ad	M	M	–20.8	13.4	0.7	300	8.0
Tuna VII, **39**	Ad	M	M	–20.4	14.1	2.5	161	5.1
Tuna VIII, **40**	Inf II	M	M	–20.2	14.3	1.0	129	2.9
		Mean		**–20.5**	**13.9**	**6.2**	**159**	**4.6**
		s.d.		**0.3**	**0.5**	**7.6**	**69**	**2.2**

buried in the same grave, as parent to child (Fig. 3) (Österholm 1993, Götherström *et al.* 1997b, Lidén and Götherström 1997).

It is also of interest to know whether the people buried within a cemetery are related and in what way, that is, whether communities were patrilocal, matrilocal or neither. It is possible to study kinship within a cemetery by using parts of the inherited genome, so called Short Tandem Repeats (STR markers), or by using maternally inherited hyper variable sequences in the mitochondrial DNA. A preliminary study on an Early Medieval cemetery in northern Sweden proved that by the use of a Y-chromosomal marker it was possible to test whether this cemetery was used by one family and if this lineage was patrilocal (Götherström *et al.* 1999). In total ten individuals were analysed and it turned out to be an 83 per cent probability that the cemetery had been used by one patrilocal family and a 92 per cent probability that the cemetery had been used by one or two patrilocal families (Götherström *et al.* 1999).

We shall now turn to the area included in the SIV project and look at some of the burials from the boat grave cemetery in Tuna in Alsike (Fig. 1; Table 1), which is interesting in this respect in that here both sexes are represented in boat graves. The general picture in Uppland otherwise is that the boat grave cemeteries are dominated by inhumed male burials, whereas the females are found in cremation graves. In Västmanland, on the other hand, we have female inhumation boat graves : by far the largest boat grave cemetery there is Tuna in Badelunda with eight boats dated from 600–1050 (Nylén 1994). The individuals from Tuna in Alsike were sex identified both by osteological and molecular methods and it is obvious that there is a slight discrepancy between the two methods, as, for example, in individuals 36 and 37 (Table 1) (Arrhenius 1990; Malmström 1995; Lidén *et al.* 1997). The molecular sex identification will be repeated, however, and the technique used will be improved. Dietary analysis of the skeletal remains from Tuna in Alsike has provided information that shows all protein digested originated from terrestrial resources and also that it came from a very high trophic level (Table 1) (Lidén *et al.* 1997). The very low variation in stable isotope values within this population also indicates that they had an equal diet regarding the protein intake. However, [bearing in mind] the trace elements which we

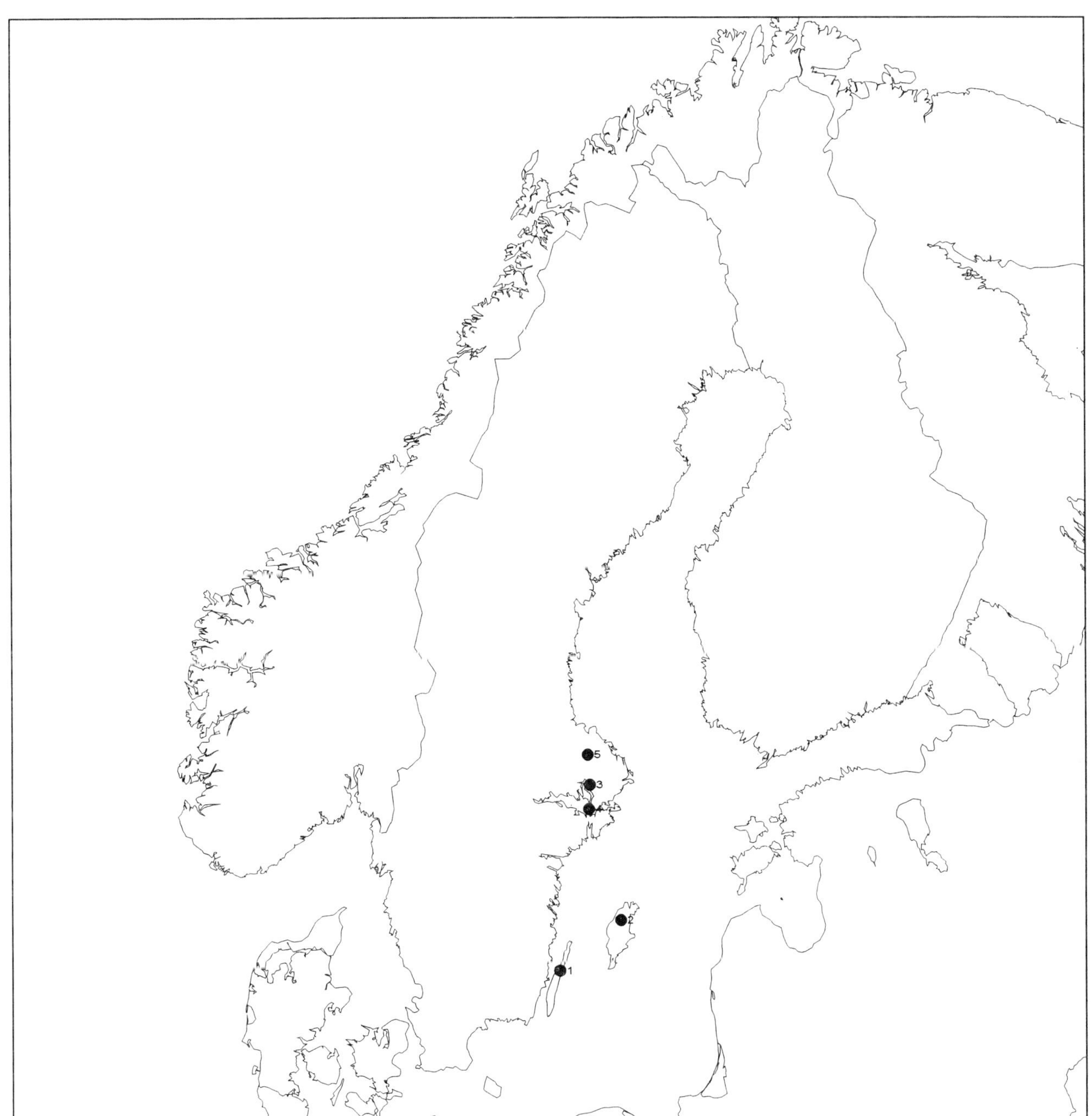

Fig. 4 Map of sites from where the horse samples for DNA analysis originated. 1) Skedemósse; 2) Halla; 3) Tuna in Alsike; 4) Birka; 5) Vendel.

can identify, the most pronounced differences are in copper and selenium. The high selenium values have previously been interpreted as an indication of trade from the north since Swedish soils are poor in selenium, while meat from reindeer, feeding on lichens, is high in selenium (Lidén and Nelson 1994). It is also noteworthy that the difference in trace element content is not correlated with sex, so this population had a gender equal diet. So far we have not been able to apply the kinship analysis to the Tuna in Alsike material but it will be applied to all the boat grave cemeteries in Vendel, Valsgärde, Tuna in Alsike as well as Tuna in Badelunda.

Preliminary positive results from DNA extractions of cremated bones might also open up the possibility of including the cremated bones from the large mounds in old Uppsala in the analysis (Götherström and Ovchinnikov 1996). Although it is necessary to work with unique sequences in kinship analysis and it is not very likely that it will ever be possible to extract those from cremated bones, it would have been of utmost interest in order to establish the relation of the kingship in old Uppsala with the rest of the Svealand. We will of course also perform dietary analyses on the same material in order to establish any rank differences. The results from the boat grave cemeteries will then be contrasted and compared to similar analyses from cemeteries within the same geographical area but of lower status.

We will only briefly mention that we also use other biological artefacts besides human remains to study rank. Horses and horsemanship is another subproject of the SIV project. Ever since the first boat graves were excavated in Vendel it was clear that the horse played an important part in the funeral ritual of the boat grave people, and the graves containing horses have always been interpreted as high status graves. Our part in this subproject is to do 'kinship' analysis on the horses to try to find if selective horse breeding existed and also to see if we can find evidence for gift exchange or trade with horses. This part of the project is a collaboration between the Archaeological Research Laboratory and the Agricultural University in Ulltuna, where they have long since been working on a molecular horse breed project. So far we have analysed five horses from five different sites within Sweden: Skedemosse, Öland; Vendel; Tuna in Alsike; Halla, Gotland, and Birka. We will also include a sample from Sutton Hoo and as a comparison we will analyse samples found in cultural layers from a number of Iron Age sites in Estonia as well as Sweden. The preliminary results so far provide evidence that there definitely existed several different breeds of horses in Sweden at this time. We also have evidence that there seems to have been the same 'kind' of race or breed of horses in Skedemosse and Alsike, whereas we have a totally new haplotype in Halla, Gotland (Fig. 4) (Götherström, Liden and Ellegren 1997).

To conclude, by studying the archaeology of rank by means of diet, molecular sex identification and molecular kinship within an archaeological context we will greatly improve our chances of saying something of the social and political structure in past societies in general. Our aim is, however, to be able to say something in particular about the power structures within the central parts of Svealand during the Vendel and Viking Periods.

Acknowledgements

We thank the Museum of National Antiquities, Professor Martin Carver, Department of Archaeology, University of York and Lembi Lõugas, Institute of History Tallinn, for providing bone samples; Hans Ellegren, The Agricultural University in Ultuna, for fruitful co-operation; Neil Schailer for help with the actin marker and we thank the SIV project who provided funding.

References

Ambrosiani, B. 1996: *Birka Vikingastaden* Vols I–V (Sveriges Radios Förlag).

Arrhenius, B. 1990: 'Trace element analysis of human skulls', *Laborativ Arkeologi* 4, 15–20.

Arrhenius, B. and Herschend, F. 1995: 'SIV-Svealand in the Vendel and Viking Periods. Settlement, society and power', unpublished application for a research programme.

Arrhenius, B. and Sjøvold, T. 1995: 'The infant prince from the East mound at Old Uppsala', *Laborativ Arkeologi* 8, 29–37.

Brown, T.A., Nelson, D.E., Vogel, J.S. and Southon, J.R. 1988: 'Improved collagen extraction by modified Longin method', *Radiocarbon* 30, 171–7.

Götherström, A., Grundberg, L. and Hårding, B. 1999: 'Kinship, religion and DNA: Y-chromosomal microsatellites used on a medieval population', *International Journal of Osteoarchaeology*. In press.

Götherström, A. and Lidén, K. 1996: 'A modified DNA extraction method for bone and teeth', *Laborativ Arkeologi* 9, 53–6.

Götherström, A., and Ovchinnikov, I. 1996: 'DNA in cremated bones', Poster, 7th Nordic Conference on the Application of Scientific Methods in Archaeology, Savonlinna, Finland 1996.

Götherström, A., Lidén, K. and Ellegren, H. 1997: 'Hästar från yngre Järnåldern i mellan Sverige, en analys av hästtyper med molekylära metoder', in Arrhenius, B. and Eriksson, G. (eds), *SIV Svealand i Vendel och Vikingatid. Studier från delprojekten vid Stockholms Universitet*, Arkeologiska Forskningslaboratoriet (Stockholm), 29–34.

Götherström, A., Lidén, K., Ahlström, T., Källersjö, M. and Brown, T. A. 1997b: 'Osteology, DNA and sex identification', *International Journal of Osteoarchaeology* 7, 71–82.

Holmquist-Olausson, L. 1993: *Aspects on Birka. Investigations and surveys 1976–1989*, Thesis and Papers in Archaeology B:3 (Stockholm).

Hummel, S., and Hermann, B. 1991: 'Y-Chromosome-specific DNA amplified in ancient human bones', *Naturwissenschaften* 78, 266–267.

Isaksson, S. 1997 'Arkeologiska boplatsundersökningar vid vendels kyrka 1996, in Arrhenius, B. and Eriksson, G. (eds.) Svealand i Vendel och Vikingatid. Rapport från utgravningarna, 5–32.

Lidén, K. 1995: 'Megaliths, agriculture, and social complexity: a diet study of two Swedish megalith populations', *Journal of Anthropological Archaeology* 14, 404–417.

Lidén, K. 1996: 'A dietary perspective on Swedish hunter-gatherer and Neolithic populations. An analysis of stable isotopes and trace elements', *Laborativ Arkeologi* 9, 5–23.

Lidén, K. and Götherström, A. 1997: 'Släktskap och genus under mellan Neolitikum på Gotland', in Åkerlund. A., Bergh, S., Nordbladh, J. & Taffinder, J. (eds.) Arkeologiska Samtal. SAR 33, 189–198.

Lidén, K. and Nelson, D. E. 1994: 'Stable carbon isotopes as dietary indicators in the Baltic area', *Fornvännen* 89,13–21.

Lidén, K., Götherström, A. and Eriksson, G. 1997: ' Diet, gender and rank', *ISKOS*, 11, 158–164.

Litt, M., and Luty, J. A. 1989: 'A hypervariable microsatellite revealed by *In Vitro* amplification of a dinucleotide repeat within the cardiac muscle actin gene', *American Journal of Genetics* 44, 397–401.

Lönnroth, E. 1977: *Scandinavians: Selected Historical Essays* (Göteborg).

Malmström, H. 1995: 'Kvinnor och båtgravar i Badelunda och Alsike.

En molekylär bestämning av de gravlagdas kön', in Arrhenius, B. (ed.), *CD-uppsatser i Laborativ Arkeologi 95/96 Del 2*, Stockholms Universitet, 3–33.

Moberg, C-A.1941: *Zonengliederungen der vorchristlichen Eisenzeit in Nordeuropa*, Gleerup (Lund).

Norr, S. and Sundkvist, A. 1997: In Herschend, F. (ed.) Svealand i Vendel och Vikingatid. Rapport från utgrävningarna i Valsgärde. Rapport från utgrävningarna 2:1–41.

Nylén, E. 1994: *Tuna i Badelunda*, Västerås Kulturnämnds Skriftserie 30.

Österholm, I. 1993: 'Jacobs/Ajvide. Undersökningar på en Gotländsk boplatsudde från stenåldern. Hemse', unpublished report.

Sawyer, P. 1991: *När Sverige blev Sverige*, Viktoria (Alingsås).

Schoeninger, M.J. 1979: 'Diet and status at Chalcatzingo: some empirical and technical aspects of strontium analysis', *American Journal of Physical Anthropology* 51, 295–310.

Schoeninger, M.J. and DeNiro, M.J. 1984: 'Nitrogen and carbon isotopic composition of bone collagen from marine and terrestrial animals', *Geochimica et Cosmochimica Acta* 48, 625–639.

Schutowski, H. 1994: 'Gruppentypische Spurenrelementmuster in Frühmittelalterichen Skelettserien Südwestdeutchlands', in Kokabi, M. and Wahl, J. (eds), *Landesdenkmalamt Baden-Würtemberg*, Beiträge zur Archäozoologie und Prähistorischen Anthropologie, Forschungen und Berichte zur Vor- und Frühgeschichte in Baden-Würtemberg 53:117–124.

Schutowski, H. and Herrmann, B. 1996: 'Geographical variability of subsistence strategies in early Medieval populations of southwestern Germany', *Journal of Archaeological Science* 23/6, 823–31.

Tuross, N., Fogel, M.L., Newsom, L. and Doran, G.H. 1994: 'Subsistence in the Florida archaic: the stable isotope and archaeobotanical evidence from the Windower site', *American Antiquity* 59, 288–303.

Wason, K.P. 1994: *The Archaeology of Rank*, Cambridge University Press (Cambridge).

Witt, M. and Erickson, R.P.A. 1989: 'A rapid method for detection of Y- chromosomal DNA from dried blood specimens by the polymerase chain reaction', *Human Genetics* 82, 271–274.

The British Church and the Emergence of Anglo-Saxon Kingdoms

Lucas Quensel-von Kalben

For many early medieval kingdoms, Christianity has been claimed to be of paramount importance for the creation of a more stable kind of political structure. The Merovingian Franks start their success story with the baptism of King Clovis in 496. Slav and Scandinavian early states also begin to emerge with the acceptance of Christianity. The formation of kingdoms in Anglo-Saxon England – starting in the sixth century – is probably also linked to Augustine's mission, even though the political process might have started earlier then the ideological one. Nicholas Higham (1997) has recently demonstrated how these two processes are interconnected. However, their coincidence might be connected to other underlying reasons and need not be causally tied to each other. It can be partly explained, for example, by the Christian monopoly of literacy in this age.

While Scandinavian and Slavic kingdoms are supposed to be converted *de novo*, the situation in Britain is more comparable to the one in the Frankish realms, where at least a part of the population had been converted long before the formation of any kingdoms. In spite of this similarity, the two regions differ in one important respect: the acceptance or rejection of the early Church. While the Frankish Church is deeply rooted in the structure of its Roman predecessor, the English Church widely ignores (Romano-)British Christianity. Why is this the case?

One answer to these alternative approaches could be the different degree of Christianization in Gaul and Britain, that is that Gaul was more thoroughly Christian than Britain. This impression is currently *en vogue* and – as I hope to show – not very probable.

A second answer relates to the demographic mixing of indigenous and Germanic populations. The number of Germanic settlers in the Frankish Kingdoms west of the Rhine has been claimed to be around 2 per cent overall, higher in the north-east and virtually non-existent in the south-west (Geary 1996, 120–121). The high number of people in Francia of Gaulish descent, potential bearers of Roman Christianity, makes a strong argument for the integration of their indigenous belief. The areas of Romano-British and Germanic settlers in Britain might have been much more exclusive. The number of the immigrating people here is much higher than on the continent. The situation in Britain is, however, far from clear, as the discussion of Nicholas Higham's influential *Rome, Britain and the Anglo-Saxons* (1992) demonstrates.

Heinrich Härke (in press) has recently discussed the different kinds of evidence (historical, linguistic, cemeteries, settlements and skeletal data) for a British survival in Anglo-Saxon England. As a result of this survey a varied and and diffuse picture emerges. The number of people of British descent seems to vary according to the sources one explores, the region and the period involved. Neither complete extinction nor complete survival can be substantiated and solutions taking social and political processes of ethnic identity into account seem most appropriate. Beside the models of other Migration Period *landnam*, a further source of information and model building should be sought in historical or ethnographic expansions and migrations.[1]

A third solution to the problem of different development in Gaul and Britain is the cultural background of Franks, on the one hand, and Angles, Saxon and Jutes, on the other. While the tribes of the Frankish confederacy had a long history of interaction with the Roman Empire, those groups that settled in Britain might have had more sporadic contacts with the Roman world.

Finally we might be misled by the written sources. Our main witness for the English conversion, Bede, argues heavily for an origin of the English Church independent from the British. This might have been overstated and Rob Meens argued in a recent article (1994) that the British Church had a lasting impact on the Anglo-Saxons and even tried (and succeeded) to mission them.[2]

Probably all of these reasons might be true for the different courses of Frankish and English conversion, but I suspect that another reason is equally responsible for the difference. The British Church might have been less attractive to the Anglo-Saxons because it increased the cultural difference between both populations and was used as the organizing principle of British resistance. To develop this argument I have to start with the state of Christianity in Late Roman Britain.

Christianity in Late-Roman Britain: An Overview

The religious world of Roman Britain is usually divided into three major groups: the Roman Pantheon, Celtic deities and the Oriental cults of Late Antiquity. One of these oriental cults won ground from 313 AD onwards and dominated by 400 AD greater parts of the Roman Empire: Christianity.

The accepted view in British archaeology of the last twenty years is that Christianity never formed a majority cult in Roman Britain. This particular view leads at times to grotesque results which I would like to call a Christianophobia.

Charles Thomas (1981) held the alternative view that Christianity in the second half of the fourth century was an important religion with a considerable number of followers. His view is mainly based on the identification of Christian churches and some kinds of object with 'Christian' symbols. In 1981 he accepted the identification of only two Christian cemeteries: Poundbury/Dorset, and a part of Winchester-Lankhills. This resulted partly from the low number of published cemeteries of Late Roman date, partly from his objections to the possibility of identifying Christian burials at all.

Ten years after Thomas, Dorothy Watts published her *Christians and Pagans in Roman Britain* (1991). In her book and a later article in the excavation report on the Butt Road cemetery in Colchester, she followed Thomas to a large degree while accepting many more Christian cemeteries than Thomas did. She suggested thirteen criteria[3] for the identification of a Christian cemetery:

1. Christian inscriptions clearly connected to the cemetery
2. West–east orientation of the skeleton
3. Undisturbed burials
4. Supine and extended position of the skeleton
5. Absence of decapitated burials
6. 'Plaster' burials
7. Neo-natal/very young infants in the cemetery
8. Mausolea or burial enclosures
9. Focal graves (graves in prominent position and used as points of reference for other graves; possibly site of pilgrimage)
10. Absence of vessels
11. Absence of animal or birds
12. Absence of hobnails
13. Absence of coins in the mouth ('Charon's fee').[4]

Three more criteria are related to the existence of contemporary pagan burial grounds close by.[5] Each of these traits gets a subjective weighting from 100 per cent down to 20 per cent. This weighting seems to be based on her impression of what is obligatory and what is just desirable for a Christian burial.[6]

A second approach to the question of identifying Christian cemeteries has been published by Ann Woodward in a report of the excavation of a large – in fact the largest at the moment – Late Roman cemetery at Poundbury near Dorchester/Dorset. Her list of criteria is a copy of Watts' list, but includes two more points:

14. Absence of gravegoods (especially unworn garments and equipment)
15. Stone cists and grave linings.

Both authors compared Roman-British cemeteries along these criteria and established an order of likelihood for a Christian burial ground. While Watts looked at twenty-nine cemeteries all over Britain, the regional context of Woodward's work is more restricted – to the Durotrigan territory of Dorset and Somerset and some other cemeteries outside this region for comparison. Woodward has a rather robust way of calculating her index, while Watts' is more finely tuned. The results are compatible with each other. Poundbury (main cemetery) (Farwell and Molleson 1993), Lankhills (burials enclosed by feature 6) (Clarke 1979) and Icklingham (West 1976) have the highest scores, followed by the Roman to sub-Roman cemeteries of Nettleton (Wedlake 1982), Henley Wood (Watts and Leach forthcoming) and Cannington (Rahtz 1977) in south-west Britain.

Watts concluded that Christianity is neither an urban nor an upper class religion (1991, 217). This point, based mainly on the non-cemetery evidence,[7] contradicts the expectation of other researchers (Radford 1971; Frend 1979 for upper class religion; Dark 1994 for lower class religion) and is highly significant for the question of the continuity of the British Church in England.

Another aspect of Watts' and Woodward's list is the even distribution of scorings from the top to the bottom: there is no major gap. Two features might be responsible for this picture: on the one hand, an approach which differentiates only between the presence and absence of a trait[8] and,on the other hand, the continuity of a burial ground from pagan to Christian (and possibly back to pagan) ritual. The latter point can be demonstrated by looking at two cemeteries and their development. At Poundbury and Winchester-Lankhills, enclosures mark areas of different burial customs, apparently of contemporaneous date.[9] The Butt Road cemetery in Colchester had two phases:[10] the first phase consists of north-south orientated graves with at least some gravegoods (often pottery), while the second phase is dominated by evenly spaced, west-east orientated graves with very few gravegoods of a completely different character.

The status of Christianity at 400

The above approaches present two problems. First, the criteria, especially those that are only indirectly or not at all confirmed by the written sources, need to be tested. Second, for the reasons discussed above (absence/presence scale; undetected burial enclosures) and the possibility of syncretism, that is the hidden continuity of pagan customs, a single grave could alter the whole picture of a cemetery from being a Christian burial ground to not. Both problems can be overcome by using a different quantitative technique, the combination table using individual graves instead of entire cemeteries. If such a table shows 'pagan' and 'Christian' traits in (more or less) mutually exclusive clusters, then we may be dealing with two seperate burial customs. And what other explanation would fit so neatly as Christianity?[11] This is not a proof in the strict sense of the word, but it puts the onus of falsification on to the 'non-believers'!

My sample has been collected from eight cemeteries across southern and eastern Britain (Fig. 1).[12] The sample size (eight cemeteries with 2020 non-disturbed graves after 280 AD) is due to the small number of published reports of Late Roman cemeteries, some of them still awaiting publication (Cannington/Somerset excavated 1962); others will be included in a later stage of my research (e.g. Queenford Farm/Oxon.). The sample is fairly mixed regionally and socially. Most of the criteria of Watts and Woodward have been integrated.[13] But before turning to the results of the analysis some examples of typical outcomes (ordered matrices) of combination tables and how they could be interpreted need to be considered.

Pattern 1, the block pattern, consists of two or more major blocks of mutually exclusive traits, an ideal which turns up quite often when comparing male and female gravegoods. It could also represent different religious, social, ethnic etc. groups with their own, mutually exclusive burial customs. Pattern 2, the stairway pattern, shows the traits arranged along a diagonal. Usually this would be interpreted as a chronological development. But of course a third possible outcome of the seriation process[14] – Pattern 3 – exists which shows no apparent ordering at all. I would call it the 'shotgun model'. This last pattern is, perhaps surprisingly, not a typical outcome of a seriation/combination table in burial analysis.

How do these ideal models compare to the real data? The first table (Fig. 2) shows the unordered entries of the different traits (column and row headings of all combination tables are in the same order). Four traits dominate the

Fig. 1 Map of Late Roman cemeteries in the sample.

	1	2	3	4	5	6	7	8	9	10	11	12	13	14	15	16
1 West-East-Orient.	**1883**	.	1828	55	334	8	31	94	31	79	20	165	72	30	159	352
2 North-South-Orient.	.	**136**	107	29	37	3	1	11	.	20	6	36	9	4	6	61
3 Supine	1828	107	**1936**	.	354	10	32	88	30	91	23	184	76	32	156	381
4 Prone or crouched	55	29	.	**84**	17	1	.	17	1	8	3	17	5	2	9	32
5 Overlapping	334	37	354	17	**371**	.	5	32	5	3	6	27	17	5	41	62
6 Decapitation	8	3	10	1	.	**11**	.	.	.	1	1	4	1	1	.	/
7 Plaster	31	1	32	.	5	.	**32**	.	4	2	.	.	.	.	18	2
8 Neonatal/Infant	94	11	88	17	32	.	.	**105**	.	2	.	1	1	.	26	4
9 Mausoleum/Enclosure	31	.	30	1	5	.	4	.	**31**	5	1	9	1	.	8	15
10 Vessels	79	20	91	8	3	1	2	2	5	**99**	6	35	9	2	2	98
11 Animal bones	20	6	23	3	6	1	.	.	1	6	**26**	12	1	1	1	26
12 Hobnails	165	36	184	17	27	4	.	1	9	35	12	**201**	19	9	17	199
13 Coins	72	9	76	5	17	1	.	1	1	9	1	19	**81**	34	10	81
14 Charon´s fee	30	4	32	2	5	1	.	.	.	2	1	9	34	**34**	4	34
15 Grave protected	159	6	156	9	41	.	18	26	8	2	1	17	10	4	**165**	34
16 Gravegoods	352	61	381	32	62	7	2	4	15	98	26	199	81	34	34	**413**

Fig. 2 Unordered combination table of 16 criteria from 8 Late Roman cemeteries (undisturbed graves only; n = 2020). The diagonal shows the absolute number of occurences in bold figures.

	1	2	3	4	5	6	7	8	9	10	11	12	13	14	15	16
1 West-East-Orient.	**1883**	-100	79	-80	-27	-68	38	-25	100	-60	-63	-58	-28	-31	33	-56
2 North-South-Orient.	-100	**136**	-81	80	26	68	-39	25	-100	59	62	57	28	30	-34	55
3 Supine	79	-81	**1936**	-100	-7	-40	100	-69	13	-37	-51	-42	-22	-19	-16	-44
4 Prone or crouched	-80	80	-100	**84**	6	39	-100	68	-14	36	50	41	21	18	15	43
5 Overlapping	-27	26	-7	6	**371**	-100	-10	34	-8	-77	14	-21	8	-14	20	-15
6 Decapitation	-68	68	-40	39	-100	**11**	-100	-100	-100	32	77	68	41	71	-100	74
7 Plaster	38	-39	100	-100	-10	-100	**32**	-100	82	13	-100	-100	-100	-100	88	-60
8 Neonatal/Infant	-25	25	-69	68	34	-100	-100	**105**	-100	-47	-100	-85	-64	-100	61	-75
9 Mausoleum/Enclosure	100	-100	13	-14	-8	-100	82	-100	**31**	58	44	58	-12	-100	60	57
10 Vessels	-60	59	-37	36	-77	32	13	-47	58	**99**	71	70	43	9	-64	99
11 Animal bones	-63	62	-51	50	14	77	-100	-100	44	71	**26**	78	-3	40	-39	100
12 Hobnails	-58	57	-42	41	-21	68	-100	-85	58	70	78	**201**	49	54	2	99
13 Coins	-28	28	-22	21	8	41	-100	-64	-12	43	-3	49	**81**	100	23	100
14 Charon´s fee	-31	30	-19	18	-14	71	-100	-100	-100	9	40	54	100	**34**	20	100
15 Grave protected	33	-34	-16	15	20	-100	88	61	60	-64	-39	2	23	20	**165**	0
16 Gravegoods	-56	55	-44	43	-15	74	-60	-75	57	99	100	99	100	100	0	**413**

Fig. 3 Unordered combination table of 16 criteria from 8 Late Roman cemeteries (undisturbed graves only; n = 2020). The diagonal shows the absolute number of occurences in bold figures. Other numbers represent Yule values.

	6	**14**	**11**	**12**	**2**	**16**	**13**	**4**	**10**	**5**	**9**	**15**	**3**	**1**	**8**	**7**
6 Decapitation	**11**	71	77	68	68	74	41	39	32	-100	-100	-100	-40	-68	-100	-100
14 Charon´s fee	71	**34**	40	54	30	100	100	18	9	-14	-100	20	-19	-31	-100	-100
11 Animal bones	77	40	**26**	78	62	100	-3	50	71	14	44	-39	-51	-63	-100	-100
12 Hobnails	68	54	78	**201**	57	99	49	41	70	-21	58	2	-42	-58	-85	-100
2 North-South-Orient.	68	30	62	57	**136**	55	28	80	59	26	-100	-34	-81	-100	25	-39
16 Gravegoods	74	100	100	99	55	**413**	100	43	99	-15	57	0	-44	-56	-75	-60
13 Coins	41	100	-3	49	28	100	**81**	21	43	8	-12	23	-22	-28	-64	-100
4 Prone or crouched	39	18	50	41	80	43	21	**84**	36	6	-14	15	-100	-80	68	-100
10 Vessels	32	9	71	70	59	99	43	36	**99**	-77	58	-64	-37	-60	-47	13
5 Overlapping	-100	-14	14	-21	26	-15	8	6	-77	**371**	-8	20	-7	-27	34	-10
9 Mausoleum/Enclosure	-100	-100	44	58	-100	57	-12	-14	58	-8	**31**	60	13	100	-100	82
15 Grave protected	-100	20	-39	2	-34	0	23	15	-64	20	60	**165**	-16	33	61	88
3 Supine	-40	-19	-51	-42	-81	-44	-22	-100	-37	-7	13	-16	**1936**	79	-69	100
1 West-East-Orient.	-68	-31	-63	-58	-100	-56	-28	-80	-60	-27	100	33	79	**1883**	-25	38
8 Neonatal/Infant	-100	-100	-100	-85	25	-75	-64	68	-47	34	-100	61	-69	-25	**105**	-100
7 Plaster	-100	-100	-100	-100	-39	-60	-100	-100	13	-10	82	88	100	38	-100	**32**

-100 to -30	-29 to 0	1 to 100

Fig. 4 Ordered combination table of 16 criteria from 8 Late Roman cemeteries (undisturbed graves only; n = 2020). The diagonal shows the absolute number of occurences in bold figures. Other numbers represent Yule values. The shading indicates different degrees of association.

table: the two main orientations of the head and the position of the body in the grave (supine or prone/crouched).

In the next step of the analysis the combinations are converted into Yule-values.[15] This value describes the degree of association between two attributes taking into account the absolute frequency of each attribute. The Yule-value falls between + 100 (complete association: trait A and B always occur together) and – 100 (no association at all). A '0' means that there is an equal chance of trait A being associated with trait B in the same grave. Figure 3 is based on the original combination table. It hints at some interesting results: mausolea or enclosures are, for example, never associated with north-south-orientated graves, while a supine position of the body tends to be associated with west-east-orientated graves.

The third table is seriated (Fig. 4): rows and columns have been shuffled to empty the lower left and top right corners (i.e. absolute number = 0; Yule value = – 100). The result does not look like the 'shotgun' model, that is it is not a random pattern. A mixture of the staircase and the block-model seems most appropiate as a description of the outcome. Some particular traits are strongly associated with others, while other traits are dispersed over all graves. Decapitation and plaster-burials are both associated traits which are grouped in two respective blocks. Overlapping and neonatal/infant graves belong to neither group exclusively, and their removal from the table would sharpen the block pattern. The clear-cut division of traits associated with one of the main grave orientations is interesting.

What does this pattern mean? I would suggest that some burial customs are gradually displaced by others, that is we see a chronological development.[16] I would call the cluster at the top left corner (north-south orientation, prone/crouched body position etc.) the type 1 ('pagan'), the cluster in the opposite corner the type 2 ('Christian').

The table does not in itself suggest a clear direction for the chronological development. It could start with the attributes which can be found at either of the two corners (top left and bottom right). Independent evidence is needed. Very few graves of the Late Roman period can be dated in absolute terms and with narrow margins of error. Only Winchester-Lankhills, a comparatively rich cemetery, has very bravely been dated. The dates cannot be used for chronological ordering because two of the main bases for dating were the grave furniture and burial customs.[17] Graves with 'Christian' attributes are spread evenly over the whole cemetery and do not suggest a horizontal stratigraphy. The Butt Road cemetery in Colchester and the temple site of Lamyatt Beacon in Somerset do show a replacement of type 1 by type 2.

What does that mean for the state of Christianity at the end of the Roman occupation? Many authors believe that it was not Christianity but a changing burial custom that was responsible for this development. Such a changing 'fashion' still needs an explanation, because burial customs are a very sensitive field of religious behaviour, which will not change without a sensible reason. I would argue that Christianity is a key factor for this change, and that it is not a sudden replacement but a slow process in which the Church growing in power, information exchange and dogmatism regulates a once highly syncretistic burial custom into normative burying behaviour.

In order to obtain some idea about the social status of the burying communities and the urban/rural divide, I subdivided the eight cemeteries into 'Christian' and 'pagan' burial grounds on the basis of the majority of the graves falling in one or the other group.[18] In the last half of the fourth century two of the urban sites (Butt Road/ Colchester; Poundbury/Dorset), and two of the rural sites (Icklingham; Bradley Hill) might have been Christian, while Winchester-Lankhills and Bath Gate/Cirencester as well as Lynch Farm/Peterborough and Ilchester are probably not. Watts' hypothesis that Christianity is not an entirely urban phenomenon seems to be confirmed. The social status of the burying community cannot be inferred from the quantity of gravegoods because of the absence of gravegoods as a Christian indicator. In Colchester silk garments in a phase 2 grave (no. 77) and the existence of (simple) burial chambers indicate that not only the lower strata of society have been buried here. The same can be concluded for Poundbury where the foundations and plaster fragments of painted mausolea have been found. The rural Christian burial grounds look more modest in character, but never appear purely as disposal areas like Lynch Farm or some parts of the heterogenous cemetery at Bath Gate/Cirencester. Some rich ('pagan') burials can be found at Winchester[19] and elsewhere, so 'pagan' does not necessarily mean lower class. The analysis of the human bone material could not find any significant differences between pagan and Christian burying communities in health and diet. The Christian community seems to be a representative cross-section of the total population.[20]

The distribution of Christian communities has been plotted by Thomas (1981, fig. 16) and – from a slightly larger database – by Watts (1991, fig. 28, here Fig. 5). Their two maps are quite compatible – with one major difference: the area of present day Somerset and Dorset – more or less the region which has been attributed to the Durotrigans – appears Christianized on Watts' map, because she includes all the cemetery evidence. Thomas ignores this type of evidence and presents a map, based on Painter (1971), which suggests a pagan revival exactly in this (and one other) area in the late fourth century. This seemingly contradictory evidence can be explained as a pagan reaction against a strong Christian community in this part of the country. Some pagan sanctuaries (Nettleton: Wedlake 1982; Lamyatt Beacon: Leech 1986) seem in the later fourth or early fifth century to be consecrated as places of Christian worship (on the evidence of rather small churches and burials).

I would therefore argue that Christianity was one of the major religions in Roman Britain around 400 AD. The eastern and southern parts of Britain, that is the

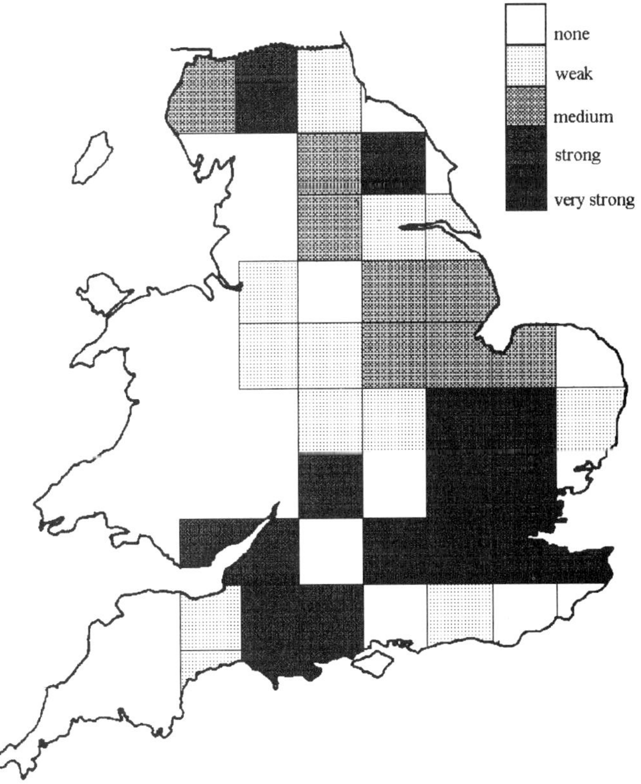

Fig. 5 Density map of indicators of Christianity (after Watts 1991).

more Romanized, urban and richer regions, seem to be more Christianized than Western Britain, an observation of fundamental importance for the rest of this paper.

The British Church in the fifth and sixth centuries in the west

There is ample evidence for the survival of the British church in western Britain in the later fifth and sixth centuries. Besides the cemeteries mentioned like Cannington, Henley Wood and Nettleton, which I would take for Christian burial grounds, we have a dense distribution of inscribed memorial stones with Christian symbols along the west coast of Britain (Nash-Williams 1950). Some or even most of these may be connected with Irish intrusions into or contacts with this area. But there is even more evidence in the written sources. In the Life of St. Germanus of Auxerre, two voyages of this bishop to Britain are mentioned. He was apparently called by a synod of British bishops to fight the Pelagian heresy in 429 and again some years later, though the reason for the second visit is not entirely clear. This case shows the survival of at least a rudimentary Church structure in Britain between 410 and 450. It also shows that the British Church was not isolated at this time but had contacts to the Gaulish Church and probably the Pope. In his lament about the state of Christianity in his own lifetime, Gildas is constantly referring to an existing hierarchical structure of the Church in an area from the Dumnonian peninsula up to North Wales and possibly further north. In his *Ruin of Britain*, dated to before the middle of the sixth century (or in Higham's (1994) short chronology at the end of the fifth), Gildas is criticizing the clergy as morally lax, but otherwise in good shape (Higham 1994, 159). The state of the British Church at the end of the sixth century is mentioned by Bede: it is very alive but following some strange and old-fashioned rituals like the 'wrong' calculation of Easter and some deviations concerning baptism. These deviations from Continental orthodox customs are a firm indication of the loss of contact. Thomas (1981) argues forcefully that the British church in the fifth century is not struggling for survival but on the contrary it is sending missions to Ireland (St. Patrick) and southern Scotland (St. Ninian). The Life of St. Patrick on the other hand shows the strong connection to the Gaulish Church where Patrick had been educated. There was a further element besides the hierarchical structure of bishops and priests who were living in rather wealthy circumstances: this is the establishment of monasteries. Bede claims that the monastery of Bangor had seven sections, with each having at least 300 monks.

The British Church seems to have flourished in fifth-century western Britain. There is no, or very slight, evidence for Roman pagan continuity or revival. This might be a result of a monopoly of literacy by the church and the apparent absence of a datable material culture in this area. In view of these conclusions, is there any evidence for (British) Christianity in the regions of Britain dominated by the Anglo-Saxons?

Evidence for the survival of the British Church in Anglo-Saxon England

The religious situation in Anglo-Saxon England in fifth and sixth centuries is far from clear. Apart from the large number of burials, which are in part the result of a religious act, there are very few indications of Anglo-Saxon paganism. The evidence (linguistic, historical and archaeological) has been usefully compiled by David Wilson (1992). The discussion of the development of Anglo-Saxon Christianity (e.g. Mayr-Harting 1972; Davis 1978; Stevenson 1992) usually starts with St. Augustine, on the assumption that British Christianity – with the exception of the later Irish branch – had no influence at all. This proposition, which is usually not tested, probably stems from Bede's statement that of the many misdeeds of the Britons their reluctance to convert the Anglo-Saxons is the worst. To my knowledge nobody has ever satisfactorily answered the question why this should have been the case. The phenomenon is not self-evident in view of the missionary efforts further west and across the Irish Sea.

The evidence for a survival of the British Church should be sought in five types of evidence: cemeteries, churches, Christian artefacts, placenames and historical sources. The two distinct burial customs in England in the Migration Period (cremation and furnished inhumation) are not compatible with the Christian burial practice as suggested in this paper. Cremation is probably an unthinkable practice for a Christian at this time, while only some 'Christian' criteria are met by the inhumations (west-east, supine position). In the supposed homelands of the Anglo-Saxons these 'Christian' traits are well established and do not presuppose British cultural influence. The average number of gravegoods and types of gravegoods in Anglo-Saxon cemeteries is much higher than those of the Late Roman period (pagan and Christian). Weapons and dress items, the main gravegoods of Anglo-Saxon men and women, are completely absent or very rare in Roman contexts. After 400 AD only some cemeteries in the Upper Thames region (Beacon Hill, Castle Hill/Little Wittenham, Queenford Farm etc.) are more comparable to the Christian burial pattern. Because of the very poor furnishing of these graves, it is rather difficult to decide if they represent Late Roman, sub-Roman or seventh/eighth century graves. Only radiocarbon dating will help to answer this problem and has already given some initial results. Queenford Farm (Chambers 1987), in particular, has a continuity from the Roman to the sub-Roman period. But outside the frontier area of the British kingdoms in the West, this kind of cemetery is very unusual.

Watts (1991) – again based on Thomas (1981) –

identifies several buildings of Late Roman date as churches. Some of them (St. Pancras/Canterbury; St. Paul-in-the-Bail/Lincoln; Richborough; Stone-by-Faversham) show some locational continuity, which might suggest a British survival; others (Icklingham; Butt Road/Colchester) have no continuity or the evidence is at least ambiguous. At first glance this seems to be a promising clue for a surviving indigenous church, but this is probably misleading because the supposed continuity is one of Watt's major criteria for identifying Romano-British churches in the first place. Taking this into account, one suspects that the majority of churches fall into disuse with the Anglo-Saxon *landnam*.

Of the many ritual paraphernalia (lead tanks, silver tableware, inscriptions, etc.) of the British church, which can mostly be identified by their Christian symbolism, only very few can be found in Anglo-Saxon contexts. Again the scarcity of objects of British production in the fifth and sixth centuries might be responsible for this. Many of these objects had even in Roman times been produced elsewhere in the Empire. Only one silver spoon in grave VII at Winterbourne Gunner might be accepted as a 'Christian' object, because of a cross-shaped symbol, but that does not mean that it accompanies a Christian person. Some of the rich gold and silver hoards with Christian connotations like Thetford (Johns and Potter 1983; Watts 1991,146–158) and Water Newton (Painter 1977; Thomas 1981, 113–120), usually dated to the fourth century, might have been deposited as late as the fifth century. Even so they are not evidence for the survival of Romano-British Christianity, but for looting and oppression.

A strong argument for the British survival are the *eccles* placenames in different Anglo-Saxon areas (especially in Kent and East Anglia: Cameron 1986). Thomas (1981) argues that these are indirect derivations of Latin *ecclesia* meaning not the physical structure of a church, but the survival of a Christian community in Anglo-Saxon territory. The *eccles* names only makes sense, if the majority of settlements are different, that is non-Christian.

The bishops and priests of the British church that Bede mentions on several occassions are very often not localized, but the context usually indicates a region outside of Anglo-Saxon control. All the evidence for survival combined is rather weak and leads to the conclusion that Christianity of British origin is indeed – as Bede already argued – not an important factor in shaping Anglo-Saxon Christianity.

A paradox and its possible explanations

If we compare the survival of the British Church in eastern, that is Anglo-Saxon territory with that in western Britain, a paradox becomes apparent. The most Christianized regions of the early fifth century in Lowland Britain are virtually without any traces of Christian survival, while the less Christianized regions in the west show the opposite development. How can we explain this paradox? Several explanations could be put forward:

(1) Most Britons emigrated from the south and east to the north and west.
(2) The entire British Church (bishops, priests, monks, Christian communities) emigrated to the west.
(3) The British Church hierarchy was destroyed by the Anglo-Saxon 'elite'; some Christian communities survived.

The extreme position of explanation 1 is difficult to believe and has already been rejected on several grounds (Härke in press). The shift of Christianity to the west is better explained by the second or third reason stated. The survival of pockets of Christian communities in Anglo-Saxon territory, as evidenced by the *eccles* placenames, tends to favour explanation 3, the movement of the church structure only. An indication of a more substantial migration of Christians to the west is the the apparent backwardness of the British Church in relation to mainstream orthodox belief and ritual, which seems to be the result of a total breakdown in communication channels to the continent.

If a combination of explanations 2 and 3 is true, what are the reasons for the disappearance of the British Church structure? The answer to this question can probably not be found in purely religious factors.[21] Instead I would argue that Christianity might have formed one focus for British resistance against Anglo-Saxon domination. The leaders of the British Church were probably part of the elite that the Anglo-Saxons meant to replace. This elite was possibly not as peaceful as one might believe. The case of St. Germanus of Auxerre who 'just by chance' led a group of Romano-Britons against an advancing Anglo-Saxon warband, the so-called 'Hallelujah' victory, illuminates the character of 'Roman' bishops as military leaders.[22] If Christianity was indeed well established in the upper class of British society, this would have been precisely the segment replaced by Anglo-Saxon dominance.

A more detailed comparison between the different attitudes of Anglo-Saxon and Frankish kingdoms to indigenous Christianity is still needed. In any case, further studies of the Christianisation process would help our understanding of the ideological and political basis of the early Anglo-Saxon kingdoms.

Acknowledgements
I would like to thank Heinrich Härke and Tania Dickinson for their help in making this paper more readable and getting rid of some German academic jargon.

Notes

1. Useful analogies for ethnic expansion can be taken from Africa, a continent with a highly dynamic ethnic history. This approach to a deeper understanding of the Anglo-Saxon *landnam* will be further developed in my doctorial thesis. Religion and religious change can been shown to reflect processes of ethnic imperialism.
2. His argument is well presented and logically coherent, but rests only on the evidence of a collection of letters between Augustine and Pope Gregory the Great called the *Libellus Reponsionum*. It has not survived directly – and is not included in the Lateran collection of Gregory's letters – but in several manuscripts (over 200) as a sythesis of the correspondence between Gregory and Augustine concerning some disputable forms of Christian worship in Anglo-Saxon England. Two of Augustine's questions relate to the polluting quality of menstruating and birth-giving women. Meens argues that this complex is best explained by a strong Christian resistance from already converted Ango-Saxons.

   Meens argument has a chain character and can be falsified or, at least, weakened at several points: is the *Libellus Reponsionum* authentic and whose religious ideas does it reflect (Augustine's own, pagan Anglo-Saxon, a Greek, Frankish, Irish or British missioned Anglo-Saxon population, or the British communities in the West)? The conversion of some Anglo-Saxons by a British mission, if a real fact, could well have happened in some border area or even to Anglo-Saxon subjects in British territory.
3. The criteria are probably based on a combination of two methods: a 'belief' in what a Christian burial should look like and an exploration of the written sources. These texts, written in Italy, Gaul and North Africa from the very beginning of Christianity to the fifth century, refer to burial rites directly and to other forms of behaviour which should have an impact on the burial rite (e.g. the different treatment of children in comparison to pagans) The specific evidence is collected by Watts (1991, 38–78). Some criteria look very promising, while others are more speculative and have to be confirmed by other means.
4. Ann Woodward (1993) includes the presence of coins anywhere in the grave as an indicator of paganism: in her opinion these coins are meant as offerings for the gods. In Winchester-Lankhills and other – mostly urban – cemeteries, coins in pottery, under the skull, in the hands or on the eyes are quite common.
5. Beside the internal evidence she includes 'external' evidence of Christian worship within a 15 km radius round the cemetery as a further indicator at a lower weighting.
6. Millett in a review of Watts' work (Millett 1992) 'remains sceptical about the value of numerical scales which gives a spurious accuracy to what are really subtle personal judgements'.
7. Viz. the identification of possible churches on rural and urban sites and the distribution of objects with a Christian connotation which range from simple grafitti on bricks and sherds to rich hoards of silver and gold.
8. Woodward is using a tripartite scale: absence, presence and rare (less than 5 per cent).
9. This should have been the rule: Cyprianus and Hilarius of Poitiers condemn the burial of a Christian inside a pagan cemetery, and even visiting a pagan cemetery is considered not appropriate.
10. The identification of these phases seemed to be based on the stratigraphy of some grave groups. Phase II graves are never cut or sealed by phase I graves. However, for the excavators this development seems so natural that it does not deserve any discussion at all.
11. Some of the criteria can claim a strong connection to Christianity by being explicitly mentioned in the church literature.
12. Poundbury/Dorset (Farwell and Molleson 1993); Winchester-Lankhills (Clarke 1979); Bath Gate Cemetery/Cirencester (McWhirr *et al.* 1982); Butt Road Cemetery/Colchester (Crummy *et al.* 1993); Bradley Hill/Somerset (Leech 1981); Icklingham/Suffolk (West 1976); Ilchester/Somerset (Leach 1982); Lynch Farm/Peterborough (Jones 1975).
13. Criteria used: west-east orientation; north-south orientation; supine position of the body; prone or crouched position of the body; overlapping of another grave; decapitation; plaster-burial; neonatal or infant burial; burial in mausoleum or enclosure; vessels; animal bones; hobnails; coins; Charon's fee; grave 'protected' (by stones, tiles, wooden markers); gravegoods. Of Watts' and Woodward's list, only the inscriptions (never in a clear grave context), the focal graves and the depositions, i.e. the unworn garments and equipment, have not been included here.
14. Combination table and seriation are from a mathematical point of view very similar; the ordering principle follows the same optimisation process.
15. Alternatively the absolute values or percentages can be used. Each of these measures has its own advantages and disadvantages; a discussion can be found in Gebühr 1970.
16. A word of caution: not all the attributes included in this statistic are really independent. A north-south orientated grave cannot at the same time be west-east orientated. The same holds true for the two groups of positioning the body in the grave. The presence of gravegoods in a grave includes, by definition, the occurrence of coins, hobnails, animal bones and vessels (but not necessarily the other way round). However, the results of the seriation are significant; this has been checked by excluding some of these traits.
17. Using Clarke's dates no chronological direction can be established. The average date for type 1 graves is between 367 and 378 (dependent on the date-span allowed), for type 2 between 362 and 379! This complete overlap is rather difficult to explain!
18. Truly 'Christian' or 'pagan' burials do consist of a combination of at least three of the defining criteria. The relation between these two classes is the deciding argument. All cemeteries could clearly be assigned to one or the other group.
19. Clarke (1979) has interpreted these graves as the burials of a partly Germanic population.
20. In this respect the British provinces do not fall outside the pattern of the other north-western provinces.
21. This has been claimed by Watts (1991: 224) on the basis of the syncretistic image of Christianity in Britain, which 'was an inherent weakness of Christianity in Britain, and one which made it unable to retain its hold ... with the withdrawal of Rome and the advent of the Saxons'.
22. The bishops in Late Antique Gaul and Spain can be seen as the legitimate successors of former civil and military leadership in these areas(van Dam 1985). In many instances the 'office' of bishopric has been seen by contemporaries as the culmination of a Roman *cursus honorum*.

Bibliography

Cameron, K. 1968: 'Eccles in English place-names', in Barley, M.W. and Hanson, R.P.C. (eds), *Christianity in Britain 300–700* (Leicester), 87–92.

Clarke, G. 1979: *The Roman Cemetery at Lankhills*, Winchester Studies 3: Pre-Roman and Roman Winchester (Oxford).

Chambers, R.A. 1987: 'The late and sub-Roman cemetery at Queensford Farm, Dorchester-on-Thames, Oxon', *Oxoniensia* 52, 35–69 and Microfiche.

Crummy N., Crummy, P. and Crossan, C. 1993: *Excavations of Roman and Later Cemeteries, Churches and Monastic Sites in Colchester, 1971–88*,Colchester Archaeological Report 9 (Colchester.)

Dark, K.R. 1994: *Civitas to Kingdom – British Political Continuity 300–800* (Leicester).

Davis, W. 1978: 'Die Bekehrung der Angelsachsen zum Christentum', in Ahrens, C. (ed.), *Sachsen und Angelsachsen* (Hamburg), 85–96.

Farwell, D.E. and Molleson, T.L. 1993: *Excavations at Poundbury 1966–80. Volume II: The Cemeteries* Dorset Natural History and Archaeology Society Monograph Series Number 11 (Dorchester).

Frend, W.H.C. 1979: 'Ecclesia Britannica prelude or dead end?, *Journal of Ecclesiastical History* 30, 129–144.

Geary, P.J. 1996: *Die Merowinger – Europa vor Karl dem Großen*, C.H. Beck (München).

Gebühr, M. 1970: 'Beigabenvergesellschaftung in mecklenburgischen Gräberfeldern der älteren römischen Kaiserzeit', in *Neue Ausgrabungen und Forschungen in Niedersachsen* 6, 93–116.

Härke, H. in press: 'Briten und Angelsachsen im nachrömischen England: zum Nachweis der einheimischen Bevölkerung in den angelsächsischen Landnahmegebieten', *Studien zur Sachsenforschung* (in press).

Higham, N. 1992: *Rome, Britain and the Anglo-Saxons* (London).

Higham, N. 1994: *The English Conquest. Gildas and Britain in the Fifth Century* (Manchester).

Higham, N. 1997: *The Convert Kings – Power and Religious Affiliation in Early Anglo-Saxon England* (Manchester.)

Johns, C.M. and Potter, T.W. 1983: *The Thetford Treasure: Roman Jewellery and Silver* (London).

Jones, R. 1975: 'The Romano-British farmstead and its cemetery at Lynch Farm, near Peterborough', *Northamptonshire Archaeology* 10, 94–137.

Leach, P. 1982: *Ilchester Vol. 1 Excavations 1974–1975*, Western Archaeological Trust Excavation Monograph No. 3 (Bristol).

Leech, R.H. 1981: 'The excavation of a Romano-British farmstead and cemetery on Bradley Hill, Somerton, Somerset', *Britannia* 12, 177–252.

Leech, R.H. 1986: The excavation of a Romano-Celtic temple and a later cemetery on Lamyatt Beacon, Somerset', *Britannia* 17, 259–328.

Mayr-Harting, H. 1972: *The Coming of Christianity to Anglo-Saxon England* (London).

McWhirr, A., Viner, L. and Wells, C. 1982: *Romano-British Cemeteries at Cirencester* (Cirencester).

Meens, R. 1994: 'A background to Augustine's mission to Anglo-Saxon England', *Anglo-Saxon England 23*, 5–17.

Millett, M. 1992: 'Review of Christian and Pagans in Roman Britain by Dorothy Watts', *Archaeological Journal* 149, 426.

Nash-Williams, V.E. 1950: *The Early Christian Monuments of Wales* (Cardiff).

Painter, K.S. 1977: *The Water Newton Early Christian Silver* (London).

Radford, C.A.R. 1971: Christian origins in Britain', *Medieval Archaeology* 15, 1–12.

Rahtz, P.A. 1977: 'Late Roman cemeteries and beyond', in Reece, R. (ed.), *Burial in the Roman World*, Council for British Archaeology, Research Report 22 (London), 53–64.

Stevenson, J. 1992: 'Christianity in sixth- and seventh-century Southumbria', in Carver, M. (ed.), *The Age of Sutton Hoo. The Seventh Century in North-Western Europe* (Woodbridge), 175–184.

Thomas, C. 1981: *Christianity in Roman Britain to AD 500* (London.)

van Dam, R. 1985: *Leadership and Community in Late Antique Gaul* (Berkeley, Ca.).

Watts, D. 1991: *Christians and Pagans in Roman Britain*, Routledge (London).

Watts, L. and Leach, P.J. forthcoming: *Henley Wood, Temples and Cemetery. Excavations by Ernest Greenfield and Others 1962–69*, Council of British Archaeology Research Report (London).

Wedlake, W.J. 1982: *The Excavation of the Shrine of Apollo at Nettleton, Wiltshire 1956–71*, Society of Antiquaries Research Report 40 (London).

West, S. 1976. 'The Romano-British Site at Icklingham', *East Anglian Archaeology* 3, 63–126.

Wilson, D. 1992: *Anglo-Saxon Paganism* (London).

Woodward, A.B. 1993: 'Discussion', in Farwell and Molleson 1993, 215–3.

Burial rites, Gender and the Creation of Kingdoms: the Evidence from seventh-century Wessex

Nick Stoodley

Introduction

It has been argued that the conditions which accompanied the emergence of Anglo-Saxon kingdoms in the late sixth and seventh century resulted in a reorganization of earlier social relations (Scull 1993). The contrasting nature of the uniform and poorly-furnished 'final phase' cemeteries and the small number of rich barrow graves is taken to be a reflection of the increasing social stratification experienced throughout England (Arnold 1988; Shephard 1979). By taking gender as the category of analysis, this paper will illustrate how this increasing polarisation within society transformed relations between men and women on different levels of society, and how this found expression via the burial rite of the seventh century. This is possible because gender is a constitutive element in human relations bound up with other aspects of social behaviour, for example status, class and ethnicity, and is therefore a powerful tool in the examination and elucidation of past social systems (Conkey and Gero 1991, 9). Moreover, gender roles and relations are historically situated, thus providing an opportunity for them to enter the archaeological record and for us to examine how male and female relations may have been altered during a period of significant change in Anglo-Saxon society. If we accept that mortuary ritual has the potential to reflect social identity, then the data from Wessex may provide a fuller understanding of the effects that increasing social stratification had on relations of gender. Rather than limiting the scope of this enquiry to just on one type of cemetery, the typical 'final phase' site, this paper studies the range of 'late' burial grounds and argues that they belong to different aspects of the same process: a process that was bound up with the emergence of the West Saxon kingdom. During this paper examples from farther afield will also be cited to enable the drawing of comparisons between Wessex and other regions.

Recognising early Anglo-Saxon gender structures

The burial evidence, in association with skeletal sexing, provides one of the strongest positions from which to observe how the *ritual* expression of gender was constructed. It can be determined whether grave goods, or any other archaeologically identifiable aspect of the mortuary ritual, are associated with sexed individuals. Traditionally, scholars have attributed weapons and tools to males, while dress accessories and jewellery have been associated with females. Based on these uncritical assumptions a dichotomous relationship thus emerged between male and female. Such static stereotypes do not encourage a critical analysis of the construction of gender during this stage of the English identity. The relationship between burial ritual and sex and its bearing on the cultural construction of gender must be examined first. Moreover, because biological sex may not always determine cultural gender, it must not be assumed *a priori* that sex and gender was linked. We must examine the mortuary data to discover whether any clusters of artefacts and/or aspects of burial mode exist that can be associated with individuals *irrespective of sex*. Following the identification of any patterning its underlying cause can be determined. Gender is, however, only one possible reason: status, kinship or ethnic affiliation, for example, may be responsible. Sex is the variable that can aid in the differentiation of gender from these other social categories (Whelan 1991, 24). Patterning that is constrained by sex is likely to be indicative of gender. But patterns in which most, but not all, members are of the same sex may also denote a gender category. In the latter case gender is shown to be a cultural category separate from biological sex (Whelan 1991, 25).

Recently some scholars have voiced warnings over the limitations of focussing primarily on gender and leaving sex as biologically given (Lesick 1997; Nordbladh and Yates 1990). It is argued that a model that views gender as a system of cultural codes inscribed on biological sex only began to predominate in the early eighteenth century (Trumbach 1994, 111). Furthermore we should accord greater emphasis to the role played in society by intersex individuals and homosexuals (Nordbladh and Yates 1990). However, we should not lose sight of the fact that in many examples adults have

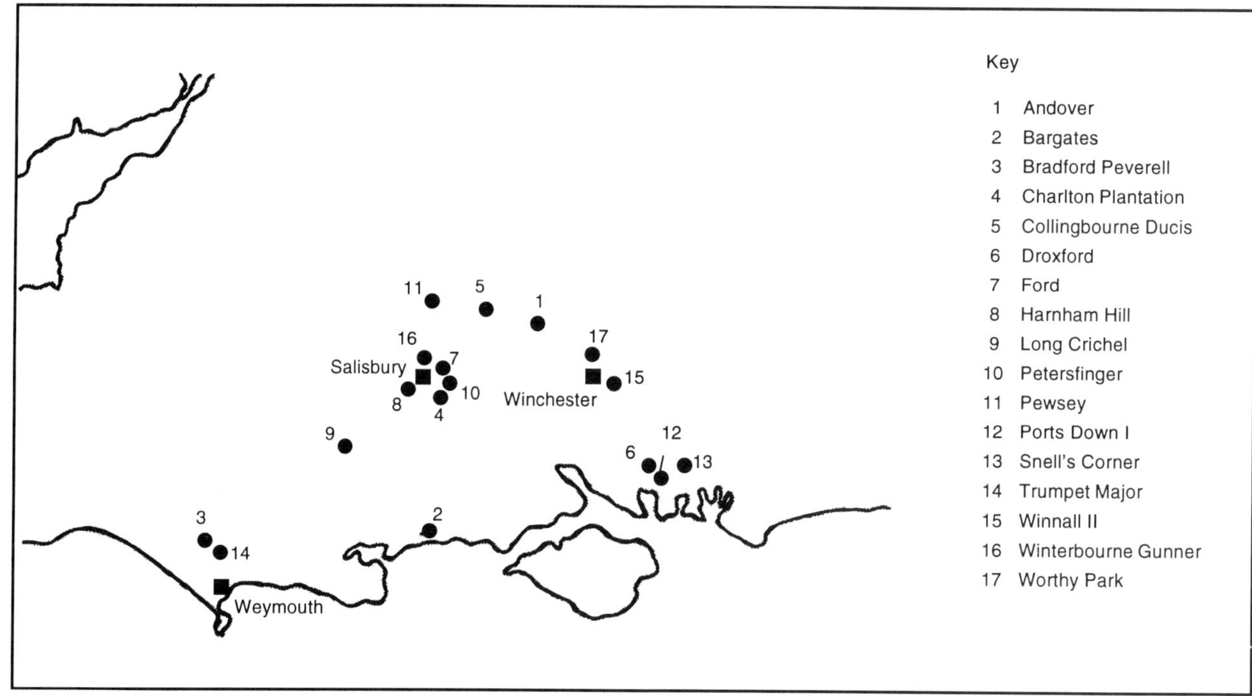

Fig. 1 Location of the principal cemeteries in the Wessex sample

structured society around a male:female polarity. Rega (1997, 3, 242) recognises the presence of intersex individuals, but argues that because biological hermaphrodites are very rare they do not form the main axis of sexual classification in society. And as Gilchrist states '...gender is firmly located within the body: a society's construction of gender is rooted in its classification of sexual difference and ideas about the body' (Gilchrist 1997, 42). In what follows a strong association between an aspect of the burial rite and biological sex will be interpreted as defining a gender structure.

The study is based on a total sample of 351 undisturbed burials of the adult age category (18 years and over) from seventeen Wessex cemeteries (see Fig. 1 for the list of sites). Of these 159 (45 per cent) are male, 122 (35 per cent) female and 70 (20 per cent) belong to unsexed adults. An examination of the grave goods interred with these individuals uncovered two dichotomous assemblages: one of weapons and the other of dress fasteners, jewellery and personal equipment (keys, chatelaines and weaving tools), hereafter dress accessories. A consideration of the sex associations of these goods revealed that both assemblages are strongly constrained by sex: weapons correlate with males and dress accessories with females (Table 1). No other aspect is unambiguously symbolic of gender. Neither is there any evidence in this sample of undisturbed burials that weapons and dress accessories were ever combined in one assemblage. The existence of two distinct sex-specific assemblages is beyond doubt.

Evidence for cross-sex gender in Wessex, that is males interred with dress accessories and females with weapons is very rare indeed. No females were granted burial with weapons and only three males (in two cases possible males: Harnham Hill burial 36 and Pewsey burial 19) had dress accessories accompanying them to the grave. The individual in burial 9 at Andover (Cook and Dacre 1985) was determined to be a probable male by two specialists but was laid to rest with a pair of annular brooches and a bead necklace. This burial is also interesting with regard to other aspects of the rite: grains of carbonized bread-wheat were discovered under the pelvis and a large flint was found on the chest. The nature of the rite accorded to this male in combination with a feminine identity suggests he was being marked out in some way as special. But it would be unwise to speculate over the status held by this individual in life. Overall the scarcity of individuals displaying a cross-sex gender further underlines the distinctiveness of gender expression.

Because these assemblages have consistent sex associations throughout the study area it is argued they served as primary indicators of gender. The mortuary ritual provided a medium for the symbolic expression of clearly defined gender boundaries. This situation is not unique to Wessex but is encountered throughout early Anglo-Saxon England (Stoodley 1997, 138–143). We have to stress that this is the situation in death. Burial ritual cannot be taken to mirror reality (Pader 1982; Parker Pearson 1982). It was meaningfully constituted and may have been used deliberately to express certain messages about particular societies. For these early Anglo-Saxon communities gender roles and relations following migration may have been much more fluid. This is the situation that ethnographic and historical sources describe as happening in frontier and settler societies (Stoodley 1997, 31–36). A

Table 1 Sex association of individual grave good types.

Type	probable male	possible male	possible female	probable female	unsexed	sample
sword	6					6
seax	3					3
axe	3					3
shield	30	5			9	44
spear	45	9			7	61
weaving tool				3	1	4
finger ring				5	4	9
necklace	1	1	3	33	14	52
brooch (>1)	1	2	2	33	12	50
bracelet			1	5	4	10
key or chatelaine			1	14	7	22

fluidity of gender may have arisen in two principal ways: first a sexual imbalance caused by the migrations may have led, out of necessity, to a blurring of roles and second there may have been a change in the organisation of gender as native and immigrant, with their own prescribed models of behaviour, interacted directly. Thus, the specific historical circumstances prevalent in early Saxon Wessex could have been responsible for the stereotypical representation of gender in the burial rite.

This symbolism is expressed through two quite separate and distinct assemblages which shall be referred to as 'standard kits.' And it is the use of different types of grave goods which results in such strong visual imagery. Objects that were themselves very different reinforced the biological differences between males and females: weapons and dress accessories. These gender kits conveyed quite different meanings: males were associated with weapons that have a very strong martial image, while the larger, and more varied group, of female-specific dress accessories pertains to aspects of bodily adornment. The result was the creation of a feminine gender in which the emphasis was squarely on the body, whereas the masculine gender was centred around the image expressed by weapons. As far as it is possible to tell, no importance appears to have been placed on the male body. It was clothed in plain trousers, a tunic and perhaps a coat (Brush 1993, 128). Throughout the period the most popular combination in burials was a spear and shield, closely followed by a spear alone. An analysis of the feminine combinations confirmed Brush's (1993, 70) observation that no clear structuring to the dress assemblage was recognisable. But, on a more general level, the most popular feminine articles in sites of the fifth and sixth century were combinations of dress fasteners and jewellery, most notably a pair of brooches and a bead necklace. To this basic configuration there were many other possible additions, such as finger rings and bracelets, but these were seldom repeated with any frequency. In the late sites (seventh and eighth century) we find marked changes, for example, pin suites, chatelaines and necklets become the main elements in the feminine kit.

Seventh-century transformations of the expression of gender

We can therefore identify gender from the assemblage which the funeral party granted an individual at burial. In the Wessex sample 74 (21 per cent) are masculine, 89 (25 per cent) are feminine, while 188 (54 per cent) have no gender based on grave artefacts. These 'gender-neutral' burials either have no grave artefacts or have articles common to the burials of both sex, for example, knives and belt buckles. It is improbable, given the size of these groups, that they constitute cross-sex gender categories made up of both males and females. At first glance these figures are intriguing, as they suggest that the practice of symbolising the deceased's gender was not particularly widespread. But the reason becomes clear if we analyse this symbolism over time. In the cemeteries in use during the fifth and sixth centuries gendered burials account for 53 per cent of all inhumations, while in the seventh and early eighth centuries they fall to just 24 per cent (Fig. 2). The remainder of this paper focuses on these late sites to attempt to explain why the practice of symbolising the deceased's gender ended and whether this was a result of wider changes in society.

The number of individuals granted a gendered burial in the seventh and eighth century had seriously declined. While the numbers are indeed very low, masculine burials interestingly now outnumber feminine: thirteen (19 per cent) compared with four (6 per cent). This is the opposite situation to that encountered in the previous century when feminine burials accounted for 31 per cent and masculine 22 per cent of the total. Except for Bargates (Jarvis 1980), which boasts eight undisturbed adult weapon burials, each site has only one or two burials expressing a gendered identity. A brief look at sites outside Wessex illustrates that the number of individuals receiving a gendered burial, though low, is higher than in Wessex. In addition, in these burial grounds either the ratio of feminine to masculine interments is roughly equal or feminine burials outnumber masculine ones. In the East Midlands at Dunstable (Mathews 1962), three feminine and five masculine inhumations were recovered, while at Leighton Buzzard III (Hyslop 1964) two weapon burials and five burials with dress accessories were found. In Kent at Polhill (Hawkes in Philp 1973),. 120 burials were excavated: fifteen individuals have weaponry and twelve have feminine articles. In East Anglia, Burwell (Lethbridge 1931) yielded only one weapon burial but thirteen adult burials satisfied the criteria for the feminine gender category; a similar pattern is also found at Shudy Camps (Lethbridge 1936). So why does the Wessex data differ from the patterns found elsewhere?

Perhaps in response to the decline of the accompanied rite, gender difference was expressed through other aspects of the burial rite, though this seems unlikely. Orientation, methods of deposition and grave size did not show any clear patterning. However, the large variety of associated grave structures, a recognised feature of later sites (Hogarth 1973), demonstrated some weak patterning. Simple internal structures such as coffins, boards and planks and the placing of stones in the grave may, in some local communities, have signalled gender identity. At Winnall II (Meaney and Hawkes 1970) one male (burial 28) had evidence for a former, now unrecognisable, wooden structure, while all the other types of structure were associated with women: three females had evidence for a wooden structure and stones. At Ports Down I (Corney *et al.* 1969) two females also had stones placed in their graves, while males went without any features. The opposite happens at Snell's Corner (Knocker 1956): three males and one unsexed adult have the remains of some former kind of wooden structure. The weapon burials at Bargates enjoyed a variety of structures: two with planks, one with a coffin and two with a bed of grass or bracken. No other burials produced any evidence for grave structures. In keeping with the artefactual evidence the numbers are small, while the meaning varied between cemeteries. Even if these practices were intended to be gender-specific, the evidence does not detract from the overall view that a much smaller number of individuals had their gender expressed via the burial rite of the seventh century.

However, the most striking observation is that within the sites of Snell's Corner, Ports Down I, Bargates and Long Crichel (Green *et al.* 1983), which are all located next to prehistoric monuments, males are marked out by the most elaborate burials. At Ports Down I, the individual in burial 6 was laid to rest with a shield. This is a large grave dug into the Bronze Age barrow. The male in burial 14 at Snell's Corner was accompanied by two weapons and a food offering (the only one in the cemetery treated in this manner) and was sited in a large grave on the eastern extremities of the site. At Bargates, two structures formally marked the grave of a weapon-bearing adult (burial 18): a penannular ditch surrounded it, while a posthole testifies to the prior existence of a marker post. This cemetery is sited next to two Bronze Age barrows and seven of the eleven individuals with weaponry were associated with these monuments. A similar situation is found outside Wessex. For instance, at Dunstable where graves were aligned in rows, burial G2 occupied an isolated position close to a Bronze Age barrow. This was the largest grave pit and also contained two pottery vessels. However, this cemetery differs from the sites in Wessex: it combines a row-grave layout with a location next to a pre-Saxon monument; further the male lacked armoury, but was the only individual to have a grave furnished with pottery vessels.

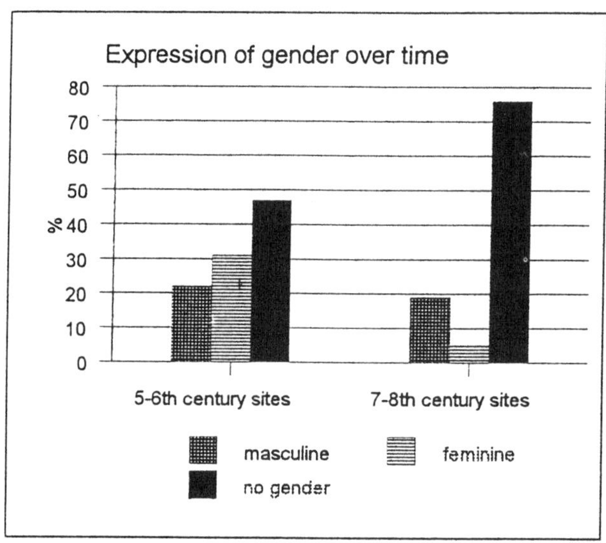

Fig. 2 Proportions of gendered adults between early and late Wessex cemeteries.

If the number of males and females in the seventh- to eighth-century sites of Wessex are examined, a very interesting pattern is noted. In the row-grave cemetery of Winnall II roughly the same number of males and females is observed: seventeen males and sixteen females. However, at those sites focussed on a prehistoric monument a disproportionate ratio of males to females is found. At Snell's Corner there are nearly twice as many males as females (15:8), and at Ports Down I there are four times as many males as females (17:4). At Bargates, while eleven individuals went to their graves with weapons, the combination of no diagnostically feminine grave goods and poor bone preservation has meant that women (if they were present), cannot by identified at this site. Unfortunately, so little of the skeletal material from the other Dorset sites has been examined. It is known, however, that the three graves from the Long Crichel barrow belonged to two males and a child. Similar imbalances occur outside the region at sites centred on pre-Saxon monuments: at Dunstable the burials of seventeen males and six females were found, and at Holborough (Evison 1957) nineteen males and eleven females were recovered (though caution is advocated here as it is estimated that only half of the burial ground was excavated).

Not only do these cemeteries have a predominance of males, but they also have evidence for the differential treatment of males and, perhaps more significantly, those with gender-signalling weapons. Females, with and without gender-signalling grave goods, are more numerous in the archetypal row-grave sites. At Winnall II three undisturbed burials were granted a feminine identity. Feminine burials are more visible in other cemeteries of this type, for example, Upper Brook Street, Winchester (Biddle 1975), Trumpet Major, Dorchester (Sparey Green 1984) and Bradford Peverell (Hawthorne 1981; Keen 1977; 1978; 1979). The pattern is also noted outside the region: at Leighton Buzzard III no burials with a masculine identity were recovered, while nine feminine ones were. Finally at Burwell thirteen feminine burials and one masculine interment were encountered, while at Shudy Camps a higher number of masculine burials are in evidence (n=5) but feminine ones still outnumber them (n=11).

Yet in the preceding two centuries a concept of 'gendered space' did not operate in the cemeteries of Wessex: no segregation of burials either by sex or age is evidenced. Some sites, and this is especially true of Wessex, for example, Andover (Cook and Dacre 1985) and Droxford (Aldsworth 1979), are arranged in individual plots. The mix of different ages, sexes and statuses in such groups suggests that they served as the burial plots of individual households. The typical 'final phase' cemetery, characterised by a row-grave arrangement, also displays the same principle with individual rows including males, females and children, for example, at Winnall II (Fig. 3). In contrast, at Snell's Corner clusters of male burials can be identified, and the central area, which is avoided by graves, is bordered by males on its northern edge and females on its southern edge (Fig. 4). At Ports Down I there are two clusters of male graves, one to the north and one to the south of the barrow, while right on the southern edge of the barrow are found the graves of two children and an infant (Fig. 5). In addition burial 9 contained the burials of three males interred in succession. This is a rare configuration and underscores the emphasis placed on the male sex in this cemetery. And let us not forget that Bargates, albeit on the basis of negative evidence, may have been a burial place given over to males. Again this evidence clearly demonstrates the difference between those sites placed next to pre-Saxon monuments and those following a row-grave layout.

Further evidence for changing attitudes towards gender is given by the breakdown of age-barriers governing the placing of gender-signalling grave goods. In the sixth century dress accessories and personal equipment were mainly found with individuals above the age twelve to fourteen years and correlates most strongly with the commencement of biological adulthood. For example, at Andover pairs of brooches and bead necklaces were placed with individuals of twelve years and over. However, at Winnall II burial 5, aged seven to ten years, had a pendant and necklet. The young individual at Snell's Corner (burial 27) was accompanied with a necklet, while a girl was interred with a necklace of beads and pendants at Bradford Peverell. The best example comes from the East Midlands site of Dunstable where three children (two are of eight years, while the precise age of the third is unknown) and an infant of one year all had assemblages similar to female adults, that is necklets. The same does not hold true of weapons. No child is encountered with weapons and in fact weapons were withdrawn from child burials before adult ones (cf. Härke 1992). Thus, while the structuring of the feminine gender according to the life cycle became more flexible, the masculine gender had become more restricted.

Set against this backdrop of changing burial customs is the phenomenon of isolated barrow burials. These are either secondary interments in Bronze Age barrows or primary Saxon tumuli sited next to prehistoric monuments. The majority do not display any great wealth, though many have weapons or cover males. From Meaney's *Gazetteer* entry for Wiltshire (Meaney 1964), fifty-one individuals were tentatively identified: 51 per cent were males or contained weapons, while only 8 per cent were females or had feminine-signalling artefacts. However, a number contained wealthy grave assemblages and are interpreted as belonging to a socially superior elite (Arnold 1988, 115–118). Examples in Wessex are at Ford (Musty 1969), Oliver's Battery (Meaney 1964, 98–99), Roundway Down II (Meaney 1964, 274), Swallowcliffe Down (Speake 1989) and Lowbury Hill (Atkinson 1916). In addition to weapons being a frequent find, objects of a wealthy nature such as bronze containers, absent from the flat cemeteries, are also present, for example, the bronze bowls at Lowbury Hill and Oliver's Battery.

The changing expression of gender: an interpretive model

It is clear that there had been a profound change in how gender was represented in death between the fifth and seventh centuries in Wessex. In the seventh century, artefacts were played down in the construction of gender, but were not totally abandoned. Instead, three types of burial ground in Wessex can be identified which each display a specific pattern of gender symbolism:

1) the 'final phase' row-grave cemetery in which females have either a similar or higher profile to males;
2) cemeteries with a prehistoric monument as the focus in which both the male sex and the masculine gender were more numerous;

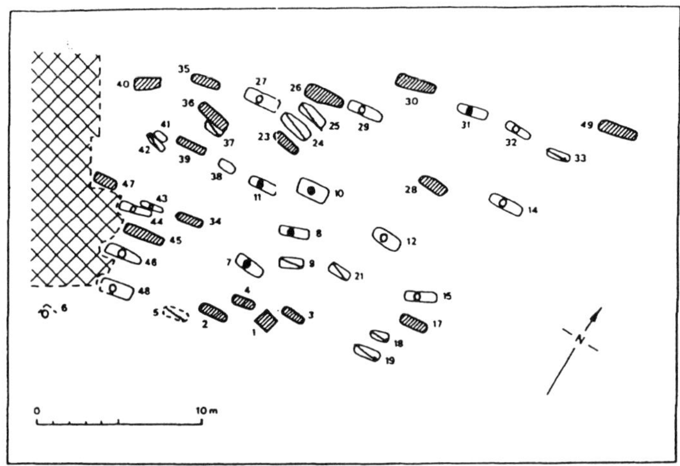

Fig. 3 Plan of Winnall II cemetery (based on Härke 1992, figure 80)

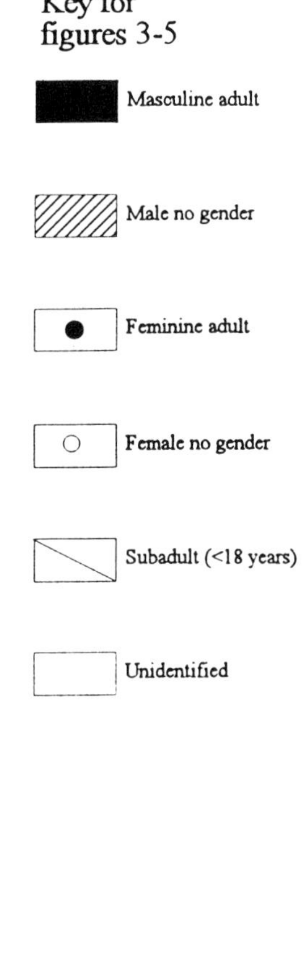

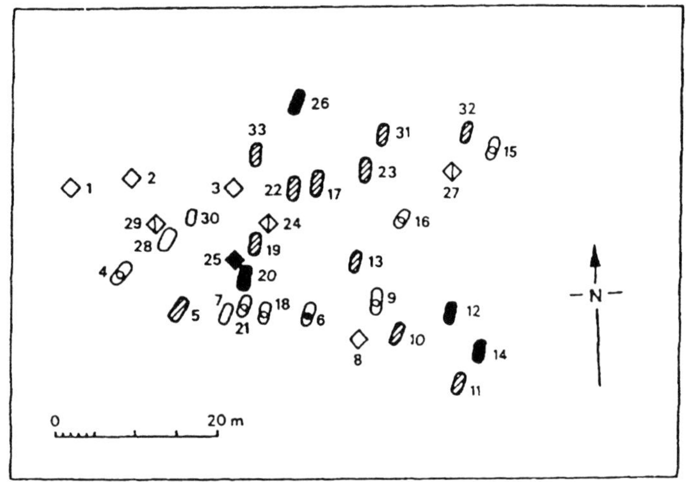

Fig. 4 Plan of Snell's Corner cemetery (based on Härke 1992, figure 74)

3) isolated barrows of both a wealthy and a more modest nature where males not only outnumber females but show a consistency in their grave goods that is lacking in the female burials of this type.

The sharp decline in the symbolism of gender cannot be interpreted merely as resulting from the ending of the accompanied rite. If this was the case, which it is not, both males and females would lose their visibility. Rather the symbols of masculinity are now reserved for a small number of individuals – a particular high status-group in society – who enjoy a degree of burial treatment not previously witnessed. But why does this group have such a strong male bias and why was it necessary to stress their gender in this way?

It is suggested that this transformation was a result of changing household structures: a direct consequence of the increasing stratification within society that foreshadowed the rise of the West Saxon kingdom. Wessex was undergoing a process in the late sixth and seventh century whereby the small communities that existed in the previous two centuries were coming together, perhaps because of military or economic forces, to merge into a larger regional unit (Yorke 1989). This would have required a change in social structure. The nature of early Anglo-Saxon kinship may have been such that relationships were traced through both the male and female line. In this context gender would have performed an important role in the maintenance of group cohesion (Brush 1988, 85). The burial ritual would have afforded the ideal

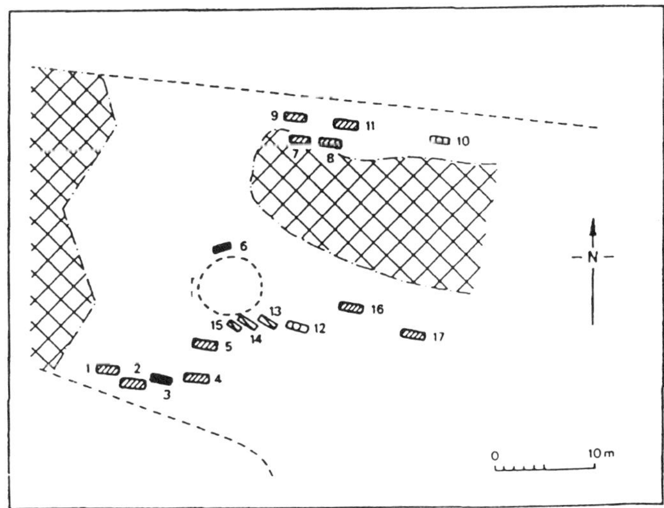

Fig. 5 Plan of Ports Down I cemetery (based on Härke 1992, figure 72)

opportunity for community leaders to validate these structuring principles. The internal layout of sites such as Andover, based on burial plots, suggests that the household unit was all important to the community structure. The strong emphasis laid on the adornment of the female body may have been a reflection of their importance in kin-connections, while the variation inherent in the feminine assemblage may echo the many different links that existed between kin-groups that required marking. In these communities, the body prior to burial must have been the focus. The symbolic messages emitted by the grave goods would have been visible to the community only during the preparation leading up to the funeral and the burial itself.

A consequence of the greater stratification witnessed in the seventh century would probably have led to the dismantling of earlier social systems. It does appear that there was no longer a role for the symbolic expression of femininity in death. According to Reiter (1978), the suppression of the kinship base of power is a common aspect of state formation. In this situation a modification of kinship probably occurred which perhaps resulted in the lines of descent no longer being traced through females. Such a transformation of society would therefore see profound changes to the expression of gender as reflected through the burial rite. In the seventh century the mortuary evidence shows not only a male elite, interred in wealthy isolated barrows, but a greater visibility for males in burial grounds centring on prehistoric monuments. Both these burial-types focus on the pre-Saxon past: they may have contained the graves of local rulers who were emulating the regional leaders. The fact that within row-grave sites weapon burials are scarce implies that the martial image of weapons was now a symbol of a largely male ruling elite who were distancing themselves from the rest of society. The segregated plan of these cemeteries and the restriction of weapons to adult burials reinforces the view that the masculine gender was now more rigidly and consistently defined.

Women expressing a feminine identity are mainly confined to row-grave cemeteries, in which the more even proportions of adults and children suggest that they served entire communities. The function of the feminine kit, unlike that of the masculine weapon-kit, does not appear to have transformed over time. Rather their small number and the appearance of an almost standardized funeral costume across England in the seventh century (Geake 1992, 85; see Geake, this volume), suggests that there no longer existed a clearly defined female role which required a ritual symbolism.

More controversially, two females appear to have been subjected to some form of mutilation either before or after death. Burial 11 at Winnall II belonged to a female in her thirties who appears to have been decapitated. She was also the only individual with her head to the east. Similarly, at Snell's Corner the neck of an elderly woman (burial 16) placed in a crouched position shows pathological changes consistent with a fracture. Again she had a unique orientation: head to the north end of the grave compared with the typical practice at this site of placing the head to the south. It is difficult to ignore the evidence from deviant burials that in Wessex some women were the victims of ritualistic abuse. Further, in all the burial grounds except for Worthy Park males enjoyed a higher average age at death than females. This pattern is usually attributed to the greater risks for women involved with early and continual pregnancy. At the late site of Winnall II the difference in mortality between the sexes is even more dramatic (Table 2). This could result from a higher pregnancy rate, but the size of the gap might suggest that the quality of life enjoyed by women had declined. Taken together the evidence points to a level of stress in society which resulted from the collapse of the old household structures and to a deterioration in the position of women. The written sources, and in particular the seventh-century laws of the West Saxon Ine (688–694), appear to concur with these changes since they describe passive women whose position is defined in relation to their menfolk (Ine 57).

Table 2 Wessex cemeteries: average age at death (number in brackets is sample size)

cemetery	male	female
Andover	41.33 (12)	36.60 (10)
Worthy Park	36.52 (25)	36.93 (15)
Pewsey	31.92 (25)	29.42 (19)
Droxford	31.00 (7)	27.44 (16)
Winnall II	38.79 (14)	28.20 (5)

Conclusion

Gender is not a constant. This study has demonstrated how its construction varied not only temporally but also spatially, permitting an insight into how the emergence of the West Saxon kingdom transformed the relations between men and women. Moreover this research has suggested how gender structures operated in an early Saxon society: why the active employment of material culture in the negotiation of male and female relations was necessary. And from a wider theoretical perspective this study is important for the insights it has given into the changes affecting gender in the move away from an egalitarian to a state society.

As a corollary, the decreasing importance of gender expression offers another reason why the accompanied grave-good rite ended. With the decline of the old household structures the role of feminine-specific kits disappeared, while weapons, for a short time the badges of those in positions of power, were ultimately to become superfluous in the early eighth century. The regional perspective has shown that Wessex does have similarities to other regions but it also differs, most notably from Kent, where the phenomenon of barrow cemeteries representing entire communities occurs (Shepherd 1979, 49). It is unlikely that the same processes were to be found in each region and this shows the strength of the regional approach with its ability to identify specific conditions.

Notes

1. This study was greatly aided by the assistance of the following people who generously allowed me access to unpublished information: K. Ainsworth and G. Denford, Winchester; K. Annable and P. Robinson, Devizes; K. Ball, Portsmouth; J. Bell, Salisbury; L. Webster, London.

References

Aldsworth, F.R. 1979: 'The Droxford Anglo-Saxon cemetery, Soberton, Hampshire', Proceedings of the Hampshire Field Club and Archaeological Society 35 (for 1978), 93–182.

Arnold, C. 1988: 'Territories and leadership: frameworks for the study of emergent polities in early Anglo-Saxon southern England', in Driscoll, S. and Nieke, M. (eds), Power and Politics in Early Medieval England and Ireland (Edinburgh), 111–127.

Atkinson, D. 1916: *The Romano-British site on Lowbury Hill, in Berkshire*, University College Reading, Studies in History and Archaeology (Reading).

Biddle, M. 1975: 'Excavations at Winchester', *Antiquaries Journal* 55, 295–338.

Brush, K.A. 1988: 'Gender and mortuary analysis in pagan Anglo-Saxon archaeology', *Archaeological Review from Cambridge* 7/1, 76–89.

Brush, K.A. 1993: 'Adorning the Dead: The Social Significance of early Anglo-Saxon Funerary Dress in England (Fifth to Seventh Centuries AD)', unpublished Ph.D thesis, University of Cambridge.

Carver, M. (ed.) 1992: *The Age of Sutton Hoo*, Boydell and Brewer (Woodbridge).

Cook, A. M. and Dacre, M. W. 1985: *Excavations at Portway, Andover 1973–1975*, Oxford University Committee for Archaeology, Monograph No 4 (Oxford).

Conkey, M.W. and Gero, J.M. 1991: 'Tensions, pluralities, and engendering archaeology: an introduction to women and prehistory', in Gero, J. M. and Conkey, M.W. (eds), *Engendering Archaeology Women and Prehistory*, Blackwell (Oxford), 3–30.

Corney, A., Ashbee, P., Evison, V.I. and Brothwell, D. 1969: 'A prehistoric and Anglo-Saxon burial ground, Ports Down, Portsmouth', *Proceedings of the Hampshire Field Club and Archaeological Society* 24 (for 1967), 20–41.

Evison, V. 1957: 'An Anglo-Saxon cemetery at Holborough, Kent', *Archaeologia Cantiana* 70, 84–141.

Geake, H. 1992: 'Burial practices in seventh- and eight-century England', in Carver (ed.) 1992, 83–94.

Gilchrist, R. 1997: 'Ambivalent bodies: gender and medieval archaeology', in Moore and Scott (eds) 1997, 42–58.

Green, C. Lynch, F. and White, H. 1983: 'The excavation of two round barrows on Launceston Green (Long Crichel 5 and 7)', *Proceedings of Dorset Natural History and Archaeology Magazine* 104, 39–59.

Härke, H. 1992: 'Changing symbols in a changing society', in Carver (ed.) 1992, 149–165.

Hawthorne, J. 1981: 'Dorset Archaeology in 1980', *Proceedings of Dorset Natural History and Archaeology Magazine* 103, 126.

Hogarth, A.C. 1973: 'Structural features in Anglo-Saxon graves', *Archaeological Journal* 130, 104–119.

Hyslop, M. 1964: 'Two Anglo-Saxon cemeteries at Chamberlains Barn, Leighton Buzzard', *Bedfordshire Archaeological Journal* 120 (for 1963), 161–200.

Jarvis, K. 1980: 'Excavations in Christchurch, 1969–1980', *Dorset Natural History and Archaeology Society Monograph* 5 (Dorchester).

Keen, L. 1977: 'Dorset Archaeology in 1976', *Proceedings of Dorset Natural History and Archaeology Magazine* 99, 120.

Keen, L. 1978: 'Dorset Archaeology in 1977', *Proceedings of Dorset Natural History and Archaeology Magazine* 100, 112.

Keen, L. 1979: 'Dorset Archaeology in 1978', *Proceedings of Dorset Natural History and Archaeology Magazine* 101, 133.

Knocker, G.M. 1956: 'Early burials and an Anglo-Saxon cemetery at Snell's Corner, near Horndean, Hampshire', *Proceedings of the Hampshire Field Club and Archaeological Society* 19, 117–171.

Lesick, K.S. 1997: 'Re-engendering gender: some theoretical and methodological concerns on a burgeoning archaeological pursuit', in Moore and Scott (eds) 1997, 31–41.

Lethbridge, T.C. 1931: *Recent Excavations in Anglo-Saxon Cemeteries in Cambridgeshire and Suffolk*, Cambridge Antiquarian Society Quarto Publications N.S. 3 (Cambridge).

Lethbridge, T.C. 1936: *A Cemetery at Shudy Camps, Cambs*, Cambridge Antiquarian Society Quarto Publications N.S. 5 (Cambridge).

Matthews, C.L. 1962: 'The Anglo-Saxon cemetery at Marina Drive Dunstable', *Bedfordshire Archaeological Journal* 1, 25–47.

Meaney, A.L. 1964: A Gazatteer of Early Anglo-Saxon Burial Sites (London).

Meaney, A. L. and Hawkes, S. C. 1970: *Two Anglo-Saxon Cemeteries at Winnall, Winchester, Hampshire*, Society for Medieval Archaeology Monograph 4 (London).

Moore, J and Scott, E. (eds) 1997: *Invisible People and Processes*, Leicester University Press (London).

Musty, J. 1969: 'The excavation of two barrows, one of Saxon date, at Ford, Laverstock, near Salisbury, Wiltshire', *Antiquaries Journal* 49, 98–117.

Nordbladh J. and Yates, T, 1990: 'This virgin text: between sex and gender in archaeology', in Bapty, I. and Yates, T. (eds), *Archaeology After Structuralism*, Routledge (London), 227–37.

Pader, E.J. 1982: *Symbolism, Social Relations and the Interpretation of Mortuary Remains*, British Archaeol. Rep. Internat. Ser. 130 (Oxford.)

Parker-Pearson, M. 1982: 'Mortuary practices, society and ideology: an ethnoarchaeological study', in Hodder, I. (ed.), *Symbolic and Structural Archaeology*, Cambridge University Press (Cambridge), 99–113.

Philp, B.1973: *Excavation in West Kent 1960–1970*, Research Reports in the Kent Series 2 (Dover), 164–214.

Rega, E. 1997: 'Age, gender and biological reality in the early Bronze Age cemetery at Mokrin', in Moore and Scott (eds) 1997, 229–247.

Reiter, R. 1975: *Towards an Anthropology of Women*, Monthly Review Press (New York).

Scull, C. 1993: 'Archaeology, early Anglo-Saxon society and the origins of Anglo-Saxon kingdoms', *Anglo-Saxon Studies in Archaeology and History* 6, 65–82.

Shephard, J. F. 1979: 'The social identity of the individual in isolated barrows and barrow cemeteries in Anglo-Saxon England', in Burnham, B.C. and Kingsbury, J. (eds), *Space, Hierarchy and Society*, British Archaeol. Rep. Internat. Ser. 59 (Oxford), 47–79.

Sparey Green, C. 1984: 'Early Anglo-Saxon burials at the "Trumpet Major" public house, Allington Avenue, Dorchester', *Dorset Natural History and Archaeology Society* 106, 149–153.

Speake, G. 1989: *A Saxon Bed Burial on Swallowcliffe Down*, English Heritage Archaeological Report 10 (London).

Stoodley, N. 1997: 'The Spindle and the Spear: a Critical Analysis of the Construction and Meaning of Gender in the early Anglo-Saxon Inhumation Burial Rite', unpublished Ph.D thesis, University of Reading.

Trumbach, R. 1994: 'London's sapphists: from three sexes to four genders in the making of modern culture', in Herdt, G. (ed.), *Third Sex, Third Gender. Beyond Sexual Dimorphism in Culture and History*, Zone Books (New York), 111–137.

Whelan, M.K. 1991: 'Gender and historical archaeology: Eastern Dakota patterns in the 19th century', Historical Archaeology 25/4, 17–32.

Yorke, B.A.E. 1989: 'The Jutes of Hampshire and Wight and the origins of Wessex', in Bassett, S. (ed.), *The Origins of Anglo-Saxon Kingdoms*, Leicester University Press (London).

Anglo-Saxon Studies in Archaeology and History 10, 1999

Towards the Kingdom of Denmark

Morten Axboe

In this paper I will try to sketch out some lines of development within the first millennium AD that may illustrate the formation of the kingdom of Denmark, using early historical sources, archaeological analyses of social processes, and scientific datings of important structures. I am not offering a strictly structured analysis, but rather an eclectic essay presenting some pieces of the puzzle.

It thus lies outside the scope of the paper to discuss the theory of state formation, apart from mentioning that the word 'state' appears to be anachronistic for the Danish Iron and Viking Age and should be reserved for the Middle Ages (Steuer 1994, 35f.). Nor will I go into any sort of detail concerning what military, legal or religious roles Iron Age kings may have had, or the economic basis for their activities. Obviously, any assumptions about the existence of 'kings' will have implications for our concept of the structure of Iron Age society, including not only the authority to order the levy necessary for the building of large defence structures as well as for active defence itself, but probably also the control of substantial landed property and other ways of gathering a considerable surplus – such as looting, controlled trade or perhaps even some sort of taxation – to explain the display of wealth, status and power that is mirrored in the finds. My aim is to present some of these finds together with some interpretations of the find material which may help to illuminate developments preceding the historically known kingdom of Denmark.

If, to start with, we go back to the Pre-Roman Iron Age, the early part of this period looks rather egalitarian when we look at the graves and the settlements. But social organization obviously went above village level, as evidenced by the Hjortspring bog find, now radiocarbon-dated to the fourth century BC (AUD 1987, 240). The weaponry found here is estimated to represent a troop of at least sixty men, needing three boats of the type found for their transportation; their defeat must also have demanded the combined forces of several villages (Kaul 1988, 22). A naval barrier at Gudsø Vig in southern Jutland has also been dated to the Pre-Roman Iron Age (AUD 1988, 219, 225; Rieck 1991, 93f.; Nørgård Jørgensen 1997, 202). The moated Borremose settlement in northern Jutland has recently been reinterpreted as a centre for the surrounding Himmerland in the fourth to second centuries BC on the basis of the unique charactér of the village, with its weak rampart and ditch appearing more symbolic than defensive, and a concentration of bog bodies and the exceptional finds of the Gundestrup and Mosbæk cauldrons within a few kilometers of the site (Martens 1994).

Towards the end of the Pre-Roman period social differences become more visible (Hedeager 1992a, 242ff.; Martens 1996, 238). A well-known example is the village at Hodde where one farm is larger than the rest, has its own fence and a concentration of the best pottery (Hvass 1985). Rich graves appear, for instance at Langå in eastern Fyn, with gold rings, a wagon, and imported Etruscan bronze vessels (Albrectsen 1954, 29ff.; Henriksen 1994). More recently a cemetery with rich graves of both the Late Pre-Roman and the Early Roman Iron Age has been found at Hedegård in central Jutland. Amongst the finds are weapons and imports, including outstanding bronze vessels, chain mail and a Roman officer's dagger with an enamelled sheath. A large associated settlement surrounded by a strong palisade has been found too, with thick culture layers (Madsen 1992;1993;1994;1995;1997).

In the Roman Iron Age the diversification of grave furnishing increases, culminating in the rich graves of the central place located in the area of Himlingøje in eastern Sjælland in the second quarter of the third century (Period C1b). It was the elite who displayed their wealth in the graves, and who controlled the connections with the Roman Empire and used the imports in a redistributive system to maintain their influence. Even early in the Roman Period there seems to have been a pattern wherein the richest graves may roughly correspond to a chieftain, leading an area like a modern *herred* and followed by a retinue of warriors. Detailed analysis suggests a social differentiation within these leading groups (Hedeager 1992a, 243; Kaldal Mikkelsen 1990, 185–191). The personal loyalty of a retinue, independent of older family ties, would have been of great importance, breaking up the earlier clan-based society (Hedeager 1992a, 248ff.). The Germanic peoples also developed their own status symbols, like snake's-head rings and Kolben armrings,

Fig. 1 Map of sites mentioned in the text. 1: Stentinget. 2: Bejsebakken. 3: Sebbersund. 4: Borremose. 5: Vendeldiget. 6: Dejbjerg. 7: Hodde. 8: Illerup. 9: Hedegård. 10: Priorsløkke. 11: Troldborg Ring. 12: Vorbasse. 13: Trælborg. 14: Trældiget. 15: Gudsø Vig. 16: Ribe. 17: Dankirke. 18: Haderslev Fjord (Dronning Margrethes Bro; Æ Lei). 19: Ejsbøl. 20: Æ Vold. 21: Olgerdiget. 22: Hjortspring. 23: Danevirke. 24: Hedeby. 25: Schlei. 26: Kanhave. 27: Langå. 28: Gudme. 29: Lundeborg. 30: Søholt/Hejrede Vold. 31: Tissø. 32: Neble/Boeslunde. 33: Hørup. 34: Lejre. 35: Himlingøje. 36: Toftegård. 37: Varpelev. 38: Uppåkra. 39: Vä. 40: Åhus. 41: Gamleborg. 42: Sorte Muld/Sylten.

apparently with the oldest finds in eastern Sjælland. Ulla Lund Hansen has demonstrated how, in its heyday, the Himlingøje area was not only able to 'filter' Roman imports and keep the unique items to itself, but was also the centre of a network covering the eastern part of present-day Denmark and possibly including Skåne too, with a concentration of the most valuable items in eastern Sjælland, surrounded by a zone of dependent areas with weapon graves and less prestigious imports (Lund Hansen *et al.* 1995, 374ff., 385ff.). But the systems based on redistribution were unstable, as demonstrated by the changing patterns and centres of wealth through the Roman Iron Age (Lund Hansen 1988).

Troubled times are also evident from the weapon sacrifices, and from ring forts, ramparts and naval barriers, some of which can be dated to the Roman or the Migration Periods. Johan Engström has estimated that the known weapon sacrifices of southern Scandinavia bear witness to around forty-nine battles during the Roman Iron Age (Engström 1997, 248). Twenty-three of these are recorded in the diagram in Figure 2 together with some Migration-period sacrifices (Ilkjær 1990, 333–339). It can be seen that twenty-one cluster within Periods C1b and C2: in other words within something like one hundred years from the early third to the early fourth century. According to the current interpretation we thus have evidence of a period of battles, won by the local defenders every four years on average. It is seldom asked what happened if the attackers

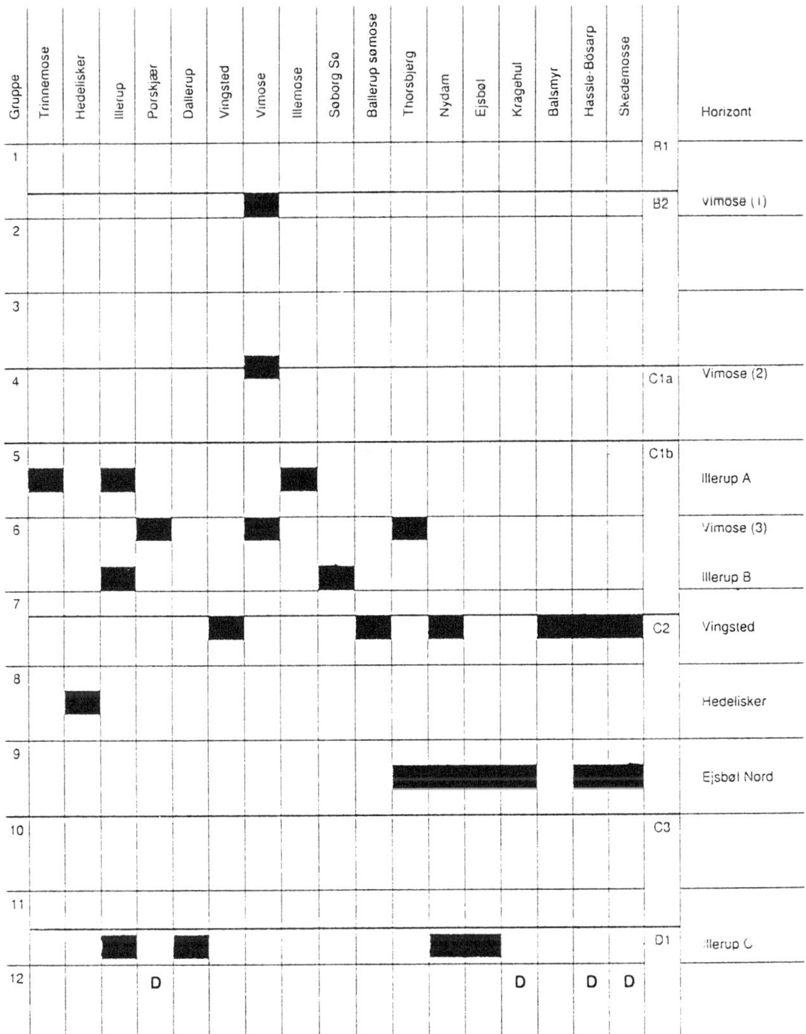

Fig. 2 Bog sacrifices of weapon and personal equipment in southern Scandinavia. D: Migration Period finds, which have not been analysed for separate depositions like the earlier finds. After Ilkjær 1990, Abb. 201, with additions from Abb. 207.

were victorious – what would they give their war gods in return, and where may we find it? Taking this and the generally fragmentary character of archaeological evidence into consideration, it must be accepted as evidence of a period of high military activity in Southern Scandinavia.

Best known is Illerup A of early C1b. The weaponry found here could equip at least about 350 men. But the force was probably larger than that: only about 40 per cent of the find-yielding area of the bog has been excavated, and, though the total annihilation of the attackers – as in the Varus-battle – cannot be excluded, a defeat would normally be considered serious if as much as 30 per cent of the force perished (Lund Hansen *et al.* 1995, 416 note 5; Albrethsen 1997, 216). So, although hypothetical, estimates of one, two or even three thousand attackers may be argued for, of course implying a defending force of at least the same size.

The strategics and logistics of prehistoric warfare is a subject of growing interest in Scandinavia (see Albrethsen 1997 and other papers in the same volume). Even the minimum Illerup force of 350 men could not have just been called together at short notice and sent abroad, nor could a defence be successful without proper training and organization. One standard weapon of the period was the lance, a weapon which demands intensive training for a closed unit to use without chaos as the immediate result (Engström 1997, 248). Similarly both archers and mounted warriors are represented in the bog finds, and a successful interplay between them and the infantry depends on discipline and training. The shields found at Illerup A seem to indicate a hierarchy: 5 silver bosses probably belonged to commanders, 30–40 bronze bosses to middle ranks, and about 300 iron bosses to common warriors (Ilkjær 1997, 58).

Ilkjær interprets the weapon sacrifices as the result of organized series of attacks from outside of present-day

Denmark (Fig. 3; Ilkjær 1993, 374–386; 1997). The focus and origin of the attacks vary with time, not like a shifting 'front-line' but rather as struggles between different regions, where both attackers and defenders had the strength and the organization for recurrent fighting.

Further evidence of organization involving larger areas are the ramparts in Jutland, too few of which have been dated hitherto. In the present context it is not particularly important whether they were built as actual defence structures or more as territorial border markers. The oldest phase of Olgerdiget in southern Jutland, which, interspersed with marshy areas, covers a distance of some 12 km, was built in 219 AD. It is thus broadly contemporary with Illerup A, but situated too far south for any direct strategic connection between the two to be necessary. The latest phase of Olgerdiget is dendro-dated to 278 or 279 AD, exactly the same year as the rampart Æ Vold some 20 km to the north (Ethelberg 1992,93; pers. comm. Steen W. Andersen. See also Wulff Andersen 1993; Axboe 1995, 223). Vendeldiget in western Jutland, a ditch 3.5 km long, has been radiocarbon-dated to 210–380 AD (cal., ±1 stand. dev., AUD 1994, 296; Mikkelsen and Helles Olesen 1997), while the 12 km-long Trældiget in southern Jutland can at present only be shown to postdate the early Pre-Roman Iron Age (AUD 1994, 203). Even more sparsely dated are the Danish ring forts, though some of them can be dated to the Roman Iron Age or the Migration Period (Andersen 1992). The fortification of the Early Roman-period village of Priorsløkke seems to demonstrate how a temporary fortress could be established in an emergency (Kaul 1997).

Finally, like the repeated sacrifices in the bogs, the naval barriers in Haderslev Fjord also demonstrate that substantial areas had to defend themselves against substantial enemies again and again: Dronning Margrethes Bro was built *ca.* 370, enlarged in 397–98 and repaired in 418–19 (AUD 1991, 260), while Æ Lei was built in 403 (AUD 1988, 233f.). It thus seems perfectly possible that the barriers played a role in delaying the attackers whose equipment was finally sacrificed in the Ejsbøl bog (Ørsnes 1988).

In the Late Roman Iron Age we thus find the Himlingøje/Varpelev area organizing Sjælland for one or two generations in the early third century, and defence structures in Jutland and weapon sacrifices scattered over the country as indications of battles throughout the period. But although the attacks appear to have come from outside, there is still nothing of a scale to suggest that the whole area of what was to be Denmark already had been united as one polity. Although eastern Sjælland was dominant in Period C1b, it soon declined, and even in the heyday of Himlingøje eastern Fyn was already establishing itself, at Gudme and Lundeborg, from *ca.* 200 AD. Interestingly enough, in Period C2 the centres on eastern Sjælland and Fyn seem to some degree to have different connections with the Continent, while Himlingøje/Varpelev also had marked influence in eastern and northern Jutland (Lund Hansen *et al.* 1995, 392).

For the time being, any comparison between the centres of Himlingøje/Varpelev and Gudme is distorted by the different finds. From eastern Sjælland we only have the graves, while the Gudme area offers a more complete cultural landscape with settlement areas, sacral place-names, gold and silver hoards, the graves of Møllegårdsmarken and the coastal site of Lundeborg.

Unique to Gudme is the complex of halls which were found in 1993 (Østergaard Sørensen 1994). One of them is amongst the largest houses known from the Danish Iron Age, 47 x 10 m, surpassed by a few metres only by the eighth-century Lejre halls, mentioned below. The Gudme hall apparently stood for some generations before it was taken down around the middle of the fourth century. South of it stood a successive series of six smaller, but still extraordinary houses, the first of which is dated to the first half of the third century and thus seems to be older than the great hall. The next of the smaller halls are contemporary to the great one, while the latest continue after it into the second half of the fifth century. Both the large and most of the smaller halls were unusually massively built, with roof-bearing posts reaching 80 cm in diameter, and the finds from the site include glass fragments, hackgold and silver, 115 denarii, and delicate jewellery, some of which was imported.

In the sixth century, the area formerly occupied by the halls appears to belong to a farm of quite usual type and dimensions for its date. The 'royal' functions may have moved to some other part of the settlement area, for Gudme as such continued and flourished with the many gold finds of the sixth century. These hoards exemplify an important change in the status display of the elite. In the Roman Iron Age it was important to demonstrate one's wealth at burials where it served to legitimize the power of the living through their connection with their ancestors. In the Migration Period wealth was displayed in the form of golden prestige objects like rings, bracteates and scabbard mounts, and it could be sacrificed within the elite settlements. This has been taken to indicate that the elite had now consolidated its status and was sacrificing to the gods as the maintainers of the established world order (Hedeager 1992a, 80f., 176f., 251). The Migration Period also saw a cessation of the collective weapon sacrifices (Fabech 1994).

Gudme is also an example of a special type of settlement with several groups of contemporary farms forming a cluster much larger than the normal rural villages of the period. Such places are known also from Stentinget and possibly Bejsebakken in northern Jutland, Neble/Boeslunde in south-western Sjælland, and the Sorte Muld/Sylten complex on Bornholm (Axboe 1991 = Axboe 1993; Watt 1991; Jørgensen 1994, 60ff.). That such settlements are not just normal villages shifting in time (like Vorbasse) is demonstrated at Gudme, where a single farmstead has been shown to have been in continuous use through twelve to fifteen phases covering the third to

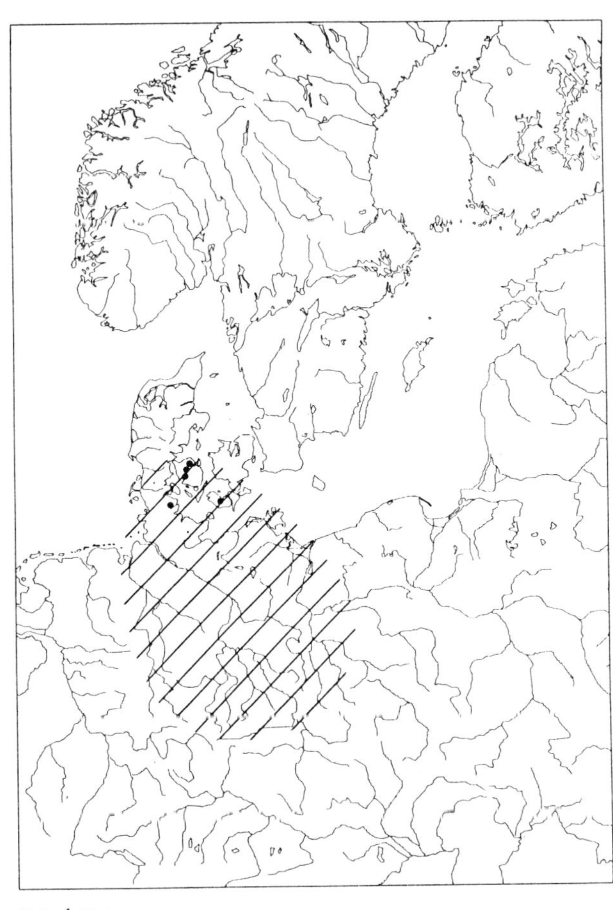

Fig. 3 Weapon sacrifices of Periods B2/C1a, C1b and C2, with indication of the attackers' origin (hatched). After Ilkjær 1993.

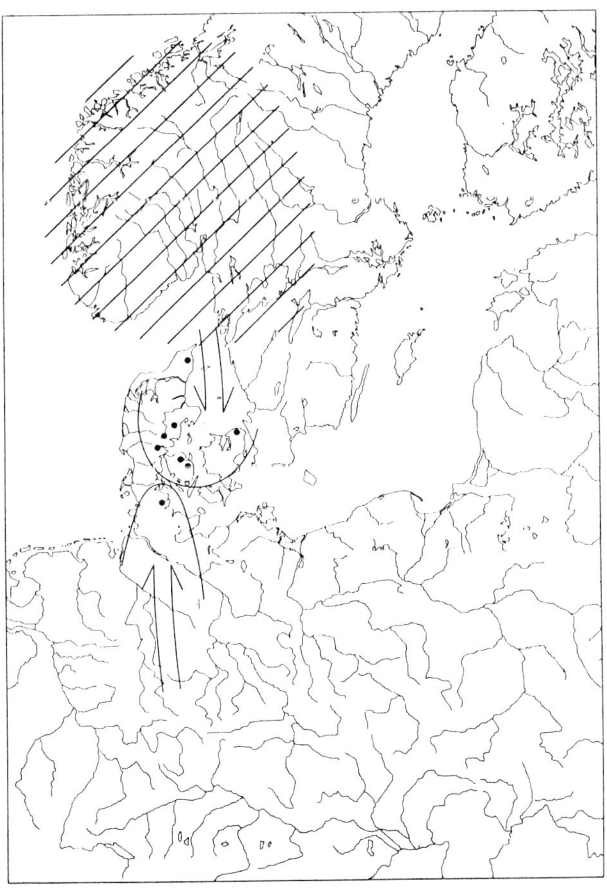

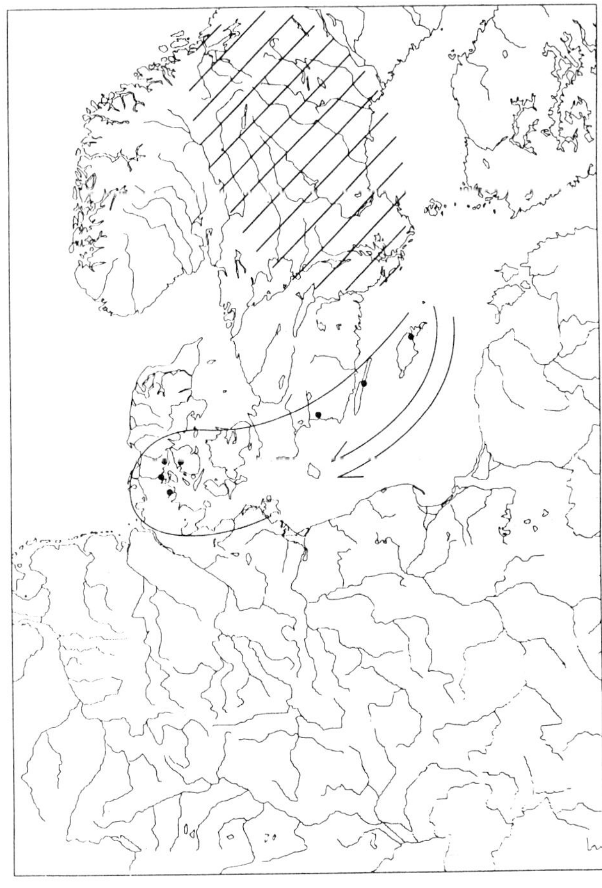

ninth centuries AD (AUD 1995, 153; Kjer Michaelsen and Østergaard Sørensen 1996). The large sites also stand out on account of their many metal detector finds, and they are interpreted as 'central places'. Outside of present-day Denmark the settlements at Vä and Uppåkra in Skåne appear to be of this type, and at Uppåkra recent metal detector surveys have added richly to the finds previously known (Stjernquist 1994).

Among the Danish 'central places' Gudme stands out through its many rich finds, including gold and silver hoards. This superiority will hardly be challenged by new finds, though the other sites are still insufficiently known for a detailed comparison. It is, however, becoming more and more evident that there is a precedence, or a range of specialization, amongst Iron Age settlements, and the diversity seems to grow towards the Viking Age. Single farms may have 'central' functions, like Dankirke and Dejbjerg in Jutland with their Migration-period imports (Jarl Hansen 1991; Jensen 1991a; Egeberg Hansen 1996), or Toftegård at Strøby in eastern Sjælland with glass, gold-foil figures *(guldgubber)*, and metal-working from the Vendel and Viking Periods (AUD 1995, 137f.; Tornbjerg 1997). At Hørup in northern Sjælland a settlement with a thick culture layer of the Late Roman Iron Age has been found, with antler and horn processing along with bronze and iron smithing, possibly including the working of bog iron (AUD 1995, 109, 1995, 118; Sørensen 1997). An important settlement complex is being excavated at Tissø in western Sjælland, with several farms, metal workshop areas, gold and silver hoards and high-quality detector finds of the sixth to tenth centuries together with weapons apparently sacrificed in the lake (Jørgensen and Pedersen 1996). Though it is difficult to estimate the representativity of the finds from sites only or mostly known from detector finds, there also seem to be significant differences between these (Axboe 1991 = Axboe 1993). Finally, there are the coastal sites, ranging from small temporary settlements of only local importance to internationally oriented sites like Lundeborg of the third to eighth centuries or later Sebbersund of the eighth to twelfth centuries (Ulriksen 1994, 1997).

Sites with trading and artisans' activities on more than a local scale would have been tempting targets for plundering and thus in need of protection and possibly also of the regulation of their functions. In return, the protecting magnate was able to tax the activities.

So the existence of 'central places' and sites with specialized functions point to kings/magnates as initiators and protectors of the activities, as generally assumed for the later foundations of Ribe and Hedeby. The contemporary existence of sites like Stentinget, Bejsebakken, Neble/Boeslunde, Uppåkra and Vä may indicate the existence of several realms, perhaps with Gudme as *primus inter pares* because of some religious precedence, but this is not the only possible conclusion. At some time kings will have been forced to a degree of itinerancy within their realm, both to consume the surplus from their landed property and for the enforcement of justice and other functions; consider the Merovingian kings traditionally travelling by ox-cart to be available to petitioners (Wood 1994, 102 and 119). Thus a king might have several 'seats', some of which may appear archaeologically as 'central places' while others may not, and it may be a misunderstanding to speak of 'Lejre kings' *vs.* 'Jelling kings' as is seen in discussions of possible Viking-period dynasties. On the other hand, we cannot be sure of distinguishing archaeologically between royal seats and seats of magnates like the members of the *Hvide* family in the twelfth century.

Some military sites can be dated to the Migration Period. These include weapon sacrifices (Fig. 2), though these seem to change character and finally disappear during the period. A few ring forts have more or less secure dates to this or the Vendel Period, including Gamleborg in Ibsker parish on Bornholm (Klindt-Jensen 1957, 152–155), the small fortresses of Trælborg and Troldborg Ring in eastern Jutland (Andersen 1992), and the immense Søholt/Hejrede Vold on central Lolland, some five times the area of Torsburgen on Gotland, with a radiocarbon-dating pointing to the period around AD 550 (Thorsen 1993; AUD 1995, 145f.; Løkkegaard Poulsen, in press).

Finally, in the sixth century we have the first historical sources mentioning the Danes, who are said to derive from the Swedes and to have driven the Heruli from their ancient homelands, and a Danish king was reportedly killed attacking Merovingian Gaul. No matter how we actually should interpret this information, the Danes by then had apparently established themselves as a power of some importance in northern Europe (Hoffmann 1992, 159ff.; Axboe 1995, 217ff.).

Then, in the seventh century, both the historical and the archaeological sources seem to let us down. The central settlements seem to continue, while graves and hoards are sparse or next to non-existent respectively (Näsman 1991), except on Bornholm, where both male and female graves are well furnished throughout the Vendel Period (e.g. Jørgensen 1990; Jørgensen and Nørgård Jørgensen 1997). One possible explanation is that after the turmoil and status-display of the preceding centuries, the winners were consolidating their power in the central part of southern Scandinavia. Lotte Hedeager has tried to illustrate this by a comparison with the historically known Merovingian realm (Fig. 4). Here it is evident that indicators of rank like ring-swords and crested helmets were deposited in graves only in the fringe zone of Merovingian influence, where personal status was uncertain and had to be demonstrated, but not in the heart of the realm where conditions were stable. The conspicuous lack of such finds in Denmark may be due to a similarly settled authority in Denmark, with areas of social and political competition on Gotland, in Uppland and in southern Norway (Hedeager 1992b). Similarly, Karen Høilund Nielsen's studies of animal art have led her to see southern Scandinavia as predominant in

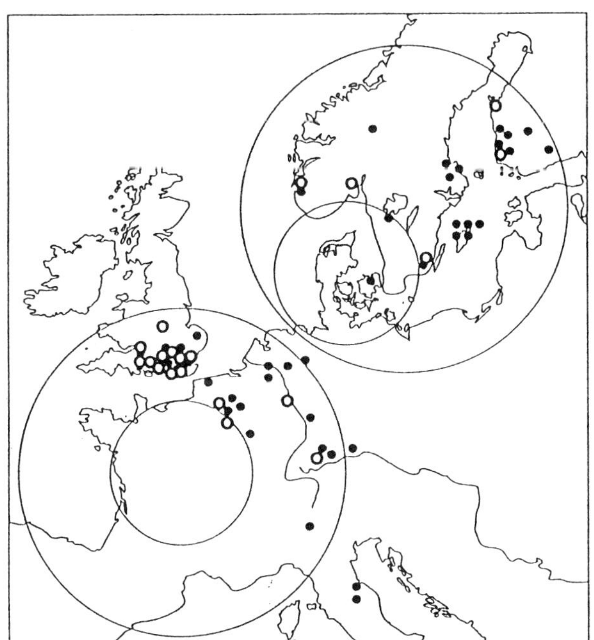

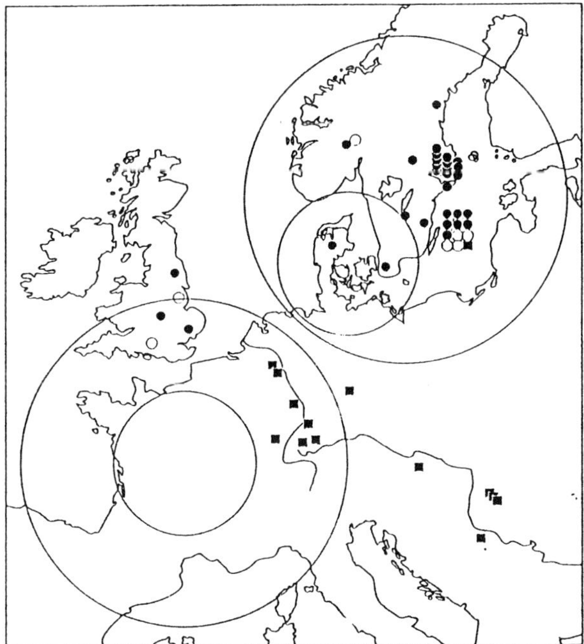

Fig. 4 Left: Distribution of ring-swords. Open signatures: Swords with traces of detached rings. Right: Squares: Frankish crested helmets from graves. Circles: Scandinavian crested helmets (open circles: uncertain). After Hedeager 1992b (adapted from Steuer 1987).

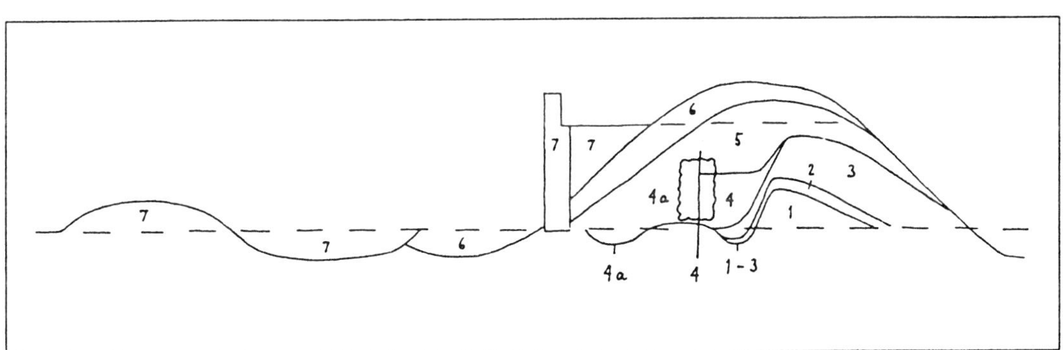

Fig. 5 The development of Danevirke, combining several sections through the Main Rampart. 1–3: Low banks with shallow ditches, seventh century. 4: Bank with palisaded front, built 737. 4a: Boulder wall with wooden front and ditch. Posts from the palisade of 737 are embedded in the wall. 5–6: Banks, phase 6 with ditch. 7: Brick wall with ditch and advanced bank, twelfth century. After Andersen 1993.

Scandinavia with a stable political structure, as opposed to the Mälar region (Høilund Nielsen 1991).

A possible centre in Denmark, apart from the 'central places' already mentioned, could be Lejre where a series of at least four great halls replaced each other on the same spot from *ca.* 700 to the later half of the tenth century. Besides the halls there are other buildings, including a smithy, cultural layers covering more than 100,000 sq. m. (Christensen 1993; 1996), and the nearby barrow of 'Grydehøj' where the large primary cremation with remains of gold-braided cloth has been radiocarbon-dated to the seventh century (Wulff Andersen 1995, 103–126).

In the early eighth century we have the foundation of the market-place at Ribe with the disputed minting of sceattas there (Jensen 1991b; Feveile and Jensen 1993 with further references; Feveile 1994); and Willibrord visiting the Danish king Ongendus (Skovgaard-Petersen 1981, 27ff.). Comparable to Ribe in date, though apparently less strictly regulated in its layout, is the non-permanent trading place at Åhus in Skåne (Callmer 1991).

The seventh and eighth centuries were not only a time of internal consolidation, however. This is shown by the new excavations at Danevirke, where the oldest phase of the Main Rampart has now been radiocarbon-dated to the middle of the seventh century. At least two more phases are prior to the posts standing in the boulder wall, which have been dendro-dated to 737 (Fig. 5; Andersen 1993). The latter date also applies to the Northern Rampart, and possibly to the massive structure recently found in the Schlei and interpreted as a naval base (dendrochronological date 'a few years after 734': Kramer 1994; Nørgård Jørgensen 1997, 207). In the first half of the eighth century we also have the Kanhave Canal, dendro-dated to 726 (Nørgård Jørgensen 1995); and broadly contemporary is one of the stake barriers at Gudsø Vig, with radiocarbon dates indicating a time frame of 690–780 (pers. comm. Anne Nørgård Jørgensen; cf. Rieck 1991, 93f.; Nørgård Jørgensen 1997 Fig. 5). Both in scale and in strategic outlook these enterprises are much larger than Olgerdiget and the other early structures. They imply rulers with the power to organize large areas, and provide a background for the Danish kings who from 777 on appear in the Frankish annals.

So this would be a convenient place to stop. The annals relate how King Godfred and his successors in the ninth century ruled over a Danish kingdom proving to be an opponent of the Frankish realm worthy of respect, and which at least at times seems to have included Skåne and parts of southern Norway. This extent of the Danish realm is confirmed by the reports of Ottar and Wulfstan from the late ninth century (Lund 1983). Even when two kings shared power over the Danes the realm was regarded as one kingdom by the Franks. Regrettably the sources fail again for the later part of the ninth and the first half of the tenth century, so that it is precarious to claim an unbroken continuity from Godfred to Harold Bluetooth who declared to have won for himself 'all Denmark, and Norway'. It is tempting to see the total dominance of one single royal family after the tenth century as having become established over a long period before that, legitimated with Odin as its divine ancestor (Axboe 1995, 232f.), but it can of course only be a guess, in view of the sparse and ambiguous historical information.

Thus the archaeological and historical sources from the first millennium can be used to compose a picture of the emergence of the Danish kingdom, evolving from possible chiefdoms of a moderate scale to the impressive Danish power of the early Viking Age. But it should be emphasized that such a generalized picture must be taken with a pinch of salt. Evolution may have gone fast at times and suffered reverses at others which we cannot be sure to discover. A king with a charismatic personality may have successfully summoned the magnates of his realm for enterprises, which weaker kings after him would fail with. Some areas may have developed separately, as I would suppose to be the case for Bornholm which, around 900, is mentioned by Wulfstan as having its own king (Lund 1983, 24) as well as because of the island's well equipped Vendel-period graves. Other interpretations may be put forward, for example, on the basis of enigmatic historical sources like Alfred's Orosius with its references to 'North-Danes' and 'South-Danes', 'Gotland' and 'Sillende' (Lund 1983; 1991).

However, the most intricate problem is that we are trying to reconstruct a story, whose end we know: a Danish kingdom as found in the Late Viking Age. To the participants in the process, the end was unknown, and perhaps not at all a concept they recognized or tried to attain. We must keep in mind that what we see as a 'process' leading to 'the kingdom of Denmark' is a construct – our construct. The lords of Himlingøje hardly set out to 'win all Denmark' – they would not have understood what we were talking about.

References

Albrectsen, E. 1954: *Fynske jernaldergrave I. Førromersk jernalder*, Ejnar Munksgaard (København).

Albrethsen, S. E. 1997: 'Logistical problems in Iron Age warfare', in Nørgård Jørgensen, A. and Clausen, B.L. (eds), *Military Aspects of Scandinavian Society in a European Perspective, AD 1–1300*, Publications from The National Museum, Studies in Archaeology and History 2 (Copenhagen), 210–219.

Andersen, H. 1992: 'De glemte borge', *Skalk* 1992/1, 19–30.

Andersen. H. H. 1993: 'Nye Danevirke-undersøgelser', *Sønderjysk Månedsskrift* 1993/11, 307–312.

AUD: *Arkæologiske udgravninger i Danmark*, 1984sq., Det Arkæologiske Nævn (København).

Axboe, M. 1991: 'Precious metals and power? Detector finds from Iron Age settlements', *Arkæologiske udgravninger i Danmark* 1991, 18–32.

Axboe, M. 1993: 'A die for a gold bracteate', in Arwidsson, G. *et al.* (eds), *Sources and Resources. Studies in Honour of Birgit Arrhenius*, PACT 38, 379–394.

Axboe, M. 1995: 'Danish kings and dendrochronology: archaeological insights into the early history of the Danish state', in Ausenda, G. (ed.), *After Empire. Towards an Ethnology of Europe's Barbarians*, The Boydell Press (San Marino/Woodbridge), 217–251.

Callmer, J. 1991: 'Platser med anknytning till handel och hantverk i yngre järnålder', in Mortensen, P. and Rasmussen, B.M. (eds), *Høvdingesamfund og Kongemagt. Fra Stamme til Stat i Danmark 2*, Jysk Arkæologisk Selskabs Skrifter 22/2 (Århus), 29–47.

Christensen, T. 1993: 'Lejre beyond legend – the archaeological evidence', *Journal of Danish Archaeology* 10 (for 1991), 163–185.

Christensen, T. 1996: 'Sagntidens kongsgård', *Skalk* 1996/5, 5–10.

Egeberg Hansen, T. 1996: 'Et jernalderhus med drikkeglas i Dejbjerg, Vestjylland', *Kuml* (for 1993–94), 211–237.

Engström, J. 1997: 'The Vendel chieftains – a study of military tactics', in Nørgård Jørgensen,A. and Clausen, B.L. (eds), *Military Aspects of Scandinavian Society in a European Perspective, AD 1–1300*, Publications from The National Museum, Studies in Archaeology and History 2 (Copenhagen), 248–255.

Ethelberg. P. 1992: 'To grave fra Højvang, Sønderjylland. Dendrodatering og absolut kronologi' *Kuml* (for 1990), 85–97.

Fabech, C. 1994: 'Reading society from the cultural landscape. South Scandinavia between sacral and political power', in Nielsen, P. O. *et al.* (eds), *The Archaeology of Gudme and Lundeborg*, Arkæologiske Studier 10, Akademisk Forlag (København), 169–183.

Feveile, C. 1994: 'The latest news from Viking Age Ribe: archaeological excavations 1993', in Ambrosiani, B. and Clarke, H. (eds), *Developments Around the Baltic and the North Sea in the Viking Age*, Birka Studies 3 (Stockholm), 91–99.

Feveile, C. and Jensen, S. 1993: 'Sceattasfundene fra Ribe – nogle arkæologiske kendsgerninger', *Nordisk Numismatisk Unions Medlemsblad 5*, 74–80.

Hedeager, L. 1992a: *Iron Age Societies: From Tribe to State in Northern Europe, 500 BC to AD 700*, Blackwell (Oxford).

Hedeager, L. 1992b: 'Kingdoms, ethnicity and material culture: Denmark in an European perspective', in Carver, M. (ed.), *The Age of Sutton Hoo*, The Boydell Press (Woodbridge), 279–300.

Henriksen, M. B. 1994: 'Kedelgrave', *Skalk* 1994/2, 28–30.

Hoffmann, E. 1992: 'Der heutige Stand der Erforschung der Geschichte Skandinaviens in der Völkerwanderungszeit im Rahmen der mittelalterlichen Geschichtsforschung', in Hauck, K. (ed.), *Der historische Horizont der Götterbild-Amulette aus der Übergangsepoche von der Spätantike zum Frühmittelalter*, Abhandlungen der Akademie der Wissenschaften in Göttingen, phil.-hist. Klasse, 3. Folge, Bd. 200, Vandenhoeck & Ruprecht (Göttingen), 143–182.

Høilund Nielsen, K. 1991: 'Centrum og periferi i 6.-8.årh. Territoriale studier af dyrestil og kvindesmykker i yngre germansk jernalder i Syd- og Østskandinavien', in Mortensen, P. and Rasmussen, B.M. (eds), *Høvdingesamfund og Kongemagt. Fra Stamme til Stat i Danmark* 2, Jysk Arkæologisk Selskabs Skrifter 22/2 (Århus), 127–154.

Hvass, S. 1985: *Hodde*, Arkæologiske Studier 7, Akademisk Forlag (København).

Ilkjær, J. 1990: *Illerup Ådal. 1: Die Lanzen und Speere. Textband*, Jutland Archaeological Society Publications 25/1 (Århus).

Ilkjær, J. 1993: *Illerup Ådal. 3: Die Gürtel. Bestandteile und Zubehör. Textband*. Jutland Archaeological Society Publications 25/3 (Århus).

Ilkjær, J. 1997: 'Gegner und Verbündete in Nordeuropa während des 1. bis 4. Jahrhunderts', in Nørgård Jørgensen, A. and Clausen, B.L. (eds), *Military Aspects of Scandinavian Society in a European Perspective, AD 1–1300*, Publications from The National Museum, Studies in Archaeology and History 2 (Copenhagen), 55–63.

Jarl Hansen, H. 1991: 'Dankirke. En myte i dansk arkæologi', in Fabech, C. and Ringtved, J. (eds), *Samfundsorganisation og Regional Variation. Norden i Romersk Jernalder og Folkevandringstid*, Jysk Arkæologisk Selskabs Skrifter 27 (Århus), 15–23.

Jensen, S. 1991a: 'Dankirke-Ribe. Fra handelsgård til handelsplads', in Mortensen, P. and Rasmussen, B.M. (eds), *Høvdingesamfund og Kongemagt. Fra Stamme til Stat i Danmark 2*, Jysk Arkæologisk Selskabs Skrifter 22/2 (Århus), 73–88.

Jensen, S. 1991b: *The Vikings of Ribe*, Den antikvariske Samling i Ribe (Ribe).

Jørgensen, L. 1990: *Bækkegård and Glasergård. Two Cemeteries from the Late Iron Age on Bornholm*, Arkæologiske Studier 8, Akademisk Forlag (København).

Jørgensen, L. 1994: 'The find material from the settlement of Gudme II – composition and interpretation', in Nielsen, P. O. *et al.* (eds), *The Archaeology of Gudme and Lundeborg*, Arkæologiske Studier 10, Akademisk Forlag (København), 53–63.

Jørgensen, L. and Nørgård Jørgensen, A. 1997: *Nørre Sandegård Vest. A Cemetery from the 6th-8th Centuries on Bornholm*, Nordiske Fortidsminder, Serie B Vol. 14, Det Kongelige Nordiske Oldskriftselskab (København).

Jørgensen, L. and Pedersen, L. 1996: 'Vikinger ved Tissø. Gamle og nye fund fra et handels- og håndværkscenter', *Nationalmuseets Arbejdsmark 1996*, 22–36.

Kaldal Mikkelsen, D. 1990: 'To ryttergrave fra ældre romersk jernalder – den ene med tilhørende bebyggelse', *Kuml* (for 1988–89), 143–199.

Kaul, F. 1988: *Da våbnene tav. Hjortspringfundet og dets baggrund*, Arnold Busck (København).

Kaul, F. 1997: 'Priorsløkke and its logistic implications', in Nørgård Jørgensen, A. and Clausen, B.L. (eds), *Military Aspects of Scandinavian Society in a European Perspective, AD 1–1300*, Publications from The National Museum, Studies in Archaeology and History 2 (Copenhagen), 137–145.

Kjer Michaelsen, K. and Østergaard Sørensen, P. 1996: 'Tusindvis af stolpehuller – uafbrudt bebyggelse i Gudme fra 3. årh. e.Kr. til vikingetid', *Årbog for Svendborg & Omegns Museum 1996*, 8–20.

Klindt-Jensen, O. 1957: *Bornholm i folkevandringstiden*, Nationalmuseets Skrifter, Større beretninger 2 (København).

Kramer, W. 1994: 'Ein Seesperrwerk des 8. Jahrhunderts in der Schlei', *Archäologie in Deutschland* 1994/3, 20–21.

Larsson, L. and Hårdh, B. (eds) 1998: *Central latsor – Centrala Fragor. Samhällsstrukturen under Järnåldern*. Acta Archaeologica Lundensia, Series in 8°, No. 28 (Stockholm).

Løkkegaard Poulsen, K. in press: '"Hejrede Wall", eine Wehranlage aus Lolland. Die Ausgrabungen 1995, 1996 und die Perspektiven', 48. Sachsensymposium, Mannheim 1997.

Lund, N. 1983: *Ottar og Wulfstan, to rejsebeskrivelser fra vikingetiden*, Oversat og kommenteret af Niels Lund, Vikingeskibshallen (Roskilde).

Lund, N. 1991: '"Denemearc", "tanmarkar but" and "tanmaurk ala"', in Wood, I. and Lund, N. (eds), *People and Places in Northern Europe 500–1600. Essays in Honour of Peter Sawyer*, The Boydell Press (Woodbridge), 161–169.

Lund Hansen, U. 1988: 'Handelszentren der römischen Kaiserzeit und Völkerwanderungszeit in Dänemark', in Hårdh, B. *et al.* (eds), *Trade and Exchange in Prehistory. Studies in Honour of Berta Stjernquist*, Acta Archaeologica Lundensia, Series in 8, Vol. 16 (Lund), 155–166.

Lund Hansen, U. *et alii* 1995: *Himlingøje – Seeland – Europa*, Nordiske Fortidsminder, Serie B Vol. 13, Det Kongelige Nordiske Oldskriftselskab (København).

Madsen, O. 1992: 'Midtjysk magt', *Skalk* 1992/2, 3–8.

Madsen, O. 1993: 'Hedegård – a wealthy village on the Skjern River', in Hvass, S. and Storgaard, B. (eds), *Digging into the Past. 25 years of Archaeology in Denmark*, Aarhus Universitetsforlag (Århus), 176.

Madsen, O. 1994: 'Midtjysk søfart', *Skalk* 1994/4, 8–12.

Madsen, O. 1995: 'Produktion, bebyggelse og samfundsorganisation i sen førromersk og ældre romersk jernalder. Et midtjysk eksempel', in Resi, H. Gjøstein (ed.), *Produksjon og samfunn*, Universitetets Oldsaksamling, Varia 30, (Oslo) 183–203.

Madsen, O. 1997: 'Pragtvåben', *Skalk* 1997/2, 5–9.

Martens, J. 1994: 'Refuge – fortified settlement – central place?', *EAZ Ethnographisch-Archäologische Zeitschrift* 35/2, 241–276.

Martens, J. 1996: 'Die vorrömische Eisenzeit in Südskandinavien, Probleme und Perspektive', *Praehistorische Zeitschrift* 71, 217–243.

Mikkelsen, P. and Helles Olesen, L. 1997: 'Vendeldiget', *Kuml* (for 1995–6), 135–47.

Näsman, U. 1991: 'Det syvende århundrede – et mørkt tidsrum i ny belysning', in Mortensen, P. and Rasmussen, B.M. (eds), *Høvdingesamfund og Kongemagt. Fra Stamme til Stat i Danmark 2*, Jysk Arkæologisk Selskabs Skrifter 22/2 (Århus), 165–178.

Nørgård Jørgensen, A. 1995: 'Nye undersøgelser i Kanhavekanalen', *Marinarkæologisk Nyhedsbrev* 5, 9–15.

Nørgård Jørgensen, A. 1997: 'Sea defence in Denmark AD 200–1300', in Nørgård Jørgensen, A. and Clausen, B.L. (eds),

Military Aspects of Scandinavian Society in a European Perspective, AD 1–1300, Publications from The National Museum, Studies in Archaeology and History 2 (Copenhagen), 200–209.

Ørsnes, M. 1988: *Ejsbøl I. Waffenopferfunde des 4.–5. Jahrh. nach Chr.*, Nordiske Fortidsminder, Serie B Vol. 11., Det Kongelige Nordiske Oldskriftselskab (København).

Østergaard Sørensen, P. 1994: 'Gudmehallerne. Kongeligt byggeri fra jernalderen', *Nationalmuseets Arbejdsmark* 1994, 25–39.

Rieck, F. 1991: 'Aspects of coastal defence in Denmark', Crumlin-Pedersen, O. (ed.), *Aspects of Maritime Scandinavia AD 200–1200*, Vikingeskibshallen (Roskilde), 83–96.

Skovgaard-Petersen, I. 1981: 'The written sources', *Ribe Excavations 1970–76* Vol. 1, Sydjysk Universitetscenter (Esbjerg), 21–60.

Sørensen, S. A. 1997: 'Hvad hånden former', *Skalk* 1997/1, 5–10.

Steuer, H. 1987: 'Helm und Ringschwert. Prunkbewaffnung und Rangabzeichen germanischer Krieger. Eine Übersicht', *Studien zur Sachsenforschung 6*, 189–236.

Steuer, H. 1994: 'Archäologie und germanische Sozialgeschichte. Forschungstendenzen in den 1990er Jahren', in Düwel, K. (ed.), *Runische Schriftkultur in kontinental-skandinavischer und -angelsächsischer Wechselbeziehung*, Ergänzungsbände zum Reallexikon der Germanischen Altertumskunde 10, Walter de Gruyter (Berlin/New York), 10–55.

Stjernquist, B. 1994: 'Uppåkra, et bebyggelsescentrum i Skåne under järnåldern', in Ganshorn, J. and Jacobsen, J.A. (eds), *Fra Luristan til Lusehøj. Festskrift til Henrik Thrane i anledning af 60-års dagen*, Fynske Minder (for 1994), 99–116.

Thorsen, S. 1993: 'Lollands virker', *Skalk* 1993/2, 3–7.

Tornbjerg, S. Å. 1997: 'Fra gubbernes verden', Skalk 1997/3, 6–10.

Ulriksen, J. 1994: 'Danish sites and settlements with a maritime context, AD 200–1200', *Antiquity* 68, 797–811.

Ulriksen, J. 1997: *Anløbspladser. Besejling og bebyggelse i Danmark 200–1100 e.Kr.* (Roskilde).

Watt, M. 1991: 'Sorte Muld. Høvdingesæde og kultcentrum fra Bornholms yngre jernalde', in Mortensen, P. and Rasmussen, B.M. (eds), *Høvdingesamfund og Kongemagt. Fra Stamme til Stat i Danmark 2*, Jysk Arkæologisk Selskabs Skrifter 22/2 (Århus),89–107.

Wood, I. 1994: *The Merovingian Kingdoms 450–751*, Longman (London/New York).

Wulff Andersen, S. 1993: 'Æ Vold', *Skalk* 1993/4, 9–13.

Wulff Andersen, S. 1995: 'Lejre – skibssætninger, vikingegrave, Grydehøj', *Aarbøger for Nordisk Oldkyndighed og Historie* (for 1993), 7–142.

Anglo-Saxon Studies in Archaeology and History 10, 1999

Evidence of Political Centralization in Westergo: the Excavations at Wijnaldum in a (supra-) Regional Perspective

Danny Gerrets

Introduction

In AD 734 the Frisians commanded by Duke Bubo were defeated by the Frankish army under the leadership of Charles the Hammer at the river Boorne. With the conquest of the Westergo and Oostergo regions in today's province of Friesland this Frisian heartland was finally incorporated in the Frankish kingdom. Some decades earlier, the Frisian kingdom had reached its largest extent. The Frisian kingdom probably stretched from what now is the Belgian border all along the North Sea coast up to the river Weser, the island of Helgoland and perhaps even up to the Danish border. In 716 Charles the Hammer was defeated by the Frisians, and the heartland of Austrasia was threatened when the Frisians appeared before the gates of the city of Cologne. How this remarkable Frisian demonstration of political and military power could take place and hence the question how political centralization came about has had to remain unanswered, because of a lack of written sources. New research offers hope that more light may be shed on Dark Age Frisia through archaeology.

The excavations on the terp Wijnaldum-Tjitsma

Between 1991 and 1993 the archaeological institutes of the universities of Amsterdam and Groningen carried out large-scale excavations of a terp near the present village of Wijnaldum in Westergo, the western part of the modern province of Friesland. Terpen (or 'wierden') are settlements on artificial mounds, typical of the northern coastal plain of the Netherlands and Germany. The footplate of a disc-on-bow brooch made of gold and red garnet was found on the terp Wijnaldum-Tjitsma in the 1950s. According to Bruce-Mitford (1974), in its craftsmanship this brooch fragment showed many similarities to jewellery found in the Sutton Hoo ship burial. Initially, this find remained curiously unnoticed by Dutch archaeologists. The Dutch research tradition at that time was mainly directed towards settlement archaeology with a special focus on man–land relationships. Material culture was only studied for typo-chronological reasons. Recently archaeological interest in material culture and its historical context has been growing. During the last decade several additional brooch fragments, together with many other metal items, have been found by amateur archaeologists using metal detectors at the terp Wijnaldum-Tjitsma; these finds suggest that this site could have been a political centre during the Early Middle Ages. The large-scale excavations were undertaken explicitly within the perspective of the historical development of the Frisian Kingdom.

Discontinuity in the terp's habitation

Occupation at Wijnaldum-Tjitsma started about AD 175 with the construction of a number of platforms made of sods (Gerrets *et al.* in prep; Gerrets 1997, 41 ff.). The site was located near the edge of tidal flats and saltmarsh in what was the former Boorne estuary. The highest platform probably bore an aisled building constructed with a roof-supporting framework of timber posts. On the lower, adjacent platform small-scale metalworking took place.

As their pottery reveals the inhabitants came from within the Westergo region and probably the site was constructed by terp dwellers from the more southerly row of terpen at Harlingen-Franeker-Dongjum. After an indigenous evolution of the handmade pottery from the Iron Age onwards, the typical 'Frisian' pottery was replaced about AD 250 by the so-called 'Eddelak' pottery, typical of the coastal plain of Groningen and Northern Germany (Taayke 1996, 194). At the same time many terpen were abandoned. This seemed to have marked the beginning of the Migration Period in Middle Roman Frisia.

Wijnaldum-Tjitsma together with some other terpen such as Hatsum in Westergo and Hoogebeintum and Driesumerterp in the Oostergo region was one of the few terpen in the coastal zone of Friesland which remained

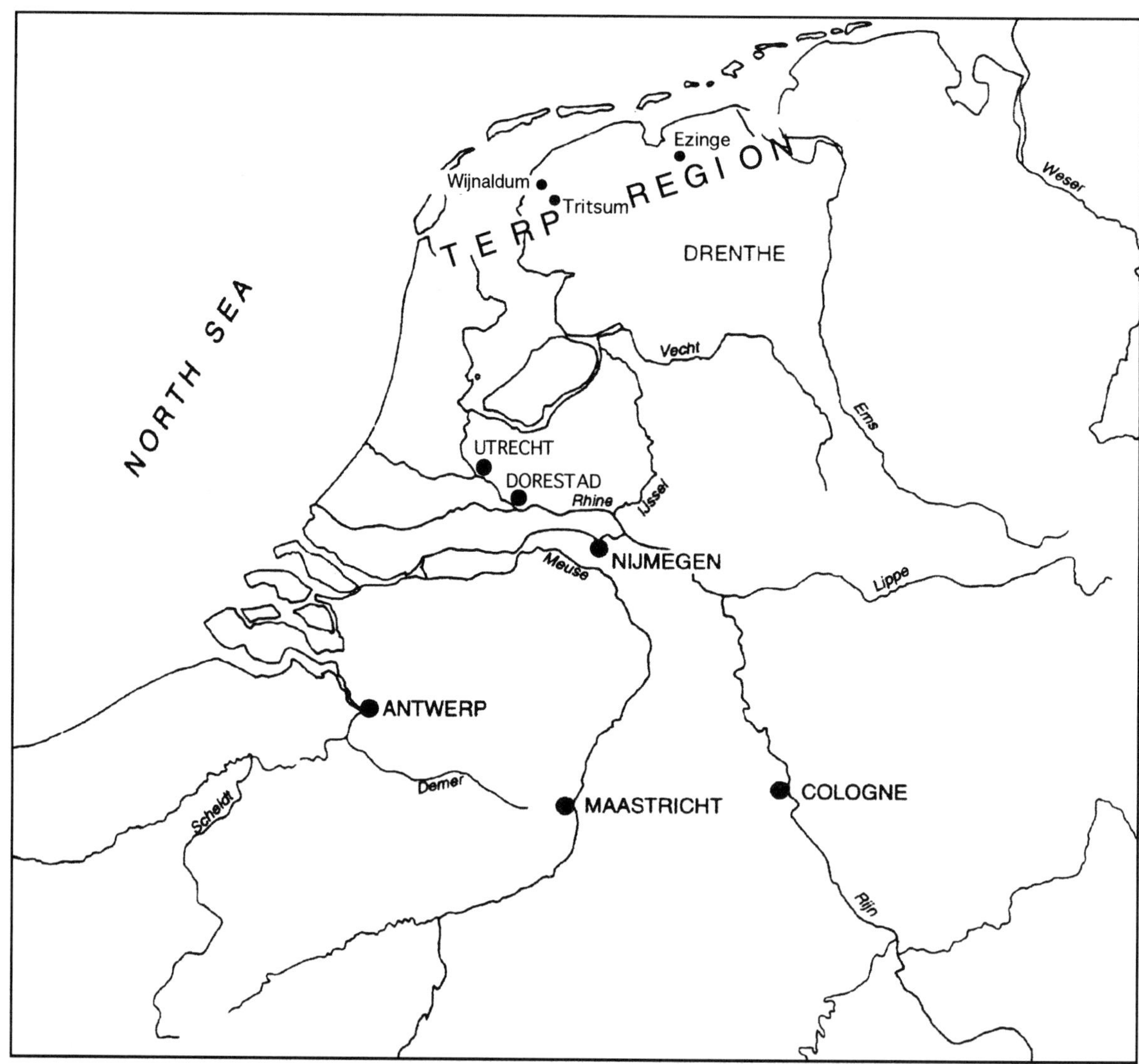

Fig. 1 Some locations mentioned in the text. Drawing J. De Koning.

occupied (Taayke, pers.comm.). Finally, at the end of the third/beginning of the fourth century AD Wijnaldum-Tjitsma was also abandoned. Careful stratigraphical analysis shows that rock-tempered Anglo-Saxon ware directly overlies the grass-tempered ware, typical of the Middle Roman Period in the region. Finds from the period between *ca.* AD 300/350 and 425 are almost completely lacking. Also elsewhere in the terp region finds from the fourth/early fifth century are scarce (Knol 1993, 110).

A change in the layout of the settlement and in house construction occurred with the arrival of new immigrants. The main orientation of the settlement in the Roman Period was NNE–SSW. In the Migration Period, however, the orientation became NNW–SSE. Buildings with a roof-bearing structure of wooden posts were replaced by sod-built structures together with pithouses apparently without a roof-supporting structure. The material culture was replaced by a new one without any immediate relationship to material from the previous period.

This has prompted a critical look at the drawings from some other terp excavations. A similar change in settlement layout could be discerned in the famous terp excavation at Ezinge (Prov. of Groningen; van Giffen 1936; de Langen and Waterbolk 1989). During the Middle Roman period (period 6) the settlement had a radial structure with aisled longhouses and barns. During the Migration Period (period 7), however, pithouses characterise the settlement, without showing any radial layout like that of the previous occupation phase. Probably the main buildings at Ezinge were sod-strutures like Wijnaldum-Tjitsma, but the Migration Period was the highest level excavated at Ezinge and preservation conditions will have been so poor that any sod walls would not have been recognized by the excavator (van Giffen 1936). At Wijnaldum-Tjitsma sod walls were recognized only under favourable conditions. Also at another, largely unpublished, terp excavation at Tritsum, a change in settlement layout and house construction seems have taken place (Waterbolk 1961). Not only the settlement layout was altered, but also burial customs changed from *Brandgruben* into a mixed ritual of cremation and inhumation (Knol 1993, 244).

From the archaeological evidence we have to conclude that the Frisians mentioned in the Roman written sources were not the Frisians that we encounter in the written sources from the Early Middle Ages. Blok (1996, 33) has recently stated that from the viewpoint of toponymy, there are no reasons to assume that there was continuity of occupation in the coastal zone of the province of Friesland, because prehistoric place-names are generally lacking.

The debate

The discussion about a possible invasion into Frisia is one of the most hotly debated subjects in archaeology. Since Boeles presented his invasion hypothesis for the first time in 1906 he has been regularly criticized (Boeles 1906). Boeles became convinced of the arrival of Anglo-Saxon immigrants when cruciform brooches and Anglo-Saxon pottery were found in the terp of Hoogebeintum in Oostergo. In 1929 the historian Gosses argued that the new material culture could very well be explained by acculturation (Gosses 1929). In 1951 Boeles repeated his opinion in his standard work *Friesland tot de 11e eeuw* (Friesland up to the eleventh century; Boeles 1951). He regarded the presence of a burnt layer together with the appearance of sunken huts in the Ezinge excavation as evidence of an Anglo-Saxon invasion. Boeles believed the majority of the population to have been killed by the invaders. With his opinion Boeles launched an emotional debate in the scientific magazine of the Frisian Academy *It Beaken*. Nationalistic feelings among the modern Frisians played an important part in this discussion. Boeles' hypothesis was rejected by some outstanding scholars from different scientific disciplines at a seminar organized by the Frisian Academy in 1953 (Sipma 1953). They admitted, however, that an influx of small numbers of people did probably take place.

Since the 1950s common opinion in archaeology has changed. Migration theories which played an important role in cultural historical archaeology were rejected and archaeologists were more concerned with long-term indigenous development. Dutch archaeologists became convinced of a continuous occupation of the terp region. When terpen were abandoned this was explained by the Dunkirk II transgression phase (Waterbolk 1979, 8 and 17; Knol, 1993 19 ff.; Taayke 1996, 194). But recent geophysical research at Wijnaldum and in northern Westergo has shown that the sea cannot have played a role of any importance in the abandonment of the region (Vos, in prep.).

With the rejection of the migration hypothesis an important aspect of Germanic and other tribal societies was ignored. Migration is a regular feature of stateless societies. When we study the historical sources about Germanic groups, we see a continuous process of fission and fusion. Some tribal entities have a short life-cycle, others have a long one. 'Tribal' names appear and disappear. This process was generated by the martial ideology which dominated Celto-Germanic society (Roymans 1996, 13 ff). Consequently, internal tribal relationships among Germanic groups are characterized by continuous raiding and warfare. The Amsivarii are a good example. They were driven from their home territory near the river Ems by neighbouring Germanic groups and tried to settle in the empty zone before the limes. The Romans would not allow this and after numerous conflicts with other groups and much reduced in number they disappear from the written sources. The Amsivarii travelled only a distance of one or two hundred kilometres at most before they tried to settle down. But even in the earliest sources, some groups (e.g. Cimbri and Teutoni) were travelling distances of hundreds and sometimes even thousands of kilometres looking for a new home territory to settle down in. This process seems to heve been intensified by political turmoil within the Roman Empire.

The inhabitants of the coastal region, probably attracted by *romanitas*, left their homesteads because of the unrest at the Roman border in the second half of the third century. After almost two centuries of relative stability, the Romans had to withdraw Roman troops from the limes about AD 250 because of internal political conflicts. Shortly after, Franks penetrated Roman territory and reached Spain. Raiding from the sea intensified to such a scale that defensive measures had to be taken to protect the Gallic coast and the east coast of Britain. About AD 290 Constantius Chlorus met Chamaves and Frisians in the central riverine area of the Netherlands or near the mouth of the river Scheldt. Perhaps other Frisians joined family members who had served in the auxiliary forces of the Roman army near Hadrian's wall, as shown by several votive stones and the so-called 'Housesteads ware' (Myres 1989, 77; Collingwood and Wright 1965, 772, 882–883, 1593–1594).

It seems unlikely that the only sound to be heard during the fourth/early fifth century in the terp region were the cries of seagulls and wading birds (Taayke 1988, 59). The emptiness of the terp region does not necessarily mean an absolute discontinuity. Although the number of finds from this period is small, it is enough to suggest that a small substrate of the old population continued to occupy certain terpen. But since their presence is hardly traceable, it is hard to believe that they were responsible for the rapid population growth later in the fifth century.

New people, new ideas

It is hard to say where exactly the new immigrants came from. There are no clear historical references to any immigration into the Dutch coastal area at that time. The

Fig. 2 Aerial photograph of the Wijnaldum-Tjitsma exacavation.

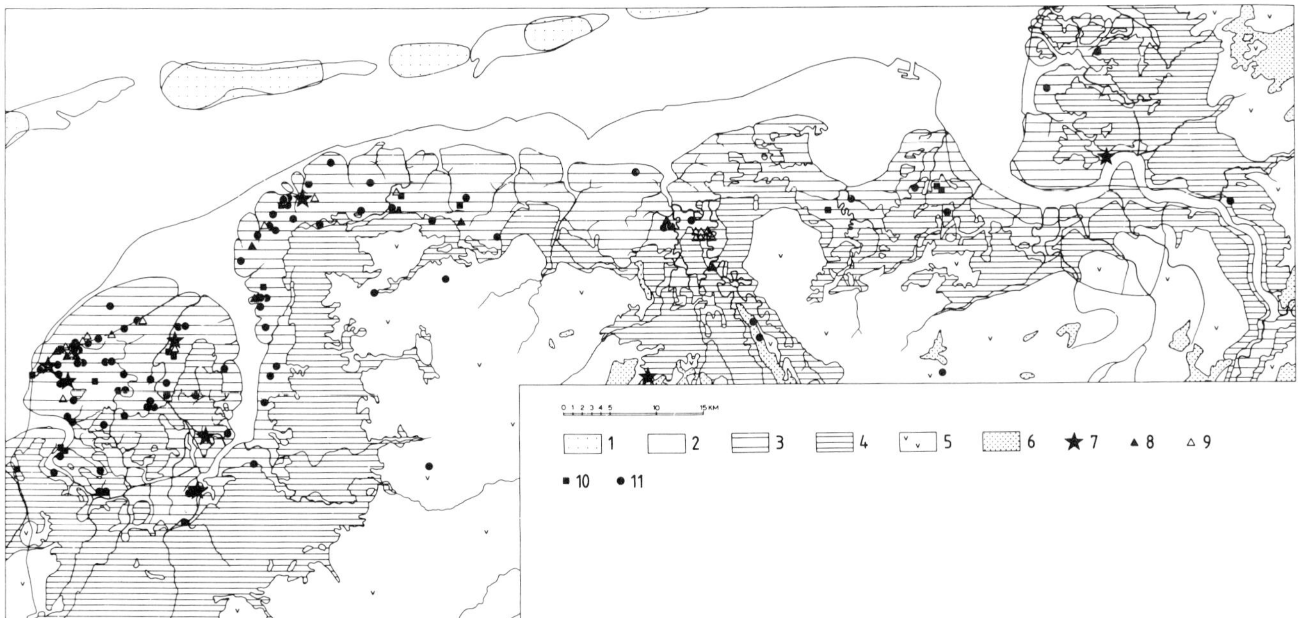

Fig. 3 The distribution of gold and silver objects and gold coins from the North Sea littoral in the Migration Period and in the Merovingian Period. 1: Sea and fresh water; 2: Beach and dunes; 3. Salt-marsh; 4: Clay; 5: peat; 6: Pleistocene hinterland; 7: Hoard with gold coins and/or precious jewellery; 8: Gold ornament; 9: Silver ornament; 10: Gold coin pendant; 11: Gold coin. Drawing H.J.M. Burgers, AIVU, after Knol 1993, 222.

only indication is a confusing statement by Procopius, who probably was informed by Anglo-Saxon envoys, that Jutes were the neighbours of the Frisians. The largest wave of immigrants must have occurred more or less simultaneously with the immigration into England in the first half of the fifth century. The earliest metal finds are similar to finds in England (Böhme 1986, 527 ff.). The material culture shows that the immigrants came from the eastern North Sea littoral. There are indications that some immigrants originated from Schleswig-Holstein, but the material culture also shows many links with the 'Elbe-Weser triangle' (Hills 1996; Taayke, pers. comm.), while other areas in the eastern North Sea littoral cannot be excluded. The reality probably will have been that the immigrants formed a heterogeneous mixture of people with a common Germanic background. They shared an ideology and a common political destiny (Hedeager 1992a, 281). The immigrants belonged to the seafaring peoples who raided the coasts of Gaul and eastern Britain from the third century onwards. They settled down on the land which historically belonged to the Frisians. These settlers with a heterogeneous ethnic background became the new 'Frisians', the people who lived on the land which once belonged to the Frisians.

The new inhabitants of the terp Wijnaldum-Tjitsma and the Westergo region brought not only a new material culture and new ideas about house construction, but also a new perception of world order. They probably belonged to retinues under aristocratic leadership. The 'Gold Horizon' of southern Scandinavia in the Migration Period reflects the development of more centralized political structures (Fabech and Ringtved 1991; Hedeager 1992b; Nielsen *et al.* 1994). It marks a far-reaching change in Germanic society, involving the disintegration of segmented lineage structures, the physical separation of an aristocratic class and the development of private landownership or private control over land (Hedeager 1992a). These developments probably will have started much earlier, but became visible archaeologically in, for instance, rich gold deposits in graves and later in votive deposits, in the physical separation of elite graves and in new symbols of power. Such features probably relate to the development of a new land-controlling aristocracy maintaining close personal relationships with each other. Gift-exchange played a crucial role in (re-) establishing personal bonds. Gold was one of the most appreciated and highly valued items, which accumulated in the hands of the people who represented the newly developed top stratum of the societal pyramid. This is best illustrated by the excessive amounts of gold apparently casually deposited at the central place of Gudme and the trading and industrial site of Lundborg on Fyn in Denmark (Thrane 1987; 1992; Nielsen *et al.* 1994; Thomsen *et al.* 1993).

International contacts

Westergo was rapidly repopulated (Knol 1993, 139). It will have been some time before new societal conditions obtained a more definite shape and new identities were created. After the arrival of new inhabitants, Wijnaldum-

Tjitsma offered a clearly different picture compared to the general settlement picture in the terp region, where the traditional aisled longhouse seemed to be the main long-lasting feature of settlements. At Wijnaldum-Tjitsma small sod houses together with pit houses are the main structures. And although only a small part of the terp was excavated it is clear that any indication that the inhabitants were cattle-breeding agriculturalists (e.g. cattle stalls and substantial dung layers) is lacking. The inhabitants seemed mainly occupied with small-scale manufacturing, such as bone and antler working, spinning and weaving and, above all, metal working. In contrast to a site such as Gudme, no great amounts of gold were found within the settlement. On the contrary, everything indicates that materials were reused over and over. But we know from indirect evidence that gold and silver were worked from the late fifth century onwards. Manufacturing took place on a very small scale, probably for a restricted group of consumers.

From the fifth century onwards, small numbers of wheel-thrown pottery were imported, mainly from the Middle Rhine area (Mayen), together with other products such as glass vessels and quernstones. Also 'Frankish' brooches and other copper objects show that there were contacts with the south. But cultural ties were strongest with the Anglo-Scandinavian world, especially England, which is true for the whole Westergo region (Knol 1993, 196 ff; Hills 1996). Although a new relationship with the Frankish south develops, inhabitants of Westergo show a remarkable indifference and perhaps even a conservative attitude towards the Roman-Christian inheritance, which was adopted by the Franks. The ties with eastern England must have been especially close. The philologist Siebs already concluded in the last century that Old Frisian and Old English (more specifically Old Kentish) showed great similarities (Sieb, 1889) and the reasons for these similarities are still frequently a subject of debate (Faltings *et al.* 1995; Looijenga and Quak 1996). Especially intriguing is the presence at Tritsum and Wijnaldum-Tjitsma of chaff-tempered 'Tritsum-ware' (Taayke and Knol 1992). This pottery displays great similarity to chaff-tempered pottery found in Belgian Flanders at Roksem/Zerkegem and in south-eastern England (Hamerow *et al.* 1994, 8 ff.). Because of the fragility of the pottery, we may assume that it was locally produced, probably by the women who used it. It does not seem very likely that this simple pottery played a role in the exchange of products. As seafaring was mainly a male activity, a possible explanation for the contemporaneous presence of this pottery in the littoral of the western part of the North Sea could be the existence of marital exchange networks.

Political centralization in Westergo

Wijnaldum-Tjitsma does not fit into the traditional picture of terp settlements as closed, corporate, peasant communities. Many aspects of the material culture excavated at Wijnaldum-Tjitsma indicate that the inhabitants maintained intensive contacts with the outside world. In the second half of the sixth century, imported pottery accounts for nearly 80 per cent of the assemblage. Wijnaldum-Tjitsma does not seem to be an exception. According to Knol's study, the Westergo region as a whole is comparatively rich in imported pottery, gold and silver finds and other prestige items (Knol 1993, 217 ff.). The overall picture is that the number of these finds diminishes further east along the North Sea coast, while this kind of find is almost absent further inland in the provinces of Drenthe and Overijssel. Numismatists believe that in Frisia the first imitation tremisses were struck even in the late sixth century, which is an indication that a more centralized power had developed in this region (Boeles 1951, 313 ff.).

The salt marsh of the Westergo region reached its largest extent during the Late Roman/Early Migration Period. It is one of the largest salt marsh areas of the North-west European plain. It offered rich pasture-land with a self-regenerating fertility, because of the occasional inundations by the sea. In view of the number of terpen, Westergo must have been densely populated. Its geographical location was excellent, midway between England and Scandinavia and connected with the Middle Rhine area by the river Vecht and the Almere lake (the predecessor of the IJsselmeer). The salt marsh was separated from the higher Pleistocene sandy soils by a wide and inaccessible peat belt. Travelling over land must have been arduous because the salt marsh was intersected by numerous smaller creeks and gullies and sometimes a larger river which drained the hinterland. The 'natural orientation' of the terp dwellers will have been towards the sea, which is shown for instance by the large number of fishbones and bones of waterfowl excavated at Wijnaldum-Tjitsma. The sea was not only a source of food or a way to obtain foreign goods by trading or raiding but also an important means of communication. All considered, we may conclude that Westergo offered the societal format for political centralization.

Kingship in Frisia?

Traditionally the constellation of Dorestad-Utrecht has been regarded as the political heart of the Frisian kingdom. It has always attracted the greatest attention of historians and archaeologists. But Utrecht and Dorestad were both in the frontier zone of the growing competition between Frisians and Franks, and as such in the spotlight of the first written sources when they started to flow again at the end of the seventh century, after centuries of absolute darkness. The new research in the Dutch North Sea littoral suggests that the political foundation for the Frisian expansion of the seventh and early eighth century had been laid earlier and further to the north.

The 'Gold Horizon' becomes visible in Friesland in

Fig. 4 Die for making gold foil used in the production of red garnet jewellery.

the first half of the seventh century. In contrast to southern Scandinavia, Friesland never saw a phase with rich graves. Although most gold objects were found during the commercial quarrying of the fertile terpsoil at the end of the nineteenth and the beginning of the present century, when about 70 per cent of the Frisian terpen were levelled, it is clear that they mainly come from a settlement context and only seldom from graves. It has often been assumed that between Frisians and Franks there was a relationship of dependency. One of the reasons for this hypothesis is that the Frisian leaders in the earliest Frankish written sources are referred to as *dux*. In the Anglo-Saxon written sources, however, the Frisian leaders are generally termed *rex*. Archaeologically there is no evidence for assuming a dependent relationship between Franks and Frisians. On the contrary, gold finds from Friesland show clearly that the cultural affinity of the Frisian aristocracy was strongest with the Anglo-Scandinavian world. Ruth Mazzo Karras in her study of seventh-century jewellery of Frisia concludes that it exhibits characteristics of Kentish and Scandinavian pieces, but that pieces which are direct copies are lacking (Mazzo Karras 1985, 170 ff.). For this reason she assumes that these were produced in Frisia itself. She regards the disc-on-bow brooches as hybrids – English in style, Scandinavian in shape. Some of the pieces show such a great familiarity with Kentish work that at least one of the craftsmen will have been trained in England (Mazzo Karras, 1985 173).

That the Frisian jewellery was probably made in Frisian workshops shows that they were not made for exchange as diplomatic gifts in the international network of the Anglo- Scandinavian aristocracy. Recently Bazelmans has added much to our knowledge on the ritual-cosmological character of the gift-exchange between lord and warrior-follower in his study of the Old English epic *Beowulf* (Bazelmans 1996; Bazelmans in press). While most of these objects probably circulated in the mutual relationship of gift-exchange between lord and warrior-follower within retinues, some of these items probably belonged to a category of goods which were inalienable (Weiner 1992; Bazelmans 1996, 72 ff.; Bazelmans in press). They were inherited from one generation to the next and the longer they remained in the possession of an aristocratic family, the more their worth increased. These objects sometimes acquired an identity of their own (e.g. swords). They were ornaments displaying the worthiness of members of an aristocratic class. Regalia will certainly have belonged to this group of inalienable objects.

Among the Frisian finds the disc-on-bow brooch of Wijnaldum-Tjitsma represents one of the most outstanding examples, because of its shape, size and craftsmanship. Amateur archaeologists with metal detectors have found additional fragments during the last decade, while one more piece was found during the excavation. Unfortunately it stems from the topsoil, so that nothing definite can be said about its context. We know, however, that gold was worked on the terp from the fifth century onwards, while a die and a small piece of unworked red garnet found in the excavation make it likely that red garnet jewellery was produced at Wijnaldum-Tjitsma (Bos and Nijboer 1997; Henk and Eva Kars, pers.comm.). Similar kinds of jewellery, executed in gold and completely covered with red garnets, are known from graves with a royal signature such as the grave of Childeric I (457/458–482) at Tournai in Belgium, the possible grave of queen Aregund, the third wife of Chlotarius I at St. Denis in Paris and the Sutton Hoo ship burial where one of the Wuffingas, possibly Rædwald, was buried (Kazanski and Périn 1988; Werner 1964; Carver 1992, 348 ff.). The Wijnaldum brooch therefore could have belonged to the regalia of a Frisian queen. Since the results of the excavation on Wijnaldum-Tjitsma revealed that in this area of the terp various products, including precious jewels, were produced for a restricted group of consumers, it seems most likely that the disc-on-bow brooch before the moment of its deposition was in the hands of a goldsmith, perhaps for repair.

The results of the excavation at Wijnaldum, together with earlier finds from the Westergo region, show that this region saw processes of political centralization similar to many other parts of North-western Europe. The Frisian aristocracy showed most cultural affinity with the Anglo-Scandinavian world, especially Kent. Knol argues that the Frankish conquest in 734 meant that Westergo lost its position as a core region in early medieval Frisia (Knol 1993, 204). Hoards and stray finds of gold and silver became more evenly distributed over the North Sea littoral of the northern Netherlands, while the close cultural relationship with England dwindled.

References

Bazelmans, J.G.A. 1996: 'Één voor allen, allen voor één. Tacitus' Germania, de Oudengelse Beowulf en het ritueel-kosmologische karakter van de relatie tussen heer en krijger-volgeling in Germaanse samenlevingen', unpublished PhD dissertation, University of Amsterdam.

Bazelmans, J.G.A. in press: 'Beyond power: ceremonial exchanges in *Beowulf*', in Nelson, J. and Theuws, F. (eds), *Rituals and Power. From Late Antiquity to the Early Middle Ages* (Leiden).

Blok, D.P. 1996: 'Das Alter der friesischen Wurtnamen', in Looyenga, T. and Quak, A. (eds), *Frisian Runes and Neighbouring Traditions*, Amsterdamer Beiträge zur älteren Germanistik 45 (Amsterdam/Atlanta), 25–35.

Boeles, P.C.J.A. 1906: 'De opgravingen in de terp Hoogebeintum', *De Vrije Fries* 20, 391–430.

Boeles, P.C.J.A. 1951: *Friesland tot de elfde eeuw. Zijn voor- en vroegste geschiedenis*, 2nd rev. ed. ('s-Gravenhage).

Boeles, P.C.J.A. 1952: 'De Angelsaksische invasie', *It Beaken* 14, 1–8.

Böhme, H.W. 1986: 'Das Ende der Römerherrschaft in Brittannien und die Angelsächsische Besiedlung Englands im 5. Jahrhundert', *Jahrbuch des Römisch-Germanischen Zentralmuseums Mainz* 33/2, 469–570.

Bos, J.M. and Nijboer, A.J. 1997: 'Koninklijke patronage: de edelsmid van Wijnaldum (Fr.)', *Paleoaktueel* 8, 108–111.

Bruce-Mitford, R. 1974: *Aspects of Anglo-Saxon Archaeology. Sutton Hoo and other Discoveries* (London).

Carver, M.O.H. 1992: 'The Anglo-Saxon cemetery at Sutton Hoo: an interim report', in Carver, M.O.H. (ed.), *The Age of Sutton Hoo* (Woodbridge).

Collingwood, R.G. and Wright, R.P. 1965: *The Roman Inscriptions of Britain I* (Oxford).

Fabech, C and Ringtved, J. (eds) 1991: *Samfundorganisation og Regional Variation. Norden i romersk jernalder og folkevandringstid*, Jysk Arkaeologisk Skrifter 27 (Aarhus).

Faltings, V.F., Walker, A.G.H. and Wilts, O. (eds) 1995: *Friesische Studien II*, =NOWELE 12 (Odense).

Gerrets, D.A. 1997: 'Continuity and change in house construction and the layout of rural settlements during the early Middle Ages in the Netherlands', in Fridrich, J. Klapšt_, J., Smetánka, Z. and Sommer, P. (eds), *Ruralia I*, =Památky Archeologické 5 (Prague).

Gerrets, D.A., Heidinga, H.A. and de Koning, J. in prep: 'Settlement development on the terp Tjitsma', in Besteman, J.C., Bos, J.M., Gerrets, D.A. and Heidinga, H.A. (eds) in prep., *The Excavation near Wijnaldum. Reports on Friesland in Roman and Medieval Times. Volume I.*

Giffen, A.E. van 1936: 'Der Warf in Ezinge, Provinz Groningen, Holland, und seine westgermanischen Häuser', *Germania* 20/1, 40–47.

Gosses, I.H. 1929: 'Friese jubileumliteratuur', *Tijdschrift voor Geschiedenis* 44, 14–39.

Haarnagel, H. 1979: *Die Grabung Feddersen Wierde, Methode, Hausbau, Siedlungs- und Wirtschaftsformen sowie Sozialstruktur* (Wiesbaden).

Hamerow, H., Hollevoet, Y. and Vince, A. 1994: 'Migration Period settlements and "Anglo-Saxon" pottery from Flanders', *Medieval Archaeology* 38, 1–18.

Hedeager, L. 1992a: 'Kingdoms, ethnicity and material culture: Denmark in a European perspective', in Carver, M.O.H. (ed.), *The Age of Sutton Hoo* (Woodbridge), 279–300.

Hedeager, L. 1992b: *Iron-Age Societies: from Tribe to State in Northern Europe 500 BC–AD 700* (Oxford).

Hills, C. 1996: 'Frisia and England: the archaeological evidence for connections', in Looijenga, T. and Quak, A. (eds), *Frisian Runes and Neighbouring Traditions*, =Amsterdamer Beiträge zur älteren Germanistik 45 (Amsterdam/Atlanta), 35–47.

Kazanski, M and Périn, P. 1988: 'Le mobilier funéraire de la tombe de Childéric Ier; état de la question et perspectives', *Revue Archéologique de Picardie 3–4 (= Actes des VIIIe Journées internationales d'archéologie mérovingienne de Soissons (19–22 juin 1986)*, 13–38.

Knol, E. 1993: 'De Noordnederlandse kustlanden in de Vroege Middeleeuwen', unpublished PhD dissertation, Free University, Amsterdam.

Langen, G.J. de and Waterbolk, H.T. 1989: 'De archeologie van Ezinge, nederzettings- en onderzoeksgeschiedenis van een Gronings terpdorp', *Jaarverslagen van de Vereniging voor Terpenonderzoek* 66–72, 78–111.

Looijenga, T. and A. Quak (eds) 1996: *Frisian Runes and Neighbouring Traditions*, =Amsterdamer Beiträge zur älteren Germanistik 45 (Amsterdam/Atlanta).

Mazzo Karras, R. 1985: 'Seventh-century jewellery from Frisia: a re-examination', *Anglo-Saxon Studies in Archaeology and History* 4, 159–177.

Myres, J.N.L. 1989: *The English Settlements*, 2nd rev. ed. (Oxford/New York).

Nielsen, P.O., Randsborg, K. and Thrane, H. (eds) 1994: *The Archaeology of Gudme and Lundeborg* (Copenhagen).

Roymans, N. 1996: 'The sword or the plough. Regional dynamics in the romanisation of Belgic Gaul and the Rhineland area', in Roymans, N. (ed.), *From the Sword to the Plough*, =Amsterdam Archaeological Studies 1 (Amsterdam), 7–127.

Sipma, P. 1953: 'Een Angelsaksische invasie in Friesland?', *It Beaken* 15, 162–186.

Siebs, Th. 1889: *Zur Geschichte der englisch-friesischen Sprache* (Halle).

Taayke, E. 1988: 'Terpenaardewerk uit de IJzertijd en de Romeinse tijd', in Bierma, M., Clason, A.T., Kramer, E. and de Langen, G.J. (eds), *Terpen en Wierden in het Fries-Groningse Kustgebied* (Groningen), 50–61.

Taayke, E. 1996: 'Die einheimische Keramik der nördlichen Niederlande, 600 v Chr. bis 300 n. Chr. Übersicht und Schlußfolgerungen', *Berichten van de Rijksdienst voor Oudheidkundig Bodemonderzoek* 42, 163–208.

Taayke E. and Knol, E. 1992: 'Het vroeg-middeleeuwse aardewerk van Tritsum, gem. Frankeradeel (Fr.)', *Paleoaktueel* 3, 84–89.

Thrane, H. 1987: 'Das Gudme-Problem und die Gudme Untersuchung, Fragen der Besiedlung in der Völkerwanderungs- und der Merowingerzeit auf Fünen', *Frühmittelalterliche Studien* 21, 1–48.

Thrane, H. 1992: 'Das Reichtumszentrum Gudme in der Völkerwanderungszeit Fünens', in Hauck, K. (ed.), *Der historische Horizont der Götterbilderamuletten aus der Übergangsepoche von der Spätantike zum Mittelalter*, Abhandlungen der Akademie der Wissenschaften in Göttingen, Philol.-hist. Klasse (Göttingen).

Thomsen, P.O., Blæsild, B., Hardt, N. and Michaelsen, K.K. 1993: *Lundborg – en handelsplads fra jernalderen*, Skrifter fra Svendborg and Omegns Museum 32 (Svendborg).

Vos, P.C. in prep.: 'The evolution of the salt-marsh ridges in Westergo, northwestern Friesland', in Besteman, J.C., Bos, J.M., Gerrets, D.A. and Heidinga, H.A. (eds), *The Excavation near Wijnaldum. Reports on Friesland in Roman and Medieval Times. Volume I.*

Waterbolk, H.T. 1961: 'Beschouwingen naar aanleiding van de opgravingen te Tritsum, gem. Franekeradeel', *It Beaken* 23/24, 216–226.

Waterbolk, H.T. 1979: 'Siedlungskontinuität im Küstengebiet der Nordsee zwischen Rhein und Elbe', *Probleme der Küstenforschung im südlichen Nordseegebiet* 13, 1–21.

Waterbolk, H.T. 1991: 'Ezinge', in Beck, H. *et al.* (eds.), *Hoops Reallexicon der Germanischen Altertumskunde* 8 (Berlin/New York), 60–76.

Weiner, A.B. 1992: *Inalienable Possessions: the paradox of keeping-while-giving*, (Berkley, Los Angeles and Oxford).

Werner, J. 1964: 'Frankish royal tombs in the Cathedrals of Cologne and St. Denis', *Antiquity* 38, 201–216.

Anglo-Saxon Studies in Archaeology and History 10, 1999

The Formation of the Anglo-Saxon Kingdom of Lindsey

Kevin Leahy

The Anglo-Saxon Kingdom of Lindsey lay on the east coast of England just south of the Humber Estuary. When first described in the twelfth century it had much the same extent as the pre-1974 Lindsey Parts of Lincolnshire, bounded by the North Sea to the east, the Humber Estuary to the north, the marshes of Thorne Waste to the west and, to the south, the river Witham and the Fossdyke, all of which effectively rendered it an island (Fig. 1). All of the places referred to by Bede as being in Lindsey lie within this area, suggesting that its form was established by the early eighth century (Stenton 1970, 133–4), although there are indications that it may have originally included lands to the south of the Witham (Bassett 1989, 2).

There is a very little documentary evidence relating to the early history of Lindsey which has led to the suggestion that it was merely a Mercian administrative unit and never a kingdom (Davies and Vierck 1974, 237). Lindsey, however, appears to have been considered a kingdom during the Anglo-Saxon period; Bede refers to it as a '*prouincia*' (HE, II,16), a term that he uses elsewhere to describe other kingdoms. It was certainly considered to be a kingdom in the seventh-century assessment known as the 'Tribal Hidage' where it was assessed, with Hatfield, at 7000 hides, placing it on a par with better known kingdoms of the South Saxons and East Saxons (Stenton 1947, 292–4).

Lindsey had its own bishops and, most importantly, its own kings. These are known from a single source, a genealogy of Aldfrith, king of Lindsey (Foot 1993, 128–40). Aldfrith's pedigree is traced back through eleven generations to Woden, the common ancestor of the Anglian kings, and unusually, back a further five generations. A major problem with this genealogy is that none of the individuals listed in it can be dated. Aldfrith had been equated with the *Ealfrid rex* who witnessed a charter of confirmation made by Offa of Mercia between 772 and 796 but it has now been convincingly argued that this should be read as *Ecgfrid* and refers to Offa of Mercia's son and brief heir, who died in 796 (*ibid.*). Dr Foot suggested a *floruit* for Aldfrith from around the last quarter of the seventh century to the first quarter of the eighth century. The kings of Lindsey never issued a coinage and the silver sceattas bearing the inscription ALDFRIDVS are now attributed to Aldfrith of Northumbria (685–704) (Grierson and Blackburn 1986, 166).

Lindsey was never a powerful kingdom being, for all of its recorded history, under the domination of either Northumbria or Mercia. In 678 the Mercians achieved a final victory at the battle of the Trent (Stenton 1947, 85) and in the years that followed Lindsey ceased to have its own king, becoming a Mercian province. In spite of its loss of independence Lindsey survived as an entity until the 1974 Local Government re-organisation when it was divided between the new administrative counties of Humberside and Lincolnshire.

In view of the dearth of documentary evidence relating to Lindsey we must turn to archaeology in an attempt to reveal its early history. During recent years there has been a massive increase in the amount of data we have on Lindsey with major excavations on cemeteries and, to a lesser extent, settlements. This has been supplemented by the work of metal detector users who have provided a large amount of useful data. Any discussion of the formation of the kingdom of Lindsey remains highly speculative but we can, at least, review the evidence and suggest a tentative interpretation.

Before discussing early Anglo-Saxon Lindsey we should consider the preceding late Roman period which shaped the process by which the Anglo-Saxon settlement occurred. Fourth-century Lindsey was prosperous. Lincoln was a successful city where it had been necessary to double the size of the walled area in order to surround its extended area (Jones 1993, 14). By the fourth century Lincoln had become the capital of the province of *Flavia Caesarensis* and probably the seat of a bishop. Our knowledge of the fourth-century city is limited but it appears to have remained active to a late date (*ibid.*, 14–27). However, whether this occupation would have been recognisable as urban life by a citizen of the first or second century remains open to doubt.

The Lindsey countryside seems to have been densely

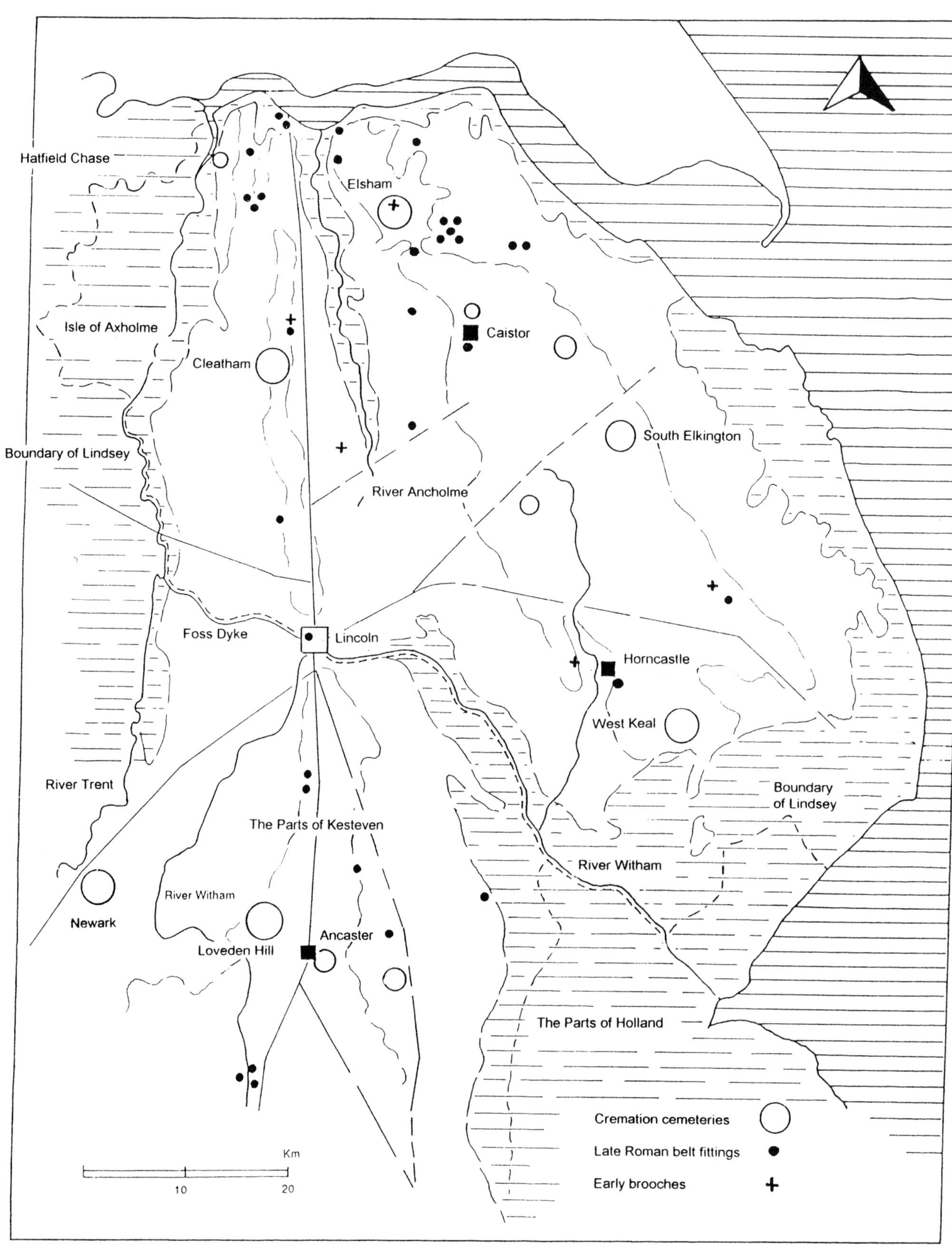

Fig. 1 The distribution of Anglo-Saxon cremation cemeteries in Lindsey and surrounding area, together with early brooches and late Roman belt fittings. Based on original data from Leahy 1993, fig. 4.1, appendix A, 39–42 and appendix B, 42. Marshland indicated by broken shading; 40 metre contour shown.

populated during the late Roman period. Pot-sherds can be found on almost every field, suggesting that very large areas were under cultivation. Many villas received new mosaic pavements in the fourth century, even in locations near the Humber which might be thought vulnerable to sea-borne attack. In spite of the confidence of the villa owners a threat was recognised. There was a significant increase in the deposition of coin hoards in the second half of the fourth century (Higginbottom 1980, 5–8). The defences of Lincoln cause no surprise but those constructed at Caistor and Horncastle were unusual. At Horncastle a two-hectare trapezoidal enclosure was surrounded by four-metre-thick walls set with interval bastions and backed by gravel ramparts (Field and Hurst 1983, 85–88). Less is known about the defences at Caistor but they, too, were four-metres thick (Rahtz 1960, 175–87). These defences are best compared to Saxon Shore forts which defended the southern and eastern coasts during the third and fourth centuries. The construction of fortifications on this scale inland suggests that the Imperial Government was particularly concerned about Lindsey. As Lindsey was well placed to supply grain to the Rhine garrison it may have warranted special protection (Leahy 1993, 29).

In 1961 Hawkes and Dunning published a paper which drew attention to a range of belt fittings which, they suggested, provided evidence for the settlement of Germanic soldier/settlers or *foederati* in late Roman Britain (Hawkes and Dunning 1961, 1–70). More recently this writer has discussed a concentration of these fittings in Lindsey (Leahy 1984, 23–32). If Germanic soldiers were settled in Lindsey during the fourth century they would have been well placed to take control when the central administration broke down. There are many difficulties with this thesis, however. The buckles and strapends cannot be said, with certainty, to be either Germanic or military. They are stylistically late Roman and formed part of official as well as military dress. Almost all of the examples found in Lindsey are not imports, but locally made copies. However, belts were not part of civilian dress in Roman Britain and it may be significant that the people of Roman Lindsey adopted a continental fashion which was, apparently, not shared by their neighbours. The distribution of these fittings (Fig. 1) shows a concentration near the Humber with a thin scatter over the rest of Lindsey (for a listing see Leahy 1993, 42, appendix B, fig. 4.1). This material is not focused around the fortified sites and has the sort of distribution one would expect from *foederati* settled in the countryside but protecting the vulnerable Estuary. Its distribution is unrelated to the locations of the cremation cemeteries, making it difficult to link the two phenomena. More work, perhaps on a national basis, is needed to understand the distribution and significance of these buckles.

The cremation cemeteries are the first real evidence we have for the Anglo-Saxon settlement of Lindsey (Fig. 1). Two of them, Cleatham and Elsham, have been excavated on a large scale yielding *c*.1100 and 625 cremations respectively. Less work has been done on the other cemeteries. At South Elkington, where it was thought that only a quarter of the cemetery was excavated, 290 urns were found (Webster 1952, 25–64). Only twenty-one urns were found at West Keal, although the scatter of urn fragments left by the plough was said to cover two acres (Thompson 1956, 189–92). The other cremation cemeteries appear to have been small with around twenty burials recorded (see Leahy 1993, 39–42 for a full listing and bibliography of all the Anglo-Saxon cemeteries in Lindsey).

The dating of the Anglo-Saxon settlement of Lindsey is very difficult to establish. While some of the pottery from the cremation cemeteries could be as early as the fourth century, it might be a century later (Eagles 1979, 142). Eagles has commented on the shortage, in Lindsey, of the early Anglo-Saxon metalwork needed to support a fourth-century dating for the pottery *(ibid.)*. There is now some indisputably early Germanic metalwork in the form of a tutulus brooch from Kirmington (Everson and Knowles 1978, 123–7) and supporting-arm brooches from Hibaldstow (Leahy 1984, 23–32), Edlington and Elsham (unpublished). Eagles' view, however, remains valid. Early cruciform brooches of Åberg's Group I are also rare, with examples known only from Glentham (Everson 1978, 85–6) and Maltby (unpublished). Roman material other than perforated coins and the occasional re-used pot is rare in the Anglo-Saxon cemeteries. This suggests that the rich culture of fourth-century Lindsey was no longer in circulation by the time of the cemeteries' inception, supporting the mid- fifth century date for the *Adventus* given by Bede (HE, I, 15). It is satisfying that Cleatham and Elsham are both early place-names with *hām* as their final element.

The cremation cemeteries have a distribution which may reflect the early stages of the Anglo-Saxon settlement, with five large, evenly spaced, sites perhaps representing original folk groupings of the settlement period. A comparative study of the pottery will, it is hoped, reveal the relationships between the cemeteries.

There are no Anglo-Saxon cemeteries to the west of the river Trent in the areas known as the Isle of Axholme and Hatfield Chase. The Trent may have been a political boundary, with the area to the west remaining in British hands or, alternatively, flooding in the late/post-Roman period may have rendered these lands uninhabitable. However, the Tribal Hidage included Hatfield with the assessment for Lindsey: *Lindesfarona ....mid Hæþfeld-lande* (Foot 1993, 128), showing that by the seventh century the kingdom included lands to the west of the Trent.

Each of Lindsey's large cremation cemeteries lies close to what was later to become an important manorial centre, Cleatham is near to Kirton in Lindsey, South Elkington near Louth, West Keal near Bolingbroke and Elsham near to Melton Ross. These places had achieved some importance in the fifth century and remained administrative centres into the eleventh. Administrative centres may also be identified by their relationship to later ecclesiastic sites. The close relationship which existed between Anglo-Saxon kingship and the Church offers a further opportunity to look at the structure of the kingdom. Stocker (1993, 116–20) has suggested pairings between Lindsey's monastic sites and secular centres, Lincoln being paired with Bardney, Kirton with Hibaldstow and Barrow with Caistor or Barton.

Although Lincoln is an obvious administrative centre there are, in contrast with other Roman cities, no cremation burials near-by, suggesting it was able to control its hinterland. Cemeteries are also absent to the south of Lincoln, suggesting that the area controlled was originally larger than the historically known kingdom (Bassett 1989, 2) and perhaps reflected the *territorium* of the Roman city. Little is known about what was happening in Lincoln at this time. Archaeological evidence for the city's survival beyond the fourth century is limited to a few sherds of early Saxon pottery (Alan Vince, pers. comm.) and a girdle-hanger (Eagles 1979, 157). In addition to this we have the enigmatic late/sub-Roman church of St Paul in the Bail, where a bronze hanging bowl found in a grave provided indisputable evidence of seventh-century activity (Jones 1994, 325–348; Bruce-Mitford 1993, 52, fig. 5.6,2, pls. 5–6).

There is other evidence for the survival of Lincoln as some form of administrative centre. It was at Lincoln where, in 628, St Paulinus met Blaecca whom Bede described as *praefectus* (HE, II, 16). Unlike many other Romano-British cities Lincoln retained its Roman name in a recognisable form (*Lin*-dum *Colon*-ia) and, furthermore, it is the only Roman city in eastern England to have given its name to an Anglo-Saxon kingdom (Yorke 1993, 141). Perhaps we should not be too concerned about the lack of early Anglo-Saxon finds from Lincoln: only small areas of the sub-Roman city have been excavated and we may be wrong in expecting to see an Anglo-Saxon material culture. Sub-Roman Lincoln may well have been culturally indistinguishable from late Roman. It is doubtful if anything resembling urban life survived in fifth century Lincoln; all that could be expected would be the headquarters of a local leader whose position was devolved from the late Roman defence force.

Links exist between the cemeteries in Lindsey and those north of the Humber in what was to become the Kingdom of Deira (Myres 1935, 250–62). Some parallels between the two areas may be a result of both drawing on the same basic Anglian tradition, but others may be more significant, particularly the urns assigned to the Sancton-Elkington potter (Myres 1969, fig. 46). These distinctive vessels occur at Sancton, East Yorkshire, and at Elkington, Elsham and Cleatham in Lindsey. Some seventh-century texts refer to the '*Humbrenses*' suggesting that there was some unity between the peoples around the Estuary and that they were only separated at a later date (Myres 1935, 250–62). It may be relevant that the dialect of medieval Lindsey is seen as part of a northern linguistic group, while the two other Parts of Lincolnshire, Holland and Kesteven, are more closely linked with the Midland dialect of English (Kristensson 1967, 241).

From the late fifth century onwards cremation was increasingly supplemented, and eventually replaced, by inhumation. At Cleatham sixty-two inhumations were found (besides *c.* 1100 cremations), but the new rite was not used on a significant scale at the other cremation cemeteries: there were no inhumations at Elkington (290 cremations) and only five at Elsham (625 cremations). It is unlikely that the cremation cemeteries were immediately abandoned in favour of the new rite as similar grave goods occur with both rites. Cremation is found as a minority rite in all of the inhumation cemeteries so far excavated with, for example, five cremations (seventy-two inhumations) from Welbeck Hill, Irby on Humber, and one from Castledyke South, Barton on Humber (196 excavated burials). Most inhumation cemeteries are small with less than 100 burials. Castledyke South, Barton on Humber is an exception with 196 excavated burials from an estimated 436 graves (Leahy 1998, 338).

The change in burial rite follows a general trend away from cremation in Anglian England, but in Lindsey it may demonstrate social changes with a move from large, regional cemeteries towards small local burial places (Fig. 2). This move may represent the breakdown of the original folk groupings and a coalescence into the Kingdom of Lindsey. However, the difficulties of transporting a body may have made local cemeteries a necessity. Perhaps as a result of more settled conditions Lincoln was no longer sacrosanct and cemeteries were established near to the city.

Claims have been made that the burial excavated beneath a large mound at Caenby may represent a princely burial (Eagles 1989, 212). Some of the metalwork from this burial can, indeed, be paralleled with finds from aristocratic burials (Speake 1980, 38–9), but we must await the re-evaluation of these finds before we can assess its importance. Everson (1993, 94–8) has drawn attention to the geographical importance of the Caenby location within Lindsey which makes it a convincing site for a royal burial. The other possible mound burials in Lindsey were reviewed by Everson (*ibid.*, 94). While some of these seem significant, it would be difficult to argue that any of them were aristocratic. Some of the seventh-century grave goods from the Roxby cemetery point to high status burials which, with the site's proximity to the rich Flixborough settlement, suggest that it was something out of the ordinary.

Roxby II is typical of what are known as 'Final Phase' cemeteries (Boddington 1990, 181). The seventh-century burials were orientated and laid in rows. In contrast to the sixth century, when grave goods were common, most of these seventh-century graves contained nothing.

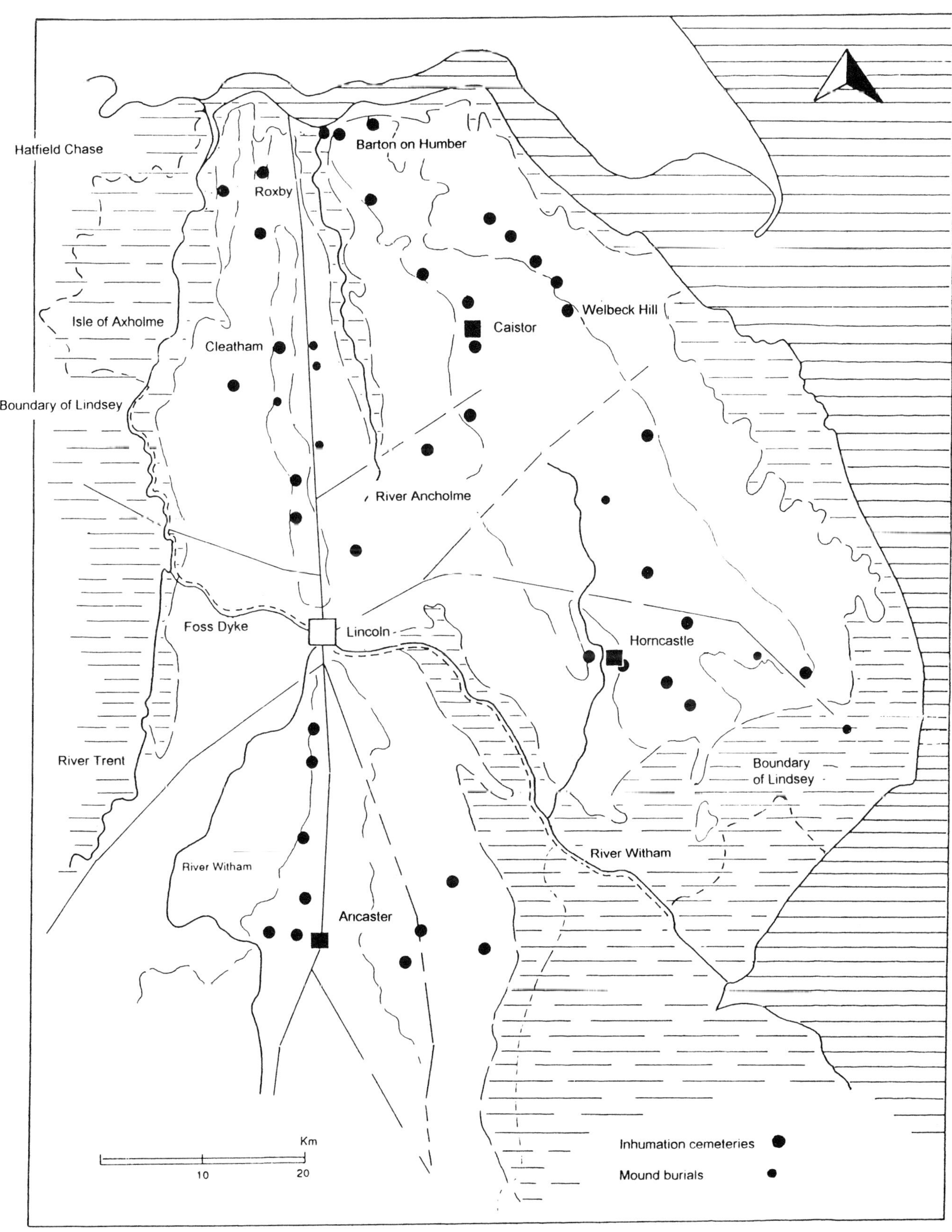

Fig. 2 Anglo-Saxon inhumation cemeteries and mound burials in Lindsey. Based on original data from Leahy, 1993, fig. 4.2, appendix A, 39–42. Marshland indicated by broken shading; 40 metre contour shown.

However, a few graves were very rich, suggesting the rise of an aristocracy and an increasing concentration of wealth and, no doubt, power into fewer hands. Roxby is a double cemetery where the sixth-century burial ground (Roxby I) was abandoned and, in the seventh century, a new cemetery opened ten metres to the south. This phenomenon has been noted elsewhere: at Chamberlain's Barn, Bedfordshire, the two cemeteries were 75 metres apart (Hyslop 1963, 160–200). Final phase burials also occurred at Cleatham and at Castledyke. The seventh-century graves at Cleatham were found in the same general area as the sixth-century burials, but were identified by their poor grave goods, east-west alignment and relative depth. Some graves had rows of stones along their sides which probably supported wooden chamber roofs.

The Castledyke cemetery (Drinkall and Foreman 1998) was very crowded with seventh-century graves cut though earlier burials. The intercutting of graves is unknown elsewhere in Lindsey, although at Cleatham graves were dug through earlier cremation burials. Any interpretation of this must remain conjectural but the inter-cutting could be a statement of political dominance. Grave 179 at Castledyke contained the bones of a youth aged around 14–16 years together with a sword and a bronze bowl (*ibid.*). This grave was cut through an earlier spear-burial and had then acted as a nucleus for other burials. The age of this young man suggests inherited rather than acquired status, pointing, again, to the rise of an aristocracy in seventh-century Lindsey.

That the Castledyke sword-burial should cut a grave containing a spear is interesting as weapon burials are uncommon in Lindsey. On average only around 7 per cent of the graves in Lindsey contain weapons as against an average of 18 per cent for southern England (Härke 1990, 30). Relatively low numbers of weapon graves are a feature of northern cemeteries which, again, places Lindsey into a northern grouping.

Although Lindsey appears to be one of the areas of England most intensively settled by the Anglo-Saxons, there is increasing evidence for what must at least have been strong contacts with British peoples if not actual cohabitation within Lindsey. Metal detecting has produced nine penannular brooches of British sixth-century type. While some of these are clearly imports from the west, others appear to be locally made copies (Susan Youngs, pers. comm.). In addition to this, Lindsey has produced more hanging bowls that any other part of England (Bruce-Mitford 1993, 45–70). These bowls with their Celtic-style decoration must have been made by British craftsmen. The inclusion in the genealogy of Aldfrith, King of Lindsey, of the British name *Caedbaed* points to some high level integration between the incoming Anglo-Saxons and the indigenous British and can be paralleled with the British name *Cerdic* in the West Saxon royal line. Barbara Yorke has drawn attention to parallels between administrative structures and religious practices in Lindsey and those in the neighbouring British enclaves of Deira and Elmet (Yorke 1993, 142), suggesting that they may have shared a similar early development based on the survival of late Roman organisation.

To conclude, the archaeological evidence has been used to construct a model in which the early stage of the Anglo-Saxon settlement was controlled, perhaps by the rump of the late Roman military command based in Lincoln. At this time burials were concentrated in five cremation cemeteries, which may represent original folk groupings with possible links with groups across the Humber. Later these groupings coalesced to form the Kingdom of Lindsey, with the cremation cemeteries being replaced by a large number of small inhumation cemeteries. There are indications of links with the British population to the west. The late seventh century saw the rise of an aristocracy as evidenced by the 'Final Phase' cemeteries.

This model offers an explanation of the evidence as it currently appears, but it is to be hoped that a detailed analysis of the cemeteries and their relationships will offer an opportunity to test the hypothesis, as will future finds. In a 1987 exhibition Lindsey was described as 'The Lost Kingdom' and, while it is still premature to say that the lost kingdom has been found, at least we now have some idea what we are looking for.

Bibliography

Bassett, S. 1989: 'Lincoln and the Anglo-Saxon see of Lindsey', *Anglo-Saxon England* 18, 1–32.

Bede, HE: Shirley-Price, L. (ed.) 1955: *A History of the English Church and People*, revised ed., Latham, R. E. 1968, Penguin (Harmondsworth).

Boddington, A. 1990: 'Models of burial, settlement and worship: the Final Phase reviewed', in Southworth, E. (ed.), *Anglo-Saxon Cemeteries: a Reappraisal. Proceedings of a Conference held at Liverpool Museum 1986*, Alan Sutton, (Stroud), 177–99.

Bruce-Mitford, R. 1993: 'Late Celtic hanging bowls in Lincolnshire and South Humberside', in Vince 1993, 45–70.

Davies, W. and Vierck, H. 1974: 'The contexts of the Tribal Hidage: social aggregates and settlement patterns', *Frühmittelalterliche Studien* 8, 222–93.

Drinkall, G. and Foreman, M. 1998: *The Anglo-Saxon Cemetery at Castledyke South, Barton on Humber*, Sheffield Excavation Reports 6, Sheffield Academic Press (Sheffield).

Eagles, B. N. 1979: *The Anglo-Saxon Settlement of Humberside*, Brit. Archaeol. Rep. Brit. Series 68 (Oxford).

Eagles, B. N. 1989: 'Lindsey', in Bassett, S. (ed.), *The Origins of Anglo-Saxon Kingdoms*, Leicester University Press (London), 202–12.

Everson, P. 1978: 'Two Anglo-Saxon cruciform brooches', *Lincolnshire Hist. Archaeol.* 13, 85–6.

Everson, P. 1993: 'Pre-Viking settlement in Lindsey', in Vince 1993, 91–100.

Everson, P. and Knowles, C. 1978: 'A tutulus brooch from Kirmington, Lincolnshire', *Medieval Archaeol.* 22, 123–7.

Field, F. N. and Hurst, N. 1983: 'Roman Horncastle', *Lincolnshire Hist. Archaeol.* 18, 47–88

Foot, S. 1993: 'The Kingdom of Lindsey', in Vince 1993, 128–40.

Grierson, P. and Blackburn, M. 1986: *Medieval European Coinage 1. The Early Middle Ages*, Cambridge University Press (Cambridge).

Härke, H. 1990: '"Warrior graves"? The background of the Anglo-Saxon burial rite', Past and Present, 126, 22–43.

Hawkes, S. C. and Dunning, G. 1961: 'Soldiers and settlers in Britain, fourth to fifth century', *Medieval Archaeol.* 5, 1–70.

Higginbottom, R. W. 1980: 'Roman coin hoards from Lincolnshire', *Lincolnshire Hist. Archaeol.* 15, 5–8.

Hyslop, M. 1963: 'Two Anglo-Saxon cemeteries at Chamberlain's Barn, Leighton Buzzard, Bedfordshire', *Archaeol. J.* 120, 160–200.

Jones, M. J. 1993: 'The latter days of Roman Lincoln', in Vince 1993, 14–27.

Jones, M. J. 1994: 'St Paul in the Bail, Lincoln: Britain in Europe?', in Painter, K. S. (ed.), *Churches Built in Ancient Times: Recent Studies in Early Christian Archaeology*, The Society of Antiquaries of London, Occasional Papers 16 (London), 325–348.

Kristensson, G. 1967: *A Survey of Middle English Dialects 1290–1350, the Six Northern Counties and Lincolnshire*, C W K Gleerup (Lund).

Leahy, K. A. 1984: 'Late Roman and Early Germanic metalwork from Lincolnshire', in Field, F. N. and White, A. (eds), *A Prospect of Lincolnshire: Essays in Honour of E.H. Rudkin*, privately printed (Lincoln), 23 32.

Leahy, K. A. 1993: 'The Anglo-Saxon settlement of Lindsey', in Vince 1993, 29–44.

Leahy, K. A. 1998: 'The demography', in Drinkall and Foreman 338–41, fig. 145.

Myres, J. N. L. 1935: 'The Teutonic settlement of England', *History* 20, 250–62.

Myres, J. N. L. 1969: *Anglo-Saxon Pottery and the Settlement of England*, Oxford University Press (Oxford).

Rahtz, P. 1960: 'Caistor, Lincolnshire, 1959', *Antiq. J.* 40, 175–87.

Speake, G. 1980: *Anglo-Saxon Animal Art and its Germanic Background*, Oxford University Press (Oxford).

Stenton, F. M. 1947: *Anglo-Saxon England*, 2nd ed., Oxford University Press (Oxford).

Stenton, F. M. 1970: 'Lindsey and its kings', in Stenton, D. (ed.), Preparatory to Anglo-Saxon England: being the Collected Papers of Frank Merry Stenton, Oxford University Press (Oxford), 127–35, previously published in Davis, H.W.C. (ed.), *Essays Presented to Reginald Lane Poole* (1927), 136–50.

Stocker, D. 1993: 'The early church in Lincolnshire: a study of the sites and their significance', in Vince 1993, 101–22.

Thompson, F. H. 1956: 'Anglo-Saxon sites in Lincolnshire: unpublished material and recent discoveries', *Antiq. J.* 36, 181–99.

Vince, A. (ed.) 1993: Pre-Viking Lindsey,. The City of Lincoln Archaeological Unit (Lincoln).

Webster, G. 1952: 'An Anglo-Saxon urnfield at Elkington, Louth, Lincolnshire', *Archaeol. J.* 108, 25–64.

Yorke, B. 1993: 'Lindsey: The Lost Kingdom found?', in Vince 1993, 141–150.

Anglo-Saxon Studies in Archaeology and History 10, 1999

The Anglo-Saxon Archaeology of the Cambridge Region and the Middle Anglian Kingdom

John Hines

The Cambridge region by the tenth century

As is well known, the process of the making of kingdoms in England reached a climax in the tenth century, when for the first time the only surviving native dynasty with truly kingly power – that of Wessex – succeeded in extending and consolidating its government of a unified England. This development involved not only the reconquest of the Danelaw but also the suppression of any ambitions to re-establish previously independent Anglo-Saxon kingdoms (Sawyer 1978, 99–131; Stafford 1989; John 1996, 83–98). The evidence for these events in the tenth century is patchy because of the selective interests of those who produced and preserved what are now our sources. The Chronicle gives a methodical account of the reconquest of the Danelaw. The struggle to incorporate English Mercia and Northumbria has to be reconstructed in a more inferential way (see Fig. 1). There is very little on East Anglia, although it is not difficult to see the political convenience of the stories of the martyrdom of a celibate Eadmund as East Anglia's final king quite apart from their relevance to the Benedictine reformation (Text: ed. Needham 1966; trans. Swanton 1975, 97–103; for the Benedictine reformation see Stenton 1947, 427–62).

No one, however, would have any good reason to suggest that the political strength and significance of the Cambridgeshire region at this date had been deviously suppressed for propagandist reasons. The minor importance of the area by this time is fairly well reflected by the history of the town of Cambridge itself. In the Roman Period it was the site of a small town which Burnham and Wacher (1990, 246–9) classify as a 'minor defended settlement'. Bede provides us with an early generic use of the term 'small town' by referring to it as a *civitatula deserta*, visited by Saxburh of Ely in the mid-690s to obtain a carved stone for the translation of the body of Æthelthryth (*HE* IV.19[17]). By the 870s, however, it was a location of sufficient prominence to attract the Danish *here* which overwintered there (*ASC*, *s.a.* 875), by or shortly after which time a bridge was presumably constructed as it is referred to in the Parker

Fig. 1 Frontispiece from a Life of Cuthbert *dated* ca. *934–938, usually believed to depict Athelstan presenting a book to the saint (representing the Lindisfarne/Chester-le-Street community and thus the Northumbrian Church). Rollason (1989) reinterprets the scene as one portraying Athelstan's devotion to the saint.* Contra *Keynes (1985, 180), however, the saint ought probably not to be interpreted as blessing Athelstan, as the sign of benediction is usually made with index and middle finger extended and the ring and little finger closed; the open palm with four extended fingers is rather a sign of showing, implying that Cuthbert recognizes the crowned Athelstan as king. Cambridge CCC MS 183, fol. 1v (290 x 190mm). Copyright. Reproduced by kind permission of the Master and Fellows of Corpus Christi College, Cambridge.*

Chronicle as *Grantebrycg* rather than *Granteceaster*. Following the Treaty of Wedmore (878) the area would have been part of the Danelaw, and in 917 the local *here* is reported to have submitted to Edward – not as a result of any direct assault, but rather outflanked in Edward's successful campaign against the army of Huntingdon on the Great North Road (Fig. 2).

The archaeological evidence from later Anglo-Saxon Cambridge not does suggest any very different picture (there is still little to be added to the summary published by Addyman and Biddle in 1965). A substantial scatter of finds, mostly haphazardly recovered and poorly curated and recorded, implies that Cambridge was the focus of considerable activity in the Early Anglo-Saxon Period (the later fifth and sixth centuries), the character of which it is very difficult to determine (Fox 1923, 242–9). The identification of a *Grubenhaus* within the site of Roman Cambridge (*Current Archaeology* 61, 1978, 57–60) is now considered unreliable (pers. comm. T. Malim), and the evidence otherwise consistently points to a slow development of the town only from the second half of the ninth century to the late tenth. This period is represented by some half-a-dozen coin finds (Blackburn and Haigh 1986), while the Cambridge mint itself seems to have come into being immediately after Edgar's coinage reform of *ca.* 973 (Jonsson 1987, 126–7). The Anglo-Saxon churches of Cambridge date from the late tenth century onwards (Addyman and Biddle 1965, 94–6; Taylor and Taylor 1965, 129–34). Although it could only be a speculative suggestion, Addyman and Biddle had good reason to identify the laying out of the King's and Cambridge Ditches as the critical moment in the establishment of the Late-Saxon town, and to propose a date after Edward's annexation of the area in 917 for this (1965, 98–100).

There is a little more evidence of activity in the local countryside in the preceding centuries. A number of eighth- and ninth-century coin finds have been made, particularly at locations along the roads and rivers to the south of Cambridge and most notably in the area around Melbourn and Royston, although in this respect again the county of Cambridgeshire would generally be characterized as one that is numismatically relatively poor (pers. comm. Mark Blackburn; see Metcalf 1984, 60–1; Bonser 1998). Highly intriguing, and seriously under-investigated, are a series of riverine deposits which may – as is the case in the Thames from Berkshire to London – cover both the Middle and the Late Saxon Periods. Possibly the earliest of these is a scramasax nearly 50 cm long, with a blade measuring approximately 31 cm by 2.5 cm, which was reportedly found after dredging in the River Rhee between Foxton and Barrington (Fox 1923, Pl. XXXVI,13; Cambs SMR 03995). It appears that this could date from as early as the late seventh or eighth centuries (Gale 1989; Härke 1993, 89–90). Shetelig (1940, IV: 64–9) also recorded a number of spearheads and axes, and one 'grappling iron', dating from the later eighth century to the end of tenth from the fen area around Ely. What was to become Cambridgeshire was, therefore, scarcely a waste or profoundly depressed area. But altogether there is no reason to regard the Cambridge region through the Middle and Late Saxon Periods as anything more than an economically viable backwater of Anglo-Saxon England.

The Cambridge region from the fifth to seventh centuries

If, however, we compare such evidence from the eighth to tenth centuries with the archaeological evidence from the fifth to seventh centuries, the Cambridge region seems to have undergone a marked change of fortune. Recent work by the Cambridgeshire Archaeology unit, with funding from English Heritage, comprising extensive excavations at the rediscovered site of the Barrington A cemetery and investigations into the Cambridgeshire Dykes, provides us with new material and a basis for an up-to-date review, to supersede the study made by Fox in his classic *The Archaeology of the Cambridge Region* (Fox 1923, 237–312; Malim 1992; Malim and Hines 1998; Malim *et al.* 1998).

Prior to Fox's book, E. T. Leeds had produced what was really the first systematic and comprehensive study of the apparent importance of the Cambridge region in early Anglo-Saxon England, in his famous analysis of the contrasts in the types of saucer brooch found in a concentration here and those of the Upper Thames region, which he also attempted to integrate with the historical traditions recorded in the Anglo-Saxon Chronicle (Leeds 1912). In essence, Leeds saw a non-Anglicized Chiltern region and the Icknield Way area as having stood as a barrier between East Anglia and the Upper Thames basin, although Anglian pressure in the east was inferred to have pushed earlier Saxon settlers there westwards into Bedfordshire and Northamptonshire. Hence the common starting-point but subsequent divergence of the saucer-brooch traditions in the two areas. Subsequently, both in response to Fox's book and as a result of his own excavations and further researches, Leeds revised his view, to emphasize ever more strongly both the role of the Icknield Way as the putative route by which Saxons settled the Upper Thames area, and the apparent capacity of archaeological evidence to overrule the 'history' of the Anglo-Saxon Chronicle (Leeds 1926; 1933).

In the 1990s archaeologists have both more evidence and different ideas, but the Icknield Way zone in early Anglo-Saxon times remains an enigmatic entity. Even along this route, however, we can point to distributions of distinctive material that reflect connexions and exchange at a level of some importance. Leeds (1912, 186) christened the 'Kempston type' of applied brooch, and a more recent corpus of these (Kennett 1971) shows them to have their greatest concentration in the South Cambridgehire area but with a distribution running out to

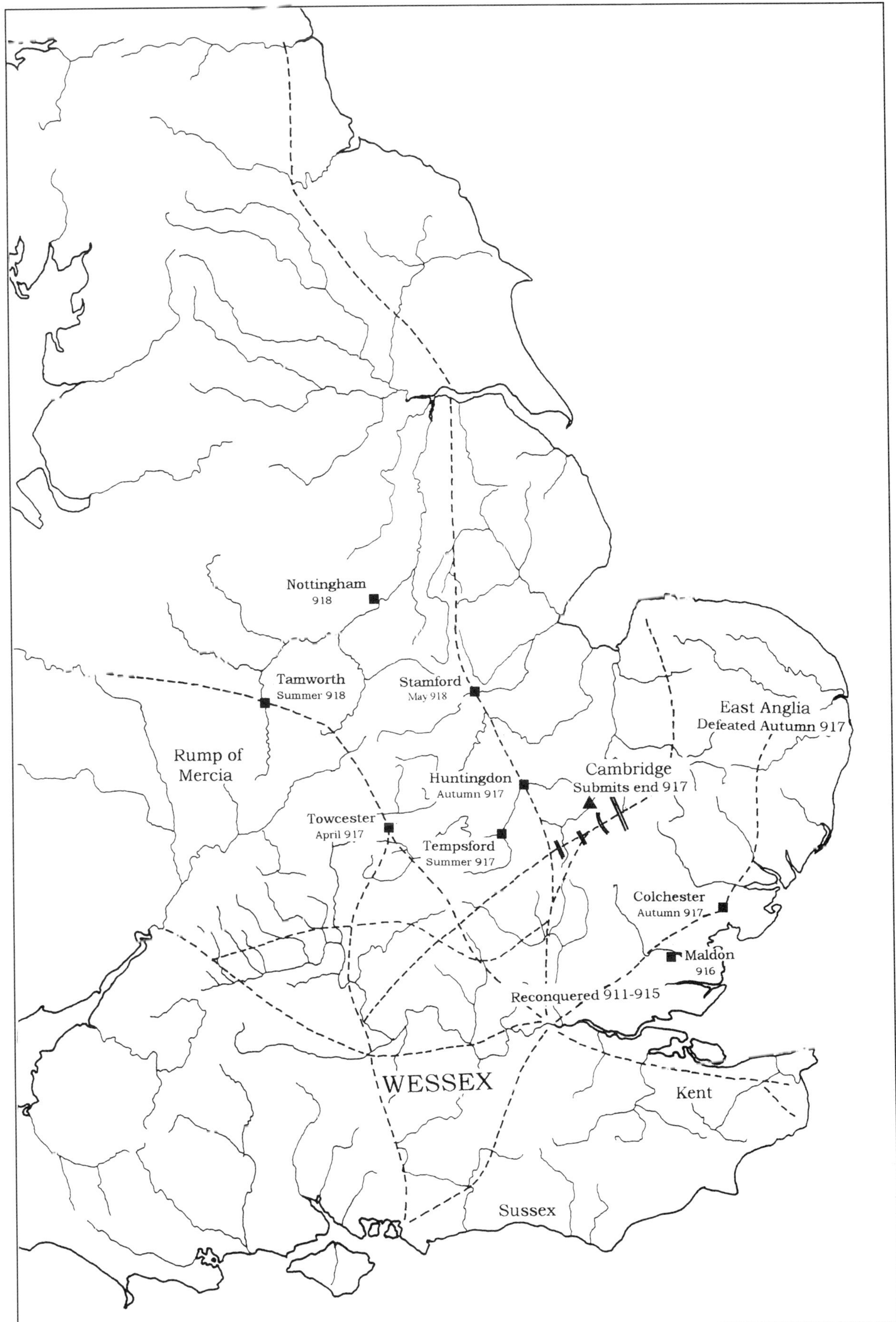

Fig. 2 Edward's reconquest of the southern Danelaw, 916–918, according to the Anglo-Saxon Chronicle MS A (Bately ed. 1986), with corrected dates. Squares: sites fortified and/or occupied, with dates.

Oxfordshire and Northamptonshire. Such links are also implied by other types of applied brooch, such as a particular zoomorphic design found in grave 95 during the recent excavations at Edix Hill (Barrington A) with distinct parallels from Abingdon and Frilford, Oxon (Malim and Hines 1998, 202; Figs. 3–4).

In his monograph of 1945, 'The distribution of the Angles and Saxons, archaeologically considered', Leeds went on to emphasize what he then perceived as the special place of the Cambridgeshire region in the development of particularly English types of small long brooch (Leeds 1945, 4–44 and 77–83). While it is still true that the volume and frequency of small long brooches is a distinctive feature of the Early Anglo-Saxon cemeteries of Cambridgeshire, there is no longer any very persuasive case to be made for attributing a special centre of development and source of influence within England to this area. Likewise with the more ordinary forms of cruciform brooch (i.e. up to Mortimer's Type D, which is virtually equivalent to Åberg's group IV: Mortimer 1990; Åberg 1926, 28–56), the studies available yield relatively little which implies distinctive local types and special regional connexions marked by such artefacts. Potentially the most significant exception in this context concerns the cruciform brooches of Mortimer's Type IC (Åberg group III) which Reichstein (1975, 44, Abb. 14, Tafn. 107–9) grouped together as Typ Islip, and which occur within an area covering Cambridgeshire and Northamptonshire (Fig. 5) that, as we shall see, is also identified as a regular area of common distribution for several other artefact-types.

Amongst those artefact-types are the various sub-types of the florid cruciform brooch (Mortimer Type Z; Åberg group V). A distribution map of the sub-types identified and catalogued by Mortimer reveals two distinct groups in terms of complementary distribution: one set occurring principally in Cambridgeshire and the central Midlands, the other in East Anglia, the north-east Midlands and further north (Fig. 6).

Essentially the same situation is revealed by the contemporary brooch-type which is functionally and qualitatively most similar to the florid cruciform brooch, the great square-headed brooch. There are differences of distribution here which can, indeed, be of such a very fine character that they are not easy to discern on a general, large-scale distribution map (e.g. Fig. 7). Great square-headed brooches of groups XV, XVI and XVII are contemporary types (of phase 3), and indeed are very numerous: more than sixty are known altogether (Hines 1997, esp. 111–41). Once again, the overwhelming majority of group XVI and XVII brooches are from sites in East Anglia (i.e. Suffolk and Norfolk) or the north-east Midlands and beyond, while group XV, by contrast, is found rather at sites in Cambridgeshire and Northamptonshire. The recurrent connexions between the Cambridge region and the central and southern Midlands are also well illustrated by the distribution of group V brooches and their derivative types (groups V, VIII, X and XI; Fig. 8). Here, attention may particularly be drawn to the recent finding of two specimens of group X – which is represented by no less than three brooches at the single site of Little Wilbraham, Cambridgeshire – along the Icknield Way zone in Buckinghamshire (Hunn *et al.* 1994; Farley and Hines 1997).

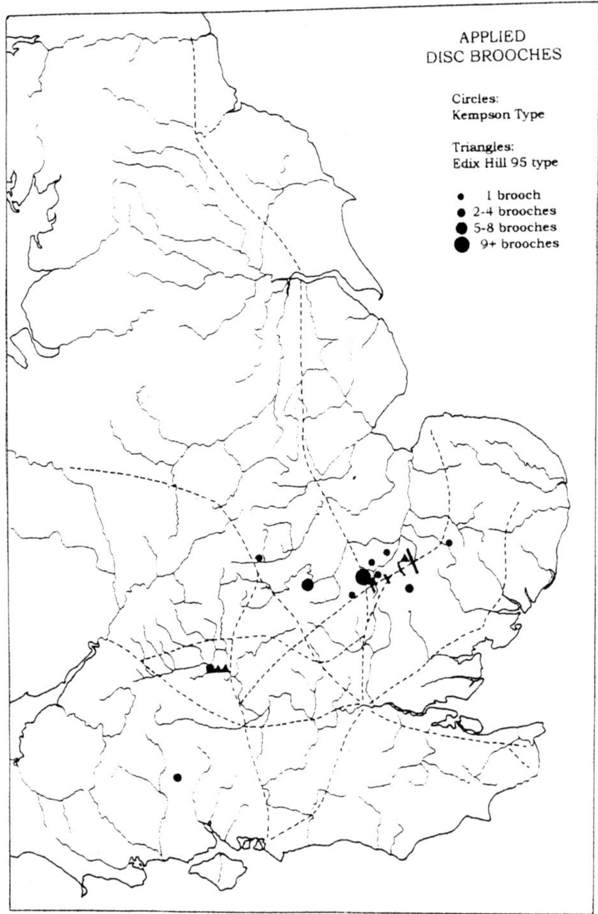

Fig. 3 Applied disc brooches. Circles: Kempston type; triangles: Edix Hill 95 type.

And so one can continue. The Cambridgeshire/southern-central Midlands zone now delineated is also home to the series of openwork disc brooches dominated by what are known as swastika brooches (Appendix 1; Fig. 9). This is particularly interesting because as – generally – relatively plain copper-alloy brooches, the openwork disc brooches appear qualitatively to be more

Fig. 4 (opposite) Applied disc brooches: Edix Hill, Cambs, grave 95 and parallels. (a)–(b) Edix Hill, Cambs, grave 95; (c) Little Wilbraham, Cambs, grave 158; (d)–(e) Abingdon, Oxon, grave B119; (f)–(g) Frilford, Oxon. (a)–(b) copyright Cambridgeshire Archaeology; (c) copyright the author; (d)–(g) copyright Ashmolean Museum, Oxford. 1:1.

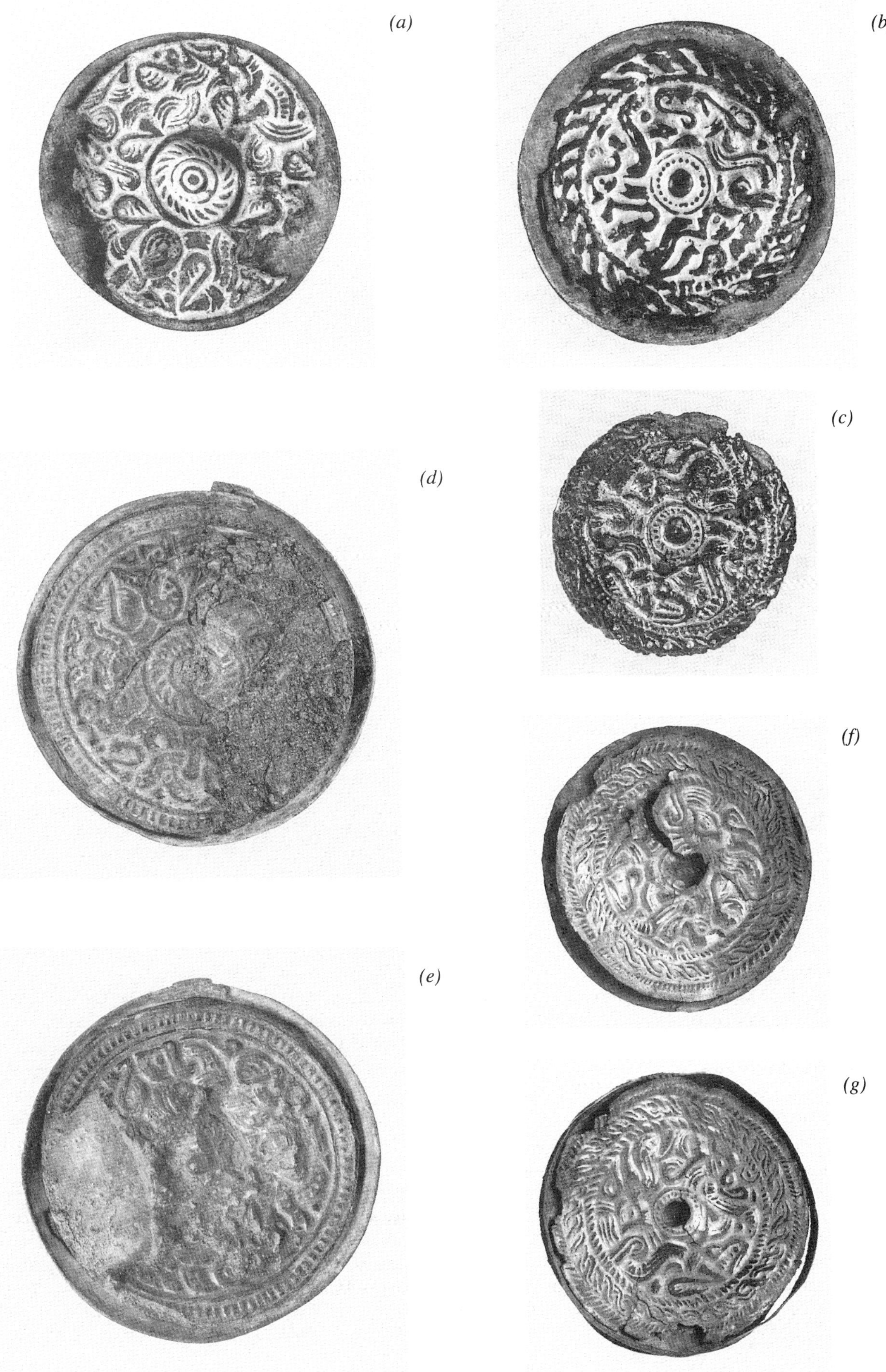
(a)
(b)
(c)
(d)
(f)
(e)
(g)

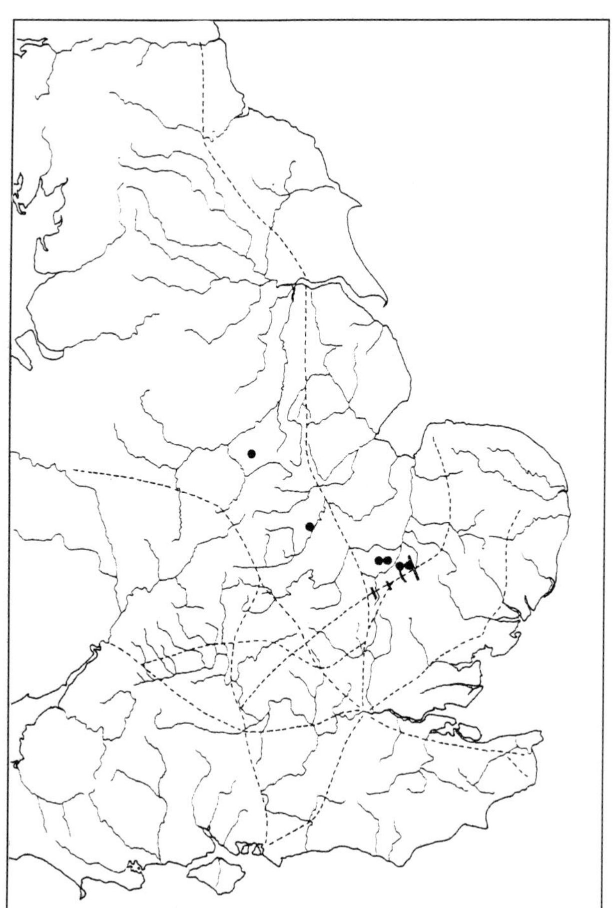

Fig. 5 Cruciform brooches, Typ Islip.

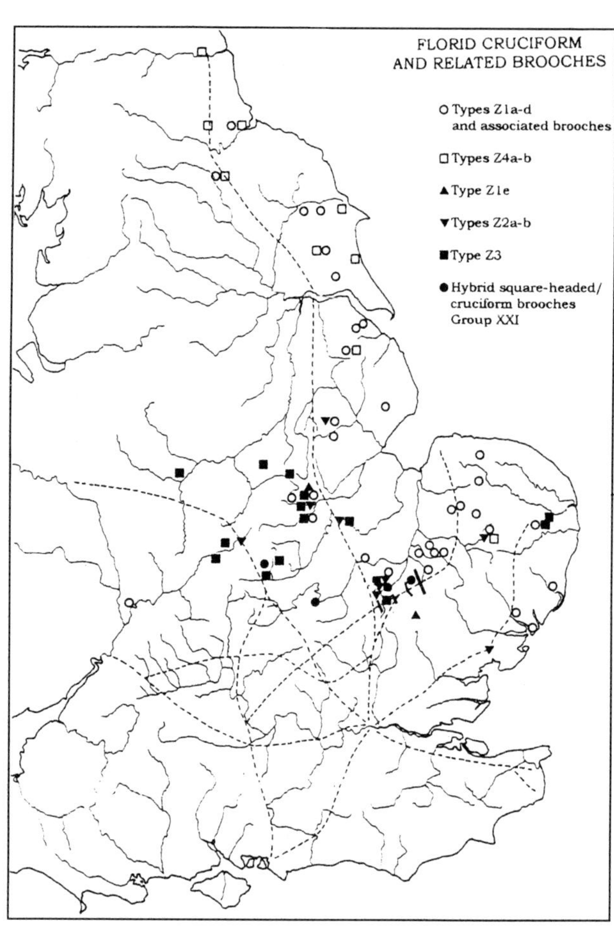

Fig. 6 Florid cruciform and related brooches.

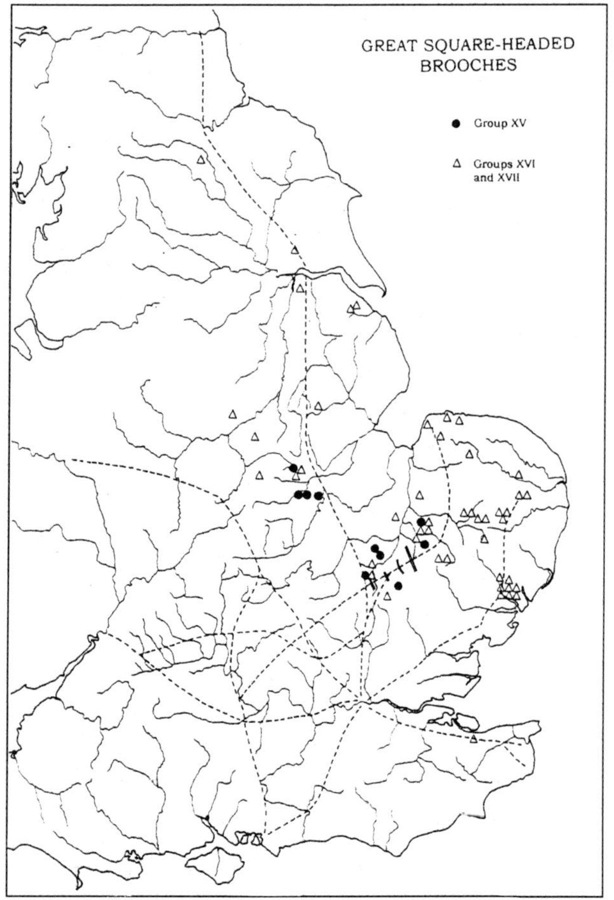

Fig. 7 Great square-headed brooches.

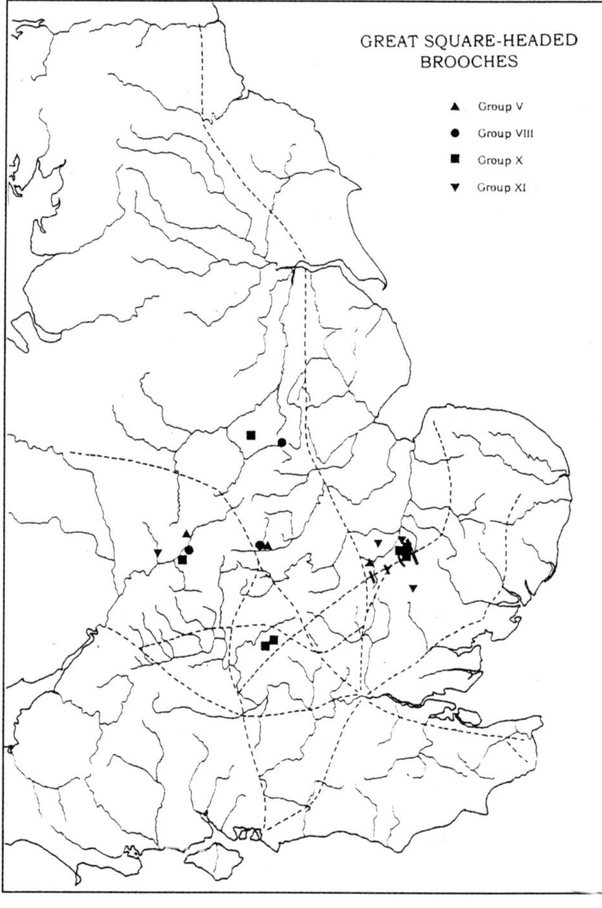

Fig. 8 Great square-headed brooches.

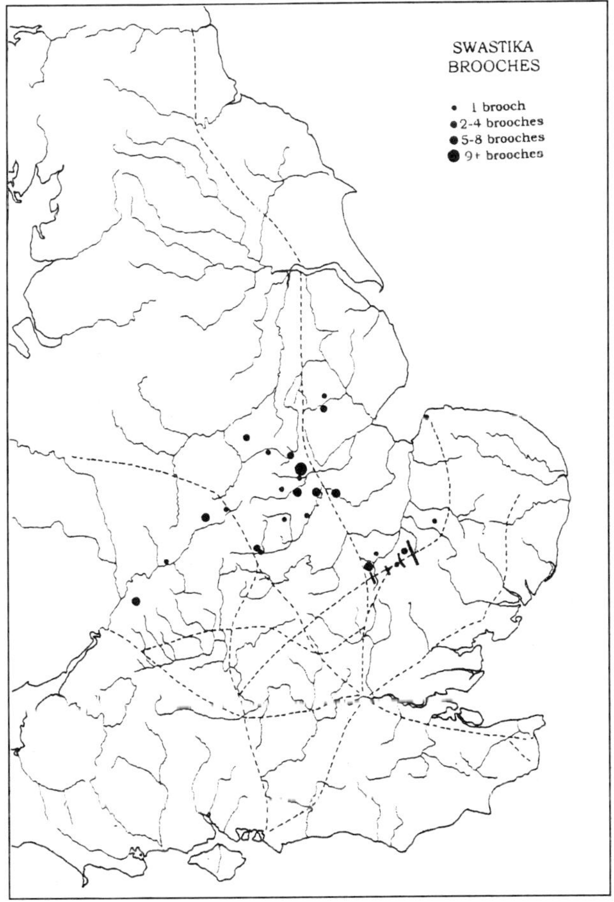

Fig. 9 Swastika brooches.

on a par with the simpler range of cruciform brooches, amongst which relevant regional groupings are far less evident, than with the showy great square-headed and florid cruciform brooches. Could, then, the distinctive form of the openwork brooches have had some symbolic significance to compensate for their lack of self-evident importance? The non-observance of the Cambridgeshire/East Anglia divide by the humbler range of artefact-types is further confirmed by the distribution of wrist-clasps (Hines 1993), practically none of which respect the boundary at all. Again there is one clear exception, in the form of the unusually elaborate clasps of form B 18g, which occur primarily within the Cambridgeshire/central Midlands zone (Hines 1993, fig. 119).

There is one quite different feature of the early Anglo-Saxon archaeology of the Cambridge region which must be considered, especially in relation to the area's wider geographical relations. This is the system of earthworks, the four Cambridgeshire Dykes (Heydon Ditch, Brent Ditch, Fleam Dyke and the Devil's Ditch), which lie across the Icknield Way over a stretch of some 30 km, at intervals varying from approximately 6 to 12 km (Fig. 10). Anglo-Saxon dates have long been suspected for some or all of these earthworks on the basis of stratigraphic relationships to Roman-period layers and recurrent associations with earlier Anglo-Saxon burials and pottery, but only recently has a convincing and useful absolute dating been achieved, in the form of radiocarbon evidence that the Fleam Dyke was constructed in the later fourth or fifth century and kept maintained or refurbished during the sixth (Fox 1923, 291–5; Lethbridge and Palmer 1929; Palmer and Lethbridge 1932; Lethbridge 1935; 1958; Hutchinson 1964; Malim *et al.*, forthcoming; cf. Axboe, this volume, for a broader comparative context).

All of the Dykes face south-west in the sense that they have their bank on the eastern side of the ditch. Although similar in design, there are sufficient differences in structural detail to suggest that they were not all built as part of a single initiative. Nonetheless, they form a system which is likely to have been operative within the Migration Period and which must have served to control movement through the southern part of the Cambridgeshire region, particularly to the benefit of the population of East Anglia. The easternmost of the Cambridgeshire Dykes, the Devil's Ditch, could practically be regarded as the boundary between the Cambridgeshire/southern-central Midlands and East Anglian/northerly Midlands zones just described (cf. Figs. 3 and 5–9). The majority of the early Anglo-Saxon burial sites – and therefore, we may infer, of early Anglo-Saxon settlement – in South Cambridgeshire lies to the flanks of the Dyke zone rather than close to the Icknield Way itself (Fig. 10). The one conspicuous exception is Little Wilbraham, situated between the Fleam Dyke and the Devil's Ditch and close to the former. It is to be hoped that it will be possible for more work to be done in the future to clarify the chronological sequence of the Dyke system in greater detail, and thus to correlate these features with the neighbouring cemeteries and their contents. At present, however, we can only report the conundrum that the rich and influential South Cambridgeshire region of the sixth century appears to have grown up in or around a broad border zone established for the benefit of the area to the north-east from which the Cambridgeshire area and associated sites in the central and southern Midlands became materially so distinctive.

Cambridgeshire and the southern and central Midlands: an interpretation

We can demonstrate that in respect of certain categories of material there was an extensive area comprising the Cambridge region and the central and southern Midlands in which common artefact-types were used in a way that implies a special network of connexions. The integrity of this zone is confirmed by the identification of an equivalent and complementary zone to the east and north, primarily in East Anglia and the territories immediately south and north of the Humber. Interestingly, the latter regional association is evidenced by very early types of wrist-clasps in England (Hines 1993, 43–6), implying that it was already in existence by the late fifth century.

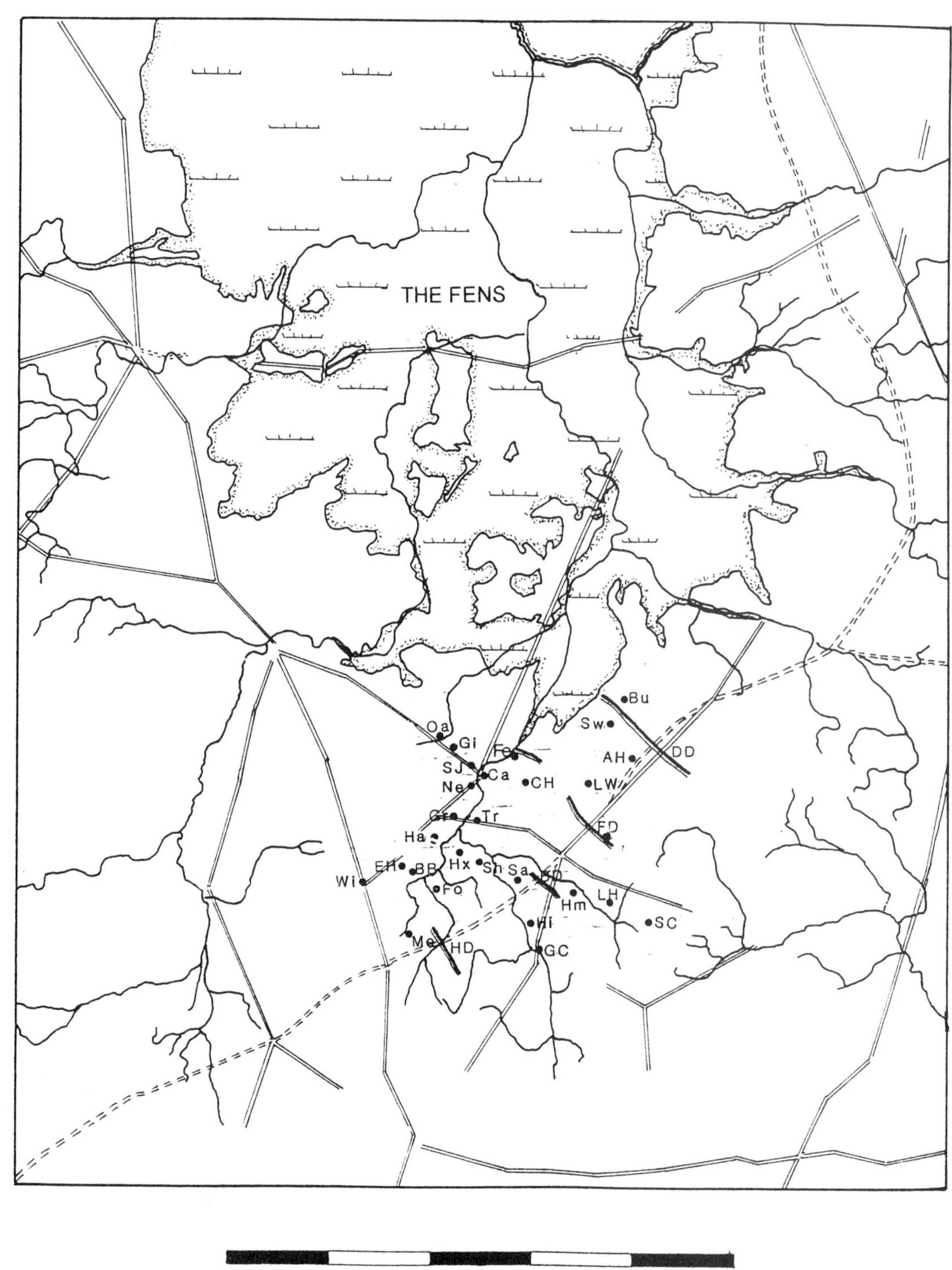

50 kilometres

Fig. 10 The Cambridgeshire Dykes and 5th- to 7th-century cemeteries in the Cambridge area. Key: Dykes – *HD: Heydon Ditch; BD: Bran Ditch; FD: Fleam Dyke; DD: Devil's Ditch.* Cemeteries – *AH: Allington Hill; BB: Barrington B; Bu: Burwell; Ca: Cambridge (scattered burials); CH: Cherry Hinton; EH: Edix Hill (= Barrington A); Fe: Fen Ditton; Fo: Foxton; GC: Great Chesterford; Gi: Girton College; Gr: Grantchester; Ha: Haslingfield; Hi: Hinxton; Hm: Hildersham; Hx: Hauxton; LH: Linton Heath; LW: Little Wilbraham; Ne: Newnham; Oa: Oakington; Sa: Sawston; SC: Shudy Camps; Sh: Shelford; SJ: St John's College Cricket Ground; Sw: Swaffham Prior; Tr: Trumpington; Wi: Wimpole.*

In some cases involving the relevant material from the Cambrigeshire/southern-central Midlands region we can point to a quantitative focus in the Cambridge area which suggests that here may be, in some sense, the source of the type (e.g. Fig. 3), while in other cases, particularly with the great square-headed brooches of group V and derivatives (Fig. 8), we can definitely state that the earliest known specimens and putative prototype forms of particular features occur in this area. This does not hold for every relevant type from the zone. Indeed the florid cruciform brooches appear quantitatively rather more characteristic of the Midlands than of the Cambrigeshire zone (Fig. 6). Nevertheless, we have clear reason to conclude that the Cambridge area occupied an important, culturally influential, place in relation to a region of considerable size in the sixth century. Our next task is to explore what the actuality of relations and organization within this zone may have been.

The simplest and therefore the safest level of reconstruction is a materialist one, remaining close to the material phenomena we are seeking to explain. An explanation in these terms looks to the economics of production and distribution, and postulates that the Cambridgeshire/Midlands region was an area supplied – predominantly if not monopolistically – from some particular source. Such an entity has in the past been referred to as a 'workshop area'. Regrettably we know very little indeed about the organization and location of production of the relevant ostentatious material: what we can infer from the distribution of artefacts most closely linked in a way that implies a common source, and from detritus of the production process such as moulds and trial or failed castings, seems to point towards local, on-site production, presumably by peripatetic craftsman, rather than centralized production at major sites such as Helgö in the Mälaren area of Sweden is widely believed to be (see Nordström ed. 1988; Ambrosiani 1992; Hines 1997, 41 n.2 and 205–22). A system of peripatetic producers certainly is not incompatible with the evidence, suggesting that our region was a zone in which high-quality jewellery production was dominated by a particular school – perhaps even family – of craftsmen.

However we cannot build an economic model solely on the supply side – we need to incorporate the market or customers of the producers into the formula. This is especially the case when we are discussing the most conspicuous jewellery, the use of which implies a claim to social rank and the deliberate demonstration of command over resources. Yet in circumstances in which there is high pressure for active display of this kind the consumers obviously had to take and use whatever they could get, and, without recapitulating the entire argument here, I would re-affirm my view that it may be appropriate, in the case of the sixth century, to allow for a high degree of independence for the producers, who were able to thrive by supplying goods that were in high demand to a (temporarily) bouyant market (see Hines 1994, but cf. also Straume 1986). At the same time we are aware that the consumption of goods in these circumstances is almost certain to have involved their exchange as well as their wearing and burial, and we have every reason to expect that female dress accessories in particular could have moved within social networks as social relationships were developed through exogamous marriage alliances.

Furthermore, while reconstruction is always ever more vulnerable the higher up the ladder of speculative inference one goes, we unquestionably have no good reason to presuppose that the folk of the sixth century acted solely as hard-headed utilitarians, devoid of imagination. The potential of material culture to develop and express ethno-cultural allegiance is always there, and the case for attributing some symbolic significance to certain major artefact classes has recently been explored and argued for, by myself in respect of wrist-clasps and their associated costume (Hines 1993, 90–3) and Tania Dickinson in respect of spiral-decorated cast saucer brooches (1991). Identities can be held at several different levels at once, of course, and can be changed. The issue to be explored here is not whether any historically recorded group-name can be assigned to any or all of the people(s) within the Cambridgeshire/southern-central Midlands network now identified. It is rather to draw attention to a particular attempt to harness the communal *potential* of this network in seventh-century Anglo-Saxon politics.

The Middle Anglian kingdom

According to Bede (*HE* III.21), a kingdom of the *Mediterranei Angli* or *Middilengli* was created by Penda of Mercia for his son Peada in the year 653 as part of a process of political manoeuvering which also saw a marriage between Peada and the daughter of Oswiu of Northumbria, and the baptism of Peada and thus conversion of the kingdom (cf. *HE* V.24; Dumville 1989a; Yorke 1990, 62–4 and 103–8; Kirby 1991, 65–6 and 88–96; Higham 1997, 231–4). Oswiu's son Alhfrith was also to marry Penda's daughter. The Middle Anglian kingdom (or kingship) itself appears to have been very shortlived, for there is no record of any king of the Middle Angles after the assassination of Peada at Easter less than three years later. As a geographical entity, however, Middle Anglia unquestionably continued not only to exist, but also to be important, especially as a separate diocese of the church, probably from the 670s onwards (cf. *HE* IV.3 and IV.12). The famous Wilfrid is recorded as having temporarily been bishop of the Middle Angles (*HE* IV.23; this claim is not explicitly confirmed by Eddius Stephanus' *Life of Wilfrid*, although there is ample evidence there of Wilfrid's good relations with the Mercian king, and his acceptance of such a position within his jurisdiction). From 737 to the later ninth century the see was located at Leicester (Dumville 1989a, 130–4).

Bede considered the Middle Anglian province to fill

up a solid block of Anglian territory between East Anglia in the east and Mercia to the west (*HE* I.15). Lindsey lay between Middle Anglia and the Humber. Various fragments of evidence combine to give us more idea of the extent of the province. The see itself seems to have been located close to the north-western border of the province with Mercia as – within what is now Leicestershire, though close to the border with Derbyshire – Breedon-on-the-Hill was apparently within Mercia proper (*HE* V.23). Lindsey stretched at least as far south as Lincoln and Partney (cf. *HE* II.16; Eagles 1989, 211), that is to the River Witham and the edge of the Fens, while to the east Bede categorically assigns 600 hides of land at Ely to East Anglia. While we cannot be certain of the fact, it seems highly plausible that this was the territory of the South Gyrwe, effectively annexed by East Anglia through the marriage of the East Anglian princess Æthelthryth with Tondberht, ruler of the minor group, that must have occurred sometime in the mid-seventh century (*HE* IV.19[17]).

To the south, Middle Anglia may have extended to the Thames in Oxfordshire. The first bishop of the Middle Angles (though not of them alone), an Irishman called Diuma, is reported as having been buried at *In Feppingum* within the province, and an eleventh-century list of the resting places of early English saints in the Liber Vitae of Hyde Abbey seems to identify this as Charlbury, Oxon (*HE* III.21; Birch ed. 1892, 89 lines 14–15). The eastern boundary between Middle Anglia and East Anglia may, of course, have moved in time, in periods either of successful East Anglian expansion or of Mercian dominance. It is, however, important to note that Chadwick's inference from a text of Felix's *Life of Guthlac*, which stated that most of the land around the Fens was regarded as belonging to Middle Anglia, is in fact based on a modified version of the text deriving from Peterborough in the tenth century, and that the probable original reading is *in meditullaneis Britanniae partibus* (in the central parts of Britain) – the possible meanings of which we need not discuss here (Chadwick 1907, 8–10; Colgrave 1956, esp. 86–7).

Discussions of the origins and character of the Middle Anglian kingdom have hitherto been the domain of historians, considering its role in the turbulent politics of mid-seventh-century England and the succeeding period of Mercian pre-eminence. Archaeology, however, may write an important introductory chapter, for the Middle Anglian kingdom coincides with, and to a very striking degree comprised, the sixth-century cultural network that has just been identified. It is also suggested, above, that this sixth-century entity existed as an economic, a social, and an ideological unit in contemporary life and thought. The Cambridge area, moreover, was clearly a centre of influence within this early network and may indeed have been its most important nucleus. Yet that area failed to share in the political developments of the seventh century in the sense that it did not continue as a political centre of any detectable significance, as we have seen. Can we account for this?

The Cambridge region in early English political history

One man's loss is proverbially another man's gain, and so it was in the struggle of early-medieval kingdoms for power and security. The eclipse of the Cambridge region on the national stage has to be accounted for within the overall pattern of English politics in the seventh century. This was a period in which three large kingdoms came to be the major players on the stage of Anglo-Saxon politics, Wessex, Mercia and Northumbria. Some smaller kingdoms in the east and south of England – East Anglia, Essex, Kent and Sussex – retained their identity and even the capacity to assert some varying degrees of independence, though the days in which any of these could aspire to national pre-eminence were gone by the close of the century (Higham 1995, esp. 112–30). Then the shift of real power and potential to the west and north was unchallengeable, and remained so until the disruptions of the Viking Age.

Sheer size is no doubt one factor that helps to explain the pre-eminence of the three large kingdoms. In the Tribal Hidage assessments, for instance, the territory of what is carefully specified as the original Mercia (*'þær mon ærest Myrcna hæt'*) is entered as 30,000 hides, the same as East Anglia, while Kent is counted only as 15,000 hides. In what is suspected to be a later addition, Wessex is assessed at 100,000 hides (Davies and Vierck 1974; Dumville 1989b). Reference to size alone, then, cannot be an adequate explanation, because both the origins of these large entities and the functional implications of their exceptional size require investigation. A very simplistic view could be that these kingdoms were able to grow because they alone were in a position to expand west- or northwards into British territory, and that it was with land that an ambitious king could both reward his military supporters and consolidate his own economic foundations. Such a view, however, implies that British territory was much more easily conquered than Anglo-Saxon in the seventh century – a situation that is far from obviously the case, whether we consider the records of seventh-century military history (such as they are) or the evidence for equivalent military organization and ideology on either side of the Anglo-Celtic cultural divide in Britain at this time (Dark 1994, 172–257; Evans 1997). It also ignores what I should now regard as the *probability* of there having been large enclaves of more British or sub-Roman character than Anglo-Saxon in fifth- to seventh-century southern and eastern Britain into which the consolidating local English polities almost certainly did expand: for example, Kent into Surrey and the Weald; Essex into the Chiltern region (Dark 1994, *passim*).

An alternative view that would allow the Celtic

populations (British and Scots) to have made a more positive and even voluntary contribution to the formation of Wessex, Mercia and Northumbria is worthy of further serious consideration: that these kingdoms arose as a result of, in a certain sense, an alliance between English and Celtic populations – or at the very least between English and Celtic aristocracies – in the relevant regions. This is hinted at by the connexions of the Northumbrian royal family with the Scottish powers, represented by the ecclesiastical centre of Iona (*HE* III.3; Dumville 1989c), and by the alliance between the Mercian Penda and Cadwallon of Gwynedd (cf. Higham 1995, 130–69). It is implied, I believe, even more strongly by the almost certainly British and Irish names occurring early on in the West Saxon dynasty – Cerdic, Cynric and Ceawlin – while an early but long-surviving name of the West Saxons as a people, OE *Gewisse*, MW *Iwis*, is widely suspected of being of Brythonic origin itself (e.g. Jenkins 1962; cf. Coates 1991). It is reasonable therefore to entertain the hypothesis that these three kingdoms in particular arose out an Anglo-Saxon/British merger, even though the visible cultural identity – that is the language and material culture – they adopted was overwhelmingly English. The basic co-operative principle would be the same even if these were really shotgun – perhaps one should say spearhead – marriages.

While, however, such a hypothesis may provide a more satisfactory general model of the origins of the three major kingdoms, it would not any more satisfactorily explain their success relative to the southern and eastern kingdoms if the presence of equivalent British populations and polities in the lowland zone is correctly postulated. Evidence of attempts by southern and eastern kingdoms to expand has already been noted, and historians have been particularly ready to infer attempts by the East Anglian kings to establish their hegemony over much of what was eventually to be the Middle Anglian zone in the early to middle seventh century (see, for instance, Kirby 1991, 63–6). Of especial relevance to the Cambridge region is the story recorded in the Anglo-Saxon Chronicle (MS A), where it is assigned to the year 571, of the Battle of *Bedcanford*, at which the West Saxon Cuthwulf is reported to have defeated a force of Britons and so to have won control of Eynsham, Benson, Aylesbury and what is probably now Limbury, within Luton.

Scholars who are optimistic about the ability of the late ninth-century Anglo-Saxon Chronicle to preserve some accurate information about events three centuries earlier, and who wish to identify elements of British survival in sub-Roman Britain, are usually willing to treat this annal seriously, and I shall cautiously align myself with them. There is a real coherency to the four sites mentioned (Fig. 11). Limbury, Aylesbury and Benson all lie on the Icknield Way, all of them on strategic crossing points: Limbury, the site of an ancient earthwork, by the source of the River Lea and where Watling Street crosses; Aylesbury where the Icknield Way crosses Akeman Street; Benson where the Icknield Way crosses the Thames, at the site of Wallingford, which etymologically seems to mean the ford of a people linked to a man called *Wealh*, 'Welshman' or 'Briton'. Eynsham is another crossing point of the Thames, giving access from the south to an area of North Oxfordshire which is linked to Aylesbury via Akeman Street and is rich in Roman-period villas.

Not surprisingly, it is also possible to construct a coherent case for dismissing this story as a later fabrication. Historians who do not believe that a British group could have controlled this area as late as the second half of the sixth century argue that if the West Saxon dynasty did conquer it then they must have done so from other Anglo-Saxon forces, and that the Chronicle version simply reflects a chronicler's assumption that any such battle should have been fought against Britons (thus Oman 1910, 229–31). This area was, moreover, disputed territory between West Saxon and Mercian kings between the mid-seventh century and the ninth, and the entry in the late ninth-century Parker Chronicle must be read as an assertion of the West Saxon dynasty's right to the land, established by primary conquest from the Britons.

If there is just one plausible historical reason to treat the record with some respect, it resides in the Saxon leader to whom the victory is ascribed, Cuthwulf. Cuthwulf is a one-hit wonder of Anglo-Saxon history; he did nothing else recorded in any other source. He appears elsewhere in Chronicle entries only as the son of Cuthwine and father of Ceolwald. If the story were a later conquest myth, why not attribute it to some more central figure in West-Saxon dynastic traditions? It is true that Cuthwulf is of historical importance as a putative ancestor of the great King Ine of Wessex, and also of Alfred the Great (*ASC*, MS A, Preface/Regnal List: Bately ed. 1986, 1–2); it is also true that Cuthwulf could have been the same person as a character known as Cutha, who has rather more to his credit in the sources. The Parker Chronicle, however, clearly thought of Cutha as a different person, giving him a different father and different son, and even placing him in a different generation.

While it is important to justify paying attention to the Chronicle entry for 571 by such arguments, one does not depend upon its truth to be able to assert that it is realistic. Evidence for at least mixed identities within the area concerned occurs in the form of place names – or, more accurately, place names which are based on personal names: for instance the **Weallingas* (of Wallingford) to the west of the area, and a Comberton, testifying to the use of the personal name *Cumbra* (which has the same root as *Cymro*, the ethnonym used for self-identification by the Britons: Charles-Edwards 1995, esp. 710–15) near Cambridge to the east. It is thus entirely credible that the population of this area could both have regarded itself, and have been regarded, as British rather than English, just as the annal implies – and this irrespective of the presence of a number of communities within it whose cultural practices were Anglo-Saxon. The most difficult problem for us is not, in fact, the nominal identity of the population of this area but rather the absence of any hard evidence either of a distinct sub-Roman or British culture there, or of any structure to the community, political or ecclesiastical. It is possible that a major British ecclesiastical centre survived at Verulamium throughout this period, and that the silence of English sources on this point reflects only their profound hostility to the British Church. But silent the sources are, and it is not a silence we can use constructively.

In this case, then, Anglo-Saxon historical tradition itself preserved the story of a lowland British enclave that was conquered and absorbed into an expanding Saxon kingdom in the late sixth century. Appropriately, in this case, it was the expansive and ultimately successful West Saxon dynasty that initially won the spoils, even if it were relatively soon to lose them to the Mercian king, only to retrieve them with the reconquest of the Danelaw and the unification of the kingdom. At this point, perhaps it would be satisfactory to invoke only the fortunes of war and the advantage of the venturesome to account for the success of a force from the west in winning control of the Icknield Way/Akeman Street zone rather than the inhabitants of the Cambridge region to the east. But the professional historian will always be happier with some more systematic explanation if any can be found. And from a slightly broader perspective it may indeed be possible to postulate a deep-seated cultural contrast between the eastern and the western communities that could give us a convincing reason why things should have turned out as they did.

An interesting parallel to the early eminence and influence of the Cambridge region can be found south of the Thames in the area immediately south of London – the southern district, or *Suðri-gē*, whose name yields modern Surrey. Here, indeed, a small but well-structured set of Anglo-Saxon sites is known from the later fifth century onwards, represented principally by cemeteries at focal points on Roman roads in the urban hinterland, for example Mitcham, Ewell, Beddington, Croydon and Orpington. Closely comparable to the influence of the Cambridge region reflected in complex sixth-century artefact-types is the position of brooches found at Dartford and Mitcham at the source of the profuse and long-lived Saxon group I of Anglo-Saxon great square-headed brooches (Hines 1997, 17–32). Yet the first time Surrey is mentioned in an Anglo-Saxon historical document, a charter of Frithuwold from 672x674, the area is designated a *regio* ruled by a *subregulus* of the King of Mercia (Blair 1989).

To attempt to account for the political eclipse of both of these early areas of influence as the Anglo-Saxon kingdoms grew, one may propose that in a certain sense they were the victims of their own early success. It is far from difficult to conceive of a situation in which early established communities – whether we call them Anglo-Saxon, British, sub-Roman or hybrid – were eventually too conservative to react to changing circumstances, or had social structures too well established for the revolutionary development of a kingship powerful enough to be successfully expansive. What is difficult, however, is to identify material or documentary evidence that could verify such a proposition.

The recent work on Anglo-Saxon cemeteries in the Cambridge region has, however, permitted us to review such evidence for social structure as can be gleaned from them. In keeping with the remainder of the country, there is evidence for increased social stratification with time, especially in the contrast between the relatively evenly furnished Migration-period graves (up to *circa* 570 AD) and the more selectively but sometimes very richly furnished Final-phase graves that succeed them. Yet the Cambridgeshire burial evidence of the seventh century scarcely supports any model of the real centralization of wealth and status in the hands of an aristocracy (Malim and Hines 1998, 319–27). The richer graves of this period are found at a number of different sites, a point nicely illustrated by the presence of the rare and certainly exclusive rite of bed burial at Cherry Hinton, Shudy Camps, and Edix Hill (Barrington A), as well as Ixworth in Suffolk (cf. Speake 1989, 98–115). Final-phase grave assemblages are known from the closely neighbouring sites of Barrington A, Barrington B, Hauxton and Melbourn, and it has proved impossible to establish any hierarchy between these communities; it is further likely that contemporary furnished burial was still being practised at Foxton, Haslingfield and possibly Trumpington too. Melbourn provides the best sample of burials that can all be dated to the Final Phase, and here there is no detectable social hierarchy of any significance within the buried population. The contemporary situation in Surrey is comparable, though different: there, rather than centralization, we face a phenomenon of diffusion, with late sixth- and seventh-century furnished burial represented at a very much larger number of (mostly small) burial sites than there are Migration-period cemeteries in the area (Poulton 1987, 197–201).

It has, admittedly, yet to be shown that the material-cultural record concurrently supports a view of greater social change and political centralization in the vital period of the late sixth and early seventh centuries in what were to be the major kingdoms. Wessex, in particular, will want careful and thorough analysis (as starting points, cf. Dickinson 1974 and Stoodley, this volume). More dramatic developments do, however, appear to be implied by the conspicuous appearance of rich barrow burials in or around the early seventh century in the Peak District, close to what must have been the heart of the original Mercia. Leslie Alcock's study of Anglian graves in Bernicia (1981), while sufficiently robust neither in terms of the samples compared quantitatively nor the consideration of chronology, nevertheless points unmistakably to the fact that the situation here in the far north of England was very

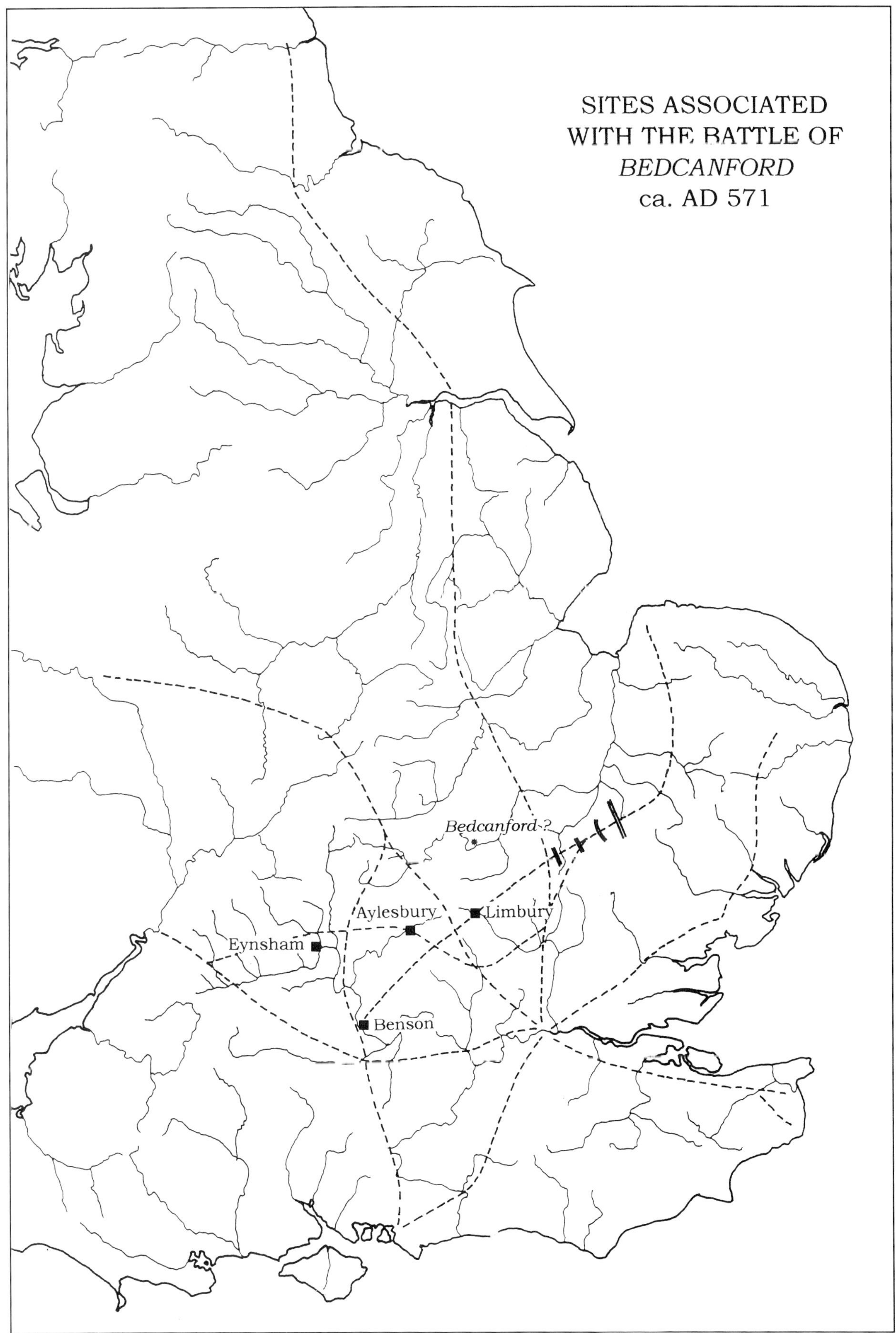

Fig. 11 Sites associated with the battle of Bedcanford ca. AD 571.

similar. If we do not have enough evidence to verify our proposition, there is at least sufficient to validate it as a hypothesis for evaluation in more detailed future work.

Reflections

If nothing else, the eclipse of the Cambridge region in Anglo-Saxon political and social history reminds us that success does not inevitably breed continuing success. A more useful general reflection to extract from this may be that progress towards state-formation under strong monarchial government may at its very source in the early Middle Ages have been more revolutionary than evolutionary, though this would not deny it some place in a consistent scheme of cultural development, especially one involving cultures in contact. It is hoped also that the foregoing study will stand as a good advertisement for the value of detailed regional and artefactual studies, even in relation to very general models of political history. The corpus of material evidence on which archaeology rests is, however, always subject to change, and archaeological reconstructions must thus always be provisional and inferential. The suggestions made above may eventually appear as misconceived as, to be honest, Leeds's earliest studies inevitably now do. Yet without Leeds's essays modern Anglo-Saxon archaeology would not have developed as far as it has, and it is in the spirit of recognition that *that* tradition is well worth preserving that the present essay is offered.

References

Åberg, N. 1926: *The Anglo-Saxons in Britain, during the Early Centuries after the Invasion* (Uppsala).

Addyman, P. V. and Biddle, M. 1965: 'Medieval Cambridge: recent finds and excavations', *Proc. Cambridge Antiq. Soc.* 58, 74–137.

Alcock, L. 1981: 'Quality or quantity: the Anglian graves of Bernicia', in Evison, V. I. (ed.), *Angles, Saxons, and Jutes* (Oxford), 168–86.

Ambrosiani, B. 1992: 'Birka – Kulturhistorisk bakgrund till ett program', in Mikkelsen, E. and Larsen, J. H. (eds), *Økonomiske og politiske sentra i Norden ca 400–1000 e.Kr.* (Oslo), 151–4.

ASC: = *Anglo-Saxon Chronicle*. See Bately ed. 1986.

Bassett, S. (ed.) 1989: *The Origins of Anglo-Saxon Kingdoms* (London).

Bately, J. M. (ed.) 1986: *The Anglo-Saxon Chronicle. A Collaborative Edition. Volume 3: MS A* (Cambridge).

Birch, W. de G. (ed.) 1892: *Liber Vitae: Register and Martyrology of New Minster and Hyde Abbey Winchester*, Hampshire Record Society (London and Winchester).

Blackburn, M. and Haigh, D. 1986: 'A Penny of Eadgar from Castle Hill, Cambridge', *Proc. Cambridge Antiq. Soc.* 75, 61–2.

Blair, J. 1989: 'Frithuwold's kingdom and the origins of Surrey', in Bassett ed. 1989, 97–107.

Bonser, M. J. 1998: 'Single finds of ninth-century coins from southern England: a listing', in Blackburn, M. A. S. and Dumville, D. N. (eds), *Kings, Currency and Alliances* (Woodbridge), 199–240.

Burnham, B. C. and Wacher, J. 1990: *The 'Small Towns' of Roman Britain* (London).

Chadwick, H. M. 1907: *The Origin of the English Nation* (Cambridge).

Charles-Edwards, T. M. 1995: 'Language and society among the Insular Celts AD 400–1000', in Green, M. J. (ed.), *The Celtic World* (London), 703–36.

Coates, R. 1991: On some controversy surrounding *Gewissae/Gewissei*, *Cerdic* and *Ceawlin*, *Nomina* 13, 1–12.

Colgrave, B. (ed. and trans.) 1956: *Felix's Life of Saint Guthlac* (Cambridge).

Colgrave, B. and Mynors, R. A. B. (eds and trans) 1969: *Bede's Ecclesiastical History of the English People* (Oxford).

Dark, K. R. 1994: *Civitas to Kingdom: British Political Continuity 300–800* (Leicester).

Davies, W. and Vierck, H. 1974: 'The contexts of Tribal Hidage: social aggregates and settlement patterns', *Frühmittelalterliche Stud.* 8, 223–93.

Dickinson, T. M. 1974: *Cuddesdon and Dorchester-on-Thames*, British Archaeological Reports 1 (Oxford).

Dickinson, T. M. 1991: 'Material culture as social expression: the case of Saxon saucer brooches with running spiral decoration', *Studien zur Sachsenforschung* 7, 39–70.

Dumville, D. N. 1989a: 'Essex, Middle Anglia, and the expansion of Mercia in the South-East Midlands', in Bassett (ed.) 1989, 123–40.

Dumville, D. N. 1989b: 'The Tribal Hidage: an introduction to the texts and their history', in Bassett (ed.) 1989, 225–30.

Dumville, D. N. 1989c: 'The origins of Northumbria: some aspects of the British background', in Bassett (ed.) 1989, 213–22.

Eagles, B. 1989: 'Lindsey', in Bassett (ed.) 1989, 202–12.

Evans, S. S. 1997: *Lords of Battle: Image and Reality of the* Comitatus *in Dark-Age Britain* (Woodbridge).

Farley, M. and Hines, J. 1997: 'A great square-headed brooch fragment from Buckinghamshire', *Medieval Archaeology* 40 (for 1996), 211–14.

Fox, C. 1923: *The Archaeology of the Cambridge Region* (Cambridge).

Gale, D. 1989: 'The seax', in Hawkes, S. C. (ed.), *Weapons and Warfare in Anglo-Saxon England* (Oxford), 71–83.

Härke, H. 1993: *Angelsächsische Waffengräber des 5. bis 7. Jahrhunderts* (Bonn).

HE: = *Historia Ecclesiastica Gentis Anglorum*. See Colgrave and Mynors (eds) 1969.

Higham, N. 1995: *An English Empire: Bede and the Early Anglo-Saxon Kings* (Manchester).

Higham, N. 1997: *The Convert Kings: Power and Religious Affiliation in Early Anglo-Saxon England* (Manchester).

Hines, J. 1993: *Clasps: Hektespenner: Agraffen* (Stockholm).

Hines, J. 1994: 'North-sea trade and the proto-urban sequence', Archaeologia Polona 32, 7–26.

Hines, J. 1997: *A New Corpus of Anglo-Saxon Great Square-Headed Brooches* (London).

Hunn, A., Lawson, J. and Farley M. 1994: 'The Anglo-Saxon cemetery at Dinton, Buckinghamshire', *Anglo-Saxon Stud. Arch. and Hist.* 7, 85–148.

Hutchinson, P. 1964: 'Finds from the Fleam Dyke, Fen Ditton', *Proc. Cambridge Antiq. Soc.* 56–57, 125–6.

Jenkins, M. G. 1962: 'Gevissae ac Iwis: dwy ddrychiolaeth', *Bull. Board Celtic Stud.* 20, 1–11.

John, E. 1996: *Reassessing Anglo-Saxon England* (Manchester).

Jonsson, K. 1987: *The New Era: The Reformation of Late Anglo-Saxon Coinage* (Stockholm).

Kennett, D. H. 1971: 'Applied brooches of the Kempston type at St John's, Cambridge', *Proc. Cambridge Antiq. Soc.* 63, 27–9.

Keynes, S. 1985: 'King Athelstan's books', in Lapidge, M. and Gneuss, H. (eds), *Learning and Literature in Anglo-Saxon England* (Cambridge), 143–201.

Kirby, D. P. 1991: *The Earliest English Kings* (London).

Leeds, E. T. 1912: 'The distribution of the Anglo-Saxon saucer brooch in relation to the Battle of Bedford, A.D. 571', *Archaeologia* 63, 159–202.

Leeds, E. T. 1926: 'The West Saxon invasion and the Icknield Way', *History*, N. S. 10, 96–109.

Leeds, E. T. 1933: 'The early Saxon penetration of the Upper Thames area', *Antiq. J.*, 13, 229–51.

Leeds, E. T. 1945: 'The distribution of the Angles and Saxons, archaeologically considered', *Archaeologia* 91, 1–106.

Lethbridge, T. C. 1935: 'The Car Dyke, the Cambridgeshire ditches, and the Anglo-Saxons', *Proc. Cambridge Antiq. Soc.* 35, 90–6.

Lethbridge, T. C. 1958: 'The riddle of the dykes', *Proc. Cambridge Antiq. Soc.* 51, 1–5.

Lethbridge, T. C. and Palmer, W. M. 1929: 'Excavations in the Cambridgeshire dykes. VI. Bran Ditch. Second report', *Proc. Cambridge Antiq. Soc.* 30, 78–93.

Malim, T. 1992: 'Barrington Anglo-Saxon cemetery, 1989', *Proc. Cambridge Antiq. Soc.* 79, 45–62.

Malim, T. and Hines, J. 1998: *The Anglo-Saxon Cemetery at Edix Hill, (Barrington A), Cambridgeshire*, CBA Research Report 112 (London).

Malim, T., Penn, K., Robinson, B., Wait, G. and Welsh, K. 1998: 'New evidence on the Cambridgeshire dykes and Worsted Street Roman road', *Proc. Cambridge Antiq. Soc.*, 85, 27–122.

Metcalf, D. M. 1984: 'Monetary circulation in southern England in the first half of the eighth century', in Hill, D. and Metcalf, D. M. (eds), *Sceattas in England and on the Continent*, BAR British Series 128 (Oxford).

Mortimer, C. M. 1990: 'Some Aspects of Early Medieval Copper-alloy Technology, as illustrated by the Anglian Cruciform Brooch', unpublised D. Phil. thesis, University of Oxford.

Needham, G. I. 1966: *Ælfric: Lives of Three Old English Saints* (London).

Neville, R. C. 1852: *Saxon Obsequies* (London).

Nordström, H.-Å. (ed.) 1988: *Thirteen Studies on Helgö* (Stockholm).

Oman, C. 1910: *England Before the Norman Conquest* (London).

Palmer, W. M. and Lethbridge, T. C. 1932: 'Further excavations at the Bran Ditch', *Proc. Cambridge Antiq. Soc.* 32, 54–7.

Poulton, R. J. 1987: 'Saxon Surrey', in Bird, J. and D. G. (eds), *The Archaeology of Surrey to 1540* (Guildford), 197–222.

Reichstein, J. 1975: *Die kreuzförmige Fibel* (Neumünster).

Rollason, D. 1989: 'St Cuthbert and Wessex: the evidence of Cambridge, Corpus Christi College MS 183', in Bonner, G., Rollason, D. and Stancliffe, C. (eds), *St Cuthbert, His Cult and His Community to A.D. 1200* (Woodbridge), 413–24.

Sawyer, P. H. 1978: *From Roman Britain to Norman England* (London).

Shetelig, H. (ed.) 1940: *Viking Antiquities in Great Britain and Ireland*, 5 parts (Oslo).

Speake, G. 1989: *A Saxon Bed Burial on Swallowcliffe Down* (London).

Stafford, P, 1989: *Unification and Conquest: A Political and Social History of England in the Tenth and Eleventh Centuries* (London).

Stenton, F. M. 1947: *Anglo-Saxon England*, 2nd ed. (Oxford).

Straume, E. 1986: 'Smeden i jernalderen, bofast–ikke bofast, høy eller lav status', *Universitetets Oldsaksamling Årbok* 1984/1985, 45–58.

Swanton, M. (ed. and trans.) 1975: *Anglo-Saxon Prose* (London).

Taylor, H. M. and Taylor, J. 1965: *Anglo-Saxon Architecture*, 2 vols. (Cambridge).

Yorke, B. 1990: *Kings and Kingdoms of Early Anglo-Saxon England* (London).

Appendix 1: List of swastika brooches (Map, Fig. 9)

'Pair' does not imply that the brooches are a matching pair. 'n.y.a.' = not yet accessioned.

Site	*Museum*
Barrington A, Cambs g. 8	Cambridge Z42255
Barrington A, Cambs	BM 76,2–12,37
Barrington A (Edix Hill), Cambs g. 19b (pair)	Cambridge [n.y.a.]
Barrington A (Edix Hill), Cambs (2 brooches)	Cambridge [n.y.a.]
Fen Ditton, Fleam Dyke, Cambs	Cambridge D1964.3
Haslingfield, Cambs	Ashmolean 1909.20
Little Wilbraham, Cambs g. 116 (pair)	Neville 1852 (present whereabouts unknown)
Little Wilbraham, Cambs	Cambridge 1883.512
Woodston, Cambs (8 brooches, including four in 2 matching pairs)	Peterborough L489–493 & 1026–7
Mildenhall, Suffolk	BM 1927,12–12,15
Hunstanton, Norfolk	Norwich
Duston, Northants (2 brooches)	Northampton
Islip, Northants	Kettering
Nassington, Northants g. 11 (pair)	Peterborough
Nassington, Northants g. 15 (pair)	Peterborough
Nassington, Northants	Oundle School
Newnham, Northants (2 brooches)	Northampton
Thorpe Malsor, Northants	Kettering
Upton, Northants	Northampton
Wakerley, Northants g. 30 (pair)	Northampton
Wakerley, Northants g. 44 (pair)	Northampton
Wakerley, Northants g. 57	Northampton
Wakerley, Northants g. 78 (pair)	Northampton
Baginton, Warwicks (6 brooches)	Coventry A/1013/30–33 & 36–7
Bidford-on-Avon, Warwicks	Stratford-upon-Avon
Churchover, Warwicks	Ashmolean 1935.618
Beckford A, Worcs g. 9 (pair)	Birmingham
Beckford B, Worcs g. 48 (pair)	Birmingham
Beckford B, Worcs g. 80	Birmingham
Ruskington, Lincs	Lincoln
Sleaford, Lincs (pair)	BM 83,4–1,175/5
Sleaford, Lincs g. 182	BM 83,4–1,387
Melton Mowbray, Leics	Melton
Empingham, Rutland g. 15	Leicester
Empingham, Rutland g. 17 (three)	Leicester
Empingham, Rutland g. 27 (pair)	Leicester
Empingham, Rutland g. 73 (pair)	[Missing]
Empingham, Rutland g. 90 (pair)	Leicester
Empingham, Rutland g. 95 (pair)	[Missing]
Empingham, Rutland g. 115 (pair)	Leicester
Empingham, Rutland g. 131 (pair)	Leicester
Glaston, Rutland g. 9	Oakham
Market Overton, Rutland (4 brooches)	Oakham OS9, 31 (two brooches), 51
North Luffenham, Rutland	Oakham OS95
Broughton Lodge, Notts g. 110	University of Nottingham
Broughton Lodge, Notts	Nottingham

Myth and art: a passport to political authority in Scandinavia during the Migration Period

Lotte Hedeager[1]

The collapse of the Roman Empire in the West had dramatic consequences for Germanic and Scandinavian societies. Among them was the collapse of political authority based on centuries-old relations with the Roman Empire. The Post-Roman World saw instead the emergence of new types of political authority rooted in a Germanic and Scandinavian cultural identity which characterised the Migration Period. I suggest in this paper that this was also based upon a new or re-invented religious cosmology.

Religions and political authority

The political landscape in the Migration Period was based on a network of invisible threads. Political power was not just a matter of military skill, landed property or the possession of gold. Even if landed property, gold objects and ability as a warrior were necessary preconditions, they were not sufficient; political power was based on more hidden structures anchored in authority, which was embedded in the cosmological order.

It meant that access to the Supernatural World, to the world of the gods and ancestors, was crucial. This contact was controlled through the ritual system and magic – the key to the Other World. Acceptance from the gods and the ancestors was necessary to get access to secret knowledge – that is wisdom – which was fundamental for exercising authority, because authority is linked up with reliability (Chang 1983). As political power is legitimized within a given cosmology, the elite always enters into a symbiotic relationship with the official religion. This is nothing new. Two things are interesting, however: first, to locate those periods of change when a new religion and political cosmology takes over and, second, to analyse the ways in which this materializes in the archaeolgical and historical evidence. From this we may gain new insight into the relationship between religion and political power and its material manifestations (de Marrais, Castillo and Earle 1996).

Such changes can be studied in the Middle Ages when kings and the warrior elite used Christianity and the Catholic Church to legitimize a new political order. But it also happened in the Migration Period, when another elite created a new political system which was legitimized in the Asir faith and the Odin cult.

Odin was king of the Asir. According to Snorri Sturluson he was gifted with all the abilities and all the skills which were necessary to be a good king: he was an excellent warrior and therefore rich in gold – that means he could create alliances and gain political power; he knew the magic of the runes and communicated with death – that means he had access to knowledge about the future; and as the last of his three main functions he was the protector of scaldic poetry because the myths and the holy stories represented the sacred – and indisputable – worldview on which the authority of the elite was based (*Ynglinga Saga*, chap. 5–8).

In the following I want to demonstrate how the old Norse Odin cult can be explained as the central religious and mythological element in the creation of political authority in Migration period Scandinavia. By confronting the written evidence from the Old Norse literature (that means roughly from the thirteenth century) and the iconography from the Migration Period, it is possible to argue for a religious universe built up around a strong shamanic tradition as the ideological anchoring of – presumably – royal power in the fifth and sixth century.[2]

'*Sejd*' and shamanism

The Old Norse literature, written in a Christian context, mostly lacks concrete information about pagan rituals, which is understandable in the light of the secrecy surrounding the magic which only a few commanded. But most of the written sources refer – whether implicitly or explicitly – to the 'operational' Nordic magic named *sejd*. The many different stories together create a picture of the course of events in Nordic magic and the mystical meaning of *sejd* (Strömbäck 1935; 1970).

It is clear that the actual process of *sejd*[3] was to pass into a state of ecstasy, the body becoming lifeless, releasing the soul to travel freely in time and space. It was then possible for the free soul to become 'wild' and cause harm, or to travel to the Other World to obtain insight and knowledge about the past or the future. This shape-changing was brought about through songs and recitation carried out by a group of assistants gathered around the one enacting the *sejd*. The transcendence could only cease through enticing the soul back to the body. This was done by a specific 'calling song'.

It is quite clear from the written sources that *sejd* and ecstasy were not separated from the shape-changing, that is the soul was released from the body to take on another form. This was always in a zoomorphic state and in this state the soul ventured upon journeys to the realm of the dead or to all corners of the world. The indisputable connection between *sejd*, ecstasy and soul-journeys is identical with the religious complex known as shamanism.[4]

Shamanism is a religious complex which traditionally is related to the so-called primitive religions (e.g. Eliade 1989; Campbell 1983, 156–269; Vitebsky 1995). But shamanism has existed as a central element in complex societies as well – among others it played a central role in ancient Chinese politics, and it is found among the Mongols and other Asiatic step-nomads (e.g. Chang 1983; Morgan 1994).

Shamanism is not in itself a well-defined religion but rather a religious complex; although there are variations there are some central ideas that recur (e.g. Eliade 1989; Bäckmann and Hultkrantz 1978; Campbell 1983). The shaman is the dominant central character – diviner and medicine-man and the only person within a society capable of contacting the supernatural world, attained through the state of ecstasy and soul-journeys.

Shamanism is unthinkable without the terms 'guardian spirits' and 'helping spirits', whose tasks are to protect the shaman on his dangerous soul-journeys (Bäckmann and Hultkrantz 1978, 43). The 'guardian spirits' are anthropomorphic; they call the shaman into service and assist him with their counsel. The 'helping spirits' have a subordinate position and are at the shaman's disposal. They are zoomorphic, and they have a number of different functions: the reindeer bull, elk or stallion are the most important and should protect the shaman's soul on its dangerous journeys by fighting the enemy spirits of other shaman; the bird is sent to the watching spirits to give the shaman advice; and the fish or snake should guide the shaman to the underworld with the souls of the dead and protect the shaman's life throughout his soul-journey. In his journey to the Other World the shaman is usually presented as riding on some bird or four-legged animal (Eliade 1989, 156; Hultkrantz 1987).

Communication with the supernatural world was accomplished through the trance, which was initiated when the shaman's helping spirit appeared.

The shaman's position in society was powerful; he was perceived to be the only one in human society that could communicate with the Other World and the ancestral spirits. His power was great and his talents feared. The shaman's initiation, that is the ritual transformation, was the decisive factor when choosing the person with the necessary transcendental powers needed to become a shaman. Initiation was usually combined with extreme physical suffering and long periods of fasting. Only through self-afflicted 'death' and return to life did a person acquire the insight necessary to become a shaman.

Odin – '*sejd*' master – the great shaman

In the Late Nordic mythology Odin appears as the Almighty Father and King of the Asir Gods, but this cannot hide the fact that he is the prototype of the original shaman, the master of *sejd* and its foremost practitioner. He is the furious ecstasy-god (his name means 'rage', 'wildness'). The nine magical acts which Snorri Sturluson ascribes to Odin in the *Ynglinga saga* (chap. 6–7) portray him as the great shaman among others; he can appear in whatever shape he chooses whilst his body lies in a death-like dormancy; he commands the magic of the weather and with words he can extinguish fire, calm the seas and turn the winds; he can communicate with the dead; he possesses oral magic – *galdrar* (spells and chants) (Halvorsen 1960) – and the magic of writing, the runes; and he is the master of *sejd*.

Other typical shamanic elements also can be found. *Hávamál* (stanza 138–140) tells how Odin, through self-sacrifice and self-afflicted torture, attained maximum power, that is made himself master of the runic magic. He sacrificed himself, by drilling himself with a spear and by hanging in the World Tree, the holy tree, for nine stormy days and nights and through such suffering he won wisdom, magic, the art of the runes and powerful spells. With help from runic letters he could force hanged men's tongues to talk, that is he could talk with the dead.

The many shapes of Odin appear to be of a particularly complicated nature. Odin is lord of the realm of the dead, he is lord of war and lord of inspiration, magic and wisdom. He is, however, more than anything the great sorcerer, the master of *sejd*. The runic letters and the magic of the mysterious belong to Odin.

Odin's connection with *sejd* is indisputable as are his shamanic characteristics, indications of which, whether deliberate, occasional or indirect can be found throughout the texts. The myths and stories about Odin and the *sejd* cannot therefore be written off as being sporadically surviving, pagan wreckage, but ought to be accepted for what they are: shadows of a powerful shamanic complex in Scandinavia during the Late Iron Age.

Myth and art

Hávamál's description of Odin where he hangs in Yggdrasil (the World Tree) for nine days and nine nights, injured and fasting, is at the same time a description of shaman initiation, with the World Tree as an important element.[5] Only through sacrificing himself to himself, by hanging, followed by self-afflicted torture and a ritual death was Odin capable of 'catching' his power, the runic letters, that is winning the insight that was necessary for him to become master of the magic. Thus the runic letters became a symbol of magic, of what in reality made Odin what he was, the greatest shaman, that is the greatest god – king of the Asir.

The myth illustrates in an archetypal way shamanism's nature, with ecstasy as the means for attaining sacred knowledge (cf. Buchholz 1971,19), and it confirms and explains *sejd* as a central magical practice in Nordic pagan life. Seen through the lenses of the myth the runic letters become something other then a primitive alphabet[6] – they represent magic, being the key to Odin's feared power because they could force dead men's tongues to talk. The word '*rún/rúnar*' then also means 'secret knowledge, knowledge of writing in verse', that is wisdom (Dumézil 1969, 52).

Over and above its phonetic importance each rune also had a symbolical value, being synonymous with a name or term connected to the mythology. Thus every rune had its own magical meaning and the runic inscriptions contained a twofold message. Magic, that is rune art, was lethal to society and had to be monopolised and controlled. In many societies, both the magic of the written word itself and the ability to read and write have often been interpreted as mystical crafts that reveal divination, open the secrets of sacred writing, provide the efficacy of amulets and holy talismans, and preserve ancestral knowledge. Literacy has been the main qualification of many holy men and learned scholars (Helms 1988:12).

Odin was the possessor and the true owner of this feared power, which the secret knowledge created (Dumézil 1969:52), and Snorri says that Odin taught the blood-gods almost everything he knew and that they were only second to him in their knowledge (*Ynglinga saga*, chap. 7). It is therefore easy to come to the conclusion that the earliest rune-art must have been connected to Odin's sacrificial priests,[7] whom Snorri later calls the blood-gods and whom anthropologists and historians of religion call shamans.[8]

The most important aspects of shamanism are identical to the central elements of the Odin cult and are possibly its oldest traces: ecstasy, the journeys to the Other World and an 'ideology of transformation'. The Old Norse sources are silent, however, about the last, central term, the zoomorphic helping spirits,[9] with the exceptions, of course, of Odin's two ravens and his steed Slejpner, which all appear in an early Viking 'disguise' (Davidson 1990,142).

But what the myths do not convey, the figurative symbolism of the Migration Period's gold bracteates reveal – the archetypal representation of the shaman's, presumably Odin's, journey to the Other World.[10] The soul is depicted as a man's head, but often in bird disguise; the hair is often styled as that of a bird's head. Odin is accompanied by his guardian spirits, the large, often horned, four-legged animal, the bird that will make the journey to the realm of the dead possible, and, on some occasions, a fish or a snake. Last but not least the specific symbol of Odin's power – the runic letters – are depicted (Figs.1–2). That the Nordic gold bracteates originated from medallions of the Byzantine Emperors adds to their strong symbolic importance by drawing a comparison between the Roman emperors and the Asir king.

Motifs that relate to the soul-journeys of Odin are the most common on the gold bracteates,[11] but other motifs known from Nordic mythology are also to be found, for

Fig. 1 Gold bracteate from Skrydstrup, Denmark (Hauck 1985–89, catalogue nr. 166). No scale.

Fig. 2 Gold bracteate from the island of Funen, Denmark (Hauck 1985–89, catalogue nr. 58). No scale.

Fig. 3 Gold bracteate from Fakse, Denmark (Hauck 1985–89, catalogue nr. 51). No scale.

Fig.4 Gold bracteate from Trollhättan, Sweden (Hauck 1985–89, catalogue nr.190). No scale.

example, Balder's death (Ellmers 1970:210; Hauck 1978:210; 1994) (Fig. 3) and Tyr who lost his hand in the jaw of Fenris-wolf (*Snorri's Edda,* chap. 24 and 33) (Oxenstierna 1956:36, Ellmers 1970:202,220; Hauck 1978:210) (Fig. 4). Both appear to belong to central myths of the fifth and sixth centuries.

Although the span in time between the written myths and the iconography are several hundred years, it does not seem too daring to regard the gold bracteates as confirmation of the central religious complex traced in the Old Norse literature, namely that the cult of Odin was built up around a strong shamanic tradition, intact from the beginning of the Migration Period to the end of the Viking Age, that is for the duration of more than 500 years.

A passport to political authority

In religious ceremonies among the Scandinavian peoples animal symbolism took a central place because the animals were the link between the living world and the supernatural. Without the helping spirits the shaman's soul-journey was judged to fail, and the animals thus came to symbolise contact with the Supernatural World. This contact was crucial for developing and keeping political authority, and therefore the iconography with the animal symbols became decisive for demonstrating political authority. It was in this environment – during the creation of political authority in the Migration Period – that the

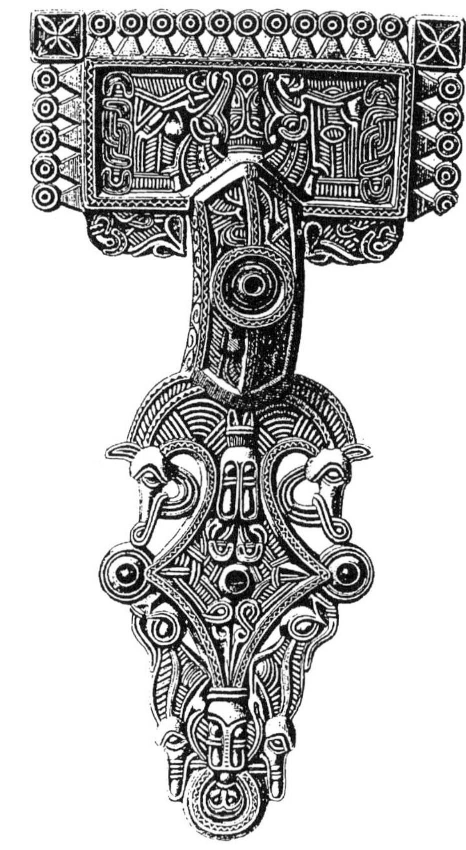

Fig. 5 Silver brooch with early animal style from Zealand, Denmark (after Åberg 1925 fig.161). No scale.

animal style was developed as a characteristic part of the elite's claim on wisdom and ideological supremacy (Fig. 5). Because of this, the animal styles continued as an important part of the symbol language among the Nordic elite up until the end of the Viking Age, when Christianity was accepted as the new ideology (Hedeager 1996; 1997; forthcoming a and b).

Thus, the passport to political power/authority was composed of the same three elements which Snorri Sturluson described as crucial for Odin to be king of the Asir (Fig. 6):

- *political alliances* were created through generosity – that is by gift giving, including gold objects, marriage and feasts – and ultimately through the fortunes of war.
- *wisdom* was created through access to the Supernatural World – that is through rituals, sacrifices, soul-journey, divination, iconography and runes. Wisdom also included the ability to judge in specific cases.
- *cosmology* was created through holy stories and origin myths – that is through scaldic poetry and performance.

All three elements can be found connected to 'the kingship in the hall', as Frands Herschend has described it (Herschend 1998), and they are represented by the symbol of sovereignty *par excellence*, the decorated bronze-and silver helmets from, for example, Sutton Hoo, Vendel and Valsgärde (Hedeager 1997, fig. 8). These stamp-ornamented helmets with figurative motifs in *Pressbleche* gather the three crucial elements for political power: the helmet itself illustrates a warrior-identity and access to political alliances; the figurative scenes illustrate the myths and holy stories, that is access to cosmology; and the animals on the helmet – the bird placed with its wings as protective eyebrows and the snake stretching from the back of the helmet to the front – mean access to the Supernatural World, that is wisdom.

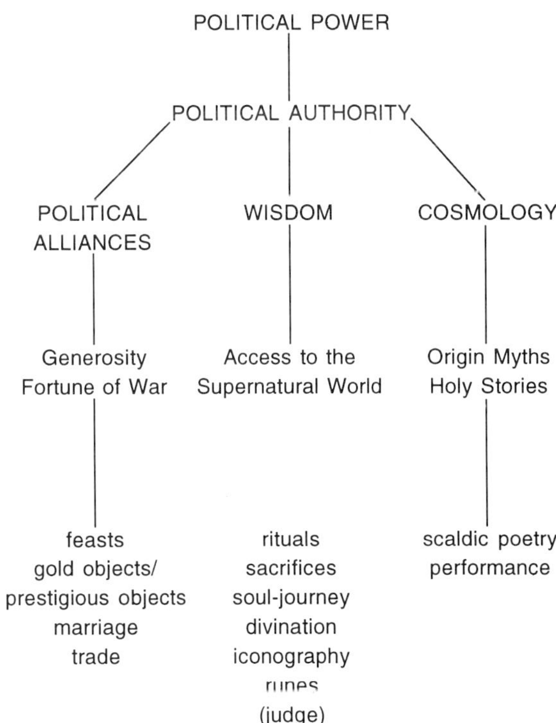

Fig. 6 Ranking of central elements and levels in creation of political power.

It was this network of almost invisible threads, so clearly illustrated on the prestigious helmets from the Late Iron Age, that together formed the ideological base for creating political authority in Migration Period Scandinavia.

Notes

1. Translation: Fiona Campbell
2. That means writen down around 1200. *The Poetic Edda* with *Hávamál* and *Voluspa* are at least several hundred years older. Concerning the use of sources from such a wide period of time, see discussions in Hedeager 1997; forthcoming a; forthcoming b.
3. The central discription is found in *Eirik saga rauda,* chap.4.
4. E.g. Strömbäck 1935; 1970; Ohlmarks 1939; Brøgger 1951; Buchholz 1971; Davidson 1988; Eliade 1989; against this explanation see Polomé 1992.
5. The self-sacrifice of Odin has in some ways certain similarities to the crucifixion of Christ. However, it is deeply rooted in the pagan line of thought and therefore not a copy of Christianity's central myth (Davidson 1990: 144).
6. This point of view has been emphasized by many scholars; cf. Nielsen 1985 with references.
7. The oldest runic inscriptions contains no secular message and must have served as communication with spirits/gods (Düwel 1978:221).
8. Cf. the inscription 'eril' on the long runic inscription on the Norwegian Eggja stone (Grønvik 1985, with references) which is interpreted as 'shaman' (Magnus 1988; 1992).
9. In *Eirik saga rauda* the animals, especially birds and cats, play an important role in the description of the *sejd*-woman's dress and the *sejd* ritual.
10. Cf. the comprehensive studies by Karl Hauck where the motifs on the A- and C-bracteates have been interpreted as being one and the same person, most probably Odin (cf. Hauck 1974; for an extensive bibliography see Hauck 1985–89). Odin is depicted as magician and shaman (Hauck 1978:211).
11. Cf. all of the so-called C-bracteates and several of the B-bracteates. The motifs on later bracteates, the D-bracteates, must be understood as the symbolic expression of the animal-motifs. The earliest bracteates, the A-bracteates, on the other hand, are still too close to their Roman model to show the significant Nordic iconography (classification after Mackeprang 1952; for the latest discussion of typology and chronology sse Axboe 1994 and Wicker 1994).

Bibliography

Sources

Sturluson, Snorre: *Nordiska Kungasagor*. Translated by K.G. Johansson (Stockholm 1991).

Sturluson, Snorre: *Edda*. Translated by Björn Collinder. (Stockholm 1983).

The Poetic Edda. Translated by L.M.Hollander. Austin, Texas 1994 (first edition 1962)

Axboe, M. 1994: 'Gudme and the gold bracteates', in Nielsen, P.O., Randsborg, K. and Thrane, H. (eds): *The Archaeology of Gudme and Lundeborg* (Copenhagen), 68–77.

Bäckmann, L. and Hultkrantz, Å. 1978. *Studies in Lapp Shamanism*. Stockholm.

Brøgger, N. C. 1951: 'Frøya-dyrkelse og seid', *Viking* 15, 39–63.

Buchholz, P. 1971: 'Shamanism – the testimony of Old Icelandic literary tradition', *Mediaeval Scandinavia* 4, 7–20.

Campbell, J. 1983: *The Way of the Animal Powers*, Historical Atlas of World Mythology 1 (London).

Chang, K.C. 1983: *Art, Myth and Ritual. The Path to Political Authority in Ancient China*, Harvard University Press (Cambridge, Mass.).

Davidson, H.R. Ellis 1988: *Myths and Symbols in Pagan Europe* (Manchester).

Davidson, H.R. Ellis 1990: *Gods and Myths of Northern Europe*, Penguin Books (first published 1964).

Dumézil, G. 1969: *De Nordiske Guder* (Copenhagen) [Danish translation of *Les Dieux des Germains. Essai sur la Formation de la Religion Scandinave (*Paris 1959)].

Düwel, K. 1978: 'Runeninschriften', in Ahrens, C. (ed.), *Sachsen und Angelsachsen*, Veröffentlichungen des Helms-Museums 32 (Hamburg), 219–230.

Eliade, M. 1989: *Shamanism. Archaic Techniques of Ecstasy*, Penguin Books.

Ellmers, D. 1970: 'Zur Ikonographie nordischer Goldbrakteaten', *Jahrbuch des Römisch-Germanischen Zentralmuseums Mainz* 17, 201 - 284.

Grønvik, O. 1985: *Runene på Eggjasteinen* (Oslo).

Halvorsen, E.F. 1960: 'Galder', in Karker, A, (ed.), *Kulturhistorisk Leksikon for Nordisk Middelalder* 5 (Copenhagen), 15–60.

Hauck, K. 1974: 'Ein neues Drei-Götter-Amulett von der Insel Fünen', in *Geschichte in der Gesellschaft. Festschrift für Karl Bosl.* (Stuttgart), 92–159.

Hauck, K. 1978: 'Götterglaube im Spiegel der goldenen Brakteaten', in Ahrens, C. (ed.) Sachsen und Angelsachsen,. Veröffentlichungen des Helms-Museums 32 (Hamburg), 185–218.

Hauck, K. 1985–89: *Die Goldbrakteaten der Völkerwanderungszeit.* Mit Beiträge von M. Axboe, C. Düwel, L. von Padberg, U. Smyra and C. Wypior, Münstersche Mittelalterschriften 24 (München).

Hauck, K. 1994: 'Gudme as Kultort und seine Rolle beim Austausch von Bildformularen der Goldbrakteaten', in Nielsen, P.O., Randsborg, K. and Thrane, H. (eds), *The Archaeology of Gudme and Lundeborg* (Copenhagen), 78–88.

Hedeager, L. 1996: Myter og materiel kultur: den nordiske oprindelsesmyte i det tidlige kristne Europa. *TOR* 28, 217–234.

Hedeager, L. 1997: *Skygger af en Anden Virkelighed. Oldnordiske Myter* (Copenhagen).

Hedeager, L. forthcoming a: 'Europe in the Migration Period. The formation of a political mentality', in Thieuws, F. (ed.), *Ritual and Power from Late Antiquity to the Early Middle Ages* (Leiden).

Hedeager, L. forthcoming b: 'Scandinavia (AD 500–700)', in Fouracre, P. (ed.), *New Cambridge Medieval History vol. I* (Cambridge).

Helms, M.W. 1988: *Ulysses' Sail*, (Princeton).

Herschend, F. 1998: *The Late Iron Age Good* (Uppsala).

Hultkrantz, Å. 1987: 'On beliefs in non-shamanic guardian spirits among the Saamis', in Ahlbäck, T. (ed.), *Saami Religion* (Uppsala), 110–123.

Mackeprang, M. 1952: *De Nordiske Guldbrakteater*, Jysk Arkæologisk Selskabs Skrifter 2 (Århus).

Magnus, B. 1988: 'Eggjasteinen – et dokument om sjamanisme i jernalderen?', in Indrelid, S., Kaland, S. and Solberg, B. (eds), *Festskrift til Anders Hagen*, Arkæologiske Skrifter, Historisk Museum, Bergen 4 (Bergen), 342–356.

Magnus, B. 1992: 'A matter of literacy or magic?', in Straume, E. and Skar, E. (eds), *Peregrinatio Gothica* 3, Universitetets Oldsaksamlings Skrifter, Ny rekke 14 (Oslo), 133–143.

Marrais, E. de, Castillo, L.J. and Earle, T. 1996: 'Ideology, materialization and power strategies', *Current Anthropology* 37/1, 15–32.

Morgan, D. 1994: *The Mongols*, The Peoples of Europe, Blackwell (Oxford).

Nielsen, K. M. 1985: 'Runen und Magie', *Frühmittelalterliche Studien* 19, 75–97.

Ohlmarks, Å. 1939: 'Arktischer Shamanismus und altnordischer *seidr', Archiv für Religionswissenschaft* 36, 171–180.

Oxenstierna, E. 1956: *Die Goldhörner von Gallehus* (Lidingö).

Polomé, E.C. 1992: 'Schamanismus in der germanischen Religion?', in Hauck, K. (ed.), *Der historische Horizont der Götterbild-Amulette aus der Übergangsepoche von der Spätantike zum Frühmittelalter*, Vandenhoeck & Ruprecht (Göttingen), 403–420.

Strömbäck, D. 1935: *Sejd*, Textstudier i nordisk religionshistoria (Stockholm).

Strömbäck, D. 1970: 'Sejd', in Karker, A. (ed.), *Kulturhistorisk Leksikon for Nordisk Middelalder* 15 (Copenhagen), 75–9.

Vitebsky, P. 1995: *The Shaman* (London).

Wicker, N. 1994: 'On the trail of the elusive goldsmith: tracing individual style and workshop characteristics in Migration Period metalwork', *Gesta* 33/1, 65–70.

Åberg, N. 1925: *Förhistorisk Nordisk Ornamentik* (Uppsala).

Anglo-Saxon Studies in Archaeology and History 10, 1999

The Bracteate of the Century – the new find of a unique Migration Period bracteate in Uppland, Sweden

Jan Peder Lamm

This brief communication concerns a newly found B-bracteate, which Professor Karl Hauck after having studied photographs of it, did not hesitate to call the bracteate find of this century. Perhaps he has made an overstatement; I hope not. Nevertheless, from the iconographic point of view its richness in detail is most remarkable. This outstanding bracteate was found recently at Söderby in Uppland in northern middle Sweden, about 70 km north of Stockholm on the outskirts of Uppsala, in a parish with the surprising name of Danmark.

Before returning to the topic promised let us have a look at a distribution map of the Migration Period gold bracteates (Fig. 1). Morten Axboe has kindly informed me that the recorded number of preserved specimens of this prestigious kind of jewellery was, in September 1996, 916. The majority of them, no less than 578, belong to 304 Scandinavian finds and another 50 are likely also to have been found in Scandinavia. Their Scandinavian distribution is restricted to Denmark, Norway and Sweden. The Swedish findplaces are most numerous, numbering 132 with 194 bracteates. The greatest number of bracteates has been found, however, in Denmark with 321, which belong to fewer but larger finds, 110 in total. In Norway 163 bracteates represent 62 finds.

In Sweden the distribution of the bracteates is uneven and mainly concentrated in the islands Öland and Gotland and in the southernmost and western parts of the country. In Uppland, where Söderby is located, they are very rare, and north of this county they are not represented at all.

The new find from Söderby, now in the Gold Room at Statens historiska museum/Museum of National Antiquities in Stockholm (SHM 33022), has its antecedents. On the 13th of October, 1876, a great find of gold bracteates was made there when digging an irrigation ditch. Four B-bracteates (IK 176) and five D-bracteates (IK 522) were found (SHM 5802) together with a cylindrical spiral, a spiral button, and a currency ring – all of gold. Also a tiny piece of half-molten silver belongs to the find (Fig. 2).

Most characteristic of the Söderby find is that the bracteates have been subject to violence; one of them is in three parts and and others have had their loops torn off. This, plus their occurrence together with odd pieces of

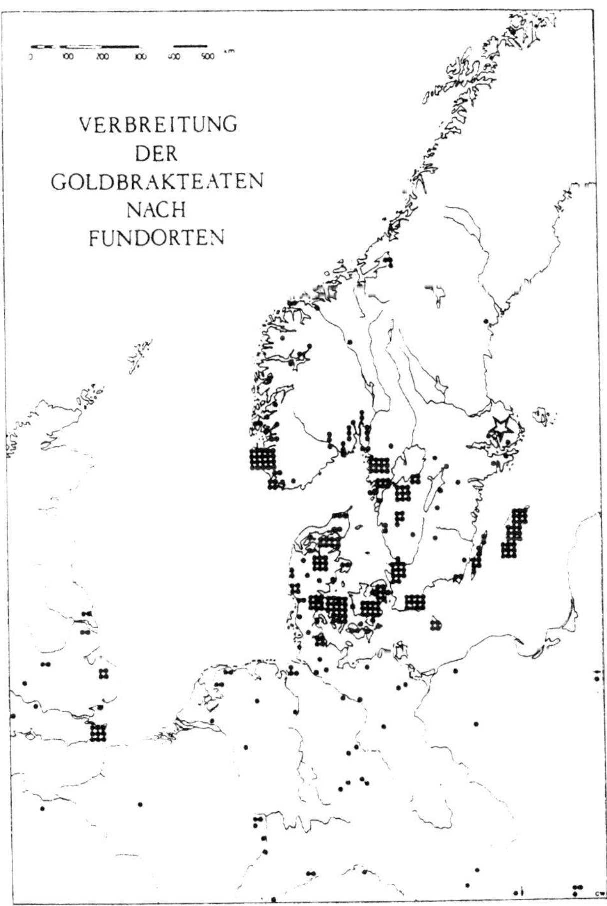

Fig. 1 Finds of Scandinavian gold bracteates (after Hauck). Söderby marked by a star.

gold and the silver fragment, makes it possible that the find might be a goldsmith's deposit of scrap material. A similar find containing five bracteates, of which four have their loops torn off, is known from west Sweden at Finnekumla in Rångedala parish, in Västergötland (IK 427–428). A plausible alternative is to consider the destruction of the objects as part of a procedure of sacrifice, an idea strengthened by the wetland character of the site. We face the same ambiguity at Vittene in Västergötland

Fig. 2 The Söderby hoard of 1876 together with the new B-bracteate to the far right. Photo SHM, Gabriel Hildebrand.

with its distorted rings from the Roman period, which were the subject of a paper by Ulf Wiking also given at the 47th Sachsensymposium (Lamm in press).

If we look at the motifs on the Söderby bracteates, we see that the B-bracteates show in profile a man resembling an acrobat turning a somersault. The figure is understood by Hauck as Odin in ecstatic rage (Hauck 1994, 262). The central motif on the D-bracteates looks like a *crux gemmata* (Arrhenius 1980, 445); between the arms of the cross we see monster heads.

Until 1945, when another B-bracteate was found at Ulvsunda (IK 195), Bromma parish, the Söderby find was the only Upplandic find containing bracteates. By the way, the Ulvsunda bracteate belongs to the same rare group as the Söderby B-bracteates. Later, in the 1960s, two fragments of bracteates were found in the workshop at Helgö (IK 270 and 271). With these, all bracteate finds from Uppland have been mentioned.

In the autumn of 1995, the site of the find of the Söderby bracteates was rediscovered by a team from Statens historiska museum working with metal detectors. The mission was to revisit and to try to rediscover the sites of some of the 'classic' precious-metal deposits found mainly during land reclamation activities in the nineteenth century. This so-called project of re-examination (*efterundersökningsprojektet*) is multifaceted. It has the explicit objective to try to discover new knowledge about the old treasure-finds and to rescue what may still remain *in situ* of the treasures. The project also aims to discover the settlements related to these high status objects, which are likely to indicate sites of high social status that played an important role in the process of founding a network of petty kingdoms during the Roman and Migration period. The project was financed by the Marcus and Amalia Wallenberg Foundation. It can be seen as a continuation of the so-called Hoard Project which in the years 1977 – 1985 was conducted on Gotland by the Gotland branch of the National Board of Antiquities/RAGU (Östergren 1989, 247).

At Söderby the project members hit a real jackpot, not only rediscovering the find place of 1876, but also finding a bracteate so remarkable that it deserved especially to be mentioned at the symposium, though its state of preservation does not allow too precise a description and discussion of its pattern.

The bracteate is completely preserved but rolled up

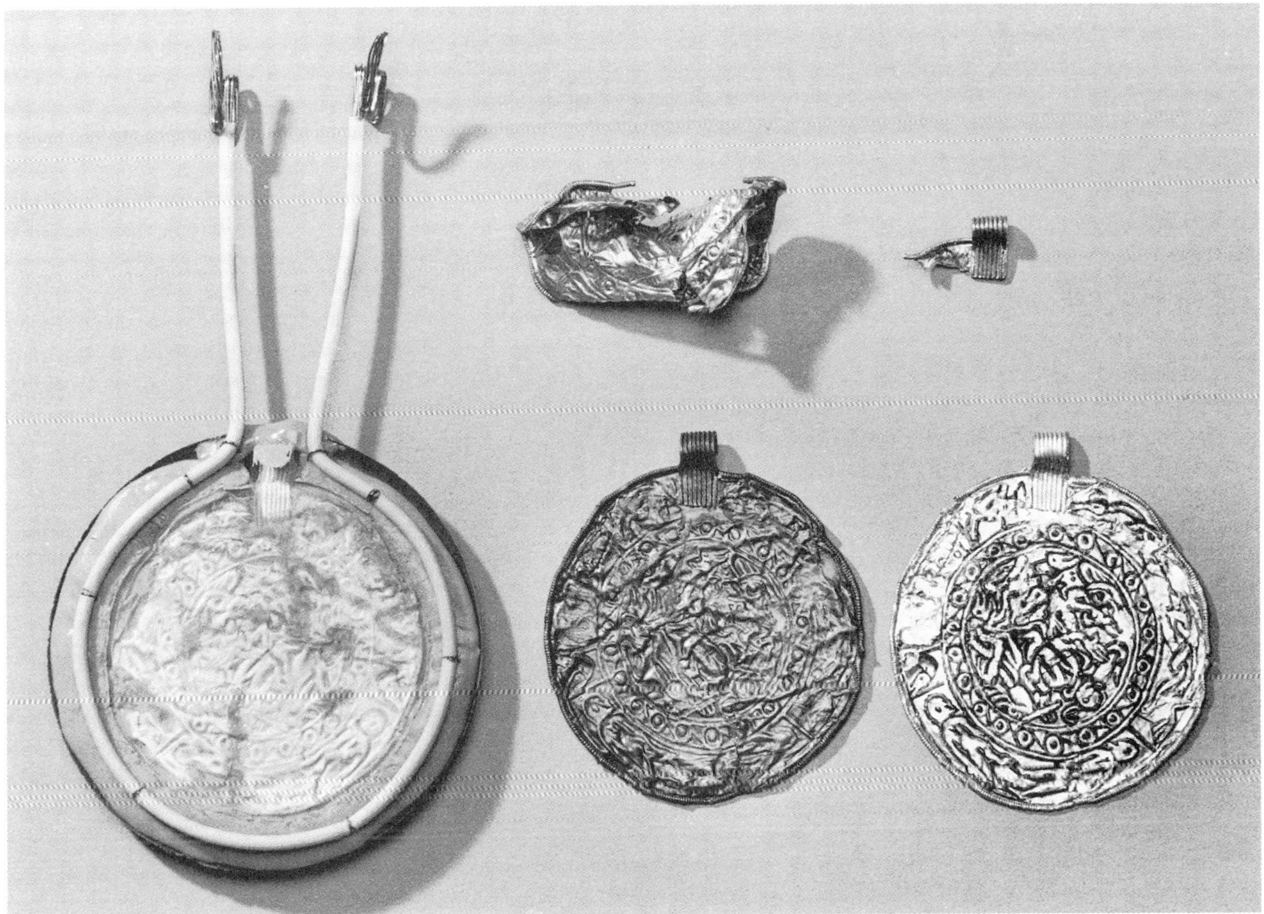

Fig. 3 Hydman's experimental series. Above the new bracteate; below from the left, the silicon form, electrotype and tinned and ink-marked electrotype. Photo SHM, Gabriel Hildebrand.

and so crumpled that we have not yet dared to try to unfold it as we fear that it can easily break into pieces. Its loop had been torn off, but was also recovered, luckily enough, about 20 m from the main part of the bracteate. The physical state of the bracteate has aroused an ethical discussion about whether it is morally defensible to try to unroll it as its defects might have been caused by actions of a sacrificial nature. If the find proves to be sacrifical, part of its character would be lost. The closest parallels which I know are from Sorte Muld on Bornholm where Margrete Watt has unfolded a series of figure foils (*guldgubbar*) and also the bracteate Sylten-C that was folded together several times into a little package (Hauck and Axboe 1990, Taf. 2). To start with, however, we have chosen to document the bracteate by making a non-damaging copy. This has been carried out by Hubert Hydman, conservator at the department of metal conservation of the technical office of the Central Board of National Antiquities in Stockholm. Hydman has succeeded in taking an astonishingly good impression of the pattern on the bracteate by applying a thin layer of silicon on to its crumpled and partly almost unavailable surface. He then has used this silicon impression to make a couple of galvanic copies of the bracteate (Fig. 3). He has tinned one of them to make a background suitable for giving contrast to the pattern of the bracteate when trying to disentangle it by stressing its readable parts with India ink. Hydman´s interpretation (Fig .4) is preliminary and details of it no doubt will be differently perceived if and when the bracteate is unfolded. In the main traits, however, Hydman´s interpretation will endure and is enlightening enough for us to get a general impression of the bracteate.

The new bracteate has a diameter of about 65 mm and weighs 15,06 g. Thus it is about 25 mm wider and three times heavier than the other individual bracteates in the hoard. As on those, its loop is very simple. And as on many other bracteates, the loop is applied in such a way that the central motif stands upside down and thus can easily be seen in its right position by the bearer of the bracteate. The bracteate is remarkable also in other respects; in particular, it is exceptionally rich in motifs which are rare or quite new in the repertoire of bracteate iconography. Its outer zone with a sequence of *entrelac* animal plaits alludes to Style II, though the details are still fairly unclear. An affinity to some Norwegian D-bracteates seems to be present (cf. IK 509, 518, 524).

Unparalleled on bracteates are the human figures which very much resemble some of the Scandinavian silhouette-cut figure foils (*guldgubbar*) but with the head in profile. The gesture of the figure in the central zone is hands up and thumbs apart. The right hand seems to hold a snake that also coils around the neck of the figure. In the left hand is a baton or a short sceptre. The lower part of the figure's body seems to be missing though its legs are pointing upwards. Under the figure there is a swarm of animal limbs, which judging from the visible heads represent at least three individuals.

Professor Karl Hauck has kindly proposed a team for further study of the bracteate and has directed my attention to its iconographic similarity with another newly found B-bracteate from Issendorf, Landkreis Stade, in Lower Saxony (Hässler *et al.*, in press). A preliminary interpretation of the central scene shows the same raging Odin as on the earlier Söderby B-bracteates and engaged in the same action; this time, however, the god's body is not seen in profile but *en face*. The winding monsters under him probably symbolize Hel. It is likely that the figure with a stick in his hand fighting the evil beasts on the new Söderby bracteate may be considered Odin trying to deliver Balder from the realms of Hel. Thus all three types of B-bracteate – the two from Söderby and one from Issendorf – seem to represent variants on the same theme.

Finally it should be stressed that Söderby lies very close to *Mora äng*, the meadow of Mora, in Lagga parish. It lies on the frontier between the former folklands, ancient Swedish districts, Attundaland and Tiundaland. Here in the medieval period kings were elected and symbolically invested by being placed on a big flat stone surrounded by other stones with inscriptions commemorating earlier investitures. By the sixteenth century the central stone had already disappeared, perhaps as a measure of precaution by someone eager to make it impossible to continue the old tradition of investing elected kings. King Gustavus I (Vasa) was interested in recovering it, perhaps with the same intention, but failed to find it. No one knows how long the meadow of Mora had had this important role. Perhaps it may even have been related to a hypothetical royal estate in the Söderby area and to the Söderby treasure?

Fig. 4 Preliminary sketch of the motif after Hydman by Cecilia Bonnevier.

Acknowledgement

I wish to express my gratitude to Professor Nancy Wicker for her kindness in checking my English text.

Bibliography

Arrhenius, B. 1980: 'Eine Untersuchungsreihe von Schwedischen Brakteatengold', *Frühmittelalterliche Studien*, 14, 438–462.

Hässler, H.J., Axboe, M., Hauck, K. and Heizmann, W. in press: 'Ein neues Problemstück der Brakteatenikonographie: Issendorf B., Lkr. Stade, Niedersachsen (Zur Ikonologie der Goldbrakteaten 54)', *Studien zur Sachsenforschung* 10.

Hauck, K. 1994: 'Das Zeugnis der uppländischen Götterbild-Amulette. In Altuppsalas Polytheismus exemplarisch erhellt mit Bildzeugnissen des 5.–7. Jahrhunderts (Zur Ikonologie der Goldbrakteaten 53)', *Studien zum Altgermanischen. Festschrift für Heinrich Beck* (Münster), 260–275.

Hauck, K. and Axboe, M. 1990: 'Zwei neue Goldbrakteaten aus Bornholm und Holstein (Zur Ikonologie der Goldbrakteaten 46)', *Frühmittelalterliche Studien* 24, 70–120.

Lamm, J.P. in press: 'The Vittene hoard: a gold-treasure from Västergötland in Sweden with a continental background', *Acta Musei Moraviæ* 81(for 1997).

IK 1985–1989: *Die Goldbrakteaten der Völkerwanderungszeit. Ikonographischer Katalog*, Münstersche Mittelalter-Schriften Band 23/1–3 (Münster).

Østergren, M. 1989: *Mellan stengrund och stenhus. Gotlands vikingatida ilverskatter som boplatsindikation*, Theses and Papers in Archaeology 2, Institute of Archaeology, University of Stockholm.

Anglo-Saxon Studies in Archaeology and History 10, 1999

Monsters and birds of prey. Some reflections on form and style of the Migration period

Bente Magnus

'The past did once exist independently of our understandings of it'
Henrietta Moore 1995

Introduction

Amongst the varied and abundant archaeological material from the Migration period in Scandinavia the large, highly decorated relief brooches hold a special position. Due to their ornamentation in Germanic animal style, their form, the technique of production, their spatial distribution and find circumstances, and their relation to Anglo-Saxon and Continental material the brooches have spurred the imagination of numerous scholars for more than a century. Consequently the number of monographs and articles on the subject is abundant but concentrates mainly on form and ornamental style as a basis for building up a chronology for the Migration period in Scandinavia. Eva Nissen Meyer's article from 1934 'Relieffspenner i Norden', based on her thesis for the Magister artium degree, still is a little gem. Regrettably it was only published in Norwegian although with a later comprehensive summary in German (Nissen Fett 1937).

Thorleif Sjøvold's *The Scandinavian Relief Brooches of the Migration Period* is the latest publication on the subject (Sjøvold 1993), John Hines' extensive monograph on the Anglo Saxon square-headed brooches appeared just as this paper was submitted for publication (Hines 1997) and other publications will appear in the near future (Kristoffersen in prep; Magnus in prep).

My fascination for relief brooches went via studies of the cultural landscape of Southwest Norway and one special location called Cross Mound. This large and conspicuous monument, which later was furnished with an early Christian stone cross, once covered a woman's grave in a cist of stone slabs with abundant and varied gravegoods, among which was a large relief brooch of gilt silver decorated in Nydam Style (Hougen 1967, fig 16). In my publication of the find I speculated freely on the woman's status and position in the local society (Magnus 1975). The Cross Mound grave is one in a row of similarly lavishly furnished women's graves from the Migration period in coastal Norway which at present form the basis for a doctoral dissertation at the University of Bergen, Norway (Kristoffersen 1995 and in prep.).

When I was asked to produce a popular and well illustrated presentation of the relief brooches found in Sweden twenty years after the Cross Mound publication I had no intention of doing more than just that. By including the relief brooches found in Finland as well as the best preserved fragments of moulds for casting relief brooches from Helgö, the material now presents a diversified picture with possibilites for interpretations other than just chronological and stylistic ones. As a side track to this work, the speculations presented in the following took form.

Objects as texts

The Danish classical archaeologist N.Hannestad's publications on Roman art as propaganda, of how art was applied and functioned in the Roman society (Hannestad 1976; 1986), have inspired my reflections on the relief brooches. By attempting a semiotic approach I was convinced that information on how the brooches may have functioned in the Scandinavian Germanic societes could be gained. If the brooches were viewed as texts or patterns of meaning it would imply that both form and ornamentation once delivered a message. This would be coupled with the status, sex and social position of the person making use of the item in question, how the object was worn and under what circumstances. The artisan smiths were designers and communicators of loosely defined messages on behalf of the ruling elite, and the contemporary public were the intended recipients (cf. K.Høilund Nielsen 1991). The fifth and sixth centuries were also times of profound structural changes in Scandinavia and a period when a distinct regionality is visible in the archaeological material (Ringtved 1988; Widgren 1988). Gold in the form of solidi 'flowed' into Southern Scandinavia, but became scarce after the first quarter of the sixth century (Kyhlberg 1986; Herschend 1980).

A time of crises?

Research on the Migration period in Scandinavia was for several decades concentrated on finding causal explanations for the obvious structural changes which occur in the archaeological material in this transitory phase. In 1933 the Swedish scholar Mårten Stenberger launched his hypothesis of the crises in his doctoral dissertation which was based on his excavations of deserted farmsteads from this period on the island of Öland in the Baltic and seen in connection with *inter alia* the numerous hoards of Roman solidi found on the island (Stenberger 1933). Continued research by several scholars on deserted agrarian settlements, hillforts and cemeteries in Scandinavia has demonstrated that profound changes in the settlement pattern had also taken place in the coastal regions of South and Southwest Norway, the Jutland peninsula, the Baltic island of Gotland and in North Sweden. Monocausal explanations like over-population resulting in exhaustion of soil and natural resources and, as a consequence, famine, migrations, wars and the Justinian Plague have given way to a more varied view. The period of change was a lengthy process where the Migration period constitutes the very transitional generations between the early and later Iron Age (Näsman 1988). Renewed studies of the Danish sacrifical war booty finds from the Roman and early Migration periods have contributed much to an altered view on the political and social development in Scandinavia (Hedeager 1992; Vang Petersen 1987; v. Carnap-Bornheim and Illkjær 1996).

One of the reasons why the label 'crises' seemed not to be in keeping with reality were the many gold hoards which have turned up in Scandinavia from just this period. The largest, from Tureholm, Sörmland in Sweden weighed 11.5 kg and was found during field work by a count in 1774. Only one tenth of the golden objects, among which were counted a neck ring of nearly one kilo of gold and sword sheath mounts decorated with filigree, were saved for posterity, the rest being melted down to improve the finder´s financial position (Lamm 1994). A hoard of golden spiral rings and ingots of gold weighing altogether 7 kg came to light in 1904 at Timboholm, Västergötland, Sweden (Gullman 1995).

In contrast the many cemeteries from the Migration period in this part of Sweden give an almost 'egalitarian' impression with their very low cairns covering cremation graves (Bennett 1987). The Danish material shows the same overall picture of modestly furnished graves contrasting with large gold hoards (Fonnesbech-Sandberg 1991). Öland and Gotland present a special picture. The Norwegian material consists of relatively few and small gold hoards and numerous richly furnished inhumation graves and monumental barrows in the same areas as numerous hillforts and deserted farmsteads. Here the regional topography makes it easier to discern former territories (Myhre 1987). The objects which constitute both hoards and grave finds are similar in Scandinavia, but regional traditions have led to different ways of deposition. More regional studies of several important find categories, settlement sites, cultural landscape and place-names, evaluated together will make the political, social and religious changes that occurred in the Migration period clearer and also give an understanding of the time aspect for these changes in the different regions.

The relief brooches

In spite of being among the most heavily decorated objects of the Migration period, the relief brooches seldom belong in any gold hoard. The reason for this may be of religious or ritualistic character as the gold hoards seem to contain mainly (but not exclusively) objects connected with display of male rank and power (Hansen in press). These are Kolben neckrings and arm rings, other types of neckrings, gold collars, large finger-rings and sword accessories, while gold bracteates may be interpreted as a more general amuletic object worn by both women and men of high rank. Only in Denmark have relief brooches been deposited with gold, mostly gold bracteates, but also solidi, gold spiral wire finger-rings and beads of glass and amber (Hedeager 1991, fig.9). In Norway and England the combination of relief brooches with gold bracteates are well known from grave finds, while the combination is not known from hoards (Bakka 1958; 1973; Hines 1989). The Swedish relief brooches stem from gravefinds and stray finds, and only in one instance has a relief brooch of gilt silver been found with gold bracteates, in Järnskogsboda, Värmland, a heavily wooded border region between Southeast Norway and West Sweden (Mackeprang 1952, 174). The Danish, Norwegian and Anglo-Saxon finds with relief brooch-cum-bracteate(s) are very similar. The brooches are of high artistic quality and mostly made of gilt silver. Some carry runic inscriptions as do some of the bracteates. The runes occur either on the gold bracteate *or* on the relief brooch in the same find. The sets must have belonged to women with a very similar high rank in the local society, but most likely of another character than high ranking men. This statement is founded *inter alia* on the observation of certain differences in the motifs and execution of ornamental style connected with women's and men's graves and on the fact that no relief brooch was ever made of pure gold (cf. below).

Two types of relief brooches.

The most common form of the relief brooches are the ones with a square head plate. They belong in the Scandinavian and Anglo-Saxon finds. In the Swedish and Danish material there are relief brooches with a semicircular headplate, which is a common feature of the Continental relief brooches. The equal-armed relief brooches, however, are not numerous but have been found in East Scandinavia (Sweden and Finland) and in Hungary. All types are represented among the mould fragments from Helgö (Holmqvist 1972). In order to test the idea of the brooches as texts I have chosen two groups of special relief brooches, the bird frieze brooches and the equal-armed brooches.

Relief brooches with a bird frieze

This group of brooches has been found mainly on the island of Gotland, with one example each from the islands of Öland and Bornholm. In addition there is a small fragment of a clay mould with a bird frieze from the workshop material at Helgö, indicating that brooches of this type may have been produced there (Lundström 1972, 227, R 642). There are nine brooches (six complete and three fragmentary) all made of gilt silver with niello inlay plus a number of related brooches (Näsman 1984). The main characteristic feature is a semicircular or omega-shaped head plate with three zoomorphic protruding knobs; the rhomboid foot is either flat or has a raised edge running the whole length of the foot. The general decoration consists of spiral ornaments executed in sharp chip-carving and mouldings emphasized with inlay of niello. Some brooches have additional embellishment in the form of mounted red garnets. The main ornamental feature is a frieze of birds, each with a long, curved neck, transversely striated and ending in a small round head with a long, curved beak. The frieze frames the head plate on both sides of a zoomorphic mask placed in the middle (Fig. 1). On four of the head plates the bovine character of the middle mask is very prominent. The foot of the brooches is either bordered by rows of the same hook-beaked birds or has a single bird's head on either side of the terminal mask. On three of the brooches the terminal mask is that of an eagle (Fig. 2), while on the others are zoomorphic heads of various forms. Ornamentation in Style I is to be seen on only one brooch, which in many ways stands out from the others (Sjøvold 1993, pl.27, S 43). Both the form of the brooches as well the frieze of birds' heads are unique in Scandinavia. They come in two groups and within each group there are a few brooches which are similar enough to have been made by the same artisan. One of them has signed his name in runes on the back of the foot of one of the brooches: 'Mik Merila worta · Merila made me' (Krause 1966, 39–40). The find circumstances are not very illucidating for any of the bird frieze brooches save for the one from Bornholm which belonged to a hoard (Klindt-Jensen 1957, 103–105). The others are stray finds or have entered the museum collections through antique dealers (Näsman 1984, 60ff)

Fig. 1 Bird frieze brooch from När, Gotland. Scale 1:1. Photo G. Hildebrand.

A row of scholars has been fascinated by the bird frieze brooches (*ibid.*). Holger Arbman wrote a small article on stylistic features in the art of the Migration period (Arbman 1945) where he, in concordance with colleagues before him, focused on the possible connection between the Gotland-Öland bird frieze brooches and two brooches found in France (Thennes, Dep. Somme, now in the Ashmolean Museum, and Douvrand, Dep. Seine-

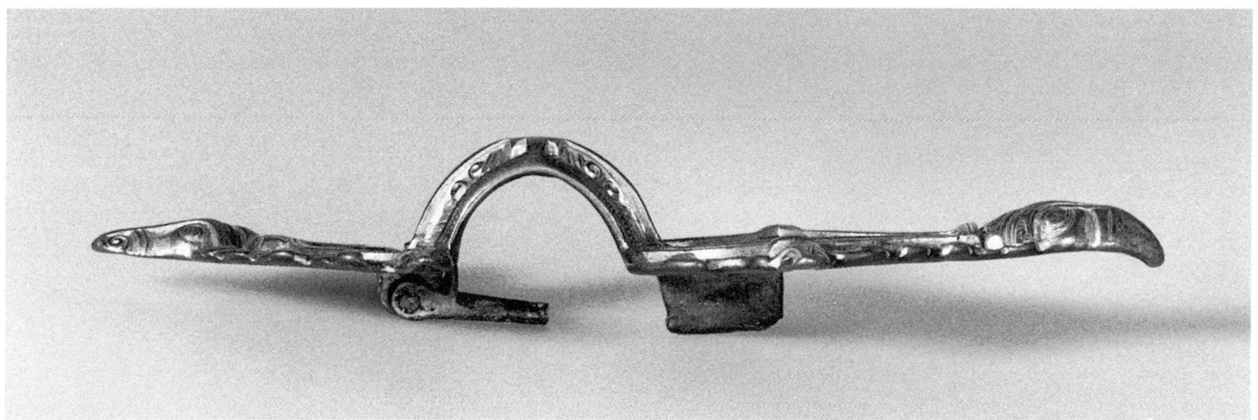

Fig. 2 Side view of the brooch from När showing the terminal eagle's head. Scale 1:1. Photo G. Hildebrand.

Inférieure, Musée de Rouen). In contrast to Åberg (1924), Arbman found that the two groups of brooches had a common origin in the Danubian kingdom of the Goths. He brought into the discussion a couple of silver buckles from Hungary with a flat, rhomboid catchment plate very close to both the Baltic bird frieze brooches and the ones from France. The bird frieze along the edges as well as the spiral ornaments executed in chip-carving come particularly close to the bird frieze brooches from När and Ethelhem, Gotland, and Dalshøj, Bornholm.

Some forty years later U. Näsman made a renewed and very thorough chronological and chorological study of the bird frieze and related brooches (Näsman 1984, 48–80). He added new finds of Continental brooches (San Andrea di Grottamare, Prov. Ascoli Piceno, and a fourth brooch of unknown provenance kept in the RGZM in Köln) and buckles (Karavukovo/Bácsordas, former Yugoslavia and Torre del Mangano, Italy) to the ones already known (Bierbrauer 1975). Näsman dated the brooches to the second half of the fifth century and maintained that the inspiration for the special motif came to Gotland from Hungary during the half century which lies between the dissolution of the Hunnic empire and the Ostrogothic conquest of Italy, AD 453 – 493. Näsman found it plausible that artisans from the eastern part of Germania may have come to work in Gotland and Öland and that the Style I elements which are to be found on a few other related buckles (Konarzew, Co. Leczyca, Poland; Gyula, Kom. Békés, Hungary; Vechiazzano, Prov. Forlì, Italy) may be a result of reciprocity (Näsman 1984, 76). The artisan's name Merila (on the brooch from Ethelhem, Gotland), being an Ostrogothic male name otherwise not known in Scandinavia (Krause 1966), lends support to his theory.

The terminal head in the form of an eagle's head on the bird frieze brooches from När and Ethelhem, Gotland, and Dalshøj, Bornholm are comparable to those on two silver gilt buckles from Hungary now at the Metropolitan Museum, New York, and two in the National Museum of Hungary (Brown 1996, 228 with references).

What message(s) do the bird frieze brooches of the western Baltic islands convey? Is it too simple to interpret the form of the brooches as a sign of group identity? The bird frieze, the terminal eagle's head and the bovine masks most likely relate to a myth, maybe an origin myth which was shared by some East Germanic (Gothic) high ranking families on the Continent and in East Scandinavia and linked them together in relation to a common identity. In a Scandinavian context a woman wearing a bird frieze brooch would thereby signal that she belonged to a special tribe different from a woman wearing a square-headed brooch. The Continental belt buckles were worn by women only. Brooches, but hardly the belt buckles, may have been worn by certain women in a ritual context and only displayed on certain occasions. No objects connected with male attire seem to be ornamented with birds of prey, but on some gold bracteates the hair-do of what is believed to be the god Odin terminates in a hook-beaked bird's head (Hauck 1985b, figs. 50, 105, 120, 142, 149).

The equal-armed relief brooches.

A very different type of brooch is the equal-armed one, which by some scholars is not classified as a relief brooch (Sjøvold 1993). Currently sixteen examples, both whole and fragmentary, are known, and in addition fragments of moulds for casting this type of brooch have come to light at Helgö (Lundström 1972, 228). The area of distribution stretches from Uppland northwards along the Swedish coast across the Bay of Bothnia to Ostrobothnia in Finland, and then across the bay of Finland via the island of Tytärsaari and down to the Theiss area in Hungary (Fig. 3). About half of the brooches stem from burials which are less than satisfactorily documented, the rest are stray finds which mostly have turned up during digging of ditches for drainage in wetland and therefore

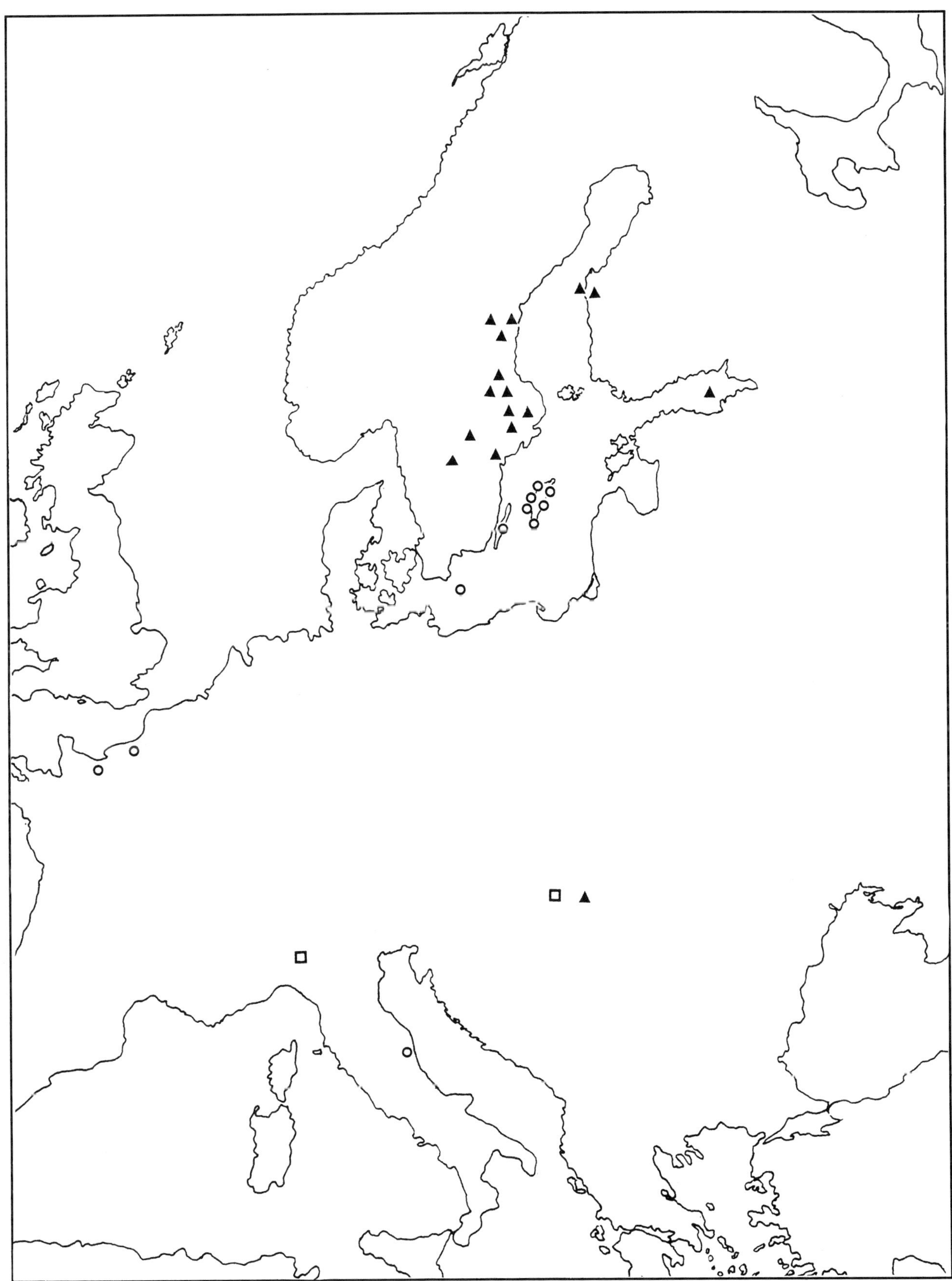

Fig. 3 Distribution map of bird frieze brooches and buckles, and equal-armed brooches. After Näsman 1984 with amendments. Key: solid triangle: equal-armed brooches; open circle: bird frieze brooches; open square: bird frieze buckles. ○ *Bird frieze brooches.* □ *Bird frieze buckles.* ▲ *Equal-armed relief brooches.*

may be ritual deposits. The majority are made of gilt bronze; only five brooches, which are the best preserved, are made of gilt silver inlaid with niello. Their characteristic form, which resembles a bow, may have been created in a milieu where experimenting with new forms was done, namely in the workshops at Helgö. Holmqvist in his conclusive chapters on the relief brooches found that equal- armed relief brooches of the best craftmanship doubtless had been made in the workshops (Holmqvist 1972, 274).

The equal-armed brooches vary in length between 10 and 24 cm (Åberg 1953: 69–75) and come in two main shapes. One is made simply by joining two footplates from small square-headed relief brooches (Sjøvold 1993, pl. 26, S15, S 20, S21) together with a bow, the other has its own distinct design (Fig. 4). The following description concerns the latter. The ornamentation is structured by way of relatively high mouldings which divide each arm into three pictorial panels: a central 'heartshaped' panel, which is bordered on both sides by a narrow panel mostly with an outer moulding, and the terminal masks. The arched bow may also function as a place for decoration. In the narrow panels, a rich biotope of Style I zoomorphic figures is to be seen in an overall pattern, crouching along the edges, each with an open jaw seemingly about to devour another. The central panel either has a rather dry spiral decoration centred around a knob or a mounted piece of coloured glass, or a mass of loose figural elements. The most characteristic ornamental features of the brooches are the terminal masks. They are mostly zoomorphic, displaying features like slanting eyes, a prominent brow and at times sculpted eyebrows or short rounded ears. The eyebrows continue in a broad nasal ridge, ending in spiral formed nostrils or in a wide open mouth, where a triangular figure protrudes. Some monsters are in the process of devouring a human head. On the equal-armed relief brooch from Ekeby, Malsta in Uppland the terminal mask is clearly meant to be a wolf-like monster (Fig. 4).

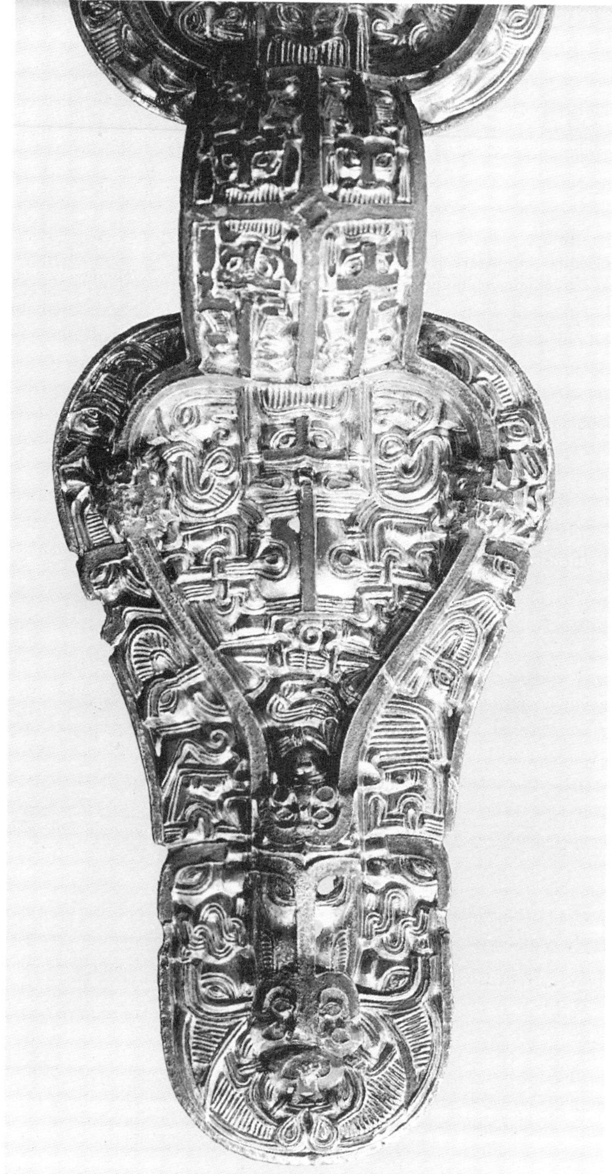

Fig. 4 Detail of the brooch from Ekeby. No scale. Photo G. Hildebrand.

Of the sixteen equal-armed relief brooches hitherto known, only three come from well documented grave finds: one fragment of a bronze brooch from a woman's cremation grave at Lovö, Uppland (Petré 1984, fig.90), one fragmentary brooch of bronze from a woman's cremation grave from Rallsta, Västmanland (Lamm 1979, 126–134) and finally a gilt silver brooch from grave 84 of the Gepidic row grave cemetery of Szentes-Nagyhegy in Hungary (Csallany 1961, 58–64, Taf. XXXIX). The (Scandinavian?) woman had been buried in an E–W position and among her rich funeral outfit is a small reliquary with a cross suspended on a chain. The brooch was found lying across her pelvis indicating an original position below the belt of the garment (Neméth 1988, 245).

Åberg dated the Gepidic equal-armed brooch to the first half of the sixth century (Åberg 1953, 102), while Csallany gave the burial a date in the Avarian period after the fall of the Gepidic kingdom in AD 567 (Csallany 1961, 322, 359). Arbman gave a date around AD 500 or the beginning of the sixth century (Arbman 1945). There is no doubt about the East Scandinavian provenance of the equal-armed brooch from Szentes-Nagyhegy and Haseloff considered it to be stylistically the oldest (phase B) of the entire group (Haseloff 1981, 189–190). Its worn surface indicates frequent use over a long period. Åberg concluded that these brooches had stylistic features which pointed to the north Swedish region as a recipient of impulses both from the east Swedish and west Norwegian regions (Åberg 1953, 75). He called special attention to the terminal masks with short upright ears which are found on a few of the Norwegian late square headed brooches (Sjøvold 1993, pl. 21). As this feature is much more common in East Scandinavia and no equal-armed relief brooch has till now turned up in Norway an influence from east to west is rather indicated.

The very easterly distribution pattern of the equal-armed brooches, with one example from the Gepidic kingdom on the Theiss, and their special form and ornamental motifs must reflect a linkage between families in the regions where the brooches were deposited. And behind this there must have been a common identity and myth of origin. The differences in size, material and the artistic execution of the brooches must indicate a difference in status between the women who once wore them. While all of the bird frieze brooches are made of gilt silver, this is the case with only five of the sixteen equal-armed ones (Gillberga, Närke; Ekeby, Uppland; Gulldynt, Ostrobothnia; Tytärsaari, Bay of Finland and Szentes-Nagyhegy, Hungary). These are of high artistic standard and must have been made for ladies of the most powerful families with a wide network of alliances over long distances. I wonder whether these ladies may not have had special ritualistic tasks in some official cult (Magnus 1995, 39). The woman buried in the Gepidic cemetery (with a reliquiary) may be once used her brooch to demonstrate her Scandinavian descent. The equal-armed brooches with their monster masks and figures in combat may relate to a destruction myth, possibly the one known from the later Sibyl's prophecy of the end of the world, Ragnarók. The terminal masks of the brooch from Ekeby would then be a representation of the Fenris wolf devouring the god Odin. Other relief brooches, which have a triangular figure only protruding from the terminal masks, may symbolize the breath of Odin (Hauck 1992,115).

The birds of the bird frieze brooches, on the other hand, have strong affinites with the terminal end of the hair-do of '*der Götterfürst*' on some of the gold bracteates, and birds of prey are among the shamanistic god's helping spirits, but may also symbolize destructive forces. As mentioned earlier three of the bird frieze brooches have the terminal head of the footplate shaped like an eagle's head with oblique protruding eyes and a broad, strong beak (Fig. 2). The golden eagle was the king of all birds and it was important among the Goths as a royal insignium in the form of eagle brooches. One of Odin's epithets is '*arnhofði*', him with head of an eagle (Falk 1924, 3). The motif of the hooked-beaked bird of prey continues into the Merovingian period and gilt bronze mounts in the form of an eagle (or a large bird of prey) decorated the shields of the helmeted warlords from Vendel, Valsgärde and the king from Sutton Hoo. The same bird is to be seen on two of the Gotlandic picture stones, Lärbro, st. Hammars I and Tingelgårda I (Lindqvist 1941, Taf. 27 and 31). It was obviously an important symbol for the warlords, and the connection between the large birds of prey tearing at the dead bodies on the battle field and the myth of Odin coming to fetch new warriors to Valhalla is well known.

The only destruction myth handed down to us in Nordic mythology is the prophecy of Ragnarok, where the Fenris wolf devours Odin, 'the masked one'. But why allude to an 'end-of-the-world' prophecy where even '*der Götterfürst*' is destroyed together with all the male gods and the giants? And why on a brooch worn by a woman if she was not acting as a sibyl? Odin was the mystical god, the all-wise always searching for new wisdom, the great shaman who could transgress all barriers – between life and death, man and woman, man and animal – and could see into the future. Could it be that the ladies wearing the gilt silver brooches had a function as 'priestesses' in a cult drama with questions and answers? Several of the Edda poems have this question and answer structure indicating that not even the mighty god Odin did possess the inner wisdom about the future of men and gods, but had to ask sibyls (*Voluspá*, Balder's Dreams). Odin seems to be the common denominator of the ornamentation of the bird frieze brooches and the equal-armed ones, but with a marked difference. In one instance as '*der Götterfürst*', the triumphant, and in the other inevitably destroyed by the forces of chaos. Did the end of the world seem closer in the early sixth than in the late fifth century?

The relief brooches were produced at a time when the final migrations and battles took place on the Continent and the connections with East Germanic tribes, which were of long standing, were more difficult to keep up. New elites with connections to the rapidly expanding Franks were during the first half of the sixth century gaining a foothold in east Scandinavia and manifested their power in the course of the following century. The numerous chieftains in Scandinavia were fighting to keep their old power over people but were doomed to lose. The new leaders, who were kings, had built the magnificent mounds of Old Uppsala and Raknehaugen at Romerike in east Norway and thus manifested their newly gained power. They displayed different symbols of power and identity from before and had different rituals where the warrior-hero was central, as demonstrated in the boat graves at Sutton Hoo, Vendel and Valsgärde. Rituals where ladies wearing large brooches played a prominent role continued for several generations all over Scandinavia as indicated by the tiny gold foils (*gullgubber*) (Fig. 7).

In the late fifth century the lines of communication seem to have been more southerly than in the early sixth century and the distribution of the equal-armed brooches shows a much more peripheral picture than the bird frieze brooches and buckles. This tendency most likely is connected with the movements of the different tribes on the Continent.

The Goths and the Gepids were two very different *gentes*. According to Cassiodorus' *Origo Gothica* the Gepids were the last to leave the '*Urheimat*' Scandza, and the Goths considered themselves to be of higher rank than the Gepids. Accordingly, it was a thorn in the Gothic flesh when, after the battle of Nedao in 453, the Gepids settled in the former Hunnic heartland while the Goths had to make do with Pannonia. The Goths were a migratory *gens* always intent on conquering new territories. With them the most successful warlord had the highest rank and their king was first and foremost a warrior king. Their most fabled *reiks*, Theoderic the Great, Roman king of Italy (d.527) was still rembered 300 years later on the rune stone of Rök in Östergötland, Sweden (Gustavson 1991 with references). At the beginning of the sixth century both Baltic and Scandinavian peoples were counted among the Goths (Wolfram 1990, 326 ff). The Gepids, on the other hand were mainly sedentary farmers and once settled in the Carpathian basin, they remained in the area for nearly a century. They were a true barbarian *gens* who had mostly lived outside of Roman influence. In the sixth century they entered a phase of expansion which troubled both the Emperor and the Lombards who were pressing on the Gepidic territory from the west. In AD 567 the Gepids were extinguished as an independent *gens* in a joint Roman-Lombardic maneuvre (Pohl 1980).

The bird frieze brooches and the equal-armed brooches are indications of contacts between east Scandinavian groups and their 'relatives', the Goths and the Gepids, in east central Europe during the generations when the mightiest barbarian *gentes* were struggling to establish themselves permanently in Europe.

A different ornamental style for women and men?

The above speculations are the results of studying two groups of relief brooches with very characteristic ornamental motifs which were worn by women. Consequently a question presents itself, whether the same motifs are found on objects connected with men, such as weapons.

Regrettably, there are very few weapon graves of the Migration period which contain decorated objects of precious metals, but a few, like graves II and V from Snartemo in South Norway, the chieftain's grave from mound 2 at Högom, Medelpad in North Sweden, as well as the so called 'smith's grave' from Vestly, Time, southwest Norway are inhumations and may serve as examples. Unfortunately only the Högom grave comes from (north-)east Scandinavia, the others come from southwest Norway.

The burial mound V at Snartemo was published by the late professor Bjørn Hougen together with other finds from grave mounds at Snartemo which were not professionally excavated and which since 1847 had been acquired by the museums of Oslo and Stavanger (Hougen 1935). The sword, the large buckle for the baldric and the gilt silver mountings for the glass beaker are pieces of high artistic standard. The ornamentation of the sword hilt demonstrates a front (Fig. 5a) and a back side (Fig. 5b), that is motifs which were displayed and could be viewed by persons being close to the man and motifs

(a)

(b)

Fig. 5 The grip of the sword from Snartemo V, V.Agder, Norway; (a) front and (b) back view. No scale.

which were turned in towards his body. The pommel made of gilt silver shows two sculpted quadrupeds resting their snouts against a triangular figure (Hougen 1967, figs. 27–28). A similar arrangement is to be seen on a sword pommel from Endre, Gotland (Nerman 1969, Taf. 52, fig. 521a) and on a silver pommel from a hoard found at Grimeton, Halland, Sweden (Haseloff 1981, Taf. 27). The top guard on the front side is decorated with two parallel rows of spiral tendrils in chip- carving divided by a narrow moulding (Fig. 5a). The back side has only grooves and mouldings (Fig. 5b). The lower guard is ornamented in the same manner. On its underside a small ring is riveted with another loose ring attached to it.

The large buckle with its deeply cut, spiral ornamentation has a thorn sculpted in round in the form of a Style I animal (Haseloff 1981, 183, Abb. 94, Taf 27). It has strong affinities with the buckles from the Sjörup deposit (Forsander 1937, Abb. 5; Hougen 1935:34 ff).

The sword grip is covered with gold foil with embossed ornaments divided into three panels by deep grooves on each side. For the sake of clarity the panels are here numbered from the pommel downwards, the frontside being F, the backside B (Fig. 5a–b). F 1 shows two zoomorphic figures entangled in combat. Panel B 1 shows two men with long hair looking very grimly away from each other, their hair joined in a common sling. Both have one arm lifted above the head with the thumbs of the hands crossing. They seem to be resting their chin on the hand of the other arm and both seem to be kneeling. According to Hauck they are to be understood as the Dioscuri. Panel B 2 has two zoomorphic figures shown in profile in a resting position with one front foot bent and one back foot streched out behind. Panel F 2 shows two doubled up figures, their confronted profiled heads forming a frontal mask. These middle panels are rectangular and about a third of the size of the other four, which have a square form. The lowest front panel F 3 shows two interlocked zoomorphic figures which have been interpreted as the horses of the Dioscuri (Hauck 1980, 533), while the B 3 panel shows a monster seen from above, with its head in profile, in the act of devouring a mixed man-animal creature, while another hybrid of a bearded man with long, straight hair and a zoomorphioc body lies back-to-back with the monster.

All the figures of the sword grip are distinctly designed in high relief with double contour lines setting the different limbs apart from each other. According to Haseloff's structure of Style I all the panels belong to style phase A except for panel F 3 which belongs to phase B (Haseloff 1981, 178, 184). Panel B 1 with the two long-haired men is mounted upside down compared to the other panels, meaning that its motif would be understandable only when the sword was placed with the blade pointing away from the viewer. B 3, however, is best viewed when the sword is resting in the sheath as is the middle panel F 2. The scenes F 1 and F 3 may be seen either way.

The glass beaker had been repaired with gilt silver fittings and a rim mount of gilt silver with rectangular panels of decoration. In one of these a human being with long straight hair is depicted in profile in a crouched position with the arm bent and the thumb of his hand pointing forward (Hougen 1935, Pl.V,2). The motif is possibly related to panel B1 on the sword grip. Another panel has a combat motive of two zoomorphic figures. According to Haseloff the metal objects from Snartemo grave V, which is to be dated to the first half of the sixth century, are ornamented in early Style I (Haseloff 1981, 175). It is possible that all the panels allude to one single Odin myth.

The motifs on the sword from mound II at Snartemo have more features in common with the relief brooches than does the gold grip ring-sword of grave V. The pommel is ornamented with two animal heads sculpted in the round with arched eyebrows and placed on either side of a rhombic figure decorated with several small single figures. Haseloff identifies the animal figures on both sides of the lower guard as griffins and he assigns them to his style phase B (Haseloff 1981, 183). Between them is a rectangular panel with four identical animal figures in a rhythmic composition (Hougen 1935, Pl. VII,2).

The well-furnished weapon grave from mound 2 at Högom contained few decorated metal objects save a sword, numerous clasp buttons and a battle bridle. The sword sheath has a mount of gold foil with an embossed motif of a human face between two Style I animal figures. Above this frieze is another with simple filigree decoration surrounding three mounts for triangular red garnets. Spirals are also the general motif of the decorative gilt silver bands of the sword grip and of the pommel (Haseloff 1981, 183, Taf 99). There is a very obvious front side and back side of the sword (Rahmqvist 1992, pl.16–22,). The man's battle bridle with its side bars which terminate in well sculpted bird's heads with long curved beak and the strap mounts shaped like long zoomorphic masks with slanting eyes and bulging nostrils give a proper martial touch to this northern chieftain's grave (Rahmqvist 1992, pl. 35 and 41).

The so-called smith's grave from Vestly in Southwest Norway was excavated in 1960 and contained a full weapon set, a gold ring and a scutiform object of gold, a Vestland cauldron and smith's tools. A glass beaker was adorned with a gilt silver ribbon with embossed decoration (Møllerop 1960). The motif consists of a row of men doing somersaults over a human head (Fig. 6). When drawn pedagogically in an upright position it becomes clear that the figures come in pairs similarly dressed with a head gear or hair-do known also from a number of relief brooches. One man wears a beard, the other is characterized by a ribbon-like figure protruding from his chest. Their hands are shown with alternatively three or four fingers in addition to the pointing thumb. Related male figures are to be seen on the few gold bracteates with a scene of three persons '*Dreigötterbrakteaten*' (Hauck 1985a, 162–171).

To sum up: there are distinct similarities between motifs found on metal objects decorated in Style I from a small number of weapon graves and motifs on relief brooches. The beast-devouring-beast or -man (or half animal-half man) of the Snartemo V sword (Fig. 5b) is also present on, for example, the equal armed relief brooch from Ekeby, Uppland (Fig. 4). But the differences are more marked. The *horror vacuii* and the monster-like masks of the relief brooches, the stylized animal figures entangled in combat or crouching with open jaw, an occasional human figure in cramped position or a human head *en face* or in profile, and staring eyes everywhere have no real counterpart from the weapon graves. The impression of chaos is contrasted to a design where the figures are easily discernible. Even the early relief brooches with much spiral decoration and relatively few, yet easily discernible, figures are more stylized than the decoration of the swords, buckle and beaker from Snartemo, Sjörup, Grimeton, Högom and Vestly. Human figures (males) are presented on swords and beakers in an early version of Style I where they still are coherent. Wilhelm Holmqvist once characterized Style I as 'the principle of partition', while the main character of Style II is the joining principle. This principle of partition and the *horror vacuii* together with extreme stylization is what constitutes the real difference between the ornamentation of high ranking warriors' decorated weapons and drinking gear and the large brooches of high ranking women. This observed difference may be due to lack of adequate comparative material from male burials, but also to the fact that women and men displayed their decorated items on different (ritualistic) occasions and in different social spheres where both form and motifs played an important role.

Fig. 6 Stamped gilt silver foil. Vestly, Rogaland, Norway (after Haseloff 1986). No scale.

The lady with the brooch

From the central places, Sorte Muld, Bornholm, Gudme-Lundeborg, Funen and Helgö, Uppland, there are known a few stamped gold foils (*gullgubber*) picturing a woman wearing a large brooch in the form of a relief brooch or (most commonly) a button-on-the-bow brooch (Fig. 7). A silver pendant of a (pregnant?) woman also wearing a large button-on-the-bow brooch comes from a Viking period grave from Aska, Östergötland (Holmqvist 1960, figs. 26 and 31; Arrhenius 1962, 79–97). These not only give us an idea of how the relief brooches were worn, but also indicate that the large gilt ones (at least) were used

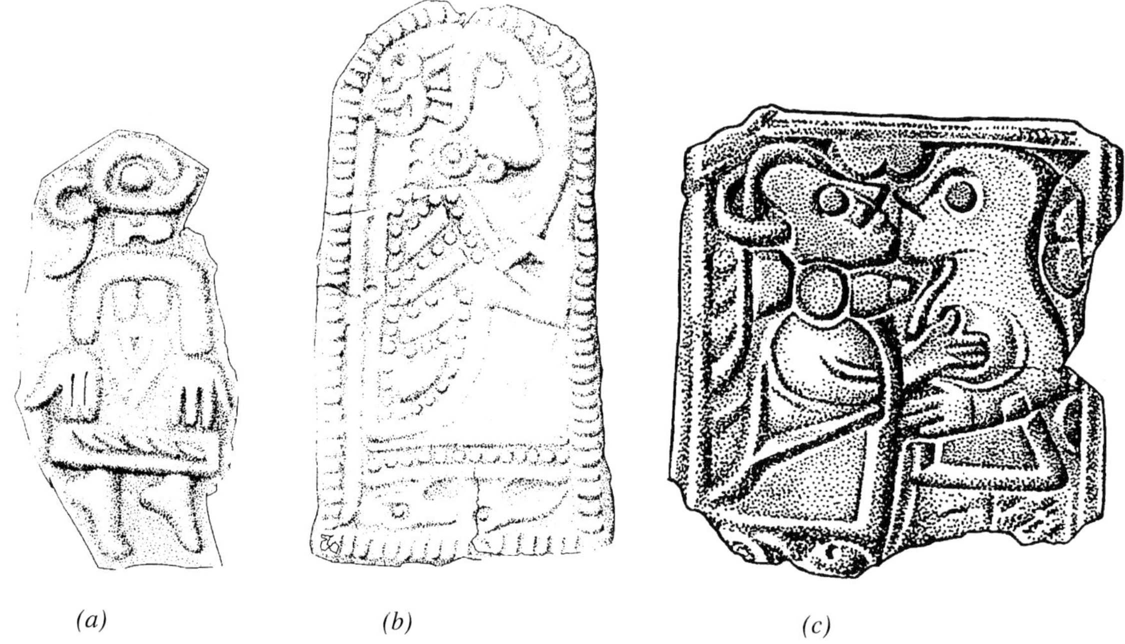

(a) *(b)* *(c)*

*Fig. 7 Gold foils (*gullgubber*) of ladies wearing large brooches: (a) and (b) from Sorte Muld, Bornholm (drawing E.Koch, after Watt 1991); (c) from Helgö, Uppland. Not to scale. Drawing B. Händel.*

in a ritualistic worship, a custom which must have begun early in the Migration period with the silver foil brooches and continued well into the Merovingian period (Watt 1991). The gold foils also demonstrate that only the form of the brooch (and the impression of golden metal) and not the complicated ornamentation was visible for persons standing at a distance from the woman wearing it (Arnold 1997, 181). In a room lit by torches and flames from the fire place, the golden relief of a large brooch would create an impression of moving light and shadow.

The large relief brooches of gilt silver with niello inlay must have been precious and important objects. They were copied in bronze and gilt to give the impression of being made of gold, and the workshop material from Helgö proves that more than two hundred relief brooches of very varied form and ornamentation were produced there during the Migration period (Holmqvist 1972). Other workshops did also exist but with a small-scale production (Rahmqvist 1983, 97–107). Early in the period very few brooches came in 'series' like the bird frieze brooches, but later it obviously became of constantly greater importance to produce several of a kind. The times were such that it seemed essential for not only the most powerful families to demonstrate their loyalties and alliances in common rituals, to distinguish between 'us and them' in social strategies to uphold land and power.

References

Arbman, H. 1945: 'Stildrag i folkvandringstidens konst', *Fornvännen* 40, 88–101.

Arnold, C.J. 1997: *An Archaeology of the Early Anglo-Saxon Kingdoms* (London).

Arrhenius, B. 1962: 'Det flammande smycket', *Fornvännen* 57, 79–97.

Arrhenius, B. 1977: East Scandinavian Style I. *Medieval Archaeology* 27, 26–42.

Bakka, E. 1958: 'On the beginning of Style I in England', *Universitetet i Bergen Årbok, Historisk- antikvarisk rekke* 3, 2–83.

Bakka, E. 1973: 'Goldbrakteaten in norwegischen Grabfunden: Datierungsfragen', *Frühmittelalterliche Studien*7, 53–87.

Bennett, A. 1987: *Graven. Religiös och social symbol. Strukturer i folkvandringstidens gravskick i Mälarområdet,* Theses and Papers in North-European Archaeology 18 (Stockholm).

Bierbrauer, V. 1975: *Die ostgotischen Grab- und Schatzfunde in Italien*, Centro italiano di studi sull'alto medioevo (Spoleto).

Brown, K.R. 1996: 'If only the dead could talk', in Calinescu, A. (ed.) *Ancient Jewelry and Archaeology* (Indiana), 224–234.

v.Carnap-Bornheim, C. and Ilkjær, J. 1996: *Illerup Ådal. Die Prachtausrüstungen,* 5–8, Jysk Arkæologisk Selskabs Skrifter 25 (Aarhus).

Csallany, D. 1961: *Archäologische Denkmäler der Gepiden im Mitteldonaubecken (454–568 u. Z.),* Archaeologia Hungarica Dissertationes Archaeologicae Musei Nationalis Hungarici, Series Nova 38 (Budapest).

Falk, H. 1924: 'Odensheite', *Skrifter Videnskapsselskapets i Kristiania*, II. Hist.-Filos Klasse 10, 1–45.

Fett, E.N. 1937: 'Nordische Fibeln der Völkerwanderungszeit', *IPEK* 11, 106–116.

Fonnesbech-Sandberg, E. 1991: 'Guldets funktion i ældre germansk jernalder', in Fabech, C. and J.Ringtved (eds.) *Samfunds-organisation og Regional Variation* (Aarhus), 233–244.

Forsander, J.E. 1937: 'Provinzialrömisches und Germanisches', *Meddelanden från Lunds Universitets Historiska Museum* 7, 11–101.

Gullman, J. 1995: 'Sveriges största guldskatt i ny belysning-Timboholmskatten undersökt med modern teknik', *Fornvännen* 90, 213–220.

Gustavson, H. 1991: *Rökstenen*, Svenska Kulturminnen 23 (Uddevalla).

Hannestad, N. 1976: *Romersk Kunst som Propaganda* (Copenhagen).

Hannestad, N. 1986: *Roman Art and Imperial Policy*, Jysk Arkæologisk Selskabs Skrifter 19 (Aarhus).

Hansen, U.L. in press: '"Goldring", Hals – und Armring. Sozial-geschichtlicher Stellenwert der Goldringe im Sinne von J.Werner und O. Kyhlberg', *Reallexikon der Germanischen Altertumskunde* (Berlin).

Haseloff, G. 1981: *Die germanische Tierornamentik der Völkerwanderungszeit,* 1–3 (Berlin).

Haseloff, G. 1986: 'Bild und Motiv in Nydam-Stil und Stil I', in Roth H. (ed.), *Zum Problem der Deutung frühmittelalterlicher Bildinhalte* (Sigmaringen), 67–110.

Hauck, K. 1980: 'Gemeinschaftstiftende Kulte der Seegermanen', *Frühmittelalterliche Studien* 14, 463–617.

Hauck, K. 1985a: 'Motivanalyse eines Doppelbrakteaten', *Frühmittelalterliche Studien* 19, 196–199.

Hauck, K. 1985b: *Die Goldbrakteaten der Völkerwanderungszeit*, IK 1, Münstersche Mittelalter-Schriften 24/1–2.

Hauck, K. 1992: 'Fünens Anteil an den Bildinhalten der Brakteaten', *Frühmittelalterliche Studien* 26, 115.

Hedeager, L. 1991: 'Gulddepoterne fra ældre germanertid – forsøg på tolkning', in Fabech, Ch. and Ringtved, J. (eds), *Samfunds-organisation og Regional Variation* (Aarhus), 203–212.

Hedeager, L. 1992: 'Kingdoms, ethnicity and material culture: Denmark in a European perspective', in Carver, M.O.H. (ed.), *The age of Sutton Hoo. The seventh century in North-western Europe*, Boydell Press (Woodbridge), 279–300.

Herschend, F. 1980: 'Myntat och omyntat guld. Två studier i öländska guldfynd. I: Det myntade guldet', *Tor* 18, 33–194.

Hines, J. 1989: 'Ritual hoarding in Migration-Period Scandinavia: a review of recent interpretations', *Proceedings of the Prehistoric Society* 55, 193–205.

Hines, J. 1997: *A New Corpus of Anglo-Saxon Great Square-Headed Brooches*, Report of the Research Committee of the Society of Antiquaries of London 51, The Boydell Press (Woodbridge).

Holmqvist 1960: 'The dancing gods', *Acta Archaeologica* 31, 101–127.

Holmqvist, W. 1972: 'Relief brooches. The Helgö workshops', in W. Holmqvist, *Excavations at Helgö IV* (Uppsala), 230–262.

Hougen, B. 1935: *Snartemofunnet. Studier i folkevandringstidens ornamentikk og tekstilhistorie* (Oslo).

Hougen, B. 1967: *The Migration Style of Ornament in Norway*, Catalogue, 2nd ed. (Oslo).

Høilund Nielsen, K. 1991: 'Centrum og periferi.i 6.–8 årh. Territoriale studier af dyrestil og kvindesmykker i yngre germansk jernalder i Syd – og Øst-Skandinavien', in Mortensen, P. and M. Rasmussen, B.M. (eds), *Fra Stamme til Stat i Danmark 2. Høvdingesamfund og Kongemagt*, Jysk Arkaeologisk Selskabs Skrifter 22,2 (Aarhus), 127–154.

Klindt- Jensen, O. 1957: *Bornholm i Folkevandringstiden*, Nat.Mus Skrifter 2 (Copenhagen).

Krause, W. 1966: *Die Runeninschriften im älteren Futhark*, (Göttingen).

Kristoffersen, S. 1995: 'Transformation in Migration animal art', *Norwegian Archaeological Review* 28/1, 1–17.

Kristoffersen, S. in prep.: 'Dyreornamentikkens sosiale tilhørighet og politiske sammenheng. Nydamstil og Stil I i S og SV Norge', Dr. dissertation, Univ. of Bergen, Norway.

Kyhlberg, O. 1986: 'Late Roman and Byzantine solidi', in Lundström, A. and Clarke, H. (eds), *Excavations at Helgö X*, (Stockholm), 13–126.

Lamm, J.P. 1979: 'De folkvandringstida reliefspännena från Hamre och Rallsta', *Västmanlands Fornminnesförening, Årsskrift* 57, 126–134.

Lamm, J.P. 1994: 'De stora ringguldsfynden', in Knape, A. (ed.), *Guldets magi i saga och verklighet*, Statens Historiska Museum (Stockholm), 35–36.

Lindqvist, S. 1941: *Gotlands Bildsteine I–II* (Stockholm).

Lundström, A. 1972: 'Relief brooches. Introduction to form element and variation', in Holmqvist, W., *Excavations at Helgö IV*, 132–229.

Mackeprang, M. 1952: *De Nordiske Guldbrakteater*, Jysk Arkeologisk Selskabs Skrifter 2 (Aarhus).

Magnus, B. 1975: *Krosshaugfunnet. Et forsøk på kronologisk og stilhistorisk plassering i 5 årh.*, Stavanger Museums Skrifter 9 (Stavanger).

Magnus, B. 1995: 'Praktspennen fra Gillberga', *Från bergslag och bondbygd. Årsbok för Örebro läns hembygdförbund och Stiftelsen Örebro läns museum 46*, 29–41.

Magnus, B. in prep: A Corpus of East Scandinavian Relief Brooches.

Meyer, E.N. 1934: 'Relieffspenner i Norden', *Bergens Museums årbok, Historisk- antikvarisk rekke* 4, 1–125.

Moore, H. 1995: 'The problems of origins. Poststructuralism and beyond', in Hodder, I. *et al.* (eds), *Interpreting Archaeology* (London), 51–3.

Myhre, B. 1987: 'Chieftains' graves and chiefdom territories in South Norway in the Migration Period', *Studien zur Sachsenforschung 6*, 169–188.

Møllerop, O. 1960: 'Foreløpig meddelelse om et smedgravfunn fra Vestly i Time', *Stavanger Museums Årbok* 70, 5–14.

Neméth, P. 1988: 'Gepidische Reihengräberfelder im Theiss-Maros-Gebiet', *Germanen, Hunnen und Awaren. Schätze derVölkerwanderungszeit*, Catalogue, Germanisches Nationalmuseum (Nürnberg), 245–246.

Nerman, B. 1969: *Die Vendelzeit Gotlands II. Tafeln*, Kungl. Vitterhet Historie och Antikvitets Akademien (Stockholm).

Näsman, U. 1984: 'Zwei Relieffibeln von der Insel Öland', *Prähistorische Zeitschrift 59/1*, 48–80.

Näsman, U. 1988: 'Den folkvandringstida ?krisen i Sydskandinavien, inklusive Öland och Gotland', in Näsman, U. and Lund, J. (eds), *Folkevandringstiden i Norden. En krisetid mellem ældre og yngre jernalder* (Aarhus), 227–25.

Petré, B. 1984: *Arkeologiska undersökningar på Lovö 2. Fornlämning RAÄ 27, Lunda*, Studies in North-European Archaeology 8 (Stockholm).

Pohl, W. 1980: 'Gepiden und Gentes an der mittleren Donau nach Zerfall des Attilareiches', in Wolfram, W. and Daim, F. (eds), *Die Völker an der mittleren und unteren Donau im fünften und sechsten Jahrhundert* (Wien), 240–305.

Rahmqvist, P. 1983: *Gene. On the Origin, Function and Development of Sedentary Iron Age Settlement in Northern Sweden*, Archaeology and Enviornment 1 (Umeå).

Rahmqvist, P. 1992: *Högom Part 1. The Excavations 1949–1984*, Archaeology and Environment 13 (Neumünster).

Ringtved, J. 1988: 'Regionalitet. Et jysk eksempel fra yngre romertid og ældre germanertid', in Mortensen, P. and Rasmussen, B.M. (eds), *Fra Stamme til Stat i Danmark 1. Jernalderens stammesamfund*, Jysk Arkæologisk Selskabs Skrifter 22, 37–52.

Sjøvold, T. 1993: *The Scandinavian Relief Brooches of the Migration Period*, Norske Oldfunn 15 (Oslo).

Stenberger, M. 1933: *Öland under äldre järnåldern. Zusammenfassung* (Stockholm).

Vang Petersen, P. 1987: 'Nydam III – et våbenoffer fra ældre germansk jernalder', *Aarbøger for nordisk oldkyndighet* (Copenhagen), 105–137.

Watt, M. 1991: 'Sorte Muld Høvdingesæde og kultcentrum fra Bornholms yngre jernalder', in Mortensen, P. and Rasmussen, B.M. (eds), *Høvdingesamfund og Kongemagt. Fra Stamme til Stat i Danmark 2*, 89–106.

Widgren, M. 1988: 'Om skillnader och likheter mellan regioner', in Näsman, U. and Lund, J. (eds), *Folkevandringstiden i Norden* (Aarhus), 273–287.

Wolfram, H. 1990: *History of the Goths* (California).

Åberg, N. 1924: *Den Nordiska Folkvandringstidens Kronologi* (Stockholm).

Åberg, N. 1953: *Den Historiska Relationen mellan Folkvandringstid och Vendeltid*, Kungl. Vitterhets historie och antikvitets akademiens handlingar 82 (Stockholm).

Anglo-Saxon Studies in Archaeology and History 10, 1999

Kings or gods? Iconographic evidence from Scandinavian gold foil figures

Margrethe Watt

Introduction

A recent find of 2345 tiny gold foil figures ('*guldgubber*') of largely Merovingian Age from the settlement site of Sorte Muld on the Baltic island of Bornholm forms the basis of a systematic analysis of the pictorial content of this unique group of finds (Fig. 1).

The Scandinavian gold foil figures ('*guldgubber*') were among the first archaeological finds to be described and discussed in detail (von Melle 1725).

The gold foil figures, which measure from 7–8 mm to over 30 mm in height, are stamped on very thin gold foil or cut out individually from a slightly thicker gold sheet.

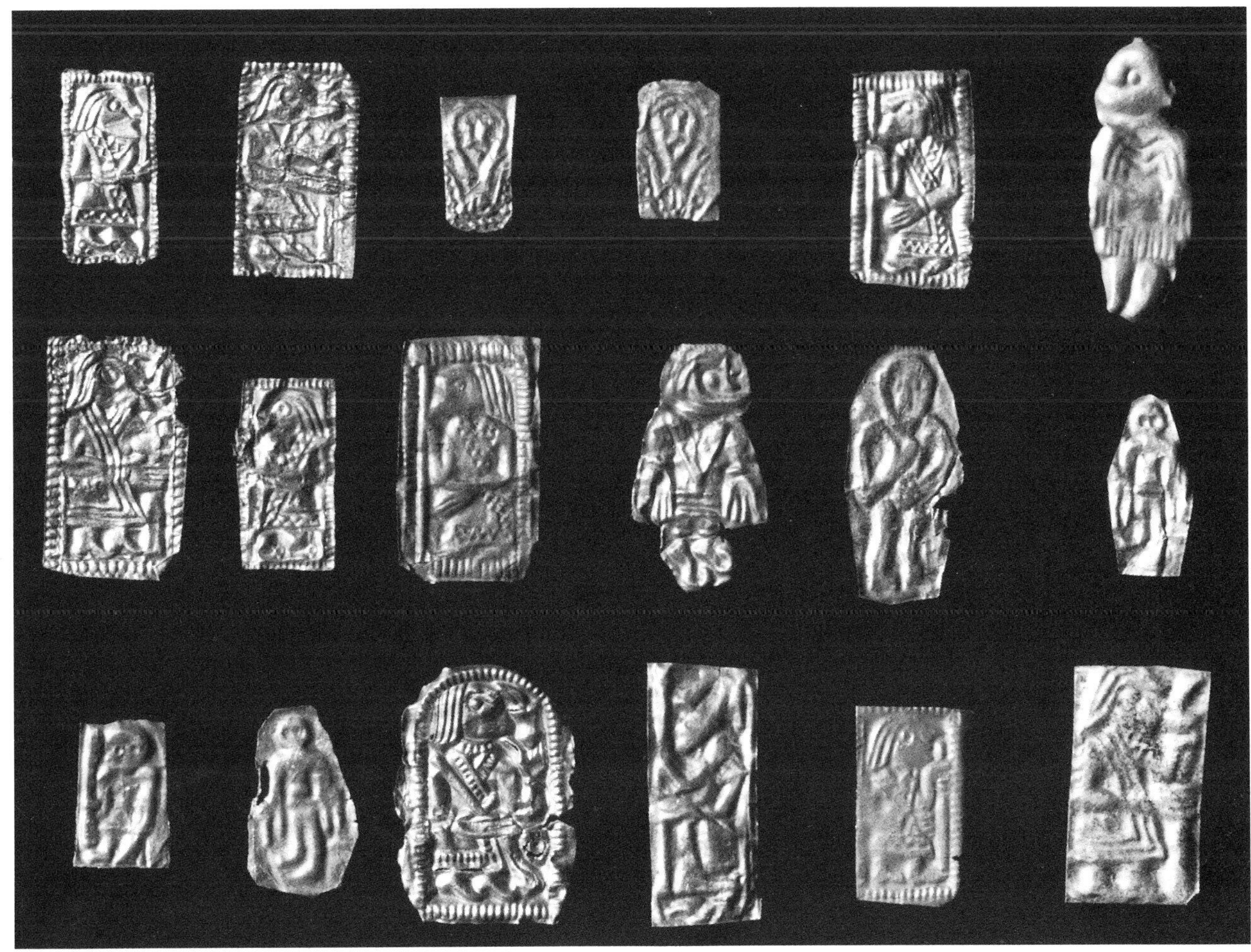

Fig. 1 Examples of typical stamped gold foil figures from the Iron Age settlement site of Sorte Muld. Phot. National Museum, Copenhagen.

The find from Sorte Muld is by far the largest and most diverse single occurrence of this type. However, for comparative purposes gold foil figures from other localities are taken into consideration. So far none has with certainty been found outside Scandinavia (Gustafson 1900; Hauck 1994; Holmquist *et al.* 1961; Lidén 1969; Lundquist 1996; Mackeprang 1943; Munch 1991; Nordén 1938; Thomsen 1993; Watt 1992; Watt in press; Zachrisson 1963).

The possibility of identifying named figures or 'professions' such as *kings, 'heroes', gods* or *priests* in otherwise anonymous iconographic material has tempted and fascinated both archaeologists and colleagues from neighbouring disciplines studying the social structure or religious rites and symbolism of Early Medieval society (e.g. Hauck 1992; 1993; 1994; Steinsland 1990).

Discoveries of new iconographic material of a magnitude such as that from Sorte Muld offers a unique opportunity for a renewed study of this fascinating group of finds from the sixth and seventh centuries. In connection with presentation and preliminary discussion of the gold foil figures from Sorte Muld I have suggested a function for these small and flimsy figures as 'temple money' (evidence of non-Christian religious activity) (Watt 1991a; 1991b; 1992).

The material

Since the appearance of the large find of figures from Sorte Muld the numbers from other Scandinavian localities have grown slowly but steadily, so that the total number of gold foil figures exceeds 2650 (to date: 1997). Of these the vast majority – at least 2374 – originate in Bornholm, 112 have been found throughout the rest of Denmark, 113 in Sweden and 43 in Norway (Fig. 2). From written accounts it is also known that many have been lost over the years, so that the totals mentioned here are minimum figures.

Of greater significance than the total numbers are the variations in die types and different motifs represented as well as their geographical distribution.

Archaeological context

Recent excavations have confirmed that the gold foil figures first and foremost are associated with what may be interpreted as central settlement or trading sites, probably the homes of petty kings or chieftains with well established political or trade contacts outside their local sphere of influence. Only exceptionally do gold foil figures appear in other contexts such as grave finds.

Results of excavations – combined with information gleaned from place names such as Gudme ('home of the gods') – suggest that pre-Christian, religious activities may have continued into Christian times at some of the sites (e.g. Lidén 1969; Zachrisson 1963). It should also be noted that nearly all find localities lie within easy access to the sea (Fig. 2).

Dating

Earlier discussions of the chronology of the gold foil figures, based largely on stylistic criteria linked to datable grave finds, suggested a date-range from the Migration Period to the Viking Age (Mackeprang 1943; Nordén 1938).

Some of the objects (attributes) depicted on figures from the recent find from Sorte Muld also give important clues as to the date: the presence of a ring sword (Fig. 3b) suggests a date not later than the early seventh century, a one-edged seax, fibulae and characteristic glass beaker types may point to dates in the sixth and seventh centuries (Figs. 3c, 3d and 3a) (Arrhenius 1983; Menghin 1983; Näsman 1986).

A number of recent excavations (Lundeborg, Sorte Muld, Ströby, Helgö, Eketorp, Borg (Lofoten) and Slöinge (Bohuslän)) have provided important new possibilities for independent archaeological dates, suggesting that the tradition of producing and using gold foil figures of this type may have existed for up to 200 years from the end of the Migration Period to the Early Viking Age. Recent excavations at Slöinge in western Sweden have provided a dendrochronologically based date for the deposition of the gold foil figures to later than 689 (Lundquist 1996).

Pictorial content of the gold foil figures

For the systematic analysis of attributes or symbols with a bearing on kingship and royal power the amount of detail shown by individual figures is of prime importance. While some figures are shown in great detail, others are stylised sometimes to a degree of being almost purely ornamental. The possible 'messages' contained in the posture, gesture and presence of attributes – and their relative frequency of occurrence – may hold important clues as to the function of the figures.

Single and double figures

The gold foil figures may be grouped in several different ways. Apart from rare animal figures, so far occurring only at Sorte Muld, the main distinction in iconographic content is between single and double figures.

Single figures (Figs. 3–4) are largely limited to southern and eastern Scandinavia (Southern Sweden, Öland, Bornholm as well as occasional occurrences from Fyn and Jutland) (Fig. 2).

The double figures (Fig. 5) have a wider distribution, occurring throughout Scandinavia from the Baltic to northern Norway. Compared to the single figures, they appear on the one hand to be quite stereotyped in their composition, but on the other to show certain regional stylistic differences.

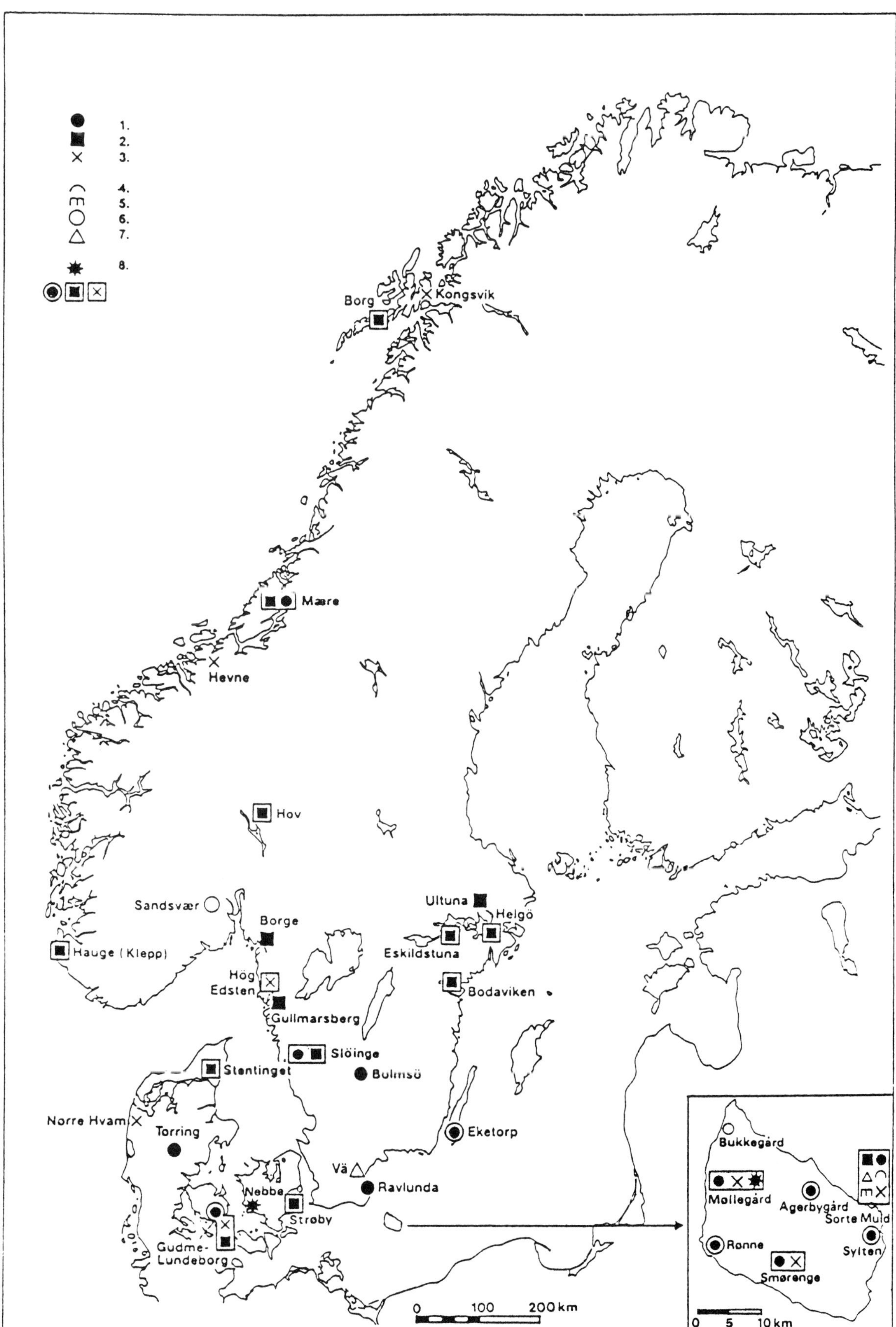

Fig. 2 Distribution of Scandinavian gold foil figures. 1. Stamped single figures; 2. Stamped double figures; 3. Individually cut or engraved figures; 4. Stamped animal figures; 5. Individually cut animal figure; 6. Uncertain figure type; 7. Stamped bronze figures; 8. Stamp for gold foil figure. Framed symbols indicate settlement context.

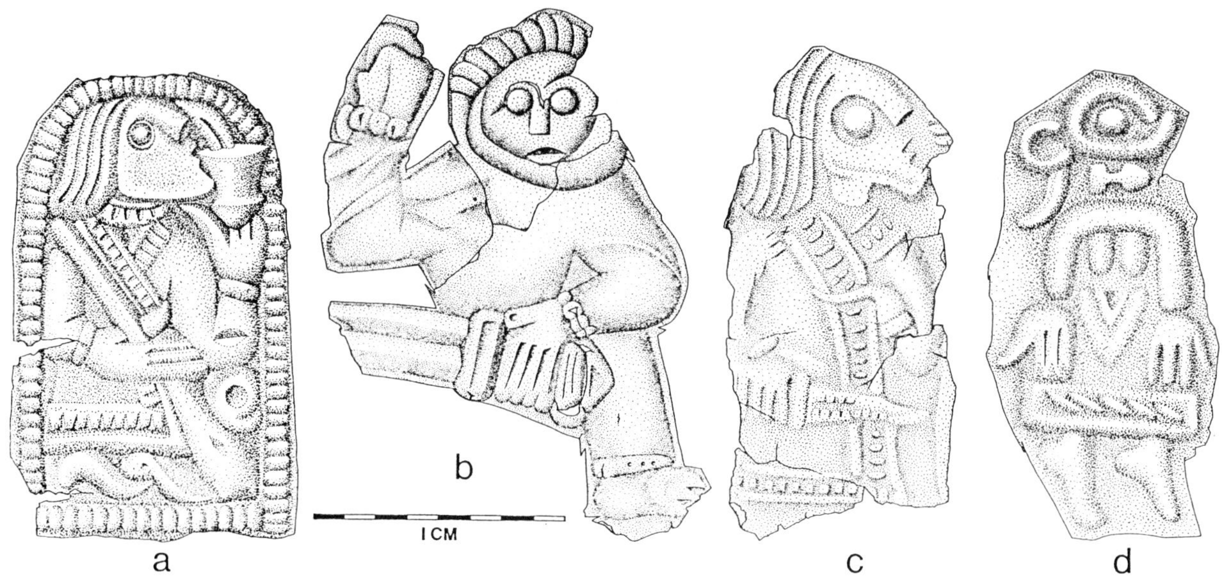

*Fig. 3 Figures from Sorte Muld with datable attributes: a. glass beaker (*Sturzbecher*); b. ring sword; c. single-edged seax; d. fibula. Drawn by Eva Koch.*

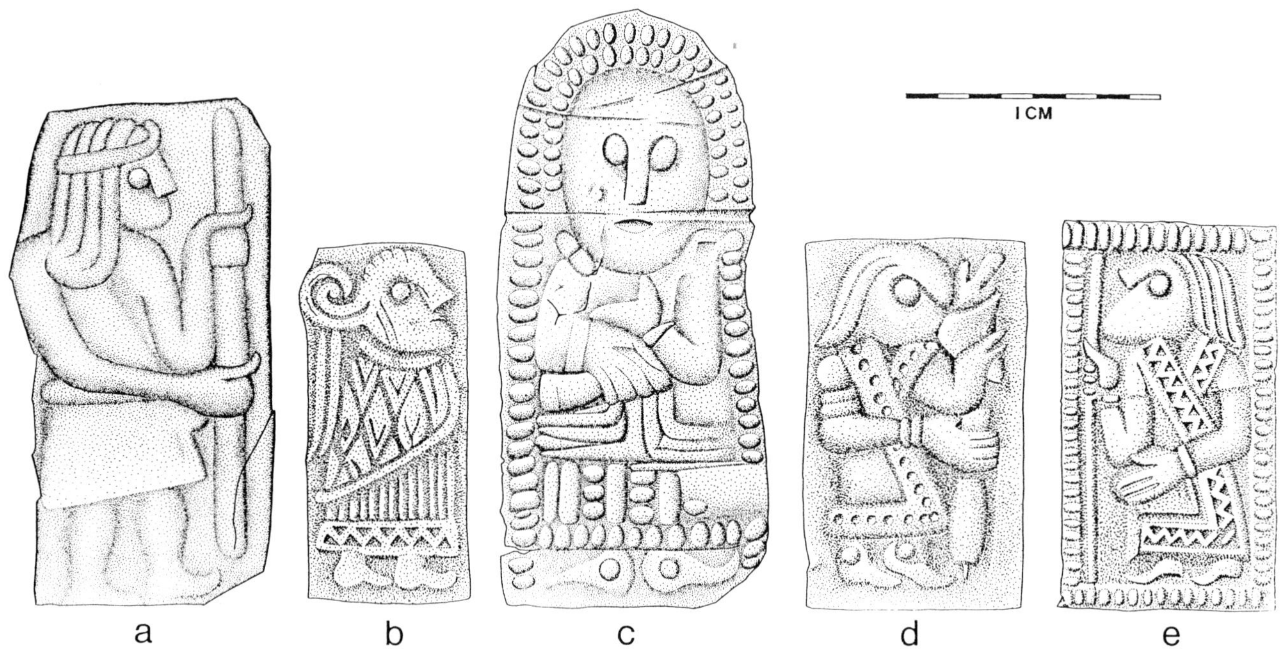

Fig. 4 Single gold foil figures from Sorte Muld. Drawn by Eva Koch.

Determination of sex

The practical distinction between male and female figures on the basis of a traditional combination of dress and hairstyle together with secondary characteristics (sex-specific attributes and posture) does not pose a major problem. Some of the very stylised types do, however, lack 'formal' sex-specific characteristics.

In a paper published in 1992 a preliminary division of the human figures into two main groups was suggested on the basis of elements such as posture, dress and attributes (Watt 1992, 217). For convenience of reference they are referred to as 'princely' or 'parading' figures and 'dancers' (i.e. figures – mostly nude – indicating movement), a term borrowed from Wilhelm Holmquist (1961).

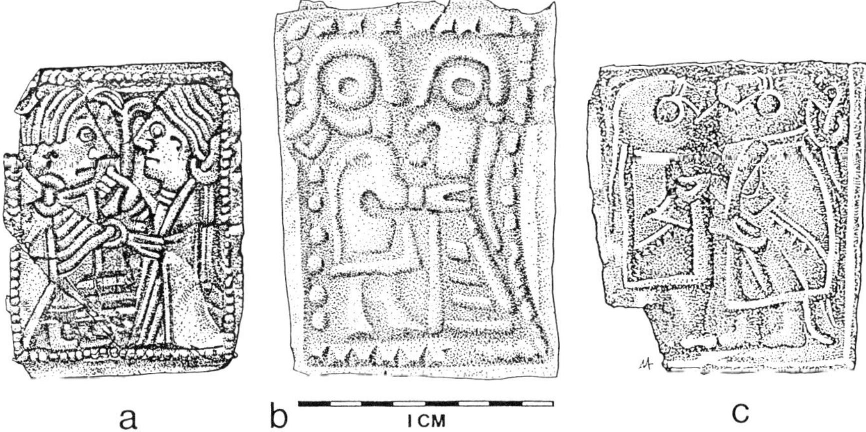

Fig. 5 Double figures from a: Klepp, Norway (drawn from photograph); b. Sorte Muld (drawn by Eva Koch); c. Slöinge, Sweden (after Lundquist and Rosengren 1992).

Dies

On the basis of the products of at least 550–600 different dies (or stamps) known up to now, the general impression is that most of them form surprisingly stereotyped groups. So far two stamps have been found on Sjælland and one on Bornholm (Fig. 6).

The greatest variation is found among the approximately 420 different dies from Sorte Muld as well as an additional 60 individually shaped (cut out) and engraved figures. Certain individual dies have produced in excess of 180 identical pieces; the majority, however, occur in ones and twos. The large number of types from Sorte Muld also show that some of the most popular motifs form 'strings' of die copies (Fig. 7).

Gold foil figures from other sites so far only occur in very small numbers of stamp-identical pieces. Long distance stamp identity has been recorded not just between Sorte Muld and other localities on the island of Bornholm, but also between Bornholm, Sjælland and Fyn.

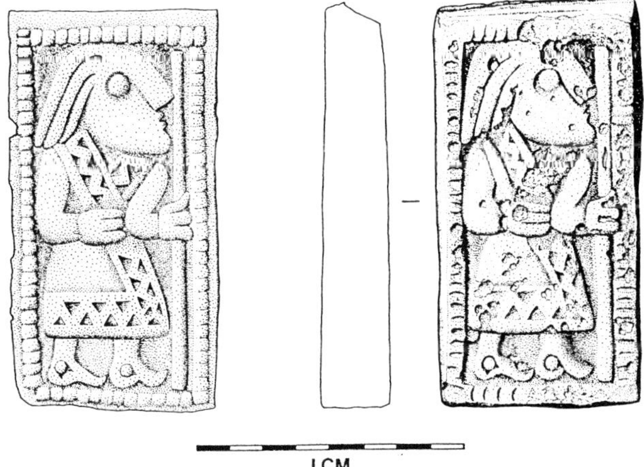

Fig. 6 A stray find of a bronze stamp (right) from the settlement site of Møllegård, Bornholm, was used for the production of at least sixty-seven gold foil figures (left) from Sorte Muld. Drawn by Eva Koch.

Iconographic and symbolic content

Analysing unique iconographic material such as the gold foil figures, one must assume that systematically occurring features such as attributes, posture and gesture have a meaning, most obviously as an expression of 'ritual' in a wide sense. Comparing details and variations within motif-related series of figures is equally important, as this suggests which specific iconographic features were regarded as important at the time.

Do the gestures represent a kind of 'liturgical language' or 'body language', a language meaningful only to the initiated? The range of gestures appear comparable to the type of 'abbreviations' most commonly seen on coins and on the closely related bracteates as well as in religious iconography in a wide sense. Even today a similar 'gesture language' is encountered in both religious and secular ceremonies, such as church ritual or in the gesture of oath-taking.

Arch ('aedicula')

The arch-shaped frame which surrounds a number of the stamped figures (Figs. 3a, 4c and 7) has close parallels in the *aedicula* of secular as well as religious (also Christian) contexts, where it signals the august position of the figure it surrounds (Fig. 8a).

Garment

The majority of figures appear to be dressed in some kind of garment, though the amount of detail shown on individual figures varies considerably. Among the more detailed representations it is possible to distinguish some

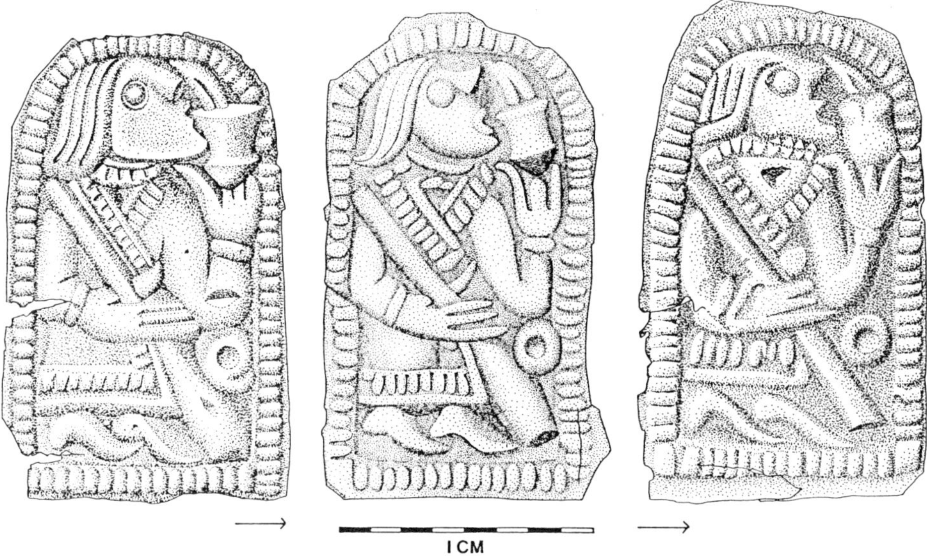

Fig. 7 String of die copies from Sorte Muld. Drawn by Eva Koch.

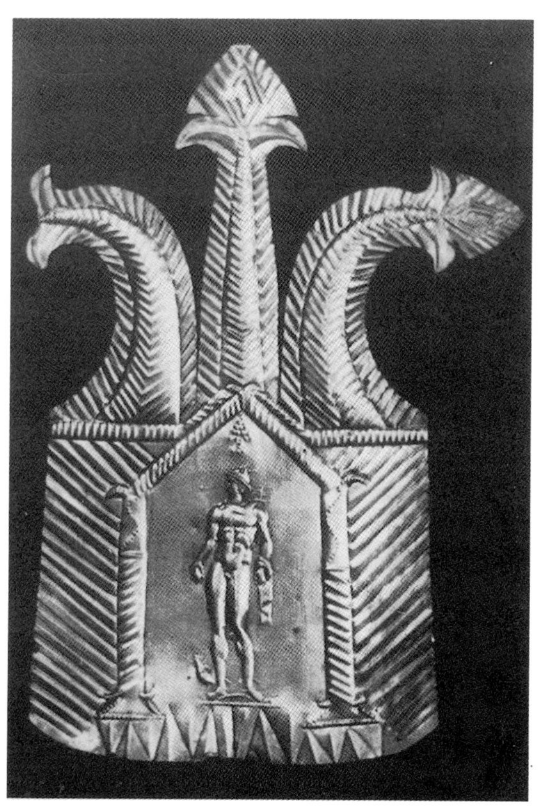

(a)

(b)

*Fig. 8 Votive plaque from the Weißenburg hoard (a) showing the god Mercurius standing inside an arch (*aedicula*) (after Kellner and Zahlhaas 1983); b. the field marshal Flavius Felix wearing ceremonial dress and carrying a 'sceptre of office' (after Garbsch and Overbeck 1989).*

standard male and female dress types (e.g. 'kaftan, 'frock and 'cape') (Figs. 4–5). While some variations in dress fashion may prove to have chronological significance, it seems likely that – at least the more elaborate – costumes also may signify rank.

'Nude' figures make up a separate group.

Hairstyle

Long hair (shoulder length or longer) is a consistent and seemingly consciously underlined feature of the majority of the male figure types (Fig.4a). The apparently consistent use of long hair as a symbol of privilege such as held by Merovingian royalty is considered important for the discussion and interpretation of the figures (Wallace-Hadrill 1982, 156–57). Figures featuring a beard are rare.

A characteristic female hairstyle with an elaborate knot or 'bun' at the top or back of the head appears to match the standard Nordic hairstyle in Late pre-Viking and Viking times (Figs. 4b and 5). However, straight 'male' hair of shoulder length is occasionally seen combined with otherwise characteristically female dress types.

Attributes

By attribute is meant any 'additional' object carried by or associated with the figures. Within the range of attributes, those relevant to the recognition and discussion of early kingship will be mentioned.

Discussing the representation of what may be regarded as *regalia* it is important to consider how contemporary Germanic society – and in particular those groups of people who lived geographically furthest removed from the Imperial frontiers – percieved the concept of rank and power symbolised by *regalia*.

Sceptre

More than half the figure types with sufficient detail appear to carry a long staff (Figs. 4a and 4e). In more than 80 per cent of these this staff or sceptre appears to be the only attribute. It is remarkable that this obviously important figure type, represented by almost 200 different dies, so far only occurs on the island of Bornholm.

An interpretation of the staff as a 'sceptre' or a symbol of high rank seems obvious, but a function as 'sceptre of office', as seen on the fifth-century consular diptych showing the field marshal Flavius Felix carrying his sceptre of office, should also be considered (Fig. 8b). Gods equipped with a sceptre are well known from Late Roman coins and medallions. Professor Karl Hauck, who has drawn attention to many interesting features, and has come forward with bold suggestions for the interpretation of the motifs on the gold foil figures in connection with his study of bracteate iconography, has argued that a short rod carried by certain figures may be interpreted as a 'sorcerer's staff' (Hauck 1994, 253).

Diadem

While the diadem is commonly depicted on Imperial coins as well as bracteate portraits, only a single occurrence has so far been registered in the group of gold foil figures (Fig. 4a). It is depicted in the form of a circlet, and although the workmanship lacks in detail, the raised knob above the forehead is clearly meant to show the mounted jewel seen above the forehead, as on solidi of the fifth and sixth centuries. The streamers at the back of the head featured on many bracteates are lacking in this case. This rare occurrence of what appears to be an Imperial diadem suggests that the craftsman was not familiar with this type of regalia.

At this point attention should also be drawn to the more surprising absence of a helmet on any of the figures. Helmets appear otherwise to be both well known and geographically widespread attributes of persons of royal or princely rank within the Germanic area. The absence is all the more surprising as figures almost identical to the most common types from Sorte Muld decorate a number of comtemporary helmets (Bruce-Mitford 1978, figs. 140, 143; Stolpe and Arne 1912).

Sword

Swords are only depicted on two of the figures, both from Sorte Muld (Figs. 3b–c). One is of the single-edged seax-type, the other – although fragmentary – is clearly two-edged with a ring attached to the hilt. Considering the importance of the ring sword as a symbol of fealty or allegiance within the Germanic '*Gefolgschaft*' (Steuer 1987), it is slightly surprising to find only a single occurrence, in this case associated with a figure of unusual posture. A possible explanation may be that the ring sword had already become a rather antiquated type at this time.

Ring

Rings occur as both neck and arm rings and in rare instances also as ankle rings. It is a difficult attribute-type to deal with as the determination of what is clearly intended to be a ring and what may equally well be regarded as an ornamental detail of the costume, will in some cases remain a matter of interpretation.

Indisputable representations of *arm rings* are limited to a few examples where one or more rings or 'bands' are placed round the upper arm (Fig. 4d).

Unquestionable *neck rings* are most commonly associated with the group of seemlingly nude figures ('dancers') (Fig. 9). This group includes not just serially stamped (matrix produced) figures, but also a number of individually cut figures with separate gold strips wound

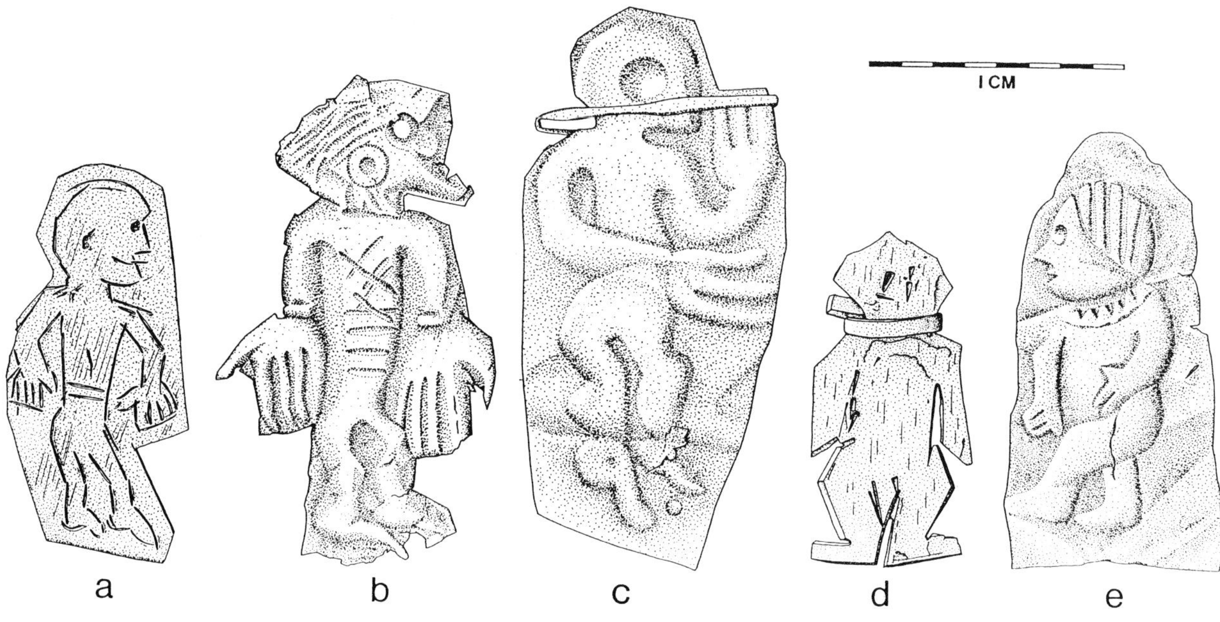

Fig. 9. 'Nude' figures from Sorte Muld. a–b with 'belt' attribute; c–e with neck rings. Drawn by Eva Koch.

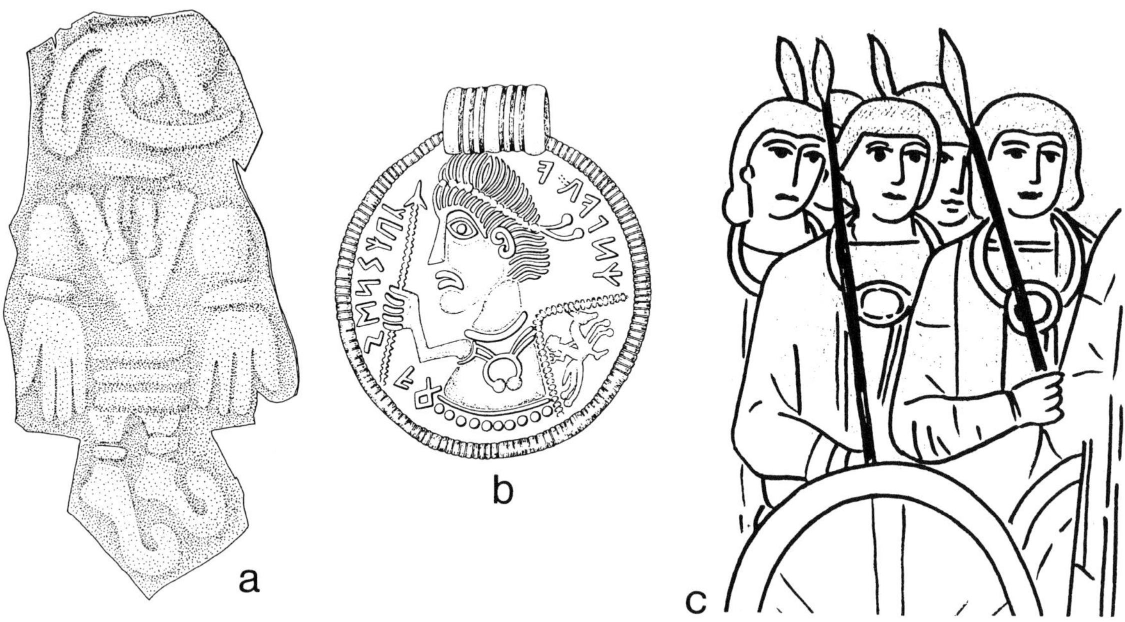

Fig. 10 Figure from Sorte Muld (a) and bracteate from Gummersmark (b) both apparently wearing 'torques' in the same manner as shown on the famous sixth-century mosaic from the church of San Vitale depicting officers of the emperor Justinian's guard (c); a. drawn by Eva Koch; b. after Hauck (ed.) 1986; c. sketched from photograph.

around the neck. The latter are considered to be particularly important as they seem to underline the presence of this attribute (Figs. 9c–d).

Torque

A small number of figures have an ornament shaped like a penannular brooch placed on the chest in the same manner as is seen on the well known 'A-type' bracteate from Gummersmark on Sjælland (Figs. 10a–b). The ornament may be interpreted as a torque similar to those worn by trusted members of the emperor Justinian's guard (Fig. 10c) (Morten Axboe, personal communication).

Space does not allow a detailed survey of all attributes and symbols associated with the gold foil figures. So far attention has been drawn only to those associated with male figures and with a bearing on 'kingship' in the widest sense. Other items depicted on the gold foils include 'clubs', drinking vessels, drinking horns, jewellery (female figures), branches or shoots (double figures), belt ('nude dancers') as well as a small number of unidentified objects or symbols.

Posture and gesture

The above review of the regalia may be supplemented with a brief presentation of the range of gestures shown by typical single figures from Sorte Muld mentioned in the introduction (Fig. 11).

The position of the hands of the single figures are of course partly controlled by the attributes attached to individual figures (Fig. 11A). But, particularly within the group of nude figures, the 'free' – and frequently oversized – hands (Fig. 11B) appear to reflect a true gesture language to which it is possible to find parallels, especially among the gold bracteates. Some gestures also have close parallels among the widespread and stereotype hand positions characteristic of prayer and blessing seen in Late Roman and contemporary Christian art. On a sixth-century mural from the church of St. Demetrius (Saloniki) the praying hands of the saint are covered in

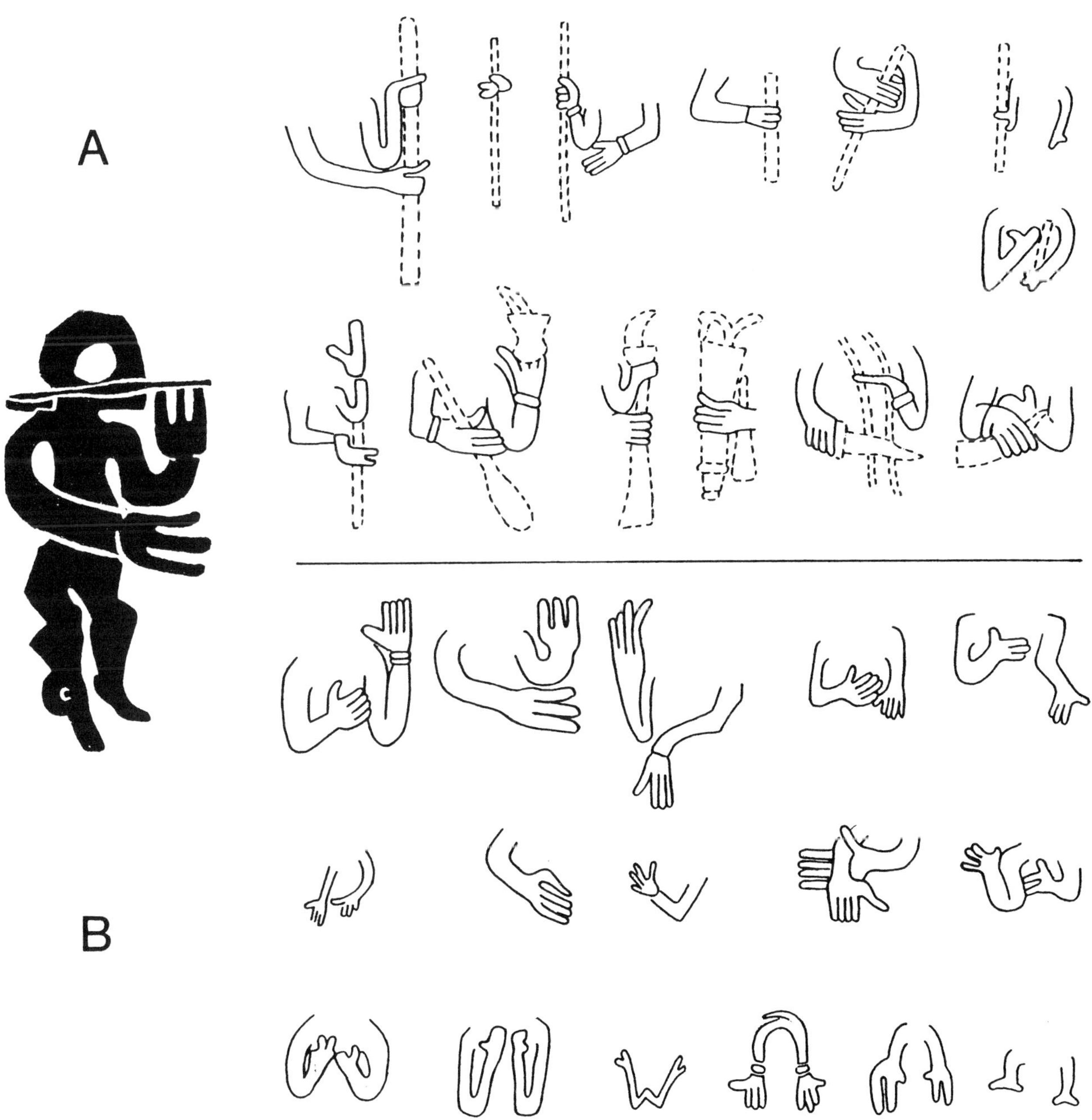

Fig. 11 Selection of hand positions (gestures) shown on single figures from Sorte Muld with attributes (A) and without attributes (B).

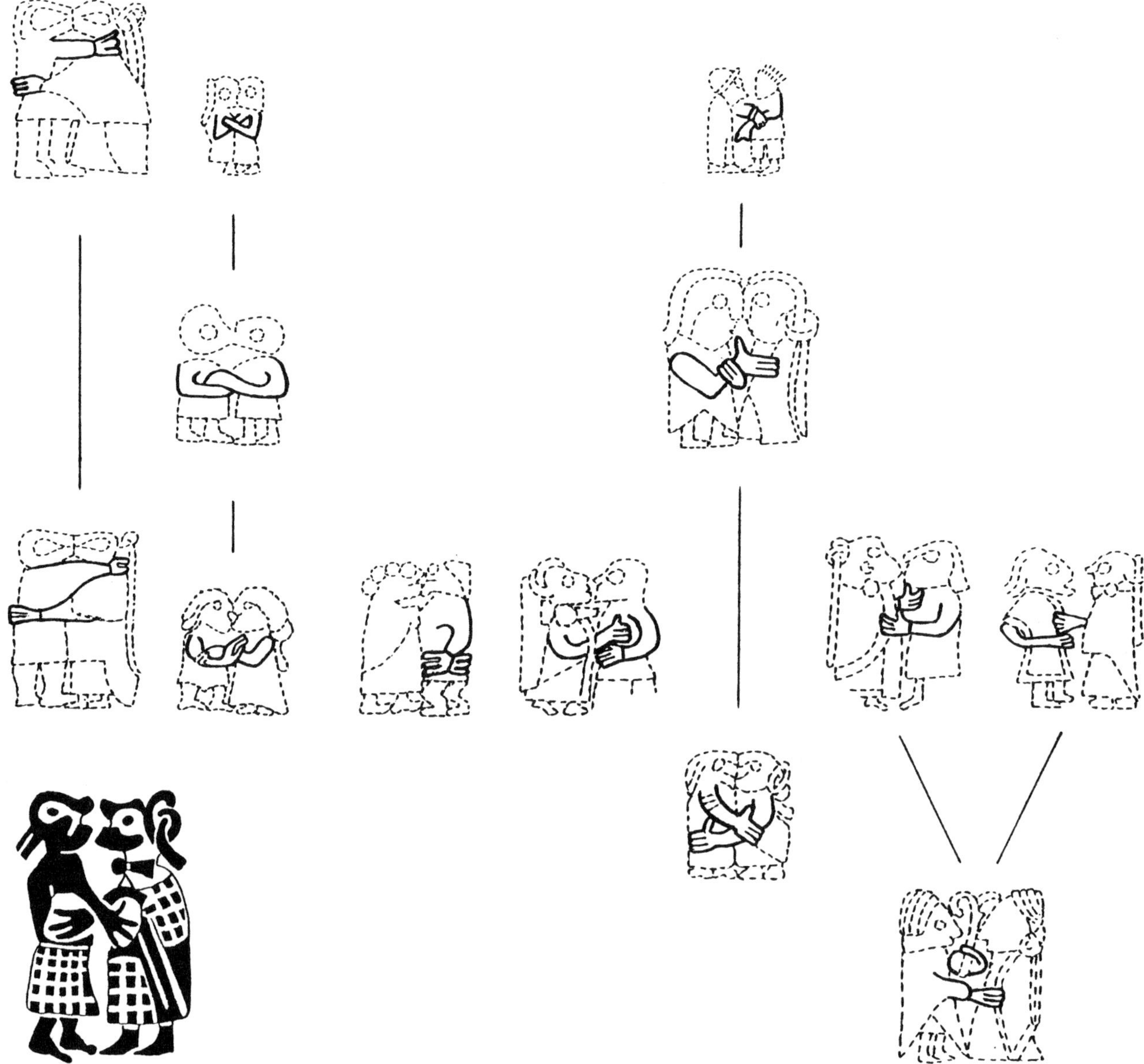

Fig. 12 Selection of hand positions shown on double figures (couples) from different Scandinavian localities.

gold to underline the importance of the gesture (Belting 1991, 101 and fig. 33).

A gesture shown by a number of figures, where one hand is seen raised in front of the face (Figs. 9c and 11 B), has close parallels within bracteate iconography (Hauck 1992, 246 and figs. 15–16). Several figures show one or both hands placed on the chest. In another common type of gesture the arms and hands are downturned with the thumbs pointing outward and the palms facing forward, presumably in a gesture of prayer or submission.

Only a single, very stylised example shows both hands raised in a gesture of 'adoration' common in Christian iconography.

Of particular interest is the gesture of one hand (the left) clasping the wrist of the other depicted on only a single figure (Fig. 11B). This gesture may be the same as that described in the Norwegian *Speculum Regale*. In this – admittedly late (thirteenth century) – educational work the father advises his son that in the company of the king it is considered good manners to approach with the right hand grasping the left wrist (Rold 1993, 199).

In a similar way the group of *embracing male and female figures*, otherwise not discussed in this paper, follows a fairly rigid pattern (Fig. 12). In these double figures the position of the arms ranges from indicating a close embrace to a light touch. Of these, one small group, in which one person appears to hold the arm or dress border of the other (Fig. 12), may possibly be a variation of the gesture described in the *Speculum Regale*.

Conclusion

Comparing the gold foil figures with their most obvious models – portraits and figures depicted on Late Roman coins (particulaly solidi), imperial medallions and their bracteate derivatives – there is a noticeable overlap in the range of attributes and symbols, but the frequency of occurrence of these appears to differ considerably among the groups.

In posture, and gesture, the group of so-called 'nude dancers' from Sorte Muld (Figs. 9 and 11) show the closest links to bracteate iconography. Although several, more or less convincing, attempts have been made to identify individual figures – or groups of figures – we are, however, still on very shaky ground. Even trying to determine the criteria for distinguishing between *king*, *god* and *man*, one is faced with the same difficulties which always set the limits when it comes to the interpretation of products of an illiterate society.

While the bracteates and the slightly younger gold foil figures appear to share a common (social) background, drawing the bulk of their symbolic content from the Late Antique imperial sphere, the tiny gold foil figures clearly owe much of their detail to a Merovingian and Frankish influence. But it is equally obvious that they have taken a definite step towards an independent Nordic tradition.

References

Arrhenius, B. 1983: 'The chronology of the Vendel graves', in Lamm, J.-P. and Nordström, H.-A. (eds), *Vendel Period Studies* 2 (Stockholm), 39–70.

Belting, H. 1991: *Bild und Kult. Eine Geschichte des Bildes vor dem Zeitalter der Kunst* (München).

Bruce-Mitford, R.L.S. 1978: *The Sutton Hoo Ship Burial* vol.2, British Museum Publications (London).

Garbsch, J. and Overbeck, B. 1989: *Spätantike zwischen Heidentum und Christentum*, Katalog, Prähistorische Staatssamlung (München).

Gustafson, G. 1900: 'Et fund af figurerede guldplader', *Foreningen til norske fornminnesmærkers bevaring. Aarsberetning* for 1899 (Kristiania), 86–95.

Hauck, K. (ed.) 1986: 'Die Goldbrakteaten der Völkerwanderungszeit', Ikonographischer Katalog (IK2, Tafeln), *Münstersche Mittelalterschriften* 2,2 (München).

Hauck, K. 1992: 'Der religions- und sozialgeschichtliche Quellenwert der völkerwanderungszeitlichen Goldbrakteaten', *Germanische Religionsgeschichte. Ergänzungsband zum Reallexikon der Germanischen Altertumskunde* 5 (Berlin/New York), 229–269.

Hauck, K. 1993: 'Die bremische Überlieferung zur Götter-Dreiheit Altuppsalas und die bornholmische Goldfolien aus Sorte Muld', *Frühmittelalterliche Studien* 17, 409–79.

Hauck, K. 1994: 'Altuppsalas Polytheismus exemplarisch erhellt mit Bildzeugnißen des 5.–7. Jahrhunderts', *Studien zum Altgermanischen. Festschrift für Heinrich Bech* (Berlin/ New York), 197–302.

Holmquist, W. 1961: 'The dancing gods', *Acta Archaeologica* 31, 101–27.

Holmquist, W. *et al.* 1961: *Excavations at Helgö I* (Stockholm).

Kellner, H.-J. and Zahlhaas, G. 1983: *Der römische Schatzfund von Weißenburg* (München/ Zürich).

Lidén, H.-E. 1969: 'From pagan sanctuary to Christian church. The excavation of Mære Church in Trøndelag', *Norwegian Archaeological Review* 3, 3–22.

Lundquist, L. 1996: 'Slöinge-projektet 1994 och 1995 – Stolpar, guldgubbar och bebyggelse', *Fornvännen* 91, 27–36.

Lundquist, L. and Rosengren, E. 1992: 'Et guldgubbefynd från Slöinge', *Halland* 75, 25–30.

Mackeprang, M. 1943: 'Om de såkaldte 'guldgubber', *Fra Nationalmuseets Arbejdsmark* 1943 (København), 69–76.

von Melle, I. A. 1725: *Commentatiuncula de simulacris aureis, quae in Boringholmia Maris Balthici insula, agris eruuntur* (Lübeck).

Menghin, W. 1983: *Das Schwert im frühen Mittelalter. Chronologisch-typologische Untersuchungen zu Langschwertern aus germanischen Gräbern d. 5. bis 7. Jahrhunderts n. Chr.* (Stuttgart).

Munch, G. Stamsø 1991: 'Hus og Hall. En høvdinggård på Borg i Lofoten', in Steinsland, G. *et. al.* (eds), *Nordisk Hedendom. Et symposium*, Odense Universitetsforlag, 321–333

Näsman, U. 1986: 'Vendel Period Glass from Eketorp II, Öland, Sweden', *Acta Archaeologica*, 55, 55–116.

Nordén, A. 1938: 'Le problèmes des "Bonshommes en or"', *Acta Archaeologica* 9, 151–63.

Rold, L. 1993: 'Takt og tone i tusind år', *Nationalmuseets Arbejdsmark* for 1993, 195–205.

Steinsland, G. 1990: 'De nordiske gullblekk med parmotiv og norrøn fyrsteideologi', *Collegium Medievale* 3, 73–87.

Steuer, H. 1987: 'Helm und Ringschwert – Prunkbewaffnung und Rangabzeichen germanischer Krieger. Eine Übersicht', *Studien zur Sachsenforschung* 6, 189–236.

Stolpe, H. and Arne, T.J. 1912: *Graffältet vid Vendel* (Stockholm).

Thomsen, P.O. 1993: 'Handelspladsen ved Lundeborg', in 'Lundeborg – en handelsplads fra jernalderen', *Skrifter fra Svendborg og Omegns Museum* 32, 68–101.

Wallace-Hadrill, J.M. 1982: *The Long-haired Kings*, University of Toronto Press (Toronto/ Buffalo/ London).

Watt, M. 1991a: 'Sorte Muld. Høvdingesæde og kultcentrum fra Bornholms yngre jernalder', in, Mortensen, P. and Rasmussen, B.M. (eds), *Fra Stamme til Stat i Danmark 2. Høvdingesamfund og Kongemagt*, Jysk Arkæologisk Selskabs Skrifter 22/2 (Højbjerg), 89–106. .

Watt, M. 1991b: 'Guldgubberne fra Sorte Muld, Bornholm. Tanker omkring et muligt hedensk kultcentrum fra yngre jernalder', in Steinsland, G. *et. al.* (eds), *Nordisk Hedendom. Et symposium*, Odense Universitetsforlag, 373–386.

Watt, M. 1992: 'Die Goldblechfiguren ('guldgubber') aus Sorte Muld, Bornholm', in Hauck, K. (ed.), *Der historische Horizont der Götterbild-Amulette aus der Übergangsepoche von der Spätantike zum frühen Mittelalter*, Abhandlungen der Akademie der Wissenschaften in Göttingen, 195–227.

Watt, M. (in press): 'Gubber', *Reallexikon der Germanischen Altertumskunde*.

Zachrisson, S. 1963: 'Från vendeltid til Vasatid', *Eskildstuna Museers Årsbok*, 17–74.

Anglo-Saxon Studies in Archaeology and History 10, 1999

Style II and the Anglo-Saxon Elite

Karen Høilund Nielsen

Since Salin first introduced the concept of Style II in 1904, in his *Die altgermanische Thierornamentik*, debate has focused on questions of its origin and spread within Europe. Opinions have fluctuated between a limited number of possibilities, of which the most important place the origins either with the Lombards, the Alamans or in Scandinavia (Haseloff 1984,114–17; Holmqvist 1955, 48).

Debate about how Style II found its way to Anglo-Saxon England and analysis of its insular forms has been more extensive. Salin's own discussion was followed by important contributions by Åberg, partly in his *The Anglo-Saxons in England* (1926) and partly in volume 1 (The British Isles) of his *From the Occident to the Orient in the Art of the Seventh Century* (1943). In the former, he concluded that Kentish Style II developed not from Anglo-Saxon Style I, but from continental Germanic and Scandinavian influences, with, however, some independent elements (Åberg 1926, 169–70). The animal style of the manuscripts developed from Style II (Åberg 1926, 177). A rather different contribution was Kendrick's *Anglo-Saxon Art to AD 900* (1938; cf. also Kendrick 1934), in which the Germanic Animal Style was divided into two, supposedly coexisting, styles, Helmet Style and Ribbon Style. Leeds' analysis of Style II in his *Early Anglo-Saxon Art and Archaeology* (1936) led to the conclusion that Style II had been introduced into England from the Continent.

The excavation of Sutton Hoo Mound 1 in 1939 had a major impact on all subsequent work on Style II; indeed it may have excessively biased our view of Anglo-Saxon Style II. Sutton Hoo not only contained a large number of objects ornamented in the style, but many of them were also of Scandinavian character (cf. Bruce-Mitford 1975; 1978; 1983, all with further references). Some of these objects were thought to be actually of Scandinavian manufacture and even the possibility of Scandinavian craftsmen working for the East Anglian court was discussed. The occurrence of similar pieces, though in less precious metals, in the Swedish Vendel and Valsgärde graves led to the conclusion that the objects from Sutton Hoo – as well as the burial type itself – were Swedish. But, despite many efforts, it has been quite hard to explain this Swedish connection.

The most recent and thorough contribution is Speake's *Anglo-Saxon Animal Art and its Germanic Background* (1980). Setting his discussion in the context of a comprehensive discussion of research history, he covered the relationship of Anglo-Saxon Style II to both Scandinavian and Continental Style II, its interpretation in relation to Norse mythology and – more vaguely – its social impact on Anglo-Saxon England. Speake argued that Style II was introduced to Kent from West Scandinavia through the same connections which had brought Style I, whereas East Anglia, lacking such preconditions for Style II, had more diverse sources: at least some of the Sutton Hoo material was imported from Sweden, some was produced in Suffolk by Swedish craftsmen and finally some by craftsmen who had come from Kent (Speake 1980, 94–6).

One might argue that after all this there is no need for a further discussion of Anglo-Saxon Style II. But perspectives and methods, and therefore the questions asked of the archaeological material, constantly change. The stylistic elements of which the animal style was composed were an important aspect for scholars like Salin and Åberg, and especially for the Danish researcher, Ørsnes, who refined the methodology for their analysis, though he examined only the South Scandinavian Style II (Ørsnes 1966). By contrast, Speake actually warned against the extended use of stylistic elements (Speake 1980, 41–2, note 18). In an age of computers, however, Ørsnes's method is particularly attractive, being well-suited to multivariate analysis. Since 1985 its revival has led to re-analysis and reassessment of European Style II, resulting in a deeper insight into the mechanisms of Scandinavian Style II (Høilund Nielsen 1991). The probable origin of Style II can be placed in South Scandinavia, and an alternative explanation can be offered for the origin of both the Style II material in some of the Vendel and Valsgärde graves and for some of the objects in Sutton Hoo Mound 1, namely that both groups derived from the Danish area (cf. Hines 1992; Høilund Nielsen 1991). The pair of drinking horns, the shield mounts and the shield boss from Sutton Hoo fitted well on the basis of their stylistic elements into the seriation of the Danish Style II; the gold buckle also fitted, though less well (Høilund Nielsen 1992). Continental Style II has also been placed in a rather different light (Høilund Nielsen 1997b; forthcoming). Its origin can also be placed in South Scandinavia and its introduction on the Continent is often followed by cultivation of a Scandinavian origin myth. The style appears among the Austrasians, the Alamans, the Lombards and the Burgundians; among the last two peoples, at least, it is followed by a Scandinavian myth of origin. The style seem to have been of use in internal socio-political conflicts between co-existing factions, representing Roman politics and culture contra Germanic.

The scope of this article will not be to make an entire assessment of Anglo-Saxon Style II, but to present some preliminary analyses and interpretations of the archaeological material, based on Ørsnes's method, and to discuss the results briefly in relation to historical sources and to comparative studies of Continental Style II.

The Style II material

Style II is found primarily on objects from Kent and Suffolk, with a scattering of occurrences in Hampshire, Buckinghamshire, Oxfordshire, Northamptonshire, Cambridgeshire, Norfolk, Lincolnshire and Northumberland (Fig. 11). Objects which share some of their stylistic elements are also found further towards the periphery, in Somerset, Warwickshire, and Yorkshire. The primary areas for Style II finds are thus either Anglian (predominantly eastern), dominated by Sutton Hoo in Suffolk, or wholly or in part linked to a so-called Jutish origin – Kent, Hampshire and the Taplow barrow from Buckinghamshire.

Style II is found on a large number of objects, but they are of restricted types (Fig. 11). Buckles with triangular plate and bracteates dominate the picture in the Kentish area, while the Sutton Hoo armour and regalia and axe-shaped and discoid mounts in general dominate the Anglian material. In addition, various models for repoussé, pins and other mounts are found in both areas. As a supplement to the present study, a handful of illuminated manuscripts has been included in order to shed light on the connections between late Style II on archaeological material and the style of the early manuscripts. These are the Book of Durrow, dated to within the seventh century, even to shortly after 600 by Roth (1987, 25–8) and the codices Paris 1587 (Alexander 1978, figs. 270–73), Köln 213 (early eighth century, Webster and Backhouse 1991, 161) and Durham A II 17 (*c.* 700, Brown 1991).

Method

Style II is characterized by its very conventional appearance. The animals are clearly distinguished in anatomical terms, and heads, legs, feet and bodies are treated almost like icons, with definite limits to the variation which these icons can display. They can therefore be treated as 'stylistic elements' and recorded for each object in the Anglo-Saxon Style II corpus. Figure 1 presents all the different stylistic elements which have been recorded so far. The stylistic elements are sorted according to whether they are heads (prefixed H), legs (L), feet (F) or bodies (B). Within these sets each identifiable element has been coded with a further letter (A-n) and a number (1-n). Note that these codes are arbitrary and carry no preconceptions about relationships within or between the sets.

Experience from analyses of the Scandinavian Style II material (Høilund Nielsen 1991) makes clear that the material may either constitute groups or may form a seriation, that is a series of continuously changing elements and objects. Groups may be interpreted as being of chronological, geographical or stylistic significance, depending on the contexts of the finds. A seriation from a restricted area is often interpreted as being of chronological significance. In this analysis, multivariate Correspondence Analysis is used (Baxter 1994, 100–39; Høilund Nielsen 1995; Jensen and Høilund Nielsen 1997, 29–61). It should reveal any structure behind the combination of stylistic elements (variables) and the objects. Only objects which include at least two stylistic elements and only stylistic elements which occur at least twice in the sample can be included in the analysis. A certain number of finds are thus left out, either because they only comprise one stylistic element or the elements are unique. Large, composite objects have been split up into smaller units for the analysis: for example, each mount of the Sutton Hoo shield has been treated separately.

As there are great differences in the types of object on which Style II occurred in the Kentish-Saxon area and in the Anglian area, and as there are also marked differences in the kinds of stylistic element used on material from the two areas, the material for analysis was divided into two, geographically-determined, groups (following the division in Høilund Nielsen 1997a, 89 and fig. 23): one is a predominantly Anglian group, with the largest number of objects coming from Suffolk, the other is predominantly Kentish-Saxon, with Kent the chief source of objects.

Analysis

The first Correspondence Analysis was done on the predominantly Anglian material together with the manuscript illustrations mentioned above (which were based on the figures in Åberg 1943, figs. 83–4). A number of objects in the sample had to be deleted because they did

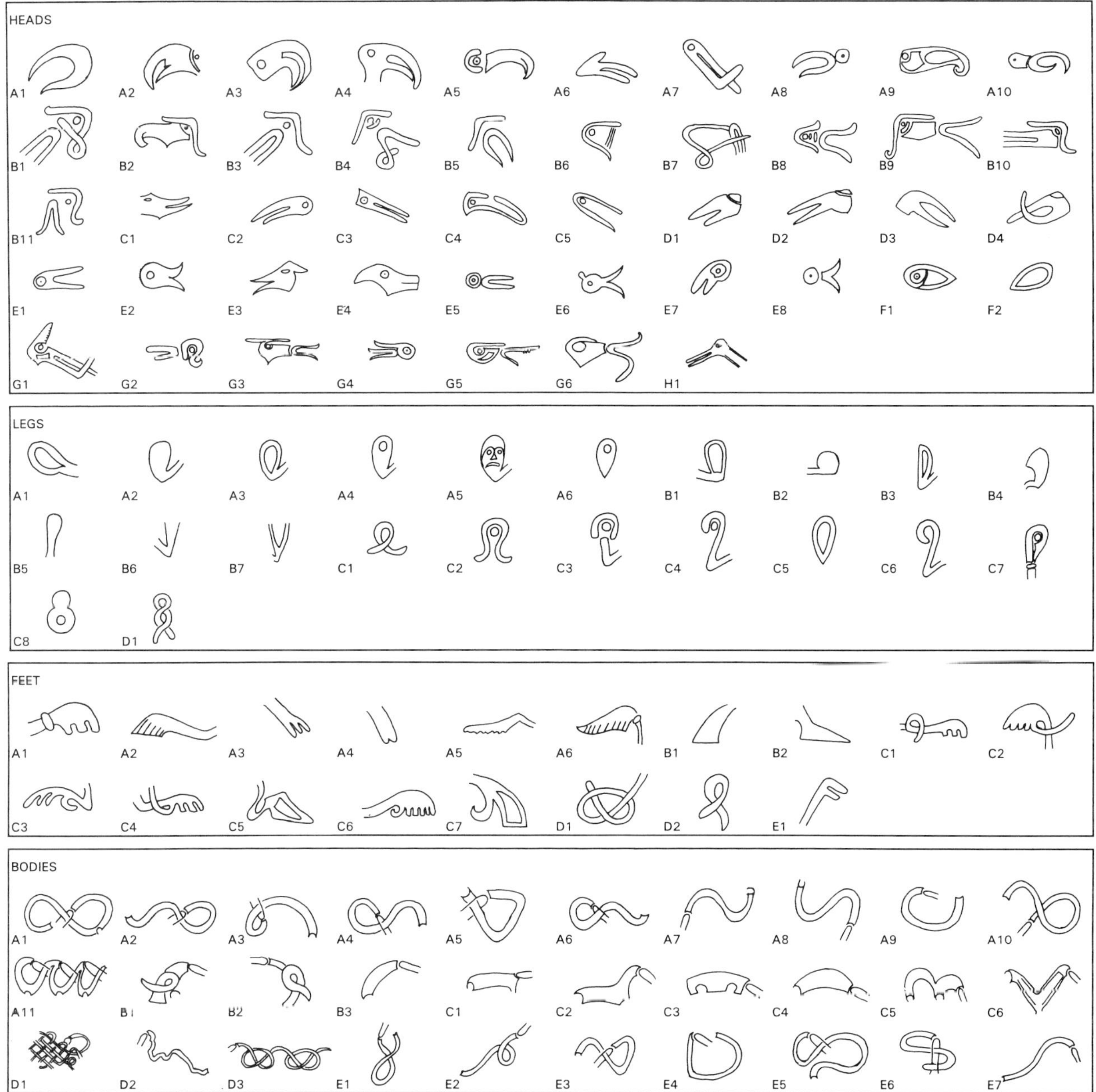

Fig. 1 Stylistic elements recorded on Anglo-Saxon artefacts. The table contains more elements than those included in Figures 3, 6, and 8. In the analyses some of the elements are combinations of several elements.

not share stylistic elements with the rest of the finds. In addition, the variables LA4 (2 occurrences), LC3 (2 occurrences), FA5+6 (2 occurrences), BA4 (9 occurrences) and BA6 (3 occurrences) had to be deleted before the second stage of the analysis. These are all rare types, which occurred at both ends of the first seriation, except for one that seemed to appear now and then throughout the entire seriation. It meant, however, that Sutton Hoo 1j (the shield boss) did not share enough variables with the other finds anymore and therefore also had to be deleted. The final result was an excellent parabola (Fig. 2), which meant that it was a well-organized seriation. It starts (on the right-hand side) with shield mounts from Sutton Hoo[1] and ends (on the left-hand side) with the manuscript Durham A II 17 from *c.* 700. The result is transferred into a sorted matrix (Fig. 3) which presents the even development of the variables between the two extremes. In spite of the even development, a phase-division can be suggested which divides the seriation into four groups or phases, called here Scandinavian (SC), Anglian 1 (A1), Anglian 2 (A2) and Manuscript (MS). All the stylistic elements of the SC group are known from Scandinavia, and analyis of the Sutton Hoo shield mounts and drinking horns together with the Scandinavian

Correspondence Analysis of Anglian Style II
Unit + Type scores
X-Axis: 1. component Correlation: 0.9901 (10.9%)
Y-Axis: 2. component Correlation: 0.9431 (9.8%)

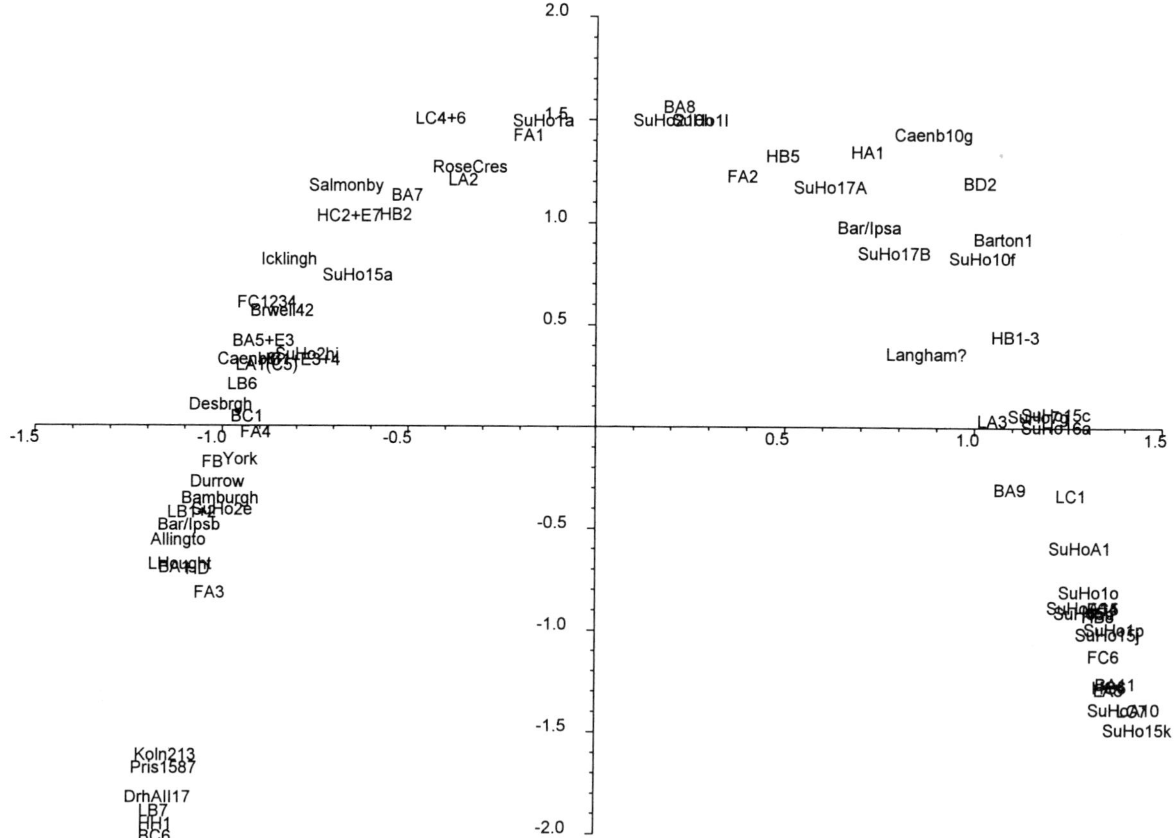

Fig. 2. Correspondence Analysis of the Anglian material. Both types and objects are included in the plot. For the Correspondence Analysis Winbasp 5.0 is used for the plots and a parallel analysis in KVARK to obtain the coordinates. The results from the two analyses are identical.

material has clearly shown that they fit into that tradition (Høilund Nielsen 1992, 282–3). There must therefore be a strong link to Scandinavia within this material, either through very close contact or the items mentioned are Scandinavian imports. A look at the subsequent development shows that the elements HB1+3 and LC1 are also found in Scandinavian 'Element-Combination-Group' 2 (EKG2: Høilund-Nielsen 1991), and the legs, LC1, are already found in Britain in the Anglian SC phase. These elements are very characteristic for a large part of the Anglo-Saxon Style II.

The two phases, A1 and A2, are also well represented by material from graves at Sutton Hoo. The first phase comprises especially axe-shaped and discoid mounts, some of which are for horse-harnesses. Front legs are often missing, which is not the case in the previous period or in the following. In phase A2 the type of animal characteristic of the subsequent MS phase is first developed. Front legs are again common. The MS phase is represented by the manuscripts and a handful of objects with very characteristic animals. The latest objects in the seriation from Sutton Hoo, the clasps, are closely followed by the Book of Durrow. Birds do not appear in this phase, although they occasionally did before and are also very common in the Book of Lindisfarne (Backhouse 1981), which is slightly later than or contemporary with the latest of the manuscripts analysed here and rather different in style.

The material from the Kentish and Saxon regions was analysed in the same way. Again objects with too few shared elements were omitted, and so were Buckland 134 and Wingham (2), which, though having more elements, still had none in common with the main body of finds. The result of the first Correspondence Analysis (Fig. 4) was a somewhat odd picture with two groups, one (to the left-hand side) small and rather concentrated and the other (to the right-hand side) forming a long series. The former group contains Crundale 3h and –8g,

	HH1	LB7	BC6	BA1	LB1+2	HD	FA3	FB	LB6	BC1	FA4	BA5+E3	LA1(C5)	FC1234	HC1+E3+4	HC2+E7	HB2	BA7	LC4+6	LA2	FA1	BA8	FA2	HB5	HA1	BD2	LA3	BA9	HB1-3	LC1	HB8	FC5	FC6	HG6	LA5	BA11	LC7
Durham A II 17	1	1					1																														
Köln 213	1	1	1			1	1																														
Paris 1587	1	1	1			1	1																														
Little Houghton				1	1	1																															
Allington Hill 8a				1	1	1		1																													
Allington Hill				1	1	1		1																													
Barham/Ipswich b					1	1		1																													
Bamburgh						1	1		1	1																											
Durrow					1	1	1					1	1																								
Sutton Hoo 1 2e						1					1																										
Desborough					1									1																							
York, Fishergate							1			1					1																						
Caenby 8i									1	1			1	1																							
Burwell 42								1	1			1				1	1																				
Icklingham												1			1	1																					
Sutton Hoo 1 2hi						1				1	1						1			1																	
Salmonby														1		1			1																		
Sutton Hoo 1 15a							1						1		1	1		1		1	1																
Rose Crescent																1	1	1		1			1														
Sutton Hoo 1 1abde																	1		1	1	1	1	1														
Sutton Hoo 2 10h																				1		1	1	1													
Sutton Hoo 1 1l																					1				1												
Sutton Hoo 17A																						1	1		1		1										
Barham/Ipswich a																							1		1		1										
Sutton Hoo 17B																							1	1			1		1								
Langham?, Field Dalling																							1				1	1									
Caenby 10g																									1	1											
Sutton Hoo 1 10f																									1	1				1							
Barton-on-Humber 1																										1			1								
Sutton Hoo 1 7g																											1		1	1							
Sutton Hoo 1 15c																													1	1							
Sutton Hoo 1 16a																													1	1							
Sutton Hoo 1 A14																											1						1	1			
Sutton Hoo 1 A1																											1			1	1	1					
Sutton Hoo 1 5b																											1	1			1		1		1	1	
Sutton Hoo 1 1o																											1			1	1		1			1	
Sutton Hoo 1 53a																														1			1			1	
Sutton Hoo 1 1p																														1	1	1					1
Sutton Hoo 1 A10																																	1	1	1	1	
Sutton Hoo 1 15k																																				1	1
sum	3	3	2	3	6	10	7	4	3	4	2	3	3	3	3	5	4	2	2	5	3	3	7	2	5	3	9	2	5	8	4	2	5	2	2	5	2
1st coordinate	-1,2	-1,2	-1,2	-1,15	-1,1	-1,09	-1,05	-1,04	-0,96	-0,95	-0,93	-0,91	-0,9	-0,9	-0,83	-0,68	-0,55	-0,51	-0,43	-0,36	-0,19	0,21	0,38	0,48	0,71	1	1,03	1,08	1,09	1,24	1,31	1,32	1,32	1,33	1,34	1,35	1,4

	Phase	sum	1st coordinate		further stylistic elements	birdhead	wing	fish	front leg	hind leg	interlace	type
Durham A II 17		3	-1,19		BC5				X	X	interlace	codex
Köln 213		5	-1,17		BA4				X	X	interlace	codex
Paris 1587		5	-1,17		HA4, LD1, BA4				X	X	interlace	codex
Little Houghton		3	-1,14	N'hants					X	X		disc brooch
Allington Hill 8a		4	-1,12	Cambs					X	X		discoid mount
Allington Hill	MS	4	-1,12	Cambs					X	X		discoid mount
Barham/Ipswich b		3	-1,1	Suff	BA4				X	X		mount
Bamburgh		4	-1,03	N'land					X	X		plaque
Durrow		5	-1,03		BC2				X	X	interlace	codex
Sutton Hoo 1 2e		2	-1,03	Suff	LB5, BA2				(?)	X		clasps
Desborough		2	-1,02	N'hants	HC3, BA6				X	X		hinged clasps
York, Fishergate		3	-0,96	Yorks	HE5				X	X		knife
Caenby 8i		4	-0,95	Lincs	HF1				X	X		disc. mount
Burwell 42		5	-0,84	Cambs	BA4	X				X		work box
Icklingham		3	-0,81	Suff								model
Sutton Hoo 1 2hi		5	-0,79	Suff	BB1	X	X		X	X		purse
Salmonby	A2	3	-0,68	Lincs	LC3				X	X		model
Sutton Hoo 1 15a		7	-0,66	Suff	FA5				X	X		cup
Rose Crescent		5	-0,35	Cambs	BA4				X	X		harness mount
Sutton Hoo 1 1abde		6	-0,16	Suff	HB9, HC4, LA4, BC4	X			X	X	open knot	buckle
Sutton Hoo 2 10h		4	0,18	Suff						X		discoid mount
Sutton Hoo 1 1l		2	0,27	Suff						X		cup
Sutton Hoo 17A		4	0,6	Suff						X		axe-shaped mount
Barham/Ipswich a		3	0,72	Suff	HA2, BA3	X				X		axe-shaped mount
Sutton Hoo 17B		4	0,76	Suff	BA4, BA6					X		axe-shaped mount
Langham?, Field Dalling		3	0,85	Norf	HE2					X		model
Caenby 10g	A1	2	0,87	Lincs							interwoven	discoid mount
Sutton Hoo 1 10f		3	1	Suff		X				X		lyre
Barton-on-Humber 1		2	1,07	Lincs								model
Sutton Hoo 1 7g		3	1,15	Suff	FD2				X	X		helmet
Sutton Hoo 1 15c		2	1,19	Suff	HG4, BE7		?					drinking horn
Sutton Hoo 1 16a		2	1,19	Suff	BA4				X	X		shield
Sutton Hoo 1 A14		3	1,25	Suff	BA4				X	X		shield
Sutton Hoo 1 A1		4	1,25	Suff	BA6					X	interwoven	shield
Sutton Hoo 1 5b		6	1,26	Suff	HG2	X	X		X	X		shield
Sutton Hoo 1 1o	SC	5	1,28	Suff	HG1, FA6, BA4				X	X		shield
Sutton Hoo 1 53a		3	1,33	Suff	HB10				X		wavy	shield
Sutton Hoo 1 1p		4	1,34	Suff	BA10				X	X		drinking horn
Sutton Hoo 1 A10		4	1,36	Suff	LA4				X	X		shield
Sutton Hoo 1 15k		2	1,4	Suff	HG5					X		shield

Fig. 3 The matrix of the objects with Anglian Style II sorted on the basis of the coordinates of the 1st axis of the plot in Fig. 2. In addition, phases, total range of stylistic elements, occurrence of other elements and interlace and types of object are included. The name of the object is in some cases followed by a combination of letter and number which refers to figures (or plates) in Speake (1980).

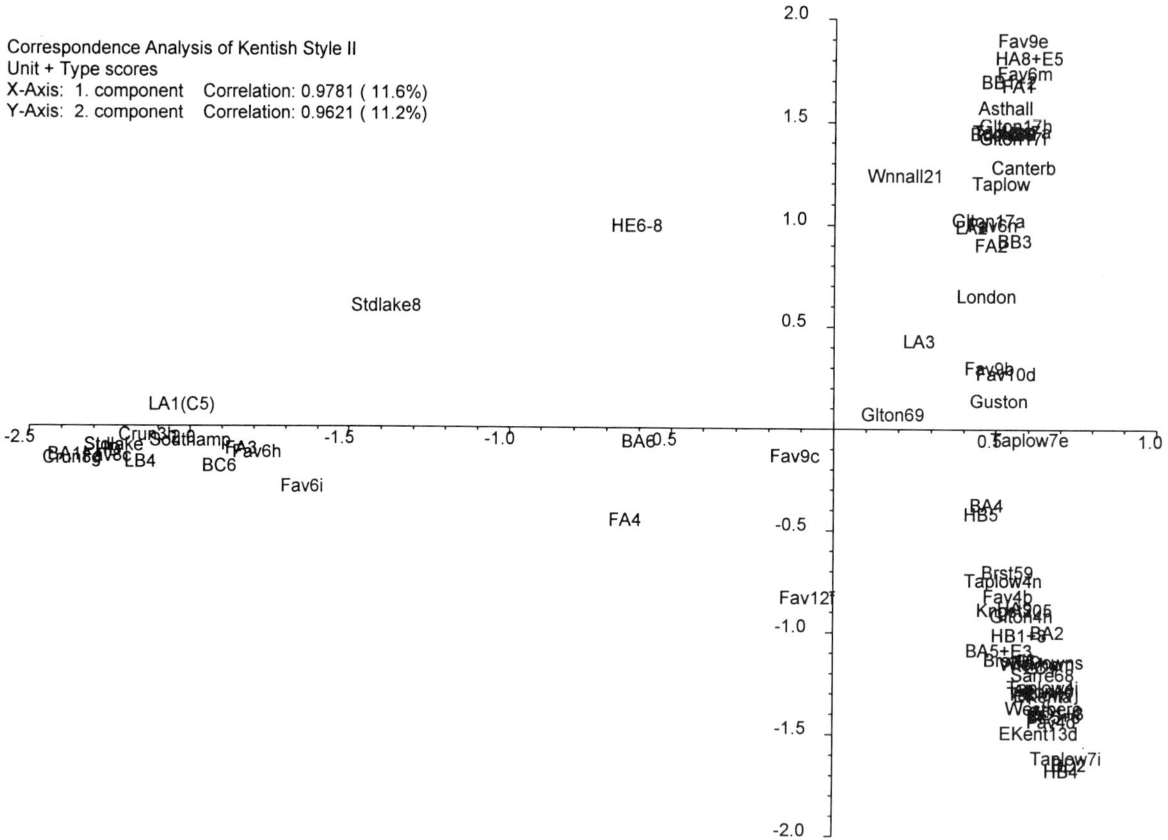

Fig. 4 Correspondence Analysis of the Kentish material. Both types and objects are included in the plot.

Faversham 6h, –6i and –8c, Southampton, Standlake and Standlake 8, and the variables HD, HE6+8, LA1(C5), LB4, FA3, BA1 and BA6. As a second stage, the objects from this group were excluded, as were East Kent 13d and variable HB4, which are outliers of the long series, and variable BA6 and Taplow 7e, Guston and Gilton 69, which had ended up in the middle between the two arms of the parabola: while these last items fitted into the analysed material, they combined elements (HB1+3 and FA2) which proved to belong at both ends of the seriation (cf. Fig. 5). With all these removed a reasonable parabola appeared (Fig. 5) and on this basis the matrix was sorted (Fig. 6), producing a fairly even development.

The orientation of the seriation is not immediately clear, unlike in the Anglian case. Buckland 29 is dated to Evison's Phase 3 and the handful of bracteates at the other end of the seriation may probably be related to Evison's Phase 5 (Evison 1987, 138–40). Faversham 9e is a keystone brooch of Avent's Class 7.2, and Faversham 9b and –9c are both of Avent's Class 7.1. Finally, Kingston 205 is a composite brooch of Avent's Class 3.2 (Avent 1975). However, the datable grave associations for these types are generally poor and therefore the only conclusion is that Kingston 205 must be later than the others. This suggests that Faversham 9e (at the right-hand side) is at the start of the seriation and East Kent a (at the left-hand side) at the end.

On the basis of the parabola and the matrix, the seriation is divided into three phases named Kent A, B and C (KA, KB, KC). There is no direct link to Scandinavian stylistic elements except for the aforementioned HB1+3 and LC1, which here appear at the end of phase KB. The objects in phase KA are dominated by winged animals; hind legs are rather rare, front legs even more rare. In the following phase, KB, hind legs are common, but the animals are already becoming stereotyped. In phase KC that is even clearer and hind legs are extremely rare. Real birds or bird-heads are almost non-existent in phase KB and KC. But interlace patterns – a phenomenon hardly seen in the Anglian material – appear in phase KC.

At this point, the small group which was excluded from the Kentish-Saxon group was added to the Anglian seriation, since it has many elements in common with that seriation and does not disturb its excellence (Fig. 7). In the sorted matrix (Fig. 8) it appears that the Kentish-Saxon objects fall within the range of the MS phase, except for Standlake 8 which appears in phase A2.

The seriations discussed above comprise about 65 per cent of the recorded Style II objects (Fig. 11). Of those not included only very few can be secondarily attached

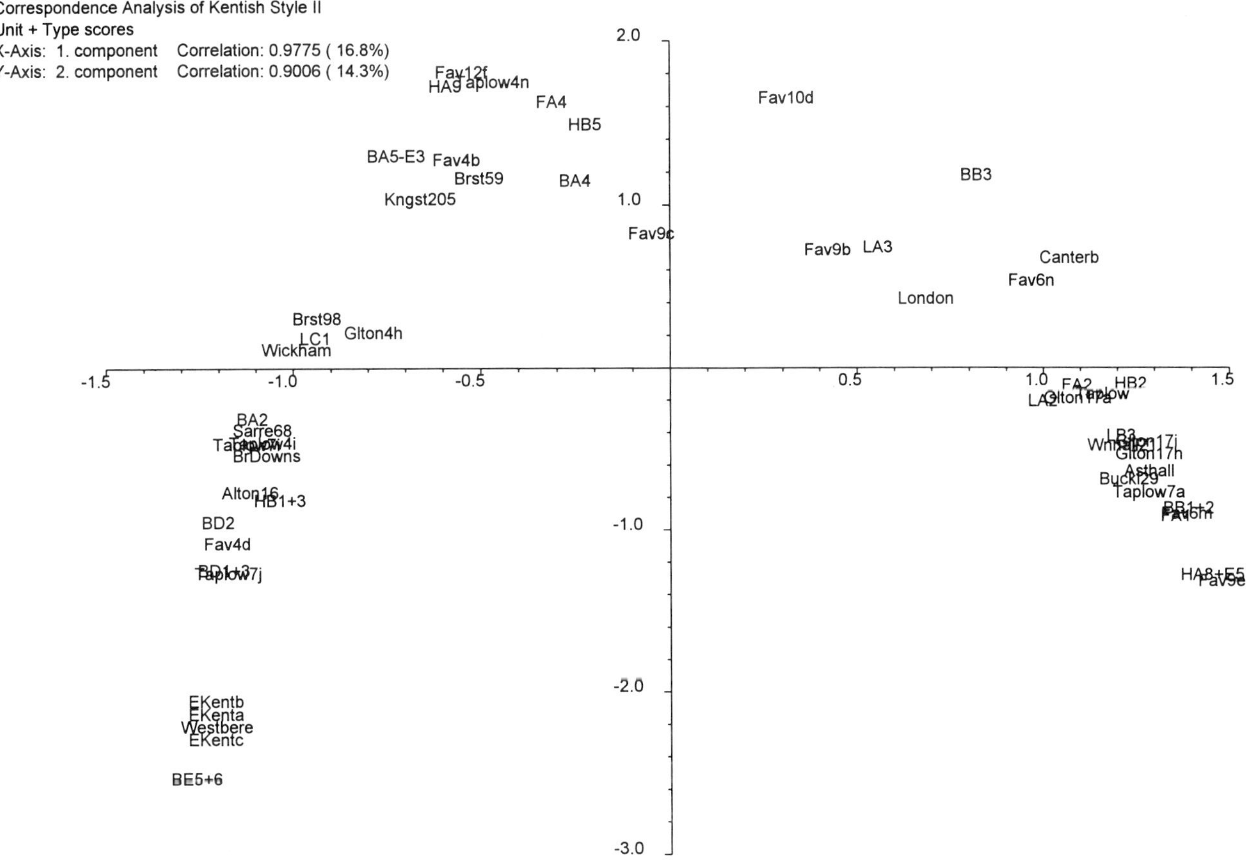

Fig. 5 Correspondence Analysis of the Kentish material. Both types and objects are included in the plot.

	BE5+6	BD2	BD1+D3	BA2	HB1+3	LC1	BA5+E3	HA9	FA4	BA4	HB5	LA3	BB3	LA2	FA2	LB3	HB2	FA1	BB1−2	HA8+E5	Phase	sum	1st coordinate		further stylistic elements	birdhead	wing	fish	front leg	hind leg	interlace	type
East Kent a	1				1																	2	-1,23	Kent								bracteate
East Kent b	1				1																	2	-1,23	Kent								bracteate
East Kent c	1				1																	2	-1,23	Kent								bracteate
Westbere	1				1																	2	-1,23	Kent								bracteate
Taplow 7j			1		1																	2	-1,19	Bucks							interwoven	cup
Faversham 4d		1			1																	2	-1,19	Kent							wavy	buckle, triangular plate
Taplow 7i		1				1																2	-1,14	Bucks	HB4	?					knots	drinking horn
Alton 16			1		1	1															KC	3	-1,13	Hants							interwoven	buckle, triangular plate
Breach Downs				1	1	1																3	-1,1	Kent							interwoven	buckle, triangular plate
Sarre 68				1	1	1																3	-1,1	Kent						X	wavy	buckle, triangular plate
Taplow 4i				1	1	1																3	-1,1	Bucks							irregular	buckle, triangular plate
Wickhambreux				1	1	1	1															4	-1,02	Kent		?				X	interwoven	buckle, triangular plate
Broadstairs 98					1		1															2	-0,94	Kent							wavy	buckle, rectangular plate
Gilton 23 4h					1	1				1												3	-0,8	Kent								buckle, triang. pl. & counter-pl.
Kingston 205					1	1	1	1		1	1											6	-0,68	Kent		X				X		composite brooch
Faversham 4b						1	1			1	1											4	-0,58	Kent						X		buckle, triangular plate
Faversham 12f							1		1													2	-0,56	Kent	HF2, LB5				X	X		bracteate
Broadstairs 59						1				1	1											3	-0,51	Kent						X		buckle, rectangular plate
Taplow 4n							1	1		1	1										KB	4	-0,49	Bucks		X					interwoven	clasps
Faversham 9c					1				1	1	1	1		1								6	-0,07	Kent	FA3, BA6				X	X		keystone brooch
Faversham 10d											1		1									2	0,29	Kent								mount for horse harness
Faversham 9b										1	1			1	1							4	0,41	Kent						X		keystone brooch
London										1		1			1	1						4	0,67	Bucks	HC2				X	X		disc brooch
Faversham 6n												1	1		1		1					4	0,95	Kent		X	?	X		X		buckle, triangular plate
Canterbury													1				1					2	1,06	Kent		X	X	X				hook
Gilton Ash 17a														1	1							2	1,08	Kent	HB6	X	X					mount
Taplow														1	1		1					3	1,14	Bucks	FC6, FC7, BA9				X	X		cup
Winnall 21														1	1				1			3	1,2	Hants	HA10, HE8		X			X		disc brooch
Buckland 29														1				1				2	1,22	Kent	HA5, BC3				X	X		bracteate
Taplow 7a														1	1			1		1	KA	4	1,26	Bucks	HB11	X			X	X	plaitwork	drinking horn
Gilton 17i															1	1	1		1			4	1,27	Kent		X	X					pin
Gilton 23 17h															1	1	1		1			4	1,27	Kent		X	X					pin
Asthall barrow														1			1	1	1			4	1,29	Oxon		X	X				interwoven	mount
Faversham 6m																1		1	1			3	1,36	Kent	HA2	X	X					buckle, triangular plate
Faversham 9e																			1	1		2	1,46	Kent			X					keystone brooch
sum	4	2	2	4	15	10	6	2	2	8	7	3	3	8	9	4	6	4	6	2												
1st coordinate	-1,28	-1,22	-1,21	-1,13	-1,06	-0,96	-0,74	-0,61	-0,33	-0,27	-0,24	0,54	0,8	0,98	1,08	1,2	1,22	1,34	1,37	1,43												

Fig. 6 The matrix of the objects with Kentish Style II sorted on basis of the coordinates of the 1st axis of the plot in Fig. 5.

Correspondence Analysis of Anglian Style II
Unit + Type scores
X-Axis: 1. component Correlation: 0.9915 (10.0%)
Y-Axis: 2. component Correlation: 0.9434 (9.0%)

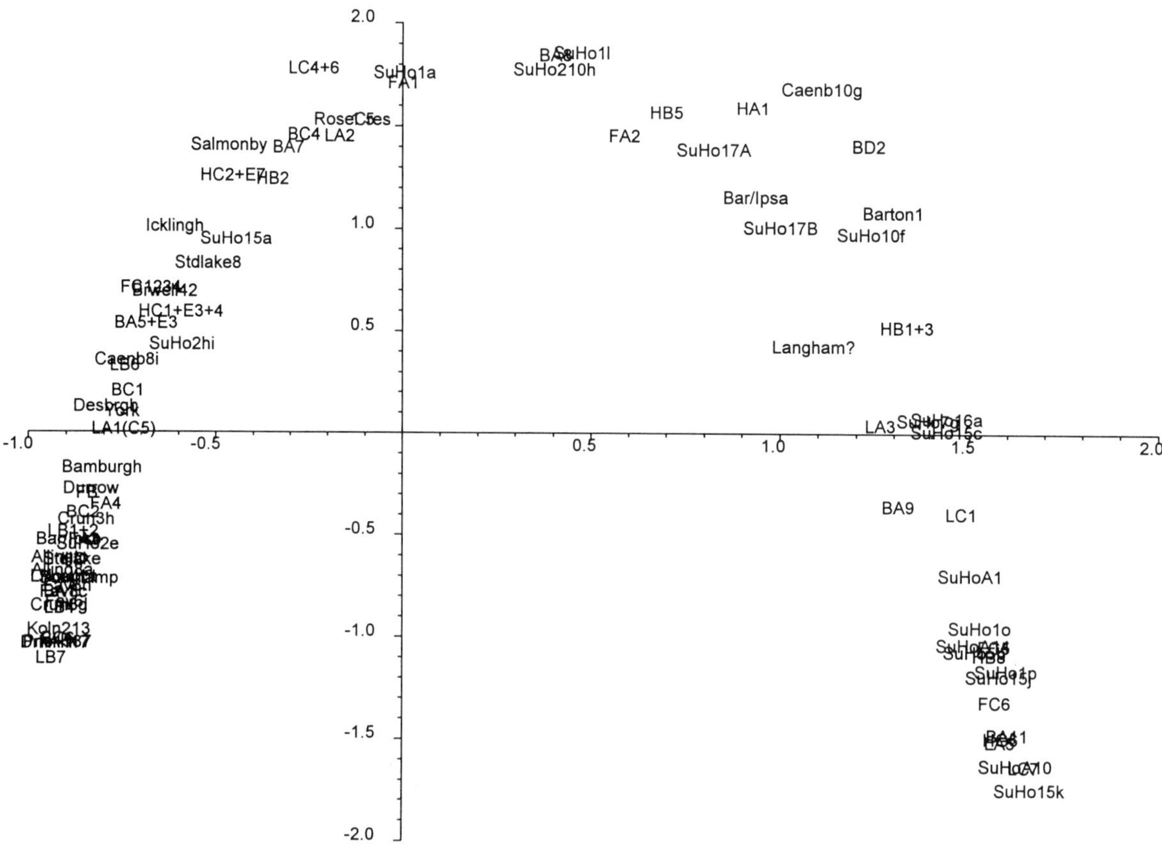

Fig. 7 Correspondence Analysis of the Anglian material including the group removed from the analysis of the Kentish material. Both types and objects are included in the plot.

to one of the series. Most of them include only a single stylistic element.

The general impression of the two stylistic series is that the Kentish series comprises rather stereotyped groups, which in the course of time lose their animal character as interlace patterns become more dominant. The Anglian series looks much more dynamic with the animal character remaining typical of most examples of the style. Interlace patterns are never especially characteristic, though they do occur now and then.

Correlation of the two stylistic schemes

To correlate the two stylistic schemes, links were drawn between shared stylistic elements (Fig. 9). Six links occur in a relatively concentrated group, two are in another, but three – HB1+3, LC1 and BD2 – seem totally out of place: they occur in the Anglian seriation at the beginning and in the Kentish at the end. At first sight this is rather alarming, but the explanation may be quite simple. The original versions of these stylistic elements are probably Scandinavian, and in the Anglian seriation there are close connections between these elements and the occurrence of Scandinavian objects or at least objects with very close Scandinavian affiliation. The occurrence of these elements in Kent may be due to secondary influence from either the Anglian area or the Continent, where the same elements occur: for instance, the combination of LC1 and HB1+3 on the disc brooch from Dienheim, Rheinland-Pfalz, Germany (Åberg 1947, Abb. 14, 1a; Klein-Pfeuffer 1993, Abb. 61,5), which dates from around the second quarter of the seventh century. Furthermore a bow-brooch from Mülhofen (Roth 1986, 140, Abb. 99) from around first quarter of the seventh century has a decoration on the foot that closely resembles that on the triangular buckle from Breach Downs (Speake 1980, Pl. 6g); here the head and body are of the same types, whilst the legs are different. Both examples show that a Continental origin for the motifs may be as likely as an Anglian/Scandinavian, and that the two areas may not necessarily have acquired the stylistic elements referred to from the same source.

	LB7	HH1	BC6	LB4	BA1	HD	LB1+2	FA3	BC2	FB	FA4	LA1(C5)	LB6	BC1	BA5+E3	FC1234	HC1+E3+4	HC2+E7	HB2	BA7	BC4	LC4+C6	LA2	FA1	BA8	FA2	HB5	HA1	BD2	LA3	BA9	HB1+3	LC1	HB8	FC5	FC6	HG6	LA5	BA11	LC7
Durham A II 17	1	1						1																																
Köln 213	1	1	1			1		1																																
Paris 1587	1	1	1			1		1																																
Crundale 8g				1	1	1																																		
Little Houghton					1	1	1																																	
Faversham 8c				1	1	1		1																																
Allington Hill					1	1	1			1																														
Allington Hill 8a					1	1	1			1																														
Faversham 6h				1		1		1																																
Faversham 6i			1	1							1																													
Barham/Ipswich b						1	1			1																														
Southampton		1	1					1				1																												
Standlake				1	1	1		1				1																												
Sutton Hoo 1 2e						1					1																													
Crundale 3h						1		1	1			1																												
Durrow						1	1	1	1			1			1																									
Bamburgh						1		1					1	1																										
Desborough							1									1																								
York, Fishergate								1						1			1																							
Caenby 8i												1	1	1		1																								
Burwell 42										1			1		1			1	1																					
Icklingham															1		1	1																						
Sutton Hoo 1 2hi						1					1			1					1				1																	
Standlake 8												1									1																			
Salmonby																1		1				1																		
Sutton Hoo 1 15a								1				1					1	1		1			1	1																
Rose Crescent																		1	1	1			1			1														
Sutton Hoo 1 1abde																			1		1	1	1	1	1	1														
Sutton Hoo 2 10h																							1		1	1	1													
Sutton Hoo 1 1l																								1				1												
Sutton Hoo 17A																									1	1		1		1										
Barham/Ipswich a																										1		1		1										
Sutton Hoo 17B																										1	1			1		1								
Langham?, Field Dalling																										1				1	1									
Caenby 10g																												1	1											
Sutton Hoo 1 10f																												1	1				1							
Barton-on-Humber 1																													1			1								
Sutton Hoo 1 7g																														1		1	1							
Sutton Hoo 1 15c																																1	1							
Sutton Hoo 1 16a																																1	1							
Sutton Hoo 1 A1																														1			1	1	1					
Sutton Hoo 1 A14																														1						1	1			
Sutton Hoo 1 5b																														1	1			1		1		1	1	
Sutton Hoo 1 1o																														1			1	1		1			1	
Sutton Hoo 1 53a																																	1			1			1	
Sutton Hoo 1 1p																																	1	1	1					1
Sutton Hoo 1 A10																																				1	1	1	1	
Sutton Hoo 1 15k																																							1	1
sum	3	4	4	5	6	15	6	12	2	4	3	7	3	4	3	3	3	5	4	2	2	2	5	3	3	7	2	5	3	9	2	5	8	4	2	5	2	2	5	2
1st coordinate	-0,96	-0,94	-0,94	-0,93	-0,93	-0,9	-0,9	-0,87	-0,87	-0,86	-0,81	-0,77	-0,76	-0,75	-0,71	-0,7	-0,63	-0,48	-0,36	-0,32	-0,28	-0,26	-0,18	-0,01	0,39	0,57	0,68	0,91	1,22	1,25	1,29	1,31	1,46	1,53	1,55	1,55	1,56	1,56	1,58	1,63

	Phase	sum	1st coordinate		further stylistic elements	birdhead	wing	fish	front leg	hind leg	interlace	type
Durham A II 17		3	-0,94		BC5				X	X	interlace	codex
Köln 213		5	-0,94		BA4				X	X	interlace	codex
Paris 1587		5	-0,94		HA4, LD1, BA4				X	X	interlace	codex
Crundale 8g		3	-0,94	Kent				X	X	X	pointed open knot	buckle, triangular plate
Little Houghton		3	-0,93	N'hants					X	X		disc brooch
Faversham 8c		4	-0,92	Kent					X	X		comp. brooch
Allington Hill		4	-0,91	Cambs					X	X		discoid mount
Allington Hill 8a		4	-0,91	Cambs					X	X		discoid mount
Faversham 6h		3	-0,91	Kent	BA6				X	X		buckle, triangular plate
Faversham 6i	MS	3	-0,91	Kent	HE2, F1D				X	X		buckle, triangular plate
Barham/Ipswich b		3	-0,9	Suff	BA4				X	X		mount
Southampton		4	-0,89	Hants					X	X		plaque
Standlake		5	-0,89	Oxon					X	X		discoid mount
Sutton Hoo 1 2e		2	-0,87	Suff	LB5, BA2				(?)	X		clasps
Crundale 3h		4	-0,87	Kent					X	X		pommel
Durrow		6	-0,85						X	X	interlace	codex
Bamburgh		4	-0,83	N'land					X	X		plaque
Desborough		2	-0,81	N'hants	HC3, BA6				X	X		hinged clasps
York, Fishergate		3	-0,76	Yorks	HE5				X	X		knife
Caenby 8i		4	-0,76	Lincs	HF1				X	X		discoid mount
Burwell 42		5	-0,65	Cambs	BA4	X				X		work box
Icklingham		3	-0,61	Suff								model
Sutton Hoo 1 2hi		5	-0,61	Suff	BB1	X	X		X	X		purse
Standlake 8		2	-0,53	Oxon	HE6, FE1					X		discoid mount
Salmonby	A2	3	-0,49	Lincs	LC3				X	X		model
Sutton Hoo 1 15a		7	-0,47	Suff	FA5				X	X		cup
Rose Crescent		5	-0,16	Cambs	BA4				X	X		harness mount
Sutton Hoo 1 1abde		7	-0,02	Suff	HB9, HC4, LA4	X			X	X	open knot	buckle
Sutton Hoo 2 10h		4	0,37	Suff						X		discoid mount
Sutton Hoo 1 1l		2	0,46	Suff						X		cup
Sutton Hoo 17A		4	0,8	Suff						X		axe-shaped mount
Barham/Ipswich a		3	0,93	Suff	HA2, BA3	X				X		axe-shaped mount
Sutton Hoo 17B		4	0,97	Suff	BA4, BA6					X		axe-shaped mount
Langham?, Field Dalling		3	1,06	Norf	HE2					X		model
Caenby 10g		2	1,08	Lincs							interwoven	discoid mount
Sutton Hoo 1 10f	A1	3	1,22	Suff		X				X		lyre
Barton-on-Humber 1		2	1,29	Lincs								model
Sutton Hoo 1 7g		3	1,36	Suff	FD2				X	X		helmet
Sutton Hoo 1 15c		2	1,41	Suff	HG4, BE7		?					drinking horn
Sutton Hoo 1 16a		2	1,41	Suff	BA4				X	X		shield
Sutton Hoo 1 A1		4	1,47	Suff	BA6					X	interwoven	shield
Sutton Hoo 1 A14		3	1,48	Suff	BA4				X	X		shield
Sutton Hoo 1 5b		6	1,49	Suff	HG2	X	X		X	X		shield
Sutton Hoo 1 1o	SC	5	1,5	Suff	HG1, FA6, BA4				X	X		shield
Sutton Hoo 1 53a		3	1,56	Suff	HB10				X		wavy	shield
Sutton Hoo 1 1p		4	1,57	Suff	BA10				X	X		drinking horn
Sutton Hoo 1 A10		4	1,59	Suff	LA4				X	X		shield
Sutton Hoo 1 15k		2	1,63	Suff	HG5					X		shield

Fig. 8 The matrix of the objects with Anglian Style II, including the group removed from the analysis of the Kentish material, sorted on the basis of the coordinates of the 1st axis of the plot in Fig. 7.

On the basis of the correlations in Figure 9, phase KA emerges as contemporary with most of A1 and half of A2; phase KB is contemporary with the remainder of A2, and KC and MS appear roughly contemporary, but may have persisted for different periods of time (Fig. 10).

Dating of the stylistic schemes

Absolute dates are not easily applied to the stylistic scheme. For the Anglian scheme, the Scandinavian origin of the style and probably even the objects of phase SC may imply a date of manufacture as far back as *c*.550 (Høilund Nielsen 1991, 130). The buckle in Sutton Hoo 17 (Carver 1998, Pl. XI) is unique but the shape ties it to Continental buckles with triangular plates with straight edges which in the Lower Rhine area date from 565 to 640 (Siegmund 1989). The version datable from 605 to 640 has a triangular, straight-edged counter-plaque. This means that the Sutton Hoo 17 buckle must be from some time after 565 but probably earlier than 605. Here a round date of 570–80 is considered not to be out of place, which would fix the middle of phase A1 to about then. The gold content of two pendants in the grave of Standlake 8, which belongs to phase A2, suggests datings between 596 and 629 for the grave, and the gold content of the Faversham 12f gold bracteate, belonging to phase KB, suggests datings between 613 and 629 for the object (Brown and Schweizer 1973), although it is doubtful whether such analyses give any precise dates at all (*ibid.*, 182–5). On the basis of Sutton Hoo Mound 1 the early part of the MS phase may be dated to just before 625. The pendant from Bacton (Fig. 11), which was not included in the seriation, is decorated with head-elements of phase MS and contains a coin dated to 585 (Campbell *et al.* 1982, 52, fig. 52), which means only that the introduction of the MS style on this object must post-date 585. The end of the MS phase is most likely to be before the production of the Lindisfarne Gospels, which are dated to *c.* 700 (Backhouse 1981, 14). Style II appears to have been introduced into the Anglian area through Suffolk, spreading to Lincolnshire, Norfolk and Cambridgeshire in the subsequent phases.

For the Kentish scheme there are few fixed points. Since buckles with triangular plates appear already at the beginning of phase KA, the phase may go back to 565, though it does not have to. Buckles with triangular plates and triangular counter-plaque occur from the middle of phase KB, which may therefore be dated to 605 or thereafter.

In short, we have a Scandinavian introduction of Style II to East Anglia some time after 550. Shortly thereafter, but in no circumstances before 565, the local versions A1 and KA appeared in the Anglian area and the Kentish area respectively. In Kent the style was most likely introduced from the Continent – there are far more links to the Continent in both style and object-type than there are to Scandinavia[2] – and developed until perhaps the middle of the seventh century with ever more stereotyped motifs dominated by interlace patterns. In the Anglian area the style lasted even longer, but it changed between 620 and 700 from a purely secular style to a style tied just as closely to sacred manuscripts produced in northern ecclesiastical scriptoria. Throughout it was primarily a style based on quadrupeds.

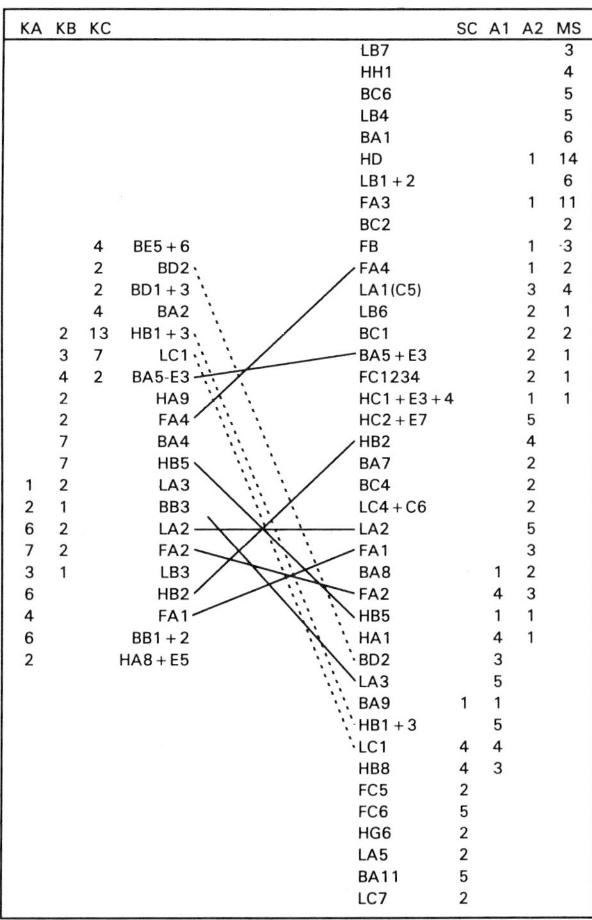

Fig. 9 Correlation of the two stylistic schemes. On the left are the Kentish phases with the number of each stylistic element in each phase; on the right the same information is presented for the Anglian phases. In the middle identical elements are connected with a line. The dotted lines indicate the elements which have totally different datings in each of the two areas.

Even though the latest objects from Sutton Hoo (the clasps) appear in the seriation close to the Book of Durrow, a date earlier than 620–25 cannot be supported for the latter. It is most likely to lie somewhat later, especially if the manuscript was made in England. Also the other richly decorated manuscripts belong to the MS phasc of the Anglian style. They were probably all created, together with the Durrow manuscript, in Northumbrian scriptoria, which means after the establishment of the monasteries in the area and, as they also have a clearly

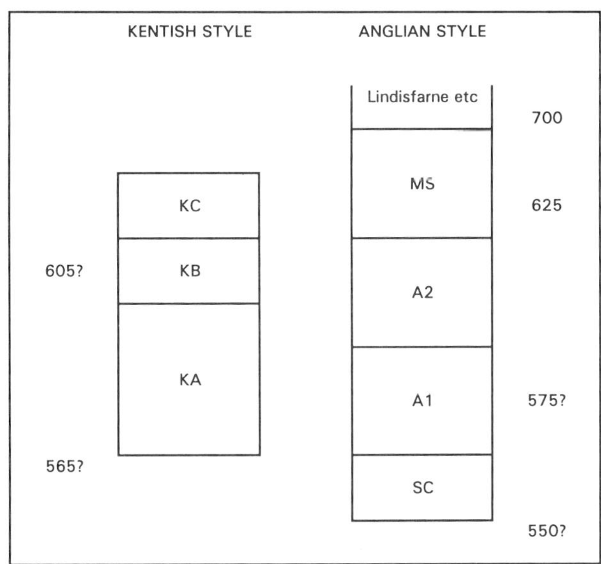

Fig. 10 Chronological scheme of the two style-developments. It must be emphasized that even though the styles are drawn here in rigid phases, they both represent very smooth and even developments.

Celtic touch, after the establishment of the Irish mission in Northumbria, which happened after 634 (Campbell *et al.* 1982, 46, 72).

The MS version of the Anglian style is not confined to the Anglian area, but is found also in the Kentish area and northwards to Northumbria, and it also appears on a clasp from Tongres, Belgium (Speake 1980, Pl. 3e). The style can be found both hidden on the reverse of objects (the Crundale buckle and a Faversham composite brooch) and presented clearly on their fronts (the Crundale pommel and one of the Faversham composite brooches).

The archaeological context

Only a few objects come from informative contexts. The earliest material from the Anglian series comes from Sutton Hoo and was buried long after it was made. There is, however, little doubt of the paramount social status of the context of this material (Bruce-Mitford 1975; 1978; 1983; Carver 1992; 1993a; 1993b). Both the Mounds 1–2 and 17 clearly express a very high social status as does also the richly furnished barrow burial from Caenby which contributes a disc to this phase and a mount to the next (Webster and Backhouse 1991, 57–8). The Standlake mount belongs to a female grave which included among other things gold pendants and a cross (MacGregor and Bolick 1993, 240) and thus constitutes a further fairly rich burial. Burwell 42 is less wealthy, but still an above-average burial of the 'Final Phase' (Lethbridge 1931, 53–7).

The Kentish examples of Anglian Style II are from rich burials and very rich cemeteries, such as King's Field, Faversham, which probably had some connection to royal circles (Crowfoot and Hawkes 1967, 65; Speake 1980, 39). It is interesting, however, that the Faversham buckles in MS style are rather simple and only of bronze, and that while the MS decoration on brooch 8c from Faversham is on the reverse, as on the Crundale buckle, on the Crundale pommel and brooch 11p from Faversham it is clearly visible. Finally, the richly decorated manuscripts are probably all created in Northumbrian scriptoria and thus tied to the ecclesiastical part of society, though clearly to the upper level. For example, Bishop Ethelwald had the Lindisfarne Gospels made in honour of Saint Cuthbert (Backhouse 1981, 7–8).

Generally, the high social context of most of the Anglian Style II persists, although there is a slight tendency for it to spread to lower levels after some time, so that the social distribution of the style widens. It is also indisputable – at least with the state of the art at the moment – that Style II is heavily linked to Sutton Hoo, which is thus differentiated, for instance, from nearby elite burial places at Snape and Pakefield, which have no Style II and which unlike Sutton Hoo are placed in pre-existing cemeteries (Carver 1992; Filmer-Sankey 1992, 50; Scull 1993, 76).

For the Kentish Style II, Faversham is well represented in all phases. As mentioned above, it is a very rich burial place with a probably royal connection. The same interpretation may also be valid for Gilton, Kingston Down and Sarre. The very rich, probably royal, barrow burial from Taplow contains material from all three Kentish style-phases and suggests a burial date some time in phase KC (see also Crowfoot and Hawkes 1967, 65–6). It is typical of princely burials too in containing gravegoods from a broad span of time which contributes to the debate over dating. Asthall barrow in Oxfordshire from phase KA is also a very rich grave belonging to the best of the magnificent Early Anglo-Saxon princely burials (Dickinson and Speake 1992, 115). In Taplow and probably Asthall a combination of Style I and Style II is found. Finally, Wickhambreux from phase KC also contained high status material (Åberg 1926, Tab. V, 79).

Two Hampshire burials appear in the Kentish scheme, Winnall grave 21, a rather poorly equipped grave, in phase KA (Meaney and Hawkes 1970), and Alton 16, a fairly rich weapon-burial with a Kentish buckle with triangular plate, which was old when buried, in phase KC (Evison 1988).

In general, Kentish Style II has a high social status too. In Kent itself there are no royal burials with Style II, but this may be due to the Christianization of Kent and a new tradition of burials within churches (Speake 1980, 39). However, there seem to be princely burials in other parts of the area throughout nearly the entire period.

The contexts of Style II in both the Anglian and Kentish areas suggest the style to be – if not exclusively – an elitist style. In the Anglian area there is a clear connection

	Phase		head (H)	leg (L)	foot (F)	body (B)	birdhead	wing	fish	front leg	hind leg	interlace	type	references	
Allington Hill	MS	Cambridgeshire	D1	B1	B	A1				X	X		discoid mount	Speake 1980	Fig. 8a-b, Pl. 15b
Allington Hill 8a	MS	Cambridgeshire	D1	B1	B	A1				X	X		discoid mount	Speake 1980	Fig. 8a-b, Pl. 15b
Alton 16	KC	Hampshire	B1	C1		D1						interwoven	buckle, triangular plate	Speake 1980	Fig. 4g, Pl. 6b
Asthall barrow	KA	Oxfordshire	B2	A2	A1	B1	X	X				interwoven	mount	Speake 1980	Fig. 6r, 17l, Pl. 2f
Asthall barrow 2		Oxfordshire	B3										repoussé mounts	Dickinson & Speake 1992	Fig. 18c
Bacton		Norfolk	D2									plaitwork	pendant	Speake 1980	Fig. 11a, Pl. 3c
Bamburgh	MS	Northumberland	D2	B6	A3	C1				X	X		gold plaque	Webster & Backhouse 1991	No 45
Barham/Ipswich a	A1	Suffolk	A1, A2	A3	A2	A3	X				X		axe-shaped mount	Webster & Backhouse 1991	No 39
Barham/Ipswich b	MS	Suffolk	D3	B1	B1	A4				X	X		mount	British Museum	
Barton-on-Humber 1	A1	Lincolnshire	B3			D2							model/die	Speake 1980	Fig. 13q, Pl. 13p
Benty Grange		Derbyshire	C1			E2							hanging-bowl escutcheon	Speake 1980	Fig. 11c
Bidford-on-Avon 81 a		Warwickshire	E1			E1							open-work axe-shaped mount	Speake 1980	Fig. 12b, Pl. 16b
Bidford-on-Avon 81 b		Warwichshire	E2										open-work discoid mount	Speake 1980	Fig. 12a, Pl. 16a
Bifrons 85		Kent	B2				X						pin	Speake 1980	Fig. 17m
Breach Downs	KC	Kent	B3	C1		A2						interwoven	buckle, triangular plate	Speake 1980	Fig. 4c, Pl. 6g
Broadstairs 59	KB	Kent	B5	C1		A4					X		buckle, rectangular plate	Speake 1980	Fig. 4m, Pl. 9c
Broadstairs 98	KC	Kent	B3			E3						wavy	buckle, rectangular plate	Speake 1980	Fig. 4l, Pl. 9a
Buckland 29	KA	Kent	A5	A2	A1	C3				X	X		bracteate	Speake 1980	Fig. 13j, Pl. 13i
Buckland 134		Kent	A6			E4							bracteate	Speake 1980	Fig. 13f, Pl. 13a
Burwell 42	A2	Cambridgeshire	B2, C2	B6	B2	A4, A5	X				X		work box	Spaeke 1980	Fig. 6o-q
Caenby 10g	A1	Lincolnshire	A1			D2						interwoven	discoid mount	Speake 1980	Fig. 10g, Pl. 15j
Caenby 8i	A2	Lincolnshire	F1	A1, B6	C1	C1				X	X		discoid mount	Speake 1980	Fig. 8i, 15e, Pl. 15k
Caenby 10j		Lincolnshire	A3				X						axe-shaped mount	Speake 1980	Fig. 10j-k, Pl. 15l
Caenby a		Lincolnshire	A1										axe-shaped mount	British Museum	
Caenby b		Lincolnshire	A1										axe-shaped mount	British Museum	
Caenby c		Lincolnshire	A3				X						axe-shaped mount	Speake 1980	Fig. 10j-k, Pl. 15l
Caenby d		Lincolnshire	A3				X						axe-shaped mount	Speake 1980	Fig. 10j-k, Pl. 15l
Camerton 5		Somerset	A4									complicated knots	bracteate	Speake 1980	Fig. 13m, Pl. 13j
Canterbury	KA	Kent	B2			B3	X	X	X				hook	Royal Museum, Canterbury	
Castle Bytham		Lincolnshire	A1?									plaitwork	annular brooch	Speake 1980	Fig. 9n, Pl. 16e
Crundale 3h	MS	Kent	D2	A1	A3	C2				X	X		pommel	Speake 1980	Fig. 3h, 8j, Pl. 14b
Crundale 8g	MS	Kent	D2	B4		A1			X	X	X	pointed open knots	buckle, triangular plate	Speake 1980	Fig. 8g, Pl. 7e
Desborough	MS	Northamptonshire	C3	B2	C2	A6				X	X		hinged clasps	Speake 1980	Fig. 6g, Pl. 8f
Durham A II 17	MS		H1	B7	A3	C5				X	X	interlace	codex	Åberg 1943	Fig. 84,7-10
Durrow	MS		D3	A1, B1	A3	A5, C2				X	X	interlace	codex	Åberg 1943	Fig. 83
East Kent a	KC	Kent	B3			E6							bracteate	Royal Museum, Canterbury	
East Kent b	KC	Kent	B3			E6							bracteate	Royal Museum, Canterbury	
East Kent c	KC	Kent	B3			E6							bracteate	Royal Museum, Canterbury	
East Kent 13c		Kent	B4?	B6, C2		A8					X		bracteate	Speake 1980	Fig. 13c, Pl. 13g
East Kent 13d		Kent	B4			E3							bracteate	Speake 1980	Fig. 13d, Pl. 13e
East Kent 13t		Kent	A7			E5							bracteate	Speake 1980	Fig. 13t, Pl. 13k
Eccles 19		Kent	E3			D3						knots	buckle, tongue-shaped plate	Speake 1980	Pl. 9e
Faversham 10d	KB	Kent	B5			B3							harness mount	Speake 1980	Fig. 10d, Pl. 15f
Faversham 12f	KB	Kent	F2	B5	A4	A5				X	X		bracteate	Spaeke 1980	Fig. 12f, 13s, Pl. 13l
Faversham 4b	KB	Kent	B5	C1		A5, A4					X		buckle, triangular plate	Speake 1980	Fig. 4b, Pl. 6e
Faversham 4d	KC	Kent	B3			D2						wavy	buckle, triangular plate	Speake 1980	Fig. 4d, Pl. 6c
Faversham 6h	MS	Kent	D4	B4	A3	A6				X	X		buckle, triangular plate	Speake 1980	Fig. 6h, Pl. 8d
Faversham 6i	MS	Kent	E2	B4	A4, D1	C6				X	X		buckle, triangular plate	Speake 1980	Fig. 6i
Faversham 6m	KA	Kent	A2	B3	A1	B1	X	X					buckle, triangular plate	Speake 1980	Fig. 6m, Pl. 8e
Faversham 6n	KA	Kent	B2	A3	A2	B3	X	?	X		X		buckle, triangular plate	Speake 1980	Fig. 6n, Pl. 2a
Faversham 8c	MS	Kent	D2	B4	A3	A1				X	X		composite brooch	Speake 1980	Fig. 8c, Pl. 11e-f
Faversham 9b	KB	Kent	B5	A2	A2	A4					X		keystone brooch	Speake 1980	Fig. 9b, Pl. 10d
Faversham 9c	KB	Kent	B3, B5	A2, A3	A3, A4	A6, A4				X	X		keystone brooch	Speake 1980	Fig. 9c, Pl. 10f
Faversham 9e	KA	Kent	A8			B2		X					keystone brooch	Speake 1980	Fig. 9e, Pl. 10e
Faversham 11p		Kent	D2										composite brooch	Speake 1980	Fig. 11p, Pl. 12b
Faversham 6a		Kent	B2				X					wavy	gold buckle	Speake 1980	Fig. 6a, Pl. 2h
Gilton 17i	KA	Kent	B2	B3	A2	B1	X	X					pin	Speake 1980	Fig. 17i
Gilton 23 17h	KA	Kent	B2	B3	A2	B1	X	X					pin	Speake 1980	Fig. 17h
Gilton 23 4h	KC	Kent	B3	C1		A4							buckle, triang. plate and counter-pl.	Speake 1980	Fig. 4h, Pl. 7a
Gilton Ash 17a	KA	Kent	B6	A2	A2		X	X					mount	Speake 1980	Fig. 17a
Gilton 69		Kent	B3	A3	A2	A6					X		discoid mount	Speake 1980	Fig. 10a, Pl. 15g
Guston		Kent	B3	A2	A2	A4					X		keystone brooch	Speake 1980	Fig. 9a, Pl. 10g
Hardingstone		Northamptonshire	E1		A2				X			plaitwork	harness mount	Speake 1980	Fig. 10e, Pl. 16d

	Phase		head (H)	leg (L)	foot (F)	body (B)	birdhead	wing	fish	front leg	hind leg	interlace	type	references	
Holborough 7		Kent	B2				X						buckle	Speake 1980	Pl. 2b
Icklingham	A2	Suffolk	C2, E3			A5							model/die	Speake 1980	Fig. 14f, Pl. 14g
Kingston 205	KB	Kent	A9, B3, B5	C1		A4, E3	X				X		composite brooch	Speake 1980	Fig. 9g, 11q, Pl. 11c-d, 12a
Kingston 13e		Kent	B7			E3							bracteate	Speake 1980	Fig. 13e, Pl. 13h
Kingston 161		Kent	B2				X						three repoussé silver mounts	Speake 1980	Pl. 2c
Kingston 300		Kent	?										open-work buckle	Speake 1980	Fig. 6l, Pl. 9h
Köln 213	MS		D3, H1	B7	A3	A4, C6				X	X	interlace	codex	Åberg 1943	Fig. 84,2-3
Langham?, Field Dalling	A1	Norfolk	E2	A3	A2	A9					X		model/die	British Museum	
Little Houghton	MS	Northamptonshire	D4	B1		A1				X	X		disc brooch	Speake 1980	Fig. 8e, Pl. 15a
London	KB	Buckinghamshire	C2	A3, B3	A2	A4				X	X		disc brooch	British Museum	
Loveden Hill		Lincolnshire	B2?				X						drinking-horn	Speake 1980	Pl. 4i
Lullingstone		Kent	E1		A4								model/die	Speake 1980	Fig. 13l
Mundford		Norfolk	B2				X					plaitwork	axe-shaped pendant	Speake 1989	Fig. 68
Occaney Beck		Yorkshire	B2				X						penannular brooch	Speake 1980	Fig. 11o
Paris 1587	MS		A4, D3, H1	D1, B7	A3	A4, C6				X	X	interlace	codex	Åberg 1943	Fig. 84,4-6
Polhill 37		Kent		A3	C3						X		keystone brooch	Speake 1980	Pl. 10h
Rose Crescent	A2	Cambridgeshire	B2, C2?	A2	A2	A4, A7				X	X		harness mount	Speake 1980	Fig. 8d, Pl. 15d
Salmonby	A2	Lincolnshire	E7	C3, C4	C4					X	X		model/die	Speake 1980	Fig. 8l, Pl. 15e
Sarre		Kent	B4?							?	?	interwoven	strap mount	Åberg 1926	Fig. 234
Sarre 68	KC	Kent	B3	C1		A2					X	wavy	buckle, triangular plate	Speake 1980	Fig. 4a, 7c, Pl. 6f
Sarre 11a		Kent	B2?				X						composite brooch	Speake 1980	Pl. 11a-b
Sewerby 24		Yorkshire	?										penannular brooch	Hirst 1985	
Sittingbourne		Kent	B7			E3							bracteate	Speake 1980	Fig. 13h, Pl. 13b
Southampton	MS	Hampshire	D3/H1	A1	A3	C6				X	X		plaque	Webster & Backhouse 1991	No 44
Standlake	MS	Oxfordshire	D2/D4??	A1, B4	A3	A1				X	X		discoid mount	Speake 1980	Fig. 8h, Pl. 15c
Standlake 8	A2	Oxfordshire	E6	A1	E1	C4					X		discoid open-work mount	MacGregor & Bolick 1993	No 47.6
Stoke Holy Cross		Norfolk	A5				X					plaitwork	open-work mount	British Museum	
Sutton Hoo 1 10f	A1	Suffolk	A1	C1		D2	X				X		yre	Speake 1980	Fig. 10f, Pl. 4b, d
Sutton Hoo 1 15a	A2	Suffolk	E3/E4, C2	A1, A2	A1, A3, A5	A7				X	X		cup	Speake 1980	Fig. 15a-b
Sutton Hoo 1 15c	A1	Suffolk	B3, G4	C1		E7		?					drinking horn	Speake 1980	Fig. 15c
Sutton Hoo 1 15k	SC	Suffolk	G5	C7		A11					X		shield mount	Speake 1980	Fig. 15k
Sutton Hoo 1 16a	A1	Suffolk	B3	C1		A4				X	X		shield-boss neck mount	Speake 1980	Fig. 16a
Sutton Hoo 1 1abde	A2	Suffolk	B2, B9, C4	A4, A2, C6	A1, A2	A8, C4	X			X	X	open knot	gold buckle	Speake 1980	Fig. 1a-b, d-e, i, 13p, Pl. 2d, 4f
Sutton Hoo 1 1j		Suffolk	G3	C3	C6	C5				X	X		shield-boss rim mount	Speake 1980	Fig. 1j
Sutton Hoo 1 1l	A2	Suffolk	A1		A1						X		cup	Speake 1980	Fig. 1l, Pl. 14l
Sutton Hoo 1 1o	SC	Suffolk	G1, B8	A3, C1	A6, C3	A4, A11				X	X		shield mount (dragon)	Speake 1980	Fig. 1o, Pl. 5a
Sutton Hoo 1 1p	SC	Suffolk	B8	C1, C7	C5	A10				X	X		drinking horn	Speake 1980	Fig. 1p, Pl. 14n
Sutton Hoo 1 2e	MS	Suffolk	D2	B5	A4	A2				(?)	X		clasps	Speake 1980	Fig. 2a-c, e, Pl. 3a
Sutton Hoo 1 2hi	A2	Suffolk	B2, D4	A2	A4	C1, B1	X	X		X	X		purse	Speake 1980	Fig. 2h-j, 17d, Pl. 3b
Sutton Hoo 1 4e		Suffolk	B2/A2				X						repair patch from hanging-bowl	Speake 1980	Pl. 4e
Sutton Hoo 1 53a	SC	Suffolk	B10	C1	C6	A11				X		wavy	shield mount	Bruce-Mitford 1978	Fig. 53a
Sutton Hoo 1 5b	SC	Suffolk	G2, B8	A5, A3	C6	A11, A9	X	X		X	X		shield mount (bird)	Speake 1980	Pl. 5b
Sutton Hoo 1 7g	A1	Suffolk	B3	C1, A3	D2					X	X		helmet mount	Speake 1980	Fig. 7g, Pl. 5c
Sutton Hoo 1 A1	SC	Suffolk	B8	A3, C1	C5	A6					X	interwoven	shield mount	Bruce-Mitford 1978	Fig. 64
Sutton Hoo 1 A10	SC	Suffolk	G6	A4, A5	C6	A11				X	X		shield-boss mount	Bruce-Mitford 1978	Fig. 39
Sutton Hoo 1 A14	SC	Suffolk	G6	A3	C6	A4				X	X		shield mount	Bruce-Mitford 1978	Fig. 61
Sutton Hoo 17A	A1	Suffolk	A1	A3	A2	A8					X		axe-shaped mount	British Museum	
Sutton Hoo 17B	A1	Suffolk	B3, B5	A3	A2	A4, A6					X		axe-shaped mount	British Museum	
Sutton Hoo 2 10h	A2	Suffolk	B5	A2	A2	A8					X		discoid mount	Speake 1980	Fig. 10h, Pl. 16f
Taplow	KA	Buckinghamshire	B2	A2	C6, A2, C7	A9				X	X		cup	British Museum	
Taplow 4i	KC	Buckinghamshire	B3	C1		A2						irregular	buckle, triangular plate	Speake 1980	Fig. 4i, 7f, Pl. 7f
Taplow 4n	KB	Buckinghamshire	B5, A9			A4, E3	X					interwoven	clasps	Speake 1980	Fig. 4n, o, 7h, Pl. 7c
Taplow 7a	KA	Buckinghamshire	B11, A8	A2	A1, A2		X			X	X	plaitwork	drinking horn	Speake 1980	Fig. 7a-b, d, Pl. 1a-b
Taplow 7i	KC	Buckinghamshire	B4	C1		D2	?					knots	drinking horn	Speake 1980	Fig. 7i, k, 14i, Pl. 14i
Taplow 7j	KC	Buckinghamshire	B3			D1						interwoven	cup	Speake 1980	Fig. 7j, m, 14h, Pl. 14k
Taplow 7e		Buckinghamshire	B10	A2	A2	A2	X				X	wavy	lyre	Speake 1980	Fig. 7e, Pl. 4a
Uncleby 62		Yorkshire	A9, E2				X						penannular brooch	Speake 1980	Fig. 11m
Westbere	KC	Kent	B3			E6							bracteate	Speake 1980	Fig. 13a, Pl. 13d
Wickhambreux	KC	Kent	B3	C1		A2, A5	?				X	interwoven	buckle, triangular plate	Speake 1980	Fig. 4e, Pl. 6d
Wingham (2)		Kent	A6			E4							bracteate	Speake 1980	Fig. 13f, Pl. 13a
Winnall 21	KA	Hampshire	A10, E8	A2	A2	B1		X			X		disc brooch	Speake 1980	Fig. 9j, Pl. 10i
York, Fishergate	MS	Yorkshire	E4, E5		A3	C1				X	X		knife handle	Webster & Backhouse 1991	No 43

Fig. 11 List of all recorded objects with Style II in England, with information on the stylistic elements which occur, other characteristics, type of interlace, object-type and references.

to the royal level; this is less clear in Kent, though still highly probable and a next-to-royal level is likely (cf. Crowfoot and Hawkes 1967, 65). In this context, it is noteworthy that the few occurrences of Anglian MS style in Kent tend to be either hidden on the reverse or on rather low-status objects. Only the pommel from Crundale and one of the composite brooches from Faversham stand out as truly conspicuous pieces.

A wider archaeological context

A broader discussion of the contexts of Anglo-Saxon Style II must depend on archaeological sources for the Anglian area, especially East Anglia, whereas for Kent archaeological material has been subject to less attention, but is supported by historical sources.

In East Anglia, the burial tradition from the second quarter of the fifth century was cremation. Late in the fifth century inhumations appeared, and it is suggested that this new burial tradition was chosen by groups or lineages wishing to distinguish themselves from the general community or to legitimize their right to a new status (Scull 1993, 75–6). In the first half of the sixth century Anglian female ornaments exhibit a fair degree of variation, but about the middle of the sixth century they become more uniform (Høilund Nielsen 1997a, 86–7), which probably reflects both acculturation of originally mixed groups of people and the creation of a new identity over larger areas.

Princely graves are not seen in East Anglia until the later sixth century. Snape and probably Pakefield may represent locally based, regional chiefs (Filmer-Sankey 1992, 50; Scull 1993, 76), whereas Sutton Hoo is exceptional and suggests a new paramount status. The burial place has no predecessor and in many ways is very peculiar (see for instance Carver 1992; 1995, 116). Ship graves in England are found only in East Anglia, at Sutton Hoo and Snape, but only at Sutton Hoo does the wealth of the graves and the character of their contents correspond to Scandinavian examples. And only here do we find Style II. The motifs of the style are clearly Scandiavian and they represent Scandinavian myths even in the late MS phase of the style. Furthermore, the ring-knob placed on the shield is of genuine Scandinavian type (though it ought to have been on the sword; Steuer 1987, 220). Perhaps someone from the lineage once had been a retainer of a Scandinavian/Danish king and thereby acquired the ring(-sword), shield and drinking horns (cf. Høilund Nielsen 1997c; Steuer 1987, 213).

Princely burial on the scale seen at Sutton Hoo is a new and apparently short-lived phenomenon, probably linked to the success of a few groups or a single dynasty in establishing a wider supremacy and eventually a regional hegemony, and to their concern to legitimize and reproduce a new status, authority and political identity (Scull 1992, 20).

The appearance of Style II in the Anglian area may thus be linked to the development of still larger kingdoms, and may be especially linked to the emerging power of one, successful lineage, centred around south-eastern Suffolk. The Scandinavian character of this power is suggested both from a stylistic point of view and from other aspects of the Sutton Hoo grave material, but it should not be forgotten that a really large part of the Sutton Hoo burial furniture is either local weaponry or, for instance, Frankish and Byzantine imports – things never found in Scandinavian contexts.

For the Kentish area richly furnished inhumation burials appear probably at least from the early sixth century. From the late fifth to early sixth centuries Scandinavian square-headed brooches and gold bracteates occur, but otherwise the material culture is of much more Frankish type. Probably Frankish ring-swords appear in Kent in an early context. Furthermore, from about 500 Frankish brooches and buckles were common in Kent together with other probably Frankish imports. The triangular buckles decorated with Style II are of the same types as used on the Continent between *c.* 565 and *c.* 640. A group of Continental inlaid iron buckles with counter-plaques with geometrical ornamentation, dated to *c.* 605–640, are also found in Kent (Hawkes 1981; cf. for the dates Siegmund 1989). As mentioned above even the Kentish Style II may have been inspired from Frankia.

Paramount burials are only seen in one example in the Kentish series, and this is Taplow in Buckinghamshire, somewhat west of Kent. It has been suggested that the missing paramount burials in Kent were due to Christianization and the subsequent burial of persons of royal rank in the churches and without gravegoods (Speake 1980, 39). People attached to the royal court or those of the royal lineages not buried in the churches may be those buried in a series of rich cemeteries such as for instance Faversham.

The Kentish Style II is much more stereotyped than the Anglian, a feature it has in common with Frankish Style II. Even in the Taplow find we do not see the clear hints of Scandinavian mythology which we do in the Sutton Hoo burial. However, a triangular buckle from Finglesham grave 95 is decorated with a warrior with two spears, horned helmet and buckle (Webster and Backhouse 1991, 22). This cemetery, situated close to the Kentish east coast, goes back to the early settlers with Jutish brooches and gold bracteates, but it is suggested that the aristocratic family left the place around 560 (Chadwick 1959; Hawkes in Campbell *et al.* 1982, 25). The Finglesham cemetery is situated close to the royal vill at Eastry (Hawkes in Campbell *et al.* 1982, 24), but it does not contain any Style II finds. A stray find from Eastry of a Gotlandic/South-Scandinavian button-on-bow brooch (dated in Scandinavia to the middle of the sixth century and in Kent to Evison's Phase 3, that is around 600) points, however, to some sort of contact with Scandinavia later than the 'Jutish' phase in East Kent (Hawkes 1979).

Faversham, situated further up the Thames estuary, probably covered the period after the aristocratic family left Finglesham. Here the proportion of exceptionally rich material and especially the many cases of gold-braid suggest royal rank for at least some of those buried and next-to-royal rank for many of the others (Crowfoot and Hawkes 1967, 65; Smith 1923). Much Style II is found here and the MS style appears at Faversham and Crundale (south-east of Faversham). Faversham lacks links to Scandinavia, but has them with the Continent.

Origin may be used to legitimize status, and the adoption of Style II in Anglo-Saxon England may be the elite families' attempt to signal descent or affiliation with elites in the 'parent-country' . The regional development of the style may have served subsequently to constitute and reproduce regional identities – Anglian and Kentish (cf. Scull 1995, 79). Of the Continental areas with which these English regions had obvious contact, Style II occurs only in Scandinavia and the Frankish area, not in the old Anglian and Saxon areas, which means that the connections must have been either with Scandinavia – or rather Denmark – or with Francia. Most likely Style II in the Anglian area was derived from the Danish area, while the Kentish Style II was primarily derived from Francia.

The historical context

Kent is best known from written sources. The oldest known pedigree from Kent presents an Eormenric as the first-named ruler, who lived in the later sixth century. His son was married to Charibert I's (561–567) daughter, Bertha, his grandson to another Frankish noble-woman, and his own name may indicate yet earlier Frankish contacts (Brooks 1989, 64; Wood 1994, 176–7; Yorke 1990, 28). Procopius even reports that the Franks claimed to rule over Brittia in the 550s (Wood 1992, 238; 1994, 176). The marriage between Eormenric's son, Æthelbert, and the Frankish Bertha was probably intended to open the possibility for a conversion of Æthelbert via the Frankish court, which would have made him subordinate to Francia. He decided, however, for a conversion through Rome (Wood 1994, 178; Yorke 1990, 28–9). Some of Bertha's grandchildren were also in exile in the Frankish Empire during Dagobert I's reign (623–639) (Wood 1994, 177). The historical material thus confirms intense contact, especially at royal level, between Kent and Francia, and supports the likelihood that Francia was the source of inspiration for Kentish Style II too.

Kentish princesses were married off to several other Anglo-Saxon kingdoms (Yorke 1990, 29). Perhaps until Æthelbert's reign East and West Kent were separate kingdoms (Brooks 1989, 69). The disappearance of the aristocratic family at Finglesham and the appearance of a royal level at Faversham may express parts of this development – a movement to a more central part of what was now Kent. Furthermore, Kent expanded into the Middle Thames region early in the seventh century (Webster and Backhouse 1991, 56) and also may have had some supremacy over Essex (Yorke 1990, 28). Archaeological material in Essex shows some Kentish affiliation (the buckle from Broomfield for instance), while the Kentish character of Taplow in the Middle Thames has already been discussed.

There are thus indications that Style II may have been spread to Kent from the Continent as part of fairly intensive contacts between the two areas, and that the style became attached to royal circles from Æthelbert onwards, that is after Kent was united into one kingdom. Furthermore it was also spread to other areas over which Kent stretched its influence and supremacy. That Kentish royal family members were buried in churches is confirmed by Bede's information of the burial place of King Æthelbert (Brooks 1989, 65), and this may explain why we do not find paramount burials like Sutton Hoo in Kent itself.

Of Kent's surviving migration myths only Bede tells about the Kentish people's origin in Jutland. The migration should have happened in the middle of the fifth century, but the information was not written down until 731. Judged on the basis of the archaeological material from Finglesham, such a myth might have been of special importance to the East Kentish kingdom. In their material culture, the people of this area show close contacts to Jutland in the late fifth century, and a myth placing their origin in Jutland might well have been cultivated. But from the shift to Faversham the situation might have been changed considerably. A united kingdom needed another myth to explain its origin: perhaps the myth of Hengist and Horsa would have been a convenient choice here, together with a Continental (Saxon) origin *and* the introduction of Style II from Francia to Kent.

No origin myth has survived for the Anglian area, and written sources are few and late, especially for East Anglia, since they were destroyed in the ninth century (Yorke 1990, 58). Information from the Tribal Hidage suggests, however, that seventh-century East Anglia was a major contemporary political unit (Scull 1992, 3; 1993, 67). Late sources place the start of the Wuffing dynasty in 571, which historically has been associated with the beginning of permanent regional overlordship in East Anglia and it seem reasonable to accept that Wuffa was a historical figure (Scull 1992, 5; 1993, 79). The introduction of the Wuffing dynasty seems contemporary with the introduction of Style II. Further, since Sutton Hoo is, so far, the only contemporaneous burial place of really paramount status, it is tempting to see it as the burial place of the Wuffingas and Style II as the signal of their descent or affiliation.

In the absence of written sources, the Lombards may serve here as an almost contemporary analogy. Lombard history was made manifest – written down (or composed)

– at the same time that Style II was adopted for extended use by the ruling Lombard elite. Both were attempts to signal descent from or affiliation with elites in Scandinavia in order to justify, through ancestral right, their rule over large parts of otherwise Roman Italy (Høilund Nielsen 1997b, 140–2; Høilund Nielsen forthcoming). Style II was, so to speak, a picture of the origin myth. Such a situation may supposedly alo have been the case in East Anglia.

A source which may give some comparable ideas is the *Beowulf* poem, though its origin and date are still very debated: the origin has been placed in Mercia, Wessex or East Anglia, and the date ranges from *c.* 700 to *c.* 1000 (cf. Chase 1981). The results of the Toronto conference (*ibid.*) preferring the late date have, however, been challenged by Newton (1993), who gives an early eighth-century date to the poem (actually he says not earlier than the middle of the seventh century) and places its origin in East Anglian royal circles (Newton 1993, 13, 133–5, 144–5). From an archaeological point of view, this early date seems most interesting as the weaponry described in *Beowulf* only fits with the material culture from the sixth and seventh centuries. Therefore *Beowulf* in Newton's interpretation may be able to give some views on the situation in East Anglia in the seventh century or even earlier. Supported by Old English royal pedigrees Newton suggests that *Beowulf* actually represents an earlier version of the history of the *Scyldings* than the one surviving in Norse sources (Newton 1993, 23–6), and furthermore that those for whom the poem was presented were well aware of dynastic concerns in Denmark whereas they were not so well informed on Norway and Sweden (Newton 1993, 132). The legend of *Scyld* acts as a dynastic myth of origin for the Danes. Newton suggests that knowledge of these concerns probably derived from the genealogical traditions of an Old English royal family which claimed descent from the *Scyldings* (Newton 1993, 133). The *Scyldings* are central for the poem, but the actors are not entirely the same as those known from Scandinavia. A Hrodmund does not actually appear in Norse sources, but is mentioned in *Beowulf* (Newton 1993, 81–2). Also in Ælfwald's pedigree a Hrodmund appears in the more mythological parts (Newton 1993, 77), and if he can be connected to the Danish *Scylding* genealogy through *Beowulf*, it may mean that the East Anglian royal family, the Wuffingas, saw themselves as originating in Denmark (for political manipulation of myths and genealogies, see Wolfram 1994).

If we compare this with the archaeological material, we see first that at Sutton Hoo there are Danish imports going back to the middle of the sixth century, while Style II with its many Scandinavian/Danish elements appears in East Anglia from the later sixth century. Style II would thus fit as the material expression of an elite family's attempt to signal descent from or affiliation with elites in the 'parent-country' – an idea perhaps also cultivated by the mythological literature.

Conclusion

In short, the conclusions of the above analyses are that there are two stylistic traditions within Anglo-Saxon Style II: a Kentish and an East Anglian. Kentish Style II may be a result of the Frankish influences in this area through both the sixth and seventh centuries, and is probably legitimizing the royal family of a united West and East Kent. In East Anglia, Style II may be due to a Danish affiliation of someone from the Wuffing lineage, perhaps a Wuffing of the middle–later sixth century who joined the Danish king as a retainer and thereby achieved the Danish part of the outfit buried with a much later Wuffing king in the Sutton Hoo Mound 1. Style II was developed locally and may have served as a signal of a mythical descent from the Danish *Scyldings,* through whom the Wuffings probably legitimized their right to paramount position in the East Anglian area.

This interpretation is thus rather different from that of Speake (1980), who saw the influence on East Anglia more literally in terms of personal contacts to Scandinavia. That he saw the influence coming from the Vendel and Valsgärde area was due to the state of the art in Scandinavian research in 1980. There are also differences in the interpretation of the Kentish material. On the basis of style and object-types there are no indications of Scandinavian contacts, while the historical sources refer exclusively to Frankish connections. The technological features, which Speake used to argue for the West Danish connection, may be due to earlier relations with Scandinavia, for some of the Danish examples actually go further back than the occurrence of Style II. That Kentish Style II was adopted from the Continent was also the general idea of Åberg and Leeds. Not until the discovery of Sutton Hoo was a real focus placed, however, on a Scandinavian origin for some of the Anglo-Saxon Style II. The origins and interpretations of Anglo-Saxon Style II thus vary within very few possibilities. Further analyses of Kentish material on a regional basis will most likely extend the possible interpretations of Kentish Style II. Changes in find material in the Anglian area over the past sixty years have already considerably changed the picture, and the possibility that new finds may totally change the picture again is obvious, especially given the impact of metal-detector finds in changing opinion of the Danish contribution to Style II.

Acknowledgements
The Style II material was recorded during early summer 1994. I am very much indebted to the staffs of the museums I visited: Royal Museum, Canterbury; The British Museum, London; York Archaeological Trust; Lincoln County and City Museum; Cambridge University Museum of Archaeology and Anthropology; Ashmolean Museum, Oxford. I especially wish to thank Birte Brugmann, Tania Dickinson, Angela Evans, Heinrich Härke, John Hines, Dafydd Kidd, Arthur MacGregor,

George Speake and Leslie Webster for attention, help, and fruitful discussions during my 1994 stay in Britain. I should also like to thank Corpus Christi College and Thomas Charles-Edwards, Oxford, for housing me during times of reading and writing in 1995. Tania Dickinson kindly improved my English. Finally I am indebted to the Danish Research Council for the Humanities for the grants that made possible the project of which the Anglo-Saxon studies are one part.

Notes

1. Some suspicion may be raised over Sutton Hoo I 16a, one of the repoussés from the Sutton Hoo shield boss. The style differs somewhat from the other objects and actually fits better into the Kentish style (see further below). Furthermore the stylistic elements would all fit into the Kentish series in late KB or early KC. If it is related to the Kent series, then it would have a date almost as late as the clasps in MS style, which suggests either a much later date for the shield or a repair of the shield. Repairs have been discussed, but questioned (Speake 1980, 31). The marked difference in style resurrects the theory of a later repair or might even suggest a remounting of older and newer mounts.
2. For instance, the buckle with similarly shaped triangular plate and with gold-foil inlay decorated in geometrical filigree from Kärlich, Mayen-Koblenz, (Hanel 1994, 27 and Tf. 15.1).

References

Åberg, N. 1926: *The Anglo-Saxons in England during the Early Centuries after the Invasion*, Almqvist & Wiksell (Uppsala).

Åberg, N. 1943: *The Occident and the Orient in the Art of the Seventh Century. I: The British Isles*, Kungl. Vitterhets Historie och Antikvitets Akademiens Handlingar, del 56:1, Wahlström & Widstrand (Stockholm).

Åberg, N. 1947: *The Occident and the Orient in the Art of the Seventh Century. III: The Merovingian Empire*, Kungl. Vitterhets Historie och Antikvitets Akademiens Handlingar, del 56:3, Wahlström & Widstrand, (Stockholm).

Alexander, J.J.G. 1978: *Insular Manuscripts 6th to 9th Century*, Harvey Miller (London).

Avent, R. 1975: *Anglo-Saxon Garnet Inlaid Disc and Composite Brooches*, BAR British Series 11(Oxford).

Backhouse, J. 1981: *The Lindisfarne Gospels*, Phaidon (Oxford).

Baxter, M.J. 1994: *Exploratory Multivariate Analysis in Archaeology*, Edinburgh University Press (Edinburgh).

Brooks, N. 1989: 'The creation and early structure of the Kingdom of Kent', in Bassett, S. (ed.), *The Origins of Anglo-Saxon Kingdoms*, Leicester University Press (London/New York), 55 74.

Brown, M.P. 1991: *Anglo-Saxon Manuscripts*, The British Library (London).

Brown, P.D.C. and Schweizer, F. 1973: 'X-ray fluorescent analysis of Anglo-Saxon jewellery', *Archeometry* 15, 175–92.

Bruce-Mitford, R. 1975: *The Sutton Hoo Ship-Burial Vol. 1: Excavation, background, the ship, dating and inventory*, British Museum Publications Limited (London).

Bruce-Mitford, R. 1978: *The Sutton Hoo Ship-Burial Vol. 2: Arms, armour and regalia*, British Museum Publications Limited (London).

Bruce-Mitford, R. 1983: *The Sutton Hoo Ship-Burial Vol. 3: Late Roman and Byzantine silver, hanging-bowls, drinking vessels, cauldrons and other containers, textiles, the lyre, pottery bottle and other items*, British Museum Publications Limited (London).

Campbell, J., John E. and Wormald, P. 1982: *The Anglo-Saxons*, Phaidon (Oxford).

Carver, M.O.H. 1992: 'The Anglo-Saxon cemetery at Sutton Hoo: an interim report', in Carver, M.O.H. (ed.), *The Age of Sutton Hoo. The Seventh Century in north-western Europe*, Boydell Press (Woodbridge), 343–371.

Carver, M.O.H. 1993a: 'Strategy and fieldwork programme at Sutton Hoo', *Bulletin of the Sutton Hoo Research Committee* 8, 5–10.

Carver, M.O.H. 1993b: 'The Anglo-Saxon cemetery: an interim report', *Bulletin of the Sutton Hoo Research Committee* 8, 11–20.

Carver, M.O.H. 1995: 'Boat-burial in Britain: ancient custom or political signal', in Crumlin-Pedersen, O. and Munch Thye, Birgitte (eds), *The Ship as Symbol in Prehistoric and Medieval Scandinavia*, Publications from the National Museum, Studies in Archaeology and History Vol. 1 (Copenhagen), 111–124.

Carver, M.O.H. 1998: *Sutton Hoo. Burial Ground of Kings?*, British Museum Press (London).

Chadwick, S.E. 1959: 'The Anglo-Saxon cemetery at Finglesham, Kent: a reconsideration', *Medieval Archaeology* 2 (for 1958), 1–71.

Chase, C. (ed.) 1981: *The Dating of Beowulf*, University of Toronto Press (Toronto).

Crowfoot, E. and Hawkes, S.C. 1967: 'Early Anglo-Saxon gold braids', *Medieval Archaeology* 11, 42–86.

Dickinson, T.M. and Speake, G. 1992: 'The seventh-century cremation burial in Asthall Barrow, Oxfordshire: a reassessment', in Carver, M.O.H. (ed.), *The Age of Sutton Hoo. The Seventh Century in North-western Europe*, Boydell Press (Woodbridge), 95–130.

Evison, V.I. 1987: *Dover: The Buckland Anglo-Saxon Cemetery*, Historic Buildings and Monuments Commission for England (London).

Evison, V. 1988: *An Anglo-Saxon Cemetery at Alton, Hampshire*, Hampshire Field Club and Archaeological Society Monograph 4 (Gloucester).

Filmer-Sankey, W. 1992: 'Snape Anglo-Saxon cemetery: the current state of knowledge', in Carver, M.O.H.(ed.), *The Age of Sutton Hoo. The Seventh Century in North-western Europe*, Boydell Press (Woodbridge), 39–51.

Hanel, E. 1994: *Die merowingischen Altertümer von Kärlich und Umgebung*, Archäologische Schriften des Instituts für Vor- und Frühgeschichte der Johannes Gutenberg-Universität Mainz, Band 4 (Mainz).

Haseloff, G. 1984: 'Stand der Forschung: Stilgeschichte Völkerwanderungs- und Merowingerzeit', in *Festskrift til Thorleif Sjøvold på 70-årsdagen*, Universitetes Oldsakssamlings Skrifter, Ny rekke. Nr. 5 (Oslo) 109–124

Hawkes, S.C. 1979: 'Eastry in Anglo-Saxon Kent: its importance, and a newly found grave', *Anglo-Saxon Studies in Archaeology and History* I, BAR British Series 72, 81–113.

Hawkes, S.C. 1981: 'Recent finds of inlaid iron buckles and belt-plates from seventh-century Kent', *Anglo-Saxon Studies in Archaeology and History* 2, BAR British Series 92, 49–70.

Hines, J. 1992: 'The Scandinavian character of Anglian England: an update', in Carver, M.O.H. (ed.), *The Age of Sutton Hoo. The Seventh Century in North-western Europe*, Boydell Press (Woodbridge), 315–329.

Hirst, S.M. 1985: *An Anglo-Saxon Inhumation Cemetery at Sewerby, East Yorkshire*, York University Archaeological Publications 4 (York).

Høilund Nielsen, K. 1991: 'Centrum og periferi i 6.–8. årh. Territoriale studier af dyrestil og kvindesmykker i yngre germansk jernalder i Syd- og Østskandinavien', in Mortensen, P. and Rasmussen, B.M. (eds), *Høvdingesamfund og Kongemagt. Fra Stamme til Stat i Danmark 2*, Jysk Arkæologisk Selskabs Skrifter XXII:2 (Højbjerg), 127–54.

Høilund Nielsen, K. 1992: 'Stylistic analyses in archaeology by means of Correspondence Analysis', in Schader, M. (ed.), *Analyzing and Modeling Data and Knowledge*, Springer-Verlag (Berlin), 277–284.

Høilund Nielsen, K. 1995: 'From artifact to interpretation using Correspondence Analysis', *Anglo-Saxon Studies in Archaeology and History* 8, 113–143.

Høilund Nielsen, K. 1997a: 'The schism of Anglo-Saxon chronology', in Jensen, C.K. and Høilund Nielsen, K. (eds), *Burial and Society. The Chronological and Social Analysis of Archaeological Burial Data,* Aarhus University Press (Aarhus), 71–99.

Høilund Nielsen, K. 1997b: 'Animal art and the weapon burial rite: a political badge?', in Jensen, C.K. and Høilund Nielsen, K. (eds), *Burial and Society. The Chronological and Social Analysis of Archaeological Burial Data,* Aarhus University Press (Aarhus), 129–148.

Høilund Nielsen, K. 1997c: 'Retainers of the Scandinavian kings. An alternative interpretation of Salin's Style II (sixth–seventh centuries AD)', *Journal of European Archaeology 5.1, 151–69.*

Høilund Nielsen, K. forthcoming: 'Animal art – the symbol of power and myth. A reassesment of Salin's Style II on a European background', *Acta Archaeologica.*

Holmqvist, W. 1955: *Germanic Art during the First Millenium AD* (Stockholm).

Jensen, C.K. and Høilund Nielsen, K. 1997: 'Burial data and Correspondence Analysis', in Jensen, C.K. and Høilund Nielsen, K. (eds), *Burial and Society.* The Chronological and Social Analysis of Archaeological Burial Data, Aarhus University Press (Aarhus), 29–61.

Kendrick, T.D. 1934: 'Style in Early Anglo-Saxon ornament', *Ipek* 9, 66–76.

Kendrick, T.D. 1938: *Anglo-Saxon Art to AD 900*, Methuen (London).

Klein-Pfeuffer, M. 1993: *Merowingerzeitliche Fibeln und Anhänger aus Pressblech*, Hitzeroth (Marburg).

Leeds, E.T. 1936: *Early Anglo-Saxon Art and Archaeology*, Clarendon Press (Oxford).

Lethbridge, T.C. 1931: *Recent Excavations in Anglo-Saxon Cemeteries in Cambridgeshire and Suffolk. A Report*, Cambridge Antiquarian Society. Quarto Publications, New Series, No. III, Bowes & Bowes (Cambridge).

MacGregor, A. and Bolick, E. 1993: *A Summary Catalogue of the Anglo-Saxon Collections (Non-Ferrous Metals)*, BAR British Series 230 (Oxford).

Meaney, A. and Hawkes, S.C. 1970: *Two Anglo-Saxon Cemeteries at Winnall, Winchester, Hampshire*, The Society for Medieval Archaeology Monograph Series: No. 4 (London).

Newton, S. 1993: *The Origins of Beowulf and the Pre-Viking Kingdom of East Anglia*, D.S. Brewer (Cambridge).

Ørsnes, M. 1966: *Form og stil i Sydskandinaviens yngre germanske jernalder*, Nationalmuseets Skrifter, Arkæologisk-historisk række XI (København).

Roth, H. 1986: *Kunst und Handwerk im frühen Mittelalter. Archäologische Zeugnisse von Childerich I. bis zu Karl dem Grossen*, Konrad Theiss Verlag (Stuttgart).

Roth, U. 1987: 'Early insular manuscripts: ornament and archaeology, with special reference to the dating of the Book of Durrow', in Ryan, M. (ed.), *Ireland and Insular Art. A.D. 500–1200*, Royal Irish Academy (Dublin), 23–29.

Salin, B. 1904: *Die altgermanische Theirornamentik. Typologische Studie Über germanische Metallgegenstände aus dem IV. bis IX. Jahrhundert, nebst einer Studie über irische Ornamentik*, K.L. Beckman (Stockholm).

Scull, C. 1992: 'Before Sutton Hoo: structures of power and society in early East Anglia', in Carver, M.O.H. (ed.), *The Age of Sutton Hoo. The Seventh Century in North-western Europe*, Boydell Press (Woodbridge), 3–23.

Scull, C. 1993: 'Archaeology, early Anglo-Saxon society and the origins of Anglo-Saxon kingdoms', *Anglo-Saxon Studies in Archaeology and History* 6, 65–82.

Scull, C. 1995: 'Approaches to material culture and social dynamics of the Migration Period in Eastern England', in Bintliff, J. and Hamerow, H. (eds), *Europe between Late Antiquity and the Middle Ages: Recent Archaeological and Historical Research in Western and Southern Europe*, BAR International Series 617 (Oxford), 71–83.

Siegmund, F. 1989: Fränkishe Funde vom deutschen Niederrhein und der nördlichen Kölner Bucht,. Inaugural-Dissertation zur Erlangung des Doktorgrades des Philosofischen Fakultät der Universität zu Köln.

Smith, R.A. 1923: *British Museum Guide to Anglo-Saxon Antiquities 1923*, reprinted by Anglia Publishing (Ipswich).

Speake, G. 1980: *Anglo-Saxon Art and its Germanic Background*, Clarendon Press (Oxford).

Speake, G. 1989: *A Saxon Bed Burial on Swallowcliffe Down*, Historic Buildings and Monuments Commission for England (London).

Steuer, H. 1987: 'Helm und Ringschwert. Prunkbewaffnung und Rangabzeichen germanischer Krieger. Eine Übersicht', *Studien zur Sachsenforschung* 6, 189–236.

Webster, L. and Backhouse, J. (eds) 1991: *The Making of England. Anglo-Saxon Art and Culture AD 600–900*, British Museum Press (London)/University of Toronto Press (Toronto, Buffalo).

Wolfram, H. 1994: 'Origo et religio. Ethnic traditions and literature in early medieval texts', *Early Medieval Europe* 3.1, 19–38.

Wood. I. 1992: 'Frankish hegemony in England', in Carver, M.O.H. (ed.), *The Age of Sutton Hoo. The Seventh Century in North-western Europe*, Boydell Press (Woodbridge), 235–241.

Wood, I. 1994: *The Merovingian Kingdoms 450–751*, Longman (London/New York).

Yorke, B. 1990: *Kings and Kingdoms of Early Anglo-Saxon England*, Seaby (London).

Invisible kingdoms: the use of grave-goods in seventh-century England

Helen Geake

Introduction

This paper will look at the kinds of grave-goods that are found in seventh and early eighth-century graves in England, and the geographical distributions of these objects. It aims to show that the same types of grave-goods are found across the whole of England, in all the early Anglo-Saxon kingdoms, and asks why this should be. The paper will suggest that the answer to this question can be found in the sources of inspiration underlying the design and selection of the objects, which in most cases can be shown to be either earlier Romano-British material or contemporary Byzantine practice.

The benefits of appealing to the heritage of Rome, visible in many aspects of early medieval life, are well-known, and must have applied to all the Anglo-Saxon kingdoms (Cramp 1972; Higgitt 1973). But what may have been missed until recently is the theoretical implications of the wide *distributions* of seventh- and early eighth-century grave-goods. If a group of neighbouring kingdoms adopt the same strategies to enhance their power, this can easily result in them using the same repertoire of material culture. Neighbouring, and perhaps competing, kingdoms are therefore rendered archaeologically invisible. This may have implications for the study of state formation in prehistoric periods (Carver 1989; Renfrew and Cherry (eds) 1986).

The paper will begin with a summary description of the grave-goods themselves and their distributions. It will then move on to look at the prototypes and parallels which may have inspired the development of the new seventh-century objects. Finally, it will examine the possible reasons why these objects were used, and look at what the grave-goods tell us about the major political changes of the time – which are, of course, the advent of kingship and the Church.

Seventh and early eighth-century grave-goods

This section draws on a study of over a thousand furnished graves from the seventh to early ninth century (Geake 1995; 1997). The study drew its data from an approximately one-third sample of all furnished and unfurnished seventh to early ninth-century graves known so far from the areas of Anglo-Saxon influence in Britain. Relatively few later eighth- and ninth-century graves were included, due perhaps to problems of identification. The study found that just under half of all the graves in the sample were furnished, and that furnished graves were virtually non-existent after the first quarter of the eighth century.

In this section, I will concentrate on a selection of grave-good types which appear, new, in the seventh century. These are mostly items of women's jewellery; as often happens in the early medieval period, the important signals are expressed by or through women.

Most noticeable among women's jewellery is a new type of necklace. Although this is shorter than the typical sixth-century necklace, the range of items worn on it increases. Some are new arrivals, such as pendants made from cabochon-cut garnets set in gold (Fig 2a top), the spherical or hemispherical 'bulla' pendants (Fig 3a top), and gold disc pendants decorated with filigree (Fig 3a third row). Disc pendants of other types are also found, with the earlier silver scutiform pendant remaining popular (Fig 3a second row). It is possible that another newly common element on the necklace, the silver wire ring (Fig 4a top), may be echoing the fashion for circular disc-shaped items. Other pendants are also found which are not easily classified and are often one-offs. These range from items such as beavers' teeth (Fig 2a second row), small crystal balls, glass beads or lumps of lignite in metal settings, to scraps of bronze with suspension holes punched through.

Most of the bead types in use in the sixth century are no longer found in the seventh. Amber beads, crystal beads and glass polychrome beads are found in few graves, and never form long strings. Instead, amethyst and shell beads, and beads made of bronze, silver or gold are found on the short necklaces, together with small glass beads in bright monochrome colours – green, blue, white, red, orange, turquoise.

The other most noticeable change in women's costume from the sixth to the seventh centuries is that brooches become very much less popular, and almost all the common sixth-century 'Germanic' types – cruciform, square-headed, small-long, saucer and button brooches – disappear entirely. The disappearance of these brooches seems to happen almost overnight and is one of the most remarkable features of this revolution in burial costume. Where a brooch is worn, it is likely, as with pendants, to be round (Fig 6a top). Annular, penannular and garnet-set disc brooches are the most often found, although even these are hardly common; only forty-nine annular, twelve disc and nine penannular brooches were found in the 1,093 graves examined in 1995 (Geake 1997). These brooches are most likely to be worn singly, showing a move away from the fashion for pairs of brooches. Annular and penannular brooches also show a trend towards a smaller and narrower loop, perhaps indicating a change in function away from securing clothing towards a more decorative use. Similarly, the only brooch form which is not round and is apparently of seventh or early eighth-century manufacture, the 'safety-pin' brooch, is small and delicate (Fig 6a bottom).

It has been suggested that as brooches declined in popularity, pins took over as clothing fasteners (Hyslop 1963, 190–91). Pairs of pins linked by a chain or perhaps a thread are a new arrival in the seventh century (Fig 4a bottom), and single pins, most commonly at the throat, remain common. They are, however, again small and delicate, and it may be that changes in costume construction meant that metal clothing fasteners were no longer required.

The revolution in decorative necklaces and brooches is accompanied by a change in the types of object which hang from a woman's belt. The knife continues to be found, but the non-functional, presumably symbolic, objects such as crystal balls and their associated sieve-spoons, and bronze girdle-hangers, disappear. In their place appear a variety of newly popular functional and non-functional object types: iron latch-lifters, small iron spoons, toilet sets, amulets, suspension devices, bags and small bronze 'workboxes'. These can be attached directly to the belt in the sixth-century manner, but are now also often found suspended from long chatelaine chains made up of linked iron loops or rods (Fig 5a top). In some cases the group of objects is found around the thighs or knees but there is no evidence for a chain; a cord or leather strap may have been used instead. Knives or shears are often found in conjunction with chatelaines, but apparently not directly attached to them; they may have been in sheaths fixed separately on to the belt.

It is not just the female-linked burial assemblage, however, which undergoes a change. There are also changes in more 'neutral' items, such as vessels, tools, combs and belt-buckles. Buckets with bronze fittings become much less common, being replaced by those with iron fittings. Glass vessels become less popular, and by the middle of the seventh century, all glass vessel types except for plain palm cups have disappeared from burials. Bronze bowls also change, with 'Coptic' bronze bowls becoming popular in the first half of the seventh century and hanging bowls in the second half. Small iron tools, mostly pointed or spatulate, make their first appearance in the grave assemblage. The double-sided comb of the sixth century is joined by the single-sided hump-backed comb, and a variety of new buckles are introduced. As with the women's jewellery, the main impression gained from neutral-gendered objects is one of delicacy, fragility and neatness of manufacture.

The familiar types of weapon are still included in male graves, but they are joined by the seax, which rises in popularity in the seventh century after first being introduced in the sixth century from Merovingian France. Weapon graves decline in numbers during the seventh and early eighth centuries, from 15 per cent to 20 per cent of all burials in the fifth and sixth centuries (Härke 1989) to 6 per cent of all seventh- and early eighth-century burials (Geake 1997, 75). Another male-linked grave-good type which appears new in the seventh century is the helmet; although these are thought to be very rare, they are possibly under-represented in the archaeological record due to poor survival.

Distributions of the grave-goods

We can now move on to look at the distributions of some of these grave-good types across England, and compare them with the regionalised distributions of sixth-century types. I will again concentrate on female jewellery types, because it is in female jewellery that sixth-century regionalisation is most apparent.

Figure 1 shows two sample maps of sixth-century female grave-goods. The first (Fig. 1a) is adapted from Hines's work on a classic 'Anglian' object, the wrist-clasp (Hines 1984; 1993). Wrist-clasps are concentrated in the north and east of England, from Yorkshire south and east to East Anglia. The second map (Fig. 1b) is adapted from Dickinson's work on a classic 'Saxon' object, the cast saucer brooch (Dickinson 1993, fig. 1). Saucer brooches are not found at all in Yorkshire, are very rare in East Anglia, and are concentrated in southern England. The difference in the distributions is emphasised by the way in which Dickinson has focussed her map on southern England, entirely removing the empty area of Yorkshire from the diagram.

In contrast, maps of seventh- and early eighth-century female-linked artefact types show a much more scattered distribution, over the whole of the area of Anglo-Saxon influence. Figures 2–6 show the occurrence of selected grave-good types within the study sample referred to above (Geake 1997). Although a very few object types retained some degree of regionalisation – disc brooches are much more common in Kent than in the rest of the country, and annular brooches (but not penannulars) are more common on the north and south banks of the Humber – in general it seems that the 'Anglian' and 'Saxon'

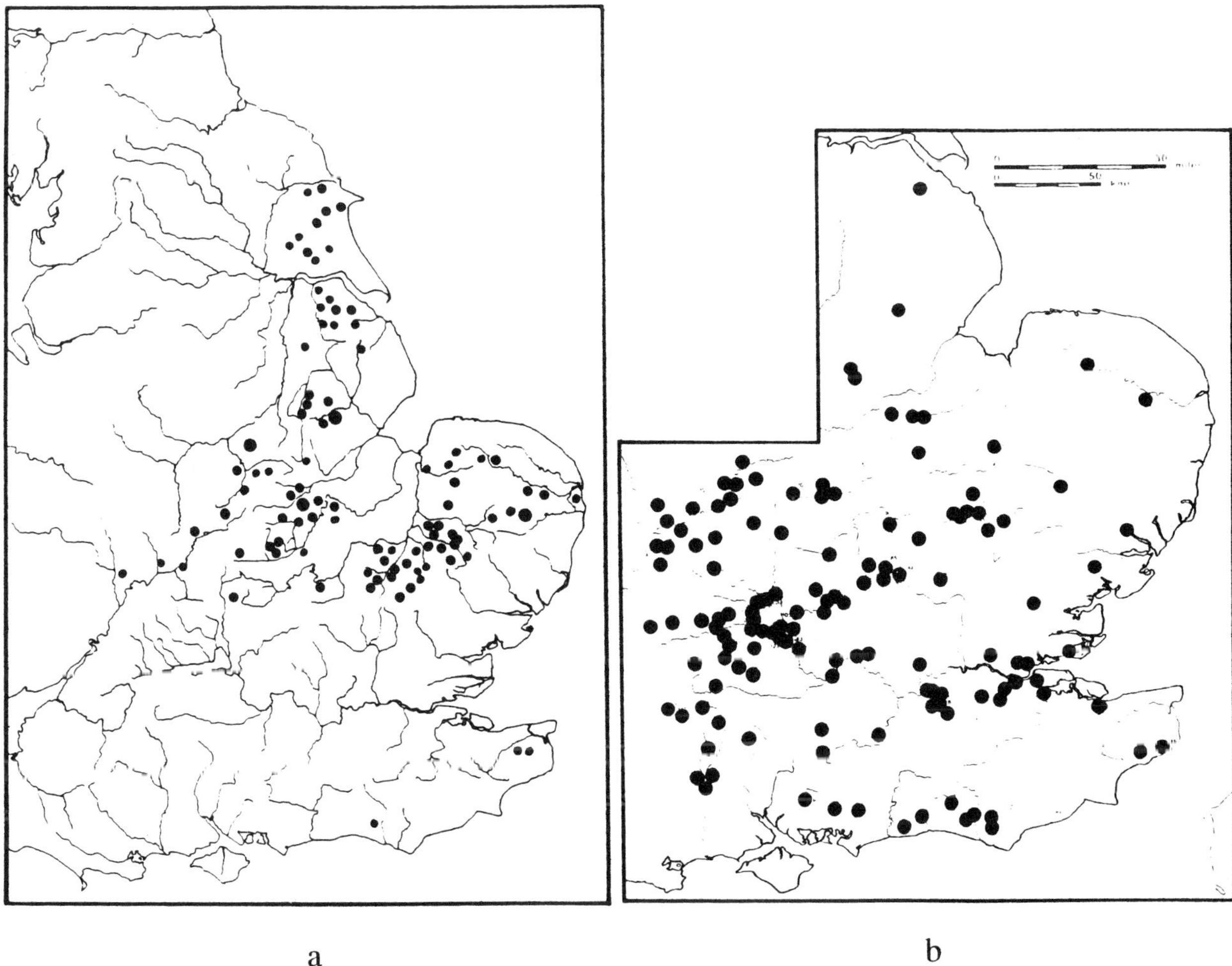

Fig. 1 (a) Distribution map of wrist-clasps in England (after Hines 1984, maps 2.8–2.16); (b) Distribution map of cast saucer-brooches in England (after Dickinson 1993, fig 1).

culture-provinces have been replaced by what one might term an 'English' culture-province.

The seventh and eighth-century homogeneity in burial artefacts has been recognised for some time (Leeds 1936, 98; Evison 1956, 108). The implications of these changes in the distributions of jewellery types have been less thoroughly studied. The problem needing explanation is best summed up by a quote from Sonia Hawkes, who with Audrey Meaney was responsible for the publication, in 1970, of one of the most famous of seventh to early eighth-century cemeteries, at Winnall in Hampshire.

> 'Whereas the cemeteries of the sixth century differ from region to region both in their modes of burial and their grave-goods, these 7th-century inhumation-cemeteries have grave-goods so strikingly similar as to suggest that culture and fashion had become almost universal, disregarding the geographical and political frontiers of their day.' (Meaney and Hawkes 1970, 45).

This succinct description of the situation might benefit from a little expansion. The conflicts between the historically known kingdoms of England during this time have been likened by Steve Bassett to the last few rounds of a knock-out contest – like England's present-day FA cup (Bassett 1989, 26–27). To expand the analogy, the kingdoms involved in these struggles (also termed 'competitive exclusion') might have been expected to attempt to assert their independence, and consolidate their nationhood, in the same way as these football teams; by selecting a strip, mascot and songs to distinguish themselves from their rivals. The observed behaviour, however, is the opposite; no sooner do they emerge into history, than the newly formed kingdoms become archaeologically indistinguishable, all using the same burial costume.

The origins of the new burial costume

One way to approach the question of why this happened is to look at what signals the seventh and early eighth-century Anglo-Saxons were sending out to observers by using these objects, and to ask where the inspiration for

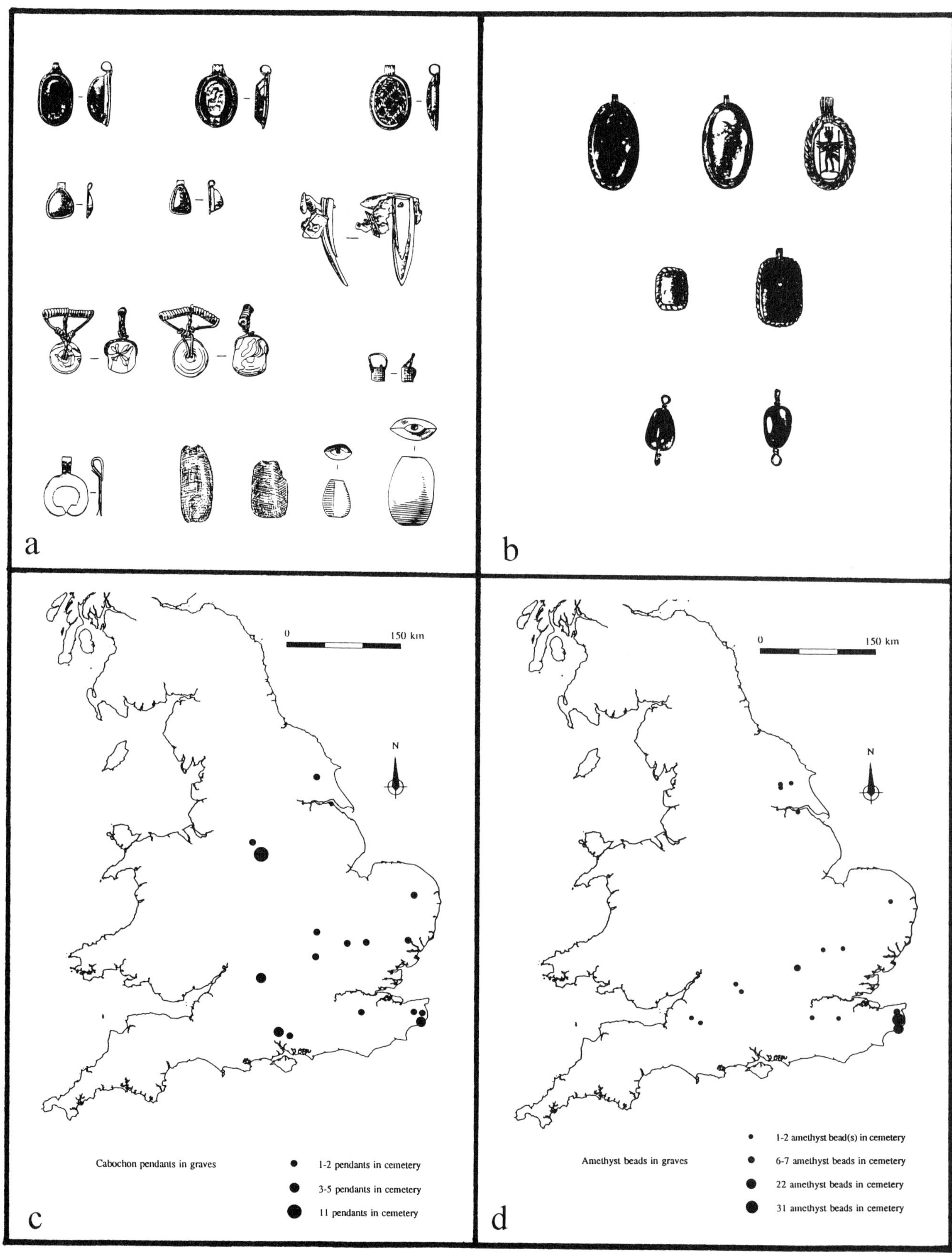

Fig. 2 (a) Pendants and amethyst beads from seventh- and early eighth-century Anglo-Saxon contexts; (b) Cabochon pendants and amethyst beads from Roman and Byzantine contexts; (c) Distribution map of cabochon pendants from sampled Anglo-Saxon contexts; (d) Distribution map of amethyst beads from sampled Anglo-Saxon contexts.

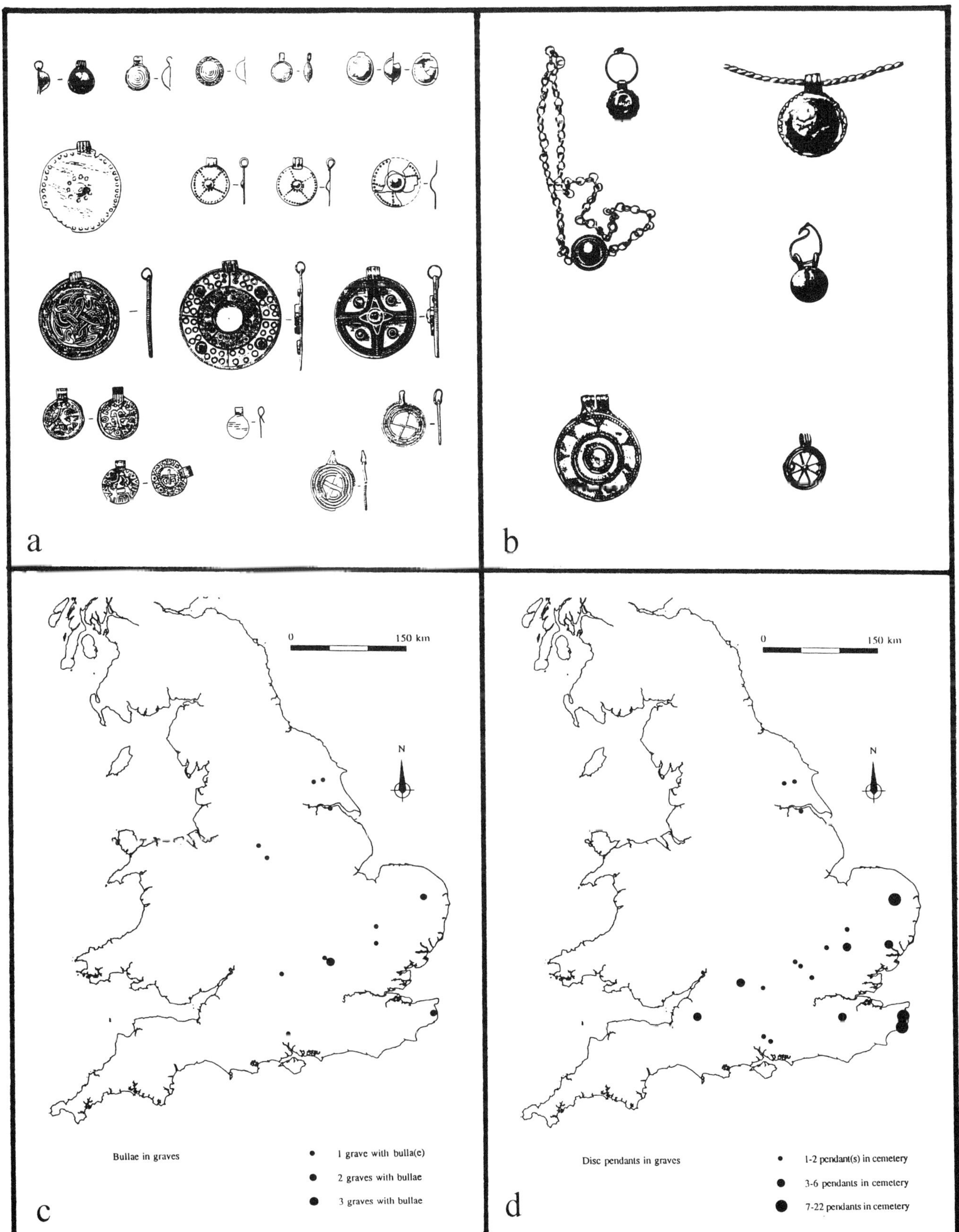

Fig. 3 (a) Bulla pendants and disc pendants from seventh- and eighth-century Anglo-Saxon contexts; (b) Bulla pendants and disc pendants from Roman and Byzantine contexts; (c) Distribution map of bulla pendants from sampled Anglo-Saxon contexts; (d) Distribution map of disc pendants from sampled Anglo-Saxon contexts.

this new sort of burial costume came from. The classic answer in the past has been that the costume was invented in Kent.

The first work on, and recognition of, seventh and eighth-century cemeteries was in the barrow cemeteries of Kent in the eighteenth century (e.g. Douglas 1793). Seventh and eighth-century burials in Kent tend to be underneath little individual mounds, making them obvious and attractive to antiquarians. During the nineteenth century, the work of the British Archaeological Association and the publication of Faussett's monumental (and still essential) *Inventorium Sepulchrale* (Faussett 1856) consolidated work in Kent. Akerman's influential *Remains of Pagan Saxondom* (Akerman 1855) also concentrated heavily on the Kentish barrows. The numerous and excellent illustrations in these books were used by archaeologists in other parts of the country to place their seventh- and early eighth-century sites in context, which naturally became a Kentish context (e.g. Smith 1912).

By the 1920s and 1930s the 'Kentish' origin of seventh and early eighth-century artefacts had become a commonplace. Lethbridge, an innovator in so much else, envisaged the women buried at Burwell in Cambridgeshire as wearing 'Kentish' objects (1931, 85); a few years later, after he had excavated the nearby Shudy Camps cemetery, he was still making casual references to the spread of objects from Kent to East Anglia (1936, 27) but, in his discussion, he uses the Kentish links for dating rather than to indicate any cultural origins (1936, 28–29). Leeds, in his 1936 survey of Anglo-Saxon art and artefacts, devoted his last chapter to the 'Final Phase' of furnished burial. He described similar objects from cemeteries as far apart as Yorkshire, Somerset, Derbyshire and Northamptonshire, but said 'that the change of fashion represented by the novelties constantly recurring in these groups was initiated in Kent we may well believe' (1936, 107). Lethbridge and Leeds were followed in this by other commentators (e.g. Ozanne 1962–63, 38).

The next influential study to appear on Conversion-period cemeteries was that of Hyslop (1963), and with her work the pattern begins to change. Hyslop noted that the importance of the new fashions *outside* Kent had been 'seriously underestimated', and that the closest parallels for many of the objects were 'not found in North Germany and Scandinavia, but in South Germany, Switzerland and, more particularly, Italy'. There were other artefacts, she suggested, 'for which the prototypes were undoubtedly Roman' (1963, 192–93). Despite this, Hyslop continued to describe seventh and early eighth-century graves as containing 'pendants, thread boxes, small buckles and other 'Kentish' objects' and commented that 'there is no difficulty in tracing the archaeological material directly to Kent' (1963, 191).

In 1970, Hawkes again combined the two approaches, describing the Roundway Down necklace as being 'in the Roman-influenced fashion which undoubtedly originated and spread from Kent' (in Meaney and Hawkes 1970, 49).

Following the decline in the use of diffusion as an explanatory device in prehistory (Renfrew 1973) it has become less and less fashionable within Anglo-Saxon archaeology to suggest putative 'origins' for artefact types. As a result, Hyslop's and Hawkes's 'Romanist' views are rarely quoted within modern cemetery reports. The 'Kentish' hypothesis lives on, however, in casual throw-away remarks found in synthetic works (e.g. Parker Pearson *et al.* 1993; Higham 1995, 96).

The theory that the burial costume was developed in Kent, the English kingdom nearest to France, has led to the suggestion that it derives from Frankish sources, which themselves ultimately drew on late Antique inspiration (e.g. Owen-Crocker 1986, 85; Hodges 1986, 72). There is little, however, in contemporary Frankish material that is comparable with the new types of English jewellery. In fact, the closest parallels can be found among Romano-British material of the first to fifth centuries and among the same models as those on which the Franks were drawing (Schulze 1976), Byzantine material of the sixth and seventh centuries.

Figures 2–6 show selected types of seventh and early eighth-century female-linked grave-goods next to possible Roman or Byzantine parallels. As far as the individual items on the necklace are concerned, cabochon pendants (Fig 2b) are known in large numbers from the classical world (Higgins 1961, 186–7), usually set with engraved gems , but after the fourth century, manufacture of these engraved stones ceased and plain settings, very like the Anglo-Saxon ones, were often used instead (Johns and Potter 1983, 20). The bulla pendant (Fig 3b top; Marshall 1911, nos. 2573, 2575, 2734, 2766) is also known from Roman and Byzantine necklaces and these, like the Anglo-Saxon examples, can be both spherical and hemispherical. Prototypes for gold filigree disc pendants, both openwork and with a sheet-gold backplate, are also plentiful in the Roman world (Fig 3b bottom; *ibid.*, no. 2975; Ross 1965, no. 179J, pl. XCVII).

The origins of wire rings on necklaces have rarely been discussed, perhaps because the design of a knotted ring is simple and common in many periods. Single finds of silver or bronze wire rings are known from a number of Romano-British sites, but unless rings are found *in situ* on a body it is difficult to assess their use. Parallels for the habit of threading small glass beads onto silver rings can also be found in Roman Britain (e.g. McWhirr *et al.* 1982, m/f fig. 65), but tend to be interpreted as earrings. The closest parallel to the necklaces of side-by-side rings known from Anglo-Saxon contexts is perhaps the group of six knotted bronze rings, three of which are linked, shown in (Fig 4b centre). These come from a first- or second-century AD grave at Sardis, Turkey, and have been interpreted as a bracelet (Waldbaum 1983, no. 809).

To go to the opposite extreme, very close parallels to the amethyst beads found in Anglo-Saxon contexts are so well-known from Roman contexts that it has been suggested that the Anglo-Saxon examples could have been looted from Romano-British sites (Leeds 1936, 131–132). The use of amethyst drops continued into Byzantine times, sometimes as pendants but more often as beads (Fig 2b bottom; Vierck 1978, 525 and 540).

The short necklaces into which these items were combined (e.g. Fig 5a) are ultimately derived from Hellenistic fashions. Precise parallels are hard to cite, as the preservation of whole necklaces is not common, but we have some evidence from very high-status items handed down through generations of collectors, and from mosaics, paintings and sculpture. Figure 5b shows a necklace with metal links and a variety of pendants from Sardinia, dated to the Byzantine period (Dalton 1901, no 282, pl. V).

Moving on to garment fasteners, antecedents for the fashion of linking pins are exceptionally rare in the Germanic world, but are found in Roman and Byzantine contexts (Fig 4b; Ross 1965, no. 1D, pl. 5). The principle of linked fasteners may also owe something to the peculiarly Romano-British fashion of wearing brooches linked by a chain (Liversidge 1968, 144). The animal heads terminating the chains of some Anglo-Saxon linked pins can also be paralleled on late Roman chains such as those found in the Thetford Treasure (Johns and Potter 1983, no. 36).

It will be clear from Figure 6 that annular, penannular and safety-pin brooches owe much to classical prototypes. The round-section annular brooches found in seventh- and early eighth-century graves are subtly different from the broad, flat-section annular brooches from sixth-century Anglo-Saxon graves, and it seems likely that here an artefact type was selected from the existing repertoire, perhaps for its slightly 'classical' flavour which could then be emphasised by a change in shape. The bronze pins which most of the seventh- and early eighth-century annular brooches possess are also characteristic of Roman rather than sixth-century Anglo-Saxon annular brooches, which tend to have iron pins (White 1988, 30).

The most common item on the chatelaine, the iron latch-lifter, clearly owes much to the form of Roman keys (Fig 5b top; Clarke 1979, fig. 84, 373; Partridge 1981, fig. 62, 98). Both the curved hook and the T-shape of Roman keys can be found among Anglo-Saxon examples.

As far as vessels are concerned, the Roman antecedents of hanging bowls are well-known, and have led a number of scholars to date their appearance in Anglo-Saxon graves (erroneously) to the fifth century onwards, rather than exclusively to the seventh and early eighth centuries (for a summary of past approaches see Brenan 1991, 7–21 and 25–26; for more recent opinion see Brenan 1991, 65–74; for arguments for a later date see Geake 1997, 85–87; Geake forthcoming). Similarly, the Mediterranean origins of 'Coptic' bowls are accepted and do not need rehearsing here (Richards 1980, 81–89).

The reader will by now, I hope, have been persuaded that there is a strong classical influence in seventh- and early eighth-century grave-goods. I am aware that almost everyone who works with early medieval artefacts can discern some classical inspiration behind their range of motifs, but I believe that it is significantly stronger in seventh-century objects than it is in late fifth or sixth-century ones. A distinct contrast can be seen between the old Germanic-style jewellery and the newer classical-style jewellery.

The causes of the renaissance of classical style

We can now turn to the underlying causes behind this revival of classical style. An obvious possible cause is the arrival of the Church, with all the political ramifications that that implies (Hyslop 1963, 192–3; Meaney and Hawkes 1970, 49). This is certainly a plausible *mechanism*, as Christianity was brought by influential visitors from Rome and the wider Mediterranean, who we know also brought books and objects bearing classical motifs (Webster and Backhouse (eds) 1991, 17–19; *HE* I, 25). But there are a few problems in citing the Church as the prime *cause* in this renaissance of classical-style objects. For a start, the conversion process in England lasted for most of the seventh century, and there is no evidence that a 'Germanic'-style grave assemblage – with saucer-brooches, long-brooches, large glass and amber beads, wrist-clasps and so on – continued to be used after *c.* 600 in those kingdoms which remained unconverted. In addition, the fact that there are no churchyard burials in England which contain any conventionally furnished burials, let alone any with classical-style objects, must argue against the Anglo-Saxons having seen these grave assemblages as in some way connected with the Church.

Despite this, it *has* been argued in the past that cemeteries with the new object-types belong to the earliest English Christians. The types of evidence used for this argument have included their predominantly west–east orientation; their careful layout implying belief in resurrection of the body; the cross and fish motifs often found on objects; and their seventh- and early eighth-century date, during and after the historically known conversion process (Lethbridge 1931, 82–84; 1936, 27–29; Meaney and Hawkes 1970, 47–48; Hawkes 1973, 186).

But other people have used other attributes of exactly the same set of graves to argue that they are the resting place of the last pagans. These attributes include the presence of grave-goods, and of weapons and amuletic grave-goods in particular; the absence of a church within the cemetery; and the use of burial mounds, particularly the re-use of prehistoric earthworks (Leeds 1936, 96–114; van de Noort 1993).

The use of these arguments to establish a Christian or pagan character for furnished graves (summarised in Boddington 1990) has been attacked many times, in Britain and in the rest of Europe and both empirically and theoretically (Morris 1983, 51–54; Young 1977 for grave-goods; Meaney 1981, 264 for amulets; Rahtz 1978 for orientations; Dierkens 1991 for 'Christian' motifs).

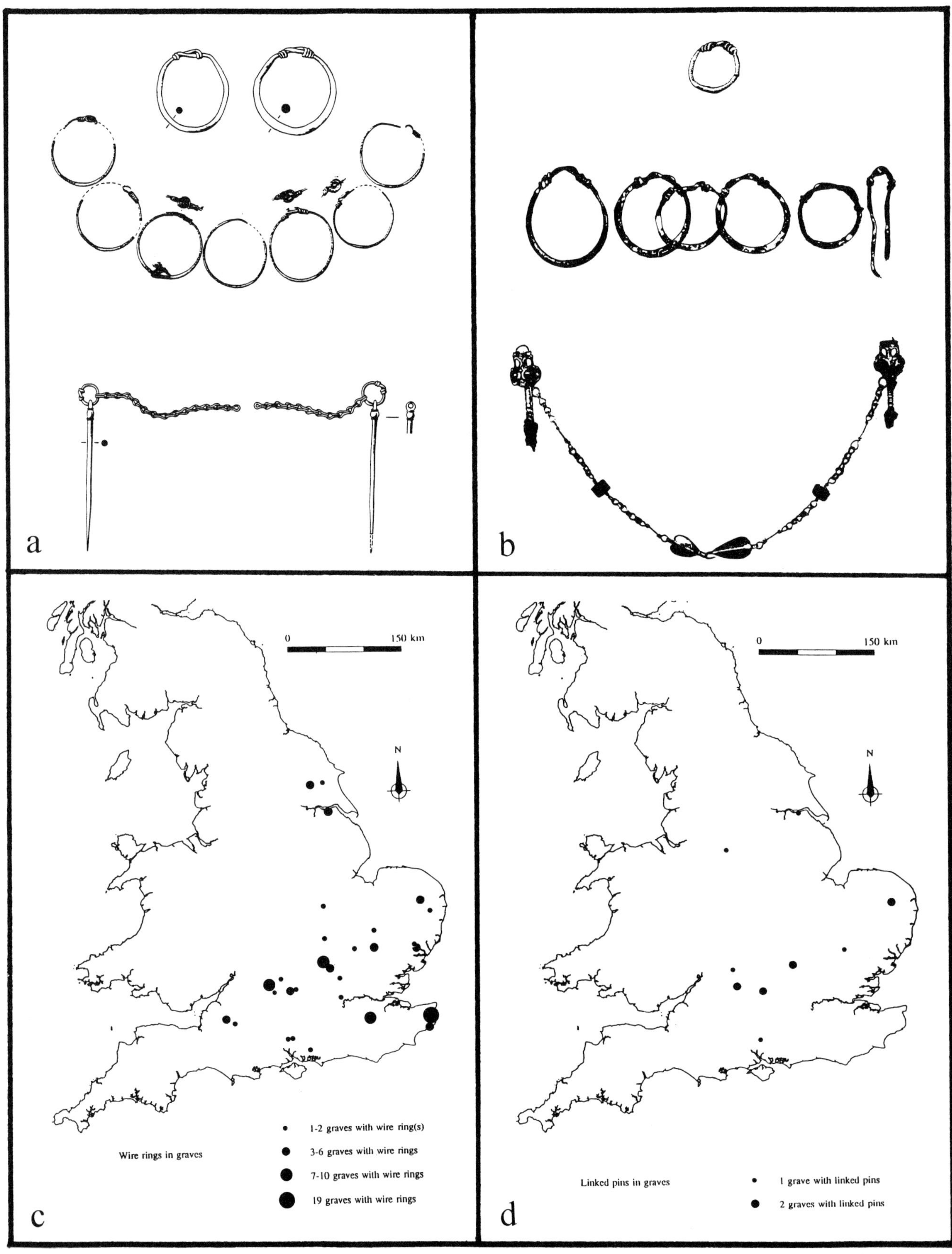

Fig. 4 (a) Wire rings and linked pins from seventh- and early eighth-century Anglo-Saxon contexts; (b) Wire rings and linked pins from Roman and Byzantine contexts; (c) Distribution map of wire rings from sampled Anglo-Saxon contexts; (d) Distribution map of linked pins from sampled Anglo-Saxon contexts.

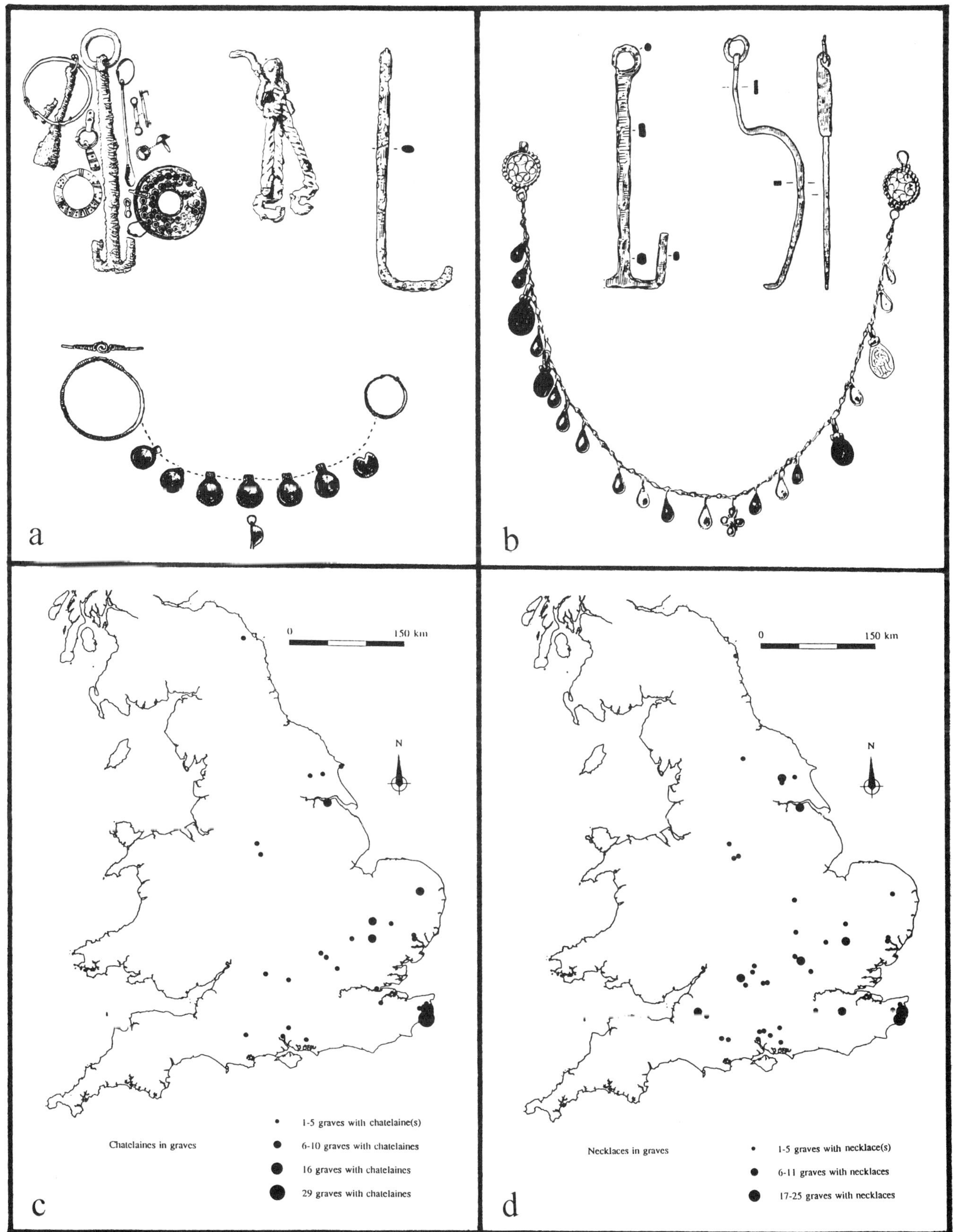

Fig. 5 (a) Chatelaines and necklaces from seventh-and early eighth-century Anglo-Saxon contexts; (b) Chatelaines and necklaces from Roman and Byzantine contexts; (c) Distribution map of chatelaines from sampled Anglo-Saxon contexts; (d) Distribution map of necklaces from sampled Anglo-Saxon contexts.

They must now be considered unusable. Moreover, if we want to look at wider social trends, it is probably unhelpful to look at whether individual graves are expressing paganism or Christianity.

Explanations based on personal beliefs can be discarded, however, while still recognising the crucial role of the Church as a political, spiritual and general all-round ideological force. After all, the Church was the cornerstone of the medieval theory of sacral kingship, and it had a pivotal role in European government, taking over many of the roles of the Empire (Brown 1971, 155–156). The arrival of its systems of power in England, as well as the arrival of its doctrines, fostered a hardening of the social hierarchy at all levels.

So, instead of seeing the use of classical-style grave-goods as a way of advertising Christian allegiance in death, we could instead see it as a way of advertising something else, but given an impetus by the presence of the Church in England. Wallace-Hadrill has argued for a similar mechanism for the development of the institution of kingship in Germanic Europe: it appears to develop within an awareness of, but not necessarily a direct relationship with, the Church (Wallace-Hadrill 1975, 181–182).

The making of kingdoms

We must therefore look for something else that all these kingdoms had in common, apart from the Church, that would lead them all at just about the same time to adopt these new burial fashions. An obvious solution is that they were all developing dynastic kingship at the same time, and needed a means to legitimise this new power.

Old, tried-and-tested arguments may be more effective as a means to legitimise power than an entirely new approach. It is very likely that the early kings deliberately looked back to the last time that there was a supreme leader in Britain – the Roman period. A 'created continuity' (Bradley 1987) may have been ideal for them all.

There are two possible ways in which this continuity could have been created. The first is for the kings to try to present themselves as the legitimate successors to the Roman state machinery. If they could do this, they could then centralise, legislate, tax and control with greater ease. So the rulers could start to rule from Roman towns, to use Roman regalia (such as Edwin of Northumbria's standard; *HE* II, 16) and to construct genealogies incorporating Caesar (such as the East Anglian dynasty; Bruce-Mitford 1975, 693–694). In other words, the kings could become Romans, and hence the natural and legitimate rulers.

The second strategy might be for the property-owning population of a territory to see themselves as inheriting the mantle of Rome. They would then of course need a ruler, taxation, the Church, stone buildings and classical jewellery as part of their civilisation package. In other words, the people would become Roman, and hence require rulers.

The two options are not, of course, mutually exclusive. The first was occasionally taken, but never wholeheartedly; if an extreme 'elite takeover' model of Anglo-Saxon acculturation (Higham 1992) is right, the perceived origins of the rulers might have been seen as so strongly Germanic that an attempt to construct 'Roman' genealogies would have failed.

The second option, the re-creation of Romanitas among the property-owning class, appears to have been adopted enthusiastically by most seventh-century kings. It can be seen in many of the archaeological and historical sources for the seventh and early eighth centuries (see, for example, Blair 1995, 20–22; Cramp 1986; Lang forthcoming).

Higham has identified similar processes at work in Bede's Ecclesiastical History, where Bede appears to assert the right of the 'English' to live in and rule the islands of Britain by describing Roman rule in Britain in terms analogous to an English imperium (Higham 1995, 9–46). As Higham comments, Bede manipulated an imperfect knowledge of Roman institutions and government to try to influence early eighth-century thought. Likewise, the classical objects copied by seventh-century manufacturers represent a slightly eccentric choice, apparently ignoring some common Romano-British artefact types.

Wormald has suggested that the Church was keen to foster a cultural unity throughout England; it wanted one Church, one people (1983, 124–126). The influence of the Church may have spurred the various kingdoms in the same direction; it is notable that the penultimate kingdom to accept the new ideological force of Christianity, Sussex, has very few of these classical-style seventh- and early eighth-century objects, and the last, the Isle of Wight, has only one single identifiable grave containing them among all its many excavated cemeteries (Geake 1997, 86, 160; Geake forthcoming). The burial costume is undemonstrative and indeed almost invisible in these areas.

Some possible problems

A few problems remain to be cleared up. It might, for example, be asked why such a strong Germanic identity remains within England, an identity observable, for example, in Bede's writings of the early eighth century; the language, the origin myths, the name for the country, and so on. Certainly there was a strong Germanic acculturation in the fifth and sixth centuries, and this could not be wiped out as if it had never happened. But the English could simply be reminded that those who live in this island are heirs to its traditions as a Roman province. They can then transfer their Germanic acculturation into an origin myth, and get on with the business of displaying their new Romanitas.

Those who work with Kentish material may also have some problems with the hypothesis put forward here. The situation in Kent is slightly different; it has strong

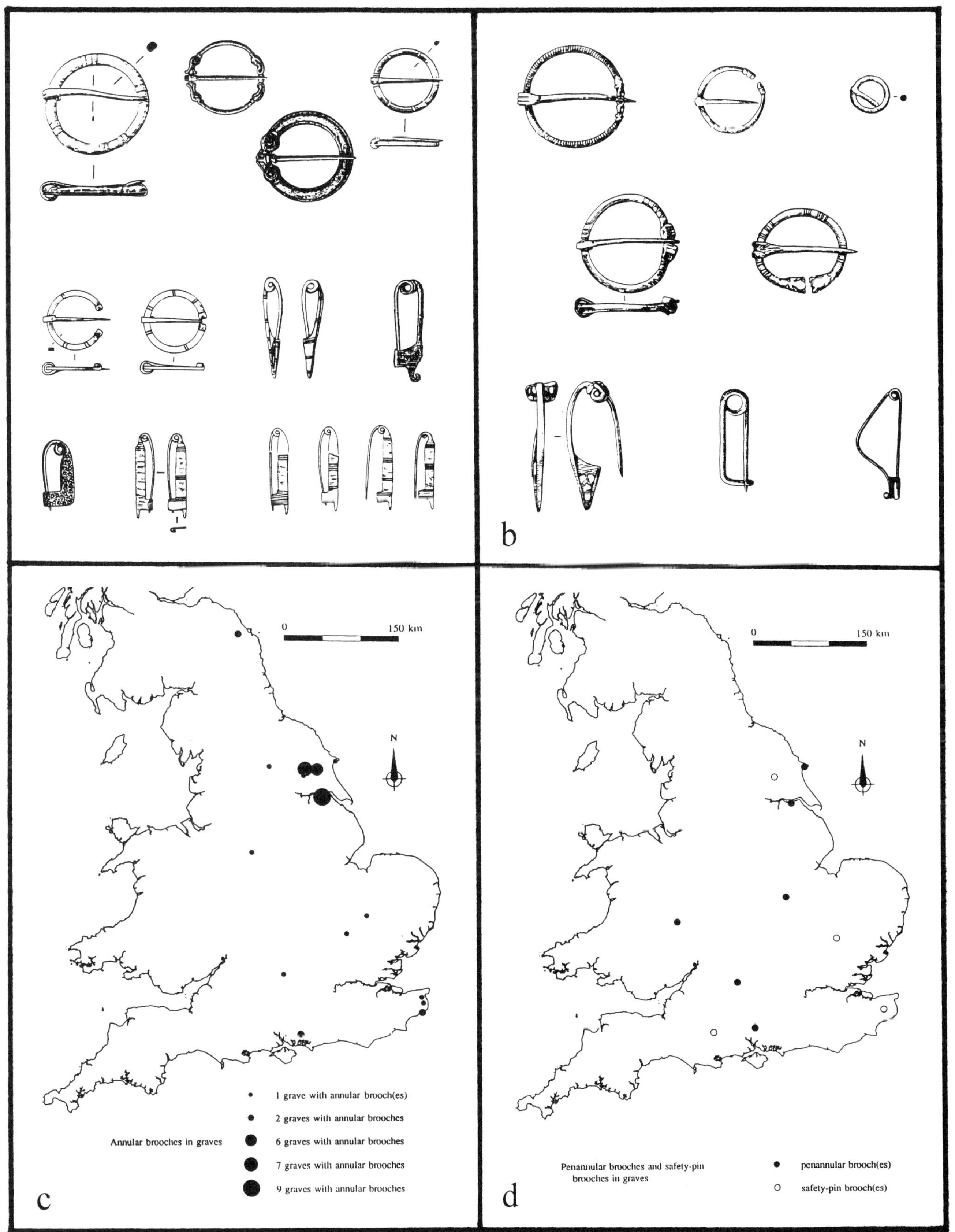

Fig. 6 (a) Annular, penannular and safety-pin brooches from seventh- and eighth-century Anglo-Saxon contexts; (b) Annular, penannular and bow brooches from Roman and Byzantine contexts; (c) Distribution map of annular brooches from sampled Anglo-Saxon contexts; (d) Distribution map of penannular and safety-pin brooches from sampled Anglo-Saxon contexts.

links with the Frankish empire, and is the only kingdom in which a different and distinctively Kentish material culture is visible, particularly in the first half of the seventh century. There may have been a brief attempt to use the notion of the Frankish empire, with its own different connection to the legacy of Rome, to legitimise power here; outside Kent, this strategy would have had no force. During the second half of the century, however, Kent does seem to join in more with the rest of England, and any differences are minimised.

It has already been noted that churchyard burials in England are virtually devoid of grave-goods. These do not at first sight fit into the model of grave-good use suggested here. There were, however, a few groups of people who did not need to be encouraged to display a particularly Roman material culture. First were those who showed a strong allegiance to the Roman church by becoming part of its hierarchy. By the fact of their taking holy orders, they were already advertising an obedience to both sacred and secular authority. And they could therefore be buried, as befits stated Christian ideology, in an ostentatiously egalitarian manner – without grave-goods. Second, it seems possible that the mere fact of burial in a churchyard, even for a lay person, showed an acceptance of the authority of church and state, with again no need for grave-goods.

Any assessment of the relationship between (more or less) furnished field cemeteries and churchyard cemeteries at this date, however, is made difficult by the fact that although conventionally furnished burials can occasionally be found in Continental and possibly in Kentish churchyards, they are never found in churchyards in the rest of England. Explanations have hitherto avoided discussion of this difference, and have played down the complete separation of furnished burial and churchyard burial (e.g. Morris 1983, 49–62). Historical sources seem to indicate that the Church did not particularly interest itself in whether or not grave-goods were used, yet the archaeological evidence from churchyards appears to suggest the opposite, and the two cannot yet be reconciled. A further complication is that the Sussex and Isle of Wight burial evidence mentioned above may indicate a concentration of unfurnished burial in the latest nominally *pagan* kingdoms.

The end of furnished burial

By the 720s or 730s, the strategy of convincing the English that they were the heirs to Rome appears to have worked. The institution of kingship was by now very secure; the population had had kings for long enough to accept them as a necessity. There was thus no need to continue to advertise a Roman identity, which equals allegiance to the king, in the grave. Grave-good usage – and with it, apparently, the use of cemeteries containing furnished burial – stops suddenly at this point all over England. It is tempting, although perhaps unwise, to link this with the tradition which credits Archbishop Cuthbert of Canterbury (740–758) with the foundation of cemeteries all over England (Morris 1983, 50).

Conclusion

It has been argued that the process of making kingdoms in Anglo-Saxon England is indicated, paradoxically, by those kingdoms becoming all very much like each other and therefore archaeologically very difficult to distinguish. They all appear to have followed the same strategy of using their material culture deliberately to construct a 'continuity' from Roman Britain, allowing their rulers to claim a legitimate power. This is observable not only in the grave-goods derived both from Romano-British and from Byzantine prototypes, but also in many other archaeological and historical sources.

In conclusion, I would therefore like to ask: if we had no documentary history for this period, would we be able to infer the existence of the separate kingdoms, and the conflicts between them? This surely has implications for the identification of separate polities in prehistory.

References

Primary Source

HE: *Historia Ecclesiastica.* In B. Colgrave and R.A.B. Mynors (ed. and transl.) 1969. *Bede's Ecclesiastical History of the English People*,Oxford University Press (Oxford).

Akerman, J.Y. 1855: *Remains of Pagan Saxondom*, John Russell Smith (London).

Bassett, S. 1989: 'In search of the origins of Anglo-Saxon kingdoms', in Bassett (ed.) 1989, 3–27.

Bassett, S. (ed) 1989: *The Origins of Anglo-Saxon Kingdoms*, Leicester University Press (London).

Blair, J. 1995: 'Anglo-Saxon pagan shrines and their prototypes', *Anglo-Saxon Studies in Archaeology and History* 8, 1–28.

Boddington, A. 1990: 'Models of burial, settlement and worship: the final phase reviewed', in Southworth, E. (ed.), *Anglo-Saxon Cemeteries: a reappraisal*, Alan Sutton (Stroud), 177–199.

Bradley, R. 1987: 'Time regained: the creation of continuity', *Journal of the British Archaeological Association* 140, 1–17.

Brenan, J. 1991: *Hanging Bowls and Their Contexts*, British Archaeological Reports 220 (Oxford).

Brown, P. 1971: *The World of Late Antiquity*,Thames and Hudson (London).

Bruce-Mitford, R. 1975: *The Sutton Hoo Ship Burial, Volume 1: excavations, background, the ship, dating and inventory*, British Museum Publications (London).

Carver, M. O. H. 1989: 'Kingship and material culture in early Anglo-Saxon East Anglia', in Bassett (ed.) 1989, 141–158.

Clarke, G. 1979: *The Roman Cemetery at Lankhills*, Winchester Studies 3, Clarendon Press (Oxford).

Cramp, R. 1972: 'The Anglo-Saxons and Rome', *Transactions of the Architectural and Archaeological Society of Durham and Northumberland* 3, 27–37.

Cramp, R. 1986: 'Anglo-Saxon and Italian sculpture', *Settimane di*

Studio del Centro Italiano di Studi sull'Alto Medioevo 32, 125–140.

Dalton, O.M. 1901: *Catalogue of Early Christian Antiquities and Objects from the Christian East in the Department of British and Medieval Antiquities and Ethnography of the British Museum*, British Museum Publications (London).

Dickinson, T.M. 1993: 'Early Saxon saucer brooches: a preliminary overview', *Anglo-Saxon Studies in Archaeology and History* 6, 11–44.

Dierkens, A. 1991: 'Interprétation critique des symboles Chrétiens sur les objects d'époque Mérovingienne', in Donnay, G. (ed), *L'Art des invasions en Hongrie et en Wallonie*, Monographes du Musée royal de Mariemont 6 (Morlanwelz), 109–124.

Douglas, J. 1793: *Nenia Britannica*, B. and J. White (London).

Evison, V.I. 1956: 'An Anglo-Saxon cemetery at Holborough, Kent', *Archaeologia Cantiana* 70, 84–118.

Faussett, B. 1856: *Inventorium Sepulchrale: an account of some antiquities dug up at Gilton, Kingston, Sibertswold, Barfriston, Beakesbourne, Chartham, and Crundale, in the county of Kent, from AD 1757 to AD 1773*, edited and with notes by C. Roach Smith, privately published (London).

Geake, H.M. 1995: 'The Use of Grave-Goods in Conversion-Period England, c. 600–c. 850 AD', unpublished DPhil dissertation, University of York.

Geake, H.M. 1997: *The Use of Grave-Goods in Conversion-Period England, c. 600–c. 850*, British Archaeological Reports 261(Oxford).

Geake, H.M. forthcoming: 'When were hanging bowls deposited in Anglo-Saxon graves?', *Med Arch* vol. 42 (1998) or vol. 43 (1999).

Härke, H. 1989: 'Early Saxon weapon burials: frequencies, distributions and weapon combinations', in Hawkes, S. C. (ed.), *Weapons and Warfare in Anglo-Saxon England*, Oxford University Committee for Archaeology Monograph 21 (Oxford), 49–61.

Hawkes, S.C. 1973: 'The dating and social significance of the burials in the Polhill cemetery', in Philp, B., *Excavations in West Kent 1960–1973*, Kent Monograph Series Research Report 2, Kent Archaeological Rescue Unit (Dover), 186–201.

Higgins, R.A. 1961: *Greek and Roman Jewellery*, Methuen (London).

Higgitt, J. 1973: 'The Roman background to medieval England', *Journal of the British Archaeological Association*, 3rd series, 36, 1–15.

Higham, N.J. 1992: *Rome, Britain and the Anglo-Saxons*, Seaby (London).

Higham, N.J. 1995: *The English Empire*, Manchester University Press (Manchester).

Hines, J. 1984: *The Scandinavian Character of Anglian England in the Pre-Viking Period*, British Archaeological Reports 124 (Oxford).

Hines, J. 1993: *Clasps, Hektespenner, Agraffen: Anglo-Scandinavian clasps of classes A–C of the 3rd to 6th centuries AD*, Kungl. vitterhets historie och antikvitets akademien (Stockholm).

Hodges, R. 1986. 'Peer polity interaction in Anglo-Saxon England', in Renfrew, C. and Cherry, J.F. (eds), *Peer Polity Interaction and Socio-Political Change*, New Directions in Archaeology, Cambridge University Press (Cambridge), 69–78.

Hyslop, M. 1963: 'Two Anglo-Saxon cemeteries at Chamberlain's Barn, Leighton Buzzard, Bedfordshire', *Archaeological Journal* 120, 161–200.

Johns, C. and Potter, T. 1983: *The Thetford Treasure*, British Museum Publications (London).

Lang, J. forthcoming: 'York and the Continent: the evidence of the monuments', in Geake, H.M. and Kenny, J. (eds) *Early Deira*.

Leeds, E. T. 1936: *Early Anglo-Saxon Art and Archaeology*, Clarendon Press (Oxford).

Lethbridge, T.C. 1931: *Recent Excavations in Anglo-Saxon Cemeteries in Cambridgeshire and Suffolk*, Cambridge Antiquarian Society Quarto Publications 3 (Cambridge).

Lethbridge, T.C. 1936: *A Cemetery at Shudy Camps, Cambridgeshire*, Cambridge Antiquarian Society Quarto Publications 5 (Cambridge).

Liversidge, J.1968: *Britain in the Roman Empire*, Routledge & Kegan Paul (London).

Marshall, F.H. 1911: *Catalogue of the Jewellery, Greek, Etruscan and Roman, in the Department of Antiquities, British Museum*, British Museum Publications (London).

McWhirr, A., Viner, L. and Wells, C. 1982: *Romano-British Cemeteries at Cirencester*, Cirencester Excavations 2 (Cirencester).

Meaney, A.L. 1981: *Anglo-Saxon Amulets and Curing Stones*, British Archaeological Reports 96 (Oxford).

Meaney, A.L. and Hawkes, S.C. 1970: *Two Anglo-Saxon Cemeteries at Winnall*, Society for Medieval Archaeology Monograph Series 4 (London).

Morris, R.K. 1983: *The Church in British Archaeology*, Council for British Archaeology Research Report 47 (London).

Owen-Crocker, G.R. 1986: *Dress in Anglo-Saxon England*, Manchester University Press, (Manchester).

Ozanne, A. 1962–63: 'The Peak dwellers', *Medieval Archaeology* 6–7, 15–52.

Parker Pearson, M., van de Noort, R. and Woolf, A. 1993: 'Three men and a boat: Sutton Hoo and the East Saxon kingdom', *Anglo-Saxon England* 22, 27–50.

Partridge, C. 1981: *Skeleton Green: a late Iron Age and Romano-British Site*, Britannia Monograph Series 2, Society for the Promotion of Roman Studies (London).

Rahtz, P.A. 1978: 'Grave orientation', *Archaeological Journal* 135, 1–14.

Renfrew, C. 1973: *Before Civilisation*, Jonathan Cape (London).

Renfrew, C. and Cherry, J.F. 1986: *Peer Polity Interaction and Socio-Political Change*, Cambridge University Press (Cambridge).

Richards, P. 1980: 'Byzantine Bronze Vessels in England and Europe', unpublished PhD dissertation, University of Cambridge.

Ross, M.C. 1965: *Catalogue of the Byzantine and Early Medieval Antiquities in the Dumbarton Oaks Collection. Volume 2: jewelry, enamels, and art of migration period*, The Dumbarton Oaks Center for Byzantine Studies (Washington, D.C.).

Schulze, M. 1976: 'Einflüsse byzantinischer Prunkgewänder auf die fränkische Frauentracht', *Archäologisches Korrespondenzblatt* 6, 149–161.

Smith, R.A. 1912: 'The excavation by Canon Greenwell, FSA, in 1868, of an Anglo-Saxon cemetery at Uncleby, East Riding of Yorkshire', *Proceedings of the Society of Antiquaries of London* 24, 146–158.

van de Noort, R. 1993: 'The context of early medieval barrows in Western Europe', *Antiquity* 67, 66–73.

Vierck, H. 1978: 'La chemise de Sainte-Bathilde à Chelles et l'influence byzantine sur l'art de cour mérovingien au VIIe sièle', *Actes du Colloque International d'Archéologie, Rouen 1975* 3, 521–64, pls. I–VI.

Waldbaum, J. 1983: *metalwork from Sardis: the finds through 1974*, Harvard U.P. (Cambridge, Mass.).

Wallace-Hadrill, J.M. 1975 *Early Medieval History*, Blackwell (Oxford).

Webster, L. and Backhouse, J. (eds) 1991: *The Making of England*, British Museum Publications (London).

White, R. 1988: *Roman and Celtic Objects from Anglo-Saxon Graves*, British Archaeological Reports 191 (Oxford).

Wormald, P. 1983: 'Bede, the *Bretwaldas* and the origins of the *gens Anglorum*', in Wormald, P., Bullough, D. and Collins, R. (eds), *Ideal and Reality in Frankish and Anglo-Saxon Society: studies presented to J. M. Wallace-Hadrill*, Blackwell (Oxford), 99–129.

Young, B. 1977: 'Paganisme, christianisation et rites funéraires mérovingiens', *Archéologie Médiévale* 7, 5–81.